PONAPEAN-ENGLISH DICTIONARY

PALI LANGUAGE TEXTS: MICRONESIA

Social Science Research Institute
University of Hawaii

Donald M. Topping
Editor

PONAPEAN-ENGLISH DICTIONARY

KENNETH L. REHG
DAMIAN G. SOHL

University of Hawaii Press
Honolulu

06   05   04   03   02   9   8   7   6

Library of Congress Cataloging in Publication Data

Rehg, Kenneth L.   1939–
   Ponapean-English dictionary.

   (PALI language texts: Micronesia)
   1.   Ponape language—Dictionaries—English.   2.   English
language—Dictionaries—Ponape.   I.   Sohl, Damian G.,
1943–   joint author.   II.   Title.   III.   Series:
Pali language texts.
PL6295.Z5R4   499'.5   79–19451
ISBN 0–8248–0562–3

The publication of this book is subsidized by the government of
the Trust Territory of the Pacific Islands.

This is one in a series of dictionaries compiled and edited with
the aid of a specially developed system of computer programs,
which also formatted the text for composition and produced the
tapes to drive a digital character-generating phototypesetter.

University of Hawaii Press books are printed on acid-free paper
and meet the guidelines for permanence and durability of the
Council on Library Resources.

CONTENTS

Preface   vii

Introduction   ix

  1. Guide to the Use of the Dictionary   ix
     1.1 The Organization of the Dictionary   x
     1.2 The Arrangement of Ponapean-English Entries   x
     1.3 Locating Affixed Words   xvi

  2. Ponapean Orthography   xviii
     2.1 Dialect Considerations   xviii
     2.2 The Alphabet   xix

  3. About This Dictionary   xx
     3.1 The Aims of the Dictionary   xxi
     3.2 Sources of Information   xxi

Chart of Abbreviations and Symbols   xxiii

Ponapean-English Dictionary   1

English-Ponapean Finder List   123

PREFACE

The Ponapean-English Dictionary is based on materials gathered primarily during the years 1971 to 1975 while its compilers were students at the University of Hawaii. This work was carried out as part of a larger project that additionally involved the development of a standard orthography and a reference grammar for Ponapean. Support for this project was provided by the government of the Trust Territory of the Pacific Islands in cooperation with the Culture Learning Institute of the East-West Center and the Pacific and Asian Linguistics Institute (now the Social Science Research Institute) of the University of Hawaii.

While this dictionary bears the distinction of being the first book-length compilation of Ponapean vocabulary to be published, it is not without a number of important predecessors. In 1880 the Reverend Luther H. Gulick published an article in the *American Oriental Society Journal* entitled "A Vocabulary of the Ponapean Dialect, Ponapean-English and English-Ponapean: With a Grammatical Sketch." This study included an estimated 2,700 Ponapean to English and 3,500 English to Ponapean entries. A dictionary of approximately 5,000 Ponapean to English entries was completed in 1950 by Fr. Paulino Cantero, a native speaker of Ponapean. Cantero's work, entitled *Ponapean-English Dictionary*, expanded considerably on Gulick's study, but unfortunately it was circulated only in a mimeographed form and copies of this important work are now rare. Another dictionary project was undertaken during the summers of 1968 and 1969 by Alan Burdick, then a Peace Corps volunteer in Ponape. The result of this effort was a highly useful booklet, also produced in perishable form, entitled *Dictionary of the Ponapean Language*. It included approximately 1,500 Ponapean to English and 750 English to Ponapean entries.

The contributions of these earlier works were invaluable in the preparation of this dictionary. Building upon the foundation they provided, it has been possible to expand this dictionary beyond the scope of its predecessors in two ways. First, a larger number of entries were included. This dictionary contains approximately 6,750 Ponapean to English and 4,200 English to Ponapean entries. Second, more information was generally incorporated into each entry. The criteria for determining which entries were included and a description of the types of information contained within entries are presented in the following Introduction.

In spite of the enlarged scope of this dictionary, it must be emphasized that it is still far from being complete. Many Ponapean words have been either intentionally or inadvertently omitted. Comparisons with dictionaries the size of those for English should therefore not give rise to comparisons about the relative complexities of these two languages. The extensive dictionaries that are available for a language like English are the result of enormous investments in time and money—far more of both than were available for this project. This dictionary must thus be understood as representing only an intermediate step toward the goal of producing a truly comprehensive dictionary of Ponapean.

The task of preparing this dictionary has been at once the source of many challenges and rewards. The challenges derived primarily from the difficulties involved in trying to document accurately the information that must be included in a bilingual dictionary. This endeavor required not only a good knowledge of the structure of both target languages, but additionally—and unrealistically—expertise in all aspects of both target cultures. The rewards resulted largely from the task of gathering the information. Eliciting new entries and trying to understand their usage provided many new and interesting insights into both languages and cultures. These activities also put the compilers in contact with many perceptive people who generously shared their time and their knowledge of Ponapean.

It would be impossible to name everyone who has played a role in the development of this dictionary, but the contributions of a number of individuals were so extensive that they merit special recognition. Marcelino Actouka invested hundreds of hours adding new entries and improving those already collected. Alan Burdick and Ewalt Joseph also offered countless valuable suggestions for improving this work. Much of the information concerning honorific speech was provided by Linter Hebel. Ioakim David also contributed information on honorific speech, house parts, and plant names. Godfred Bartolome and Santiago Edmond provided many fish names, and Lotis Seneris was especially helpful in the investigation of Ponapean numerals. Additional assistance in checking entries as well as in adding new ones came from Hanover Ehsa, Oliper Joseph, Rodrigo Mauricio, Paulino Rosario, Casiano Shoniber, Gideon David, and Weldis Welley. James Abrams, William Hubbard, Terry Malinowski, and Ellen Zunino also shared data on Ponapean they collected while serving as Peace Corps volunteers on Ponape. The Reverend Harold Hanlin suggested a number of improvements, as did Elaine Good, Sheldon Harrison, and Hiroshi Sugita. The latter also served as the consultant for identifying Japanese loanwords. Robert Hsu and Ann Peters were responsible for the design of the computer programs that ordered the mass of linguistic data out of which this dictionary grew, and, in addition, they provided much valuable help throughout the production of this work. Assistance in proofreading was given by James Tharp. Cynthia Dalrymple, Doreen Yamamoto, and Melody Actouka did most of the keypunching, and Mrs. Actouka additionally suggested many improvements in format and content. Donald Topping served as general editor and as the director of the project which sponsored this dictionary. To all of these individuals and to any others whose names we may have inadvertently omitted, we wish to express our sincere appreciation. For the faults of this work, we alone accept full responsibility.

INTRODUCTION

Ponapean is the native language of the indigenous people of the island of Ponape. Ponape is located approximately halfway between Hawaii and Indonesia at 6°54′ north latitude and 158°14′ east longitude within the geographic area known as Micronesia. Ponape and its two satellite atolls, Pakin and Ant, are also known as the Senyavin Islands. On older maps, Ponape alone is sometimes called Ascension Island.

Ponapean is a Nuclear Micronesian member of the large family of languages named Austronesian. At present, there are approximately 15,000 native speakers of Ponapean. Along with English, this language serves as a lingua franca for the linguistically diverse Ponape District of the Trust Territory of the Pacific Islands. While no detailed language variation studies have been conducted in this area, on the island of Ponape itself two major dialects of Ponapean may be easily discerned. These are: (1) the Kiti dialect, spoken primarily in the municipality of that name, and (2) the Main or Northern dialect, spoken on the rest of the island. The varieties of speech spoken on three neighboring atolls—Ngatik, Pingelap, and Mokil—are very closely related to Ponapean and, along with Ponapean, are to varying degrees mutually intelligible. Collectively, the language of all these speech communities is called *Ponapeic*. Other languages classified as Nuclear Micronesian are Gilbertese, Marshallese, Kusaiean, the Trukic languages, and probably Nauruan.

The major grammatical features of Ponapean have been described in the companion volume to this work, entitled *Ponapean Reference Grammar*, henceforth abbreviated PRG. Consequently, the scope of this introduction will be limited to providing information helpful in using this dictionary. Where it is necessary to employ grammatical terminology that may be unfamiliar to the reader, cross references to the PRG are provided.

The introductory materials that follow are divided into three main sections. The first section serves as a **Guide to the Use of the Dictionary**. It describes the organization of the dictionary, explains the arrangement of Ponapean-English entries, and includes advice on locating affixed words. The second section briefly comments on **Ponapean Orthography**. Dialect considerations in spelling and the Ponapean alphabet are the topics of this section. The third section is captioned **About This Dictionary**. It sets forth the aims of the dictionary and the major sources of entry information. Every user of this dictionary is urged to read these materials.

1. Guide to the Use of the Dictionary

Because the mass of information that must be included within a dictionary is so great, special procedures for organizing and arranging the information must be employed. The purpose of this guide is thus to acquaint the user with these procedures so that he will be able to employ this dictionary with maximum efficiency and understanding.

1.1 The Organization of the Dictionary

The main body of this work is divided into two parts. The first part consists of a **Ponapean-English Dictionary** and the second part of an **English-Ponapean Finder List**. The distinction that is made between the terms *dictionary* and *finder list* is important. Whereas the Ponapean-English dictionary attempts to list at least all high-frequency lexical items that occur in Ponapean, the finder list includes only those key English words that are used in the definitions of Ponapean entries. Therefore, this list is designed as a supplement to the dictionary to help the user find Ponapean-English entries. A typical entry that might occur in the finder list is illustrated by the following example.

> **accent**
> accent, dialect, tune, tone: *ngohr.*
> to speak with an accent: *sis*₁

Further information about the usage of the Ponapean words *ngohr* and *sis*₁ is presented in the Ponapean-English entries for these words.

1.2 The Arrangement of Ponapean-English Entries

A Ponapean-English entry may be divided into as many as eight parts, each of which contains a different kind of information. The order of presentation of these eight parts is: (1) headword, (2) alternate spellings, (3) usage label, (4) grammatical label, (5) definitions, (6) phrase or sentence examples, (7) loan source, and (8) cross reference. The conventions employed for these parts are described below.

(1) **Headword.** Every entry begins with a headword printed in boldface type. All headwords, including proper nouns, compounds of two or more words, and affixes, are entered in the following alphabetical order: a(h), e(h), i(h), o(h), oa(h), u(h), k, l, m, mw, n, ng, p, pw, r, s, d, t, w. Conventional Ponapean alphabetical order is therefore employed except that long vowels, signaled by writing *h* after a vowel, are alphabetized immediately after corresponding short vowels. This procedure is employed to assist the user who may be uncertain about vowel length in a word he is attempting to locate. The following words illustrate this alphabetical practice.

au	kehse
ahu	par
id	pahr
ihd	dau
kese	dahu

Proper nouns begin with a capital letter. A hyphen before or after a headword indicates that the headword can never occur alone and must always be used in combination with another word or an affix. Headwords that are spelled the same way, but are unrelated in meaning, are entered separately with subscript numerals, as in the following examples.

Headword	*Meaning*
ah_1	'name of the letter *a*'
ah_2	'his, her, its'
ah_3	'however, and'
ah_4	'shark mullet'
ah_5	'Oh!'

Further information about headwords is given in section 1.3.

(2) **Alternate Spellings.** Some headwords in this dictionary are listed with alternate spellings. These alternate spellings are listed after the headword, as in the following examples.

> **ahia**, also **iahia**
> **aine**, also **ainih**
> **akadahn**, also **kaladahn** or **lakadahn**

Alternate spellings are given for headwords that have two or more common pronunciations that are not simply regular dialect variants of each other. If two or more variant spellings of a word exist, each is entered as a headword in its proper place.

(3) **Usage Label.** Headwords that are limited in usage to a particular time or social situation are identified by the use of one of the following labels printed in small capitals.

ARCHAIC. This label indicates that the headword is rarely used except in certain restricted contexts, such as legends, chants, or historical narratives.

HONORIFIC. The term *honorific* is used to label headwords that are part of the Ponapean *meing* (or high language) that is used to convey respect when speaking to or of one's superiors. Finer distinctions of usage within honorific speech—such as what words should be used when addressing a holder of a particular traditional political title—are not specified by this label. Occasionally such distinctions are indicated in the definition, but a complete and accurate description of honorific speech awaits further research.

POLITE. This term is used to label headwords that are not part of the honorific system, but are used in formal situations in place of words that might be considered common or vulgar.

SLANG. This label is used for headwords or usages that are not regarded as standard, but are commonly employed in informal contexts. Such words or usages are often short-lived, but some become part of the common vocabulary.

A few users of an earlier draft of this dictionary have suggested that certain headwords should be excluded because they are vulgar. Following the advice of the Ponapean Orthography Committee, such headwords have not been omitted. Further, the label *vulgar* has not been employed, since meaningful criteria for such a label must almost always be based upon contextual usage, rather than intrinsic meaning.

(4) **Grammatical Labels.** Every Ponapean entry contains a label printed in italics that specifies the grammatical function of the headword. The abbreviations and conventions used for these labels are described below. Definitions for all the grammatical terms used in these labels may be found by consulting the index of the PRG.

Nouns

n.   noun

n (3s: _____).   noun that may occur with possessive suffixes

The form of the noun enclosed in parentheses and preceded by *3s:* is the third person singular form of the possessed noun. For example, the headword *mahs* is labeled *n(3s: mese)*; *mahs* means 'face' and *mese* means 'his, her, or its face'. Native speakers consider the third person singular form of nouns of this class to be the basic possessed form.

n3s.   noun that always occurs with possessive suffixes

The headword is given in the third person singular form, but 'his, her, or its' is not included in the definition. For example, *sepe* is labeled n3s and is defined as 'cheek', not as 'his, her, or its cheek'.

poss. cl.   possessive classifier

The headword is given in the third person singular form, except for the two common classifiers *ah* and *nah*, for which all possessed forms are entered as headwords.

prep. n.   prepositional noun

The headword is given in the third person singular form or in a bound form.

rel. n.   relational noun

The headword is given in a bound form.

Verbs

adj.   adjective

vi.   intransitive verb

Active and resultative distinctions for these verbs are specified by the nature of the definition. Therefore, the active intransitive verb *mwenge* is translated 'to eat' while the resultative intransitive verb *lop* is translated 'to be cut'.

vi. neut.   neutral intransitive verb

Neutral intransitive verbs are defined in their active form. They may also occur with a resultative meaning. Therefore, the verb *les* is defined 'to split', but it may also mean 'to be split'.

vt.	transitive verb
Pronouns	
pron.	pronoun
ind. pron.	independent pronoun
obj. pron.	object pronoun
subj. pron.	subject pronoun
Numerals	
num.	numeral
num. cl.	numeral classifier
Demonstratives	
dem.	demonstrative
	These words are identified as pointing demonstratives in the PRG.
dem. mod.	demonstrative modifier
dem. pron.	demonstrative pronoun
Prepositions	
prep.	preposition
Conjunctions	
conj.	conjunction
Interrogatives	
interr.	interrogative
Negators	
neg.	negator
Adverbs	
adv.	adverb
conj. adv.	conjunctive adverb
sent. adv.	sentence adverb
Interjections	
interj.	interjection
Affixes	
aff.	affix
verb. pref.	verbal prefix
verb. suff.	verbal suffix

Several additional grammatical labels are employed in this work but, because of their very low frequency, they have been written out in full and involve no special conventions.

(5) **Definitions.** Definitions or glosses of headwords are given in English and printed in roman type. Since words from different languages rarely have precisely equivalent meanings, the range of meaning of a Ponapean headword may be conveyed by listing several English words. For example,

the headword *ahlap* is defined 'bulky, stocky, thick, large in girth'. When
the meaning of a headword can easily be divided into several related meanings, these meanings are separated by semicolons. Therefore, *ketihnain* is
defined 'to revitalize, to nourish; to augment, as a point in an argument'. In
such definitions the most frequently encountered meaning of the headword
is listed first, with less common meanings following. Definitions may also
include cross references to other entries that will be useful in helping the
user understand the headword in question. Thus, the headword *emen* is
defined 'one; see *men₃*'. Under *men₃*, additional information will be found
about the use of the numeral *emen*.

(6) **Phrase or Sentence Examples.** Ponapean phrase or sentence examples
are included in some entries to illustrate the meaning or grammatical function of the headword. These examples are printed in italics and are followed
by English translations printed in roman type, as illustrated below.

Headword	Phrase or Sentence Example
-long	*alu* walk, *aluhlong* walk into
kai-	*Kaido dahlen.* Move the dish toward me.

To limit the size and consequently the cost of this dictionary, the use of
phrase and sentence examples has largely been restricted to headwords that
occur in a bound form, or to those in which such examples are important in
understanding the usage of the headword.

(7) **Loan Sources.** The names of source languages for borrowed words are
printed in roman type and are enclosed within square brackets; for example, [Eng.]. Language names rarely employed in this work are written out in
full. The names of the four common source languages are abbreviated as
follows:

Eng.	English
Ger.	German
Jap.	Japanese
Span.	Spanish

When the source of a word believed to be borrowed is unknown, a question
mark is used. When the source of a borrowed word is uncertain, the name
of the probable source language is followed by a question mark, as [Eng.?].
A word borrowed into Ponapean from a language which in turn borrowed
the word from another Ponapean source language is labeled as follows:

Headword	Loan Source
ampangia	[Jap.<Eng.]
komi	[Jap.<Ger.]

Thus, the word *ampangia* 'umpire' was borrowed into Ponapean from
Japanese, which in turn borrowed the word from English. The left-pointing
wedge (<) may thus be read as 'borrowed from'. A left-pointing wedge may

also be used to signal that part of a headword has been borrowed from another language, as in the following examples.

Headword	Loan Source
mahlenih	[*mahlen*<Ger.]
pepen kairu	[*kairu*<Jap.]

Mahlen 'to paint or to draw' was borrowed from German, but it occurs in the headword above in combination with the Ponapean transitive suffix *-ih*. Note that within the loan source label, loan words are spelled as they occur in Ponapean, not in the source language.

(8) **Cross-References.** Entries wherein the headword is grammatically labeled as a verb (*adj.*, *vi.*, *vi. neut.*, or *vt.*) may end with a cross-reference to another related verb form. For example, if the headword is an intransitive verb and it has a related transitive form, that transitive form will be cross-referenced at the end of the entry. Cross-references may also be made to the adjectival or intransitive forms of a headword that is a transitive verb. These cross-referenced verb forms are preceded by a dash, are printed in boldface type, and are followed by a comma and a label that identifies the grammatical function of the related form. For example:

> **audaud** *vi.* To be filled, to be loaded. —**aude**, *vt.*
> **aude** *vt.* To fill, to load. —**audaud**, *vi.*

Only the grammatical labels *adj.*, *vi.*, and *vt.* are used after these cross-referenced forms. Whether a cross-referenced intransitive verb is active, resultative, or neutral may be determined by looking at the main entry for that verb.

While it is rare for an entry to contain all eight kinds of information described above, many entries are divided into subentries, each of which may contain separate alternate forms, usage labels, grammatical labels, definitions, and phrase and sentence examples. Examples of entries divided into subentries follow.

Example 1.	**engieng 1.** *adj.* Windy. **2.** HON-ORIFIC. *adj.* Angry. —**angi-angih**, *vt.*
Example 2.	**irail 1.** also **re.** *subj. pron.* They, plural. **2.** also **ihr**$_1$. *ind. pron.* They, plural.
Example 3.	**dakadopi**, also **daka. 1.** *vi.* To high jump. **2.** *n.* High Jump. [Jap.]

Note that each subentry is numbered. Information presented before numbered subentries may be interpreted as being applicable to all subentries. Therefore, in example 3, *daka* is an acceptable alternate form of *dakadopi* both when it is being used as a noun and as a verb. In example 2, however, the alternate form *re* is possible only as a subject pronoun, and *ihr* only as an independent pronoun. Loan source information, as in example 3, is applicable to the entire entry. Cross-references, as in example 1, are always given at the end of the entry, regardless of the number of subentries.

1.3 Locating Affixed Words

Ponapean is a language in which it is possible to form thousands of new words from a single root word through the use of prefixes, suffixes, and reduplication. In most cases, however, it is possible to understand the meanings of these new words if one knows the meaning of the root word and the individual affixes. For example, a word like *doudi* 'to climb down' can be easily understood as a combination of the meanings of the verb *dou* 'to climb' and suffix *-di* 'down'. Thus, for purposes of economy, a decision was made by the compilers of this work to include root words and affixes, but generally to exclude affixed words with predictable meanings. The verb *dou* is consequently included in this work, and so is the suffix *-di*, but the word *doudi* is not.

This practice does not mean that root words in combination with affixes are never included in this dictionary. In a few instances affixed words with predictable meanings are entered because of their extremely high frequency. Root words in combination with affixes are regularly included in this work when (1) the addition of the affix results in an unpredictable meaning, (2) the potential of the root word to combine with a particular affix is unpredictable, or (3) the root word always occurs in combination with a particular affix. Therefore, a verb like *rukihdi* is included as a headword, since its meaning 'to ambush, to catch in the act' cannot be accurately predicted from the combined meanings of *rukih* 'to peep' and *-di* 'down'. A transitive verb such as *deiadih* 'to embroider' is entered since it is not possible to predict that the intransitive form of this verb, *deiad*, may combine with the transitive suffix *-ih*. And, a verb like *koasoandi* 'to be organized' is entered with the suffix *-di*, because this verb always occurs in combination with this affix.

A consequence of not listing affixed words with predictable meanings is that many words a user might ordinarily encounter in speech or in writing are not listed as headwords in this dictionary. To be able to locate the root words, it is therefore necessary that the user be familiar with Ponapean processes of affixation. A detailed account of affixation in Ponapean is given in the PRG, and most Ponapean affixes are listed separately in this dictionary. A brief summary of the common affixes of Ponapean is also included here as a reference for recognizing affixed words.

Reduplication. Reduplication involves the complete or partial repetition of a word. It is used productively in Ponapean to signal durative aspect. Examples of eleven common patterns of reduplication are listed below.

Root Word	Root Word Reduplicated
lal	lallal
pa	pahpa
el	elehl
ahn	aiahn
wal	wewal
duhp	duduhp
alu	alialu
liahn	lihliahn
luhmwuhmw	luluhmwuhmw
mmwus	mmwummwus
siped	sipisiped

Prefixes. Six common prefixes are employed in Ponapean. These are listed below for quick reference in locating root words. An entry for each of these prefixes is given in the dictionary.

Prefixes

ak-	sa-
ka-	sou-$_1$
li-	sou-$_2$

Suffixes. Twenty-nine suffixes are listed below. As with the prefixes, a full entry for each of these suffixes is given in the dictionary.

Suffixes

-ehng or -ieng	-long
-ehr or -ier	-n$_1$
-ie$_1$	-n$_2$
-ie$_2$	-niki
-iei	-nge
-ira	-pe
-irail	-pene
-iuk or -uhk	-peseng
-ki	-sang
-kit	-seli
-kita	-da
-kitail	-di
-kumwa	-do
-kumwail	-wei
-la	

For a discussion of the possessive pronoun suffixes, not listed in the preceding chart, see chapter 4 of the PRG.

Enclitics. In addition to the affixes listed above, four enclitics are also conventionally written attached to the word they follow. These are:

-et or -e	-o
-en	-te

Introduction

2.0 Ponapean Orthography

Ponapean has been written for well over one-hundred years. Out of this experience has evolved a relatively systematic spelling system. However, as anyone who has had occasion to read or write Ponapean knows, many areas of indecision concerning the spelling of this language still remain. In an effort to deal with these problems, a Ponapean Orthography Workshop was organized in 1972 under the auspices of the Trust Territory government and the Pacific and Asian Linguistics Institute of the University of Hawaii.

The initial meeting of this workshop was conducted in Kolonia, Ponape. Participating were Paulino Cantero, Godaro Gallen, Linter Hebel, Santiago Joab, Ewalt Joseph, Pensile Laurence, Martiniano Rodriguez, and Leonard Santos. Attending as consultants were Harold Hanlin, Kenneth Rehg, and Damian Sohl. The outcome of this first workshop was a set of tentative recommendations regarding spelling practices for Ponapean. The practical implications of these recommendations were studied for one year and, in 1973, a majority of the above-named participants met again in consultation with Harold Hanlin, William McGarry, and Damian Sohl to draft a final set of spelling recommendations. That set of recommendations has served as the basis for the spelling procedures employed both in this work and in the PRG. Details are presented in the PRG, but for the convenience of the user, those recommendations serving as the basis for the alphabet employed in this work are summarized here.

2.1 Dialect Considerations

Ponapean has traditionally employed a basically *phonemic* writing system—that is, with a few exceptions, one symbol is used to represent one sound. The way words are spelled, therefore, mirrors the way they are pronounced. One difficulty with this procedure, however, is that the pronunciation of words in Ponapean sometimes varies from one area of the island to another. One question that faced the participants in the orthography workshop was which dialect would serve as a standard for spelling, or if indeed any standard at all should be established.

How much dialect variation actually exists in Ponapean has never been fully studied. However, as previously pointed out, two major dialects are easily recognized—the Kiti and the Northern. These two dialects are distinguished from each other primarily on the basis of their vowel systems. In the Northern dialect, a distinction is made between the vowels /e/ (as in /pel/ 'to steer a canoe') and /ɛ/ (as in /pɛl/ 'to be in a taboo relationship'). In the Kiti dialect, these two vowels are not distinctive. Therefore, it is impossible to find a pair of words where the difference between the vowels /e/ and /ɛ/ results in a difference in meaning. Further, many words that contain /ɛ/ in the Northern dialect are pronounced with the vowel /ɔ/ in the Kiti dialect. It is this characteristic distribution of vowels which most speakers of Ponapean recognize as being the distinguishing feature of the Kiti dialect. The remaining sounds of the two dialects are the same. (See section 2.6.7 of the PRG for further details.)

Since both dialects have served as standards for spelling in the past, and since neither may lay claim to being the prestige dialect of Ponapean, the selection of a spelling standard for Ponapean required careful consideration. Three alternatives were explored. The first was to employ one symbol that could variously stand for /ɛ/ in the Northern dialect and /ɔ/ in the Kiti dialect, to be used in those words where there was dialect variation. The second was to allow all speakers of Ponapean to spell in accordance with their own pronunciation, and the third was to select one of the two dialects as a standard.

The first alternative was rejected because it had been unsuccessfully tried before. The second alternative, which would allow all speakers to write words as they pronounce them, was also rejected because the committee felt that to accept this solution would be to abandon the goal of standardization. Alternative three remained, and the Northern dialect was chosen as the standard. The most important reason for choosing the Northern dialect was that the majority of Ponapeans speak this dialect. In accordance with this recommendation, then, the spellings in this dictionary mirror Northern pronunciation. More specifically, Kolonia area pronunciation has usually served as the model.

2.2 The Alphabet

The alphabet recommended by the workshop participants employs twenty symbols—sixteen single letters and four digraphs. These symbols are listed in Ponapean alphabetical order below.

a e i o oa u h k l m mw n ng p pw r s d t w

It should be noted that this alphabet, or one similar to it, had already gained widespread acceptance prior to the time the workshop was held. It represents a synthesis of at least six alphabetic traditions in Ponape.

A guide to the sounds (or phonemes) these symbols represent is given in the following chart. The symbols of the alphabet are listed in column one. The phonetic norms of the sounds represented by the symbols are described in column two, and example words containing these symbols are listed in column three.

Symbol	Description	Example
a	[a] low central unrounded vowel	kak
e	[e] mid front unrounded vowel	esil
	or	
	[ɛ] lower-mid front unrounded vowel	med
i	[i] high front unrounded vowel	ni
	or	
	[y] high front glide	iahd
o	[o] mid back rounded vowel	rong

oa	[ɔ] lower-mid back rounded vowel	*oa*le
u	[u] high back rounded vowel	pw*u*ng
	or	
	[w] high back glide	dah*u*
h	[:] signals vowel length	a*h*, e*h*, i*h*,
		o*h*, oa*h*, u*h*
k	[k] unaspirated voiceless velar stop	*k*a*k*
l	[l] voiced dental lateral	*l*aid
m	[m] voiced bilabial nasal	*m*e
mw	[mʷ] velarized voiced bilabial nasal	*mw*ein
n	[n] voiced dental nasal	*n*ih
ng	[ŋ] voiced velar nasal	*ng*ih
p	[p] unaspirated voiceless bilabial stop	*p*eh
pw	[pʷ] unaspirated velarized voiceless	
	bilabial stop	*pw*ihn
r	[ř] voiced alveolar trill	*r*ahn
s	[sʸ] palatalized voiceless	
	alveolar fricative	*s*ahpw
d	[t] unaspirated voiceless dental stop	*d*uhp
t	[ʈ] voiceless retroflexed affricate	*t*ih*t*i
w	[w] high back glide	*w*ini

Note that:

1) The letter *e* is used to represent both /e/ and /ɛ/. Therefore, /seysey/ and /sɛysɛy/ are both spelled *seisei*. Since such ambiguous spellings are comparatively rare, and since these two sounds do not contrast in Kiti speech, it was recommended that both these sounds be spelled *e*.

2) The letters *i* and *u* are used to represent both vowels and glides. This practice is a long-standing one in Ponapean. The procedures for writing and reading these glides was outlined at the workshop as follows:

a) /y/ is always written *i*. In reading, whenever *i* is (1) preceded by a vowel or *h*, or (2) is at the beginning of a word and is followed by a vowel, it represents /y/. Elsewhere it represents /i/.

b) /w/ is written *w* before vowels and *u* elsewhere. In reading, *u* represents /w/ after vowels or *h*. Elsewhere it represents /u/.

It now seems clear, however, that these spelling principles are based on an oversimplified analysis of Ponapean glides and that, in some cases in word final position, the letters *i* and *u* ambiguously represent both vowels and glides. For a further discussion of this problem see section 2.7.3 of the PRG.

3) Ponapean consonants may occur doubled. In this case they are written as they are pronounced, except that /mwmw/ is written *mmw*. By analogy, /mwpw/ is written *mpw*.

3.0 About this Dictionary
Since this work represents only an intermediate step toward the goal of producing a comprehensive dictionary of Ponapean, it is important that the

user know something about the way it was prepared. The aims of the dictionary and the sources of information it is based on need to be examined to understand what the compilers have tried to accomplish, and, more importantly, what they have left unaccomplished.

3.1 The Aims of the Dictionary

The principal aim of this work is to present an accurate and economical account of the major lexical facts of Ponapean. Therefore, while an attempt has been made to include at least all the commonly used root words and affixes in Ponapean, the number of entries has been a less important consideration than their nature and quality. Certain types of entries have been deliberately excluded. As previously stated, affixed words with predictable meanings are left out, and so are personal names, place names, and most foreign words that have not been fully assimilated into the language. It may be useful to include some entries of these types in future dictionaries, but the immediate purpose of this work is to provide reliable information on the core vocabulary of Ponapean.

A second aim is to provide a linguistic document that, in conjunction with the PRG, will be of use to educators in Ponape. Hopefully, both of these volumes will have value as reference works in designing Ponapean language arts programs. To a lesser extent, they should also prove to be useful in programs for teaching English in Ponape. Additionally, these works may be beneficial to English-speaking students of Ponapean and to scholars of other Pacific languages and cultures.

A final aim is to stimulate interest in the continuation of the dictionary-making process for Ponapean. Many Ponapeans have expressed considerable interest in this work, and some have assisted in its preparation. It is hoped that, as a consequence of circulating this volume in the Ponapean community, still others will be willing to contribute to a second and improved edition.

3.2 Sources of Information

The major source for the information included in this dictionary has been the spoken language. Most of the data came from elicitation sessions with native speakers. Informal conversations and tape recordings of legends, narratives, and radio broadcasts were also monitored for new vocabulary.

The dictionaries of Gulick, Cantero, and Burdick, cited in the Preface, were a second major source of information. Although some of the entries in these dictionaries did not meet the criteria for inclusion in this work, many did, and the compilers owe a great debt to the labors of their predecessors. Also of considerable assistance was a large file of Ponapean words compiled by past employees of the Ponape Department of Education.

Articles and books on Ponape written by other scholars also proved to be of value in this compilation. Three studies were especially valuable. Most of the plant names came from Sydney F. Glassman's book, *The Flora of*

Ponape (Honolulu: Bishop Museum Press, 1952). Many terms relating to traditional Ponapean culture came from Saul H. Riesenberg's *Native Polity of Ponape* (Washington, D.C.: Smithsonian Institution Press, 1968), and some of the honorific vocabulary came from Paul L. Garvin and Saul H. Riesenberg's article "Respect Behavior on Ponape: An Ethnolinguistic Study" (*American Anthropologist* 54[2]. Part 1 [201–220].). Publication details of other works consulted in the preparation of both this dictionary and the grammar are listed in the bibliography of the PRG.

To insure the quality of the data collected from all sources, every potential entry in this dictionary was checked by at least two native speakers. Information reported by one speaker or one written source that could not be further verified was excluded. When conflicting information was given, additional speakers were consulted. In all cases, preference was given to the way speakers actually used the language, as opposed to how they thought it should be used. In this respect, descriptive rather than prescriptive accuracy has been the guiding principle in the preparation of this dictionary.

CHART OF ABBREVIATIONS AND SYMBOLS

adj.	adjective
adv.	adverb
aff.	affix
conj.	conjunction
conj. adv.	conjunctive adverb
dem.	demonstrative
dem. mod.	demonstrative modifier
dem. pron.	demonstrative pronoun
Eng.	English
Ger.	German
ind. pron.	independent pronoun
interj.	interjection
interr.	interrogative
Jap.	Japanese
n.	noun
neg.	negator
num.	numeral
num. cl.	numeral classifier
obj. pron.	object pronoun
poss. cl.	possessive classifier
prep.	preposition
prep. n.	prepositional noun
pron.	pronoun
rel. n.	relational noun
sent. adv.	sentence adverb
Span.	Spanish
subj. pron.	subject pronoun
verb. pref.	verbal prefix
verb. suff.	verbal suffix
vi.	intransitive verb
vi. neut.	neutral intransitive verb
vt.	transitive verb
3s	third person singular
<	'borrowed from'

PONAPEAN-ENGLISH DICTIONARY

A

ah₁ *n.* Name of the letter *a*.

ah₂, also e₂. *poss. cl.* His, her, its; third person singular form of the general possessive classifier.

ah₃ *conj.* However, and. *I sukuhl ah e doadoahk.* I went to school and he worked.

ah₄ *n.* Shark mullet, at a growth stage of approximately twelve inches.

ah₅ *interj.* Oh!; often used as an expression of approval.

ahi₁ *n.* Fire.

ahi₂, also ei₁. *poss. cl.* My; see *ah₂*.

ahia, also iahia. *n.* Rainbow.

aiau *n.* Banyan tree, *Ficus carolinensis*, used in the treatment of tetanus and as a hemostatic in menstruation.

aio *n.* Yesterday.

aikiu 1. *vi. neut.* To ration. 2. *n.* Ration. [Jap.] —aikiuih, *vt.*

aikiuih *vt.* To ration. [Jap.] —aikiu, *vi.*

ain₁ 1. *n.* An iron. 2. *vi. neut.* To iron clothing. [Eng.] —aine or ainih, *vt.*

ain₂ *n.* Handcuff, shackle. [Eng.]

aine, also ainih. *vt.* To iron. [*ain*<Eng.] —ain₁, *vi.*

ainih₁ *vt.* See *aine*.

ainih₂ *vt.* To handcuff. —ainpene, *vi.*

ainoko *n.* Half-caste. [Jap.]

ainkot, also angkot. *n.* Strand, as of sennit, hair, etc..

ainpene *vi.* To be handcuffed. —ainih₂, *vt.*

ainpwoat 1. *n.* Cooking pot. 2. *vi.* To prepare food in a pot; to prepare a small informal feast or party. [Eng.] —ainpwoate, *vt.*

ainpwoate *vt.* See *ainpwoat*.

aip 1. *n.* Drum. 2. *vi.* To play the drum.

air *vt.* To draw out, to pull out, of any string-like object.

airas, also aida. *vi.* To drop into a hole, of a marble in the game *anaire*. [Jap.]

ais₁ *n.* Tree sp., *Parinarium glaberrimum*, used for poles, paint, and caulking canoes; medicine taken before eating food prepared by another to avoid the effects of magic.

ais₂ *n.* Ice. [Eng.]

aisara *n.* Ash tray. [Jap.]

aiso *n.* Food cabinet. [Jap.]

aiskehki *n.* Popsicle, frozen confection. [Jap.<Eng.]

aiskurihm *n.* Ice cream. [Eng.]

aispiring *n.* Aspirin. [Jap.<Ger.]

aispwoakus *n.* See *aispwoaks*.

aispwoaks, also aispwoakus. *n.* Icebox, refrigerator. [Eng.]

aida, also airas. *vi.* To drop into a hole, of a marble in the game *anaire*. [Jap.]

au *adj.* Of an *uhmw*, to be reduced to glowing coals.

ahu *n (3s: ewe)*. Mouth.

aulaud *adj.* Given to exaggeration, loud mouthed, boisterous.

auleng₁ *n.* Grass sp., *Curcuma sp.*.

auleng₂ *n.* Water taken on a trip.

aulikamw *adj.* Lying, untruthful.

aumat 1. *adj.* Bad breathed. 2. SLANG. *interj.* An insult, You have bad breath!

aun, also oun. *num.* Six; see *ehd*.

aupah *n3s.* Jaw, of an animal.

aupwal 1. *vi.* To have a harelip. 2. *n.* Harelip.

aupwahpw *adj.* Toothless.

aupwet 1. *adj.* Scarred around the mouth by yaws. 2. *n.* A scar by the mouth caused by yaws.

ausaledek *adj.* Employing gross or inappropriate speech, speaking openly of sex, usually said of women.

auselpat 1. *adj.* Scarred severely around the mouth by yaws. 2. *n.* A large scar by the mouth caused by yaws.

ausuwed *adj.* Displaying crude speech manners, foulmouthed.

aud *vi.* To be out, in baseball. [Eng.]

audaud *vi.* To be filled, to be loaded; to know almost everything. —aude, *vt.*

audapan *adj.* Capacious, holding a lot; knowledgeable.

aude *vt.* To fill, to load. —audaud, *vi.*

audepe *n3s.* Content, subject matter.

audokahp *n.* Outside curve, in baseball. [Jap.<Eng.]

audsapahl *vi.* To refill; to start over, as in the preparation of kava. —**audsapahlih**, *vt.*

audsapahlih *vt.* See *audsapahl.*

ak- *verb. pref.* A prefix meaning to demonstrate or demonstrating. *lemei* cruelty, *aklemei* demonstrating cruelty.

ahk₁ *n.* Mangrove sp.; hoe or any implement for digging; pointed piece of mangrove used for husking coconuts.

ahk₂ *interj.* An expression of disgust.

aka₁, also ka₁, akat, or kat. *dem. mod.* These, by me.

aka₂ *num.* One; see *ka₂.*

ahka *interj.* Of course!

akau, also kau₂. *dem. mod.* Those, away from you and me.

akahk *vt.* To demonstrate, to act as if. *E akahk me e kommwad.* He demonstrated that he was brave.

akamai 1. *vi.* To argue, to quarrel. 2. *n.* Argument, quarrel, dispute.

akan, also kan. *dem. mod.* Those, by you.

akap *num.* One; see *kap.*

akapa *n.* Mangrove sp., *Rhizophora apiculata*; often used in the building of a feasthouse.

akadahn, also kaladahn or lakadahn. *n.* A variety of banana. [Tagalog]

akat, also aka₁, kat, or ka₁. *dem. mod.* These, by me.

akatantat *vi.* To abhor.

akelel *n.* Mangrove sp., *Rhizophora mucronata.*

aker- *vt.* To move a group of things. *Akerodo mwangas akan.* Move the coconuts here.

akerpene *vt.* To gather.

akedei 1. *n.* A throwing contest. 2. *vi.* To engage in a throwing contest.

ahki *conj.* Because, because of, in answer to a question. *Dahme ke pwandiki? Ahki e keteu.* Why were you late? Because it rained.

Ahkos, also Oakos. *n.* August. [Eng.]

akuh *adj.* Boastful.

akupwung *adj.* Petty, desirous of being correct at all times, disagreeable.

akupwungki *vt.* To complain about the unfairness of something; to resent something, as a critism or a jest taken seriously.

akutuhwahu *adj.* Proud, competitive, unwilling to be humbled.

akka *interj.* An exclamation of pleasant surprise.

aklapalap *adj.* Proud, self-assertive, cocky.

akmanaman 1. *vi.* To make a display of magic, spiritual power, or authority. 2. *n.* A display of magic, spiritual power, or authority; a trick, as a card trick.

akpapah *adj.* Polite.

aksuwei *adj.* Boastful.

aktikitik *adj.* Humble, unassuming, meek.

ahl₁ *n.* Road, street, trail, path, line.

ahl₂ *n.* Fish sp., wahoo, *Acanthocybium solander.*

alahl *adj.* Striped.

alahldi *vi.* To be taken or gotten. —**ale**, *vt.*

ahlap *adj.* Bulky, stocky, thick, large in girth. *Lukopen Souliko me ahlap.* Soulik has a large waist.

alasang *vt.* To copy, to imitate.

alasapw 1. *vi.* To conquer; to play the game *alasapw.* 2. *n.* A game, similar to steal-the-flag.

ale *vt.* To take or get. —**alahldi**, *vi.*

ahlek *n.* Reed sp., *Saccharum spontaneum*, used as a building material and for medicinal purposes.

alem *num.* Five; see *ehd.*

alemengi *adj.* Said of one who copies or imitates fashions or behavior. —**alemengih**, *vt.*

alemengih *vt.* To copy, to imitate, to mimic, to learn from. —**alemengi**, *adj.*

alesop *n.* Side path, a small path off the main one.

alehdi *vt.* To be awarded or to receive votes, a degree, title, etc.; to have sexual intercourse with.

alis *n (3s: elise).* Beard, mustache.

alu *vi.* To walk.

aluhmwur 1. *vi.* To formally acknowledge the presence of visitors, done as a respect gesture by individuals travelling after or with the recipients. 2. *n.* The name of the associated feast. —**aluhmwurih**, *vt.*

aluhmwurih *vt.* See *aluhmwur.*

aluweluwe HONORIFIC. *n3s.* Leg.

alkeniken *adj.* Said of one who tries to exalt himself by flattering or presenting gifts to his superiors.

allap *n.* Main road, usually one for vehicular traffic.

alminiom *n.* Aluminum. [Eng.]

aldo *vi.* To sing alto. [Eng.]

ahm *n.* Slip noose or snare for catching animals.

ama, also ahmwe. *n.* Hammer. [Eng.]

amas *adj.* Raw, uncooked; sober.

ahmen *interj.* Amen. [Eng.]

Amerika *n.* America, United States of America. [Eng.]

ami *n.* Screen. [Jap.]

ampaia, also ampangia. *n.* Umpire. [Jap.<Eng.]

ampangia, also ampaia. *n.* Umpire. [Jap.<Eng.]

amper *n.* Umbrella. [Eng.]

ahmw₁, also liahmw or omwinwel. *n.* A tiny flying insect, commonly found in the forest.

ahmw₂, also omw. *poss. cl.* Your, singular; see *ah₂.*

amwa *poss. cl.* Your, dual; see *ah₂.*

amwail *poss. cl.* Your, plural; see *ah₂.*

ahmwadang *n.* Food or kava served prior to a formal meal or kava ceremony.

ahmwe, also ama. *n.* Hammer. [Eng.]

amwer *vt.* To crumple, to wrinkle. —emwirek, *adj.*

amweredi *vt.* To pick, pull, or cut down in entirety. —emwiemwidi, *vi.*

amwin *vt.* To wash one's hands. —emwiemw, *vi.*

amwise *n.* Mosquito.

ahn₁ *vt.* To be used to or accustomed to. *I ahn mwohd nantat.* I'm used to sitting on the floor.

ahn₂ *interj.* Well then?, Then what?, So what?

anaire 1. *n.* Japanese marble game, the object of which is to shoot a marble in proper order into five holes. 2. *vi.* To play this game. [Jap.]

anahn 1. *adj.* Necessary, indispensable. 2. *n.* Need. —anahne, *vt.*

anahne *vt.* To need, to require. —anahn, *adj.*

anapi *n.* Firecracker. [Jap.]

ahne *vt.* To heed, to pay attention to, to agree with.

ahnek *vi.* To have a boyfriend or girlfriend.

ahnepe *n3s.* Custom, way of doing things.

anien *n.* Onion. [Eng.]

aniket *vi.* To take pleasure in seeing one receive his comeuppance. —aniketih, *vt.*

aniketih *vt.* See *aniket.*

ahniki *vt.* To own, to have, used with nouns occurring with the classifier *ah.*

anihn *n.* The bitter part of a clam, used for medicine; the black part of the spider conch, believed to be poisonous.

ansou *n.* Time, a period of time. *Mie ansou sohla keteu Pohnpei.* There was a time when there was no rain in Ponape. *I kilele oh ansowohte e mwekid.* I took his picture and at that very moment he moved.

ansu *n.* Tree sp., star fruit tree. [Jap.]

andasiro 1. *vi.* To throw underhanded. 2. *n.* In baseball, an underhand pitch. [Jap.<Eng.]

andehna *n.* Antenna. [Eng.]

ahng₁ 1. *n.* Air, wind. 2. HONORIFIC. *n.* Message from the *Nahnmwarki.*

ahng₂ *vt.* To pass along physical objects from one person to another. *Menlau ahngodo mahs soahlen.* Please pass me the salt.

ahng₃ *vt.* To pay attention to; to take another's speech or actions seriously. *Ke dehr ahngada e koasoi, pwe e me likamw.* Don't pay attention to what he says, because he is lying.

angahng *adj.* Gigantic, spacious.

anged *adj.* Long, tall.

angiangih HONORIFIC. *vt.* To be angry at, to scold. —engieng, *adj.*

angiangin *adj.* Energetic.

angkasi *n.* Handkerchief. [Jap.<Eng.]

angke *n.* Anchor. [Eng.]

angkehlail 1. *vi.* To take by force; to rape. 2. *adj.* Said of one who shows off his power or strength.

angkesip *n.* Handkerchief. [Eng.]

angkot, also ainkot. *n.* Strand, as of sennit, hair, etc..

apa *num.* One; see *pa₃.*

apak *num.* One; see *pak₁.*

ahpako *n.* Fish sp., shark mullet.

apali *num.* One; see *pali₁.*

apalipeseng *vi.* To be divided into groups or sections.

apar *num.* One; see *par₂*.

ahpada *vi.* To become pregnant.

apadopi 1. *n.* Broadjump, longjump. 2. *vi.* To broadjump, to longjump. [Jap.]

ape₁ 1. *n.* Thing; etcetera. 2. *interj.* Hey you!

ape₂ *vi.* To cause or perform some action or motion; to have sexual intercourse. —**apehne**, *vt.*

ape- HONORIFIC. *vi.* To come or go. *Komw apehdo.* Come here.

apel *n.* Tree sp., mountain apple, *Syzygium malaccense; apple.* [Eng.]

apehne *vt.* To cause or perform some action or motion; to repair, to fix; to have sexual intercourse with. —**ape₂**, *vi.*

apere HONORIFIC. *n3s.* Shoulder.

apehdo *n.* In Net, the titles from eight down in the *Nahnmwarki* line and from six down in the *Nahnken* line.

apih *vt.* To pull something, usually with a rope. —**ep**, *vi.*

apin SLANG. *vt.* To spank or beat.

apis *n.* Outrigger support, extending from the side of the hull to the ends of the outrigger.

apid *vt.* To carry on one's side, to carry under one's arm. —**epid**, *vi.*

apkahs *n.* Half-caste. [Eng.]

apw *conj. adv.* And then; really. *Irail doadoahk lao nek, irail apw kohla Kolonia.* They worked until finished, and then they went to Kolonia. *I apw pahn men iang.* I really would like to come.

ahpw *conj.* But. *I men kang kehp, ahpw sohte nei kehp.* I want to eat yam, but I don't have any.

apwal 1. *adj.* Difficult, hard, troublesome, impossible. 2. *n.* Hard times, difficulty. 3. *interj.* Used with *I en* to mean I'll be damned if.... *Apwal i en doadoahk.* I'll be damned if I'll work.

apwalih *vt.* To take care of.

apweda *interr.* What else? What other alternative is there? Why not? *Kitail pahn tuhweng ohlo? Apweda?* Are we going to meet that man? What else?

apwin *vt.* To wash one's face. —**epwinek**, *vi.*

apwid *n.* Tree sp., *Macaranga carolinensis*, used for medicinal purposes.

ahpwide, also **ahpwte**. *adv.* Used in combination with adjectives suffixed by *-la* to indicate that the quality described will be intensified. *Ke dehr mwenge laud, pwe ke pahn ahpwide mworouroula.* Don't eat a lot, because you will get even fatter.

apwraiasi *n.* A variety of palm. [Jap.]

ahpwte *adv.* See *ahpwide*.

ahpwtehn *adv.* Just, in a temporal sense. *E ahpwtehn kohdo.* He just came.

ahr₁, also **arail**. *poss. cl.* Their, plural; see *ah₂*.

ahr₂ *n.* Foul ball; foul, in any sport. [Jap.<Eng.]

ara₁ *poss. cl.* Their, dual; see *ah₂*.

ara₂ *num.* One; see *ra*.

arail, also **ahr₁**. *poss. cl.* Their, plural; see *ah₂*.

aramas *n.* People, person, human being, mankind.

aramas mwahl *n.* Commoner.

aramas sarawi *n.* Saint.

are, also **ari**. *num.* Two; see *ehd*.

arekarek *adj.* Gritty.

Arem *n.* Class of people of the past.

arehn sakau *n.* Second cup of kava in the kava ceremony.

arep *n.* Spear, arrow.

arepe, also **pwurien arepe**. *n.* Hibiscus pole, after the bark has been stripped.

arer, also **sikarer**. *vi.* To spray or blow inside, of windblown rain.

arewella *vi.* To return to the wild state, of animals.

ari, also **are**. *num.* Two; see *ehd*.

arih *vt.* To stir, to probe. —**erier**, *vi.*

arimaki *n.* Bellyband, sash. [Jap.]

aririh *vt.* To attend or serve a dignitary during a feast. —**erir**, *vi.*

ahrkohl *n.* Alcohol. [Jap.<Eng.]

ahs *n.* Ass, donkey. [Eng.]

asamwan *n.* Male turtle; male mangrove crab.

asapein *n.* Female turtle; female mangrove crab.

asi₁ *vi.* To sneeze.

asi₂ *n.* Chopsticks. [Jap.]

asimel *n.* Fish sp..

asiper *n.* Hair swirl, two of which are said to be the mark of a naughty child.

asmaki 1. *n.* Headband, worn to keep perspiration out of one's eyes. 2. *vi.* To wear a headband. [Jap.]

ahd₁ *n (3s: ede).* Name; noun.

ahd₂ *n.* Current.

ahd- *vi.* To drift, to flow. *Pihlo ahdodo paliet.* The water flowed towards this side.

adamwahu *adj.* Having a good reputation.

adamwahl *n.* A non-baptismal name.

adaru *adj.* Lucky; skillful as a batter in baseball. [Jap.]

adasi *vi.* To go barefoot. [Jap.]

adahd *vi. neut.* To sharpen, to put an edge on something. —**ede₂**, *vt.*

adi *n3s.* Vapor, smoke, mist.

adih *vt.* To take by force, of any kind. *Ke dehr adih naipen rehn serien.* Don't take that knife away from that child.

ahdin mehla *n.* The throes of death. *Ahdin mehla saikinte lel liho, ah re tepida mwahiei.* That woman hadn't yet reached the throes of death and they started wailing.

aditik *n.* Nickname, abbreviated name.

aditikih *vt.* To nickname.

adohl *n.* A variety of coconut palm, having nuts with a sweet, juicy husk.

ahdomour *adj.* Of a stream, rising and fast flowing.

adu *num.* Nine; see *ehd*.

adsuwed *adj.* Having a bad reputation.

Adwendo *n.* Advent. [Span.]

aht₁ *poss. cl.* Our, exclusive; see *ah₂*.

aht₂ *n.* Heart, in cards. [Eng.]

ata *poss. cl.* Our, dual; see *ah₂*.

atail *poss. cl.* Our, plural; see *ah₂*.

ataut *n.* Joist, the timber to which floorboards are attached.

ahtikitik *adj.* Thin, slender, of small girth.

ahtikitik en neh *n3s.* Area of the leg just above the ankle.

awa *n.* Hour. [Eng.]

awih *vt.* To wait.

awihala *vt.* To anticipate, to expect.

awihodo *vt.* To await.

E

e₁ *subj. pron.* He, she, it.

e₂, also **ah₂**. *poss. cl.* His, her, its; third person singular form of the general possessive classifier.

e₃ *interj.* What, in response to being called.

-e, also **-et**. *dem. mod.* This, by me. *pwihke* this pig.

eh₁ *n.* Name of the letter *e*.

eh₂ *n3s.* Liver.

eh₃ *interj.* A particle used after names of people when calling them.

eh₄ *interj.* An interjection signifying comprehension.

ei₁, also **ahi₂**. *poss. cl.* My; see *ah₂*.

ei₂ *sent. adv.* Yes.

eieri, also **eierima**. *interj.* An exclamation, used when one makes a mistake. [Jap.?]

eierima, also **eieri**. *interj.* An exclamation, used when one makes a mistake. [Jap.?]

eikek *vi.* To pout.

eiker *n.* Acre. [Eng.]

eilepe *n3s.* Midst, of an activity.

eimah *adj.* Uninhibited.

eimwolu HONORIFIC. **1.** *vi.* To be surprised, astonished, or shocked; to wonder. **2.** *n.* Amazement.

einiar *n.* Whirlwind; gust of wind containing rain.

eipahi **1.** *adj.* Walking with swinging hands. **2.** *vi.* A command during the pounding of kava to keep the rhythm going.

eirek *adj.* Pliant.

eirekpene *vi.* To shrink; to gather, as when a string is pulled in a piece of cloth.

eirekpeseng *vi.* To expand.

eis *num.* Seven; see *ehd*.

eisek *num.* Ten.

eisel *vi.* To gather *iol* vines to be used as training ropes for yams.

eidak **1.** *vi.* To have a serious case of asthma in which one gasps for breath. **2.** *n.* Serious case of asthma in which a person gasps for breath.

eidik *vi.* To throw an object so that it will skip, as on the surface of the water. —**eidikih**, *vt.*

eidikih *vt.* To skip an object at something. —**eidik**, *vi.*

ehu *num.* One; see *-u*.

ehk₁ *num.* Ten.

ehk₂ *interj.* Ouch, an exclamation of pain.

ekei₁ *num.* Some; several. *Ekei uht kau tikitik.* Some of those bananas are small.

ekei₂ *interj.* An interjection, often conveying a feeling of surprise or wonder; also used in a scolding or teasing manner.

eker *vt.* To call, to summon.

eki *n.* Fish sp., milkfish, *Chanos Chanos.*

ekiek *vi.* To be hidden or concealed. —**ekihla**, *vt.*

ekihla *vt.* To hide or conceal. —**ekiek**, *vi.*

ekipir *n.* Eave of a building.

Ekipten *n.* Egypt. [Eng.]

ekis **1.** *num.* One; see *kis₁*. **2.** *adv.* A bit. *Sehtet ekis mwerekirek.* This shirt is a bit wrinkled.

ektahr *n.* Hectare. [Eng.]

el₁ *vt.* To rub, to massage. —**eliel**, *vi.*

el₂ *num. cl.* Used in counting garlands. *elin kapwat pahiel* four garlands.

ehl₁ *n.* Garland; string of flowers or beads.

ehl₂ *num.* One; see *el₂*.

ehl₃ *n.* Hell. [Eng.]

ele₁ *vt.* To draw a line; to inscribe.

ele₂ *sent. adv.* Perhaps, maybe, possibly. *Ele e soumwahu.* Perhaps he is sick.

elen pillap *n.* Bed of a river.

elenwel **1.** *n.* Part, in the hair. **2.** *vi.* To part, of the hair.

elep *num.* Half, of objects divided horizontally or by their width; one; see *lep.*

eliel *vi.* To rub, to massage. —**el₁**, *vt.*

elielpaidoke HONORIFIC. *vt.* To hear.

eliman HONORIFIC. **1.** *vi.* To dream. **2.** *n.* Dream. —**elimene**, *vt.*

elimene HONORIFIC. *vt.* To dream about.
—**eliman**, *vi.*

elimoang *n.* Mangrove crab.

elin katieu *n.* The royal wreath placed on the head of a *Nahnmwarki* at his coronation.

elinpwur *n.* Garland of *pwuhr, Fagraea sair.*

elinge HONORIFIC. *n3s.* Voice, sound.

elingek, also **delingek**. *vi. neut.* To carry something requiring repeated trips, as numerous bags of copra. —**elingeki**, *vt.*

elingeki *vt.* See *elingek.*

elipant *n.* Elephant. [Eng.]

elipip *n.* Whirlwind, whirlpool.

elisenket *n.* Bush sp., *Orthosiphon stamineus.*

eliwahki *vt.* To confront.

eluwenpwong *vi.* To go out at night for the purpose of a sexual liaison.
—**eluenpwongih**, *vt.*

eluwenpwongih *vt.* See *eluenpwong.*

eluwentek *vi.* To waddle. [*tek*<Eng.]

emen *num.* One; see *men3.*

Eminalau Lapalap *n.* Title of the wife of a *Souwel Lapalap.*

emp1 *n.* Coconut crab.

emp2, also **omp**. *n.* Vine sp., *Ipomoea gracilis.*

empwoatol 1. *n.* A game in which one attempts to pick up a bottle with a nail tied to a line which is attached to a stick. 2. *vi.* To play this game. [*pwoatol*<Eng.]

emwih *n3s.* Bunch, of palm nuts.

emwiemw *vi.* To wash one's hands.
—**amwin**, *vt.*

emwiemwidi *vi.* To be picked, pulled, or cut down in entirely.
—**amweredi**, *vt.*

emwirek *adj.* Crumpled, wrinkled.
—**amwer**, *vt.*

emwodol *num.* One; see *mwodol.*

emwut *num.* One; see *mwut2.*

en1, also **-n1**. *construct particle.* Of; see *-n1.*

en2 *infinitive marker.* To be to. *Ohlo nda I en kohla.* That man said I am to go.

-en *dem. mod.* That, by you. *pwihken* that pig by you.

eni *n.* Ghost, usually considered malicious.

eni aramas *n.* Ancestral ghost.

eni lapalap *n.* Ancestral ghost of a *Nahnmwarki.*

enihep 1. *adj.* Mildewy, mildewed. 2. *n.* Mildew, stain caused by mildew.

enihwos *n.* Clan deity; ever-existing ghost.

ehnta *n.* Fish sp..

eng- *vi.* To reach for. *E engalahng uhpw akau.* He reached for the coconuts.

ehng *sent. adv.* Yeah, an informal affirmative response.

-ehng, also **-ieng**. *verb. suff.* To, toward, in relation to, for; This form of the suffix occurs after a verb root ending in a consonant. *nehk* to distribute, *nehkehng* to distribute to.

enge *n3s.* Chela, the claw of a crab, lobster, shrimp, etc..

engeir *n.* South wind, shifting wind, believed to bring bad weather.

engieng 1. *adj.* Windy. 2. HONORIFIC. *adj.* Angry. —**angiangih**, *vt.*

engila SLANG. *vi.* To die.

engimah *adj.* Windy with accompanying rough seas.

enginpar *n.* Trade wind.

engipip *n.* Whirlwind.

engida SLANG. *vi.* To spend the night with a woman.

engidek SLANG. *adj.* Gluttonous.

engidi SLANG. *vi.* To lie down.

engitik *adj.* Breezy, airy.

engk *n.* Landslide.

engkidi *vi.* To slide or fall, of a pile of non-living objects, as a landslide.

engmwahukihla *vt.* To take advantage of.

ep *vi.* To be pulled, usually with a rope.
—**apih**, *vt.*

epeng *num.* Four; see *ehd.*

epetik *n.* A small *ah*, a fish sp..

epiep 1. *vi.* To fish with line. 2. *n.* Line fishing.

epil *n.* Fish sp., goatfish, *Mulloidichthys vanicolensis.*

epini 1. *vi.* To jump rope; to engage in a tug-of-war. 2. *n.* A jump rope.

epid *vi.* To be carried on one's side, to be carried under one's arm. —**apid**, *vt.*

epidipe *vi.* To cross one's arms.

epit *num.* One; see *pit2.*

Epreil *n.* April. [Eng.]

epweh *n3s.* Customary manner.

epwel₁ *vi.* To be unable to sleep, to have insomnia.

epwel₂ *n.* Fish sp..

epwelseri *vi.* To baby-sit.

epwiki *num.* One hundred.

epwinek *vi.* To wash one's face. —apwin, *vt.*

epwidik *num.* A little bit of, a small piece of, a fragment of. *Kihdo kenei epwidik mwahmwen.* Give me my small piece of fish.

er *adj.* Thoroughly knowledgeable.

-ehr, also -ier. *verb. suff.* Used to signal perfective aspect; This form of the suffix occurs after a verb root ending in a consonant. *mwadong* play, *mwadongehr* have already played.

erala *vi.* To be concluded; to be ended.

eralahr *interj.* The end!

erein *prep. n.* During the time, for a period of, while, within a distance. *E wadengki pwuhko erein awa riau.* He read that book for a period of two hours. *Nan erein mwail riau sang Pohnpei, sohte sohpen Sapahn kak laid.* Within a distance of two miles from Ponape, no Japanese ship can fish..

ereki *vt.* To know thoroughly, to master.

erekiso HONORIFIC. *n.* Body, of a person.

eremen, also ieremen. *interj.* Forget it!, Better not!

eretik *adj.* Knowledgeable about many things.

eri 1. *sent. adv.* Well, then, thus. *Eri, ohlet mehla.* Well then, this man died. 2. *conj. adv.* Then, so. *I doadoahk lao nek oh ngehi eri kohla.* I worked until finished and then I went there. 3. *interj.* Enough!, Stop!

eria *interj.* I warned you!

erier *vi. neut.* To stir; to probe. —arih, *vt.*

erimeddo *n.* Helmet. [Jap.<Eng.]

ering₁ *n.* Ripe coconut, syn. with *mwangas.*

ering₂ HONORIFIC. *n.* Tooth.

eripit *adj.* Wise, knowledgeable.

erir 1. *vi.* To serve as a cup bearer in the drinking of kava. 2. *n (3s: erire).* Cup bearer. —aririh, *vt.*

eruwahn *vi.* To completely understand.

erpehs *vi.* To spread the stones of an *uhmw* too thin, so that the earth shows.

ehs₁ *interj.* An expression of much pain.

ehs₂ *n.* Ace, in cards. [Eng.]

ese *vt.* To know, to understand.

esel *num.* One; see *sel₂.*

eseng HONORIFIC. *n.* Tooth.

esil *num.* Three; see *ehd; third cup of kava in the kava ceremony.*

esingek 1. *vi.* To breathe. 2. *n.* Breath.

esingekida *vi.* To breathe a sigh of relief.

esou *num.* One; see *sou₄.*

eskorpion *n.* Scorpion. [Span.]

esse *interj.* Ouch, an exclamation of pain.

esdasion *n.* Station of the cross. [Span.]

ed- *interr.* An interrogative verb meaning 'to proceed by what means'. *Re edala?* How did they go there?

ehd₁ *num.* One; this numeral and others in this series are part of a general counting system used to enumerate things in the sense of counting them off; they never occur as part of larger grammatical constructions.

ehd₂ *n.* Bag, sack.

ehd₃ *vt.* To strip off water, to strip the leaves off a vine; to clean out intestines, to remove something from a rope-like object.

ede₁ *n3s.* Gill.

ede₂ *vt.* To sharpen, to put an edge on something. —adahd, *vi.*

edenpwel *n.* Burial name given to a chief after his death.

edi₁ *n3s.* Core, of a boil or pimple.

edi₂ *n3s.* Bile, of the liver.

edied *adj.* Cloudy, blurred, smoky.

ediedila *vi.* To have blurred vision, to go blind.

ediedin nahnmwarki *n. Uhmw* prepared in the presence of a *Nahnmwarki.*

edila *vi.* To have sexual intercourse for the first time, of a male.

ehdila *vi.* To have an experience for the first time.

edin kent *n.* Bladder.

edin marer *n.* Fontanel.

edin mwenge *n.* Stomach.

ediniei 1. *n.* Smoke. 2. HONORIFIC. *vi.*
To call.

edinieng *n.* Swim bladder of a fish.

edinperen HONORIFIC. *n.* Eye.

edip *num.* One; see *dip.*

editoal 1. *n.* Feast given upon
completing the roof of a new *nahs.* 2.
vi. To prepare this feast.

-et, also -e. *dem. mod.* This, by me.
pwihket this pig.

ete *num.* One; see *te.*

eten *n.* This evening.

ehtik *n.* Spleen.

ewel₁ *num.* One; see *wel₂.*

ewel₂ *num.* Eight; see *ehd.*

ewen mwenge, also owen mwenge. *adj.*
Selfish with food.

ewen neminem *adj.* Selfish with food,
used in an extremely derogatory sense.

ewen sawi *n.* Fish sp..

ewenkel *n.* Gate, entry.

ewetik *adj.* Abstemious, temperate in
eating and drinking.

I

i *subj. pron.* I. *I duhdu ni mensenget.* I bathed this morning.

ih₁ *n.* Name of the letter *i*.

ih₂ *ind. pron.* He, she, it.

ih₃ 1. *n.* Bunch, of bananas. 2. *num.* One; used for counting bunches of bananas.

ih₄ ARCHAIC. *n3s.* Belly.

ia *interr.* Where, what. *Ke pahn kohla ia?* Where are you going?

iahia, also ahia. *n.* Rainbow.

iau *interj.* How's it coming?, What's up?; I warned you!; So there!

iahk *adj.* Mentally disturbed, crazy, insane.

iakiu 1. *n.* Baseball. 2. *vi.* To play baseball. [Jap.]

iakumehda 1. *n.* One hundred meter dash. 2. *vi.* To run a one hundred meter dash. [Jap.]

iang *vt.* To accompany, join, or go with, to participate, to attend.

iangahki *vt.* To add or include.

iangala *vt.* To adhere to; to join the other side.

iahnge *interr.* Where, plural. *Iahnge kepwe kan?* Where are those things?

Iap *n.* Yap.

iasai *n.* Vegetable. [Jap.]

iasada *vi.* To be risen, to be resurrected, used biblically.

iasenei HONORIFIC. *adj.* Fortunate.

iahd *interr.* When. *Ke kohdo iahd?* When did you come?

iaht *n.* Yard, the unit of measurement. [Eng.]

iawasa *interr.* Where. *Iawasa me re pahn ketla ie?* Where are you going?

ie₁ *locative pronoun.* Occurs in the original position of a focussed locative phrase. *Ruk me ohlo mwemweitla ie.* Truk is where that man visited.

ie₂, also iet. *point. dem.* Here, by me (singular).

-ie₁ *obj. pron.* Me. *Kidio ngalisie.* That dog bit me.

-ie₂ *verb. suff.* Superlative suffix. *lingan* beautiful, *lingahnie* most beautiful.

iei *sent. adv.* Yes, as a response to a negative question; indeed. *Ke sohte pahn laid? Iei.* Aren't you going to fish. Yes. *Iei duwe.* Indeed this is the way it is.

-iei *verb. suff.* Outwards. *lus* jump, *lusiei* jump outwards.

ieias HONORIFIC. *vi.* To be alive.

ieu *num. cl.* See -u.

ieuieu, also iouiou. *n.* Plant sp., *Alpinia carolinensis.*

iehkan, also ietakan. *point. dem.* Here, by me (plural).

ien₁ *point. dem.* There, by you (singular).

ien₂ *n.* Yen, Japanese currency. [Jap.]

ienakan *point. dem.* There, by you (plural).

ienlam *n.* Clam sp., giant clam.

ienpwong 1. *vi.* To eat a late night snack, usually of a woman who is breastfeeding a child. 2. *n.* Such a late night snack.

-ieng, also -ehng. *verb. suff.* To, toward, in relation to, for; This form of the suffix occurs after a verb root ending in a vowel. *wa* to carry, *wahieng* to carry to.

ienge *n3s.* Companion, follower, complement.

iengen seri *n.* Placenta.

-ier, also -ehr. *verb. suff.* Used to signal perfective aspect; This form of the suffix occurs after a verb root ending in a vowel. *nehne* distribute, *nehnehier* have already distributed.

ieremen, also eremen. *interj.* Forget it!; Better not!

iehroas *n.* Only child.

Iesus, also Sises. *n.* Jesus.

iet, also ie₂. *point. dem.* Here, by me (singular).

ietakan, also iehkan. *point. dem.* Here, by me (plural).

iheteng *vi.* To be constipated.

ihieng *interj.* Pardon me!, used when one passes in front of another.

io *point. dem.* There, away from you and me (singular).

iou *adj.* Sweet, delicious, tasty.

iouiou, also ieuieu. *n.* Plant sp., *Alpinia carolinensis.*

iouioun wai *n.* A variety of torch ginger, *Canna indica.*

iohkan *point. dem.* There, away from you and me (plural).

iokoioko *n.* Name of two of the holes in the marble game *anaire.* [Jap.]

iol *n.* Vine sp..

iohla 1. *vi.* To miscarry. 2. *n.* Miscarriage.

iomo *n.* Fish sp., goatfish, *Parupeneus indicus.*

iopwou *n.* Barren female, usually of pigs.

iohsep *n.* Gardenia, *Gardenia jasminoides.*

-iuk, also **-uhk.** *obj. pron.* You; This form of the suffix occurs after vowels or the glide *y* (written *i*). *doakoa* to spear, *doakoaiuk* to spear you.

ius *vt.* To use. [Eng.]

ihk *vt.* To inhale, to breathe in deeply, to absorb.

ikel *n.* Eagle. [Eng.]

ikem *n.* Mangrove jack.

ikem asimel *n.* A medium sized *ikem*, a fish sp..

ihkenpwong *vi.* To feel sleepy during the daytime as a result of staying up at night.

iki *n3s.* Tail, end, extreme.

ikih *vt.* To avenge.

ikiala *vt.* To be at the end of.

ikiepw *n.* Fish sp., snapper, *Lethrinus kallopterus.*

ikimwang *n.* Scorpion.

ikimweng *n.* Fish sp., a mature *pehioang.*

ikintangih *vt.* To glance at; to look out of the corner of one's eye at. —**ikinteng,** *vi.*

ikinteng 1. *vi.* To glance; to look out of the corner of one's eye. 2. *adj.* Shifty-eyed. —**ikintangih,** *vt.*

ikipak *adj.* Small-hipped.

ikidewe *vt.* To decorate, to give an elaborate description of.

ikidiki *vt.* To blame, to lay the blame to.

ihkos *vi. neut.* To pleat, as a dress; to gather material, in sewing. —**ihkose,** *vt.*

ihkose *vt.* See *ihkos.*

ihkosen iouiou HONORIFIC. *n.* Hair.

ikoaik *vi.* To eat only meat, to eat only one thing. —**ikoaike,** *vt.*

ikoaike *vt.* See *ikoaik.*

ikmwir *vi.* To be last in a sequence. —**ikmwiri,** *vt.*

ikmwiri *vt.* See *ikmwir.*

ikdasi *n.* Drawer. [Jap.]

ila *vt.* To carry in the mouth. —**ilail,** *vi.*

ilail *vi.* To carry in the mouth. —**ila,** *vt.*

ilail en likend *n.* Basket for the wives of the *Nahnmwarki* and *Nahnken* in which *lihli* is presented.

ilail en sounlih *n.* Basket in which *lihli* is presented to the pounder of the breadfruit.

ilail en sounpiah *n.* Basket in which *lihli* is presented to the preparer of the coconut cream.

ilau *n.* Plant sp., *Clerodendrum inerme.*

ilakih *vt.* To send on an errand, to send to deliver a message. —**ilek-,** *vi.*

ilapas *vi.* To make a nest.

ile 1. *adj.* Elevated. 2. *n.* Elevation.

ile- *rel. n.* Location some distance in relation to (somewhere or something). *E mi iledio.* It's at a location some distance downward (from it).

ilek$_1$ *n.* Fish sp..

ilek$_2$ *n.* Dispatch or message.

ilek- *vi.* To send a dispatch or message. *E ilekilahng ah pwoudo.* He sent a message to his wife. —**ilakih,** *vt.*

ilekitik *adj.* Bossy, demanding.

ilewe *vt.* To secure a canoe by placing a pole between the outrigger and the hull and sticking it into the ocean bed.

ili *n3s.* Sucker of banana, breadfruit, taro, etc..

ilihl 1. *vi.* To steer a vehicle. 2. *n.* Steering paddle. —**ilihlih,** *vt.*

ilihlih *vt.* See *ilihl.*

ilisapw 1. *vi.* To give a party or gift to a medicine maker the fourth day of taking medicine. 2. *n.* The name of this party or gift.

ilok *n.* Wave, as in the ocean.

ilok sawa *n.* Breaker, a wave that breaks into foam.

impiokai *n.* Agricultural fair. [Jap.]

impwal *n.* Tent.

ihmw *n (3s: imwe).* Building, house, home, dwelling.

ihmw sarawi *n.* Church.

ihmwalap *n.* Family dwelling.

imwe *poss. cl.* A possessive classifier used for buildings.

13

imwen kainen *n.* Outhouse.

imwen kaudok *n.* Temple, house of worship.

imwen keiru *n.* Inn. [*keiru*<Jap.]

imwen kepwe *n.* Warehouse.

imwen kopwung *n.* Courthouse.

imwen kuk *n.* Cookhouse. [*kuk*<Eng.]

imwen mwenge *n.* Restaurant.

imwen net *n.* Store.

imwen padahk HONORIFIC. *n.* Cabinet, particularly one in which food is stored.

imwen sukuhl *n.* Schoolhouse. [*sukuhl*<Eng.]

imwen wini *n.* Hospital.

imweteng *n.* Jail, prison.

imwi *n3s.* Top, summit, end, outcome.

imwioas *n.* Thatch house.

imwilap *n.* Large end of a canoe.

imwinsapw *n.* Cape of land.

imwintihti 1. *vi.* To be adversaries or enemies. 2. *n.* Adversary, enemy, feud.

imwisekila *vi.* To be finished, to be accomplished.

imwitik *n.* Small end of a canoe.

in, also **ino**. *n.* Mother, mom, a term of familiarity.

ihn₁ *n (3s: ine).* Mother; any person one's mother or father would call sister.

ihn₂ *n.* The quantity of kava placed in the hibiscus bast.

ihn kahlap *n (3s: ine kahlap).* Grandmother, sometimes one's spouse's grandmother.

ihn wini *n.* Medicine wrapped in coconut cloth.

inaur *vt.* To lash. —**inou₂,** *vi.*

inahme *n.* Fish sp..

inangih *vt.* To arouse any feeling, to arouse sexually.

inap *n (3s: inepe).* Anything which is sat upon; hot pad for pots.

inahpwed *vi.* To have a mouthful. —**inahpwede,** *vt.*

inahpwede *vt.* See *inahpwed.*

inapwih *vt.* To forbid or prohibit something taboo or illegal.

Inahs *n.* A ghost of the *Sounkawad* clan.

inasio *n.* A variety of banana.

inadi HONORIFIC. *n.* Tooth.

inen *adj.* Straight.

inen- *vi.* To come or go directly. *E inenla Pohnpei.* He went directly to Ponape.

inen oaroahr *n.* A feasthouse having three center posts, located on the shore.

inenen *adv.* Very. *Mehn Pohnpei inenen kadek.* Ponapeans are very kind.

ineng₁ *n.* Desire or wish.

ineng₂ *n.* Abnormal hair, course and rapid growing.

inengiada *vt.* To desire or wish.

inengida *vi.* To desire to have sexual intercourse.

ini *vi. neut.* To carry two bundles of things with a pole across the shoulders. —**inie,** *vt.*

inie *vt.* See *ini.*

inim *vt.* See *inihn.*

inimpene *vt.* To weld.

inihn *vi.* To cook, roast, broil, toast, etc.. —**inim,** *vt.*

inipal *n.* The fibrous, cloth-like material of the coconut palm; a container made of this material, used to squeeze medicine through.

ino, also **in**. *n.* Mother, mom, a term of familiarity.

inou₁ 1. *n.* Contract, promise, agreement, covenant. 2. *vi.* To promise.

inou₂ *vi.* To lash. —**inaur,** *vt.*

inou sarawi 1. *vi.* To marry in the church. 2. *n.* Spouse, married in church.

inoande *n3s.* Main tuber of a yam plant.

inkahp *n.* Inside curve, in baseball. [Jap.<Eng.]

ins *n.* Inch. [Eng.]

insens *n.* Incense. [Eng.]

insis *n.* Hinge. [Eng.]

ihnda *vi.* To place kava in the hibiscus bast.

ingi *n3s.* Pectoral fin of a fish.

ingin 1. *n.* A painful infection. 2. *vi.* To have a painful infection.

inginsoi *adj.* Easily bothered or upset by trivial matters, demanding, dependent.

ingihng₁ 1. *vi. neut.* To braid. 2. *n.* Braid. —**ingid,** *vt.*

ingihng₂ 1. *vi.* To whisper; to cry very softly. 2. *n.* Any very soft sound.

ingir HONORIFIC. *vt.* To smell.

ingirek *adj.* Smelly.

ingid *vt.* To braid. —ingihng₁, *vi.*

ingidpene *vt.* To squeeze.

ingitik *vi.* To whisper, to hum, to groan.

ingitingkihdi *vt.* To say something under one's breath.

ingk *n.* Ink. [Eng.]

ip, also ipa. *n.* Father, dad, a term of familiarity.

ipa, also ip. *n.* Father, dad, a term of familiarity.

ipe *poss. cl.* A possessive classifier used for things to cover with, as sheets.

ipihp 1. *vi.* To blow, as the wind. 2. *n.* Lightning without thunder. —ipir, *vt.*

ipir *vt.* To blow at. —ipihp, *vi.*

ihpw *n.* Spear handle.

ipwa *interj.* I warned you!

ipwadeke, also pwendeke. *sent. adv.* Is it correct to assume that. *Ipwadeke kowe mehn Ruk?* Is it correct to assume that you are Trukese?

ihpwe *n3s.* The upper half of the human body, the torso.

ipwerek *adj.* Ornamented.

ipwieng *vt.* To be paternally descended from.

ipwin nenek *n.* Child born of an adulterous relationship.

ipwihpw 1. *vi.* To be of mixed blood lines, to be of a mixed breed. 2. *n.* Paternal descendant. *ipwihpw en mehn wai* descendant of an American man.

ipwidi 1. *vi.* To be born. 2. *n.* Birthday.

ir- *vi.* To penetrate, to sink, to dig in. *Elimoango iridi nan pwelmatak.* The crab dug into the mud.

ihr₁ 1. also irail. *ind. pron.* They, plural. 2. HONORIFIC. *ind. pron.* You.

ihr₂ 1. *n.* A string of something, as of flowers or fish. 2. *vi. neut.* To string, as flowers or fish. —ihre, *vt.*

ira *subj. pron., ind. pron.* They, dual.

-ira *obj. pron.* Them, dual.

irail 1. also re. *subj. pron.* They, plural. 2. also ihr₁. *ind. pron.* They, plural.

-irail *obj. pron.* Them, plural.

irair *n.* Portion; event; topic.

irairdi *vi.* To be forbidden; to be divided. —irehdi, *vt.*

iralaud *n.* Chapter, of a book; book, of the Bible; title, in the legal code.

iranai *vi.* To pass, in a card game. [Jap.]

irap HONORIFIC. 1. *n.* The meat or fish part of a meal; any complement to the main course of a meal. 2. *vi.* To eat meat or fish.

iraparap *vi.* To be spread, as a sheet or blanket. —irepe, *vt.*

irar HONORIFIC. 1. *n.* Cane. 2. *vi.* To walk with a cane.

iraramwar 1. *n.* Feast of public acceptance of a *koanoat* title. 2. *vi.* To prepare this feast.

irareileng HONORIFIC. *n.* Cane, of the *Nahnmwarki.*

irareiso HONORIFIC. *n.* Cane, of the *Nahnken.*

ire₁ *n3s.* Condition or state of a person or thing.

ire₂ *n3s.* Border or limit; section or article.

ihre *vt.* See *ihr₂.*

irek *n.* Series, line.

irekila *vi.* To be lined up, to be ordered.

ihrekiso HONORIFIC. *n.* Skin.

irekidi *vi.* To place in successive order.

iren sehd *n.* Sea level.

irepe *vt.* To spread, as a sheet or blanket; to drape, as with a sheet or blanket.

irepen sehd *n.* Horizon at sea.

irepeseng *vt.* To separate.

irere *vt.* To support.

irehdi *vt.* To forbid. —irairdi, *vi.*

iretikitik *n.* Detail; verse of the Bible.

irip *vt.* To fan. —irihr, *vi.*

irihr *vi.* To fan. —irip, *vt.*

irihrla *vi.* To be erased. —iris, *vt.*

iris *vt.* To rub; to erase. —irihrla or irisek, *vi.*

irisek *vi.* To be rubbed. —iris, *vt.*

iroir 1. *vi.* To look or peer in the distance; to see one's own reflection; to inspect one's own appearance. 2. *adj.* Positioned to have a beautiful view. —irong, *vt.*

irong *vt.* To look or peer in the distance; to see one's own reflection; to inspect one's own appearance. —iroir, *vi.*

irlapiso HONORIFIC. *n.* Fan.

ihs₁ *interr.* Who, whoever. *Ihs ohlo?* Who is that man? *Walahng ihs me men ale.* Carry it to whoever wants it.

ihs₂ *n.* Yeast, the alcoholic beverage prepared from yeast. [Eng.]

isais 1. *vi. neut.* To pay tribute, to repay a service or good deed. 2. *n.* Tribute, gift, reward. —ise, *vt.*

isaniki *vt.* To take immediate action on something because the opportunity is right.

ise *vt.* To pay tribute, to repay a service or good deed. —isais, *vi.*

isek ARCHAIC. *n.* Coconut shell container, calabash.

isepe *n3s.* Fee, rental payment.

isih *vt.* To hiss at.

isiakan *num.* Seventy; see *ehk.*

isiel *num.* Seven; see *el₂.*

isik *vt.* To burn, to light, to set fire to, to burn off feathers or hair. —isida or isihs or mwasik, *vi.*

isika *num.* Seven; see *ka.*

isikap *num.* Seven; see *kap.*

isikis *num.* Seven; see *kis₁.*

isilap HONORIFIC. *n.* Forehead.

isilep *num.* Seven; see *lep.*

isimen *num.* Seven; see *men₃.*

isimome *n.* Game involving bouncing a ball, usually played by girls. [Jap.]

isimwas 1. *n.* Feast given upon completion of a new feasthouse. 2. *vi.* To prepare this feast.

isimwodol *num.* Seven; see *mwodol.*

isimwut *num.* Seven; see *mwut₂.*

isinge *interr.* Who, plural.

isingoul *num.* Seventy; see *ngoul.*

isipa *num.* Seven; see *pa₃.*

Isipahu *n.* Title of the *Nahnmwarki* of Madolenihmw.

isipak *num.* Seven; see *pak₁.*

isipali *num.* Seven; see *pali₁.*

isipangpiri *n.* Last player in playing marbles. [Jap.]

isipar *num.* Seven; see *par₂.*

isipit *num.* Seven; see *pit₂.*

isipoar *num.* Seven; see *poar.*

isipwong *num.* Seven; see *pwong.*

isipwoat *num.* Seven; see *pwoat.*

isipwuloi *num.* Seven; see *pwuloi.*

isira *num.* Seven; see *ra.*

isihs 1. *vi.* To burn off. 2. *n.* Bonfire; forest fire; burning landscape. —isik, *vt.*

isihsek *num.* Seventy; see *eisek.*

isisel *num.* Seven; see *sel₂.*

isisou *num.* Seven; see *sou₄.*

isisop *num.* Seven; see *sop.*

isida *vi.* To be burned, to be lit, to be set fire to. —isik, *vt.*

isidip *num.* Seven; see *dip.*

isidun *num.* Seven; see *dun.*

isite *num.* Seven; see *te.*

isitumw *num.* Seven; see *tumw.*

isiwel *num.* Seven; see *wel₂.*

Iso *n.* A term of address to titled people in the *Nahnken* line.

Isoeni *n.* Old title of the *Nahnmwarki* of Sokehs.

isou *n.* Tree sp., *Calophyllum inophyllum*, used for lumber.

isol 1. *vi.* To go without food, or without feasting. 2. *n.* Scarcity, famine.

Isohlap *n.* A title.

Isohpahu *n.* A title.

isuh *num.* Seven; see *-u.*

isuhmw *num.* Seven; see *umw.*

issohping *n.* Sauce bottle, with a capacity of 1.8 liters. [Jap.]

id₁ *vi. neut.* To make fire by rubbing a stick in a trough of wood. —iding₂, *vt.*

id₂ *vi.* To rise, of the tide.

id- *vi.* To point. *E idila peilongo.* He pointed inland. —idih, *vt.*

ihd₁, also uhd. *vt.* To take one's turn to.

ihd₂ *n.* Plant sp..

ihd₃ *vt.* To fetch or draw liquids.

ihd₄ ARCHAIC. *n.* Salt water eel, a generic term.

ida *n.* Stem of the ivory nut palm, used for mending thatch roofs.

idaid *vi.* To be under pressure, to be mashed. —idang, *vt.*

ihdak *vi.* To drive fish into a net.

idan *vt.* To carry in a vehicle. —peidaid, *vi.*

idahnwel *n.* Rattan, *Flagellaria indica.*

idang *vt.* To apply pressure to, to mash. —idaid, *vi.*

idawarih HONORIFIC. *vt.* To say, to see.

idawehn *vt.* To follow, to go after, to pursue, to obey.

idek *vt.* To ask. —peidek, *vi.*

idemei *vi. neut.* To turn a canoe in the direction of the outrigger.

idengek *vi.* To lean, of animate beings.

idi *n3s.* End, limit.

idi- *vi.* To reach a limit or boundary.

idih   vt. To point at. —id-, vi.

idihada   vt. To point out, to identify; to appoint. —idihdida, vi.

idier   HONORIFIC. vi. To be full, after eating.

iding$_1$ vt. To grate; to force. —idihd$_1$, vi.

iding$_2$ vt. To rub to make a fire. —id$_1$, vi.

idip   vt. To draw or fetch water. —idipil, vi.

idipek   adj. Strong, capable of moving steadily and with force.

idipen pihl   n. Implement for drawing water.

idipil   vi. To draw or fetch water. —idip, vt.

idihd$_1$ 1. vi. neut. To grate, as taro. 2. n. Grated taro, yam, or banana mixed with coconut milk and wrapped in leaves. —iding$_1$, vt.

idihd$_2$ 1. n. Feast involving yams, usually given in December. 2. vi. To prepare this feast.

idihdida   vi. To be pointed out, to be identified; to be appointed. —idihada, vt.

ido   n. Well. [Jap.]

iddai   interj. Ouch! [Jap.]

it   adj. Stuffed; too tight, as of clothing.

iht   n. Fish sp..

itait   adj. Limited, just sufficient.

itar   vi. To be enough, adequate, ample.

ihte   interj. That's it!, That's all!

itiek   vi. To bend, to droop.

itiekidi   vi. To bow.

itier   HONORIFIC. vi. To be full, after eating.

itik   vt. To shake. —itiht, vi.

itikek   adj. Shaky, wobbly.

itipe   vi. To shake hands.

itiht   vi. To be shaken. —itik, vt.

itoit   1. vi. To be forceful. 2. n. Force, duress. —iton, vt.

iton   vt. To force. —itoit, vi.

O

-o *dem. mod.* That, away from you and me. *pwihko* that pig away from you and me.

oh₁ *n.* Name of the letter *o*.

oh₂ *conj.* And. *Wein Uh oh Net tikitiksang wein Madolenihmw.* The municipalities of Uh and Net are smaller than the municipality of Madolenihmw.

oh₃ *n (3s: owe).* Sprout of a yam.

oh₄ *interj.* Oh!

oh tier *interj.* Oh dear!, Oh my! [Eng.]

ohi *interj.* A response employed when one is being called.

ohio *n.* Reef, deep below the surface, but visible.

Ou *n.* A title.

Ou Ririn *n.* A title, in the *Nahnken* line.

oukanehu *interj.* Are you kidding?.

oulaid 1. *n.* Feast for returning fishermen. 2. *vi.* To prepare this feast.

oumw *num.* One; see *umw₂*.

oun, also aun. *num.* Six; see *ehd.*

Oun Pohnpei *n.* A title, in the *Nahnken* line.

Oun Sapawas *n.* A title.

ounsouna *n.* A variety of yam.

Oundol *n.* A title.

Oundol en Ririn *n.* A title.

Oundolen Ririn *n.* A title, in the *Nahnmwarki* line.

ouraman *vt.* To dream about. —ouremen, *vi.*

ouremei *vi.* To use a kava stone for the first time.

ouremen 1. *vi.* To dream. 2. *n.* Dream. —ouraman, *vt.*

oudek *n.* Punishment; destruction at the order of a chief.

ok *vi.* To start or to burn, of a fire; to burn, of a light.

okasi *n.* Candy. [Jap.]

okei *interj.* Okay. [Eng.]

oko, also ko. *dem. mod.* Those, away from you and me.

okoteme, also mehkot. *pron.* Something, anything (singular). *Wahdo okoteme.* Bring something.

ohl *n.* Man, male.

ohla 1. *vi.* To be broken, ruined, destroyed, spoiled. 2. *n.* Ruin, damage, wound.

olenei ARCHAIC. *n.* Good man.

ohlet *vi.* To halt, to stop; to hold, in a card game. [Eng.]

oloiso HONORIFIC. *n.* Royalty.

olohdi *n.* Widower.

ohlsehl *n.* Wholesale store. [Eng.]

omp, also emp₂. *n.* Vine sp., *Ipomoea gracilis.*

ompwu *vi.* Of a person, to be carried on another's back. [Jap.]

omw, also ahmw₂. *poss. cl.* Your, singular; see *ah.*

ohmw *n.* Home plate, in baseball. [Jap.<Eng.]

omwi HONORIFIC. *poss. cl.* Your, singular; see *ah.*

omwinwel, also ahmw₁ or liahmw. *n.* A tiny flying insect, commonly found in the forest.

ohmwrang *n.* Home run. [Jap.<Eng.]

ohn *adj.* Hung over.

ohn kehp *n.* Vine, of a yam.

ohn sakau *adj.* Hung over from kava or alcohol.

one *vt.* To mend or repair, used principally with native objects. —onohn, *vi.*

onepek *n.* Peace, tranquility, good feelings.

onohn *vi.* To be mended or repaired, used principally with native objects. —one, *vt.*

onop *vi.* To study, to prepare. —onopada, *vt.*

onopada *vt.* To prepare, to get ready. —onop, *vi.*

ondol en luwi *n.* A variety of yam.

ohntile *n3s.* Attached handle, as of a basket, suitcase, lamp, etc..

ong *prep.* To, toward, in relation to, for.

ohpalawasa HONORIFIC. *vi.* To wake up.

opampap *adj.* Humble, unassuming, meek.

ohpis *n.* Office, government. [Eng.]

opohn *n.* Harpoon. [Eng.]

ohpweisou HONORIFIC. *n.* Hat.

ohpwet *n.* A variety of yam.

ohpwet en pohnpei *n.* A variety of yam.

ohpwet en wai *n.* A variety of yam.

opwong₁ *num.* One; see *pwong*.

opwong₂ *n.* Carrying tray. [Jap.]

opwuloi *num.* One; see *pwuloi*.

orens *n.* Orange, the fruit. [Eng.]

os *vi.* To sprout, to grow.

ohs *n.* Hose. [Eng.]

ose *n3s.* New shoot or sprout of a tuber; spur of a chicken.

osime *n.* Diaper. [Jap.]

osihre *n.* Locker, cabinet. [Jap.]

osiroi *n.* Baby powder. [Jap.]

osop *num.* One; see *sop₂*.

ohd, also **wehd.** *n.* Taro, *Alocasia macrorrhiza*.

ohdai *n.* Bandage, gauze. [Jap.]

ohdou HONORIFIC. *n.* Basket.

odopai *n.* Scooter, motorcycle. [Jap.<Eng.]

odun *num.* One; see *dun*.

oht ARCHAIC. *n.* Reef.

ohtehl *n.* Hotel. [Eng.]

otoht *adj.* Of food, appetizing due to the manner in which it is eaten by another.

otumw *num.* One; see *tumw*.

owen mwenge, also **ewen mwonge.** *adj.* Always hungry.

owen wedei *adj.* Talkative.

OA

oah *n.* Name of the digraph *oa*.

oail *n.* Oil. [Eng.]

Oakos, also Ahkos. *n.* August. [Eng.]

Oakotope *n.* October. [Eng.]

oale *vt.* To wave, to signal. —oaloahl, *vi.*

oaloahl *vi.* To wave, to signal. —oale, *vt.*

oaloahd *n.* Seaweed sp., *Blyxa muricata.*

oaloahdenpil *n.* Plant sp., *Enhalus acoroides*, found in fresh water.

oahng *n.* Turmeric.

oangalap *n.* Turmeric sp..

oange *n3s.* Yolk, of an egg.

oangen palau *n.* Turmeric sp..

oangen pelle *n.* Turmeric sp., *Zingiber zerumbet.*

oangitik *n.* Turmeric sp., a variety of *Curcuma.*

oangoahng 1. *adj.* Yellow. 2. *n.* Yellow.

oapoar *num.* One; see *poar*.

oapwoat *num.* One; see *pwoat*.

oaralap 1. *adj.* General, summarized. 2. *n.* General idea; summary. —oarelepe, *vt.*

oare *vt.* To scrape together and pick up a pile of something, such as dirt, kava, etc.. —oaroahr₁, *vi.*

oarelepe *vt.* To give the general idea of, to give a summary of. —oaralap, *adj.*

oaritik 1. *adj.* Detailed. 2. *n.* Detail. —oaritikih, *vt.*

oaritikih *vt.* To give a detailed account of. —oaritik, *adj.*

Oaron Maka *n.* A title.

Oaron Pwutak *n.* A title.

oarong *n.* Fish sp., blue jack crevally, *Caranx melampygus.*

oarong en pwong *n.* Fish sp., jack, *Caranx sexfasciatus.*

oaroahr₁ *vi. neut.* To scrape together and pick up a pile of something, such as dirt, kava, etc.. —oare, *vt.*

oaroahr₂ *n.* Shore, land near the ocean, landing place for canoes or boats.

oahs₁ *n.* Ivory nut palm, *Coelococcus amicarum; roof, thatch.*

oahs₂ *n.* Horse. [Eng.]

oasmete *n.* Tin roofing. [*mete*<Eng.]

oaht *vi. neut.* To order. [Eng.] —oahte, *vt.*

oatalaud SLANG. *adj.* Big mouthed, boastful.

oate SLANG. *n3s.* Mouth.

oahte *vt.* To order. [Eng.] —oaht, *vi.*

oatilikamw SLANG. *adj.* Lying, untruthful.

oatwalek SLANG. *adj.* Having a large mouth.

U

-u *num. cl.* Used in the general counting system; occurs as *ieu* when used like an indefinite article. *uhpw riau* two drinking coconuts, *pwuhk ieu* a book.

uh$_1$ *n.* Name of the letter *u*.

uh$_2$ *vi.* To stand.

Uh$_3$ *n.* Name of a municipality in Ponape.

uh$_4$ *vi.* To boast.

uh$_5$ *n.* Tide.

uh$_6$ *n.* Fish trap.

uh$_7$ *n.* Sharpening stone.

uh$_8$ *adj.* Entire, whole, as in *Pohnpeiuh.*

uk *adj.* Fast, speedy.

uhk$_1$ *n.* Net.

uhk$_2$ *vt.* To urge; to lead.

-uhk, also -iuk. *obj. pron.* You; This form of the suffix occurs after consonants. *duhp* to bathe, *duhpuhk* to bathe you.

ukalap *n.* Large seine or net.

ukada *adj.* Steep, uphill.

uke *vt.* To roll, of objects too heavy to lift.

ukedi *adj.* Steep, downhill.

uketik *n.* Small seine or net.

uhki *vt.* To stand for; to support.

ukinlekidek *n.* Throw net.

ukouk 1. *n.* A type of net fishing, where the fisherman uses a *naik* in each hand. 2. *vi.* To fish in this manner.

ukulehle *n.* Ukulele. [Eng.]

uliunleng HONORIFIC. *n.* Hair.

uluhl 1. *n.* Pillow; small hill. 2. *vi.* To use a pillow. —ulung, *vt.*

ululin neh *n3s.* Upper shin bone.

ulung *vt.* To use a pillow. —uluhl, *vi.*

ulunge *poss. cl.* A possessive classifier used for pillows or things used as pillows.

ulungen kieil *n.* Vine sp., *Davallia solida.*

ulungen wehi *n.* New Guinea starfish.

ullap *n (3s: ullepe).* Uncle, of the same clan; any person one's mother would call brother.

umepwosi *n.* Pickled plum. [Jap.]

umpang *vt.* To carry something requiring repeated trips, as numerous bags of copra; to carry. [Jap.]

umw$_1$ *vi. neut.* To bake in an *uhmw.* —umwun$_1$, *vt.*

umw$_2$ *num. cl.* Used in counting yams and bananas. *kehp isuhmw* seven yams.

uhmw *n.* A traditional Ponapean oven made of loose stones which are heated and placed around the food to be baked.

umwulap 1. *n.* Heat treatment. 2. *vi.* To receive a heat treatment.

umwule *n.* Fish sp., rabbitfish, *Siganus canaliculatus.*

umwun$_1$ *vt.* To bake in an *uhmw.* —umw$_1$, *vi.*

umwun$_2$ *n.* Fish sp., a kind of parrotfish.

umwun edied 1. *n.* Feast given upon completion of a building. 2. *vi.* To give this feast.

umwun kepinwar 1. *n.* Feast given for one departing, a farewell feast. 2. *vi.* To give this feast.

umwun luhwen mei 1. *n.* Feast given at the end of the breadfruit season. 2. *vi.* To give this feast.

umwun mwurilik 1. *n.* Death feast, given after the burial. 2. *vi.* To give this feast.

uhn- *n.* Group, cluster of, bunch of.

une *n.* Mounded row, as in a garden. [Jap.]

uhnpeh *n3s.* Forearm.

unsek *adj.* Entire, whole, unanimous, complete; normal.

undeng *vi.* To drive. [Jap.] —undengih, *vt.*

undengih *vt.* See *undeng.* [*undeng*<Jap.]

undohkai *n.* Athletic meet. [Jap.]

up *vt.* To cover or shield oneself from the weather. —upuhp, *vi.*

uhp *n.* Plant sp., *Derris elliptica*, used for poisoning fish.

uhp kitik *n.* Vine sp., used for poisoning fish.

uhpa *vt.* To serve.

uhpaup *vi.* To poison fish. —**uhpe,** *vt.*

uhpal *vi.* To take sides with. —**uhpalih,** *vt.*

uhpalih *vt.* See *uhpal.*

uhpe *vt.* See *uhpaup.*

uhpeiuh *n.* One of the principal kava stones in a *nahs.*

uhpeileng *n.* One of the principal kava stones in a *nahs.*

uhpeimwahu *n.* One of the principal kava stones in a *nahs.*

uhpen iap *n.* Vine sp., used for poisoning fish.

uhpen palau *n.* Bush sp., used for poisoning fish.

uhpene *vi.* To compete.

upenei *n.* Vine sp., used for poisoning fish.

uhpoar *vi.* To protect.

upuhp *vi.* To cover or shield oneself from the weather. —**up,** *vt.*

uhpw *n.* Drinking coconut.

uhpwel *vi. neut.* To mound earth around the roots of a plant. —**uhpwelih,** *vt.*

uhpwelih *vt.* See *uhpwel.*

ur *vi.* To wade, as in water or tall grass. —**urak₁,** *vt.*

ur- *vt.* To gather palm fronds for thatch. *I pahn urodo ei parem.* I'll gather nipa palm fronds.

uhr₁ *n.* Lobster.

uhr₂ *n.* Post.

urak₁ *vt.* To wade, as in water or tall grass. —**ur,** *vi.*

urak₂ *vt.* To lap up.

urak₃ HONORIFIC. *vt.* To drink.

uramai 1. *n.* Feast to celebrate the first usage of a new kava stone. 2. *vi.* To give this feast.

uhramwahu *adj.* Having good timing; having arrived at the proper time.

uhran *vi.* To wait for an event.

uhrahn *vi.* To have sexual intercourse during daylight hours.

urahdek, also **ruwahdek.** 1. *vi.* To be pulled, to be dragged. 2. *adj.* Not quite cooked, of food items that are tested for being cooked by inserting a fine stick. —**urahdeki,** *vt.*

urahdeki, also **ruwahdeki.** *vt.* To pull, to drag. —**urahdek,** *vi.*

uhre *n3s.* Muscle of a clam, used for closing the shell.

uhrelleng HONORIFIC. *n.* Sheet, as for bedding.

uhren uhpw *n.* The soft upper part of the shell of the coconut, at a certain growth stage.

urenna *n.* Lobster.

uridi *vt.* To cut palm fronds for thatch.

urohs 1. *n.* Skirt, half-slip. 2. *vi.* To wear a skirt or half-slip. [Jap.<Eng.]

uruhr ARCHAIC. *n.* Laughter, happiness.

us₁ *vt.* To pull out, to pluck.

us₂ *vt.* To vote for. —**usuhs,** *vi.*

uhs *n.* Float, as for a fishing net.

usalis HONORIFIC. *vi.* To remove whiskers.

use *n.* Grass sp., *Cyperus javanicus.*

uhse *vt.* To continue to completion.

uhsehiong *vt.* To convey information.

uhsepe *n3s.* Continuation.

usepehi *n.* Cork-like wood.

usu *n.* Star.

Usuhn Rahn, also **Usuhrahn.** *n.* Venus, the morning star.

usup, also **usupih.** *vt.* To splash water towards an object.

usupih, also **usup.** *vt.* To splash water towards an object.

Usuhrahn, also **Usuhn Rahn.** *n.* Venus, the morning star.

usuhs 1. *vi.* To vote. 2. *n.* Election, raffle, lottery. —**us₂,** *vt.*

usuwarih *vt.* See *usuwer.*

usuwer *vi.* To strain one's neck to see. —**usuwarih** or **usuwere,** *vt.*

usuwere *vt.* See *usuwer.*

uskomwkomw HONORIFIC. *vi.* To remove gray hair.

uspwetepwet HONORIFIC. *vi.* To remove gray hair.

uhd, also **ihd₁.** *vt.* To take one's turn to.

uhdak *n.* Native, one indigenous to an area.

uhdahn *sent. adv.* Certainly, really, definitely, truly. *Sahpwet uhdahn lingan.* This area is really beautiful.

uhdi *vi.* To stop, of moving objects.

udiahl POLITE. *vt.* To watch, to behold, to observe. —**poudiahl,** *vi.*

udong *n.* Noodle. [Jap.]

uduk *n (3s: uduke).* Meat, flesh, muscle; biblically, human or sex.

uht *n.* Banana, *Musa paradisiaca.*

uht mwot *n.* A variety of banana, said to be native to Ponape.

uter 1. *n.* Any food prepared with grated coconut. 2. *vi.* To prepare food with grated coconut, to mix things together. —**utere**, *vt.*

utere *vt.* To prepare food with grated coconut, to mix things together. —**uter**, *vi.*

utiak *n.* A variety of banana.

utimwas *n.* A variety of banana.

utin iap *n.* A variety of banana, from Yap.

utin kuam *n.* A variety of banana, from Guam.

utin menihle *n.* A variety of banana, from Manila.

utin palau *n.* A variety of banana, from Palau.

utin pihsi *n.* A variety of banana, from Fiji.

utin ruk *n.* A variety of banana, from Truk.

utin seipahn *n.* A variety of banana, from Saipan.

utin wai *n.* A variety of banana.

utindol *n.* A variety of banana.

utisel *n.* A variety of banana, *Musa textilis.*

uhtohr 1. *adj.* Independent. 2. *n.* Independence.

utumwot *n.* A variety of banana.

utun ngih *n3s.* Gums, of the teeth.

utuhn pihl *n.* Source, of a river or a stream.

utung *vt.* To prop. —**utuht**, *vi.*

utuht *vi.* To be propped. —**utung**, *vt.*

utuwi *n.* Upstream.

uwako, also **wako.** *vi.* To gag.

uwe$_1$ *n3s.* Size.

uwe$_2$ *n3s.* Residue.

uhweng *vt.* To oppose, to disagree with; to go against.

uweng kosonned *vi.* To be illegal, to do something illegal.

uhwoas *vi.* To cut ivory palm fronds for thatch.

K

ka₁, also aka₁, kat, or akat. *dem. mod.* These, by me.

ka₂ *num. cl.* Used in counting rows or lines of things. *kahngen nih weneka* six rows of coconut palms.

ka₃ *interj.* Wow!

ka- *verb. pref.* Causative prefix, also used in forming ordinal numerals. *pweipwei* stupid, *kapweipwei* cause to be stupid; *pahieu* four, *kapahieu* fourth.

kah- *n.* Row, always appears with the construct suffix. *Mie kahn nih riau.* There are two rows of coconut trees.

kai- *vt.* To move. *Kaido dahlen.* Move the dish toward me. —kei-, *vi.*

kaiahn 1. *vi.* To drill, to train, to exercise. 2. *n.* Drill, training, exercise. —kaiahne, *vt.*

kaiahne *vt.* To drill, to train someone. —kaiahn, *vi.*

kahiep *vi.* To be unburdened or empty-handed; to travel without provisions.

kaiot HONORIFIC. *n.* Chin.

kaik, also saik₂. *neg.* Not yet. *E kaik kohdo.* He hasn't yet come.

kaikai *n3s.* Chin.

kaikes *n.* Tree sp., *Abrus precatorius.*

kaikinte, also saikinte. *neg.* Not yet.

kaiko 1. *n.* Guard, sentry. 2. *vi.* To guard. [Jap.?]

kailok *n.* Hatred.

kailongki *vt.* To hate or dislike, of people.

kain *n.* Kind, sort, type. [Eng.]

kainen *vi. neut.* To straighten; to inventory; to defecate. —kainene, *vt.*

kainene *vt.* To straighten; to inventory; to aim. —kainen, *vi.*

kaingun *n.* Navy. [Jap.]

kaipw HONORIFIC. *n.* The lower half of the human body.

kaipwihdi *vt.* To give birth, used biblically.

kair *n.* News.

kairehki *vt.* To inform.

kairu *n.* Toad, frog. [Jap.]

kaisa *n.* Company, corporation, group. [Jap.]

kaisihsol *vi.* To fast or abstain from food, voluntarily or on direction from a superior. —kaisihsolih, *vt.*

kaisihsolih *vt.* See *kaisihsol.*

kaidehkin, also kaidehn. *neg.* Not; used to negate equational sentences.

kaidehn, also kaidehkin. *neg.* Not; used to negate equational sentences. *Kaidehn ih mehn Ruk.* He's not a Trukese.

kaidehn mwamwahl *interj.* That is impressive!

kaidih *vt.* To wait for high tide.

kait *n.* A variety of yam.

kau₁ *vt.* To erect, to raise; to drink directly from a container. —kokou, *vi.*

kau₂, also akau. *dem. mod.* Those, away from you and me.

kau₃ *n.* Harmful magic, sorcery.

kahu *n (3s: kahwe).* Buttocks; bottom.

kahula *vi.* To take an oath.

kaulim 1. *adj.* Querulous, critical. 2. *n.* Criticism.

kaun 1. *n.* Ruler, boss, leader, director. 2. *vt.* To boss, to rule, to lead, to direct.

kauna, also kahwina. *vt.* To scale or pluck. —kahwin, *vi.*

kaunehdi, also kawenehdi. *vt.* To lay someone or something down; to change the position of something from vertical to horizontal.

kaunop- *vt.* To prepare; to warn, to remind. *Kitail kaunopada mwenge!* Let's prepare food!

kaup *vt.* To peel, as a banana. —kokoup, *vi.*

kaupe *n3s.* Disadvantage.

kaurere *vt.* To sprinkle water, as on clothing prior to ironing.

kaururi ARCHAIC. *n3s.* Mouth.

kaus *vt.* To eject, to banish. —pokous, *vi.*

kaud *adv.* Right?; isn't it true that?. *Kaud ih me nda?* Isn't it true that he said it?

kaudok 1. *vi.* To worship, to pray. 2. *n.* Worship, religion, prayer.

kautoke HONORIFIC. *vt.* To send on an errand, to send to deliver a message.

kak *vt.* Can. *Ke kak uhda?* Can you stand up?

kahk₁ *vi.* To step.

kahk₂ 1. *n.* Riddle. 2. *vi.* To ask a riddle.

kahka 1. *adj.* Desiring peace and quiet while under the influence of kava. 2. *vi.* Biblically, to show respect, to honor.

kakairada *vt.* To provide guidance for children.

kakau *n.* Cacao, *Theobroma cacao.* [Eng.]

kahke *n.* Bird sp., fairy tern.

kakehlail *n.* Confirmation.

kakehle *vt.* To strengthen.

kakerepil *n.* Fish sp., an immature sweetlips porgy, *Plectorhynchus celebicus.*

kahki, also **pohkahki.** 1. *n.* Khaki, tan. 2. *adj.* Khaki, tan. [Eng.]

kakil *vt.* To stare. —**pekekil,** *vi.*

kakiles *n.* Sp. of large black ant.

kakipwel *n (3s: kakipweli).* Banana flower.

kakihr *vt.* To submerge; to strip off clothes; to unsheathe a knife or hidden weapon; to slide, as on a cable; to tight-line fish.

kahkirek *n.* Tree sp..

kakonepene *vt.* To reassemble; to fit together.

kakonehda *vt.* To assemble, to put together; to start a rumor.

kakosih *vt.* To bend, to bend to one's will; to imprison.

kakureiso HONORIFIC. *vi.* To close one's mouth.

kakus *vt.* To spray, to cause to flow; to drain. —**kokus,** *vi.*

kakudai *n.* Marching band. [Jap.]

kakko *adj.* Putting on airs, showing off. [Jap.]

kala₁ *adj.* Boastful.

kala₂ *n.* Collar. [Eng.]

kalaimwun 1. *adj.* Large. 2. *n (3s: kalaimwuni).* Magnitude.

kalaidong ARCHAIC. *n.* Kava, *Piper methysticum.*

kalak *n.* Tree sp., *Palaquium karrak.*

kalamwir *vt.* To water, to cool with water. —**kelemwir,** *vi.*

kalahngan 1. *adj.* Kind, generous, merciful. 2. *n.* Kindness, generosity, mercy.

kalahngan en komwi *interj.* Thank you.

kalahp *n.* Pacific green back turtle.

kahlap 1. *n (3s: kahlepe).* Original; main part. 2. HONORIFIC. *n.* Body, of a person.

kalapada *adj.* Having thin legs and a large torso.

kalapw *adv.* Frequently. *E kin kalapw seiloak.* He frequently travels.

kalapwuk HONORIFIC. *vi.* To be alone. *E kalapwuk.* He is alone.

kalapwuhs *n.* Jail, prison; prisoner. [Span.]

kaladahn, also **akadahn** or **lakadahn.** *n.* A variety of banana. [Tagalog]

kalahdiki HONORIFIC. *vt.* To disdain.

kalawahda *vt.* To scare off.

kale, also **kaleke** or **kalekehte.** *sent. adv.* Don't dare. *Kale ke tangasangie.* Don't you dare run away from me.

kaleu, also **kalo.** *n (3s: kalewe).* Root.

kalehk *vi.* To fast or abstain from food. —**kalehki,** *vt.*

kahlek 1. *vi.* To dance. 2. *n.* A dance.

kahlek pwoaloapwoal 1. *n.* A Western style dance. 2. *vi.* To dance any Western style dance.

kaleke *sent. adv.* See *kale.*

kalekehte *sent. adv.* See *kale.*

kalehki *vt.* See *kalehk.*

kalelapak *vi.* To check, to inquire, to ask.

kalemwei *n.* Sp. of shellfish, found in fresh-water.

kalender *n.* Calendar. [Eng.]

kalewiala *vt.* To finish cooking food not done.

kalikasang *vt.* To wean; to train not to do something.

kalipe *vt.* To banish, to exile. —**kalipilip,** *vi.*

kalipilip *vi.* To be banished, to be exiled. —**kalipe,** *vt.*

kahlipw *n.* Pit, area for storing preserved breadfruit.

kalitopw *adj.* Causing a feeling of intoxication, of kava, alcohol, or sex.

kalo, also **kaleu.** *n (3s: kalewe).* Root.

kaloke *vt.* To punish; to antagonize. —**kalokolok,** *vi.*

kalokolok 1. *vi.* To be punished. 2. *n.* Punishment. —**kaloke,** *vt.*

kalon *n.* Gallon. [Eng.]

kaloalamwahu 1. *vi.* To comfort. 2. *n.* Native medicine used for a jealous spouse. —kaloalamwahwih, *vt.*

kaloalamwahwih *vt.* To comfort. —kaloalamwahu, *vi.*

kahlu 1. *n.* A marching dance. 2. *vi.* To perform a marching dance.

kaluhlu HONORIFIC. *vi.* To vomit.

kalupwur *vt.* To scrape the surface of something. —koalupwulupw, *vi.*

kaluhsih *vt.* To defeat; to waste. [*luhs*<Eng.] —koaluhs, *vi.*

kahluwa *vt.* To lead or guide.

kaluwanda *vt.* To remove some part of something so that it is no longer whole or complete.

kaluwenta 1. *n.* A kind of magic applied to blood from a wound, believed to cause death. 2. *vi.* To employ this kind of magic.

kama₁ *n.* Pot. [Jap.]

kama₂ *n.* Sickle. [Jap.]

kama₃ *n.* Comma. [Eng.]

kamair *vt.* To put to sleep.

kamaurada *vt.* To start, of an engine.

kamakam *vi. neut.* To spank or beat. —keme, *vt.*

kamakamala *vi.* To be killed; to be executed. —kemehla, *vt.*

kamala *vi.* To be killed. —kemehla, *vt.*

kamalaulau 1. *vi.* To be reduced in number. 2. *n.* Reduction. —kamalaulawih, *vt.*

kamalaulawih *vt.* To reduce in number. —kamalaulau, *vi.*

kamam *vt.* To enjoy, of any intoxicating drink.

kahmahm 1. *adj.* Given to denial, contradictive. 2. *n.* Denial, initial refusal out of politeness.

kamana *vt.* To make official, to authorize, to give official approval to. —kamanaman, *vi.*

kamanaman *vi.* To be made official, to be authorized, to be given official approval. —kamana, *vt.*

kamantik *vt.* To cautiously persuade; to move slowly, physically or mentally.

kamang *vt.* To kill a tree, by any method.

kamangaila *vt.* To simplify, to arrange in a simple manner, to delete some part of task.

kamangaida *vt.* To request; to get, to use.

kamara₁ *vt.* To lighten a burden, either physical or mental.

kamara₂ *n.* Camera. [Eng.]

kamarainih *vt.* To enlighten.

kamasak *vt.* To scare.

kamasriaparih *vt.* To double, as roofing or paper.

kamadal *vt.* To smooth out; to finish, as of concrete.

kamadamad *adj.* Insincere in the refusal of food, prompted by the dictates of hospitality.

kamadipw 1. *vi.* To feast. 2. *n.* Feast, party. —kemedipwe, *vt.*

kamadipw en peneinei 1. *n.* Family feast. 2. *vi.* To prepare this feast.

kamadipw en wahu 1. *n.* Feast given annually to pay tribute to the *Nahnmwarki*. 2. *vi.* To prepare this feast.

kamat *vi. neut.* To age, of food; to let get ripe. —kamata, *vt.*

kamata *vt.* See *kamat.*

kameimeiso HONORIFIC. *vi.* To pluck out whiskers.

kamel *n.* Camel. [Eng.]

kamehlel 1. *vi.* To be verified, to be believed to be true. 2. *n.* Final proof; final heat of a race. —kamehlele, *vt.*

kamehlele *vt.* To verify; to believe to be true. —kamehlel, *vi.*

kamedek *adj.* Painful, physically or mentally.

kampare *interj.* An exhortation, Do your best!. [Jap.]

kampio *vi.* To care for an invalid in the hospital. [Jap.] —kampioih, *vt.*

kampioih *vt.* See *kampio.*

kampilein *vi.* To file a complaint in court. [Eng.] —kampileinih, *vt.*

kampileinih *vt.* See *kampilein.*

kampos *n.* Compass. [Eng.]

kampwul *n.* Source of light.

kamwait *vt.* To entertain; to baby-sit, to pamper.

kamwahu₁ 1. *n.* Improvement; community improvement tax or labor. 2. *vi.* To do community improvement work.

kamwahu₂ *vi.* To settle a quarrel. —kamwahwih, *vt.*

kamwakel *vi.* To clean. —kamwakele, *vt.*

kamwakele *vt.* See *kamwakel.*

kamwakid *vt.* To move, to shake; to make a motion, as in a legislative proceeding. —**kemwekid,** *vi.*

kamwahl *vi.* To double-cross; to fool. —**kamwahlih,** *vt.*

kamwahlih *vt.* See *kamwahl.*

kamwamw *vt.* To exhaust, of a supply.

kamwan 1. *n.* Joke. 2. *vi.* To joke or tease. —**kemwene,** *vt.*

kamwarak *vt.* To spread out, as a mat; to sow, as seed.

kamwatau, also **kamwataur.** *vt.* To dangle; to hang, as the legs from a chair.

kamwataur, also **kamwatau.** *vt.* See *kamwatau.*

kamwahwih *vt.* To improve; to settle a quarrel; to say good things about someone. —**kamwahu₂,** *vi.*

kamweng 1. *vi.* To be fed; to make a small feast; to provide food. 2. *n.* Fertilizer. —**kamwenge,** *vt.*

kamwenge *vt.* To feed. —**kamweng,** *vi.*

kamwer 1. *n.* Seed bed; bait arranged on the ocean floor to lure turtles. 2. *vi.* To make a seed bed; to arrange bait on the ocean floor to lure turtles.

kamwetel *n.* Earthworm; hair roots of kava.

kamwot *vi.* To be shortened, to be abbreviated.

kamwotial 1. *n.* A kind of magic, performed to shorten a distance, as when carrying a heavy load. 2. *vi.* To employ this kind of magic.

kan, also **akan.** *dem. mod.* Those, by you.

Kahn Sapwen Kohwa Likilik en Dekehn Pacific *n.* Trust Territory of the Pacific Islands.

kana *vi.* To win. [Span.]

kanai *vt.* To cherish; to add small stones to an *uhmw.* —**keneinei,** *adj.*

kanaiehng *vt.* To take care of, to watch out for.

kanakan ARCHAIC. *adj.* Good.

kanahng *interj.* Hurry up!, Come on!

kanahng- *vt.* To continue on. *Kanahngala omw mwengehn!* Continue your eating!

kaneng *adj.* Having contents; well developed, of the tuber of a plant; having a large clitoris.

kaneng en uhmw *vi.* To provide food to be prepared in the *uhmw* at a *kamadipw.*

kanengamah *adj.* Patient.

kanenge *n3s.* Substance; inside of something, contents.

Kanep *n.* Title of the wife of a *Kaniki Ririn.*

Kaniki *n.* A title.

Kaniki Ririn *n.* A title, in the *Nahnken* line.

Kanikihn Sapawas *n.* A title.

kahnihmw *n.* City.

kanu *adj.* Ripe, before the stage called *mat.*

kahnsapw *n.* Group of sizeable islands.

kansenoh₁ *adj.* Important.

kansenoh₂ 1. *vi.* To confess. 2. *n.* Confession.

kanser 1. *n.* Cancer. 2. *vi.* To have cancer. [Eng.]

kansohpa *n.* Copra drying shed. [Jap.]

kahndeke *n.* Archipelago; group of islands.

kandehla *n.* Candle. [Span.]

kandoku *n.* Watchman. [Jap.]

kanti *n.* Hard candy. [Jap.<Eng.]

kang *vt.* To eat.

kahng₁ *vt.* To dislike, to refuse.

kahng₂ *n.* Row; mountain range; small stream.

kahng₃ *vt.* To visit door by door.

kangid *vt.* To pound or press something into a thick, heavy mass; to chew into fine particles.

kangidirawi *vi.* To be falsely accused; to be a scapegoat.

kangkohdang *n.* Tourist party. [Jap.]

kangkuru *n.* Kangaroo. [Eng.]

kap *num. cl.* Used in counting bundles or sheaves. *kepen tuwi riakap* two sheaves of firewood.

kahp *n.* Curve. [Jap.<Eng.]

kapa *n.* Copper. [Eng.]

kapahieu *num.* Fourth.

kapaik *vt.* To carry on one's shoulder. —**kepeik,** *vi.*

kapailok 1. *adj.* Insulting. 2. *n.* Insult. —**kapailoke,** *vt.*

kapailoke *vt.* To insult. —**kapailok,** *adj.*

kahpaido *n.* Carbide, carbide lamp. [Jap.<Eng.]

kapaidok HONORIFIC. *vi.* To hear, to listen. —**kapaidoke,** *vt.*

kapaidoke *vt.* See *kapaidok.*

kapakap₁ 1. *vi.* To pray. 2. *n.* Prayer.

kapakap₂ *n.* Bundle, sheaf.

kapal *vt.* To knead, as of dough. —**kepel,** *vi.*

kapang *n.* Suitcase. [Jap.]

kapapeseng *vt.* To extend one's arms; to train a hibiscus tree in order to direct the growth of a yam vine.

kapar 1. *vi.* To march. 2. *n.* A march or a procession. —**kapara₁,** *vt.*

kapahr *vi.* To look for wild mountain yams.

kapara₁ *vt.* To walk together with physical contact; to associate with. —**kapar,** *vi.*

kapara₂ *vt.* To breed. —**kaparapar,** *adj.*

kaparapar *adj.* Fertile, procreating prolifically. —**kapara₂,** *vt.*

kapahrek 1. *vi.* To give a speech or sermon; to align, to equalize, to level. 2. *n.* Speech or sermon.

kapas 1. *n.* Feast made for a fishing party. 2. *vi.* To prepare this feast.

kapasa *vi.* To fasten, to affix.

kapasmwar 1. *n.* Feast of public acceptance of a title. 2. *vi.* To prepare this feast.

kapat 1. *vi.* To add. 2. *n.* Addition. —**kapata,** *vt.*

kapata *vt.* See *kapat.*

kapatau, also **kopatau.** *n.* Phlegm.

kapahtou *adj.* Sad.

kape *vt.* To play with a toy canoe or boat.

kapei *n.* A cure for blindness caused by magic.

kapeilokaia *vi.* To talk back.

kapel 1. *n.* Feast to welcome someone coming or returning to Ponape. 2. *vi.* To prepare this feast.

kapehme *vt.* To make someone realize his mistake.

kapehr *n.* A variety of torch ginger, *Geocardia herbacea.*

kaperen *adj.* Amusing, pleasant, funny.

kaped *vi.* To deflower, to cause a girl to lose her virginity. —**kapede,** *vt.*

kapehd *n (3s: kapehde).* Belly, guts.

kapede *vt.* See *kaped.*

kapehden neh *n3s.* Arch of the foot.

kapi *n3s.* Bottom, the lowest part of yam or taro.

kapil *vt.* To encircle, to go around; to circle.

kapir *vt.* To turn or twist. —**kepir₂,** *vi.*

kapirada *vt.* To wake someone up.

kapisel *vt.* To shoot, to perform the action which discharges a weapon.

kapiser *vt.* To hasten.

kapihdi *vt.* To influence or prejudice another's opinion.

kapidolong₁ *vt.* To submit; to admit.

kapidolong₂ 1. *n.* Feast for a new dwelling house. 2. *vi.* To prepare this feast.

kapit₁ HONORIFIC. *vi.* To talk, to speak.

kapit₂ *vt.* To pry out; to relax a wire or stick under tension. —**kepit₁,** *vi.*

kapit₃ *vt.* To rescue, to loose an animal or a person; to salvage.

kapitih *vt.* To joke with, to tease. —**kepit₂,** *adj.*

kapose *vt.* To detonate; to pop, as a balloon.

kapw *adj.* New.

kapwai *vt.* To criticize or insult another, usually of women.

kapwaiada *vt.* To fulfill.

kahpwal *n.* Undesirable result, problem, difficulty.

kapwala *vi.* To visit a place for the first time; to refurbish or make like new again.

kapwang *adj.* Tiresome, boring.

kapwarsou HONORIFIC. 1. *vi.* To eat breakfast. 2. *n.* Breakfast.

kapwad *vt.* To insert or retract.

kapwadala *vt.* To leak, as a secret; to reveal.

kapwat 1. *n.* Decoration, ornament, or new outfit of clothing; flower, used generically; garland. 2. *vi.* To decorate or ornament. —**kapwata,** *vt.*

kapwata *vt.* See *kapwat.*

kapwatapwat *adj.* Ornamented, outfitted in new clothing.

kapweiek *vt.* To stop some action.

kapwer 1. *vi.* To be the smallest. 2. *n.* Runt, of a litter; smallest one, as of a bunch of coconuts.

kapwie *n.* Cafe. [Jap.<French]

kapwoi *n.* Sp. of pepper plant, the leaves of which are used as a wrapping for betel nut. [Yapese]

kapwonopwon *adj.* Mysterious.

kapwowiala *vt.* To postpone or cancel.

kapwur *vi. neut.* To repound kava.
—**kapwure**, *vt.*

kapwuhr *vt.* To scare someone by surprising him.

kapwur moahl *vi. neut.* To repound kava with a small stone.

kapwur peh *vi. neut.* To repound kava with the fist.

kapwure *vt.* To repound kava.
—**kapwur**, *vi.*

kapwus *n.* Any of a number of ceremonies performed to bring luck to a fishing net.

kapwusenleng *n.* A net ceremony given to the *enihlap*.

kapwusenlimw *n.* A net ceremony requiring the performance of sexual intercourse prior to use of the net.

kapwusenmaraki *n.* A net ceremony introduced from the East.

kapwude *vt.* To remove a yam by cutting it below the vine so that another yam will develop.

kapwudong *adj.* Itchy or irritating.

kapwkapwewasa *interj.* It's useless!, It's in vain!.

kapwkapwung *n.* Discussion.

kar₁ *vt.* To comb. —**keriker₂**, *vi.*

kar₂ *vt.* To gather reeds; to cut down vines.

karaun 1. *vi.* To make an accusation. 2. *n.* Accusation. —**karaunih**, *vt.*

karaun likamw 1. *vi.* To make a false accusation. 2. *n.* False accusation.
—**karaun likamwih** or **karaun likemwe**, *vt.*

karaun likamwih, also **karaun likemwe**. *vt.* To falsely accuse.
—**karaun likamw**, *vi.*

karaun likemwe, also **karaun likamwih**. *vt.* See *karaun likamwih*.

karaunih *vt.* To accuse. —**karaun**, *vi.*

karahk *vi.* To move with a low profile, as in a squatting or bent over position; short legged.

karakar *adj.* Warm, hot; angry.

karakarahk *adj.* Low, respectful, humble.

karakaramwahu HONORIFIC. *vi.* To warm oneself by a fire.

karahkidi *vi.* To crouch down; to descend from the sky, as thunder or an airplane.

karanih *vt.* To be near or close to.
—**keren**, *adj.*

karang *vt.* To dry by heat, as copra or tobacco. —**kereng**, *vi.*

karangahp *n.* Fish sp., yellowfin tuna, *Neothunnus macropterus*.

karapahu *n.* Carabao, water buffalo. [Span.]

karapih *vt.* To creep up to; to sneak up to. —**kerep**, *vi.*

karara *n.* Tree sp., *Myristica hypargyraea*.

kararan *adj.* Having a tickling effect.

kararanda *vi.* To be sexually stimulated by petting.

karasapene *vt.* To compare.

karasaras *vi.* To give an example; to make an analogy; to point out a paradox.

karasepe *n3s.* Example.

karada *vi.* To board, to step up onto, to climb aboard.

karat *n.* A variety of banana.

karateniap *n.* A variety of banana.

karawan *vt.* To chase away; to shoo.

kahre *vt.* To lead or guide; to take someone to some place. —**pakahr**, *vi.*

kahrepe *n3s.* Cause, reason, purpose.

karer 1. *adj.* Sour. 2. *n.* Citrus, lime, lemon.

karerrer *adj.* Frightening.

kahrehda *vt.* To cause, to be the reason for. *Ih me karehda liho sengiseng.* That's the cause of that woman's crying.

kariau *num.* Second.

karindong *n.* A kind of sugar-coated cookie. [Jap.]

karipin *n.* Carbine. [Eng.]

karipwude *vt.* To scratch, as when itching. —**keripwud**, *vi.*

karis *vi.* To march.

karihs *vt.* To snap off. —**kerihri**, *vi.*

karisihn *n.* Kerosene. [Eng.]

karonge, also **koaronge**. HONORIFIC. 1. *vt.* To hear, to listen. 2. *n.* Ear.

karongorong 1. *vi.* To hold a hearing. 2. *n.* A hearing.

karongorongki *vt.* To hint.

karuwaru *adj.* Hurried, rushed.
—**keruwa**, *vt.*

karmihna *n.* Bush sp., *Angelonia gardneri*.

kahs₁ *vi.* To speak in anger; to boast.

kahs₂, also **kahsilihn**. *n.* Gasoline. [Eng.]

kahs₃ *n.* Deck of playing cards. [Eng.]

kasah *n3s.* Side of a canoe opposite the outrigger.

kasahi *vi. neut.* To turn a canoe away from the outrigger.

kasaing *vt.* To meet, to meet by chance.

kasau *vt.* To transfer, to move or change location; to postpone. —**kosou,** *vi.*

kasak *n.* Bowl, used in the preparation of food.

kasakas HONORIFIC. **1.** *vi.* To pray. **2.** *n.* Prayer.

kasale- *vt.* To show or expose; to introduce or make something known. —**kasansal,** *vi.*

kasaloh *adj.* Nerve-wracking.

kasalowe *vt.* To cause another to be nervous.

kasamwoh *vt.* To welcome; to lead one's aim when shooting birds. —**koasoamw,** *vi.*

kasansal **1.** *vi.* To be exposed, to be exhibited. **2.** *n.* Exhibition. —**kasale-,** *vt.*

kasahnwar *vi.* To exchange information.

kasang₁ *n (3s: kesenge).* Fork, as of a tree, road, etc.; spaces between the fingers and toes;.

kasang₂ HONORIFIC. *n.* Neck.

kasangat *adj.* Failing to provide entertainment, causing loneliness.

kasap *n.* Bird sp., frigate bird.

kasapal *n.* Fish sp., silverfish, *Gerres abbreviatus* or *Gerres kapas.*

kasapahl *vi.* To return an action in kind.

kasapwil *vt.* To change the status of someone or something, to graduate. —**kesepwil,** *vi.*

kasapwurupwur *adj.* Complicated.

kasar **1.** *n.* A type of net fishing, where fish are chased into the net. **2.** *vi.* To fish in this manner.

kasarawi₁ *vt.* To celebrate; to observe a holiday; to dedicate; to bless, to consecrate.

kasarawi₂ *vi.* To be taboo.

kasare *vt.* To send away, to cast out; to drive fish into a net. —**pakasar,** *vi.*

kasaroh pwunan *interj.* You lose!, Too bad!, Tough luck!; often shortened to *kasaroh.*

kasawa *vi.* To hatch.

kasawih *vt.* To examine, to diagnose, to make a choice, to guess. —**keseu,** *vi.*

kahsekir *vi.* To walk backwards.

kaselel **1.** *adj.* Precious, beautiful, perfect, fine. **2.** *interj.* An informal greeting or leave taking expression, as Hi! or Bye!.

kaselehlie *interj.* A formal greeting or leave taking expression, as hello or goodbye.

kasik *vt.* To expect, to await.

kasikih *vt.* To shoot. —**kesik,** *vi.*

kahsilihn, also **kahs₂.** *n.* Gasoline. [Eng.]

kasingai *n.* Large staple, as used in building. [Jap.]

kasoutik HONORIFIC. **1.** *vi.* To eat dinner. **2.** *n.* Dinner.

kasouwas HONORIFIC. **1.** *vi.* To eat lunch. **2.** *n.* Lunch.

kasokamai *vi.* To build a fish trap of coral or stone on a reef.

kasongosong *vt.* To tempt, to entice.

kasohre *vt.* To make vanish; to dismiss, as a court case; to abolish. *Kowe me kak kasorehla ah nsensuwedo.* You are the one who can make his unhappiness vanish.

kasosohng *vt.* To equate, to compare in terms of size; to imitate.

kasohtik *adj.* Conservative, not wasteful, conserved; sparing. —**kasohtikih,** *vt.*

kasohtikih *vt.* To conserve. —**kasohtik,** *adj.*

kasohwe *vt.* To consider of no consequence; to disregard; to hold in contempt, as in court.

kasuwo *n.* Fish sp., skipjack tuna, *Katsawonus pelamis.* [Jap.]

kasuwopwisi *n.* Dried skipjack tuna. [Jap.]

kassoku *vi.* To train for an athletic event. [Jap.]

kasdo *n.* Movie, motion picture. *I men kilang kasdohn palapal.* I want to see a sword fighting movie. [Jap.]

kadaileng *vi.* To sing in a loud falsetto.

kadau *adj.* Tiresome, physically.

kadauluhl *vt.* To cause to move further; to pass along; to go on; to kill or finish off, of something wounded.

kadaur₁ *vt.* To recall the past history of. —**kadoudou** or **kodoudou,** *vi.*

kadaur₂ *vt.* To throw with a hip toss.

kadaudok *n.* Descendant, offspring, of humans.

kadall *vi.* To swallow. —**kadalle** or **kadanle,** *vt.*

kadalle, also **kadanle.** *vt.* To swallow. —**kadall,** *vi.*

kahdaneki *vt.* To name.

kadanle, also **kadalle.** *vt.* To swallow. —**kadall,** *vi.*

kadang *vt.* To stretch, to make taut; to tense, of the muscles. —**kedeng,** *vi.*

kadangada *vt.* To press or iron. —**kedengida,** *vi.*

kadar *vt.* To send; to let go, to release. —**pekeder,** *vi.*

kadahr 1. *vi.* To roll a toy wheel. 2. *n.* Toy wheel. —**kadahre,** *vt.*

kadahre *vt.* To slide or roll, as a toy wheel. —**kadahr,** *vi.*

kadawahl *n.* Food given to guests to take to their parents as a token of respect.

kadawado 1. *vi.* To sing a song to soothe a restless child. 2. *n.* Song to soothe a restless child, often one which tells a story of a child of antiquity.

kadeik 1. *vt.* To ask about, to inquire, to question; to judge. 2. *n.* A judgment. —**pakadeik,** *vi.*

kadeikpen loale *n3s.* Conscience.

kadek₁ *adj.* Kind, generous.

kadek₂ *adj.* Good at something, clever.

kadek₃ *n.* Fish sp..

kadekedek *vi.* To shout in a falsetto voice, either when carrying kava or to challenge another to a fight.

kahdeng *n.* Curtain. [Eng.]

kadehde 1. *vt.* To witness, to observe or hear something with certainty, to testify. 2. *n.* Testimony.

Kadehde Kapw *n.* New Testament.

Kadehde Mering *n.* Old Testament.

kading₁ *vt.* To tickle. —**kediked,** *vi.*

kading₂ *vt.* To cut open, for the purpose of removing the contents. —**ked,** *vi.*

kadip 1. *vi.* To accuse. 2. *n.* Accusation. —**kadipa,** *vt.*

kadipa *vt.* To accuse. —**kadip,** *vi.*

kadipadip *n.* Criminal or civil complaint.

kadipw *vt.* To trace or track, as the spoor of an animal.

kadipw nta 1. *n.* A kind of magic applied to blood from a wound, believed to cause death. 2. *vi.* To employ this kind of magic.

Kadipwan *n.* Title of the wife of a *Nahn Pohnpei.*

kadiring *n.* Plant sp., the leaves of which are used as a spice.

kadoukeinek, also **kodoukeinek.** *vi.* To trace one's ancestry according to clan.

kadoudou, also **kodoudou.** *vi.* To trace one's ancestry, to recall past history. —**kadaur₁,** *vt.*

kadoke *n3s.* Tip, of anything high.

kadokehla *vt.* To complete by adding to. —**kadokodokala,** *vi.*

kadokenmei HONORIFIC. *n.* Head.

kadokodokala *vi.* To be complete, as a consequence of being added to. —**kadokehla,** *vt.*

kahdolik *n.* Catholic. [Eng.]

kadongodong *adj.* Unlikeable, obnoxious, despicable.

kadorsingko *n.* Mosquito coil. [Jap.]

kaduh *vt.* To submerge.

kat, also **ka₁, aka₁,** or **akat.** *dem. mod.* These, by me.

kaht₁ *n.* Ant.

kaht₂ *n.* Cat. [Eng.]

kataiau *adj.* Dilatory, said of a child who stalls before carrying out instructions.

katairong *vi.* To be noisy; a command to Shut up! or Be quiet! —**kataironge,** *vt.*

kataironge *vt.* To disturb with noise. —**katairong,** *vi.*

Katau ARCHAIC. *n.* Kusaie.

Katau Peidak ARCHAIC. *n.* Kusaie.

Katau Peidi ARCHAIC. *n.* Yap.

katauk HONORIFIC. *n.* Canoe house.

kataul *n (3s: kataule).* Gizzard.

kataur *n.* Sp. of shellfish, found in fresh and salt water.

kataman 1. *vt.* To remember or recollect; to carry a number, as in the process of addition. 2. *n.* Recollection.

katamaniki *vt.* To remind.

katapan *adj.* Useful, worthwhile, valuable, advantageous.

katar *n.* Fern sp., *Cyathea ponapeana* or *nigricans,* a tree fern.

kate *vt.* To stone, to throw rocks at.

kateng 1. *n.* Belt. 2. *vi.* To wear a belt.

31

katengenei *vi.* To start to fly, of a young bird.

katep₁ *n.* Pile of leaves or banana stems placed on the ground to cushion the fall of breadfruit being picked.

katep₂ *n (3s: katepe).* Worth.

katepeik 1. *n.* Feast given to celebrate the first fishing trips with a new canoe. 2. *vi.* To prepare this feast.

katepweke *vt.* To throw at.

katiasang *vt.* To miss an event; to lose one's footing.

katik₁ *adj.* Bitter tasting, of anything.

katik₂ *n.* Fish sp..

katik₃ *vt.* To underestimate.

katikala *vt.* To take in, as clothing; to discourage. —**ketikila,** *vi.*

katoutoupe *n3s.* Burden.

katokiedi *vt.* To stop.

katop *n.* Sp. of sea cucumber.

katohre *vt.* To subtract; to separate. —**katohrohr,** *vi.*

katohrepeseng *vt.* To sort or separate; to segregate. —**katohrohrpeseng,** *vi.*

katohrohr 1. *vi.* To subtract; to be separated; to be segregated. 2. *n.* Subtraction. —**katohre,** *vt.*

katohrohrpeseng *vi.* To be sorted or separated. —**katohrepeseng,** *vt.*

katuk *vt.* To stab.

katwelwel ARCHAIC. *n.* Tail.

kawa₁ *n.* Long ago. *Irail mehn kawa ko me kehlail.* Those people of long ago were strong.

kawa₂, also **kawakusu.** *n.* Leather shoes. [Jap.]

kawai *vt.* To move something slowly and quietly; to snatch, to steal, to do something illegal.

kawahki *vt.* To depend on.

kawakusu, also **kawa₂.** *n.* Leather shoes. [Jap.]

kawaluh *num.* Ninth.

kawe *vt.* To criticize.

kaweid *vt.* To lead or guide; to set an example for; to advise.

kaweidsuwed *vi.* To lead someone to do wrong. —**kaweidsuwedih,** *vt.*

kaweidsuwedih *vt.* See *kaweidsuwed.*

kawehla *vt.* To break, to destroy, to ruin.

kawenehdi, also **kaunehdi.** *vt.* To lay someone or something down; to change something from a vertical to a horizontal position;.

kawehdi *vt.* To double-cross one member of a married couple, as a consequence of participation in an extra-marital affair.

kawehwe *vt.* To explain, to translate.

kahwin *vi. neut.* To scale or pluck. —**kahwina** or **kauna,** *vt.*

kahwina, also **kauna.** *vt.* To scale or pluck. —**kahwin,** *vi.*

ke₁ *subj. pron.* You.

ke₂ *vt.* To bite. —**keikei,** *vi.*

kei 1. *vi. neut.* To anoint; to apply to the skin, as medicine. 2. *n.* Oil, lotion. —**keie,** *vt.*

kei- *vi.* To move. *Ohlo keido limwahi.* That man moved near me. —**kai-,** *vt.*

kehi *n.* A large yam tied to a pole, requiring two men to carry it.

keie *vt.* To anoint. —**kei,** *vi.*

keieu 1. *num.* First. 2. *adv.* Most.

keielekda *vi.* To start, of a court case; to convene, of a meeting.

kehieng *vt.* To be allergic to, to easily contract, as an illness.

keik *n.* Cake. [Eng.]

keikei *vi.* To bite. —**ke₂,** *vt.*

keilahn aio *n.* Long ago. *Wahr oapwoat seisang sekeren wai keilahn aio.* A canoe traveled from a foreign shore long ago.

keile *n3s.* Edge.

keimw *n (3s: keimwi).* Corner, angle; close clan relations.

keimwinneh *n3s.* Heel.

keimwinpeh *n3s.* Elbow.

keimwinwar *n (3s: keimwinwere).* End of a canoe.

keimwisak *vt.* To finish; to accomplish something. —**keimwisek,** *vi.*

keimwisek *vi.* To be finished; to be accomplished. —**keimwisak,** *vt.*

kehimwidi *vi.* To become very ill, incapacitated, bed-ridden.

keimwoale *vi.* To be oiled, to be shiny with oil.

keimwpahieu 1. *n.* Rectangle. 2. *vi.* To be rectangular.

keimwsiluh 1. *n.* Triangle. 2. *vi.* To be triangular.

keinahki *vt.* To blame.

keinapwih *vt.* To prohibit. —**keinepwi,** *vi.*

keinek *n.* Lineage, extended family, clan.

keinemwe HONORIFIC. *vt.* To ask.

keinepwi *vi.* To be prohibited.
—**keinapwih**, *vt.*

keinimek *adj.* Uninformed.

keinihn HONORIFIC. *vi.* To be
intoxicated.

keinuhnu HONORIFIC. *n.* Nose.

keingihng *adj.* Tilted, listing.

keipwekidi HONORIFIC. *vi.* To sit down,
to lower oneself.

keipweni HONORIFIC. *interj.* An
expression commonly used when
making a speech in the presence of
important people, asking forgiveness
for one's unworthiness.

keirek *adj.* Dense, tightly woven or
packed.

keirida *vi.* To grow up, to progress.

keiru *vi.* To stay temporarily.

keisar *n (3s: keisere)*. Pancreas.

keisek *num.* Tenth.

keisuh *num.* Seventh.

keid, also **weid₂**. *vi.* To walk in a
specific direction.

kehid *n.* Plant sp., useful in starting
fires.

keidek HONORIFIC. *vt.* To ask.

keidisol 1. *n.* Feast given at the end of
the yam season. 2. *vi.* To prepare this
feast.

keidu *n.* Central post of a *nahs*.

keidupwus *adj.* Hairy, of the navel.

kehoaroahr *n.* Plant sp., with a pink
flower.

kehu *n.* Mast, of a canoe or ship.

keus ARCHAIC. *interr.* Who goes there?

kehk *vi.* To give out from exhaustion.

kehke *n (3s: kehkeh)*. Stem of a fruit.

kehkei *n.* Any frightening thing or
person, used with children.

kekel 1. *adj.* Hard, not soft. 2. *vi.* To
have an erection. 3. *n.* Erection.

kehkehlik *vi.* To give instructions
before leaving or dying; to make a
will.

kekeluwak *adj.* Hard, not soft; tough, as
of meat.

kekihr 1. *n.* A type of taut line fishing,
done off the bottom. 2. *vi.* To taut
line fish off the bottom.

kehl₁ *n.* Strength.

kehl₂ *n.* Enclosure, pen, fence, wall, as
of a fort.

kehl₃ 1. *adj.* Very hot, of objects. 2. *n.*
Heat.

kehlail *adj.* Strong, powerful, healthy.

keleu, also **kolou**. *n.* Hibiscus sp.,
Hibiscus tiliaceus, the inner bark of
which is used as a bast in the
preparation of kava.

keleun and *n.* Hibiscus sp., *Kleinhovia
hospita*, used for making outriggers.

keleun wai *n.* Hibiscus sp., *Hibiscus
rosa-sinensis*.

keleunleng *n.* Hibiscus sp..

kelek *n.* A large basket made from a
palm frond.

kelemwed *n.* A small sp. of bat.

kelemwir *vi.* To be watered; to be
cooled with water. —**kalamwir**, *vt.*

kelen mahn *n.* Cage.

kelehpw *vi.* To be alone. *E kelehpw.*
He was alone;

kelepwiki *vi.* To kneel.

keliali, also **kiliali**. HONORIFIC. *vi.* To
vomit.

kelikemwe *vt.* To disbelieve.

kelimau *num.* Fifth.

kelimwed *n.* A small sp. of bat.

kelingeringer *adj.* Irritating,
bothersome, annoying.

kelipa HONORIFIC. *vi.* To joke or tease.

keluhla *vt.* To do something, either
that one knows is wrong or that turns
out to be wrong; to repent.

kehma *n.* Tree sp., *Terminalia
carolinensis*.

keme *vt.* To spank or beat.
—**kamakam**, *vi.*

kemei *n.* Sp. of shellfish.

kehmei 1. *n.* Second feast of the
breadfruit season. 2. *vi.* To prepare
this feast.

kemeik *n.* Fish sp., humphead
parrotfish, *Bolbometopon muricatus*.

kemehla *vt.* To kill, to execute.
—**kamala** or **kamakamala**, *vi.*

kemenkouruhr *adj.* Funny, amusing.

kemenseng₁ HONORIFIC. 1. *vi.* To eat
breakfast. 2. *n.* Breakfast.

kemenseng₂ *n.* A kava planting; area
where kava is planted.

kemenda *vt.* To tame.

kemed *n.* Sp. of sea cucumber.

kemedipwe *vt.* To make a feast for.
—**kamadipw**, *vi.*

kemisik *n.* Fresh water eel.

kehmmarepe *n.* A variety of yam.

kehmmarepehn kehpwetik *n.* A variety of yam.

kemmad, also **kiemmad. 1.** *vi.* To put on dry clothes. **2.** *n.* Dry clothes one puts on, extra clothes taken on a trip. **—kemmade,** *vt.*

kemmade *vt.* To give someone dry clothes. **—kemmad** or **kiemmad,** *vi.*

kehmmeirkelik *n.* A variety of yam.

kehmmeirkelik mwotomwot *n.* A variety of yam, slow in maturing.

kehmmeirkelik pwetepwet *n.* A variety of yam, slow in maturing, having white flesh.

kehmmeirkelik weitahta *n.* A variety of yam, slow in maturing, having red flesh.

kehmmwas *n.* A variety of yam, thin, with fibrous roots.

kehmmwot *n.* A variety of yam, bearing seeds.

kehmmwot en namwanamw *n.* A variety of yam.

kehmmwot en pohnpei *n.* A variety of yam.

kehmmwuterek *n.* A variety of yam.

kehmpahini *n.* A variety of yam.

kempak *adj.* Shallow as a consequence of being flat-bottomed, as a canoe.

kehmpalai *n.* A variety of yam, producing fruit on the vine.

kehmpekehi *n.* A variety of yam.

kempenial *n.* Bush sp., *Psychotria carolinensis.*

kempoake *adj.* Pitiful, saddening.

kehmpuwalap *n.* A variety of yam, non-native.

kehmpuwetik *n.* A variety of yam, non-native.

kehmpwedawel *n.* A variety of yam.

kemwekid 1. *vi. neut.* To be made to move or shake. **2.** *n.* A motion, as in a legislative proceeding. **—kamwakid,** *vt.*

kemwene *vt.* To joke with, to tease. **—kamwan,** *vi.*

kemwetemwet *vi.* To make an insincere offer of food, prompted by the dictates of hospitality.

kemwurala *vt.* To say farewell to a traveler or a dying person.

kemwurumwur *vi.* To make a final statement or perform a final action.

kehn₁ *adv.* Easily. *E kehn lingeringer.* He's easily angered.

kehn₂ *vt.* To feel, to experience.

kehnaramas *adj.* Of a place, attracting many people.

kene *poss. cl.* A possessive classifier for edibles. *E sohte kang kene dohnaso.* He didn't eat his doughnut.

kenei sakau 1. *vi.* To eat after drinking kava. **2.** *n.* Meal after kava.

keneinei *adj.* Cherished, well cared for. **—kanai,** *vt.*

kehnek *adj.* Prone to premature ejaculation.

-kenen *aff.* Suffix used to form singular emphatic pointing and demonstrative pronouns. *iet* here, by me, *ietkenen* here by me!; *met* this one, by me, *metkenen* this one, by me!.

-kenenkan *aff.* Suffix used to form plural emphatic pointing and demonstrative pronouns.

keniken *adj.* Favorite.

kehnmant *n.* Tree sp., *Randia cochinchinensis.*

kehnpap *n.* Tree sp., *Syzygium carolinense.*

kehnpwil *n.* Tree sp., *Garcinia ponapensis.*

kens 1. *n.* Yaws. **2.** *vi.* To be infected; to ulcerate.

kensa *vi.* To examine, to have a physical examination. [Jap.]

kehndake *n.* Ladder, steps, stairs.

kehndawih *vt.* See *kehndou.*

kendip₁ *vi.* To spit.

kendip₂ *n.* Fish sp..

kendo 1. *vi.* To estimate. **2.** *n.* Estimate, estimation. [Jap.]

kehndou 1. *n.* A line or pole placed between a yam planting and the branches of a tree in order to direct the growth of the yam vine upward. **2.** *vi.* To employ a line or pole for this purpose. **—kehndawih,** *vt.*

kent *n (3s: kenti).* Urine.

kehnti *n.* Part of the outrigger support of a canoe.

kehntik *adj.* Easily awakened.

kehnwasa *adj.* Easily awakened; conscious.

keng *adj.* Sharp, of an edge or point.

kehng *n.* Fish sp., sweetlips porgy, *Plectorhynchus goldmani* or *Plectorhynchus chaetodontoides.*

kengir　n. Belt.

kehngid　n. Mango.

kehngid en pohnpei　n. Tree sp., a variety of mango.

kehngitik　vi. To move to a cooler area.

kengk　n. Coconut, containing no nut.

kengkang　n. Porch; covered stoop of a Japanese style house. [Jap.]

kep$_1$　vi. To consume something, especially medicine, before kava.

kep$_2$　n. Cup. [Eng.]

kehp　n. Yam, generic term.

kehp kos　n. A variety of yam.

kehp lapwed　n. A variety of yam.

kehp send　n. A variety of yam.

kehp silik　n. A variety of yam, having red flesh.

kehp tipaker　n. A variety of yam, cigar-shaped.

kehp tuhke　n. Cassava, manioc, tapioca.

kepe　n3s. Thigh.

kepe-　vt. To carry in a bundle. *Liho kepehla arail tuwi.* That woman carried their bundle of firewood.

kehpei　n. Tree sp.; very light driftwood; cork.

kepeia　vt. To consider fortunate.

kepeiahda　vt. To make one rich. *Mwangas me kepeiahda ohlo.* Copra is what made that man rich.

kepeik　vi. To carry on one's shoulder. —kapaik, vt.

kepeira　vi. Of a yam vine, to put out runners in all directions.

kepehiso　HONORIFIC. n. Thigh.

kepeukuhk　HONORIFIC. n. Sennit.

kepel　vi. To be kneaded, as of dough. —kapal, vt.

kepelipel　adj. Taboo.

kehpenei　n. A variety of yam.

kehpeneikesu　n. A variety of yam.

kepennok　n. Broom made from the inner ribs of palm fronds.

keper　adj. Dangerous.

keperepere　n3s. Descendant, offspring, usually of animals.

kepikirot　vi. To be in the dark without a source of light.

kepiloal$_1$　1. vi. To take medicine or magic for protection or to instill certain qualities in the one taking it. 2. n. The medicine or magic employed for this purpose.

kepiloal$_2$　adj. Deep, of the hull of a canoe.

kepin　n. Captain. [Eng.]

kehpin and　n. A variety of yam, from And.

kehpin awai sohkatepe　n. A variety of yam, from Hawaii.

kehpin kipar　n. A variety of yam, from Kipar, fruit-bearing.

kehpin kipar weitahta　n. A variety of yam, having red flesh.

kehpin lohd　n. A variety of yam, from Lohd.

kehpin lupwu　n. A variety of yam.

kehpin mweli　n. A variety of yam, sweet-smelling.

kehpin na kitik　n. A variety of yam.

kehpin namwo kepeu　n. A variety of yam.

kehpin namwo kepsu　n. A variety of yam.

kehpin namwo pwetepwet　n. A variety of yam, having sweet-smelling, white flesh.

kehpin namwo weitahta　n. A variety of yam, having sweet-smelling, red flesh.

kehpin nanpeilam　n. A variety of yam, from Peilam.

kehpin palau pwetepwet　n. A variety of yam, from Palau, having white flesh.

kehpin palau weitahta　n. A variety of yam, from Palau, having red flesh.

kehpin peisaper　n. A variety of yam.

kehpin pehleng　n. A variety of yam, from Pehleng.

kehpin penieu　n. A variety of yam, from Penieu.

kehpin pisi　n. A variety of yam, from Fiji.

kehpin pwahr　n. A variety of yam, having a sweet flavor.

kehpin sapahn　n. A variety of yam, from Japan.

kehpin seini　n. A variety of yam, from China.

kehpin seipahn　n. A variety of yam, from Saipan.

kehpin dolen pohnpei　n. A variety of yam.

kehpin dolen wai pwetepwet　n. A variety of yam, having white flesh.

kehpin dolen wai weitahta　n. A variety of yam, having red flesh.

kepin dowehlap HONORIFIC. *vi.* To drink kava from the same cup immediately after the *Nahnmwarki*.

kepin tihn peh *n3s.* Shoulder joint.

kehpin tomwara *n.* A variety of yam, from Tomwara.

kehpin wai *n.* A variety of yam.

kepina *n.* Governor, district administrator. [Eng.]

kepinan 1. *vi.* Full of pus, pussy. 2. *n.* A pus filled infection.

kehpineir *n.* A variety of yam, surface rooted.

kehpineir en wai *n.* A variety of yam.

kehpinou *n.* A variety of yam.

kepinpaiki *n3s.* Lower part of the back of the head.

kepinpil *n.* Mouth of a river.

kepinsinoangi *n.* Original branch of kava that is planted.

kepinwar *n.* Provisions taken on a trip; gift taken on a trip; good deeds, used biblically; advice taken to heart.

kepinwarih *vt.* To share, either food or advice.

kepinwer *n (3s: kepinwere).* Throat.

kepinga *vt.* To praise.

kepir₁ 1. *n.* Paddle dance. 2. *vi.* To dance the paddle dance.

kepir₂ *vi.* To be turned or twisted. —**kapir,** *vt.*

kepir meliek 1. *vi.* To run the hurdles. 2. *n.* The hurdles.

kepirek *vi.* To turn one's head in contempt.

kepised *vi.* To be infected by salt water.

kepidau *n.* Large pass in the outer reef and the area inside the lagoon adjacent to the pass; harbor.

kepidak *vt.* To pass around, to pass indirectly; to get around, as a problem. —**kepidek,** *vi.*

kepidek *vi.* To be passed around, to be passed indirectly; to be gotten around, as a problem. —**kepidak,** *vt.*

kepit₁ *vi. neut.* To pry out; to relax a wire or stick under tension. —**kapit₂,** *vt.*

kepit₂ 1. *adj.* Said of one who likes to tease or make fun of others. 2. *n.* Joke. —**kapitih,** *vt.*

kehpit HONORIFIC. *n.* Knife, machete.

kepsakau 1. *vi.* To eat before kava. 2. *n.* The meal before kava.

kehpsel *n.* A variety of yam, having fibrous flesh.

keptakai *adj.* Very stubborn.

kehpwallal *n.* A variety of yam, having no particular season.

kepwe *n.* Thing, possession; internal organs or guts of larger mammals; genitals.

kepweikeng *adj.* Sharp-tongued.

kehpwel *n.* A growth stage of a yam.

kepwehn doadoahk *n.* Tool.

kepwehpwe *adj.* Rich, wealthy, having many possessions.

kehpwetik *n.* A variety of yam, having no particular season.

kehpwetik en kehmpwalap *n.* A variety of yam.

kepwil, also pwekil. *n (3s: kepwili).* Corner of the mouth.

kepwilipwet *adj.* Scarred at the corner of the mouth by yaws.

ker₁ *vi.* To run, as of water; to flow or trickle.

ker₂ *n (3s: kari).* A derogatory term for face.

kehr *vi.* To call, as in to call someone a bad name; to badmouth.

kereilik HONORIFIC. *n.* The two doors in the rear of a feast house, used by the *Nahnmwarki* and *Nahnken*.

kereiso HONORIFIC. *n.* Bathing spot in a stream.

kereu SLANG. *vi.* To run; to flee; to swim, of fish.

kereker *n.* Gutter; bamboo or pipe used to channel a flow of water.

keremwel HONORIFIC. *adj.* Happy, joyful.

keremweliso HONORIFIC. *adj.* Happy, joyful.

keren *adj.* Near, close. —**karanih,** *vt.*

Kerenis *n.* Kapingamarangi, also known as Greenwich. [Eng.]

kereng 1. *vi.* To be dried by heat, as of copra or tobacco. 2. *n.* Tobacco. —**karang,** *vt.*

kerengireng *adj.* Peppery, spicy, hot.

kerep *vi.* To creep; to crawl on all fours. —**karapih,** *vt.*

kerepwel HONORIFIC. *vi.* To bow.

keredi *vi.* To alight or step down.

keriker₁ *n.* Fish sp..

keriker₂ *vi.* To comb one's hair. —**kar₁,** *vt.*

kerilel *n.* A small *keriker*, a fish sp..

keripwud *vi.* To scratch, as when itching. —**karipwude**, *vt.*

kerir *n.* Secret sweetheart.

kerihri *vi.* To be snapped off. —**karihs**, *vt.*

kerismei 1. *n.* First feast of the breadfruit season. 2. *vi.* To prepare this feast.

kehrourou *n.* A feasthouse having three center posts with pits for kava stones on the main platform.

keruwa *vt.* To hurry, to rush. —**karuwaru**, *adj.*

kerkala SLANG. *adj.* Pretentious, proud, boastful.

kerlikamw *adj.* To be a character.

kersuwed *adj.* Ugly.

kehrdipaur *adj.* Engaging in the pot calling the kettle black kind of name calling.

kertakai *n.* A large *keriker*, a fish sp..

kehs₁ *n.* Hook.

kehs₂ *n.* Case. [Eng.]

kese *vt.* To throw; to drop. —**kos₁**, *vi.*

kehse *vt.* To hook.

keseirahk *vi.* To laugh in a boisterous manner.

keseu *vi.* To be examined, to be diagnosed, to be figured out. —**kasawih**, *vt.*

kehsek *vi.* To mate, of animals. —**kehsekih**, *vt.*

kehsekih *vt.* To mate with, of animals. —**kehsek**, *vi.*

kehsehki *vt.* To notify, to inform, to hint at, to let someone know.

kesehkida *vi.* To be shocked, as by bad news.

kesehla *vt.* To throw away, to get rid of; to divorce.

kesempwal 1. *adj.* Important, valuable. 2. *n (3s: kesempwale).* Importance, value.

keseng 1. *vi.* To play music. 2. *n.* Anything capable of producing music, a musical instrument, radio, tape recorder, etc..

keseng popouk *n.* Harmonica.

keseng tiati *n.* Organ.

kesengenpil *n.* Tributary of a stream.

kesepweke *vt.* To drop; to defeat in competition.

kesepwil 1. *vi.* To change status; to graduate. 2. *n.* Promotion; demotion; graduation. —**kasapwil**, *vt.*

keses ARCHAIC. *adj.* Cruel, belligerent, tough.

kesik 1. *vi.* To shoot. 2. *n.* Gun, as a rifle or speargun. —**kasikih**, *vt.*

kesik lapalap *n.* Cannon.

kesik pos *n.* Any weapon employing gun powder.

kesileng *adj.* Disdainful.

kesiluh *num.* Third.

kesihnen *vi.* To stand. —**kesihnenih**, *vt.*

kesihnenih *vt.* See *kesihnen.*

kesingketieu *n.* Bow, of a bow and arrow.

kesingkomi *n.* Slingshot. [*komi*<Jap.<Ger.]

kesihpwong *vi.* To remain awake all night, as at a wake.

kesoulikilik *adj.* Untrustworthy.

kesso 1. *vi.* To run or swim the final lap in a race. 2. *n.* The final lap in a race. [Jap.]

ked *vi.* To be cut open, for the purpose of removing the contents. —**kading₂**, *vt.*

kehd *vi.* To have smoke in one's eyes.

kedei *n.* A variety of palm, *Ponapea ledermanniana.*

kedekede *sent. adv.* Time passed.... *Kedekede oh rahn ehu...* Time passed and one day....

kedeng *vi.* To be stretched; to be made taut. —**kadang**, *vt.*

kedengida *vi.* To be pressed, to be ironed. —**kadangada**, *vt.*

kedengideng *vi. neut.* To stretch, to make taut. —**kadang**, *vt.*

kedepwidepw 1. *vi.* To sing a song written in memory of a deceased person or a person who has permanently left Ponape. 2. *n.* A song of this nature.

kederwahwa HONORIFIC. *n.* Conch shell.

kederwin *vi. neut.* To scale or pluck. —**kederwina**, *vt.*

kederwina *vt.* To scale or pluck. —**kederwin**, *vi.*

kediked *vi. neut.* To tickle. —**kading₁**, *vt.*

kedilahs *n.* Sword, cutlass, bayonet. [Eng.]

Kedinikapw *n.* Title of the wife of a *Kuloap.*

Kedindel *n.* Title of the wife of a *Saudel.*

kedingiding *n.* Part of a *nahs*, the poles at the edge of the thatch under the eave.

Kedipwan *n.* Title of the wife of a *Soupwan*.

kedirepw 1. *adj.* Busy; bothersome. 2. *n.* Busybody.

kedirepwe *vt.* To bother.

keduwara SLANG. *vt.* To glare at.

kedda *n.* Japanese clogs. [Jap.]

kedwerer *vi.* To fish for *werer*, a sp. of sea cucumber.

ket- HONORIFIC. *vi.* A high language verbal root of motion. *Komw pahn ketla ia?* Where are you going?

keteu 1. *vi.* To rain. 2. *n.* Rain.

ketel *n.* Kettle. [Eng.]

ketemenpe *n3s.* Memorial, recollection, souvenir.

ketewe *vt.* To fool, to tease, to kid, to joke with.

keti *interj.* How about that!; Wow!; may be used either approvingly or disapprovingly.

ketia₁ *vt.* To reveal verbally. —**ketihti**, *vi.*

ketia₂ 1. *n.* Boat pole. 2. *vi.* To pole a boat or canoe.

ketia₃ HONORIFIC. *n.* Kava pounding stone.

ketiamau *adj.* Disagreeable.

ketieu₁ *n.* Spear, harpoon.

ketieu₂ *n.* Tree sp., *Ixora casei*.

ketieni 1. *adj.* To be superstitious. 2. *n.* Superstition.

ketiket₁ *adj.* Numb; asleep, as when one's leg falls asleep.

ketiket₂ *adj.* Insistent.

ketikila *vi.* To be taken in, as clothing. —**katikala**, *vt.*

ketihna *vt.* To revitalize.

ketihnain 1. *vi.* To revitalize, to nourish; to augment, as a point in an argument. 2. *n.* Food, nourishment.

ketihnepe *n3s.* Food, nourishment.

keting *n.* Payment or reward; food provided in return for labor; food provided for a hunting or fishing trip.

keting en inou wahr 1. *n.* Second feast for a new canoe, when it is lashed together. 2. *vi.* To prepare this feast.

keting en taht 1. *n.* Third feast of a new feasthouse. 2. *vi.* To prepare this feast.

keting en wahr 1. *n.* First feast for a new canoe. 2. *vi.* To prepare this feast.

ketipin *n.* Sun.

ketipinipin *adj.* Tingly, as when the circulation is shut off in one's leg.

ketipwehl 1. *adj.* Bratty. 2. *n.* Brat.

ketihti *vi.* To reveal verbally. *Pwuksarawi ketihti...* The Bible says... —**ketia₁**, *vt.*

ketitik *n.* Sp. of small ant.

ketitoal *n.* Sp. of small black ant.

ketiweita *n.* Sp. of small red ant.

ketihwo *adj.* Mischievious, naughty, difficult, frustrating.

ketkeikamedek *n.* Sp. of small red ant, known for its bite.

kewelik, also **kowelik**. *n.* Bird sp., heron-like.

keweneu *num.* Sixth.

-ki *verb. suff.* Instrumental suffix; with active verbs it permits the expression of an instrument; with adjectives of emotion it means 'about', with other adjectives it means 'to consider'; also used in 'why' questions, see *dahme*. *inou* lash, *inouki* lash with (something); *nsensuwed* sad, *nsensuwediki* sad about; *dehde* clear, *dehdehki* to consider clear.

kih₁ *n.* Name of the letter *k*.

kih₂ *n.* Fish sp..

kih₃ *n.* Key. [Eng.]

kih₄ *n.* Tree sp., known for its hard wood, commonly found on the low islands.

kih₅ ARCHAIC. *n.* Shell adze, made from the shell of the giant clam.

kih- *vt.* To give. *Kihdo mahs ehu masis.* Please give me a box of matches.

kiai *n.* A strut supporting the outrigger of a canoe.

kiauk *vi.* To be disfigured by yaws.

kiam *n.* Basket made from a palm frond.

kiamoro *n.* Basket, suspended from a pole and carried by two or more people.

kiarameru *n.* Caramel. [Jap.<Eng.]

kiassi 1. *n.* Catcher, in baseball. 2. *vi.* To be a catcher. [Jap.<Eng.]

kiahweliwel *adj.* Appearing physically out of shape or unfit; limp, flexible, springy, disjointed, used to describe a manner of walking.

kie₁ *poss. cl.* A possessive classifier for things to sleep on.

kie₂ *n.* Gear. [Eng.]

kieil *n.* Sp. of large brown lizard; any large lizard, alligator, or crocodile.

kielek *vi.* See *kiedek*.

kiemmad, also **kemmad.** 1. *vi.* To put on dry clothes. 2. *n.* Dry clothes one puts on, extra clothes taken on a trip. —**kemmade,** *vt.*

kiepw *n.* Lily sp..

kied *vt.* To scramble, to put out of order.

kiedek, also **kielek.** *vi.* To burst forth, of something built up, as emotions or flood waters; to collapse, of a pile of objects.

kiewek *n.* Hybrid plant; tree sp., a variety of mango.

kiewek en kakonehp *n.* A variety of yam.

kiewek en kehpin kipar *n.* A variety of yam.

kiewek en kehpin namwu pwetepwet *n.* A variety of yam.

kiewek en kehpin namwu weitahta *n.* A variety of yam.

kiewek en mahnd *n.* A variety of yam.

kiewek en pasahnpwehk *n.* A variety of yam.

kihou *n.* Old work clothes.

kioak *n.* Fish sp., rabbitfish, *Siganus doliatus.*

kioakomwot *n.* Fish sp..

kioaroahr *vi.* To collapse with a crashing noise; to rumble, as of one's stomach.

kiuhri *n.* Cucumber. [Jap.]

kik₁ *n (3s: kiki).* Newly sprouted roots; hanging roots, as of a banyan tree.

kik₂ *vi.* To kick. [Eng.] —**kikim,** *vt.*

kihk *n (3s: kiki).* Nail, as a finger or toenail.

kik suwed *adj.* Said of a plant which leaches all nutrients from the soil.

kikansu *n.* Machine gun. [Jap.]

kihkieng *vt.* To assume; to make a show of doing something.

kikim *vt.* To kick. [Eng.] —**kik₂,** *vi.*

kikin neh *n3s.* Toenail.

kikin peh *n3s.* Fingernail.

kil 1. *n.* Yam disease, causing small black spots on the yam. 2. *vi.* To have this disease.

kihl₁ *n (3s: kili).* Skin, bark, hide₁, any outer covering; any skin disease; dandruff.

kihl₂ *n.* Keel. [Eng.]

kilamp *n.* Clamp, vise. [Eng.]

kilang *vt.* To see, discern, look at, observe, examine.

kilahpwada *n.* Incest.

kilahs *n.* Glass, drinking glass, glasses, goggles, mirror. [Eng.]

kilahs toantoal *n.* Sunglasses, dark glasses. [*kilahs*<Eng.]

kilahsenirongin *n.* Mirror. [*kilahs*<Eng.]

kilahsoupwa HONORIFIC. *n.* Incest.

kilel 1. *vi. neut.* To photograph. 2. *n.* Sign, mark, picture, camera, movie, motion picture. —**kilele,** *vt.*

kilel en peidek *n.* Question mark.

kilel mwekid *n.* Movie, motion picture.

kilele *vt.* To photograph. —**kilel,** *vi.*

kilelehdi *vt.* To mark; to recognize; to take note of.

kihlenuwo 1. *vi.* To perform some action or to say something that is interpreted as an omen of death. 2. *n.* Omen of death.

kiles *vi.* To disdain.

kiliali, also **keliali.** HONORIFIC. *vi.* To vomit.

kilikil *n.* Fish sp., a kind of parrotfish.

kilikilengsuwed 1. *adj.* Incestuous. 2. *n.* Incest.

kilimenip en kakonehp pwetepwet *n.* A variety of yam.

kilimenip en kakonehp weitahta *n.* A variety of yam.

kilimenip en kehmmeirkelik *n.* A variety of yam.

kilimenip en kehmmwuterek *n.* A variety of yam.

kilimenip en kehpenei *n.* A variety of yam.

kilimenip en kehpinamwu pwetepwet *n.* A variety of yam.

kilimenip en kehpinamwu weitahta *n.* A variety of yam.

kilimenip en kiewek en mahnd *n.* A variety of yam.

kilimenip en lukenaisais *n.* A variety of yam.

kilimenip en pasahnpwehk *n.* A variety of yam.

kilimenip en pohnpei *n.* A variety of yam.

kilin kihs *n.* A disease of taro, causing discoloration of the plant.

kilin kutuwa *n.* A skin infection resembling a burn.

kilin mese *n3s.* Eyelid.

kilin moange *n3s.* Scalp.

kilin wai 1. *n.* A disease of the skin, causing continual peeling. 2. *vi.* To have this disease.

kilinau *n (3s: kilinewe).* Lip.

kilisou *vi.* To be naked, to be nude.

kilitepw 1. *n.* Smallpox, chicken pox. 2. *vi.* To have smallpox or chicken pox.

kiluh *n.* Glue. [Eng.]

kilsarawi 1. *n.* A disease of the skin, characterized by a light discoloration of the skin, usually on the trunk of the body. 2. *vi.* To have this disease.

kimsi *n.* Kimchee. [Korean]

kin *aspect marker.* Used to signal habitual aspect. *I kin pirada kuloak isuh.* I (habitually) get up at seven o'clock.

kinaka *n.* Native, used derogatorily. [Eng.<Hawaiian]

kinehda *vt.* To make up a lie, to start a rumor.

kinih *vt.* To pinch. —kinikin, *vi.*

kinikin *vi. neut.* To pinch. —kinih, *vt.*

kiniwed *n.* Bird sp., crimson crowned fruit dove.

kinsipakudang *n.* Atomic bomb. [Jap.]

kinte *vi.* To provide bedding or clothing for someone.

kihng₁ *n.* Rooster. [Eng.]

kihng₂ *n.* King, in cards. [Eng.]

kingko *n.* Safe, cash box. [Jap.]

kipar *n.* Any of a number of varieties of pandanus.

kiparamat HONORIFIC. *vi.* To laugh, to smile.

kiparenwel *n.* Pandanus sp., *Pandanus tolotomensis.*

kipada HONORIFIC. *vi.* To get up.

kipe *vt.* To surround, to enclose, to spread everywhere. *Lehk kipe sahpw koaros.* Famine spread over the land.

kihpeseng *vt.* To spread.

kipedi HONORIFIC. *vi.* To lie down.

kihr₁ *adj.* Nonbuoyant.

kihr₂ *n.* Fish sp., snapper, *Lutjanus malabaricus.*

kihr en eiwel *n.* Fish sp., red snapper, *Lutjanus bohar.*

kirahka *n.* Candy, cookie, cracker. [Eng.]

kirakahu *adj.* Worn low on one's hips, as of trousers.

kirawih *vt.* To economize on; to use wisely.

kirek *n.* Smegma.

kirekinwel *n.* Tree sp., malay apple, *Syzyguim stelechanthum.*

kirer *vi.* To burp, to belch.

kiresek SLANG. *n.* Penis.

kirehdi *vi.* To peel off; to pull down an eyelid, a lip, or the foreskin of the penis.

kiried *adj.* Murky, as of muddy water or a cloudy sky.

kirikir *n (3s: kirikiri).* Stem.

kirimwot *n.* A variety of breadfruit.

kiriniol HONORIFIC. *adj.* Warm, hot.

kiripw *vi.* To be single, to be unmarried.

kiris *vi.* To slip, to slide.

kirihs *n.* Grease, fat. [Eng.]

Kirismas *n.* Christmas. [Eng.]

Kiroulikihak *n.* A title.

Kiroun *n.* A title.

Kiroun Dolehtik *n.* A title.

kihrsal *n.* Fish sp..

kis₁ *num. cl.* Used in counting small pieces or fragments of things. *kisin kehp riakis* two small pieces of yam.

kis₂ *vi.* To kiss. [Eng.]

kihs *n.* Octopus.

kisa *n.* Train. [Jap.]

kisakis 1. *n.* Gift, present, prize. 2. *vi.* To give a gift, present, or prize. —kisikise, *vt.*

kiseh *poss. cl.* A possessive classifier used for relatives.

kisetikmei, also pisetikmei. *n.* Bush sp., *Melastoma marianum.*

kisikis *n.* Fraction.

kisikise *vt.* To give a gift, present, or prize. —kisakis, *vi.*

kisim *vi.* To sic an animal.

kisin ihr *n.* Any grater, other than a coconut grater.

kisin leh *n.* Oil, perfume; pond; deep pocket of water in the reef.

kisin likou   n. Letter, correspondence.

kisin metehn popouk   n. Police whistle.

kisiniei   n. Fire.

kisinieng   n. Air, wind.

kisinioang   n. Turmeric sp., edible.

kisinnin   n. Child affianced by a parental arrangement.

kisinpwil   n. Chewing gum.

kisinsel   n. String.

kisingai   adj. Crazy, mad, mentally retarded. [Jap.]

kid   num. Thousand.

kid-   vi. To litter, to make untidy. E kidala likin ihmwo. He littered outside that house. —kide, vt.

kihd   n. Garbage, waste, debris.

kida   n. Guitar. [Eng.]

kidalap   adj. Many. Aramas kidalap ese ohlo. Many people know that man.

kidahwe   vt. To scold or reprimand.

kide   vt. To litter, to make untidy. —kid-, vi.

kideidei   adj. Fishy, greasy.

kideu   n. Vine sp., Polypodium phymatodes.

kidi   n. Dog.

kidienleng   n. A large sp. of caterpillar.

kidienmal   n. Plant sp., Selaginella kanehirae.

kidienwet   adj. Incorrigible.

kidikid   1. vi. neut. To wrap.   2. n. Wrapper, cover. —kidim, vt.

kidilipes   n. Wolf, used biblically.

kidim   vt. To wrap. —kidikid, vi.

kidipe   n3s. Cover, wrapper.

-kit   obj. pron. Us, exclusive.

kiht   ind. pron. We, exclusive.

kita   subj. pron., ind. pron. We, dual.

-kita   obj. pron. Us, dual.

kitail   subj. pron., ind. pron. We, plural.

-kitail   obj. pron. Us, plural.

kitei   1. adj. Moldy.   2. n. Mold.

kitel   n. Fish sp., small and found in fresh water.

kitentel   adj. Smooth or slippery, as of silk.

Kiti   n. Name of a municipality in Ponape.

kitik   n. Rat, mouse.

ko, also oko.   dem. mod. Those, away from you and me.

koh, also kowe.   ind. pron. You.

koh-   vi. To come or go. Irail kohla Kiti aio. They went to Kiti yesterday. E

pahn kohdo lakapw. He will come tomorrow.

koiasi   n. Fertilizer. [Jap.]

koikoi₁   vi. To be shaved, of the head.

koikoi₂   vi. neut. To grate on a coconut grater. —kohke, vt.

koikoi₃   n. Bird sp., Micronesian broadbill, Myagra oceanica.

koid   n. Sp. of sea cucumber.

kou   n. Cow. [Eng.]

koul   1. vi. To sing.   2. n. Song.

koul sarawi   1. n. Christian hymn.   2. vi. To sing a Christian hymn.

koulin sampah   1. n. A love song.   2. vi. To sing a love song.

kounsup   adj. Frowning, unsmiling.

koupahleng   n. A feasthouse having five center posts.

koupe   vi. To vote by a show of hands.

kourahpw   vi. neut. To cook fish with coconut milk and turmeric. —kourahpwih, vt.

kourahpwih   vt. See kourahpw.

kouruhr   vi. To laugh.

kousapw   n. A political unit of land, consisting of a number of private homesteads, smaller than a wehi.

kousoan   1. vi. To reside.   2. n. Residence.

koudiahl   1. vi. To be spectacular.   2. n. Revelation, used biblically.

kout, also kuht.   n. Goat. [Eng.]

kohkang   vi. To exchange. [Jap.]

kohke   vt. To grate on a coconut grater. —koikoi₂, vi.

kohko   n. Fish sp., dolphin, Coryphaena hippurus.

kokou   vi. To be erected, to be raised. —kau₁, vt.

kokoup   vi. neut. To peel, as a banana. —kaup, vt.

kohkohlahte   adv. Forever.

kokus   vi. To be sprayed; to be drained. —kakus, vt.

kol   vt. To hold.

kohl sisel   n. Cold chisel. [Eng.]

kolou, also keleu.   n. Hibiscus sp., Hibiscus tiliaceus, the inner bark of which is used as a bast in the preparation of kava.

kolukol   vi. To hold the cup during the preparation of kava.

koluhla   1. vi. To repent; to do reluctantly.   2. n. Repentance.

41

koluhs *adj.* Wasteful. [*luhs*<Eng.]
—**kaluhsih,** *vt.*

koluwar *vi.* To remain aboard a boat or canoe while others are diving for fish.

koll, also **kull.** *n.* Roach.

kom *vt.* To pull in a net.

komi, also **kumi.** *n.* Rubber, plastic. [Jap.<Ger.]

komou *n.* Tree sp..

kommoal *vi.* To rest; in combination with the suffixes *-di* and *-sang* (*kommoaldihsang*) this verb means to retire or to quit one's work.
—**kommoale,** *vt.*

kommoale *vt.* See *kommoal.*

kommwad *adj.* Brave, fierce.

kompani *n.* Company, friend; fish sp., rabbitfish, *Siganus vulpinus.* [Eng.]

kompoakapah *n3s.* Dear friend, close buddy.

kompoake *adj.* Emotionally moving, causing pity.

kompwal *vt.* To cover an *uhmw* with leaves. —**kompwel,** *vi.*

kompwel *vi. neut.* To cover an *uhmw* with leaves; of a hen, to sit on eggs just prior to their hatching.
—**kompwal,** *vt.*

komw HONORIFIC. *subj. pron.* You.

kohmw *n.* Comb. [Eng.]

komwaropwidi HONORIFIC. *vi.* To be covered up.

komwi HONORIFIC. *ind. pron.* You.

kohmwowe *vt.* To be first in line or in order; to start an activity. *I pahn kohmwowe atail doadoahk.* I'll start our work.

kohn *n.* Corn. [Eng.]

kona *n.* Powder of any kind, tooth powder or tooth paste. [Jap.]

konehng *adj.* Appropriate, proper.

konok *n.* Vine sp., *Piper ponapense,* used in the treatment of toothache.

konuhr *vi.* To wrinkle up one's nose.

konpene *vi.* To fit, to go together well.

kons *adj.* Dull, blunt.

kontirak 1. *n.* Contract. 2. *vi.* To make a contract. [Eng.]

kohntutuk *vi.* To squat.

kongkiri *vi., vt.* To concrete. [Jap.<Eng.]

kohp *vt.* To prophesy.

kopatau, also **kapatau.** *n.* Phlegm.

kohper HONORIFIC. *vi.* To cough.

kopil *n.* Clam sp..

kopou *adj.* Cold, cool, chilly.

kopokop 1. *vi.* To cough. 2. *n.* Cough.

kohpwa₁ *n.* Fish sp..

kohpwa₂ *n.* Box, chest, coffin, casket.

kopwenadi *n3s.* Breast, as of a chicken.

kopwou, also **kupwu.** *n.* Basket, purse, handbag.

kopwukopw₁ *adj.* Weak, soft, easily broken, fragile.

kopwukopw₂ *n.* Gristle, cartilage.

kopwung 1. *vi.* To go to trial. 2. *n.* Trial.

kopwungloal HONORIFIC. *adj.* Kind, merciful.

kopwkopwenadi *n3s.* Solar plexus.

korehd *vt.* To scrape, as the meat out of a coconut. —**koroiroi,** *vi.*

kohri *n.* Shave ice, snow cone. [Jap.]

korila *n.* Gorilla. [Eng.]

korinta 1. *n.* Blood blister; reddening of the white of the eye. 2. *vi.* To have a blood blister; to have reddening of the white of the eye.

koro *n.* Grounder, in baseball. [Jap.]

koroikot *vi.* A command from the director of a *kamadipw* to bring more hibiscus bast for the kava.

koroiroi *vi. neut.* To scrape, as the meat out of a coconut. —**korehd,** *vt.*

koronihda *n.* Cornet, trumpet, bugle. [Span.]

koropwung *n.* A small waterfall.

koruk *n.* Parcel.

kos₁ *vi.* To throw; to drop. —**kese,** *vt.*

kos₂ *adj.* Bent; humped.

kohs *n.* Navigational course. [Eng.]

kosetipw *vi.* To foretell the future; to locate lost objects through the use of magic. —**kosetipwih,** *vt.*

kosetipwih *vt.* To foretell the future about. —**kosetipw,** *vi.*

kosou *vi.* To be transferred, to be moved; to be postponed. —**kasau,** *vt.*

kosolong *n.* Cove, inlet.

kosonned *n.* Law.

kosdang *vi.* To put in reverse, of a vehicle. [Jap.] —**kosdangih,** *vt.*

kosdangih *vt.* See *kosdang.* [*kosdang*<Jap.] —**kosdang,** *vi.*

kode *n3s.* Animal's horn.

kodie *n3s.* End of kava ceremony, end, last one.

kodoukeinek, also **kadoukeinek.** *vi.* To trace one's ancestry according to clan.

kodouluhl *adv.* Extremely. *E pwangada kodouluhl.* He got extremely tired.

kodourur *n.* Small wood shavings for starting a fire, dry wood for the *uhmw.*

kodoudou, also **kadoudou.** *vi.* To trace one's ancestry, to recall past history. —**kadaur**₁, *vt.*

kodokenmei HONORIFIC. *n.* Head, temple.

kodokod *vi. neut.* To husk with a stick; to gore; to engage in sexual intercourse in a female superior position. —**kodom,** *vt.*

kodom *vt.* To husk with a stick; to gore; to engage in sexual intercourse in a female superior position. —**kodokod,** *vi.*

kodon *n.* Giant.

koduhpwal *vt.* To cover up. —**koduhpwel,** *vi.*

koduhpwel 1. *vi.* To be covered up. 2. *n.* Veil. —**koduhpwal,** *vt.*

koduhsou HONORIFIC. 1. *vi.* To eat dinner. 2. *n.* Dinner.

kot *adj.* In good condition, young looking; slow in maturing; stuck.

Koht₁ *n.* God. [Eng.]

koht₂ *n.* Hibiscus fiber.

kotala *vi.* To relieve oneself, to defecate or urinate.

kote *vt.* To cross to the other side; to cut down; to cut a girl's hair straight across at the bottom.

kotekehp 1. *n.* First feast of the yam season, usually in October. 2. *vi.* To prepare this feast.

koten wini 1. *n.* A party or gift given to a *sounwini* the fourth day of taking medicine. 2. *vi.* To prepare this party or give this gift.

kotokot HONORIFIC. 1. *vi.* To be given a haircut. 2. *n.* A haircut.

kotop *n.* Tree sp., *Exorrhiza ponapensis.*

kotuhwahu *adj.* Belligerent, easily angered.

kohwa *n.* Trusteeship; lease.

kowahlap *adj.* Extensive, large.

kowarak, also **kowaraki.** *vt.* To copulate with, to have sexual intercourse with. —**kowerek,** *vi.*

kowaraki *vi.* See *kowarak.*

kowe, also **koh.** *ind. pron.* You.

kowel *n.* Bud of the coconut flower.

kowelik, also **kewelik.** *n.* Bird sp., heron-like.

kowerek *vi.* To copulate, to have sexual intercourse. —**kowarak,** *vt.*

kowet HONORIFIC. *vi.* To shout in a falsetto voice, either when carrying kava or to challenge another to a fight.

kowih SLANG. *vt.* To chase.

koahiek *adj.* Competent, capable, well versed; able to take care of one's self; large or spacious, of inanimate objects.

koaik *vi. neut.* To turn away from the wind when sailing.

koail *n.* Fish sp., a mature sweetlips porgy, *Plectorhynchus celebicus.*

koait *adj.* Crowded, lacking space.

koakon *n.* Small box; joint; fitting; knuckle; a small plot of land, a house lot.

koakone *vt.* To join; to fit. —**koakonokon,** *vi.*

koakonehmpwetepwet *n.* A variety of yam, white.

koakonehp *n.* A variety of yam.

koakonehp weitahta *n.* A variety of yam, red.

koakonokon *vi. neut.* To join; to fit. —**koakone,** *vt.*

koakorot *vi.* To crow, of a rooster.

koakos *adj.* Stern, of parents or spouses; causing others difficulty because of the desire to have everything one's way. —**koakose,** *vt.*

koakose *vt.* To be stern with. —**koakos,** *adj.*

koahkoa *vt.* To sweep; to shave. —**koakoahk,** *vi.*

koakoahk *vi.* To sweep; to shave. —**koahkoa,** *vt.*

koal *vi.* To wear a grass skirt.

koahl *n.* Grass skirt.

koale *vt.* To make sennit. *I pahn koale ei kisin pwehl.* I'm going to make my sennit. —**ngkoal,** *vi.*

koalupwulupw *vi. neut.* To scrape the surface of something. —**kalupwur,** *vt.*

koamoatoar *vi.* To be oiled or lubricated. —**koamoatoare,** *vt.*

koamoatoare *vt.* To oil or lubricate. —**koamoatoar,** *vi.*

koamwosod HONORIFIC. *vi.* To urinate.

koamwoamw *vi.* To be destructive, to be wasteful.

koamwoamwala *vt.* To lay waste to.

koamwoamwasang *vt.* To exhaust a supply of something.

koamwoadoaloan *vt.* To await an event.

koahnek *vi.* To stir in one's sleep.

koanoa *vt.* To catch up with; to be on time for an event.

koanoat HONORIFIC. **1.** *poss. cl.* A possessive classifier used for edibles with all title holders of *koanoat* rank. **2.** *vi.* To eat.

koansop *n.* An ornamentally wrapped ball of sennit.

koangoangehki *vt.* To talk someone into doing something.

koahpi *n.* Coffee. [Eng.]

koapwoaroapwoar **1.** *vi.* To have faith, trust, or hope. **2.** *n.* Faith, trust, hope.

koapwuroaloat ARCHAIC. *vi.* To have something stuck between the hull and the outrigger of a canoe.

koahr *n.* A barbed piece of wood, used as a tool for tying thatch onto a roof.

koaramahd *n.* Bush sp., *Coleus scutellarioides.*

koahre₁ *n.* Tree sp., *Northiopsis hoshinoi*, known for its strong wood.

koahre₂ *vt.* To scrape together with the hands.

koarompwa *vt.* To delay, to impede.

koarong HONORIFIC. *n (3s: koaronge).* Ear.

koaronge, also **karonge.** HONORIFIC. *vt.* To hear, to listen.

koaros *num.* All. *Pillap koaros lapakehda.* All the rivers flooded.

koaruhsie *num.* Every. *Ohl koaruhsie pokonpene Kolonia.* Every man gathered in Kolonia.

koasok *vi.* To pile up. —**koasoke,** *vt.*

koasoke *vt.* To pile up. —**koasok,** *vi.*

koasoai **1.** *vi.* To talk, to discuss, to tell a story. **2.** *n.* Talk, discussion, rumor, story, adage, parable. —**koasoaia,** *vt.*

koasoaia *vt.* See *koasoai.*

koasoakoahiek *adj.* Inappropriate, awkward because of unfamiliarity, difficult to learn.

koasoamw **1.** *vi.* To welcome; to lead one's aim when shooting birds. **2.** *n.* A welcoming. —**kasamwoh,** *vt.*

koasoamwoasoamw *vi.* To make an insincere request for assistance.

koasoane *vt.* To organize, to structure; to settle, to decide. —**koasoandi,** *vi.*

koasoandi **1.** *vi.* To be organized, to be structured; to be settled, to be decided, to be agreed upon. **2.** *n.* Organization, structure, rule, plan, agreement. —**koasoane,** *vt.*

koasuk *vt.* To weigh down, to anchor something in place by placing an object on top.

koaskoasok *n.* A pile; stone wall.

koade *vt.* To assist someone by carrying part of his load.

koadia *vt.* To fill up with a liquid; to pour in. *Koadiahda mahs stohp karisihnen.* Please fill the stove with kerosene. —**koadiadi,** *vi.*

koadiadi *vi.* To be filled. —**koadia,** *vt.*

koadoke *n3s.* Top, peak, summit, ridge.

koadokehla *vt.* To bring to completion. —**koadokodokala,** *vi.*

koadokodokala *vi.* To be brought to completion. —**koadokehla,** *vt.*

koadoahke *vt.* To work on.

koadoangoul *num.* Ten; see *ehd.*

koadoadoahki *vt.* To hire.

koato *adj.* Durable, having the ability to survive either time or circumstance.

koatop *n.* A variety of palm.

koatoa *n.* Mangrove sp..

koatoanehng *vt.* To suppress, as a cry of pain, a cough, laughter, or a bowel movement.

koatoahnien *vi.* To visibly show one's displeasure at a request.

koatun *n.* Cotton; kapok tree. [Eng.]

kuair *n.* Choir. [Eng.]

kuahpa *n.* Guava, *Psidium guajava.* [Eng.]

kuk *vi.* To cook. [Eng.] —**kukih,** *vt.*

kukih *vt.* To cook. [*kuk*<Eng.] —**kuk,** *vi.*

kukusuh *n.* Air gun. [Jap.]

kul *vi. neut.* To grab, to seize. —**kulih,** *vt.*

kuhl *vi.* To suck on, as a cigarette or sugar cane.

kuhleid *n.* Kool-Aid, any similar drink. [Eng.]

kulih *vt.* To grab, to seize. —**kul,** *vi.*

kuloak *n.* Time, clock, watch, hour. [Eng.]

Kuloap *n.* A title.

kulu *n.* Bird sp., Pacific golden plover, *Pluvialis dominica.*

kulup *n.* Used leaves of the *uhmw.*

kull, also **koll**. *n.* Roach.

kumi, also **komi**. *n.* Rubber, plastic. [Ger.]

kumw *vi. neut.* To disturb or alert by making a pounding noise. —**kumwur**, *vt.*

kumwa *subj. pron., ind. pron.* You, dual.

-kumwa *obj. pron.* You, dual.

kumwail *subj. pron., ind. pron.* You, plural.

-kumwail *obj. pron.* You, plural.

kumwisekala *vi.* To fall.

kumwitin kidi *n.* A variety of the yam *kehpineir*, shaped like a dog's paw.

kumwukumw₁ *n.* A thudding noise.

kumwukumw₂ *n.* Small hill.

kumwur *vt.* To disturb or alert by making a pounding noise. —**kumw**, *vi.*

kumwus HONORIFIC. *vi.* To tease.

kumwusek *vi.* To thud.

kumwut *n (3s: kumwuti).* Fist.

kumwut en peh *n3s.* Wrist.

kumwutik *vi.* To sneer.

kun *vi.* To be extinguished; to be turned off, of lights and motors.

kuhpene *vi.* To close or to shut any round object, as a pipe or one's mouth.

kupwel *vt.* To bend, of something rigid. —**kupwelek**, *adj.*

kupwelek *adj.* Bent, of something rigid. —**kupwel**, *vt.*

kupwu, also **kopwou**. *n.* Basket, purse, handbag.

kupwur₁ *n.* Albatross.

kupwur₂ HONORIFIC. *n (3s: kupwure).* Wish, intention, plan, decision, desire, heart.

kupwur peren HONORIFIC. *adj.* Happy, joyful.

kupwurehiong HONORIFIC. *vi.* To think, to feel.

kupwurekeng HONORIFIC. *adj.* Wise, knowledgeable.

kupwurehda HONORIFIC. *vi.* To decide, to determine.

kupwuriso HONORIFIC. *n.* Stomach.

kupwurohki HONORIFIC. *vt.* To care about.

kupwuropwon HONORIFIC. *adj.* Stupid, silly, idiotic, simple, dumb.

kupwurki HONORIFIC. *vt.* To agree, to like.

kupwud *n (3s: kupwude).* New leaf.

kur *vi.* To move one's hips in the manner characteristic of sexual intercourse. —**kurih**, *vt.*

kurando *n.* Baseball field. [Jap.<Eng.]

kureiong *n.* Crayon. [Eng.]

kurih *vt.* To move one's hips against another's in the manner characteristic of sexual intercourse. —**kur**, *vi.*

kuro *n.* Common dog's name, from the Japanese word for black. [Jap.]

kurodong *n.* Croton. [Eng.]

kuroamw **1.** *n.* Bait thrown around a canoe to attract fish. **2.** *vi.* To throw bait around a canoe to attract fish.

kuroap *n.* Baseball glove. [Jap.<Eng.]

kuruma *n.* Cart. [Jap.]

kurupdoloina HONORIFIC. *n.* Penis.

kurupw *n.* Immature coconut before reaching the growth stage called *uhpw.*

kus *vi.* To gush; to climax or ejaculate.

kuhs *n.* Goose. [Eng.]

kudud *n.* A variety of banana.

kuht, also **kout**. *n.* Goat. [Eng.]

kutian *n.* Accordion. [Eng.]

kutohr *n.* Egg; a small yam that can be carried by hand.

kutohr en mese *n3s.* Eyeball.

kutoahr *n.* Bird sp., with bluish wings.

kuwa *n.* Hoe. [Jap.]

kuwai *vi.* To whistle.

klopis *n.* Club, of cards. [Eng.]

L

-la *verb. suff.* There, away from you and me; used with adjectives to indicate that a new state exists that has come about as a result of a gradual change from some previous state; used with verbs of loss or disappearance to signal an action has been carried through to its logical conclusion; also used with some verbs to indicate the action or activity they denote is carried out without undue delay. *tang* run, *tangala* run there; *tihti* skinny, *tihtihla* become skinny; *sar* faded, *sarala* completely faded; *kohla* go there, *kohlahla* go ahead and go there.

Laiap *n.* A traditional lesser priest.

laiohn *n.* Lion. [Eng.]

laikihk *adj.* Bitter, of kava.

lain *n.* Line, boundary; a piece of property. [Eng.]

laisin *n.* License. [Eng.]

laid *vi.* To fish. —**laidih,** *vt.*

laid kapw 1. *n.* Third feast given to celebrate the use of a new net. **2.** *vi.* To prepare this feast.

laidih *vt.* To fish for. —**laid,** *vi.*

laidiniki *n.* Porpoise.

lait *n.* Cigarette lighter. [Eng.]

lao₁ *n.* Dear, a term of affection used by parents with their children.

lao₂ *conj. adv.* Until. *Kita awih ira lao kohdo.* Let's wait until they come.

lahu, also **loh₁.** *n (3s: lewe).* Tongue.

laumwaumw *adj.* Disrespectful, usually said of children.

laud 1. *adj.* Big, old. **2.** *n (3s: laudi).* Bigness, greatness.

lahk *n (3s: lake).* Penis, of an adult.

lakapw *n.* Tomorrow.

lakadahn, also **akadahn** or **kaladahn.** *n.* A variety of banana. [Tagalog]

laki *adj.* Lucky. [Eng.]

lakiot ARCHAIC. *n.* Highly prized cloth made from breadfruit bark.

lakid *vt.* To drop; to discard. —**lekidek,** *vi.*

lakohn *n.* A round of kava.

lal *vi.* To make a sound.

lahlahwe *vt.* To blaspheme.

lallal *vi.* To speak incessantly; to run, said of a machine.

lamai *vt.* To be cruel, belligerent, or tough to. —**lemei,** *adj.*

lamalam *n.* Thought, idea, opinion; common sense; religious belief.

laman *n.* Lime. [Eng.]

lamisih, also **lemisih.** *vt.* To arrange one's hair in a chignon or bun. —**lemis,** *vi.*

lammwin *adj.* Majestic, inspiring fear and awe.

lamp *n.* Lamp. [Eng.]

Lampein *n.* Title of the wife of a *Lepen.*

Lampein Ririn *n.* Title of the wife of a *Lepen Ririn.*

lampwon *adj.* Stupid, stupified.

lampwoatol *n.* Bottle lamp, made with a wick in a bottle of kerosene. [Eng.]

lamwahk *n.* Plant sp., *Galeola ponapensis,* a kind of orchid.

lamwahk en wai *n.* Plant sp., a kind of orchid.

lamwer, also **limwoahr.** *n.* Gecko.

landana, also **randana.** *n.* Lantana, *Lantana camara.* [Eng.]

lanten *n.* Lantern. [Eng.]

lang *vi.* To be hung up. —**langa,** *vt.*

lahng₁ *n.* Sky, heaven.

lahng₂ *n (3s: langi).* Bad weather.

lahng₃ *n.* Spider conch sp..

langa *vt.* To hang up. —**lang,** *vi.*

langilangih HONORIFIC. *vt.* To give a title, to crown; to wear a garland.

lap *adj.* Large in stature; important or physically large.

lahp *n.* Guy or gal; sweetheart (with *ah*).

lapake 1. *vi.* To flood. **2.** *adj.* Flooded. **3.** *n.* A flood.

lapala *adj.* Physically big.

lapalap *adj.* High ranking.

lapalapala *vi.* To be exalted, to be promoted.

Lapango *n.* A legendary male ghost, said to have dug the channel at *Sapwalap* with his penis.

lapwa, also lapwad or lawad. *vt.* To open or untie, as a bag. —lapwedek, *vi.*

lapwad, also lapwa or lawad. *vt.* To open or untie, as a bag. —lapwedek, *vi.*

lapwada *vi.* To be released; to be forgiven, in a religious sense. —lapwahda, *vt.*

lapwahda *vt.* To release. —lapwada, *vi.*

lahpweseisei *n.* Waterspout.

lapwed *n.* Salt water eel, a generic term.

lapwedek *vi.* To be untied. —lapwa or lapwad, *vt.*

lapwedehlam *n.* Salt water eel, commonly found in deep water.

lapweden pahniak *n.* Salt water eel, commonly found along the edge of mangrove swamps.

Lasialap *n.* A clan name.

lahd *n.* Fish sp., jack, *Atule mate.*

ladu *n (3s: laduwi).* Male servant, either politically or domestically.

latok *n.* Anything short or stubby.

lawalo *adj.* Wild, not domesticated; disobedient.

lawarourou HONORIFIC. *vi.* To visit.

lawad, also lapwa or lapwad. *vt.* To open or untie, as a bag. —lawadek, *vi.*

lawadek *vi.* To be opened or untied, as of a bag. —lawad, *vt.*

lawi *n.* Fish sp., yellow-tailed brown parrotfish *Cetoscarus bicolor.*

leh$_1$ *n.* Oil, for cooking or as a lotion; perfume.

leh$_2$ *n.* Pool, lake.

leu *vi.* To be cooked.

lek 1. *vi.* To be slashed, lanced, or cut; to have an incision made; to be castrated. 2. *n.* Incision; medical operation, on the legs or arms. —leke, *vt.*

lehk 1. *n.* Any period of famine. 2. *adj.* Selfish.

leke *vt.* To slash; to make an incision; to castrate. —lek, *vi.*

lekelek *n.* Castrated animal; a scar inflicted to demonstrate one's manhood.

lekidek *vi.* To be dropped; to fish with a th.owing net. —lakid, *vt.*

lekidekla *vi.* To be discarded, to be neglected; to be cast out or damned.

lel$_1$ *vi.* To reach or arrive at.

lel$_2$, also leltih. SLANG. *adj.* Perfect, just right. *Omw suhten udahn lel!* Your shoes look great!

lel$_3$ *vi.* To be wounded, as a consequence of fighting.

lel- *vi.* To smell. *Mehkot lelada wasaht.* Something is smelling up this place.

leleki *vt.* To bring to the attention of an authority, to report.

lelepek *adj.* Reliable.

leles *n.* Plant sp., the leaves of which cause itching.

leltih, also lel$_2$. SLANG. *adj.* Perfect, just right.

leme *vt.* To believe or suspect.

lemei *adj.* Cruel, belligerent, tough. —lamai, *vt.*

lemelemehk *adj.* Suspicious.

lemehda *vi.* To decide, to figure out.

lemis *vi.* To arrange one's hair in a chignon or bun. —lamisih or lemisih, *vt.*

lemisih, also lamisih. *vt.* See *lemis.*

lemmw, also lommw. *adj.* Afraid of ghosts.

lempahntamw *n.* Main rear platform of a feasthouse.

lempe *n.* Unripe fallen fruit.

lempehdi 1. *vi.* To fall, of unripe fruit. 2. HONORIFIC. *vi.* To fall.

Lempwei Lapalap *n.* A title, in the *Nahnmwarki* line.

Lempwei Ririn *n.* A title.

lempweileng HONORIFIC. *n.* Duster.

lemwedek SLANG. 1. *vi.* To eat. 2. *n.* Food.

lemwlemwur *adj.* Cool, cold, damp.

lehn kei *n.* Coconut oil for the skin.

lehn pwelmatak *n.* Puddle.

lehn wai *n.* Perfume.

lehn wisoar *n.* Coconut oil for the hair.

lehnawahu HONORIFIC. *n.* Coconut oil for the hair.

lehnkalangi HONORIFIC. *n.* Coconut oil for the skin.

lehnmwese *vt.* To check on, to keep on eye on.

lengelenge *n3s.* Hip.

lengen *n.* Sp. of small crab.

lengileng HONORIFIC. *n (3s: lengilengi).* Any high title; garland.

lengilengih *vt.* To give a high title.

lengk *adj.* Acrophobic.

lep *num. cl.* Used in counting oblong pieces. *lepin tuhke sillep* three oblong pieces of wood.

lehp 1. *n.* A marching dance. 2. *vi.* To dance a marching dance. [Eng.]

lepalep *vi.* To doze.

lepel, also **mepel**. *n.* Level, a carpenter's tool. [Eng.]

Lepen *n.* A title.

Lepen Madau *n.* A title.

Lepen Ririn *n.* A title, in the *Nahnken* line.

lepi- *rel. n.* Section, piece.

lepin *vi.* To be approximately half full, of a container of a liquid.

lepin kahs *n.* Saying, proverb.

lepin keidu *n.* King post.

lepin likou *n.* Material, cloth.

lepin lokaia *n.* Word.

lepin mahsen HONORIFIC. *n.* Word.

lepin pil *n.* Pool, pond, puddle.

lepin rausis 1. *n.* Short pants, shorts. 2. *vi.* To wear short pants or shorts.

lepin sed *n.* Ocean, sea, as the Pacific Ocean, or the Philippine Sea.

lepin seht 1. *n.* Blouse. 2. *vi.* To wear a blouse.

lepin tuhke *n.* Log, stick.

lepdahla *n.* Windward.

lepdihla *n.* Leeward.

lepdo *n.* Left field, in baseball. [Jap.<Eng.]

lehpwel *n.* Taro patch, marsh, bog; large swamp.

les₁ *vi.* To have it coming. *Ke les.* You had it coming.

les₂ *vi.* To be split, of a husked coconut; to be rung, of a bell. —**leser**, *vt.*

leser *vt.* To split a husked coconut; to ring a bell. —**les₂**, *vi.*

lesikihla *vi.* To be shamed, to be humbled.

lesila *vi.* To receive one's comeuppance.

lesihpwong 1. *vi.* To eat a late night snack, usually of a woman who is breastfeeding a child. 2. *n.* Such a late night snack.

Ledek *n.* A clan name.

ledin *n.* Female pigeon.

let *vi. neut.* To flick. —**leteng**, *vt.*

leht *n.* Lead; bullet, cartridge. [Eng.]

letek *n.* Sp. of cane grass.

letelet *vi.* To knock or rap. —**leteng**, *vt.*

lehtemp *n.* A variety of breadfruit.

leteng *vt.* To flick; to knock or rap. —**let** or **letelet**, *vi.*

leter *n.* Letter, of the alphabet. [Eng.]

lewair *n.* A flash flood from the mountains.

li- *verb. pref.* Prefix meaning given to. *pirap* steal, *lipirap* given to stealing.

lih₁ *n.* Name of the letter *l*.

lih₂ *n.* Woman; lady; female of any species.

lih₃ *n.* Boom sheet, sail rope.

lih kadek *n.* Nun.

liaid *vi.* To pick lice from one's own head. —**liaide**, *vt.*

liaide *vt.* See *liaid*.

liaudan *adj.* Capacious, able to hold a lot.

liakotohrohr *adj.* Uncooperative, unsociable, acting alone, selfish.

liahmw, also **ahmw₁** or **omwinwel**. *n.* A tiny flying insect, commonly found in the forest.

liahn *adj.* Outgoing, friendly, knowing no stranger, usually said of children and pets.

liapiap *n.* Noose for snaring rats.

liapwahpw *vi.* To place a wrap over one's shoulders so that the front of the torso is covered.

Liarkatau *n.* A clan name.

lielehle ARCHAIC. *n.* Good woman.

liemeir *n.* Grass sp..

lienei *n.* The favorite female child of a *Nahnmwarki* or *Nahnken*.

lienseisop *n.* Woman who goes aboard visiting ships for sexual reasons.

liengimat 1. *n.* Filariasis. 2. *vi.* To have filariasis.

liep 1. *n.* Cord, looped around one's ankles and used for climbing. 2. *vi.* To loop a cord around one's ankles for climbing trees. —**liepih**, *vt.*

liepe HONORIFIC. *vt.* To trick; to lie to.

liepih *vt.* To loop a cord around one's ankles for climbing trees. —**liep**, *vi.*

lieraran *n.* Nymphomaniac.

lierikik *adj.* Restless, with reference to a child.

lierpwater *n.* Fish sp., butterfly fish.

48

liesengou *n.* Woman desiring sexual intercourse.

liedepwen *n.* Childless woman.

liedipan *n.* Prostitute, used biblically.

liet₁ *adj.* Full of milk, of the breasts.

Liet₂ *n.* Class of people of the past, believed to be cannibals.

Liou *n.* Title of the wife of an *Ou.*

Liou Ririn *n.* Title of the wife of an *Ou Ririn.*

Liounpei *n.* Title of the wife of an *Oun Pohnpei.*

Lioundol *n.* Title of the wife of an *Oundol.*

liourehre 1. *vi.* To mutter indistinctly during sleep; to be delirious. 2. *n.* Muttering; delirium.

lioli *n.* Fish sp., trigger fish.

liohdi *n.* Widow.

lioakoahk *adj.* Troublesome, hotheaded, defective.

lioal *n.* Lightning, electricity.

lioaroahrpwohtik *n.* Small green insect with a powerful odor.

lioasoahs *adj.* Pretentious; desirous to get something impossible to attain.

lik₁ *num.* Billion.

lik₂ *vi.* To be satisfied; of animals, to come out of heat; to stop bearing fruit, as of a coconut tree.

likaut *n.* Joker, in cards.

likamisik 1. *adj.* Horrible in appearance. 2. *n.* Anything peculiarly sacred. —**likamisikih,** *vt.*

likamisikih *vt.* To horrify. —**likamisik,** *adj.*

likamw 1. *vi.* To lie. 2. *adj.* Untruthful. 3. also **likamwete.** *sent. adv.* Apparently, it seems that.

likamwala *vt.* To seem to have the attributes of.

likamwada *vi.* To be made a liar of; to be humiliated.

likamwete, also **likamw.** *sent. adv.* Apparently, it seems that. *Likamwete e kohdo aio.* Apparently he came yesterday.

likamwohd *n.* Bride.

likan *n.* Spider sp..

likangkangenihmat 1. *adj.* Incestuous. 2. *n.* Incest.

likarak *n (3s: likereke).* Louse, flea.

likarahs *n.* Rock crab.

likahs 1. *n.* Swing, hammock, seesaw. 2. *vi.* To swing.

likahde *vt.* To caress.

likawih *vt.* To wear. —**likou,** *vi.*

likawihada *vt.* To dress oneself. —**likouda,** *vi.*

likeikiris, also **likekiris.** *adj.* Slippery, slick.

likeilap *adj.* Old, decrepit, of people; big.

likekehu *adj.* Always standing.

likekiris, also **likeikiris.** *adj.* Slippery, slick.

likelikad *vi.* To sigh.

likehmw *n.* Vine sp., *Ipomoea digitata.*

likend HONORIFIC. *n.* Wife, usually referring to wives of high chiefs; title of the wife of a *Nahnmwarki,* in Uh and Madolenihmw.

likendinkep *n.* Stingray.

Likendlap *n.* Title of the wife of an *Isohlap.*

likepip *vi.* To flap, as a bird flaps its wings.

likepisir *n.* Bird sp., with a wide fanning tail.

likerwaite *adj.* Deformed, of the eyelids.

likesekeseu *adj.* Critical, of people.

likedepw *n.* Freshwater shrimp.

likediked *adj.* Given to tickling others.

likedipwuhpwu *n.* Bird sp..

liki *prep. n.* Outside (him, her, or it).

likih *vt.* To trust. —**likilik,** *adj.*

likier HONORIFIC. *vi.* To be full, after eating.

likilik *adj.* Trustworthy. —**likih,** *vt.*

likimwei, also **mweilik.** *vi.* To throw or punch forcefully.

likinioar HONORIFIC. *n.* Back of the head.

likinleng HONORIFIC. *n.* Back of the head.

likinmwoale HONORIFIC. *n3s.* Cheek.

likinpaiki *n3s.* Back of the head or neck.

likinsap *n (3s: likinsepe).* Cheek.

likinsekiri HONORIFIC. *n.* Back of the head.

likirikirir *adj.* Disdainful.

likisang *vt.* To abstain, from anything.

likid₁ *n.* Sp. of shellfish.

likid₂ *vt.* To accompany and assist.

likidal *n.* Hibiscus sp..

likidar *adj.* Scavenger-like. —**likidere,** *vt.*

likidek *adj.* Irreconcilably or deeply hurt, of one's feelings.

likidere *vt.* To scavenge, of people. —**likidar**, *adj.*

likidi HONORIFIC. *vi.* To spit.

likidmeliehla HONORIFIC. *vt.* To forget or abandon.

likou 1. *n.* Cloth, anything made of cloth, material, clothes. 2. *vi.* To wear clothing. —**likawih**, *vt.*

likouli 1. *n.* Dress. 2. *vi.* To wear a dress.

likoumeimei 1. *n.* Lava-lava, made of the bark of the breadfruit tree. 2. *vi.* To wear such a lava-lava.

likouda *vi.* To dress. —**likawihada**, *vt.*

likoutei 1. *n.* Lava-lava. 2. *vi.* To wear a lava-lava.

likokohunsop *adj.* Stern-faced, unsmiling.

likokouruhr *adj.* Happy-looking, smiling.

likommwei *n.* Fish sp., snapper, *Lutjanus fulviflamma.*

likoserek 1. *n.* Slip knot. 2. *vi.* To tie a slip knot.

likoht *n.* Owl.

likotkotuhwahu *adj.* Short-tempered, self-conscious.

likuwer *vi.* To call. —**likuwerih**, *vt.*

likuwerih *vt.* See *likuwer.*

liksansalamwahu *adj.* Hypocritical.

lil *vi.* To lower a sail.

lihli 1. *n.* Pounded food, as breadfruit, taro, yams, and bananas. 2. *vi. neut.* To pound food.

lihli karer *n.* Fermented pounded food.

lilikoio *n.* Portuguese man-of-war, the jellyfish.

lim *vt.* To fold. —**limilimpene**, *vi.*

lihm *n.* Bailer.

limaile *n.* A ghost.

limau *num.* Five; see *-u.*

limak *vt.* To bail. —**limalim**, *vi.*

limakap *num.* Five; see *kap.*

limakis *num.* Five; see *kis₁.*

limalim *vi.* To bail. —**limak**, *vt.*

limanokonok *adj.* Absent-minded, forgetful.

limara *num.* Five; see *ra.*

limarepeileng HONORIFIC. *n.* Pupil, of the eye.

limasaweirek HONORIFIC. *vi.* To blink.

limadip *num.* Five; see *dip.*

limadun *num.* Five; see *dun.*

limatumw *num.* Five; see *tumw.*

lime HONORIFIC. *n3s.* Arm, hand.

limeirpwong *n.* Grass sp., *Phyllanthus niruri.*

limeisek *num.* Fifty; see *eisek.*

limeiso HONORIFIC. *n.* Hand.

limeidihd *adj.* Opressive.

limek *adj.* Bent, smashed, mashed, dented.

limehk *num.* Fifty; see *ehk.*

limelep *num.* Five; see *lep.*

limenimeninseri *n.* Sp. of lizard, light blue with dark blue stripes, *Perocheirus.*

limengimeng 1. *n.* Tuberculosis. 2. *vi.* To have tuberculosis.

limengoul *num.* Fifty; see *ngoul.*

limesel *num.* Five; see *sel₂.*

limehda *vt.* To pick up, to carry, to take along.

limedek *adj.* Outgoing, forward, of women.

limedramin SLANG. *adj.* Forward, uninhibited, outgoing.

limete *num.* Five; see *te.*

limewel *num.* Five; see *wel₂.*

limiel *num.* Five; see *el₂.*

limika *num.* Five; see *ka₂.*

limilimpene *vi.* To be folded. —**lim**, *vt.*

limisou *num.* Five; see *sou₄.*

limisop *num.* Five; see *sop₂.*

limoumw *num.* Five; see *umw₂.*

limmen *num.* Five; see *men₃.*

limmwer *n.* Fish sp., a small *ah.*

limmwot *vi. neut.* To wrap kava in a bast with many twists.

limmwut *num.* Five; see *mwut₂.*

limpa *num.* Five; see *pa₃.*

limpak *num.* Five; see *pak₁.*

limpali *num.* Five; see *pali₁.*

limpar *num.* Five; see *par₂.*

limpahr *n.* Plant sp., *Lycopodium cernuum* or *phlegmaria.*

limpit *num.* Five; see *pit₂.*

limpoak 1. *n.* Love. 2. *adj.* Kind, loving. *Lahpo limpoak.* That guy is kind. 3. *vi.* To be in love. *Ira limpoak.* They are in love.

limpoar *num.* Five; see *poar.*

limpwel *n.* Sp. of small crab.

limpwo *n.* Limbo. [Eng.]

limpwong *num.* Five; see *pwong.*

limpwoat *num.* Five; see *pwoat.*

limpwuloi *num.* Five; see *pwuloi.*

limrei *vi. neut.* To wrap kava in a bast with a minimal number of twists.

lihmw *n.* Sponge; moss or lichen.

limwah *prep. n.* Next to (him, her, or it).

limwakarakar *adj.* Sensitive, temperamental.

limwakatantar *n.* Millipede.

limwahnsaleng *n.* Salt water eel, commonly found in muddy areas.

limwasahsa *adj.* Voyeuristic.

limwahdek *vi.* To crawl on one's belly.

limwadong *n.* Sea anemone sp..

limwesou ARCHAIC. *adj.* Obnoxious, disgusting, irritating; lusty.

limwehdi *n.* A small sp. of bat; caterpillar.

limwih *vt.* To sponge off, to wipe dry. —**limwilimw,** *vi.*

limwilimw *vi. neut.* To sponge off, to wipe dry. —**limwih,** *vt.*

limwinpwudo *n.* Handkerchief.

limwomwodol *num.* Five; see *mwodol.*

Limwohdeleng *n.* A ghost, said to take on various female forms, that dwells in the Kolonia area.

limwoahr, also **lamwer.** *n.* Gecko.

linenek *adj.* Always willing to engage in sexual intercourse, of a woman.

lingaling *adj.* Bright, clear, shiny.

lingan *adj.* Beautiful, shiny.

lingada *vi.* To appear on the horizon, of land.

linge *n3s.* Beam of light.

lingelingel *adj.* Given to biting.

lingeringer *adj.* Angry.

lingkiri *n.* Oyster.

lingkorot *n.* Sp. of shellfish, black in color.

lip *vi.* To leave a usual living area; to leave in haste because of displeasure.

lipahned *vi.* To gossip. —**lipahnede,** *vt.*

lipahnede *vt.* To gossip about. —**lipahned,** *vi.*

lipahrourou *n.* Butterfly.

lipahrok *vi.* To spy. —**lipahroke,** *vt.*

lipahroke *vt.* To spy on.

lipahdopwonla *vi.* To die while pregnant, also resulting in the death of the fetus.

lipeiahk, also **peiahk.** *adj.* Oval.

lipekekil *adj.* Looking in a begging manner.

lipengipeng *vi.* To sigh in one's sleep.

liper$_1$ *n.* Fish sp., halibut.

liper$_2$ *adj.* Skinny; sick, weak.

lipes *adj.* Ferocious, rabid.

lipet *n.* A variety of breadfruit.

lipilipil *adj.* Choosy.

lipirap *adj.* Thievish, given to stealing.

Lipitahn *n.* A clan name.

lipopohn *adj.* Vain.

Lipopohnwel *n.* A ghost, of the jungle.

lipoahrok *n.* Bird sp., a sea bird having a twisted beak.

lihpw$_1$ *n (3s: lipwe).* Trace or track.

lihpw$_2$ *n.* Large hole in the ground.

lipwan *adj.* Having an impact, effective, efficient.

lipwanapwan *vi. neut.* To suspend from one shoulder or both with a strap or rope, as a bag or purse or knapsack. —**lipwene,** *vt.*

lipwei *n.* Clam sp..

lipwene *vt.* To suspend from one shoulder or both with a strap or rope, as a bag or purse or knapsack. —**lipwanapwan,** *vi.*

lipwesepwes *adj.* Frequently engaging in sexual intercourse.

lipwongmas *vi.* To faint.

lipwoar 1. *vi.* To scold. 2. *adj.* Deprecative. —**lipwoare,** *vt.*

lipwoare *vt.* To scold. —**lipwoar,** *vi.*

lipwusinger *adj.* Unpleasant, always in a bad mood; harsh acting.

lirau *n.* Reed sp., used for weaving.

lirop *n.* Mat.

lirohro *adj.* Protective, mother-hen-like.

liroaridi HONORIFIC. *adj.* Bashful, embarrassed, ashamed.

lisaimwer *adj.* Loosely attached; limp looking, of people.

lisalseliwi, also **liseliseliwi.** HONORIFIC. *adj.* Hypocritical.

lisap *n.* Fish sp..

lisarapat *n.* Fish sp..

liseian *adj.* Pregnant.

liseirkopw *adj.* Always crying, of a child.

liseiseipahini, also **liteiteipahini.** *n.* Sp. of green lizard.

liseliping *adj.* Chaotic.

liseliseliwi, also **lisalseliwi.** HONORIFIC. *adj.* Hypocritical.

lisoi *vi.* To doze off, to nod when falling asleep.

lisouduhdu *n.* Sp. of crab.

lisongapwo *n.* Parlaysis.

lisop *n.* Sp. of shellfish.

lisosipil *adj.* Said of one who consistently puts too much water in kava or *lihli.*

lisoapwoar *n.* Sp. of crab.

lisoarop 1. *n.* Hat. 2. *vi.* To wear a hat.

lida *n.* Fish sp., a kind of parrotfish.

lidangalangal *n.* Sickness of a pig after giving birth.

lidep *n.* Fertile female of any species.

lider₁ 1. *n.* Food or drink employed as a chaser after drinking kava. 2. *vi.* To take a chaser after drinking kava.

lider₂ *vi.* To be intentionally bothersome. —**lidere,** *vt.*

lidere *vt.* To intentionally bother; to interfere with; to intervene. —**lider**₂, *vi.*

liderewes *adj.* Butt-in, pesky.

lidik *n.* Sea urchin.

lidip 1. *n.* An animal trap. 2. *vi.* To trap. —**lidipih,** *vt.*

lidipih *vt.* To trap. —**lidip,** *vi.*

lidoi *n.* Fish sp., a kind of parrotfish, *Scarus rubroviolaceus.*

lidokodok pwise *n.* Fish sp., a kind of needle fish.

lidu 1. *n.* Female servant, either politically or domestically. 2. *vi.* To serve as a slave. —**liduih,** *vt.*

liduih *vt.* To serve as a slave. —**lidu,** *vi.*

liht *n.* Jellyfish.

litak *n.* Fish sp., mudskipper.

litapwih *vt.* To paint. —**litepw,** *vi.*

liteh *n3s.* Two or more breadfruit at the end of a branch.

liteiteipahini, also **liseiseipahini.** *n.* Sp. of green lizard.

litehlapalap *adj.* Wide and flat.

litepw 1. *n.* Paint; initial effects of kava or alcohol. 2. *vi.* To paint; to feel the initial effects of kava or alcohol. —**litapwih,** *vt.*

litepwitepw HONORIFIC. *vi.* To look for lice.

litok *n.* Hen.

litokmwanger *n.* Reed sp., a variety of *ahlek* with reddish spots on the stem.

liwair₁ 1. *n.* A flash flood from the mountains. 2. *vi.* To flash flood.

liwair₂ *n.* A small sp. of bat.

liwaisisik *vi.* To hop on one foot.

lo *vi.* To be caught.

loh₁, also **lahu.** *n (3s: lewe).* Tongue.

loh₂ *vi.* To have something stuck in one's throat.

loh₃ *n.* Seat, in a canoe.

loi *vi.* To collide.

loi- *vi.* To arrive at a specific location, to appear on the scene.

loiloitik HONORIFIC. *vi.* To whisper.

loipehs *vi.* To tap ashes from a cigar, cigarette, or pipe.

lou *adj.* Cool, cooled off.

loulou HONORIFIC. 1. *vi.* To pray. 2. *n.* Prayer.

lok *vi.* To suffer, physically or mentally; to be tired; to give up.

lohk *vi.* To spread news around. —**lohki,** *vt.*

lokaia 1. *vi.* To talk, to speak. 2. *n.* Language, speech; dispatch.

lokaia suwed *adj.* Foulmouthed.

lokaia tohto *adj.* Argumentative.

lokala *vi.* To be sated, to have had it with something or someone.

lokalok *adj.* Restless; uncomfortable, causing minor discomfort.

lohki *vt.* See *lohk.*

lohkinned HONORIFIC. *vi.* To call in food, by a *Nahnmwarki* prior to a feast.

lokolok *n.* Suffering.

lokulok, also **lukuluk.** 1. *vi.* To have a serious case of asthma; to breathe in an agitated manner. 2. *adj.* Asthmatic. 3. *n.* A serious case of asthma; agitated breathing.

lohlo *n.* Crossbeam in a house.

lolok *vi.* To frown.

lolong *n.* Stone burial chambers.

lommw, also **lemmw.** *adj.* Afraid of ghosts.

lohmwei 1. *n.* A disease of infants, attributed to the mother's becoming pregnant while a child is still nursing. 2. *vi.* To have this disease.

lohnwar *n.* Seat, in a canoe.

-long *verb. suff.* Inwards, into. *alu* walk, *aluhlong* walk into.

lohng *n.* Termite.

longenmwet *n.* Termite.

lop *vi.* To be cut crosswise. —**lopuk**, *vt.*

lopidi *n.* District, precinct; cut in a hill or mountain made for a road.

lopuk *vt.* To cut crosswise. —**lop**, *vi.*

lopw₁ *num.* Hundred thousand.

lopw₂ *vi.* To clap. —**lopwor**, *vt.*

lohpwelipwel *vi.* To make a good catch with a net.

lopwolopw *vi.* To wash clothing, to do laundry, literally the action of pounding clothing. —**lopwor**, *vt.*

lopwon *n.* Any soft object which is made into a ball; a ball of kava root fibers set aside during the first pounding; one of the cups of kava in the kava ceremony.

lopwor *vt.* To wash clothing, to launder; to clap; to applaud. —**lopw₂** or **lopwolopw**, *vi.*

lohpwu *n.* Cross or crucifix; floor beam; a carrying pole with a cross pole attached; a kava plant large enough that it requires being carried on such a carrying pole.

lohpwuala, also **lohpwuhla**. *vi.* To be crucified.

lohpwuhla *vi.* See *lohpwuala.*

lohs *n.* Mat.

losolos *adj.* Lush, as of foliage; thick, as a coat of hair.

lohdi *vi.* To be conquered, captured, overcome.

lohteng *adj.* Mute, dumb, stuttering.

lohtik *n (3s: lohtiki).* Uvula.

loak *vi.* To be locked. [Eng.] —**loakehdi**, *vt.*

loahk *n.* Lock. [Eng.]

loakehdi *vt.* To lock. [*loak*<Eng.] —**loak**, *vi.*

loakewel HONORIFIC. *vi.* To defecate.

loakipil HONORIFIC. *vi.* To bathe.

loakiso HONORIFIC. **1.** *vi.* To bathe. **2.** *n.* Water for bathing.

loal *adj.* Deep.

loalamwahu *adj.* Good-hearted.

loale *prep. n.* Inside (him, her, or it).

loaleid, also **loaloid**. *vi.* To miss a person or a place, to be homesick.

loalekeng, also **loalokong**. *adj.* Intelligent, smart.

loalehng, also **loalohng**. *vt.* To be devoted, reliable, persevering.

loaloh *adj.* Heartsick, of a man who has lost his wife.

loaloid, also **loaleid**. *vi.* To miss a person or a place, to be homesick.

loalokong, also **loalekeng**. *adj.* Intelligent, smart.

loalohng, also **loalehng**. *vt.* To be devoted, reliable, persevering.

loalopwon *adj.* Stupid, silly, idiotic, simple, dumb.

loaloapwoat *adj.* Faithful, persevering, single-minded, diligent.

loallap **1.** *adj.* Daring, reckless, bold, adventurous. **2.** *n.* Thief, murderer, rascal.

loalloale *vt.* To hide one's feelings.

loalmasarang *adj.* Indecisive when confronted with a number of appealing choices.

loang *vi.* To be passed in the traditional manner of respect; to be placed across another thing. —**loange**, *vt.*

loahng *n.* Fly.

loangalap *n.* Wasp.

loange *vt.* To pass in the traditional manner of respect; to place one thing across another thing. —**loang**, *vi.*

loangen pwise *n.* A bluish colored fly.

loangen suke *n.* Honeybee. [*suke*<Eng.]

loangenmeiso HONORIFIC. *n.* Toothpick.

loangon *n.* Sp. of sea cucumber.

loangoapahpa *vi.* To put one's leg over a sleeping partner.

loangkoait *vi.* In Uh, to serve the *Nahnmwarki* by carrying kava directly from the pounding stone.

luh *vi.* To be incomplete, as a consequence of some part being removed.

Luhennos *n.* A title.

luk *vi.* To be invited; to be towed; to troll for fish. —**luke**, *vt.*

luhk₁ *n.* Invitation.

Luhk₂ *n.* Lord, used to refer to a number of traditional Ponapean gods.

Luhk Pohnpei *n.* A title.

luke *vt.* To invite; to tow. —**luk**, *vi.*

lukenaisais *n.* A variety of yam.

lukepenpwong *n.* Midnight, middle of the night.

lukiamwas *n.* A variety of breadfruit.

lukielel *n.* A variety of breadfruit.

lukouk *n.* Small hand net.

lukom *vi.* To wrap around.

lukope *n3s.* Middle, either in a spatial or temporal sense; waist or trunk of the body.

lukuluk, also **lokolok. 1.** *vi.* To have a serious case of asthma; to breathe in an agitated manner. **2.** *adj.* Asthmatic. **3.** *n.* Serious case of asthma; agitated breathing.

lukuwal *n.* A variety of breadfruit.

lul 1. *vi.* To flame. **2.** *n.* Flame.

luhl *interj.* An exclamation, said to drive away sharks.

luhmwuhmw HONORIFIC. **1.** *vi.* To be sick. **2.** *adj.* Sickly. **3.** *n.* Sickness, disease, illness.

luhpes *n.* Louver. [Eng.]

lupwoluwo *n.* A large octopus-like creature, said to live in the mouth of rivers, possibly mythical.

luhr *n.* Small sp. of shrimp.

lus *vi.* To jump. —**lusuk,** *vt.*

luhs *vi.* To lose. [Eng.]

lusiam *vi.* To commit suicide by hanging oneself.

lusida *vi.* To jump up; to be surprised.

lusuk *vt.* To jump; to catch a ride with. —**lus,** *vi.*

lusulus 1. *adj.* Contagious; wandering, of speech. **2.** *n.* Fever.

lususuhr *adj.* Soft, easy to sink in, as a swampy place.

luwaikehk *vi.* To call by shouting.

luwak *adj.* Jealous, envious.

luwakahk *adj.* Jealous, usually with reference to one's spouse.

luwaruhru HONORIFIC. *vi.* To travel.

luhwe *n3s.* Remains, remnant; change, as of money; the one remaining.

luhweiso HONORIFIC. *n.* Leftover food.

luwehs *n.* Plant sp., having a sticky sap.

luhwehdi *vi.* To be leftover.

luwet *adj.* Weak, feeble, sickly.

luwetakahu *adj.* Weak, feeble, sickly.

luwou *n.* Bracelet.

M

ma *conj.* If. *Ma ke idih iahia, sendin pehmwen pahn kensda.* If you point at a rainbow, your finger will ulcerate.

mah *adj.* Old, aged; ripe.

mai₁ *n.* Stone or coral fish trap.

mai₂ *adj.* Skillful. [Jap.]

mahi *n.* Breadfruit.

maiai *adj.* Unlucky, unfortunate.

maiauda, also maiouda. *vi.* To be relieved, to be free from encumbrances.

maiouda, also maiauda. *vi.* To be relieved, to be free from encumbrances.

maikol *n.* Overripe breadfruit.

maing *n.* Sir, madam.

maingih, also meingih. *vt.* To speak to another using respect forms of speech. —meing, *vi.*

maoakani *n.* Mahogany. [Eng.]

mahu *n.* Fish sp., any bluish parrotfish.

mahuenmoar *n.* Fish sp., a kind of parrotfish.

mauk SLANG. *vi.* To cry, to weep.

mahulik *n.* A mature *mahu.*

maun *vi.* To be right-handed.

maud *n.* Fish sp..

maudel *vi.* To yawn.

mahk₁ 1. *adj.* Reserved, containing one's feelings for fear of self-embarrassment or embarrassing others, constrained in one's action by a social situation, formal in one's relations with others. 2. *n.* Deference.

mahk₂ *n.* Insignia, sign. [Eng.]

mahkada *vi.* To stop, of rain.

mahkenwol *vi.* Extreme form of *mahk.*

mahkehngie *interj.* Excuse me!, Forgive me!.

mahkete *conj.* Otherwise. *Omw lehken, mahkete aramas poakoapoakeiuk.* It's your selfishness; otherwise people would like you.

makiaki *vi.* To sob.

makinet *n.* Magnet. [Eng.]

makirehl *n.* Canned mackerel. [Eng.]

mahkoneidi *vi.* To cease, resulting in a return to normalcy.

makoroni *n.* Macaroni. [Eng.]

makunai *adj.* Stupid, incapable of learning. [Jap.]

mahl 1. *adj.* Excessively bright. 2. *n.* Temporary blindness induced by excessive light.

malau *adj.* Far apart.

malaulau *adj.* Few.

malamal *adj.* Slow, referring to long intervals between some repetitious activity. *Ohlo lokaia malamal.* That man speaks slowly.

malangalang *adj.* Discomforted, by filth or something unpleasant looking; prissy.

malek *n.* Chicken.

malekelek *n.* Fish sp..

malekenwel *n.* Bird sp., jungle fowl, *Gallus.*

mahlen 1. *vi.* To draw or paint, as a picture. 2. *n.* Painting, drawing. [Ger.] —mahlenih, *vt.*

mahlenih *vt.* To draw or paint, as a picture. [*mahlen*<Ger.] —mahlen, *vi.*

mahlengida HONORIFIC. *vi.* To wash one's face.

maledek *adj.* Roomy; free, at ease in doing something.

mahliel *n.* An eye condition caused by exposure to glare, resulting in sensitivity to light.

mahliok *adj.* Calm and overcast, with no rain, used in describing the weather.

malimalih HONORIFIC. *vt.* To blow with air expelled from the mouth.

malipe HONORIFIC. *vt.* To call.

mall *n.* Natural clearing in the forest, a grassy, unfertile area; an area with little topsoil.

mamahd *vt.* To maximize the volume of one's voice. *Serepeino mamahd ah wer.* That girl screamed as loud as she could.

mame *n.* Beans. [Jap.]

mamenoki *n.* Tree sp.. [Jap.]

man *vi.* To take hold, to stick; to be effective.

mahn *n.* Animal, insect.

manaida n. Chopping board. [Jap.]

manaman 1. adj. Magical, mysterious, spiritual; official. 2. n. Magic, mysterious or spiritual power; miracle; authority.

manih vt. To wink at. —men₄, vi.

mahnien adj. Calm, cool, not easily disturbed, of people.

manokehla, also mankonehla. vt. To forget. —manokonokla, vi.

manokonokla vi. To be forgotten. —mankonehla or manokehla, vt.

mankonehla, also manokehla. vt. To forget. —manokonokala, vi.

mannaka n. Name of one of the holes in the marble game anaire. [Jap.]

mansu n. A kind of dumpling stuffed with a red bean jam. [Jap.]

mand adj. Tame.

manda n. Next day.

mandaken aio n. Day before yesterday.

mandolihn n. Mandolin. [Eng.]

manterihn, also manterihng. n. Mandarin orange, tangerine. [Eng.]

manterihng, also manterihn. n. Mandarin orange, tangerine. [Eng.]

mangarangar vi. To be sickened by too much greasy food.

mangat n. Plantain.

mangil n (3s: mangile). Handle of a tool.

manguro n. Fish sp., dogtuna, Gymnasarda unicolor. [Jap.]

mangnga 1. n. Cartoon, comic strip; character, clown. 2. vi. To be a character, to be a clown; to be foppish. [Jap.]

map n. Map. [Eng.]

mahr₁ n. Preserved breadfruit.

mahr₂ n. Fish sp., rabbitfish, Siganus puellus.

marain 1. adj. Bright, either with reference to light or intelligence; civilized, enlightened. 2. n. Civilization.

maram n. Moon; moonlight.

maram mat n. Full moon.

maram pwul n. New moon.

marapat n. Fish sp..

marahra adj. Fast, swift, of a moving object; light, in weight.

marasau n. Tree sp., Aglaia ponapensis.

maradahn n. Old preserved breadfruit.

mahrek n. Fern sp., Cyclosorus adenophorus.

marekeiso HONORIFIC. vi. To anoint.

marekeng adj. Dry, of the hair or skin.

marekileng HONORIFIC. n. In a nahs, the area where the Nahnmwarki sits.

marep₁ vi. To blink.

marep₂ n. Fish sp., goatfish, Upeneus arge.

marer vi. To hiccough.

maresed n. Preserved breadfruit soaked in salt water prior to placing it in the pit.

marop vi. To be smashed, to be broken.

marosong 1. n. A marathon. 2. vi. To run a marathon. [Jap.<Eng.]

marungurung adj. Faded.

mahrdi vi. Of leaves, to turn or begin to dry.

mahs₁ n. In the past, a long time ago. Mahs mehn Pohnpei kin pelipel. In the past, Ponapeans did tatooing. Mahs mahs mie ohl emen. Once upon a time there was a man.

mahs₂ n (3s: mese). Face.

mahs₃ adv. Please. Kihdo mahs. Give it to me please.

mahs₄ n. First. I pahn kohla Pohnpei mahs. I will go to Ponape first.

Mahs₅ n. March, the month of the year. [Eng.]

masak vt. To be afraid of, to fear.

masal vi. To blossom, to bloom; to fray, as of ropes.

masamas adj. Beloved, favored.

masamwahu adj. Good-looking, pretty, handsome.

mahsanih HONORIFIC. vt. To say, to see.

masapang adj. Cross-eyed.

mahsahs adj. Cleared, as of vegetation.

masaht n. Small black mangrove crab.

mahsen HONORIFIC. 1. vi. To speak. 2. n. Language, speech.

masepwehk adj. Afraid, frightened, cowardly, bashful.

masinoki n. Ironwood. [Jap.]

masis n. Match. [Eng.]

masokod n. Fish sp..

masomwomw n. Cataract, opacity of the crystalline lens of the eye.

masuku n. Catcher's mask. [Jap.<Eng.]

masukun adj. Blind.

maskala *adj.* Pretentious, proud, boastful.

masliki *n3s.* Outer side, outer surface.

masloale *n3s.* Inner side, inner surface.

maspali *adj.* One-eyed.

massuwed *adj.* Ugly; sad-looking.

masduwarawar *adj.* Large-eyed.

mad$_1$ *n.* Reef; large coral head.

mad$_2$ *vi.* To be dry.

mada *n.* Forked stick part of a slingshot. [Jap.]

madau$_1$ *n.* Ocean, beyond the reef.

madau$_2$ *n.* Thought.

madamadau 1. *vi.* To think. 2. *n.* Thought. —**medewe**, *vt.*

madap *adj.* Uneven, of an edge.

madeu *n.* Tree sp., *Cinnamomum.*

madekeng *adj.* Very dry.

madep *n.* Sp. of sea cucumber.

madepei *n.* Large submerged coral head.

mahdire *n.* Nun. [Span.]

madires *n.* Mattress. [Eng.]

madol *n.* Space between things; time between events.

Madolenihmw *n.* Name of a municipality in Ponape.

mat *adj.* Ripe, overripe, rotten, spoiled, decayed.

maht *n.* Pimple, acne.

matala HONORIFIC. *vi.* To die.

matamat$_1$ *adj.* Pliable, resilient.

matamat$_2$ *n.* Ginger, *Eleocharis laxiflora.*

matenei *adj.* Ripe, ready to eat, of fruit.

materek *adj.* Supple, limber; easily persuaded; lucky.

mahwin 1. *vi.* To be at war. 2. *n.* War, battle.

me$_1$, also **met.** *dem. pron.* This one, by me; here; now.

me$_2$ *pron.* One; also used in relative and finite clauses. *Me toantoalo ohla.* The black one is broken. *Kowe me wiahda.* You are the one who did it. *Mwahmw me e wahdo aioh mat.* The fish that he brought yesterday is spoiled. *I manokehla me ke kohsang Ruk.* I forgot that you came from Truk.

me$_3$ *stative marker.* Used to emphasize the factuality of a state named by an adjective. *E me kehlail.* He is strong (no doubt about it).

meh$_1$ *n.* Thing.

meh$_2$ *vi.* To bleat, of a goat.

Mei$_1$ *n.* May, the month of the year. [Eng.]

mei$_2$ 1. *adj.* Blue. 2. *n.* Blue.

meiais *n.* A variety of breadfruit.

meiapaup *n.* A variety of breadfruit.

meiarepe *n.* A variety of breadfruit.

meiuhpw *n.* A variety of breadfruit.

meikalak *n.* A variety of breadfruit.

meikimwer *n.* A variety of breadfruit.

meikidi *n.* A variety of breadfruit.

meikole, also **meipa.** *n.* A variety of breadfruit.

meikuwet *n.* A variety of breadfruit.

meimei *n.* A clothlike material made from the bark of breadfruit.

meimwed *n.* A variety of breadfruit.

mein padahk *n.* A variety of breadfruit.

mein peimwas *n.* A variety of breadfruit.

mein pohn sakar *n.* A variety of breadfruit.

mein pohnle *n.* A variety of breadfruit.

mein pwahr *n.* A variety of breadfruit.

mein pwuht *n.* A variety of breadfruit.

mein sahrek *n.* A variety of breadfruit.

meinuwe *n.* A variety of breadfruit.

meinpwuhten sokehs *n.* A variety of breadfruit.

meing 1. *n.* High language, respect forms of speech. 2. *vi.* To speak using respect forms of speech. —**maingih** or **meingih**, *vt.*

meingih *vt.* See *meing.*

meingtoal *vi.* To be left-handed.

meipa, also **meikole.** *n.* A variety of breadfruit.

meipwiliet *n.* A variety of breadfruit.

meipwon *adj.* Virgin, pure, undefiled.

meipwuhleng *n.* A variety of breadfruit.

meir *vi.* To sleep.

meiroang 1. *n.* Sacrifice, offering, contribution. 2. *vi.* To sacrifice, to make an offering or contribution.

meirkelik *adj.* Deep in sleep.

meisaip *n.* A variety of breadfruit.

meise *n.* A variety of breadfruit.

meisei *n.* A variety of breadfruit.

meiserihseng *n.* A variety of breadfruit.

meid 1. *adv.* Truly. *Ke meid roson!* Aren't you truly lucky! 2. *vi.* To be blessed, used biblically.

meitehid *n.* A variety of breadfruit.

meiti *n.* A variety of breadfruit.

meitoal *n.* A variety of breadfruit.

meiweke *n.* A variety of breadfruit.

mek 1. *adj.* Dented. 2. *n.* Dent.

mehkan, also **metakan.** *dem. pron.* These, by me.

mehkei *pron.* Something, anything (plural).

mehkot, also **okoteme.** *pron.* Something, anything (singular).

mehla *vi.* To die; to stop, of a mechanical object.

meleilei 1. *adj.* Peaceful, easygoing, unenthusiastic, slow moving, passive, lethargic. 2. *n.* Peace.

mehlel 1. *adj.* True, honest. 2. *sent. adv.* Truly, honestly.

melengileng *adj.* Shiny, glistening, polished.

meliek *vi.* To move rapidly.

meliehla HONORIFIC. *vt.* To forget.

melikahka HONORIFIC. 1. *n.* Song. 2. *vi.* To sing.

melimel 1. *n.* Windstorm, typhoon. 2. *vi.* To be struck by a windstorm or typhoon.

mem *adj.* Sweet.

mehme₁ *n.* Wart.

mehme₂ 1. *vi.* To eat, said only of infants. 2. *n.* Premasticated food for infants.

memiap *n.* Papaya, also called mummy apple. [Eng.]

men₁ *vt.* To want. *I men kilang kasdo.* I want to see a movie.

men₂ 1. *dem. pron.* That one, by you; there, by you. 2. *interj.* That's it!, from *Ih men.*

men₃ *num. cl.* Used in counting animate beings. *pwihk limmen* five pigs.

men₄ *vi.* To wink. —**manih,** *vt.*

mehn₁ *n.* One of, thing of.

mehn₂ *vi.* To kiss, to rub noses.

mehn akinen *n.* Target.

mehn adahd *n.* File, sharpening stone, razor strop.

mehn eringi *n.* Toothpick.

mehn ersaleng *n.* A pick used for the ear, as a Q-tip.

mehn kapas *n.* Glue.

mehn kataman *n.* Reminder.

mehn kawa *n.* People of olden times.

mehn kisetik 1. *vi.* To have the measles. 2. *n.* Measles.

mehn kodu *n.* Dye.

mehn koadi *n.* Funnel.

mehn loipehs *n.* Ash tray.

mehn madau 1. *vi.* To be seasick. 2. *n.* Seasickness.

mehn mwadong *n.* Toy.

mehn namwanamw *n.* Low islander; any islander, Micronesian or Polynesian, of non-Ponapean origin.

mehn pahn kadip *n.* Defendant, in a criminal case.

mehn pahn repenpwung *n.* Defendant, in a civil case.

mehn pwuropwur *n.* Drill, brace.

mehn rar *n.* Flat piece of wood used to pry off the charred skin of roasted breadfruit.

mehn roh *n.* Stretcher.

mehn rokumw 1. *n.* Nosebleed, occurring spontaneously. 2. *vi.* To have a spontaneous nosebleed.

mehn sahmwa *interj.* Thank you, used only with younger people.

mehn seipinsel *n.* Pencil sharpener.

mehn sohng *n.* Ruler, tape measure.

mehn suhs *n.* Jew.

mehn doadoahk *n.* Tool; gift or contribution to a party.

mehn tang 1. *vi.* To have diarrhea. 2. *n.* Diarrhea.

mehn windeng *n.* Steering wheel. [*windeng*<Jap.]

menakan *dem. pron.* Those, by you.

menemen en pahsu *n.* Pearl.

mehnia *interr.* Which. *Mehnia likou me ke mwahuki?* Which material do you like?

menioak *n.* Cassava, manioc, tapioca.

menihke *n.* Any non-swimming marine organism, i.e. shells, starfish, sea cucumbers, etc.; sex organs of a female.

menin kahlipw *n.* Dragonfly.

menin lohsapw *n.* Sand flea.

menin douioas *n.* Insect sp., walking stick.

meninrahn *n.* Centipede.

menindeiuh *n.* Director of a feast.

menipinip *adj.* Thin, of flat objects as paper.

menipinipi *n3s.* Sideburn.

menuwa *n.* Man-of-war, an armed naval vessel; warship. [Eng.]

menkerep *n.* Any four-legged animal.

menkumwo *vi.* To be hungry for meat.

menlau *interj.* Thanks, informal.

menmwenge *vi.* To be hungry.

mennei *n.* The favorite male child of a *Nahnmwarki* or *Nahnken.*

mennim *vi.* To be thirsty.

menpihr *n.* Bird.

mehnsahk 1. *n.* A kind of sickness, producing dizziness. 2. *vi.* To have this kind of sickness.

menseiren *vi.* To comply; to do something against one's will.

menseker 1. *vi.* To want to fart. 2. *interj.* Used to excuse oneself prior to farting.

menseng *n.* Morning.

mensiek *n.* Grasshopper.

mehnda 1. *interr.* Why, to what purpose. *Mehnda ke sohte iang?* Why didn't you go along? 2. *interj.* Never mind!

mentikitik *n.* Early morning.

meng *adj.* Withered, dry, dead, of vegetation.

mengei *adj.* Easy.

menger *n.* Fish sp., flying fish.

mengiloal *vi.* To talk to oneself.

menginpeh *n3s.* Result of one's work; writing, handwriting, signature.

mengihtik *n.* Detail.

mepel, also lepel. *n.* Level, a carpenter's tool. [Eng.]

mer *adj.* Rusty, corroded.

merei *n.* Place for wrestling or fighting.

merepwinsed *n.* Mangrove sp., *Heritiera littoralis.*

merer *n.* Fish sp., wrasse, *Cheilinus undulatus.*

merimer *adj.* Almost ripe, as of bananas and mangoes; light, of a color.

mering *adj.* Old, of inanimate objects.

Mesaia *n.* Messiah. [Eng.]

mesarawi POLITE. *n.* Genitals.

mese *n3s.* Face; facade; upper part of yam, taro, pineapple, etc.; edge of a reef.

mesehl 1. *n.* A kind of magic, employed to romantically attract another; a love potion or charm. 2. *vi.* To employ

magic to romantically attract another. —mesehlih, *vt.*

mesehlih *vt.* To employ magic to romantically attract another. —mesehl, *vi.*

mesenedi *n3s.* Solar plexus.

mesenih *n.* First-born child.

mesenlam *n.* Boundary between the shallow and deep part of a lagoon.

mesenmwomw *n.* Wart, corn.

mesenpek *n.* Head of a yam.

mesendid *n.* A large upright in the framing of the walls of a building.

mesiha *n.* Fire.

mesiek *vi.* To move swiftly up and down.

med *vi.* To be full, after eating.

medakahn *adj.* Talkative, outgoing.

medahlia *n.* Medal, usually a catholic religious medal. [Span.]

mede *n.* Ripe breadfruit.

medeu *n.* A kind of adze.

medek *vi.* To hurt; to be painful; to ache.

medendel *adj.* Smooth and flat.

medehde *n.* Coconut leaves upon which food which is to be distributed at a feast is placed; leaves upon which freshly caught fish are placed.

medewe *vt.* To think. —madamadau, *vi.*

medi *n.* Fish sp., snapper, *Lethrinus lentjan.*

met, also me₁. *dem. pron.* This one, by me; here; now.

metakan, also mehkan. *dem. pron.* These, by me.

mete *n.* Metal, nail, badge, spear for a speargun. [Eng.]

meteitei *adj.* Slimy.

metel *n.* Medal, non-religious. [Eng.]

metik, also mitik. *vt.* To kiss.

mehwo *adj.* Voracious.

mi *vi.* To exist, a locative verb. *Pwuhko mi pohn tehpelo.* That book is on the table.

mih *n.* Name of the letter *m.*

mie *vi.* To exist, an existential verb. *Mie aramas nan ihmwo.* There is someone in that house.

mihk *vt.* To suck, to absorb.

milik *n.* Milk. [Eng.]

milikkang *n.* Milk can. [Jap.<Eng.]

milikpil *n.* Evaporated milk. [*milik*<Eng.]

milikten *n.* Condensed milk.
[*milik*<Eng.]

min *adj.* Neat, clean.

mihn *adj.* Mean. [Eng.]

minimin 1. *adj.* Cooperative. 2. *n.*
Union, association, any cooperative
venture; cooperation.

minit *n.* Minute; minutes, as of a
meeting. [Eng.]

mihsa *n.* Mass. [Span.]

misiohn *n.* Catholic mission. [Span.]

misin *n.* Protestant mission. [Eng.]

misihn *n.* Machine, engine, outboard
motor. [Eng.]

misihn en lioal *n.* Generator.

misihn tiati *n.* Treadle operated sewing
machine.

miso *n.* Bean paste. [Jap.]

mihding, also mihting. 1. *n.* Meeting.
2. *vi.* To meet. [Eng.]

middo *n.* Catcher's mitt. [Jap.<Eng.]

mitik, also metik. *vt.* To kiss.

mihting, also mihding. 1. *n.* Meeting.
2. *vi.* To meet. [Eng.]

mo *vi.* To heal.

mour₁ *n (3s: mouri).* Life.

mour₂ *adj.* Alive, raw; undried or
green, of wood; fresh.

mol 1. *vi.* To catch with a slip noose.
2. *n.* Slip noose.

molomol *adj.* Of plants, to be a deep
healthy green; of the skin, sleek.

mohn ohla *n.* Scar.

mohn pakudang *n.* Bomb crater.

mohngiong *n (3s: mohngiongi).* Heart.

mohngiong mwakelekel *adj.* Free from
sin; charitable.

mohr *n.* Small kava plant, one
remaining after the larger plants have
been removed.

moromor *n.* War, battle, dispute.

moron *adj.* Large, in quantity.

mohs *n.* Field, open area.

mosul *adj.* Thick.

mowe *n3s.* Scar, trace, ruins.

moahk *n.* Fish sp..

moakoan *n.* Curdled coconut milk.

moahl₁ *n.* Kava pounding stone.

moahl₂ 1. *vi.* To pass by; to be caught
sight of; to visit. 2. *n (3s: moahle).*
Appearance, at a place.

moahloahl *adj.* Always bumming
around, always on the go.

moamoar *vi.* To snore.

moahng₁ *n (3s: moange).* Head.

moahng₂ *adj.* Ill intentioned.

moangamad *adj.* Bald.

moangen kateng *n.* Belt buckle.

moangepwet *adj.* Gray headed;
flowering, of mango trees.

moangkoikoi *vi.* To shave one's head.

moangmedek 1. *vi.* To have a
headache. 2. *n.* Headache.

moangtakai *n.* Fish sp., a growth stage
of *ah.*

moaralap HONORIFIC. *vi.* To yawn.

moarungurung *adj.* Dull or old-looking,
of inanimate objects.

moahd *n (3s: moahde).* Echo; barely
discernable sound from a distant
source.

moatoar₁ *adj.* Oily, greasy.

moatoar₂ HONORIFIC. *n (3s: moatoare).*
Mat; sleeping place.

moatoare HONORIFIC. *poss. cl.* A
possessive classifier used in honorific
speech in place of the common
language classifier *kie.*

mmwen *n.* Fish sp..

mmwus 1. *vi.* To vomit. 2. *n.* Vomit.

mpahi *adj.* Submissive, modest, self-
effacing.

mpe *prep. n.* Next to (him or her), with
animate relationships.

mpei *adj.* Buoyant.

mpek *vi.* To look for lice. —pakid, *vt.*

mpehn *n.* Two large logs at the base of
the fire for an *uhmw.*

mpeng *vi.* To be awakened. —pangin,
vt.

mpereng *vi.* To burn brightly, of a
source of light having a flame, as a
lamp.

mpoake *vi.* To kiss, to rub noses.

mpwa *n.* Hermit crab.

mpwe *n.* Curve, bend.

mpwei *n.* Ball; stomach; sphere.

mpwein kent *n.* Bladder.

mpwein tenek *n.* The spongy substance
found in a sprouting coconut in its
early stage of development.

mpwek *n.* Bud of a flower.

mpwekin ripwiripw *n.* Fish sp..

mpwel₁ *n.* Blister, from sunburn.

mpwel₂ *vi.* Of a traditional oven, to be
at a stage where food has been placed
in it.

mpwel₃ *n.* A variety of palm.

mpwel₄ *n.* Female pig before it is bred.

mpwel₅ *n.* Sp. of crab.

mpwelehdi *vi.* To unexpectedly converge upon a place, of a large number of people.

mpwer *n.* Twins; also used to refer to multiple births, as *mpwer silimen* , triplets.

mpwer- *vi.* To come or go in pairs. *Ira mpwerlongodo nan wenihmwo.* They came in the door together (in a pair).

mpwet **1.** *vi.* To blister. **2.** *n.* Blister.

mpwi **1.** *adj.* Leaky, as of a roof. **2.** *n.* Drop.

mpwokos *adj.* Humpback.

mpwos *n.* Boil, swelling, infection.

mpwosada *vi.* To swell; to rise, as of bread.

mpwoampw *n.* Rise, low hill.

mpwul **1.** *n (3s: mpwule).* Flame. **2.** *vi.* To burn with a flame.

mpwulapwul **1.** *adj.* Pink. **2.** *n.* Pink.

mpwun *n.* Barnacle.

MW

mwah *n.* The opposite sex sibling of one's spouse, the spouse of one's opposite sex sibling.

mwahi *n.* Color; pattern or design, as of material; stain, mark; freckle, mole, or any skin discoloration.

mwahiei *vi.* To wail, at a funeral.

mwail *n.* Mile. [Eng.]

mwahu *adj.* Good.

mwahuki *vt.* To like or love, to consider good, to desire sexually.

mwaur *vt.* To douche. —mwoumwou, *vi.*

mwakar *vi.* To be slighted, to be displeased.

mwakelekel *adj.* Clean; innocent, honest.

mwakereker *n.* Constellation, possibly the particular constellation Pleiades.

mwahkohko *vi.* Of women, to sway the body and head while dancing.

mwahl *adj.* Common, useless, of no consequence.

mwalaun *adj.* Devious, deceptive. —mwalaunih, *vt.*

mwalaunih *vt.* To fool or deceive. —mwalaun, *adj.*

mwalekuluk ARCHAIC. *adj.* Wrinkled, as the face of an old person.

mwahliel 1. *n (3s: mwahlieli).* Brain. 2. *adj.* Dizzy.

mwalusulus *n.* Fish sp., bass-grouper, *Cephalopholis argus.*

mwahmw *n.* Fish.

mwamwahl *adj.* Not respected.

mwahn ARCHAIC. *n.* Man, male.

mwahnakapw 1. *n.* Young man. 2. *adj.* Young, of males.

mwand *n.* Trace of movement either seen or heard, as made by a person sneaking around. *Mie mwand limwahn wenihmwo.* There was a trace of movement near the door.

mwahng *n.* A variety of wet land taro, *Cyrtosperma chamissonis.*

mwahng kieil *n.* A variety of taro with a stalk colored like the sp. of lizard *kieil.*

mwahng suwain *n.* A variety of taro with lacy edged leaves.

mwangaingai *adj.* Bumpy, rough, not smooth.

mwangas *n.* Ripe coconut; copra; ripe betel nut.

mwanger *n.* Fish sp..

mwanger en mwoanipil *n.* Fish sp..

mwanger en nanipil *n.* Fish sp..

mwanger en nannamw *n.* Fish sp..

mwanger ripwiripw *n.* Fish sp..

mwangerenger *adj.* Spotted, splotched.

mwahngih HONORIFIC. *vt.* To know.

mwahngieng *adj.* Giddy, dizzy.

mwahngin meir *n.* A variety of taro from Meir.

mwahngin moar *n.* A variety of dry land taro.

mwahngin namwanamw *n.* A variety of taro from the outer islands.

mwahngin nukuwer *n.* A variety of taro from Nukuoro.

mwahngin ngetik *n.* A variety of taro from Ngatik.

mwahngin palau *n.* A variety of taro from Palau.

mwar, also mwahr. *n (3s: mware).* Title, name.

mwahr, also mwar. *n (3s: mware).* Title, name.

mwarak *vt.* To fall on, as of rain on leaves.

mwaramwar 1. *vi.* To wear a garland, necklace, or lei. 2. *n.* Garland, necklace, lei. —mware, *vt.*

mwaramwer *n.* Small yam; anything that comes in round forms, as *mwohni mwaramwer,* meaning change.

mwarahntik- *vi.* To break or shatter, especially of glass. *Dahlo pwupwidihte mwarahntikpeseng.* The dish fell and shattered.

mware₁ *poss. cl.* A possessive classifier for garlands, titles, or names.

mware₂ *vt.* To wear a garland, necklace, or lei. —mwaramwar, *vi.*

mwareiso HONORIFIC. *n.* Chest.

Mwarekehtik, also Mwarikihtik. *n.* A title.

Mwarikihtik, also Mwarekehtik. *n.* A title.

mwarmware *n3s.* Chest.

mwahs 1. *n.* Worm, bacteria, germ. 2. *vi.* To have worms.

mwasakoil *n.* Maggot.

mwasahl *n (3s: mwasahle).* Intestine.

mwasahn *vt.* To watch out for, to look out for, to observe.

mwasenger *n.* Intestinal worm.

mwasik *vi.* To be burned, of anything. —isik, *vt.*

mwaso, also mwesot. *n.* An eel, commonly found in mangrove swamps.

mwasod, also mwosod. *adj.* Rotten, of wood.

mwadang *vi.* To go fast, to be quick, to hurry.

mwadangete *adv.* Quickly, suddenly. *E mwadangete aluhla.* He quickly walked there.

mwadik *n.* Trickery, chicanery.

mwadong 1. *vi.* To play; to take recreation. 2. *n.* Game, recreation, drama. —mwadonge, *vt.*

mwadonge *vt.* To play with. —mwadong, *vi.*

mwaht *n.* Clearing, field, plantation, garden, farm.

mwahtakai *adj.* Failing to observe the proper *mwah* relationship.

mwatal *n.* Any of a number of varieties of pandanus.

mwataliniak *n.* Pandanus sp., *Humata banksii.*

mwate *vi.* To move vertically, of something flexible.

mwatih *vt.* To clear an area; to cut or pull grass; to clean and prepare kava for pounding. —mwet, *vi.*

mwei₁ *n.* Spot, stain.

mwei₂ *vi.* To be broken, of a string; to be divorced; to finish defecating. —mweid₁, *vt.*

mwehi *n.* Reign, era.

mweilik, also likimwei. *vi.* To throw or punch forcefully.

mweimwei 1. *vi.* To allow or permit. 2. *n.* Permission. —mweid₃, *vt.*

mwein *sent. adv.* Probably, maybe, perhaps. *Mwein ohlo pahn mwahula.* Probably that man will get better.

mweinlihamwahu *n.* Mole.

mweinlikou *n.* Remnants, small pieces of cloth.

mweinliroar *n.* Birthmark, any skin discoloration present from birth.

mweir, also mwer₁. *adj.* Loose, as of a knot or lashing.

mweid₁ *vt.* To break, as a string. —mwei, *vi.*

mweid₂ *n.* Hollow, ravine.

mweid₃ *vt.* To allow or permit. *I mweidehng ira en kohla kasdo.* I allowed them to go to the movie. —mweimwei, *vi.*

mweidpeseng *vt.* To grant a divorce; to cause a divorce.

mwek *n.* Hammock for children.

mwehk *n.* Tree sp., *Glochidion ramiflorum,* the terminal buds of which are used for increasing the appetite of young children.

mweker *vi.* To make an explosive or slapping noise.

mwekimwek *n.* Plant sp., *Tacca leontopetaloides,* arrow plant.

mwekid *vi.* To move.

mwehl₁ *adj.* Red hot, of objects; angry, furious.

mwehl₂ *n.* Ripe breadfruit wrapped in leaves and prepared in an *uhmw.*

mwele *adj.* Calm, of the weather.

mwelekih *vt.* To suspect.

mweleng *n.* Area below the peak of a roof.

mwelengen sakau *n.* Dried skin from drinking too much kava.

mweli *n.* Rocky area.

mwelimwel ARCHAIC. *n.* A kind of hair-do worn by women in which the hair is tied in knots at the nape of the neck or lower.

mwell *n.* A sp. of *Nudibranch.*

mwemmwan *vi.* To bulge, of something covered, the shape of which is discernible.

mwehmwe *n.* A yam that develops on the vine, not edible.

mwemweit *vi.* To visit.

mwenemwenei *vi.* To jiggle up and down, as of the fat on a fat person.

mwenge 1. *vi.* To eat. 2. *n.* Food.

mwengehn menseng 1. *vi.* To eat breakfast. 2. *n.* Breakfast.

mwengehn pwong 1. *vi.* To eat a late night snack. 2. *n.* A late night snack.

mwengehn soutik 1. *vi.* To eat dinner. 2. *n.* Dinner.

mwengehn souwas 1. *vi.* To eat lunch.
2. *n.* Lunch.

mwenginingin *vi.* To whisper.

mwengintik *n.* Side platform of a *nahs.*

mwengki 1. *n.* Monkey. 2. *adj.* Silly,
given to monkeying around. [Eng.]

mwer₁, also mweir. *adj.* Loose, as of a
knot or lashing.

mwer₂ *vi.* To fall in quantity, as rain or
fruit.

mwer₃ *n.* Deception.

mwerek *adj.* Slack, as of a rope;
wrinkled.

mwerekirek *adj.* Wrinkled.

mwersuwed, also mworsuwed. *adj.*
Dishonest, crooked, malicious, wicked.
—mwersuedih, *vt.*

mwersuwedih *vt.* To cheat; to be
dishonest or crooked to.
—mwersuwed or mworsuwed, *adj.*

mweseisei *vi.* To make noise; to disturb.

mweseu *adj.* Lusty.

mwesel *vi.* To leave or depart.

mwesen ntahkereker 1. *n.* Dysentery.
2. *vi.* To have dysentery.

mwesenloang *n.* Maggot.

mwesot, also mwaso. *n.* An eel,
commonly found in mangrove swamps.

mwehdi *n.* Caterpillar.

mwet *vi. neut.* To clear an area; to cut
or pull grass; to clean and prepare
kava for pounding. —mwatih, *vt.*

mweteh *n3s.* Shade.

mweteu *vi.* To hang down.

mwetida *vi.* To be in heat, to be ready
for breeding, of female dogs and pigs.

mwetiwel 1. *vi.* To make a clearing,
plantation, garden, or farm. 2. *n.*
Clearing, plantation, garden, farm.

mwih *n.* Name of the digraph *mw.*

mwir 1. *n.* A kind of magic to delay an
action. 2. *vi.* To perform this kind of
magic.

mwidihlihk *n (3s: mwidihlihki).* Kidney.

mwo *dem. pron.* That one, away from
you and me; there, away from you and
me.

mwoh *vi.* To moo, of a cow.

mwou *adj.* Bruised; abused.

mwoumwou *vi.* To douche. —mwaur,
vt.

mwohkan *dem. pron.* Those, away from
you and me.

mwokuhku HONORIFIC. *vi.* To whisper.

mwokuhr 1. *n.* Rotten fruit. 2. *adj.*
Rotten, of fruit.

mwoluhlu HONORIFIC. *vi.* To whisper.

mwompwon, also mwomwalis. *n.* Fish
sp., goatfish, *Parupeneus cyclostomus.*

mwohmw *n (3s: mwomwe).*
Appearance; kind, sort, type.

mwomwala *vi.* To be exhausted, of a
supply.

mwomwalap *adj.* Impolite.

mwomwalis, also mwompwon. *n.* Fish
sp., goatfish, *Parupeneus cyclostomus.*

mwomwadahn kosonned *n.* Bill,
proposal, in legislative proceedings.

mwomwawas *adj.* Impertinent, rude.

mwomwehda *vt.* To pretend; to imitate;
to intend.

mwomwitik *adj.* Shy; embarrassed,
usually of girls.

mwomwohdiso *n.* Congregation, parish,
a gathering in the presence of a
Nahnmwarki.

mwomwohdmwahl *vi.* To be idle.

mwomwmei *n.* Fish sp., a kind of
parrotfish.

mwomwsang *vi.* To be annihilated or
destroyed.

mwohn wahr *n.* Bow of a canoe.

mwohnawar 1. *n.* Paddler who sits in
the bow of a canoe. 2. *vi.* To paddle
from the bow of a canoe.

mwohni *n.* Money. [Eng.]

mwohniki *vt.* To consider most
important.

mwohnmei *n.* First breadfruit
harvested, which are taken to a chief.

Mwohnsapw *n.* Lord, chief of the
highest order.

mwohndi *vi.* To sit down.

mwongoungou *adj.* Attractive,
attracting admiration or interest.

mwopw *vi.* To be out of breath, to be
unable to catch one's breath; to be
shut off from a source of air.

mworourou *adj.* Fat, stout.

mworopw, also mwoaroapw. *n.*
Polynesian chestnut, *Inocarpus
fagiferus.*

mworopwinsed *n.* Tree sp., *Heritiera
littoralis.*

mworsuwed, also mwersuwed. *adj.*
Dishonest, crooked, malicious, wicked.
—mwersuwedih, *vt.*

mwohso 1. *n.* Appendicitis. 2. *vi.* To have appendicitis. [Jap.]

mwosod, also **mwasod.** *adj.* Rotten, of wood.

mwohd *vi.* To sit. —**mwohdang,** *vt.*

mwohdang *vt.* To sit in on, as a meeting. —**mwohd,** *vi.*

mwohdenpwong *vi.* To remain awake all night, as at a wake.

mwohdipwisou 1. *vi.* To offer first fruits, of produce not traditionally important in Ponape. 2. *n.* Such a first fruits offering.

mwodol *num. cl.* Used in counting small, rounded objects. *kisin kehp riemwodol* two small round yams.

mwotomwot *adj.* Short.

mwotkoloi *adj.* Very short.

mwowe₁ *prep. n.* Ahead of, in front of, before (him, her, or it).

mwowe₂ *vt.* To offer as a first fruit.

mwowihdi *vi.* To be swamped, of canoes and boats.

mwoahl HONORIFIC. *n (3s: mwoale).* Sacred place, altar, throne; sleeping place, sitting place, house.

mwoalehlap HONORIFIC. *n.* Platform upon which the *Nahnmwarki* and *Nahnken* sit, in a *nahs*.

mwoalehle *adj.* Shiny with oil or grease.

mwoalen kopwung *n.* Court.

mwoalehda HONORIFIC. *vt.* To dress oneself; to wear a grass skirt.

mwoalehdi HONORIFIC. *vi.* To sit.

mwoaloal *n.* Dent, depression.

mwoaloaldi *vi.* To be dented; to squat down in the water.

mwoalus *n.* Cinder, ember, charcoal, coal of a fire.

mwoanipil *vi.* To peep at people bathing in a river. —**mwoanipilih,** *vt.*

mwoanipilih *vt.* See *mwoanipil.*

mwoanok *vt.* To peep at.

mwoarok en sakau *n.* Residue at the bottom of a cup of kava.

mwoarosala *vi.* To lose one's will to succeed, to lose all hope.

mwoaroang *vi.* To be noisy.

mwoaroangoaroang *adj.* Noisy.

mwoaroapw, also **mworopw.** *n.* Polynesian chestnut, *Inocarpus fagiferus.*

mwoasoangidi *vi.* To be decayed, of wood.

mwoasoahngot *adj.* Decayed, of wood; termite ridden.

mwoator 1. *vi.* To wilt, to lose muscular control. 2. *adj.* Limp; paralyzed.

mwukumwuk *vi.* To rinse one's mouth, to gargle.

mwulepene *vt.* To twist or wind together.

mwuledek *n.* Excessive amount.

mwuhmwu 1. *n.* Muumuu, an ankle length dress. 2. *vi.* To wear a muumuu. [Eng.<Hawaiian]

mwuhn *n.* Fish sp., squirrelfish, *Myripristis adustus.*

mwur *adv.* A little; a bit. *I mwur soumwahuda aio.* I became a little sick yesterday.

mwuhr *n.* Later.

mwuri *prep. n.* After, behind (him, her, or it).

mwurilik 1. *n.* Death feast, given after the burial. 2. *vi.* To prepare this feast.

mwurinwar 1. *n.* Paddler who sits in the stern of a canoe. 2. *vi.* To paddle from the stern of a canoe.

mwuroi *n.* Pigeon.

mwuserehre HONORIFIC. *vi.* To think.

mwusikek *vi.* To initiate movement of the whole body, as when one starts to rise, walk, run, etc..

mwusiko *n.* Marching band. [Jap.<Eng.]

mwusing 1. *n.* Pool of money, the combined wagers of betters. 2. *vi.* To form a pool. [Jap.]

mwusihrer *vi.* To shiver, to shudder.

mwut *adj.* Pulverized, crushed, mashed.

mwut₂ *num. cl.* Used in counting heaps or piles. *mwutin dihpw pahmwut* four piles of grass.

mwuterek *adj.* Soft.

mwutumwut *n.* Bunch, group, clump.

N

-n$_1$, also en$_1$. *construct suffix*. Of; This suffix is written together with the preceding word if that word is one syllable long or ends in a vowel; otherwise, it is written as the separate word *en*. *olen Pohnpei* man of Ponape.

-n$_2$ *aff*. Derivational suffix, used to form adjectives from nouns, meaning 'having', 'full of', or 'characterized by'. *dohl* mountain, *dolon* mountainous; *ilok* wave, *ilokin* wavy.

na *interj*. O.k., so, well, now.

nah *poss. cl.* His, her, its; third person singular form of the dominant classifier.

nahi$_1$ *n*. Child, any person called child in the Crow kinship terminology.

nahi$_2$ *n*. The small stick attached to the end of a breadfruit picking pole.

naik **1.** *n*. A type of net fishing, employing a net attached to a curved stick. **2.** *vi*. To fish in this manner.

nain *adj*. Having many offspring.

nainai *n*. Title of a *Nahnmwarki*. *Nainain Nahnmwarki en Kiti Soukise*. The title of the *Nahnmwarki* of *Kiti* is *Soukise*.

nainiki *vt*. To own, to have, used with nouns occurring with the classifier *nah*.

naip *n*. Knife, machete. [Eng.]

naipokos *n*. Pocketknife.

nair, also **neirail**. *poss. cl.* Their, plural; see *nah*.

naisi *n*. Name of one of the holes in the marble game *anaire*. [Jap.]

nait *poss. cl.* Our, exclusive; see *nah*.

naitikihdi *vt*. To give birth. —**neitik**, *vi*.

nahk *n*. Storeroom, storage area; any woman in one's wife's clan except one the wife calls mother.

Nahlaimw *n*. The second ranking title in the *Nahnken* line, formerly the highest priestly title.

Nahleo *n*. Title of the wife of a *Nahnawa*.

nahliam *n*. Fish sp., barracuda.

nahlik en sokele *n*. A variety of yam.

Nahlik Lapalap$_1$ *n*. A title, in the *Nahnmwarki* line.

nahlik lapalap$_2$ *n*. A variety of yam.

Nahlikiei Lapalap *n*. Title of the wife of a *Nahlik Lapalap*.

Nahlikiroun Pohn Dake *n*. Title of the wife of a *Kiroun Pohn Dake*.

Nahlisahu Ririn *n*. Title of the wife of a *Nahnsahu Ririn*.

nahluhk$_1$ *n*. Spider sp..

Nahluhk$_2$ *n*. A title.

nam SLANG. *vt*. To eat, to taste, used derogatorily. —**neminem**, *vi*.

namaiki *adj*. Impudent, conceited. [Jap.]

namanam *n*. Taste.

namari *n*. Lead. [Jap.]

Nahmadau *n*. A title.

Nahmadoun Oare *n*. A title.

namenek *adj*. Bashful, embarrassed, ashamed.

nampil *adj*. Bland, tasteless, watery.

nahmw, also **nehnamw**. *n*. Deep place within the barrier reef, lagoon.

nan *prep*. In. *Kilelo mi nan kapango*. That picture is in that suitcase.

nahn$_1$ *n*. Buddy, honey, pal, used in addressing one's spouse, or peers or children of the same sex; an attention getting exclamation, Hey!.

nahn$_2$ *n*. Pus.

nahn$_3$ *interj*. Behold!. *Nahn! Iei Ih sapwillimen Koht*. Behold! He is the son of God.

nahn$_4$ *sent. adv.* Actually. *Nahn kowe me wia*. Actually you are the one who did it.

Nahn Kirou *n*. A title.

Nahn Kirou Ririn *n*. A title.

Nahn Kiroun Pohn Dake *n*. A title, in the *Nahnmwarki* line.

Nahn Pohnpei *n*. A title, in the *Nahnken* line.

nahna *n*. Mountain.

Nahnalek *n*. Title of the wife of a *Nahnmwarki*, in Net, Kiti, and Sokehs.

Nahnalosomw *n*. A house ghost or spirit.

Nahnapas *n*. A title, in the *Nahnken* line, formerly of the second highest priest.

Nahnapasepei *n.* Title of the wife of a *Nahnapas.*

Nahnado *n.* Title of the wife of a *Noahs.*

Nahnawa *n.* A title, in the *Nahnmwarki* line.

Nahnawa Iso *n.* A title.

Nahniau *n.* A title.

naniak *n.* Mangrove swamp.

Nahniek *n.* A clan name.

nanisol *n.* Season of scarcity, when yams and breadfruit are not bearing.

Nahnihd Lapalap *n.* A title, in the *Nahnmwarki* line.

Nahnidipei Lapalap *n.* Title of the wife of a *Nahnihd Lapalap.*

Nahnullap *n.* A net ghost or spirit.

nankapehd *n.* Guts, in the sense of fortitude or the seat of the emotions.

nankapi *n3s.* Bottom, lower part, referring to the inside of an object.

Nahnkar *n.* Title of the wife of a *Mwarekehtik.*

Nahnkei *n.* A title.

Nahnken *n.* Title of the highest chief in one of the two title lines.

Nahnkeniei *n.* Title of the wife of a *Nahnken.*

nankep *n.* Inlet.

Nahnkedin Idehd *n.* Title of the wife of a *Nahnmadaun Idehd.*

nankisiniei *n.* Hell.

nankoakonmedek **1.** *n.* Arthritis, rheumatism. **2.** *vi.* To have arthritis or rheumatism.

Nahnku *n.* A title, in the *Nahnken* line.

Nahnkulai *n.* Title of the wife of a *Nahlaimw.*

Nahnkuhpei *n.* Title of the wife of a *Nahnku.*

nanmadau *n.* Ocean, beyond the reef.

Nahnmadaun Idehd *n.* A title, in the *Nahnken* line.

Nahnmadaun Pehleng *n.* A title.

nanmadola- *prep. n.* Area between. *nanmadolara* area between them.

nahnmwal *n.* A variety of breadfruit.

Nahnmwarki *n.* Rank of the highest chief in one of the two title lines.

nanmwoale HONORIFIC. *vi.* To fart.

nanmwoalehdi HONORIFIC. *vi.* To rest.

Nahnnep *n.* Title of the wife of a *Wasai.*

nanpar *n.* Trade wind season.

nanparas *n.* Pit, formerly the pit in the middle of the main platform of a *nahs* where a fire was kept burning from which the first of the *uhmws* were lit.

Nahnpei *n.* A title, in the *Nahnmwarki* line.

Nahnpei Ririn *n.* A title.

Nahnpweipei *n.* Title of the wife of a *Nahnpei.*

nanpwunga- *prep. n.* Location between. *nanpwungara* location between them.

nanras *n.* Ground level of a feasthouse.

nanrek *n.* Season of plenty, breadfruit season.

Nahnsahu Ririn *n.* The third ranking title in the *Nahnken* line.

Nahnsaumw en Ririn *n.* A title.

Nahnsaumw en Wehi *n.* A title.

nansapw *n.* Land under cultivation.

nahnsapwe *n.* Thunder; a god of Ponapean religion.

Nahnsahwinsed *n.* A ghost of the sea, said to cause illness.

Nansehlang *n.* Demigod of canoe building and carpentry.

nansed *n.* Ocean, sea.

Nahnsou *n.* A title.

Nahnsou Sed *n.* A title.

Nahnsou Wehi *n.* A title.

nandenge *n3s.* Groin.

Nahnte *n.* Title of the wife of a *Dauk.*

nanti *adj.* Said of one who tries hard.

nantihnsewe *n3s.* Back.

Nahntu *n.* A title.

Nahntuhpei *n.* Title of the wife of a *Nahntu.*

nanwel *n.* Jungle, forest, area overgrown with trees.

nanwerenge *prep. n.* Middle, center, or midst of (him, her, or it).

nanwehwe *n3s.* Slit, crack, small opening, empty space, outer space.

nappa *n.* Chinese cabbage. [Jap.]

nahri *n.* Reef, with many large stones or coral heads protruding above the surface of the water.

nahs *n.* Feasthouse.

nasepwel *n.* An informally built feasthouse.

nasupi *n.* Eggplant, *Solanum melongena.* [Jap.]

natih *vt.* To attempt to gain favor, to
bribe.

natihada *vt.* To buy.

ne *vi.* To be divided, to be distributed.
—nehk, *vt.*

neh *n3s.* Leg.

nei₁ *poss. cl.* My; see *nah.*

nei₂ *adj.* Neat, clean.

neinsokihn *n.* A variety of yam.

neipi *vi.* To go without underwear.
[Eng.]

neira *poss. cl.* Their, dual; see *nah.*

neirail, also nair. *poss. cl.* Their, plural;
see *nah.*

neidam *vi.* To sail with the outrigger
lifted from the water.

neita *poss. cl.* Our, dual; see *nah.*

neitail *poss. cl.* Our, plural; see *nah.*

neitik *vi.* To give birth; to be a parent;
to possess, to draw interest, of money.
—naitikihdi, *vt.*

nehu *n.* Fish sp., a kind of frog fish.

nek₁ *vi.* To be finished; to climax or
ejaculate.

nek₂ *conj. adv.* Could, alternatively. *Ke
nek kohdo lakapw.* You could
alternatively come tomorrow.

nehk *vt.* To divide, to distribute. —ne,
vi.

nekinek *vi.* To store, to put away.
—nekid, *vt.*

nekinekidi *vi.* To be buried, used
Biblically.

nekidala *vt.* To save, keep, store, put
away.

nekidedi *vt.* To bury, to put in a safe
place.

nektait *n.* Necktie, tie. [Eng.]

neme *n3s.* Taste, flavor.

nemilo *vi.* To French kiss, literally, 'to
eat the tongue'.

neminem SLANG. 1. *vi.* To eat. 2. *n.*
Food. —nam, *vt.*

nempe *n.* Number. [Eng.]

nen *num.* Ten thousand.

nehn troahli *n.* The two wheels and the
axle of a narrow gauge train.
[*troahli*<Jap.<Eng.]

nehnamw, also nahmw. *n.* Deep place
within the barrier reef, lagoon.

nehne 1. *vi.* To do division. 2. *n.*
Division, in arithmetic.

nenek *vi.* To commit adultery, to
fornicate. —nenekih, *vt.*

nenekih *vt.* See *nenek.*

nenne *vi.* To sleep, of children.

nennen *adj.* Quiet, silent.

nengi, also ningi. *n.* Green onion. [Jap.]

ner *adj.* Sensitive, susceptible to stimuli.

ned *vt.* To smell.

net₁ *vi.* To buy, sell, or trade, to shop.

Net₂ *n.* Name of a municipality in
Ponape.

ni, also nin. *prep.* At, to. *E kohla ni
sidohwaho.* He went to the store.

nih₁ *n.* Name of the letter *n.*

nih₂ *n.* Coconut palm, *Cocos nucifera.*

niaul *n.* Slope.

Nialem *n.* Friday.

Niare *n.* Tuesday.

Niepeng *n.* Thursday.

Niesil *n.* Wednesday.

Niehd *n.* Monday.

niondo *n.* Bayonet. [Jap.]

Nikaunop *n.* Saturday.

nihkarat *n.* A variety of coconut palm,
with round nuts.

nihkengk *n.* A variety of coconut palm.

nihkerehs *n.* Cigar; originally
Negrohead tobacco. [Eng.]

-niki *aff.* Derivational suffix, used to
form transitive verbs from nouns
which may be directly possessed,
meaning 'to own' or 'to have'. *sahpw*
land, *sapweniki* to own (of land).

nihl *n.* Nail, spike. [Eng.]

nillime HONORIFIC. *poss. cl.* A possessive
classifier employed in honorific speech
in place of the common language
classifier *sapwe.*

nim *vi., vt.* To drink.

nime *poss. cl.* A possessive classifier for
drinkable things. *Kihdo mahs nimei
uhpwo.* Please give me my drinking
coconut.

nin, also ni. *prep.* At, to.

nihn 1. *n.* Tree sp., *Ficus tinctoria*; a
belt worn by women made of the bark
of the *nihn* tree. 2. HONORIFIC. *n.* A
garland worn by high title holders.

ninih HONORIFIC. *vt.* To be crowned
with.

nihnihrek HONORIFIC. *n.* Eyelash.

ninlengida HONORIFIC. *vi.* To stand.

nindokon *n.* While; time of. *Irail lelodo
nindokon mentikitik.* They arrived
while it was early in the morning.

nintapi *n.* In the beginning. *Nintapi re pwungki, ah met re sapwungki.* In the beginning they agreed with it; however, now they don't agree with it.

ningi, also **nengi.** *n.* Green onion. [Jap.]

ningkapwan, also **ngkapwan.** *n.* A while ago.

nireng *vi.* To hit two marbles with one shot. [Jap.]

nihrir *n.* A variety of coconut palm.

nihd *vt.* To slide into or out of. —**nihdek,** *vi.*

nihdek *vi.* To be slid into or out of. —**nihd,** *vt.*

nihdwel, also **wel₁.** *vi.* To molt a shell.

nihtahta *n.* Fish sp..

nihtik *n.* A variety of coconut palm.

nihtoal *n.* A variety of coconut palm, bearing green nuts.

nihweita *n.* A variety of coconut palm, bearing red nuts.

noumw *poss. cl.* Your, singular; see *nah.*

noumwa *poss. cl.* Your, dual; see *nah.*

noumwail *poss. cl.* Your, plural; see *nah.*

nok *adj.* Smoothed; creased, as of trousers.

nohk *n.* Main rib of the stem of a palm frond; any hard straw-like object.

nohkin, also **nohn.** *adv.* Too.

nokonok *n.* Vine sp..

nokonokon *adj.* Matted, of hair or feathers.

nohlik *n.* The Genesis flood.

nompe *adj.* Alcoholic, always drunk. [Jap.]

nohn, also **nohkin.** *adv.* Too. *Ke dehr nohn doadoahk laud.* Don't work too hard.

nono *vi.* To snore.

nohno *n.* Mother; any person one's mother or father would call sister.

nohno kahlap *n.* Grandmother, sometimes one's spouse's grandmother.

Nopempe *n.* November. [Eng.]

nohpwei **1.** *n.* Feast of tribute, first fruits offering; the first four cups of kava in the kava ceremony. **2.** *vi.* To make a traditional feast of tribute, to make a first fruits offering.

nohd *n.* Musical note. [Eng.]

noahrok **1.** *adj.* Greedy. **2.** *n.* Greed. —**noahroke,** *vt.*

noahroke *vt.* To covet, to be greedy for. —**noahrok,** *adj.*

Noahs *n.* A title, in the *Nahnmwarki* line.

nuhkaledohnia *n.* A variety of yam, from New Caledonia. [Eng.]

nur **1.** *vi.* To contract; to flinch, to jerk away; to twitch. **2.** *adj.* Said of something which will shrink, as cloth.

nuhs *n.* News. [Eng.]

nuhspehpa *n.* Newspaper. [Jap.<Eng.]

nuhd *n.* Squid.

nsar *vi.* To be trapped in a leg noose. —**nsere,** *vt.*

nsen *n (3s: nsene).* Will, feelings.

nsehn *vt.* To snare with a slip noose.

nsenamwahu **1.** *adj.* Happy, contented, enjoying the good life. **2.** *n.* Happiness.

nsenoh *adj.* Concerned.

nsenohki *vt.* To take care of; to be concerned about, to be interested in, to worry about.

nsensuwed **1.** *adj.* Sad, sorry. **2.** *n.* Sadness.

nsere *vt.* To trap with a leg noose. —**nsar,** *vi.*

nsoange *vt.* To probe the earth to find yams.

nda *vt.* To say.

ndand *adj.* Famous, celebrated.

ndape *n.* Girt, a beam connecting the corner posts of the exterior frame of a building at the roof level.

ndil **1.** *vi.* To torch fish. **2.** *n.* Torch made of dried coconut palm fronds; source of light; torch fishing.

nta *n (3s: ntah).* Blood.

ntahpwilipwil **1.** *n.* A disease in which women bleed from the vagina. **2.** *vi.* To have this disease.

nting *vi.* To write; to tattoo. —**ntingih,** *vt.*

nting en peneinei *n.* Census.

nting sarawi ARCHAIC. *n.* A sacred tattoo placed just above the knee on females.

ntingih *vt.* To write; to tattoo. —**nting,** *vi.*

NG

ngai *vi.* To bay, of dogs when hunting.

ngalangal *adj.* Dry, of something which commonly has a moisture content, i.e., wood, one's throat, dirt, but not clothing or dishes; low, of the tide when the bottom is exposed.

ngalis *vt.* To bite. —ngelingel₁, *vi.*

ngap *vi.* To draw back one's arm.

ngahp *n.* Fathom, the distance between outstretched arms, approximately six feet.

ngapada *vi.* To draw back one's arm as if to strike a blow.

ngar SLANG. *vt.* To see, discern, look at, observe, examine, with a derogatory connotation.

ngarahk *vi.* To laugh heartily.

ngarangar *n.* Empty half of coconut shell; coconut cup used for drinking kava.

ngat *vi.* To choke, as a consequence of food lodging in the trachea.

ngat- *vi.* To be bored or tired of something repetitious. *I ngatasangehr kang rais.* I've gotten tired of eating rice.

-nge *aff.* Enumerative suffix. *ihs* who, *ihsnge* who (plural).

ngehi *ind. pron.* I. *Ngehi mehn Pohnpei.* I am a Ponapean.

ngelingel₁ *vi.* To bite. —ngalis, *vt.*

ngelingel₂ *adj.* Stinking, foul-smelling.

ngehn *n (3s: ngeni).* Soul, spirit, shadow.

Ngensarawi *n.* Holy Ghost.

ngensuwed *n.* Devil.

ngengngersuwed 1. *adj.* Incestuous. 2. *n.* Incest.

ngepe *vt.* To measure with outstretched arms.

ngeder *num.* A great many, an uncountable number. *Aramas ngeder iang doadoahk.* A great many people participated in the work.

nget 1. *vi.* To pant. 2. *n.* Mild case of asthma.

ngetengete *n3s.* Roof of the mouth.

ngih₁ *n.* Name of the digraph *ng.*

ngih₂ *n3s.* Tooth.

ngih₃ *n.* Tree sp., *Pemphis acidula.*

ngih pasapas *n.* False teeth.

ngiau *vi.* To meow, the sound that a cat makes.

ngiangi *adj.* Diligent or persevering because of enthusiasm.

ngihl *n (3s: ngile).* Voice; tune.

ngihlap *n (3s: ngihlepe).* Molar.

ngilawas *adj.* Grating or unpleasant, of the voice; employing an offensive tone of voice.

ngilekeng *adj.* Derisive.

ngilekir *adj.* Husky, hoarse, of the voice; also used to describe a change of voice, as in adolescents.

ngilepwet *adj.* Said of someone unable to correctly say the Ponapean *r* or *t* sound.

ngihnwer *adj.* Overly talkative, protesting too much, all talk and no action.

ngihpit *adj.* Buck-toothed.

ngihpwar *n.* Tusk; large boar with tusks.

ngir HONORIFIC. *vi.* To be tired.

ngiringir *vi.* To growl or snarl, to quarrel. —ngiringirih, *vt.*

ngiringirih *vt.* To growl or snarl at. —ngiringir, *vi.*

ngirisek *vi.* To resound.

ngis *vi.* To chant; to be boisterous.

ngihs *n.* Chant, often one relating the oral history of Ponape.

ngisingisido *n.* A variety of yam.

ngidar *vt.* To clamp, to crush.

ngidingid *adj.* Adherent, cohesive, gummy, sticky; insistent.

ngihtehte 1. *adj.* Strenuous, diligent. 2. *vi.* To grind one's teeth.

ngihtuk *adj.* Gap-toothed, having missing or broken teeth.

ngoul *num.* Ten.

ngolungol *n (3s: ngolungoli).* Lung.

ngong *vi.* To bark. —ngongih, *vt.*

ngongih *vt.* To bark at. —ngong, *vi.*

ngopw *vi.* To oink, to grunt, of a pig.

ngopwungopw *n.* The oinking or grunting sound of a pig.

ngohr *n (3s: ngore).* Accent, dialect, tune, tone.

ngoang *adj.* Concerned, anxious, eager.

ngoapwur *vt.* To snap, of dogs or pigs.

ngoatamah *adj.* Overly talkative, protesting too much, all talk and no action.

ngutoar *vi.* To sniff, to draw in air sharply through the nose.

ngkapwan, also **ningkapwan.** *n.* A while ago. *E kohdo ngkapwan.* He came a while ago.

ngkad *vt.* To roof a building; to attach a piece of roofing material. —**ngked,** *vi.*

ngke₁ *n.* Water container made of a leaf of *sepwikin.*

ngke₂ HONORIFIC. *n.* Provisions taken on a trip; water for the *Nahnmwarki.*

ngkel *adj.* Of breadfruit or bananas, still green but ready to eat.

ngken *vi.* To start or to burn, of a fire; to glow as of embers.

ngked *vi.* To roof a building with thatch. —**ngkad,** *vt.*

ngkopw *n.* Sp. of small crab.

ngkoak **1.** *n.* Fresh banana, breadfruit, or taro leaves used to cover an *uhmw.* **2.** *vi.* Of an *uhmw,* to be covered with fresh leaves. —**ngkoake,** *vt.*

ngkoake *vt.* Of an *uhmw,* to cover with fresh leaves. —**ngkoak,** *vi.*

ngkoal *vi. neut.* To make sennit. —**ngkoale** or **koale,** *vt.*

ngkoale *vt.* See *ngkoal.*

P

pa$_1$ *conj. adv.* Since (contrary to
expectations); suddenly. *Mwein e sohte
nda, pwe i pa sehse.* Maybe he didn't
say, since (contrary to your
expectations) I don't know. *Se
mwomwohd a mwangaso pa
pwupwidi.* We were sitting and
suddenly the ripe coconut fell.

pa$_2$ *vt.* To weave. —peipei$_2$, *vi.*

pa$_3$ *num. cl.* Used in counting fronds.
pahn nih riapa two coconut palm
fronds.

pah$_1$ *prep. n.* Below, under (him, her,
or it).

pah$_2$ *n3s.* Leaf of any large leaved
plant, such as taro or a palm.

pai$_1$ 1. *vi.* To weigh down with stones;
of an *uhmw*, to cover with hot
stones. 2. *n.* The stones used in an
uhmw.

pai$_2$ 1. *adj.* Fortunate. 2. *n.* Fortune,
wealth, happiness, grace.

pahi$_1$ *n.* Coral.

pahi$_2$ *n.* Sling, for throwing.

paiamwahu 1. *adj.* Lucky. 2. *n.* Luck,
good fortune.

paiahn *vi.* To be used to one another.

pahieu *num.* Four; see -u.

pahiel *num.* Four; see el$_2$.

paiente, also paiete. *sent. adv.* Luckily,
fortunately. *Paiente ke kanengamah.*
Luckily you are patient.

pahieng *vi.* To be elegant, to look good
in one's clothing.

paiete *sent. adv.* See *paiente.*

paiolihn *n.* Violin. [Eng.]

paiker *vi.* Of a liquid, to be channeled
into a container with a trough, gutter,
etc.. —paikere, *vt.*

paikere *vt.* To channel a liquid into a
container with a trough, gutter, etc..
—paiker, *vi.*

paiking *n.* Infection. [Jap.]

pailol HONORIFIC. 1. *vi.* To eat after
drinking kava. 2. *n.* Meal after kava.

pain *vt.* To incite.

pahina *n.* Barrier reef.

pahini *n.* Coconut palm frond.

pahini pokon *n.* Fish sp..

paip$_1$ *n.* Large boulder of basalt.

paip$_2$ *n.* Pipe, as a water pipe. [Eng.]

paip$_3$ *n.* Pipe, for smoking. [Eng.]

Paipel *n.* Bible. [Eng.]

pairuk$_1$, also dairuk. *vi.* To bend
forward from the waist; to walk in a
stooped position; to bow.

pairuk$_2$ *n.* A kind of adze.

pahisek *num.* Forty; see *eisek.*

paisuwed 1. *adj.* Unlucky. 2. *n.* Ill
fortune.

paid *interj.* And who else?, an
interrogative noun. *Koh paid?* You
and who else?

paidi *vt.* To make a small *uhmw.*

paiwed *n.* Plant sp..

pahumw *num.* Four; see *umw$_2$.*

paun 1. *n.* Pound; food. 2. *vi.* To eat.
[Eng.]

paur *vi.* To defecate.

paud$_1$ *vt.* To lash with hibiscus bark for
carrying.

paud$_2$ SLANG. *vt.* To say.

pahudaud *vi.* To be given information.

paute *n.* Powder of any kind;. [Eng.]

pauwehs *n.* Plant sp., a flowering plant.

pak$_1$ 1. *n.* Occurrence, time. 2. *num.
cl.* Used in counting occurrences or
times. *pak riapak* two times.

pak$_2$ 1. *vi.* To be smashed, as of a fallen
ripe fruit. 2. *adj.* Flat, of something
normally rounded.

pahk *vt.* To lift up something hinged or
moveable on one side, as a page , lid,
or hanging cloth;.

paka *vt.* To move aside stones used for
an *uhmw* in the act of cleaning it.

pahka *num.* Four; see *ka$_2$.*

pakair 1. *n.* Notice, announcement. 2.
vi. To notify, to announce.

pakalong *adj.* Abnormal, deformed,
odd.

pahkap *num.* Four; see *kap.*

pakahr *vi.* To be lead or guided, to be
escorted. —kahre, *vt.*

pakaraun 1. *vi.* To make an
accusation. 2. *n.* Accusation.

pakas *n.* Fish sp., surgeonfish,
Acanthurus xanthopterus.

pakasar *vi.* To send away, to cast out. —**kasare**, *vt.*

pakad *vt.* To defecate on something. —**pek**, *vi.*

pakadanah *interj.* Alas, you are a fool! [Jap.]

pakadeik *vi.* To be questioned. —**kadeik**, *vt.*

pakatei *vi.* To fish by driving fish into the rocks on the reef.

pakehng *vi.* To be attached.

paker 1. *vi.* To punch. 2. *n.* Punch, boxing. —**pakere**, *vt.*

pakere *vt.* To punch. —**paker**, *vi.*

pakehro *interj.* You fool! [Jap.]

paki₁ *n3s.* Replantable part of a plant; butt, as of a cigarette.

paki₂ *n.* Second cup of kava after the squeezing of the kava is initiated.

pahkis *num.* Four; see *kis₁*.

pakid *vt.* To look for lice. —**mpek**, *vi.*

pako, also **poake**. *n.* Shark.

pako lohpwu *n.* Fish sp., hammerhead shark.

pakudang *n.* Bomb, shell. [Jap.]

pakking 1. *n.* Fine, punishment. 2. *vi.* To be fined, to be punished. [Jap.]

pal *vi. neut.* To hack with a knife. —**pele**, *vt.*

pala *sent. adv.* As if. *Pala kowe me ese.* As if you are the one who knows.

palahi *n.* A variety of wild yam, *Dioscorea bulbifera.*

palaiau *n.* Fish sp., small and found in fresh water.

palang₁ *vt.* To dry, to expose objects to the sun in order to dry them. —**peleng**, *vi.*

palang₂ HONORIFIC. *n.* Basket.

palangk *n.* Porch.

palapal *n.* Fish sp., rabbitfish, *Siganus punctatus.*

palas *n.* Ballast. [Eng.]

pahle *n3s.* Base of the stem of a palm.

palek, also **palesek**. *adj.* Skillful in tree climbing.

pahlep *num.* Four; see *lep.*

palepwohl 1. *n.* Volleyball. 2. *vi.* To play volleyball. [Eng.]

palesek, also **palek**. *adj.* Skillful in tree climbing.

pali₁ 1. *n.* Part, side; division, section; day after tomorrow. 2. *num. cl.* Used in counting body extremities and sections. *peh riepali* two hands, *pelien mete limpali* five sheets of tin roofing.

pali₂ *n.* Navigational skill.

palih₁ *vt.* To peck, of birds or of fish nibbling bait. —**pel₁**, *vi.*

palih₂ *vt.* To tattoo. —**pelipel**, *vi.*

palieir *n.* South.

paliepeng *n.* North.

paliet *n.* Life on earth as opposed to the afterlife, literally this-side.

palikapi *n.* West.

palikasa *n.* Side of a canoe opposite the outrigger.

palikir *vt.* To carry a child on one's back. —**pelikilik**, *vi.*

palilaud *n.* The larger part, majority.

palimaun *n* (3s: *palimauni*). Right side.

palimeing *n* (3s: *palimeingi*). Left side.

palimese *n.* East.

palimoron *n.* Majority.

palingehn *n* (3s: *palingeni*). Soul, spiritual side of a being.

palisal- *rel. n.* Side exposed to. *E mi palisalodohng sapwen Soulik.* It's on the side exposed to Soulik's land.

palihdam *n.* Outrigger side of a canoe.

paliwar *n* (3s: *palinwere*). Body, of a person.

palodou *n.* Pole, used to train yam vines.

pahmaru *n.* A variety of yam.

pahme *n.* Fish sp., a kind of parrotfish.

pahmen *num.* Four; see *men₃*.

pampei *n.* Security guard. [Jap.]

pahmwodol *num.* Four; see *mwodol.*

pahmwut *num.* Four; see *mwut₂*.

pan *n.* Pan. [Eng.]

pahn₁ *aspect marker.* Used to signal unrealized aspect. *Ke pahn mwesel iahd?* When will you leave?

pahn₂ *n.* Bait, lure.

pahn₃ *n.* Times. *Irail tuhpene pahn pak limau.* They met five times.

pahnangi *n3s.* Downwind, lower.

pahnadi *n3s.* Chest; the area immediately in front of one.

panawih *vt.* To advise. —**peneu**, *vi.*

pahnepwel HONORIFIC. *n.* Sole of the foot.

pahnediwo *vi.* Nauseous.

pahniak *n.* Seaward edge of the mangrove swamp.

pahnisou HONORIFIC. 1. *vi.* To eat lunch. 2. *n.* Lunch.

pankeik *n.* Pancake. [Eng.]

pahnkopwul HONORIFIC. *n.* Night.

pahnkupwur HONORIFIC. *n.* Chest.

pahnneh *n3s.* Sole of the foot.

pannukas *vi.* To shoot a marble into the wrong hole in the game *anaire.* [Jap.]

pahnpeh *n3s.* Armpit.

pahnpwoal HONORIFIC. *n.* Armpit.

pansahi 1. *n.* Victory; a game, similar to steal-the-flag. 2. *vi.* To play this game. [Jap.]

pahnta *n.* A variety of taro.

pang *vi.* To be tilted, crooked, cock-eyed.

pahng₁ *vt.* To enumerate.

pahng₂ *vi.* To be distributed, to be spread around.

pangala *vt.* To betray; to give away, without motivation or compensation. —**pengipengla,** *vi.*

pangapang 1. *vi.* To lie crosswise. 2. *n.* Incline.

pangin *vt.* To awaken. —**mpeng,** *vi.*

pangid *vt.* To blow one's nose. —**pengidek,** *vi.*

pahngoul *num.* Forty; see *ngoul.*

pahngok, also **poahngok.** HONORIFIC. 1. *vi.* To speak or command. 2. *n.* Speech or command. —**pahngokih,** *vt.*

pahngokih *vt.* See *pahngok.*

pangk₁ *n.* Bench. [Span.]

pangk₂ *n.* Bank. [Eng.]

pangku *vi.* To have a flat tire. [Jap.<Eng.]

pap *vi.* To swim, of people, non-marine animals, and turtles. —**pepe,** *vt.*

papah *vi.* To assist, to serve.

pahpa₁ *n.* Father; any person one's father would call brother.

pahpa₂ *num.* Four; see *pa₃.*

pahpa kahlap *n.* Grandfather, spouse's grandfather, father's mother's brother.

pahpa sarawi *n.* Pope.

pahpak *num.* Four; see *pak₁.*

pahpali *num.* Four; see *pali₁.*

pahpar *num.* Four; see *par₂.*

pahpei *n.* Place of the *uhmw.*

pahpit *num.* Four; see *pit₂.*

pahpoar *num.* Four; see *poar.*

pahpwong *num.* Four; see *pwong.*

pahpwoat *num.* Four; see *pwoat.*

pahpwuloi *num.* Four; see *pwuloi.*

par₁ *vt.* To cut, trim, or sharpen with any large cutting tool. —**periper,** *vi.*

par₂ *num. cl.* Used in counting flat things. *pelien mete silipar* three sheets of tin roofing.

par₃ *adj.* Aerodynamically unsound, not suitable for throwing.

par₄ *adj.* Abnormal sounding, as of the voice or an instrument.

par₅ *vi.* To be fecund; to spread from one area to another.

par₆ *vi.* To sprout, of coconuts.

pahr₁ *n.* Year.

pahr₂ *n.* Tree sp., *Erythrina.*

pahr₃ *n.* Sprouting coconut palm; spongy center of a sprouting coconut.

pahr₄ *n.* Bar, tavern. [Eng.]

pahra *num.* Four; see *ra.*

parakapw *n.* New year.

parakus *n.* Fish sp..

parap *n.* Outrigger platform.

parapar *n.* Fish sp..

parapar en lik *n.* Fish sp..

paradais *n.* Paradise. [Eng.]

pahrek *adj.* Equal, even, flush.

parem *n.* Nipa palm, *Nipa fruticans.*

pahrehre HONORIFIC. *n.* Jaw.

paret *n.* Tern, a black sea bird.

parikang *n.* Hair clipper. [Jap.]

pariki *vi.* To go fast. [Jap.]

pahris HONORIFIC. *n.* Lower lip.

Parisehr *n.* Pharisee. [Eng.?]

pahro *n.* Pomade.

pahrourou *n.* A feasthouse having three center posts without pits for kava stones on the main platform.

parok *vt.* To catch something animate; to arrest. —**poaridi₁,** *vi.*

parohl 1. *n.* Parole, probation. 2. *vi.* To be on parole or probation. [Eng.] —**parohlih,** *vt.*

parohlih *vt.* To parole, to place on probation. [*parohl*<Eng.] —**parohl,** *vi.*

pahru *n.* Crowbar, bar. [Jap.<Eng.]

pas₁ *vi.* To arrive by sea; to return from fishing.

pas₂ 1. *adj.* Sticky. 2. *vi.* To be tagged, as in the game of *wie eni.*

pas₃, also **peis.** *vi.* To sing bass. [Eng.] —**peisih,** *vt.*

pahs₁ *n (3s: pese).* Nest.

pahs₂ *n.* Litter, requiring four or more men to be carried, used for carrying large yams, etc.; a large yam, kava plant, etc. that is carried on such a litter.

pahs₃ *vi.* To pass, in a card game. [Eng.]

pasakapw *vi.* To visit a place for the first time.

pahsan *vt.* To wait on; to depend on.

pasahnpwehk *n.* A variety of yam.

pasapas *n.* Series of long objects placed together side by side; platform; copra drying platform; shelf.

pasapeng 1. *vi.* To respond, to answer. 2. *n.* Response, answer.

pahsel *num.* Four; see *sel₂.*

pahsed *n.* Underworld, below the ocean.

pasete *n.* Fish sp..

pahsinse *n.* Passenger. [Eng.]

pahsou *num.* Four; see *sou₄.*

pahsop *num.* Four; see *sop₂.*

Pahsohpa *n.* Lent. [Eng.]

pahsu *n.* Clam sp.; slang for vagina.

pasur, also poasur. *vt.* To hammer. —pos₁ or pospos, *vi.*

passai *vi.* To cut grass. [Jap.]

pahsdo *n.* First base, in baseball. [Jap.<Eng.]

pasdohng *vi.* To visit a church for the purpose of praying, used by Catholics. [Span.]

pad *adj.* Dented.

pahd₁ *n.* Dent, depression; puddle.

pahd₂ *vt.* To push with one's foot.

padahk 1. *vi.* To preach. 2. *n.* Lesson, teaching.

padahk en lamalam *n.* Christian teachings.

padahkih *vt.* To teach, to instruct.

padi *n3s.* Eyebrow.

padik *vt.* To squeeze or press, to push, as a switch. —ped, *vi.*

padil *n.* Paddle, dance paddle.

pahdil *n.* Dried palm frond.

pahdip *num.* Four; see *dip.*

pahdire *n.* Catholic priest. [Span.]

padiri *n.* Battery. [Eng.]

pahdun *num.* Four; see *dun.*

padda *n.* Baseball bat. [Jap.<Eng.]

pat₁ *vi.* To be together.

pat₂ *adj.* Scarred.

pahtakai *n.* Bush sp..

patapat 1. *adj.* Flat, of a surface. 2. *n.* A plain, level ground.

pate *vi.* To have a hole that results in a leak, as in a canoe, roof, or tire tube.

pahte *num.* Four; see *te.*

patehla *vi.* To lose one's composure.

patehn neh *n3s.* Foot; hoof.

patehn nehn kewelik *n.* Plant sp., *Taeniophyllum petrophilum.*

paterek *adj.* Close together, side by side.

pato- *vi.* Humilative verb stem of motion.

pahtou₁ *adj.* Disappointed, sorrowful.

pahtou₂ *n.* Bush sp., *Allamanda cathartica.*

patukul SLANG. *adj.* Very bad.

pahtumw *num.* Four; see *tumw.*

patpene *vi.* To mix, to mingle.

pahwel *num.* Four; see *wel₂.*

-pe *aff.* Derivational suffix used to form directly possessed nouns from verbs; *-pe* is the third person singular form. *akamai* argue, *akamaipe* argument concerning him.

peh *n3s.* Arm, hand; foreleg, as of a dog; wing, of a bird.

pei₁ *vi.* To float.

pei₂ 1. *vi.* To play a reed throwing game. 2. *n.* The name of this game.

pei₃ 1. *vi.* To fight. 2. *n.* A fight.

pei₄ *vi.* To be full, of a cup of kava.

pei₅ *vi.* To be anchored or tied up, of a boat; to be parked, of a car.

pehi₁ *n.* A big seed, as in a mango.

pehi₂ *n.* Altar; any ancient structure of stones; a pile.

peiai *vi.* To exchange the lead, as in racing.

peiahk, also lipeiahk. *adj.* Oval.

peian *vt.* To be next to.

peiei- *rel. n.* Seaward. *E mi peieio.* It's seaward.

peiek *vi.* To be slid, usually of light objects. —peieki, *vt.*

peieki *vt.* To slide, usually of light objects. —peiek, *vi.*

peien *conj. adv.* Happen to. *Ma e peien kohdo, ke kak pakairiki.* If he happens to come, you can announce it.

pehioang *n.* Fish sp., a kind of mullet.

peik₁ *adj.* Skillful, of a diver able to go deep or hold his breath for a long period of time.

peik₂ *adj.* Obedient, respectful.

peikasal 1. *adj.* Hesitant, indecisive. 2. *n.* Hesitation, indecision.

peikieng *vt.* To be dedicated to.

peikini *n.* Large basket carried by four or more people; a litter of wood with coconut leaves laid over it to carry large amounts of food.

peikopw *n.* Fish sp..

peilah *n.* Two days after tomorrow.

peilong- *rel. n.* Inland. *E mi peilongo.* It's inland.

pein₁ *sent. adv.* On one's own; self. *Ohlo pein diarada ah sapwung.* That man found his mistake on his own;

pein₂ ARCHAIC. *n.* Woman; female of any species.

peinakapw 1. *n.* Young woman. 2. *adj.* Young, of females.

peinar *n.* Pestle, for pounding breadfruit.

pehinen *adj.* Accurate, in shooting or throwing.

peined 1. *n.* Cursing, foul language. 2. *vi.* To curse, to use foul language.

peinikid *n.* Pile of debris, dump.

peipei₁ *n.* Small black sp. of sea urchin.

peipei₂ *vi. neut.* To weave. —**pa₂**, *vt.*

peipei₃ HONORIFIC. *n.* Head, temple.

peipei aramas *n.* Fern sp., *Histiopteris incisa*.

peipei eni *n.* Fern sp..

peipeseng *vi.* To melt.

peirin *adj.* Extremely envious or jealous.

peiruhru *n.* Clay.

peis, also **pas₃**. *vi.* To sing bass. [Eng.] —**peisih**, *vt.*

peisarawi *n.* Holy altar.

peisenge *n3s.* Complement.

peisih *vt.* To sing bass. *I pahn peisih koulet.* I'll sing bass in this song. [Eng.] —**pas₃** or **peis**, *vi.*

peisin *n.* Basin. [Eng.]

peisipal *vi.* To alternate, to exchange, as a load or position.

peisihr 1. *n.* A reed throwing game. 2. *vi.* To play this game.

peidaid 1. *vi. neut.* To transport in a vehicle. 2. *n.* Transportation. —**idan**, *vt.*

peidak *n.* Upland, land to the east; windward.

peidek 1. *vi.* To ask. 2. *n.* Question. —**idek**, *vt.*

peidepe *n3s.* Transportation.

peidi *vi.* To arrive, by means of transportation.

peidi- *rel. n.* Leeward. *E mi peidio.* It's leeward.

peidihsang *vi.* To be lower than, to be younger or smaller than.

peidlakid *adj.* Careless with physical possessions, likely to lose or misplace belongings.

peitehl *n.* Large flat pounding stone employed in the preparation of kava or pounded foods.

peuk *vt.* To blow on, with air expelled from the mouth. —**pepeuk**, *vi.*

peukpe *vi.* To whistle through one's fingers.

peunmoang SLANG. *adj.* Empty-headed.

pek *vi.* To defecate. —**pakad**, *vt.*

pehk *num.* Forty; see *ehk*.

pekehi 1. *n.* Polygamy; any wife besides the principal wife. 2. *vi.* To commit polygamy.

pekehilek *adj.* Always sending others on an errand.

pekekil *vi.* To stare at one another. —**kakil**, *vt.*

pekeder *vi.* To be sent; to be let go, to be released. —**kadar**, *vt.*

peki *vt.* To ask for, to request. —**pekipek**, *vi.*

pehkiek 1. *vi.* To be summoned; to be called to the presence of a *Nahnmwarki*. 2. *n.* Subpoena, summons.

pekinpwel *n.* Overused, unproductive soil.

pekindihdi *n.* Youngest child.

pekipek 1. *vi.* To request, to ask a favor, to beg. 2. *n.* Requisition. —**peki**, *vt.*

pekid *n.* Bucket, barrel. [Eng.]

pel₁ *vi.* To peck, of birds or of fish nibbling bait. —**palih₁**, *vt.*

pel₂ *vi.* To be in a taboo relationship with someone or something.

pel₃ *vi.* To steer a canoe with a paddle. —**peliki**, *vt.*

pel₄ *vi.* To place a cup under the hibiscus bast during the process of preparing kava.

pehl₁ *vi. neut.* To reheat, to warm over, as food. —**pehle**, *vt.*

pehl₂ *n.* Bell. [Eng.]

pele *vt.* To hack with a knife. —**pal**, *vi.*

pehle *vt.* To reheat, to warm over, as food. —**pehl₁**, *vi.*

peleu *n.* Fish sp., a small *pakas.*

pelekenna *n.* Oyster.

peleng *vi.* To be dried, to be exposed to the sun in order to be dried. —**palang₁**, *vt.*

pelepel en sikaliwi *n.* A notch cut into a coconut tree, used as a step in climbing.

peliali *vi.* To match in competition; to be a member of a matched pair; to be on opposing sides. —**pelian**, *vt.*

pelian *vt.* To compete with; to be a member of a matched pair. —**peliali**, *vi.*

pelianda *vt.* To resist.

pelie *n3s.* Member of a matched pair; peer; counterpart, opponent.

pelien kadip *n.* The prosecution, a court term.

pelien lamalam *n.* Religious denomination.

pelien mete *n.* Tin roofing. [*mete*<Eng.]

pelien pwoson *n.* Religious denomination.

pelien serek *n.* Canvas.

pelik *n.* The shell of the clam sp. called *lipwei;* coconut grater.

pelik wahu HONORIFIC. *n.* Back wall of a feast house.

pelikie HONORIFIC. *n3s.* Upper part of the back.

pelikilik 1. *vi. neut.* To carry a child on one's back. 2. *n.* Two in a row; alternative title. *Pelikilik en Nahnmwarki en Uh Sangoro.* The alternative title of the Nahnmwarki of Uh is Sangoro. —**palikir**, *vt.*

pelikipe *vi.* To hold one's hands behind one's back.

pelikiso HONORIFIC. *n.* Back.

pelipel 1. *vi. neut.* To tattoo. 2. *n.* Tattoo. —**palih₂**, *vt.*

pelipelien *vi.* To go around in a group.

peluhs *n.* Bird sp., brown and white in color.

pehm *vi.* To perceive; to feel, think, or sense.

pehmitik *adj.* Easily awakened, early rising.

pehn₁ *n.* Pen, for writing. [Eng.]

pehn₂ HONORIFIC. *n.* Drinking coconut.

-pene *verb. suff.* Together, toward each other; with adjectives naming qualities it is used with a reciprocal meaning or to indicate 'totality'; with adjectives of size, it signals a decrease in size. *pihr* fly, *pihrpene* fly together; *mwahu* good, *mwahupene* good to each other; *mat* ripe, *matpene* all ripe; *tihti* skinny, *tihtipene* get skinnier.

peneinei 1. *n.* Family, relative. 2. *vi.* To be related.

peneu 1. *n.* Advice. 2. *vi.* To be advised. —**panawih**, *vt.*

peniaida *n.* Plywood; originally from 'veneer' plus the Japanese word *ida* meaning 'plank'. [Jap.<Eng.]

penipen *n.* Sp. of sea cucumber.

pens, also **pihns**. *n.* Beans. [Eng.]

pensi *n.* Needle nose pliers. [Jap.<Eng.]

peng- *vi.* To lean. *Uhto pengila pohn ihmwo.* That banana tree is leaning over that house.

pengepenge *n3s.* Side.

pengipengla *vi.* To be betrayed; to be given away, without motivation or compensation. —**pangala**, *vt.*

pengidek *vi.* To blow one's nose. —**pangid**, *vt.*

pengohsi *n.* Attorney, lawyer, defender. [Jap.]

pepe *vt.* To swim to, of people, non-marine animals, and turtles. —**pap**, *vi.*

pehpe *n.* Flower of the breadfruit tree.

pepeuk *vi.* To be blown on, with air expelled from the mouth. —**peuk**, *vt.*

pepehm 1. *vi.* To sense. 2. *n.* Feeling, thought.

pepen kairu *vi.* To dog-paddle. [*kairu*<Jap.]

pepen lamwer *vi.* To dog-paddle.

peper *n.* Pepper. [Eng.]

pepehd *vi.* To stay awake.

pehpoahrok *n.* A large ray.

pepdais 1. *vi.* To be baptized. 2. *n.* Baptism. [Eng.] —**pepdaisih**, *vt.*

pepdaisih *vt.* To baptize. [*pepdais*<Eng.] —**pepdais**, *vi.*

Pepweri *n.* February. [Eng.]

per *adj.* Cautious, hesitant, fearful.

pehr *n.* Bear. [Eng.]

pere 1. *vt.* To cover, to screen from view. 2. *n.* Room; cover; protection.

perek *vi. neut.* To unroll, as a mat. —**pereki**, *vt.*

pereki *vt.* To unroll, as a mat. —**perek**, *vi.*

peren₁ *adj.* Happy, joyful.

peren₂ *n.* Citrus plant or fruit.

peren tikitik *n.* Hibiscus sp..

pehri *n.* Bamboo, *Bambusa vulgaris.*

perin mahi *n.* Breadfruit tree sprout.

periper *vi. neut.* To cut, trim, or sharpen with any large cutting tool. —par₁, *vt.*

pehris *n.* Fish sp..

permasepeng 1. *n.* Quadrangle, square. 2. *vi.* To be quadrangular, to be square.

persent, also piresent. *n.* Percentage, percent. [Eng.]

persona *n.* Person, Catholic biblical term, one of the trinity. [Span.]

pehrdi *vi.* To lose. [Span.]

pehs₁ *n.* Ashes.

pehs₂ *n.* Land boundary. [Eng.]

pehsas 1. *n.* Thief. 2. *vi.* To be a thief.

pehse *vi.* To be acquainted with one another.

pesen likan *n.* Spider web, cobweb.

pesenkoahte *n.* Sound made by the rubbing of crossed branches.

-peseng *verb. suff.* Apart, away from each other; with adjectives of size, it signals an increase in size. *sei* paddle, *seipeseng* paddle away from each other; *lapala* large, *lapalapeseng* get larger.

peserek *vi.* To be yanked or jerked. —sereki, *vt.*

pehsehs 1. *adj.* Gray, grayish; dust covered. 2. *n.* Gray.

pesnes, also pisnis. 1. *n.* Business. 2. *vi.* To do business. [Eng.]

ped *vi.* To be squeezed or pressed, to be pushed, as a switch. —padik, *vt.*

pedala *vi.* To have sexual intercourse for the first time, of a female; to be deflowered.

pedeli 1. *n.* The sibling of opposite sex by whom one would swear. 2. *interj.* I swear!

peden were *n3s.* The area between the collarbone and the neck.

pedenpil *n.* Puddle.

pedeped *adj.* Shallow.

pedehde *n.* Potato, sweet potato *Ipomea batatas.* [Eng.]

pediang *vi.* To paddle or pole against the wind.

pedilik₁ *n.* Canoe part, the vertical sheer strake that ordinarily extends above the central portion of the leeward gunwale.

pedilik₂ *n.* Fish sp., a kind of parrotfish.

pedilukop *vi.* To stand with one's hands on one's hips, to stand with one's arms akimbo.

pehdinpwong *vi.* To stay up late; to have a wake.

pediped *n.* Fish sp..

pedidi *vi.* To pound with rhythmical beats prior to the pounding of kava.

pedihdi *n.* Fish sp., pompano, *Selar crumenopthalmus.*

Pedlem *n.* Bethlehem. [Eng.]

pehdmour *vi.* To take by force, in a greedy manner.

pehdpeseng *vi.* To open one's eyes.

pehdsel *vi.* To engage in a tug-of-war.

pet *vi.* To bid; to bet. [Eng.]

peht *n.* Bed. [Eng.]

pehtakai *n.* Hibiscus sp..

pehwehwe *n.* Manta ray.

pewi *n3s.* Empty shell, as of a coconut, a crab, etc..

pih *n.* Name of the letter *p.*

piah *vt.* To flavor with coconut milk. —piahia, *vi.*

piahia 1. *vi. neut.* To flavor with coconut milk. 2. *n.* Food flavored with coconut milk. —piah, *vt.*

pie *n3s.* Vagina.

pihe, also pihru. *n.* Beer. [Eng.]

pioing *n.* Hospital. [Jap.]

piokiok *adj.* Ugly, matted looking, as wet feathers.

pihk *n.* Sand.

pihkahkis *n.* Pickaxe. [Eng.]

pikapik *adj.* Sandy.

pikila *vi.* To be transformed by supernatural power.

pikipas *vi.* To have nothing left.

pikipik *vi. neut.* To pat; to slap affectionately. —pikir, *vt.*

pikir *vt.* To pat; to slap affectionately. —pikipik, *vi.*

pikos *adj.* Curly.

pikmasaht *vi.* To catch the kind of mangrove crab called *masaht.*

pikser *n.* Picture, snapshot. [Eng.]

pil₁ *adv.* Also. *Liho pil neksang University of Hawaii.* That woman also graduated from the University of Hawaii.

pil₂ *vt.* To choose, to pick out, to select. —pilipil, *vi.*

pil₃ *n.* Bill. [Eng.]

pihl *n.* Water, liquid.

pilaik *n.* Flag. [Eng.]

pilakai 1. *n.* Black eye; punch. 2. *vt.* To punch. [Eng.]

pilampwoia *n.* Tree sp., acacia. [Eng.]

pilampwoia weitahta *n.* Tree sp., flame tree.

pilahn 1. *n.* Plan. 2. *vi.* To plan. [Eng.] —pilahne, *vt.*

pilahne *vt.* To plan. [*pilahn*<Eng.] —pilahn, *vi.*

pilangkes *n.* Blanket. [Eng.]

pilasdik *n.* Plastic. [Eng.]

pilat₁ *n.* Record, a sound recording. [Ger.]

pilat₂ 1. *n.* Flat tire. 2. *vi.* To be intoxicated to the point of being immobile. [Eng.]

pilawa *n.* Bread. [Eng.]

pilawa amas *n.* Flour. [*pilawa*<Eng.]

pile, also pilede. *vt.* To pick fruit with a pole.

pilei 1. *vi.* To play cards. 2. *n.* Playing cards. [Eng.]

pilein 1. *n.* Plane, a carpenter's tool. 2. *vi.* To plane. [Eng.] —pileinih, *vt.*

pilein mwohni *vi.* To gamble. [Eng.]

pileinih *vt.* To plane. [*pilein*<Eng.] —pilein, *vi.*

pileit *n.* Plate. [Eng.]

pilen ewe *n3s.* Saliva.

pilen mese *n3s.* Tear, teardrop.

pilen pahnmweli HONORIFIC. 1. *n.* Gossip. 2. *vi.* To gossip.

pilen dawas HONORIFIC. *n.* Saliva.

pilerehre HONORIFIC. *vi.* To promise.

piled *n.* Pole for picking breadfruit.

pilede, also pile. *vt.* To pick fruit with a pole.

piledek *adj.* Of a man, effeminate; of a woman, masculine.

pilim *n.* Photographic film. [Eng.]

piling *vt.* To break apart, of food.

pilingek *vi.* To limp.

pilipil 1. *vi.* To choose, to pick out, to select. 2. *n.* Election, selection. —pil₂, *vt.*

pilihs *n.* Wallet, purse, valise. [Eng.]

pilisimen *n.* Policeman. [Eng.]

pilitik₁ *vi.* To be broken into small pieces with the hands, as breadfruit. —pilitikih, *vt.*

pilitik₂ *n.* Stream.

pilitikih *vt.* To break into small pieces with the hands, as breadfruit. —pilitik₁, *vi.*

pihlohlo *n.* Ground food mixed with ripe bananas.

piloak *n.* Pulley, block, of a block and tackle. [Eng.]

pillap *n.* River.

pilloak *vi. neut.* To twist off breadfruit with a pole and let it fall to the ground. —pilloake, *vt.*

pilloake *vt.* See *pilloak.*

pimpip *vi.* To speak incessantly.

pimpong 1. *n.* Ping-pong. 2. *vi.* To play ping-pong. [Eng.]

pihn *n.* Pin, tack, bobbypin. [Eng.]

pina *vt.* To patch; to block; to seal a bottle or end of a tube. —pinapin, *vi.*

pinapin 1. *vi.* To be patched; to be blocked; to be sealed. 2. *n.* Stopper. —pina, *vt.*

pihnas *n.* Peanut. [Eng.]

pihnas pwete *n.* Peanut butter. [Eng.]

pinepe *n3s.* Stopper.

pinike *n.* Vinegar. [Eng.]

pinipin *adj.* Closely twisted or curled, kinky, tangled.

piniwer *vi.* To choke on something.

pinpene *vt.* To wrap around.

pihns, also pens. *n.* Beans. [Eng.]

pinsel *n.* Pencil. [Eng.]

pindi *vi.* To be stranded in shallow water.

pintat *vi.* To convulse.

ping *adj.* Confused, disordered, messy.

pingin likou *n.* Remnant of cloth; rug.

pingiping *n.* Confusion, disorder, mess.

pingko 1. *n.* Bingo. 2. *vi.* To play bingo. [Eng.]

pip *vi.* To be worn around the waist, of a weapon. —pipih, *vt.*

pihp 1. *vi.* To beep or honk a horn. 2. *n.* Horn of an automobile. [Eng.] —pihpih, *vt.*

pipih *vt.* To wear around the waist, of a weapon. —pip, *vi.*

pihpi *n.* Vagina.

pihpih *vt.* To beep or honk a horn. —pihp, *vi.*

pipihs *vi.* To urinate. —**pihs,** *vt.*

pir₁ *vi.* To turn, to spin, to twist. —**pirer,** *vt.*

pir₂ *vi.* To flash.

pihr *vi.* To fly.

pirain 1. *vi. neut.* To fry. 2. *n.* Frying pan, skillet. [Eng.] —**piraine,** *vt.*

piraine *vt.* See *pirain.*

piraipang *n.* Frying pan, skillet. [Jap.<Eng.]

pirap *vi.* To steal. —**pirapa,** *vt.*

pirapa *vt.* See *pirap.*

pirapir 1. *vi. neut.* To tie; to wear a belt. 2. *n.* Belt. —**pire,** *vt.*

pirahs *n.* Brass. [Eng.]

pire *vt.* To tie. —**pirapir,** *vi.*

pirek *adj.* Crooked, off target, inaccurate.

pirekek *vi.* To turn one's head.

pirepe *n3s.* Binding, wrapper.

pirepira *n.* Propeller. [Jap.<Eng.]

pirer *vt.* To turn, to spin, to twist. —**pir₁,** *vi.*

piresent, also **persent.** *n.* Percentage, percent. [Eng.]

pirien 1. *n.* Sibling; brotherhood. 2. *vi.* To be siblings; to establish a close friendship.

piris *n.* Bridge. [Eng.]

pirida *vi.* To wake up.

piroski *n.* A cloth, used as a wrapper to carry objects. [Jap.]

piroas 1. *n.* Brush. 2. *vi.* To brush one's teeth. [Eng.]

pihru, also **pihe.** *n.* Beer. [Jap.<Eng.]

piruwek *vi.* To be rolled over, of inanimate objects.

pihrda *vi.* To become suddenly excited, to fly off the handle.

pis *n.* Pitch, tar. [Eng.]

pihs *vt.* To urinate on. —**pipihs,** *vi.*

pisalap *adj.* Coarse.

pisek *adj.* Free, idle; unconcerned, untroubled.

pisel *vi.* To slip off, to lose one's grip when climbing; to be discharged, of a weapon; to miss one's chance.

pisella *vi.* To happen to. *Ma i pisella iang, I pahn nsenamwahu.* If I happen to participate, I'll be happy.

piselpeseng *vi.* To be dislocated, of a joint; to come apart, of things joined together.

piser- *vi.* To come or go in a hurry, often in response to a leader's demands or an emergency. *Lahpo piserala Kolonia.* That guy hurried to Kolonia.

piserwar *vi.* To ascend.

pisetik *adj.* Fine, not coarse.

pisetikmei, also **kisetikmei.** *n.* Bush sp., *Melastoma marianum.*

pisiken *vi.* To push each other. —**siken,** *vt.*

pisilei *vi.* To guard; to maintain a vigil. —**sile₁,** *vt.*

pisin *n.* Pidgin, as Pidgin English. [Eng.]

pisirop 1. *n.* A game, hide-and-seek. 2. *vi.* To play this game.

pisop *n.* Bishop. [Eng.]

pisnis, also **pesnes.** 1. *n.* Business. 2. *vi.* To do business. [Eng.]

pispohra 1. *n.* Jacks. 2. *vi.* To play jacks. [?]

pissa 1. *n.* Pitcher. 2. *vi.* To be a pitcher. [Jap.<Eng.]

pisdong *n.* Piston, of an engine. [Eng.]

pisdor *n.* Pistol, revolver. [Jap.<Eng.]

pid₁ *vt.* To wrap around; to roll a cigarette.

pid₂ *vt.* To pertain to; to concern.

pidakih *vt.* To go around. —**pidek,** *vi.*

pidakihpene *vt.* To surround.

pidek *vi.* To go around. —**pidakih,** *vt.*

pidekila HONORIFIC. *vi.* To defecate.

pidekilik *n.* Fish sp..

pidilin *vi.* To pull each other's hair, as in a fight. —**dilin,** *vt.*

pidohi *vi.* To exit.

pidolong *vi.* To enter.

pit₁ *vi.* To spring back.

pit₂ *num. cl.* Used in counting strips or strands. *piten peilirop riepit* two strips of pandanus for weaving mats, *pitenwel isipit* seven strands of hair.

pit- *vi.* To escape. *Pwihko pitsang nan kehlo.* That pig escaped from that pen.

piht₁ *n.* Cheat, lie.

piht₂ *n.* Foot, measurement. [Eng.]

piht₃ *vi.* To conduct music. [Eng.] —**pihtih,** *vt.*

pitakatak 1. *adj.* Pasty, mashed. 2. *n.* Any mashed or pasty mass.

pitenmoang *n (3s: pitenmoange).* Hair, of the head.

pitenpeipei HONORIFIC. *n3s.* Strand of hair.

pitentepwitepw HONORIFIC. *n (3s: pitentepwitepwi).* Hair, of the head.

pitenwel *n (3s: pitenwali).* Strand of hair.

pitih *vt.* To trick; to lie to.

pihtih *vt.* See *piht₃.*

pitik *vt.* To sting, as of jellyfish.

pitikan *adj.* Fast, in bodily movement.

pitikek, also **pitirek.** *vi.* To flap, of a fish; to move rapidly.

pitikihda *vi.* To be itchy from something.

pitiniau *adj.* Lying, untruthful, said of a person.

pitipit *adj.* Fast, in the ability to perform actions.

pitirek, also **pitikek.** *vi.* To flap, of a fish; to move rapidly.

poh *n.* Color.

poisin *n.* Poison. [Eng.]

pou *adj.* Feeling cold, cool, chilly.

poula *vi.* To spoil, of cooked food.

poupit *n.* A stage of development of the coconut before it turns brown.

poupoulap₁ *adj.* Too familiar.

poupoulap₂ *n.* A variety of banana, having a large trunk but small fruit.

poupoar *vi.* To take sides.

pous 1. *vi.* To be connected, to be fastened together; to be passed on, of verbal information. 2. *n.* Connection. —**pouse,** *vt.*

pouse *vt.* To connect, to fasten together; to pass on verbal information. —**pous,** *vi.*

poudek *n.* Anchor; rope used for tying boats or canoes.

poudiahl *vi.* To watch, to behold, to observe. —**udiahl,** *vt.*

pok *vi.* To be hit with an object; to take one's turn at bat, in baseball. —**poakih,** *vt.*

pohk *n.* Whip.

pohkahki, also **kahki.** 1. *adj.* Khaki, tan. 2. *n.* Khaki, tan. [*kahki*<Eng.]

pokaraun 1. *vi.* To play a dirty trick. 2. *n.* A dirty trick. [Eng.] —**pokaraunih,** *vt.*

pokaraunih *vt.* To play a dirty trick. [*pokaraun*<Eng.] —**pokaraun,** *vi.*

pokous *vi.* To be ejected, to be banished. —**kaus,** *vt.*

pohkomwokomw *adj.* Grinning, without opening the mouth.

pokon 1. *vi.* To be assembled together in a crowd. 2. *n.* Meeting.

pokune *vi.* To hoe. [*une*<Jap.]

pohl *adj.* Delighted, overjoyed.

pohlemei *adj.* Arrogant; mean looking.

polo *n.* Crowd, fleet, school of fish.

pohmarungurung *adj.* Dull colored.

pon *adj.* Stuffed up, clogged.

pohn kepehmwahu *adj.* Skillful in making sennit.

pohn ntahn mwell 1. *adj.* Purple. 2. *n.* Purple.

pohn pwehl 1. *adj.* Brown. 2. *n.* Brown.

pohn sowe *n3s.* Back.

pohn delen pwukie *n3s.* Kneecap.

pohn tihn sowe *n3s.* Back.

pohnangi *n3s.* Above, upper, upwind, windward side; older sibling relationship.

pone *n.* Tree sp., *Thespesia populnea.*

pohnese *vt.* To acknowledge; to show consideration.

pohnihr HONORIFIC. *n.* Back of the neck.

pohnkahke *adj.* Lazy.

pohnkares *n.* Casing of a bullet.

pohnkoiohlap HONORIFIC. *vi.* To eat with the *Nahnmwarki* or *Nahnken.*

pohnkodoul SLANG. *vi.* To be naked, to be nude.

pohnlik *n.* Area on the beach or along the reef where the waves break.

pohnmwahso *adj.* Proud, with a negative connotation.

pohnpe *adj.* Successful in growing things, having a green thumb; successful in seeking a spouse.

Pohnpei *n.* Ponape.

Pohnpeiuh ARCHAIC. *n.* Ponape.

pohnsehse *vt.* To ignore.

pohndal *n.* Coconut shell.

pohndele HONORIFIC. *n3s.* Knee.

pohndihpw 1. *adj.* Green. 2. *n.* Green.

pohntehndipw 1. *adj.* Green. 2. *n.* Green.

popoki *vi.* To be whipped. —**poakih,** *vt.*

popohl *n.* Peace, tranquility; joy.

popohn *adj.* Aloof, indifferent.

popohnli *adj.* Pretending to be womanly.

popohnwol *adj.* Pretending to be manly.

popohr *vi.* To be slapped in the face. —**pohr,** *vt.*

pohr *vt.* To slap someone's face. —**popohr,** *vi.*

pohrehre HONORIFIC. *n.* Upper part of the mouth.

pohris HONORIFIC. *n.* Upper lip.

poros *n.* Fish sp..

poros en merer *n.* Fish sp..

pos₁ *vi.* To be hammered. —**pasur** or **poasur,** *vt.*

pos₂ *vi.* To explode.

posoke 1. *n.* Story, of a building. 2. *vi.* To be stacked.

pospos *vi.* To hammer. —**pasur** or **poasur,** *vt.*

pohtou *adj.* Gloomy, downcast.

powe *prep. n.* Above, upon, on (him, her, or it).

powehdi *vt.* To conquer; to overcome.

powi *n3s.* Empty casing, as of a coconut, cartridge, or shell.

poak 1. *vi.* To be in love; to be close. 2. *adj.* Loving. —**poakpoake,** *vt.*

poake, also **pako.** *n.* Shark.

poakehla *vt.* To pity.

poakepoak *n.* Love; affection.

poakih, also **woakih.** *vt.* To whip, to spank, to beat. —**pok** or **popoki,** *vi.*

poakpoake *vt.* To love, to like, to sympathize with. —**poak,** *vi.*

poans *n.* Shoot, of a plant.

poahngok, also **pahngok.** HONORIFIC. 1. *vi.* To speak or command. 2. *n.* Speech or command. —**poahngokih,** *vt.*

poahngokih *vt.* See *poahngok.*

poangot *n.* A rough area in the ocean caused by converging currents.

poar *num. cl.* Used in counting long, thin pieces or strips of something. *poaren dinapw rioapoar* two pieces of board, *poaren karangahp silipoar* three strips of tuna.

poahr *vi.* To wipe, after defecation.

poaridi₁ *vi.* To be caught, of something animate; to be arrested. —**parok,** *vt.*

poaridi₂ *vi.* To bow or sit as a respect gesture.

poaron HONORIFIC. 1. *vi.* To be commanded; to be summoned or dispatched. 2. *n.* Errand; task. —**poarone,** *vt.*

poarone HONORIFIC. *vt.* To command; to summon or dispatch. —**poaron,** *vi.*

poarongorong *adj.* Said of one who eavesdrops.

poasen kaun *n.* Capital, of a place.

poahsoan *n (3s: poahsoane).* Foundation, purpose; home; uterus.

poasur, also **pasur.** *vt.* To hammer. —**pos₁** or **pospos,** *vi.*

poad *vi.* To be planted. —**poadok,** *vt.*

poahd *n.* Individual planting, of any plant.

poaden *adv.* Incessantly, always. *E poaden kapakap.* He's always praying.

poadok *vt.* To plant. —**poad,** *vi.*

poadoahk *vi.* To fight each other. —**doahke,** *vt.*

poadoandoar *vi.* To separate a fight. —**doare,** *vt.*

poadoapoad 1. *n.* History, sacred story. 2. *vi.* To tell the history of something, to tell a sacred story.

poadoar 1. *vi.* To wrestle. 2. *n.* Wrestling.

poadoarepe₁ *n3s.* Protector, protection.

poadoarepe₂ 1. *vi.* To arm wrestle. 2. *n.* Arm wrestling.

poatoapoat *adj.* Everlasting, constant, permanent.

pu *adj.* Bent, crooked, curved.

plaias *n.* Pliers. [Eng.]

plakpwoht *n.* Blackboard. [Eng.]

preik₁ *vi.* In pool, to break, i.e. to shoot first. [Eng.]

preik₂ 1. *n.* Brake, as on an automobile. 2. *vi. neut.* To brake. [Eng.]

preisihl *n.* A variety of banana. [Eng.]

preisis₁ 1. *n.* Suspenders. 2. *vi.* To wear suspenders. [Eng.]

preisis₂ *n.* Brace, bracket. [Eng.]

pringihnas *n.* Eggplant, *Solanum melongena.* [Span.]

Prohs *n.* Protestant. [Eng.]

proadkahs *n.* Broadcast station. [Eng.]

PW

pwa₁ *sent. adv.* Really, indeed; used to signal emphasis. *Ke pai pwa!* You are really fortunate!

pwa₂ ARCHAIC. *vi.* To say.

pwai₁ *n.* Wooden implement for splitting breadfruit.

pwai₂ *n.* Oyster.

pwaik *vt.* To split. —pwepweik, *vi.*

pwail 1. *n.* File. 2. *vi. neut.* To file. [Eng.] —pwaile, *vt.*

pwaile *vt.* See *pwail.*

pwailet *n.* Pilot. [Eng.]

pwain *vt.* To buy, to pay, to hire. —pweipwei₂, *vi.*

pwaindi *vt.* To cover. —pweipweidi, *vi.*

pwais *n (3s: pweise).* Responsibility; share of food; task.

pwaisikel 1. *n.* Bicycle. 2. *vi.* To ride a bicycle. [Eng.]

pwakan SLANG. *adj.* Perfect, just right.

pwakanakan *adj.* Muddy, sloppy.

pwakel₁ *interj.* What a knockout!, of someone or something exceptional.

pwakel₂ *n.* Belt loop. [Eng.]

pwakih *vt.* To chase. —pwepweki, *vi.*

pwakihdi *vt.* To catch up to, to chase down, to overtake. —pwekidi, *vi.*

pwal 1. *vi.* To be slit, to be cut open; to be operated on; to be divided. 2. *n.* Surgery; medical operation, in which the body cavity is entered. —pwalang, *vt.*

pwahl *n.* Crack.

pwahlahl *n.* Fish sp., snapper, *Lutjanus gibbus.*

pwalang *vt.* To slit, to cut open; to operate on; to divide; to shatter, as glass. —pwal, *vi.*

pwalapwal *n.* Crack; vagina.

pwalasapw 1. *vi.* To divide land. 2. *n.* Division of land.

pwallap 1. *vi.* To divide land into large areas. 2. *n.* Region, large area of land.

pwand *adj.* Late, slow.

pwang *adj.* Tired, lazy.

pwangahki *vt.* To be tired of, to be disinterested in, to be bored by.

pwangih *vt.* To flirt. —pwengipweng, *vi.*

pwar *vt.* To appear; to go through; to pass, in a race.

pwahr *n.* Hole, for planting yams; a yam planting.

pwarapwar *n.* Ridge cap.

pwarek *vt.* To visit.

pwarer *n.* Well, spring.

pwahrih *vt.* To dig a hole for a yam; to poke.

pwarosohs *vi.* To manifest itself, of a ghost.

pwadai, also pwadaiki. *n3s.* Tail.

pwadaiki, also pwadai. *n3s.* Tail.

pwadik₁ *vt.* To retrieve from a hole with one's hand; to gag oneself with one's finger. —pwedipwed, *vi.*

pwadik₂ *vt.* To add water to pounded kava. —pwed₂, *vi.*

pwaten, also pwatin. *n.* Button. [Eng.]

pwati *n.* Putty. [Eng.]

pwahtiet *adj.* Active, peppy.

pwatin, also pwaten. *n.* Button. [Eng.]

pwe *conj.* Because, since, but, so that. *E sohte kohla laid, pwe e soumwahu.* He didn't go fishing, because he was sick.

pwei *adj.* Hardy, of crops and domesticated animals.

pweiek *vi.* To move backwards; to backslide; to stop suddenly.

pweiekidi HONORIFIC. *vi.* To remain overnight, to go to bed, to bed down.

pweikoar *n.* Taro leaves placed around the base of a kava stone to catch fallen pieces of kava.

pweilaud *adj.* Expensive, costly.

pweinaper *n.* Pineapple, *Ananas comosus.* [Eng.]

pweine₁ *n3s.* Cost.

pweine₂ *n3s.* Lid, cover.

Pweipei Lapalap *n.* Title of the wife of a *Lempwei Lapalap.*

pweipwand 1. *n.* Debt, credit, account. 2. *vi.* To be in debt.

pweipwei₁ *adj.* Stupid, silly, idiotic, simple, dumb.

pweipwei₂ 1. *vi.* To be bought; to be paid; to cost money. 2. *n.* Cost, wage, reward. —pwain, *vt.*

pweipweidi *vi.* To be covered.
—**pwaindi,** *vt.*

pweirengid *adj.* Extremely stupid, silly, idiotic, simple, dumb.

pweisaniki *vt.* To be responsible for providing something or doing a task.

pweisang *vt.* To release.

pweisenwair *n.* Rotten egg.

pweisou 1. *n.* Hat; sun visor made from coconut fronds, used while fishing. 2. *vi.* To wear a hat or a sun visor.

pweida *vi.* To be successful.

pweidi *vi.* To remain overnight, to go to bed, to bed down.

pweitikitik *adj.* Inexpensive, cheap.

pwehu₁ *n.* Fish sp., snapper, *Lutjanus semicinctus.*

pwehu₂ *n.* A kind of magic used to halt an activity or to inhibit an emotion.

pweula 1. *vi.* To be postponed; to be canceled; to fail, of a project. 2. HONORIFIC. *vi.* To die.

pwek₁ *vt.* To lift; to adopt.

pwek₂ *adj.* Short of a competitor's distance, as in throwing or jumping.

pwek₃ *vi.* To be chased.

pwek₄ *vt.* To formally distribute food at a *kamadipw.* —**pwekipwek,** *vi.*

pwehk *n.* Bat.

pwehki *conj.* Because; on account of. *Limwei sohte mwahukinira pwehki ara lehko.* Limwei doesn't like them because of their selfishness.

pwekil, also **kepwil.** *n (3s: pwekeli).* Corner of the mouth.

pwekipwek *vi. neut.* To formally distribute food at a *kamadipw.* —**pwek₄,** *vt.*

pwekid *n.* Pocket. [Eng.]

pwekida *interr.* Why?; used as a one word sentence.

pwekidah *n3s.* Share of food formally received at a *kamadipw.*

pwekidi *vi.* To catch up with. —**pwakihdi,** *vt.*

pwekmwar *vi.* To give a title.

pwehl₁ *n.* Dirt, soil, earth, ground; first cup of kava in the kava ceremony.

pwehl₂ *n.* Sennit.

pweleng *n.* Ridge area of a house or land.

pwelih *vt.* To drink the first cup of kava.

pwelipar 1. *n.* Dust. 2. *adj.* Dusty.

pwelipwel *adj.* Dirty, soiled.

pwelmatak 1. *n.* Mud. 2. *adj.* Muddy.

pwelmwahu *adj.* Fertile, of the soil.

pweltoal *n.* Black soil.

pwelweita *n.* Red soil.

pwenieu *n (3s: pweniewi).* Food for the wives of all *koanoat* title holders.

pwendeke, also **ipwadeke.** *sent. adv.* It was thought that.

pwengilih *vi.* To court a woman.

pwengipweng *vi. neut.* To flirt.
—**pwangih,** *vt.*

pwengkin *n.* Pumpkin; also used to describe one who has an unfaithful spouse. [Eng.]

pwengwol *vi.* To court a man.

pwepweik *vi.* To be split. —**pwaik,** *vt.*

pwepweki *vi.* To chase one another.
—**pwakih,** *vt.*

pwepwengi *vi.* To be well matched in a competitive endeavor.

pwer *vi.* To appear; to blossom, of fruit trees.

pwere₁ *vt.* To take a drink and hold it in the mouth without swallowing.

pwere₂ *n3s.* Lower abdomen.

pwereht *n.* Biscuit. [Eng.]

pwerik ARCHAIC. 1. *vi.* To dance. 2. *n.* Dance.

pwerila *vi.* To be fascinated, by someone or something new.

pweriniak *n.* Hole, for planting yams; a yam planting.

pwerinmwomw *n.* Fish sp., rabbitfish, *Siganus doliatus.*

pwerisek *adj.* Industrious, hard working.

pwerkidipw *n.* Fish sp..

pwes *vi.* To have sexual intercourse.

pwehs *n.* Sexual intercourse.

pwed₁ *adj.* Fast growing.

pwed₂ *vi.* To add water to pounded kava. —**pwadik₂,** *vt.*

pwed- *vi.* To go through an entrance or opening. *Lapwedo pwedilong nan pwoahro.* That eel went into that hole.

pwehd *n.* Labia, of the vagina.

pwehde *conj.* Since.

pwedehk *vi.* To buzz.

pwedila *vi.* To be lucky.

pwedipwed *vi.* To catch fish from holes in the coral by hand; to grab at a woman's vagina. —**pwadik₁,** *vt.*

pwet$_1$ *n.* Light colored scar.

pwet$_2$ *vi.* To flower, of mango trees.

pweht$_1$ *n.* Lime, made from coral.

pweht$_2$ *n.* Tortoise shell.

pwete *n.* Butter. [Eng.]

pwetenleng *n.* Horizon.

pwetepwet 1. *adj.* White. 2. *n.* Gray hair.

pwewih *vt.* To employ a kind of magic used to halt an activity or to inhibit an emotion.

pwih *n.* Name of the digraph *pw.*

pwihk *n.* Pig, swine, pork. [Eng.]

pwil$_1$ *vt.* To put down; to put aside, of one's beliefs or emotions. —pwilidi, *vi.*

pwil$_2$ *vi.* To flow; to rise or flood, of a stream.

pwihl *n (3s: pwili).* Gum, of a tree.

pwilel *n.* Calabash, gourd.

pwihleng HONORIFIC. *n.* Drinking coconut.

pwili *n.* Cowrie; any species of sea shell.

pwiliet *n.* Bird sp., black and red in color.

pwilipeipei HONORIFIC. *n3s.* Long hair of a woman.

pwilipwil *adj.* Sticky.

pwilis *n.* Chewing gum.

pwilisang *vi.* To come from; to originate from, of a person.

pwilidak *adj.* Native, aboriginal.

pwilidi *vi.* To be put down; to be put aside, of one's beliefs or emotions; to make regular payments or deposits. —pwil$_1$, *vt.*

pwihn *n.* Group, team, grade level.

pwihnen kaiahn *n.* Training group, kindergarten.

pwinik *vt.* To select or choose from a group of animate beings, to pick out an animal.

pwinimas *adj.* Greedy, always wanting the biggest or the best.

pwiningining *adj.* Tiny, minute.

pwirar *vi.* To make a splattering noise.

pwise *n (3s: pwiseh).* Feces; internal organs or guts of smaller animals and fish.

pwishen karapahu *n.* Bush sp..

pwisehn ketipin *n.* Algae.

pwisehn kou *n.* Bush sp.. [*kou*<Eng.]

pwisik *vt.* To pry out, to pry off, as a nail or bottle cap.

pwisinger *adj.* Cross or tough, of a person.

pwisirek *adj.* Sassy, impudent, saucy.

pwidikidik *adj.* Tiny, small, little.

pwidingeu *adj.* Roguish.

pwoh *n (3s: pwowe).* Smell, odor, aroma.

pwohi *n.* Buoy. [Eng.]

pwou *n.* Fishing pole.

pwourda *vi.* To get up; to sit up from a supine position; to wake up.

pwoud *n.* Spouse, husband or wife; any clansmate of one's spouse of the same sex and same generation as the spouse.

pwoudiki *vt.* To marry. —pwopwoud, *vi.*

pwohk *n.* Fork, the eating utensil. [Eng.]

pwohkungo *n.* Man-made cave, air-raid shelter. [Jap.]

pwohlap *adj.* Smelly.

pwolismasda *n.* Policeman. [Jap.<Eng.]

pwolol 1. *vi.* To bubble. 2. *n.* Bubble.

pwolkeno *n.* Volcano. [Eng.]

pwomakirant *n.* Bush sp..

pwohmaria *n.* Plant sp., *Plumeria rubra*, plumeria.

pwohmat *interj.* You stink!, derogatory exclamation used principally by women.

pwompwomw *n.* Vine sp., *Passiflora foetida.*

pwon *adj.* Whole, entire, intact.

pwone *n3s.* Hip.

pwonopwon 1. *adj.* Round; circular. 2. *n.* Circle.

pwonopwoniki *vt.* To find something confusing, difficult to understand, or mysterious.

pwong *num. cl.* Used in counting nights. *pwohng silipwong* three nights.

pwohng *n.* Night.

pwongiedi *vi.* To have darkness descend upon one before reaching one's destination.

pwongitik HONORIFIC. *vi.* To be hungry.

pwopwe *n3s.* Shoulder.

pwohpwo$_1$ *n.* Affectionate name for baby girls.

pwohpwo$_2$ *adj.* Strong smelling, stinking.

pwopwoud 1. *n.* Married couple. 2. *vi.* To get married. —pwoudiki, *vt.*

pwohr *n.* Carton of cigarettes. [Jap.<Eng.]

pworen timwe *n3s.* Nostril.

pworou *vi.* To be wet under the arms from sweat, or in the crotch from urine or sweat.

pworu *n.* Sp. of crab.

pwohs *n.* Boss. [Eng.]

pwohsensen *adj.* Moldy smelling.

pwosou *n.* A large fishing net.

pwoson 1. *n.* Faith, belief, creed. 2. *vt.* To believe in, to have faith in.

pwohsdo *n.* Post office. [Jap.<Eng.]

pwohdaka 1. *n.* Pole-vaulting. 2. *vi.* To pole-vault. [Jap.]

pwoht₁ *n.* Boat. [Eng.]

pwoht₂ *n.* Bobbin, of a sewing machine.

pwoht₃ *vi.* To lose, in the card game *pilein epwiki.*

pwoht kisiniei *n.* Steamboat.

pwohtik *adj.* Fragrant.

Pwohtiki *n.* Portugal.

pwoton HONORIFIC. *n.* Married couple.

pwoaik *n.* Dew.

pwoaikentehine HONORIFIC. *adj.* Cold, cool, chilly.

pwoail *vi.* To boil. [Eng.] —pwoaile, *vt.*

pwoaile *vt.* See *pwoail.* [*pwoail*<Eng.]

pwoaki *n.* Grass sp., *Thoracostachyum pandanophyllum.*

pwoalehdi *vt.* To embrace, to hug. —pwoaloapwoal, *vi.*

pwoalos *n.* Large bundle.

pwoalosolos *adj.* Of clothing, too large at the waist; baggy.

pwoaloapwoal *vi.* To embrace, to hug each other. —pwoalehdi, *vt.*

pwoampwoamw₁ *n.* Plant sp., a kind of vine.

pwoampwoamw₂ *n.* A Japanese boat with a diesel engine. [Jap.]

pwoamw *vi.* To be pumped. [Eng.] —pwoamwih, *vt.*

pwoamwih *vt.* To pump. [*pwoamw*<Eng.] —pwoamw, *vi.*

pwoapw *vi.* To crack, to break, to come apart, of an object fastened to something.

pwoar *vi.* To have a hole.

pwoahr *n.* Hole, cave.

pwoaren kahwe *n3s.* Anus.

pwoaren pwise *n3s.* Anus.

pwoarenmas *n (3s: pwoarenmese).* Eye.

pwoarukus *n.* Spring of water.

pwoat *num. cl.* Used in counting long objects, also used metaphorically with nouns like *kohl* 'song' and *koasoai* 'story'. *tuhke rioapwoat* two trees, *kohl rioapwoat* two songs.

pwoaht *n.* Can, tin. [Eng.]

pwoatol *n.* Bottle. [Eng.]

pwuh₁ *n.* Betel nut, *Areca cathecu.*

pwuh₂ *n.* Ship or work whistle.

pwuhk *n.* Book. [Eng.]

pwuka, also pwukat. *dem. mod.* These here, by me (emphatic).

pwukau, also pwuko. *dem. mod.* Those there, away from you and me (emphatic).

pwukan *dem. mod.* Those there, by you (emphatic).

pwukapwuk *adj.* Reddened, of the skin.

pwukat, also pwuka. *dem. mod.* These here, by me (emphatic).

pwuke *vt.* To knot. —pwukopwuk, *vi.*

pwukekeimw *n.* Cornerstone.

pwukel *n (3s: pwukele).* Knot, joint, as in a stalk of bamboo.

pwukelekel *adj.* Knotty.

pwuken eni 1. *n.* Any non-slip knot. 2. *vi.* To tie, with any knot other than a slipknot.

pwuken nting *n.* Notebook. [*pwuhk*<Eng.]

pwukeneu *vi.* To be tied, with any knot other than a slipknot.

pwukenwilia *n.* Plant sp., bougainvillia. [Eng.]

pwukepe *n3s.* Responsibility.

pwuker *n.* Gravel, pebbles, crushed coral, any rock-like material used as a ground cover.

pwukere *vt.* To spread gravel or coral, as on the road.

pwukesok *vi.* To blush; to flush, of the face.

pwuki *n.* A swelling wave; the prominence of anything.

pwukie *n3s.* Knee.

pwuko, also pwukau. *dem. mod.* Those there, away from you and me (emphatic).

pwukopwuk 1. *n.* Knot. 2. *vi. neut.* To knot. —pwuke, *vt.*

pwukoa *n.* Responsibility, obligation, duty.

Pwuksarawi *n.* Bible. [*pwuhk*<Eng.]

pwul *adj.* Immature, of fruit.

pwulak *n.* Fish sp., unicorn fish, *Naso unicornis.*

pwulahk *vi.* To come or go, used in a derogatory way.

pwulangking *n.* Fish sp., surgeonfish, *Naso lituratus.*

pwuloi 1. *n.* Of cane-like plants, the part of the stem between the joints; stanza of a song. 2. *num. cl.* Used in counting sections from joint to joint of cane-like plants or stanzas in songs. *sehu pahpwuloi* four sections of sugar cane, *pwuloin koul riopwuloi* two stanzas.

pwulok *n.* Mangrove sp., *Xylocarpus granatum.*

pwulopwul *adj.* Young.

pwull₁ *adj.* Loose fitting.

pwull₂ *vi.* To have something in one's eye.

pwuldohser *n.* Bulldozer. [Eng.]

pwuhn *n.* Fish sp..

pwunan 1. *n.* Sleep, the crust around the eyes formed during sleep. 2. *vi.* To have sleep in one's eyes.

pwunod *adj.* Worried.

pwundosi 1. *n.* Loincloth. 2. *vi.* To wear a loincloth. [Jap.]

pwung₁ *adj.* Correct, right, just.

pwung₂ *vi. neut.* To swell, of waves; to splash. —**pwungur,** *vt.*

pwuhng *n.* Justice, right.

pwungen sahpw *n.* A traditional ritual to maintain the fertility of the soil.

pwungih₁ *vt.* To worship, to adore.

pwungih₂ *vt.* To hem, as shirts, pants, dresses, etc..

pwungiari *vi.* To be indecisive.

pwungidek *vi.* To break, of waves; to splash. —**pwungur,** *vt.*

pwungidekida *vi.* To be washed up on the reef or shore; of water, to be agitated. —**pwungur,** *vt.*

pwungur *vt.* To splash; to wash up on the reef or shore. —**pwung₂** or **pwungidek** or **pwungidekida,** *vi.*

pwupw *vi.* To fall.

pwuhpw *n.* Fish sp., trigger fish, *Rhinecanthus aculeatus.*

pwupwula *vi.* To be lost, of objects; to fail to complete a competitive activity.

pwupwuda *vi.* To be intoxicated by kava to the point of losing one's self-control.

pwur *vi.* To return.

pwuhr *n.* Tree sp..

pwuhr- *vi.* To descend into, to fall into, to step into, as a hole. *Misihno pwuhrla nansedo.* The outboard motor fell into the ocean.

pwuraia *n.* Pliers. [Jap.<Eng.]

pwurak *vt.* To spit out.

pwure *vt.* To drill a hole in; to make a hole in a coconut. —**pwuropwur,** *vi.*

pwuremas *vi.* To open at the top, of a drinking coconut.

pwurenwai *n.* Tree sp., *Cananga odorata,* having fragrant flowers.

pwurehng *vi.* To repeat; to do again.

pwurepwur en eni *vi.* To offer a drinking coconut to someone before tasting it.

pwuri *n (3s: pwurie).* Stomach, of certain fish like tuna; core, as of breadfruit; protrusion of the large intestine from the anus.

pwuriamwei 1. *vi.* To be surprised, astonished, amazed, or shocked; to get excited; to be disappointed. 2. *n.* Surprise, astonishment, amazement, shock.

pwuriamweikihla 1. *vt.* To be sorry. 2. *interj.* Too bad!.

pwuriemwot, also **pwuriemwotomwot.** *adj.* Short-tempered.

pwuriemwotomwot *adj.* See *pwuriemwot.*

pwurien arepe, also **arepe.** *n.* Hibiscus pole, after the bark has been stripped.

pwuhrieng *vi.* To dress.

pwurok₁ *n.* Chick, just after hatching.

pwurok₂ *adj.* To be broke, to be out of money. [Eng.]

pwurokiram *n.* Program, especially a radio program. [Eng.]

pwuropwur *vi.* To drill a hole. —**pwure,** *vt.*

pwurur 1. *adj.* Hasty. 2. *vi.* To struggle.

pwurkadorio *n.* Purgatory. [Span.]

pwuhrsang *vi.* To undress.

pwuhs₁ *n (3s: pwuse).* Navel.

pwuhs₂ *vt.* To push. [Eng.]

pwuhseng *n.* Balloon. [Jap.]

pwusukoal   *vi.* To throw a temper
tantrum.

pwudau, also pwudo.   *n (3s: pwudowe).*
Perspiration, sweat.

pwudo, also pwudau.   *n (3s: pwudowe).*
Perspiration, sweat.

pwuhdo   *n.* Envelope. [Jap.]

pwudoniap   *n.* Wart.

pwudong   1. *adj.* To be itchy.   2. *n.*
Rash.

pwudopwud   *n.* Foam, scum.

pwudowado   *adj.* Sweaty.

pwut   *adj.* Joyous, lusty.

pwuht   *n.* Boot. [Eng.]

pwutak   *n.* Boy.

pwuteletel   SLANG. *adj.* Sensuous,
beautiful.

pwutemei   1. *n.* Second feast of the
breadfruit season.   2. *vi.* To prepare
this feast.

Pwuton   *n.* A clan name.

pwuwak   1. *adv.* Frequently. *E pwuwak
keteu.* It frequently rains.   2. *adj.*
Having a special affinity for growing
certain species of yams.

pwuwalok   *adj.* Swollen or puffed up as
a consequence of a wound or blow.

pwuwas   *n.* Fish sp., half beak,
Hemiramphus guoyi.

R

ra *num. cl.* Used in counting branches. *rahn tuhke limara* five tree branches.

rah *n3s.* Branch; tentacle, as of an octopus.

rais *n.* Rice. [Eng.]

raido *n.* Right field, in baseball. [Jap.<Eng.]

rahu *n.* Reed sp., *Phragmites karka*; a minor rafter to which pieces of thatch are attached.

rauk, also sauk. *vi.* To fall down, of standing objects.

raun *vi.* To make the rounds. [Eng.]

rausis 1. *n.* Trousers, pants. 2. *vi.* To wear trousers. [Eng.]

rausis mwotomwot 1. *n.* Short pants, shorts. 2. *vi.* To wear short pants or shorts.

rausis preisis 1. *n.* Bib overalls. 2. *vi.* To wear bib overalls. [Eng.]

rak *vi.* To rack, as in pool. [Eng.]

rahk₁ *n.* Season of plenty, breadfruit season.

rahk₂ *n.* One of the outrigger supports on a canoe.

rakih *vt.* To scratch with the fingernails; to claw. —rekirek, *vi.*

rakied *n.* Gravel, pebbles.

rakudai *vi.* To flunk, to fail. [Jap.]

ramen *n.* Chinese-style noodle soup. [Jap.]

ramin *adj.* Smudged, faultily washed.

ramwune 1. *n.* Marble; glass fishing ball. 2. *vi.* To play marbles. [Jap.]

rahn *n.* Day.

Rahn en Santi *n.* Sunday. [*santi*<Eng.]

Rahn en Sapwad *n.* Sunday, Sabbath. [*sapwad*<Eng.]

Rahn Kaunop *n.* Saturday.

rahn kuloak *n.* Hands of a clock or watch. [*kuloak*<Eng.]

Rahn Sarawi *n.* Sunday.

Rahn Sarawi Lapalap *n.* Catholic holy day.

rahnmwahu 1. *vi.* To greet. 2. *n.* Greeting. —rahnmwahwih, *vt.*

rahnmwahwih *vt.* To greet. —rahnmwahu, *vi.*

rahnmwoalehdi HONORIFIC. *vi.* To rest.

ranning 1. *n.* Undershirt. 2. *vi.* To wear an undershirt. [Jap.<Eng.]

ransi *n.* A motor launch. [Jap.<Eng.]

randana, also landana. *n.* Lantana, *Lantana camara.*

rahnwet *n.* Today.

rap *n.* A salt water eel, commonly found on the barrier reef.

rahp *n.* Raft, barge. [Eng.]

rapahki *vt.* To search for, to look for. —repen₁, *vi.*

rapit *n.* Rabbit. [Eng.]

rappa *n.* Bugle. [Jap.]

rar₁ 1. *vi.* To make a cracking, crunching, or static-like noise. 2. *n.* A noise of this kind.

rar₂ *num.* Million.

rar₃ *vi. neut.* To skin or peel. —rere, *vt.*

rahr *n.* Finger coral.

rara *n.* Pandanus sp..

rarahni *n.* Crown of thorns starfish.

rarenei HONORIFIC. *vi.* To laugh.

rarkapwudong *n.* Fire coral.

ras₁ *vi.* To be equal; to be the same as.

ras₂ *adj.* Of the tide or of bodies of fresh water, to reach a low point where much of the bottom is exposed.

rahs *n.* Place of the *uhmw*; small stones used for making an *uhmw.*

rasaras 1. *n.* Saw. 2. *vi. neut.* To saw. —rese, *vt.*

rawahn *n.* Tree sp., durian, *Pangium edule*, edible fruit.

re 1. also irail. *subj. pron.* They, plural. 2. HONORIFIC. *subj. pron.* You.

reh₁ *prep. n.* Location of (him, her, or it).

reh₂ *n.* Grass, any of a number of grasses.

rei *vi.* To be stained; to be dyed. —reid, *vt.*

reirei₁ *adj.* Long, tall.

reirei₂ *adj.* Runny, of colors in materials; pale, of the face as after a sudden shock; blue, of the face as when cold; puckered up, of the mouth as after eating unripe bananas.

reise *n.* Razor; razor blade. [Eng.]

reisuwan *adj.* Tall.

reid *vt.* To stain; to dye;/. —**rei**, *vi.*

reidi *vi.* To rhythmically pound a kava stone at the beginning of the kava ceremony.

rehu *n.* Beam or rafter of a roof.

reulap *n.* Rafter.

rek *adj.* Abundant, plentiful.

rekeleng, also **rekenleng**. HONORIFIC. *n.* Finger.

rekenleng, also **rekeleng**. HONORIFIC. *n.* Finger.

rekenpwel, also **rekepwel**. HONORIFIC. *n.* Toe.

rekepwel, also **rekenpwel**. HONORIFIC. *n.* Toe.

rehki 1. *n.* Rake. 2. *vt.* To rake. [Eng.]

rekipwel *vi.* To clear land by pulling up grass or weeds, to bare the earth.

rekirek *vi. neut.* To scratch with the fingernails; to claw. —**rakih**, *vt.*

rekidi *vi.* To bend down to pick something up.

rekohdo *n.* Record, a sound recording. [Jap.<Eng.]

rehl *n.* Rail. [Eng.]

rehmaikol *n.* Grass sp., *Axonopus compressus.*

remek *n.* Tree sp..

rempwidi *vi.* To calm down after a time of excitement, as after a fight.

rehn sehmen *n.* Grass sp..

rens *n.* Wrench. [Eng.]

rensed *n.* Salt water.

rensuh *vi.* To practice for an athletic event, to warm up for an athletic event. [Jap.]

rehnta *n.* Grass sp., *Andropogon glaber* or *Paspalum orbiculare.*

reng *vi.* To be dried, as of copra or tobacco.

renged *adj.* Dark, of colors.

rengireng *vi.* To warm oneself by a fire.

rengk 1. *vi.* To slide, of rocks. 2. *n.* Rock slide.

rehpadil *n.* Grass sp., *Ischaemum chordatum.*

repen$_1$ *vi. neut.* To search. —**rapahki**, *vt.*

repen$_2$ *n.* Ribbon, lace. [Eng.]

repwirepw *adj.* Mixed, of bananas and any other food.

rer 1. *vi.* To tremble or shake; to be on edge, of the teeth. 2. *adj.* Shaky.

rere *vt.* To skin or peel. —**rar**$_3$, *vi.*

rehre *vt.* To kill a tree by banding, to band a tree.

rerei 1. *vi.* To run a relay race. 2. *n.* The name of this race. [Jap.<Eng.]

rereiso HONORIFIC. *n.* Cane.

rerehd wasa *vi.* To bawl, to cry loudly.

rerinmwoalu HONORIFIC. *vi.* To sigh in one's sleep.

rerinpehiso HONORIFIC. *n.* Pillow.

rese *vt.* To saw. —**rasaras**, *vi.*

resires *n.* Shoal.

redio *n.* Radio. [Eng.]

rehdil *n.* Fern sp., *Nephrolepis acutifolia.*

rehtakai *n.* Grass sp., *Chrysopogon aciculatus* or *Eleusine indica.*

rih *n.* Name of the letter *r.*

riai *num.* Two; used for counting bunches of bananas.

riau *num.* Two; see -*u.*

riaka *num.* Two; see *ka*$_2$.

riahka *n.* Small two-wheeled cart, pulled or pushed by hand. [Jap.<Eng.]

riakap *num.* Two; see *kap.*

riakis *num.* Two; see *kis*$_1$.

riahla 1. *vi.* To be cursed, resulting in illness or misfortune. 2. *n.* Curse.

riapa *num.* Two; see *pa*$_3$.

riapak *num.* Two; see *pak*$_1$.

riapali *num.* Two; see *pali*$_1$.

riapar *num.* Two; see *par*$_2$.

riara *num.* Two; see *ra.*

riasop *num.* Two; see *sop*$_2$.

riadip *num.* Two; see *dip.*

riadun *num.* Two; see *dun.*

rie *poss. cl.* A possessive classifier used for siblings or any person called sibling in the Crow kinship terminology.

rieisek *num.* Twenty; see *eisek.*

riehk *num.* Twenty; see *ehk.*

riehl *num.* Two; see *el*$_2$.

rielep *num.* Two; see *lep.*

riemen *num.* Two; see *men*$_3$.

riemwodol *num.* Two; see *mwodol.*

riemwut *num.* Two; see *mwut*$_2$.

riengoul *num.* Twenty; see *ngoul.*

riepit *num.* Two; see *pit*$_2$.

riesel *num.* Two; see *sel*$_2$.

riesou *num.* Two; see *sou₄*.

riete *num.* Two; see *te*.

riewel *num.* Two; see *wel₂*.

rioumw *num.* Two; see *umw₂*.

riopwuloi *num.* Two; see *pwuloi*.

riotumw *num.* Two; see *tumw*.

rioapoar *num.* Two; see *poar*.

rioapwong *num.* Two; see *pwong*.

rioapwoat *num.* Two; see *pwoat*.

rik *vt.* To gather, of objects on the ground, or of people.

rimpio 1. *n.* Gonorrhea. 2. *vi.* To have gonorrhea. [Jap.]

rinso *n.* Powdered soap. [Eng.]

rihng *n.* Ring, as for the finger. [Eng.]

rihp *n.* Dried out leaves of the *uhmw*.

ripe *vt.* To move, of covers, lids, tops, louvers, etc., generally of flat items parallel to the ground.

rihpe 1. *n.* A kind of magic used to render powerless one's opponent in a fight. 2. *vi.* To employ this kind of magic. —rihpehih, *vt.*

rihpehih *vt.* See *rihpe*.

rihpw *n.* Fungus, fungus infection.

ripwiripw₁ *adj.* Covered by a fungus infection.

ripwiripw₂ *n.* Fish sp..

rir *adj.* Difficult to locate or understand; hidden, concealed; vague. —ririh, *vt.*

rihr *n.* Line of debris such as seaweed, twigs, leaves, etc. floating in the ocean.

ririh *vt.* To hide behind, to conceal. —rir, *adj.*

ririnmas *n (3s: ririnmese).* Eyelash.

ririnmen *n.* Flock of birds located over a school of fish.

ririnmwomw *n.* School of fish.

ririnpaiso HONORIFIC. *n.* Speech of a chief; heart.

ririnderihleng HONORIFIC. *n.* Eyelash.

rihs *vt.* To break a long object by hand.

risiht *n.* Receipt. [Eng.]

rit- *vi.* To be opened or closed, of anything hinged. *Wenihmwo ritidi.* The door is closed. —riting, *vt.*

riting *vt.* To open or close anything hinged or attached, as a door or window. —rit-, *vi.*

ro *vi.* To be carried on a litter between forward and rear carriers. —rowe, *vt.*

roh *n.* Carrying litter requiring two or more people to carry.

roi *adj.* Of a place, unsuitable for planting because of being shaded by larger plants.

roik *vi.* To cringe.

rohk *vt.* To gather up, to catch with the hands.

rokumw *n.* Sp. of small land crab.

rokupadda 1. *vi.* To play the game, fly-take-a-bat. 2. *n.* The name of this game. [Jap.]

rokpahs *n.* Incense holder. [?]

rohlikedepw *vi.* To fish for shrimp.

rommwidi *vi.* To appear withdrawn; to calm down.

rong *vt.* To hear, to listen; to examine with a stethoscope.

rohng *n.* News.

rongamwahu *n.* Good news; good reputation; gospel, biblically.

rongkapw *n.* Current news, recent information.

rop *vi. neut.* Of Micronesian canoes, to change direction by repositioning the sail.

rohpapiso HONORIFIC. *n.* Carrying litter, for the *Nahnmwarki* or *Nahnken*.

ropwe *n3s.* Rooster's comb.

ropwen malek *n.* Plant sp., *Celosia argentea*.

rorok *adj.* Contrary to one's expectations.

rorong SLANG. *vi.* To sleep, of children.

ros *vi.* To be consumed or used up.

rohs *n.* Flower, any flowering plant. [Eng.]

rosario 1. *n.* Rosary. 2. *vi.* To say the rosary. [Span.]

roson *adj.* Healthy, of human beings.

rohsopwou *vi.* To fish for the sp. of fish, *soupwou*.

rosotakai 1. *n.* A game, involving teams in a game of catch. 2. *vi.* To play this game.

rot *adj.* Dark.

roht *n.* Darkness.

rotala *vi.* To become dark; to act irrationally; to have defective vision.

rotama *n.* Grated taro mixed with bananas and sweetened.

rotapwahk *adj.* Pitch-black; in the dark, as of one who doesn't know something.

rotensowas 1. *n.* A kind of magic that enables the user to go unnoticed, as if invisible. **2.** *vi.* To employ this kind of magic.

rotorot *adj.* Pagan, uncivilized, uneducated, uncultured.

rowe *vt.* To carry on a litter between forward and rear carriers. —**ro,** *vi.*

roake *vt.* To take in handfulls; to make a fist.

roam *n.* Rum. [Eng.]

roang *adj.* Burned, crisp, of something overcooked.

roapoahnge *vt.* To cradle something in one's arms.

roahs *n.* Whale.

Ruk₁ *n.* Truk.

ruk₂ *vi.* To hide; to take shelter.

rukih *vt.* To peep; to observe from a hidden position.

rukihdi *vt.* To ambush; to catch in the act.

rukoa *vt.* To chew; to crush. —**rukoaruk,** *vi.*

rukoaruk **1.** *vi. neut.* To chew; to crush. **2.** *adj.* Chewable, as of a soft bone. —**rukoa,** *vt.*

ruksaku *n.* Rucksack. [Jap.<Eng.]

ruhl *n.* Ruler, for measuring. [Eng.]

ruhdo *n.* Coarsely grated tapioca.

ruwahdek, also **urahdek.** *vi.* To be pulled, to be dragged. —**ruwahdeki,** *vt.*

ruwahdeki, also **urahdeki.** *vt.* To pull, to drag. —**ruwahdek,** *vi.*

ruwek *vi.* To be sprained.

ruwes *vi.* To command, to order. —**ruwese,** *vt.*

ruwese *vt.* See *ruwes.*

S

sa- *verb. pref.* A negative prefix meaning not. *pwung* correct, *sapwung* incorrect.

sah *n.* Crock. [Eng.]

saih *vt.* To paddle to. —sei$_1$, *vi.*

sahi *n.* Fleet of canoes; trip by sea, ocean voyage.

saik$_1$ *vt.* To catch, as fish.

saik$_2$, also kaik. *neg.* Not yet.

saike, also sangke. 1. *n.* A game, paper-scissors-stone. 2. *vi.* To play this game. [Jap.]

saikinte, also kaikinte. *neg.* Not yet.

saim *vt.* To sharpen to a point. —seisei$_1$, *vi.*

sain 1. *vi., vt.* To sign. 2. *n.* Signature, poster, sign, notice. [Eng.]

saingo *n.* The final activity in a competition. [Jap.]

saip *n.* Sardine.

sair *vt.* To come in contact with, to touch, to touch upon.

saireng *n.* Siren, as on a police car or ambulance. [Eng.]

sais 1. *n.* Size, as of clothing. 2. *vi.* To be the right size. [Eng.]

saida *n.* Soda, soft drink. [Jap.<Eng.]

sauk, also rauk. *vi.* To fall down, of standing objects.

saun *vt.* To make a fire; to add wood to an existing fire. —sou$_3$, *vi.*

sahused *n.* Fish sp., a sp. of shark.

Saudel *n.* A title, in the *Nahnmwarki* line.

saut *adj.* Disgusting because of filthy or unsanitary conditions.

sak HONORIFIC. *vi.* To eat. —sakan, *vt.*

sahk HONORIFIC. *n.* Food.

sakau 1. *n.* Kava, *Piper methysticum*; any intoxicating beverage. 2. *vi.* To be intoxicated, to be drunk. [Polynesian]

sakau kepeik *n.* A kava plant, requiring one person to carry it.

sakau lohpwu *n.* A kava plant, large enough that it requires being carried on a *lohpwu.*

sakau pahs *n.* A kava plant, large enough to be carried on a *pahs.*

sakau ro *n.* A kava plant, requiring two persons to carry it.

sakan HONORIFIC. *vt.* See *sak.*

sakana *n.* Fish sp.. [Jap.]

sakanakan *adj.* Bad.

sakando *n.* Second base, in baseball. [Jap.<Eng.]

sakar *n.* A boat docking or landing area used by a particular family.

sakarahl HONORIFIC. *vi.* To greet the *Nahnmwarki* or *Nahnken* when passing by.

sakarada *vi.* To request permission to leave; to confess.

sahkas 1. *n.* Circus. 2. *vi.* To walk on a tightrope. [Eng.]

sake *n.* Japanese rice wine. [Jap.]

saki 1. *n.* Jack, as an automobile jack. 2. *vi.* To jack. [Jap.<Eng.] —sakih, *vt.*

sakih *vt.* See *saki.*

sakier *n.* Bird sp., a sea bird.

sakon, also soakon. *adj.* Self-centered, demanding; of children, spoiled; of an infant, always crying. —sakone, *vt.*

sakone *vt.* To force someone to do something, to impose one's will upon another. —sakon or soakon, *adj.*

sakot 1. *n.* Breadfruit disease. 2. *vi.* Of breadfruit, to have this disease.

sakura *n.* A card game. [Jap.]

sal *vt.* To gather rope, to haul in a line.

sahl *n.* Rope, cord, line, string.

salamalam *adj.* Unconcerned about imposing on others.

salada *vi.* To be exposed; of commoners, to be seated facing the main platform in a *nahs.*

salelepek *adj.* Unreliable, inept, incompetent.

saleng *n (3s: salenge).* Ear.

salehng *vt.* To face, of inanimate objects.

saleng en eni *n.* Mushroom.

saleng medek 1. *n.* Earache. 2. *vi.* To have an earache.

saleng walek 1. *n.* A variety of taro. 2. *adj.* Having a distended, pierced earlobe in the style of the Trukese.

salenge *n3s.* The angular protrusion on either end of the hull of a Ponapean canoe.

salengopon *adj.* Deaf.

saledek *adj.* Free, relieved, unrestrained, licentious.

saledi *vi.* Of nobles, to be seated facing the commoners.

sali 1. *vi.* To eat meat or fish. 2. *n.* The meat or fish part of a meal; any complement to the main course of a meal. —selie, *vt.*

salih *vt.* To tie; to be affiliated with. —sel₁, *vi.*

sahliel *adj.* Dizzy; mentally ill or retarded.

saliokda *vt.* To suddenly realize.

salihdi *vt.* To tie up; to imprison; to detain. —selidi, *vi.*

saloh *adj.* Nervous.

salong *adj.* Hard to find.

sall *vi.* To be angry.

salla *vi.* To accidentally expose one's genitals.

sallong *n.* Tree sp., a variety of mango.

sahm₁ *n (3s: seme).* Father; any person one's father would call brother.

sahm₂ *n.* Jam, jelly. [Eng.]

sahm kahlap *n (3s: seme kahlap).* Grandfather, spouse's grandfather, father's mother's brother.

samani *vt.* To be expert at. —semen, *adj.*

samin *adj.* Messy, unsanitary, filthy.

saminimin *adj.* Uncooperative.

samurai *n.* Japanese warrior. [Jap.]

samusi *n.* Rice paddle. [Jap.]

samma *n.* Fish sp., mackerel pike. [Jap.]

sammenip *n.* Fish sp..

sampah *n.* World, earth.

sampakihda *n.* Plant sp., Arabian jasmine, *Jasminum sambac.*

sampei *n.* Any island off the coast of a main island.

sampion 1. *n.* Champion. 2. *vi.* To be a champion. [Jap.<Eng.]

sampwil *n.* Grated green banana with coconut oil.

sampwo 1. *n.* Mumps. 2. *vi.* To have the mumps.

samwa₁ *num.* Plus some. *I pwainiki tala rieisek samwa.* I bought it for twenty some dollars.

samwa₂ *n.* A term of affection used by parents with their children.

samwalahr *vi.* To depart.

samwei *n.* Fish sp., snapper, *Lethrinus ramak.*

samwei medi *n.* Fish sp., a mature *samwei.*

Samworo, also Soumwaroh. *n.* A traditional high priest.

samwodohr *vi.* To have arrived at or departed from an area.

sahn *vt.* To be unaccustomed to.

sanek *n.* Coil of sennit.

sansal 1. *adj.* Clear, evident, obvious. 2. *n.* Portrait; poster.

sansar₁ *vi.* To be sliced, to be peeled. —sere₁, *vt.*

sansar₂ *vi.* To duck, to dodge. —sarek₁, *vt.*

sansarada *vi.* To be uprooted. —sarek₃, *vt.*

sansing *vi.* To strike-out, in baseball. [Jap.]

sandangdopi 1. *n.* A game, hop-skip-jump. 2. *vi.* To play this game. [Jap.]

sandepehpa *n.* Sandpaper. [Eng.]

-sang *verb. suff.* From, in opposition to; *-sang* occurs as a separate word before locative or temporal phrases. *I aluhlahsang ohlo.* I walked away from that man. *Pwihke laudsang pwihko.* This pig is big in opposition to that pig. or This pig is bigger than that pig. *Soulik sohte pahn doadoahk sang Niehd lel Niepeng.* Soulik will not work from Monday until Thursday.

sangat *adj.* Lonesome, lonely.

Sahngoro 1. *n.* Title of the *Nahnmwarki* of Uh. 2. *vi.* To hold this title.

sangk *vi.* To come and go early in the morning; to commute.

sangke, also saike. 1. *n.* A game, paper-scissors-stone. 2. *vi.* To play this game. [Jap.]

sangkenei *vi.* To arrive or depart early in the morning.

sap *vi.* To cut into pieces. —sepe₂, *vt.*

sapa₁ *adj.* Inappropriate, bizarre, incongruous, not fitting.

sapa₂ *n.* Male pigeon.

sapak *vt.* To harvest, of bananas. —sapasap₁ or sapidi, *vi.*

sapakaris *adj.* Sexually unattractive.

sapal *vi.* To walk, implying to a destination a considerable distance away.

sapahl 1. *vi.* To repeat an activity; to do again. 2. HONORIFIC. *vi.* To return.

sapan *adj.* Generous, kind.

Sapahn *n.* Japan. [Eng.]

sapahrek *adj.* Unequal, uneven, not flush.

sapasap₁ *vi.* To be harvested, of bananas. —**sapak**, *vt.*

sapasap₂ *n.* Grass sp..

sape *vt.* To carry in one's arms.

sapei 1. *n.* Woman's sitting dance. 2. *vi.* To perform this dance.

sapeik₁ *adj.* Disobedient.

sapeik₂ *adj.* To be unable to hold one's breath for a long time under water.

sapeleng *n.* Reed sp., *Miscanthus floridulus.*

sapeng *vt.* To respond to, to answer.

sapede *n3s.* Area of a palm tree where the leaves begin to emerge from the trunk.

sahpis *n.* Service, as in a restaurant. [Jap.<Eng.]

sapidi *vi.* To be harvested, of bananas. —**sapak**, *vt.*

sapw₁ *vi.* Of kava, to reach the stage where, depending on the municipality, the fourth or fifth cup is served; of Ponapean medicine, to reach the fourth, eighth, twelfth, etc. day of taking it.

sapw₂ *num.* Hundred million.

sahpw *n (3s: sapwe).* Land, farmstead, homestead.

sapwake *n.* Hawksbill turtle.

sapwasapw *vi.* To own land; to homestead. —**sapweniki**, *vt.*

sapwad *vt.* To untie, to untangle. —**sapwedek**, *vi.*

sapwe 1. *n3s.* Depending on the municipality, the fourth or the fifth cup of kava in the kava ceremony; of Ponapean medicine, that which is taken on the fourth, eighth, twelfth, etc. day. 2. *poss. cl.* A possessive classifier used for land.

sapwel 1. *n.* Shovel. 2. *vi.* To shovel. [Eng.] —**sapwele**, *vt.*

sapwele *vt.* To shovel. [*sapwel*<Eng.] —**sapwel**, *vi.*

sapwellime HONORIFIC. *poss. cl.* A possessive classifier employed in honorific speech in place of the common language classifiers *ah* and *nah.*

sapweniki *vt.* To own, of land. —**sapwasapw**, *vi.*

sapwedek *vi.* To be untied; to be untangled. —**sapwad**, *vt.*

Sapwetan *n.* A title.

sapwung 1. *adj.* Incorrect, wrong, erroneous. 2. *n.* Mistake, error.

sapwtehn *n.* Desert.

sar *vi.* To peel, of the skin after being sunburned; to fade, as of a color; to bleach out; to let up.

sahr *n.* Mangrove crab hole.

sara₁ *vi.* To open one's mouth.

sara₂ *n.* Fish sp., squirrelfish, *Adoryx spinifer.*

sarau *n.* Fish sp., barracuda, *Sphyraena langsar* or *Sphyraena bleekeri.*

sarang *n.* Roots of kava or of the wild yam, *kehpineir.*

sarasi *n.* Bleach. [Jap.]

sarasko *n.* Bleach, especially powdered bleach. [Jap.]

sarada₁ *vi.* To look upwards.

sarada₂ *vi.* To cease, resulting in a return to normalcy.

sarawi 1. *adj.* Holy, sacred. 2. *n.* Religious service; magic; taboo.

Sarawihn Iasada *n.* Easter.

sarek₁ *vt.* To duck, to dodge. —**sansar₂**, *vi.*

sarek₂ *vt.* To relieve another of his burden.

sarek₃ *vt.* To uproot, to peel, to pry. —**sansarada**, *vi.*

saretep *vi.* To be uprooted.

sarikik *vi.* To cut one's nails.

sarip *vt.* To root, while looking for something. —**senser₁**, *vi.*

saripidi *vt.* To bury. —**seridi**, *vi.*

saroh *n.* Shame, embarrassment.

sarongorong *adj.* Pigheaded, refusing to accept advice or follow instructions.

sarohdi *vi.* To be embarrassed or humiliated.

saruwaru *adj.* Errant; always in a hurry.

sarmada 1. *n.* Underwear. 2. *vi.* To wear underwear. [Jap.]

sas₁ *vi.* To stagger.

sas₂ *adj.* Confused, said of one who misidentifies his possessions.

sasairiki *vt.* To be unaware of; to be uninformed about.

sasimi 1. *n.* Raw fish, raw meat of any kind. 2. *vi.* To eat raw fish or raw meat of any kind. [Jap.]

sadak *n.* Tree sp., *Elaeocarpus carolinensis.*

sahdo *n.* Third base, in baseball. [Jap.<Eng.]

sawa₁ *n.* A variety of taro, *Colocasia esculenta.*

sawa₂ *vi.* To be broken, of anything containing liquid, granular objects, or gas; to break, of waves; to rapidly change for the worse, of the weather or emotions.

sawahn awai *n.* A variety of taro from Hawaii, *Xanthosoma saittifolium.*

sawahn wai *n.* A variety of taro, *Xanthosoma sp..*

sawang *n.* Soup bowl. [Jap.]

sawas 1. *vi.* To help, assist, aid. 2. *n.* Help, assistance, aid. —**sewese,** *vt.*

sawi₁ *poss. cl.* A possessive classifier for clan members.

sawi₂ *n.* Fish sp., grouper, *Plectropomus leopardus, Plectropomus melanoleucus,* or *Plectropomus truncatus.*

sawi pwiliet *n.* Fish sp..

se₁ *subj. pron.* We, exclusive.

se₂ *n.* Sandy place inside the barrier reef.

se₃ *vi.* To shout in a falsetto voice, either when carrying kava or to challenge another to a fight.

sei₁ *vi.* To paddle. —**saih,** *vt.*

sei₂ *n.* Fish sp., porcupine fish.

sei₃ *n.* Soursop, *Annona muricata.*

seikan *adj.* Successful, in fishing or hunting.

seike *poss. cl.* A possessive classifier for a catch, as of fish.

seikihs *vi.* To fish for octopus.

seilipwei *vi.* To gather *lipwei,* a species of clam.

seiloak 1. *vi.* To go on a trip, to travel. 2. *n.* Trip.

seiloakoaloak *vi.* To troll while paddling. [Mokilese]

seiloangon *vi.* To gather *loangon,* a species of sea cucumber.

seimek *adj.* Fast, in walking.

seimenihke *vi.* To gather any non-swimming marine organism.

seimwoak HONORIFIC. *vi.* To sleep.

sein *n.* Chain. [Eng.]

Seini *n.* China. [Eng.]

Seipahn *n.* Saipan.

seipahsu *vi.* To gather *pahsu,* a species of clam.

seipeng *vi. neut.* To cover picked, green bananas to hurry their ripening.

seipwok 1. *n.* Breadfruit or grated banana cooked with coconut milk. 2. *vi.* To cook breadfruit or grated banana with coconut milk.

seir *n.* Generic term for *Seirin pohnpei* and *Seirin wai.*

seiren *vi.* To comply, to acquiesce, to do something against one's will.

seirin pohnpei *n.* Tree sp., *Fagraea sair,* having fragrant flowers.

seirin wai *n.* Tree sp., *Cananga odorata,* having fragrant flowers.

seisei₁ *vi.* To be sharpened to a point. —**saim,** *vt.*

seisei₂ 1. *vi.* To be given a haircut. 2. *n.* A haircut. —**sehk₁,** *vt.*

seidi HONORIFIC. *vi.* To lie down; to spend a night at.

sehu *n.* Sugar cane, *Saccharum officinarum.*

seualahl *n.* A variety of sugar cane.

seukauti, also **seukoahti.** *adj.* Carefree, happy-go-lucky.

seukoahti, also **seukauti.** *adj.* Carefree, happy-go-lucky.

seun nukini, also **seutoal.** *n.* A variety of sugar cane.

seun nta *n.* A variety of sugar cane.

seun palau *n.* A variety of sugar cane.

seun wai *n.* A variety of sugar cane.

seuneir *n.* A variety of sugar cane.

seupwet *n.* A variety of sugar cane.

seuseu *n (3s: seusewi).* Smaller tuber of a yam plant.

seutoal, also **seun nukini.** *n.* A variety of sugar cane.

sek *vi.* To ring, to bump into. —**seker,** *vt.*

sehk₁ *vt.* To cut, to give a haircut. —**seisei₂,** *vi.*

sehk₂ *n.* Jack, in cards. [Eng.]

sekeh, also **sekehn.** *adv.* Not easily.

seken *n.* Second, as a unit of time; second, in a sequence. [Eng.]

sekehn, also **sekeh.** *adv.* Not easily. *Mahr sekehn ohla.* Preserved breadfruit doesn't easily spoil.

sekenpwoud HONORIFIC. *vi.* To ask for forgiveness.

seker *vt.* To strike or hit something that makes noise; to ring, as a bell. —**sek,** *vi.*

sekere *adv.* Maybe, perhaps. *I pahn sekere laid lakapw.* I will perhaps go fishing tomorrow.

sekerehki HONORIFIC. *vt.* To inform.

sekerou *adj.* Wasteful.

sekesekere *vt.* To be most likely to be.

seked 1. *n.* Checkers. 2. *vi.* To play checkers. [Eng.]

sekid 1. *n.* Jacket. 2. *vi.* To wear a jacket. [Eng.] —**sekidih,** *vt.*

sekid welpeseng *n.* Suit coat. [*sekid*<Eng.]

sekihda *n.* Form, for the pouring of concrete. [Jap.]

sekidih *vt.* To wear a jacket. [*sekid*<Eng.] —**sekid,** *vi.*

sekpene 1. *vi.* To come into conflict. 2. *n.* Conflict, confrontation.

sekteri *n.* Secretary. [Eng.]

sel₁ *vi.* To be tied. —**salih,** *vt.*

sel₂ *num. cl.* Used in counting rope or sennit. *kisin pwehl pahsel* four balls of sennit.

sehla *n.* Sailor. [Eng.]

sele *n.* Chili pepper, *Capsicum frutescens.*

-seli *verb. suff.* Here and there, without definite direction; about. *tang* run, *tangseli* run here and there.

selie *vt.* To eat meat or fish. —**sali,** *vi.*

selin mour *n (3s: selin mouri).* Major blood vessel.

selin nta *n (3s: selinintah).* Blood vessel.

selin peleng likou *n.* Clothesline.

selidi *vi.* To be imprisoned; to be shutdown as a consequence of being in violation of the law. —**salihdi,** *vt.*

selitilit *adj.* Restless.

sellap *n.* Vine sp..

selmete *n.* Cable.

semen *adj.* Expert. —**samani,** *vt.*

Sehmen *n.* Germany.

semihs, also **simihs.** 1. *n.* Slip, chemise. 2. *vi.* To wear a slip or chemise. [Eng.]

sempoak *adj.* Unloving.

sempwe *vi.* To turn or point into the wind when sailing.

semwek 1. *adj.* Of breadfruit, overripe. 2. *n.* A breadfruit disease.

semwehmwe *adj.* Poor.

sehmwida *n.* Tree sp., *Poinciana pulcherrima.*

sens, also **sent.** *n.* Cent, money. [Eng.]

sensen 1. *n.* Skin disease caused by a fungus. 2. *vi.* To have this disease. 3. *adj.* Moldy or old tasting.

senser₁ *vi.* To root, while looking for something; to scratch, as of a chicken. —**sarip,** *vt.*

senser₂ *vi.* To weave reeds or cane, as for a fish trap.

senserek *n.* Fish sp., angelfish.

sensuh *n.* Player, athlete. [Jap.]

send *n.* Appendage, finger, toe.

senda 1. *n.* Center field, in baseball. 2. *vi.* To play center field. [Jap.<Eng.]

sendilepe *n3s.* Thumb.

sendimesemese *n3s.* Index finger.

sendin neh *n3s.* Toe.

sendin peh *n3s.* Finger.

sendohki *n.* Fighter plane. [Jap.]

sent, also **sens.** *n.* Cent, money. [Eng.]

sent mwaramwer *n.* Change, of money; coin.

Senweri *n.* January. [Eng.]

seng *vi.* To cry, to weep, to moan.

sehng *vt.* To go look for someone or something whose presence is expected.

sengeu *adj.* Lusty.

sengiseng *n.* Fish sp..

sehp *vi.* To be safe, in baseball. [Eng.]

sepe₁ *n3s.* Cheek.

sepe₂ *vt.* To cut into pieces. —**sap,** *vi.*

sepeimwekid *adj.* Quiet, not talkative, passive in a confrontation.

sepehl *adj.* Unstable, as of a canoe.

sepehlda *vi.* To capsize or turn over, of any vehicle.

seper *n.* Zipper. [Eng.]

sepit HONORIFIC. *vi.* To wait.

sepitipit *adj.* Unhurried or slow at an activity.

Septempe *n.* September. [Eng.]

sepwere *vt.* To predict the success of an activity while it is still in progress, believed to bring bad luck.

sepwikin *n.* A variety of mountain taro, *Alocasia macrorrhiza.*

sepwil- *vi.* To move; to change status. *Wasai pahn sepwilida Nahnmwarki.* The Wasai will be promoted to Nahnmwarki.

sepwiliras *interj.* An expression used to claim food dropped by another.

sehpwong 1. *n.* A type of net fishing, done at night. 2. *vi.* To do this type of net fishing.

sepwurek *vi.* To tear easily, to wear out easily, of clothing.

ser$_1$ 1. *vi.* To walk with a source of light. 2. noun form also **sehr**$_1$. *n.* A portable light source, as a torch or flashlight. —**sere**$_2$, *vt.*

ser$_2$ *vi.* To run aground.

ser$_3$ *interj.* An exclamation used to attract the attention of two or more people.

sehr$_1$, also **ser**$_1$. *n.* A portable light source, as a torch or flashlight.

sehr$_2$ *n.* Chair, seat. [Eng.]

sehr$_3$ *n.* Share, as of stock. [Eng.]

ser pahdil *n.* Palm frond torch.

serala *vi.* To happen to.

sere$_1$ *vt.* To slice, to peel with an instrument. —**sansar**$_1$, *vi.*

sere$_2$ *vt.* To provide a source of light for. —**ser**$_1$, *vi.*

sehre *vt.* To bring along.

sereu SLANG. *n.* Guy or gal.

serek 1. *vi.* To sail. 2. *n.* A sail.

serekeileng *adj.* Rude, discourteous.

sereki *vt.* To yank or jerk. —**peserek**, *vi.*

serepein *n.* Girl.

serere *vt.* To hint about something; to employ irony.

serehd *n.* Bird sp., resembling a parrot.

seri *n.* Child.

seri nenek *n.* Child born of an adulterous relationship.

seri pwelel *n.* Infant.

serien pirap *n.* Child born of an adulterous relationship.

seringiring *adj.* Almost ripe, ready to harvest.

serihso$_1$ HONORIFIC. *n.* Child of the *Nahnmwarki* or *Nahnken.*

serihso$_2$ *n.* A tiny flying insect, commonly found in the forest; another name for an *ahmw*$_1$.

serida 1. *n.* Feast given at the time the construction of a feasthouse is initiated. 2. *vi.* To prepare this feast.

seridi *vi.* To be buried. —**saripidi**, *vt.*

sero *num.* Zero. [Eng.]

serpwoatol *n.* Bottle lamp, made with a wick in a bottle of kerosene.

sehse *vi.* To not know.

sed *vi.* To place the rotten stem of *ohd* or sea water in breadfruit in order to make it soft. —**sedih**, *vt.*

sehd *n.* Ocean, sea.

Sehdan *n.* Satan, devil. [Eng.]

sedei *n.* A type of garland worn by the nobility.

sedih *vt.* See *sed.*

sehdokon *adj.* Careless about where one defecates.

set *interj.* Shit!, a mild explicative in Ponapean. [Eng.]

seht 1. *n.* Shirt. 2. *vi.* To wear a shirt. [Eng.] —**sehtih**, *vt.*

seteu *n.* Fish sp., rabbitfish, *Siganus corallinus.*

sehtih *vt.* See *seht.* [*seht*<Eng.]

setik *adj.* Quick, in performing an action.

sewe *vt.* To mix liquids with non-liquids; to exchange agricultural products for fish.

sewen mwomw 1. *n.* An exchange of agricultural products for fish. 2. *vi.* To exchange agricultural products for fish.

sewese *vt.* To help, assist, aid. —**sawas**, *vi.*

sewi *n.* Conch shell, conch shell trumpet.

sih *n.* Name of the letter *s.*

siai 1. *n.* Contest, competition. 2. *vi.* To engage in a contest.

siai en padok kehp 1. *n.* Yam raising competition. 2. *vi.* To engage in a yam raising competition.

siamwed *n.* A large *ah*, a fish sp..

siar *vi.* To sizzle or crackle.

siemen 1. *n.* A kind of magic, used to destroy agricultural products. 2. *vi.* To employ this kind of magic.

siepil 1. *n.* A kind of magic, performed upstream from a bather which results in blindness. 2. *vi.* To employ this kind of magic.

sioahk *n.* Bird sp., black in color.

sik *vi.* To bounce, to skip.

sik- *vi.* To protrude; to surpass previous performance or behavior. *Meteho sikilahsang dinapwo.* The nail protruded from the board. *Ma ke likawih likowen, ke pahn siksang mahs.* If you wear that clothing, you will surpass (your appearance) in the past.

sihk₁ *n.* Bird sp., a white sea bird.

sihk₂ *n.* Penis of an infant.

sika *n.* Cigarette, cigar. [Eng.]

sikaliwi *n.* The liquid gathered from the coconut flower, sometimes used to make molasses or fermented to make an intoxicating beverage.

sikamwerada HONORIFIC. *vi.* To wash one's hands.

sikarer, also **arer.** *vi.* To spray or blow inside, of windblown rain.

sikasik *adj.* Bouncy.

sike *n3s.* Top and bottom fins of a fish.

sikel *vi.* To tiptoe.

siken *vt.* To push. —**pisiken,** *vi.*

sikeng 1. *vi.* To take a test or examination. 2. *n.* Test, examination. [Jap.]

sikinkihri *n3s.* Lower back, tailbone area.

sikihr *n (3s: sikihri).* Tailbone area.

sikongki *n.* Phonograph. [Jap.]

sihl *n.* Seal, the sea mammal. [Eng.]

silasil 1. *n.* Magical protection against another's harmful magic, medicine, or spirits. 2. *vi.* To obtain such magical protection.

sile₁ *vt.* To guard. —**pisilei,** *vi.*

sile₂ *n.* Clam sp.; adze, axe.

sile moahl *n.* A kind of adze.

sileimw *vi.* To be left behind to guard a house.

sileit₁ *n.* Slate. [Eng.]

sileit₂ *n.* Breech birth.

sihleng HONORIFIC. *n (3s: sihlangi).* Face.

siliakan *num.* Thirty; see *ehk.*

siliel *num.* Three; see *el₂.*

silik *n.* Silk. [Eng.]

silika *num.* Three; see *ka₂.*

silikap *num.* Three; see *kap.*

silikis *num.* Three; see *kis₂.*

silimen *num.* Three; see *men₃.*

silimwodol *num.* Three; see *mwodol.*

silimwut *num.* Three; see *mwut₂.*

silinder *n.* Cylinder, of an engine. [Eng.]

silingoul *num.* Thirty; see *ngoul.*

silipa *num.* Three; see *pa₃.*

silipak *num.* Three; see *pak₁.*

silipali *num.* Three; see *pali₁.*

silipar *num.* Three; see *par₂.*

siliper *n.* Silver. [Eng.]

silipit *num.* Three; see *pit₂.*

silipoar *num.* Three; see *poar.*

silipwong *num.* Three; see *pwong.*

silipwoat *num.* Three; see *pwoat.*

silipwuloi *num.* Three; see *pwuloi.*

silira *num.* Three; see *ra.*

silihsek *num.* Thirty; see *eisek.*

silisel *num.* Three; see *sel₂.*

silisou *num.* Three; see *sou₄.*

silisop *num.* Three; see *sop₂.*

silidip *num.* Three; see *dip.*

silidun *num.* Three; see *dun.*

silite *num.* Three; see *te.*

silitumw *num.* Three; see *tumw.*

siliwel *num.* Three; see *wel₂.*

siluh *num.* Three; see *-u.*

siluhmw *num.* Three; see *umw₂.*

sillep *num.* Three; see *lep.*

sim *vt.* To gather up rope, to coil rope.

simaht *adj.* Smart, intelligent. [Eng.]

simekiri *vi.* To be closed, of a charge account. [Jap.]

simend, also **siment.** *n.* Cement, concrete, mortar; filling, of a tooth. [Eng.]

siment, also **simend.** *n.* Cement, concrete, mortar; filling, of a tooth. [Eng.]

simihs, also **semihs.** 1. *n.* Slip, chemise. 2. *vi.* To wear a slip or chemise. [Eng.]

simihden *n.* A variety of swamp taro.

simpung *n.* Newspaper. [Jap.]

simw *vi. neut.* To swarm; to seize food at a feast, done by a large group of people. —**simwih,** *vt.*

sihmw *n.* The seizing of yams at a funeral feast.

simwih *vt.* To swarm on; to seize food at a feast, done by a large group of people. —**simw,** *vi.*

sihn *n.* Chain. [Eng.]

sinakoke *n.* Synagogue; chapel, used by protestants. [Eng.]

sineipw *n.* An island in a river or stream.

sinek *n.* Snake. [Eng.]

sino *n.* Snow. [Eng.]

sinom *vi.* To sink in; to penetrate, to pierce.

sinopwunopw *adj.* Fat, healthy looking, of infants or young domestic animals.

sinter *n.* Any species of ginger plant. [Eng.]

sing *vi.* To fart. —singid, *vt.*

singiles *n.* T-shirt, singlet. [Eng.]

singid *vt.* To fart at. —sing, *vi.*

sihp₁ *vi.* To shave. [Eng.] —sihpih₁, *vt.*

sihp₂ 1. *n.* A sieve. 2. *vi. neut.* To strain in a sieve. [Eng.] —sihpih₂, *vt.*

sipal *vi.* To cross over an obstacle; to skip, as a grade in school or a title.

sipalla HONORIFIC. *vi.* To die.

Sipein *n.* Spain. [Eng.]

sihpek HONORIFIC. *vi.* To sneeze.

sipel *vi.* To spell. [Eng.] —sipelih, *vt.*

sipele *vt.* To go beyond, to exceed, to surpass, to overtake.

sipelih *vt.* To spell. [*sipel*<Eng.] —sipel, *vi.*

siped *vt.* To shake out with a snapping motion; to brush off. —sipisip, *vi.*

sihpih₁ *vt.* To shave. [*sihp₁*<Eng.] —sihp₁, *vi.*

sihpih₂ *vt.* To strain in a sieve. [*sihp₂*<Eng.] —sihp₂, *vi.*

sipiring₁ *n.* Spring, as a coil spring. [Eng.]

sipiring₂ *n.* T-shirt, singlet. [Jap.]

sipisip 1. *vi.* To fish with a throw line; to be shaken out with a snapping motion; to be brushed off. 2. *n.* Throw line fishing. —siped, *vt.*

sipihdo *adj.* Speedy, fast. [Jap.<Eng.]

sipuwer ARCHAIC. *vi.* To trim hair at or below the base of the neck.

sippwu *n.* Tip, in baseball. [Jap.<Eng.]

sihpw₁ *n.* Chief magistrate. [Eng.]

sihpw₂ *n.* Sheep. [Eng.]

sipwe *vt.* To hold in contempt; to refuse to obey.

sihr *n.* A throwing stick, typically a reed, used in the game *peisihr.*

siraik *n.* Strike, in baseball. [Jap.<Eng.]

sirang *adj.* Ray-like, fanning, kinky.

sirangarang *adj.* Ray-like, pointing in all directions.

sirangk *n.* Cabinet, particularly one in which food is stored. [Ger.]

sirangkau *adj.* Said of one who ignores others. [Jap.] —sirangkawe, *vt.*

sirangkawe *vt.* To ignore. [*sirangkau*<Jap.] —sirangkau, *adj.*

sirei *vi.* To smile.

siring *vt.* To shout at someone to stop him from doing something.

sirkumsais *vi.* To be circumcised. [Eng.] —sirkumsaisih, *vt.*

sirkumsaisih *vt.* To circumcise. [*sirkumsais*<Eng.] —sirkumsais, *vi.*

sis₁ *vi.* To speak with an accent.

sis₂ *vi.* To shiver.

sihs *n.* Cheese. [Eng.]

sisel 1. *n.* Chisel. 2. *vi.* To chisel. [Eng.] —sisele, *vt.*

sisele *vt.* See *sisel.* [*sisel*<Eng.]

Sises, also Iesus. *n.* Jesus. [Eng.]

siset *n.* Scissors. [Eng.]

sisipwai HONORIFIC. *n3s.* Nose.

sispando 1. *n.* Brassiere, bra. 2. *vi.* To wear a brassiere or bra. [Jap.<Eng.]

sidail *n.* Style. [Eng.]

sidakin 1. *n.* Stockings, socks. 2. *vi.* To wear stockings or socks. [Eng.]

sidamp 1. *n.* A stamp, trademark. 2. *vi.* To be stamped. [Eng.] —sidampih, *vt.*

sidampih *vt.* To stamp. [*sidamp*<Eng.] —sidamp, *vi.*

sidahs 1. *n.* Starch. 2. *vi. neut.* To starch. [Eng.] —sidahsih, *vt.*

sidahsih *vt.* See *sidahs.* [*sidahs*<Eng.]

sidihma *n.* Steamer. [Eng.]

sihdiro *vi.* To be embarrassed by the unexpected.

sidohp *n.* Stove. [Eng.]

sidohsa *n.* Automobile, car. [Jap.]

sidohwa *n.* Store. [Eng.]

sihdnaip *n.* Sheath knife, hunting knife, diving knife, dagger. [Eng.]

so *vi.* To be saturated.

soh *sent. adv.* No.

soepwel *adj.* Irresponsible.

soher *neg.* No longer. *I soher pahn kohla.* I no longer will go.

sohiahia 1. *n.* Heartburn. 2. *vi.* To have heartburn.

sohiak *n.* The second sprouting of a yam, after the vine dies off the first time.

soiu₁ *n.* Soy sauce. [Jap.]

soiu₂ *n.* Tree sp..

soik *vi.* To politely refuse an offer.

soire *adj.* Unlimited, infinite.

soisoi *adj.* Favored, well-loved, of a child or pet.

sou₁ *n (3s: sowi, sawi).* Exogamous, matrilineal clan.

sou₂ *vi.* To move, to change residence.

sou₃ *vi.* To be made, of a fire. —**saun,** *vt.*

sou₄ *num. cl.* Used to count piles of feces. *pwise pahsou* four piles of feces.

sou₅ *neg.* Not, used in negative questions. *Ke sou pwangadahr?*Haven't you gotten tired?

sou₆ ARCHAIC. *n.* Sun.

sou-₁ *aff.* Derivational prefix meaning 'an expert at' or 'a practioner of', used to form nouns from verbs. *kohp* to prophesy, *soukohp* prophet.

sou-₂ *verb. pref.* A negative prefix meaning not or 'the opposite of'. *mwahu* good, *soumwahu* ill.

souapwal *n.* Blood brother, one fed at the same breast as a child.

soukautih *adj.* Unconcerned.

Soukise *n.* Title of the *Nahnmwarki* of Kiti.

soukohp *n.* Prophet.

soulap *n (3s: soulepe).* Wife's mother, all women one's wife calls mother; for women, the husband of all females called child.

Souleng *n.* Christian.

Soulik *n.* A title.

soulikilik *adj.* Distrustful.

Soulikin Sapawas *n.* A title.

Soulikin Soledi . A title.

Soulikin Dol *n.* A title.

soulipilipil *adj.* Not choosy.

soumahk *adj.* Bold, brazen, insensitive.

Soumaka *n.* A title.

soumaleu *vi.* To prepare an *uhmw*, so that it is ready to be lit. —**soumalewe,** *vt.*

soumalewe *vt.* See *soumaleu.*

Soumas *n.* Chief of a section of land; member of the clan of the *Nahnmwarki* or *Nahnken.*

Soumadau *n.* A title.

soumoahl *n.* The principal kava stone in a *nahs*, from which the *Nahnmwarki* is served.

soumwahu 1. *n.* Sickness, disease, illness. 2. *adj.* Sick, diseased, ill.

soumwahu en lih 1. *n.* Menstruation. 2. *vi.* To menstruate.

soumwahu en mpwei 1. *n.* Ulcers. 2. *vi.* To have ulcers.

soumwahu en mwasahl 1. *n.* Hernia. 2. *vi.* To have a hernia.

soumwahu en wai 1. *n.* Cold, flu. 2. *vi.* To have a cold or the flu.

soumwahn *neg.* Not at all. *I soumwahn kak kilang.* I can't see at all.

Soumwaroh, also Samworo. *n.* A traditional high priest.

soumwet *n.* Farmer.

soun *n.* Practitioner of; this word is typically written attached to the word it precedes.

sounapwalih *vt.* To care for.

souneliel *n.* Masseur, masseuse, one who practices the art of massage for its healing powers.

sounet *vi.* To play a game involving pretending.

Souniap *n.* A clan name.

sounkamehlel *n.* Witness; judge, except in court.

sounkanekid *n.* Treasurer.

sounkapakap *n.* Prayer leader.

sounkapahndil *n.* An intermediary for a boy and a girl.

sounkaraun *n.* False accuser.

sounkadeik *n.* Biblically, the role of God as judge in the last judgement; judgement.

sounkadehde *n.* Witness.

sounkadip *n.* Prosecutor, accuser, tattletale.

Sounkawad *n.* A clan name.

sounkaweid *n.* Advisor.

sounkawehwe *n.* Interpreter.

sounkeneitik *n.* Midwife.

sounkeseu *n.* Inspector; laboratory technician.

sounkoul *n.* Singer; in the Protestant church, a song leader.

sounkolukol *n.* The person who holds the cup during the preparation of kava.

sounkomour *n.* Savior.

sounkopwung *n.* Judge, in court.

sounkohwa *n.* Deacon.

sounlaid *n.* Fisherman.

sounlih *n. Lihli* maker.

sounlokaia *n.* Spokesman.

sounmahlen *n.* Painter.

Sounmaraki *n.* A clan name.

sounmwadong *n.* Player, athlete.

sounne *n.* One who is in charge of distributing food at a *kamadipw.*

sounnet *n.* Store clerk.

sounpar 1. *n.* Year. 2. *n (3s: sounpere).* Age.

sounpadahk *n.* Teacher; preacher.

sounpei *n.* Soldier.

sounpei nansapw *n.* Army.

Sounpelienpil *n.* A clan name.

sounpiah *n.* Maker of coconut cream for *lihli.*

sounpok *n.* Batter, in baseball.

Sounpwok *n.* A clan name.

sounpwong *n.* Month; moon.

sounpwong weneu *n.* A variety of wet land taro.

sounrar *n.* One who peels the breadfruit in the preparation of *lihli.*

Sounrohi *n.* A clan name.

Sounsamaki *n.* A clan name.

sounsawas *n.* Attorney, lawyer, defender.

sounsenoh *adj.* Unconcerned.

soundeisakau *n.* Director of a feast.

soundeidei *n.* Tailor.

soundolung *n.* Harvester.

soundoar *n.* Savior.

sountomw *n.* Propitiator.

sounwielioal *n.* Electrician.

sounwiemisihn *n.* Mechanic.

sounwiengi *n.* Dentist.

sounwinahni *n.* Shaman, sorcerer.

sounwini *n.* Practitioner of native Ponapean medicine.

soupal *n.* Expert; expert canoe builder.

Soupeidi, also Sohpeidi. *n.* Title holder in the *Nahnmwarki* line.

soupisek *adj.* Busy.

soupoad *n.* Historian, one known for his knowledge of Ponapean history.

Soupwan *n.* A title.

soupwerik *n.* Dance master, one known for his knowledge of Ponapean dances.

souse *n.* Master carpenter.

soused *n.* Expert fisherman.

sousou *n (3s: sousowi).* Grave, cemetery.

soudi *vi.* To bury in the mud, of crabs.

soutik *n.* Evening.

soutuk *adj.* Everlasting.

souwas *n.* Noon.

Souwel en Wasai *n.* A title.

Souwel Lapalap *n.* A title, in the *Nahnken* line.

Souwene *n.* A title.

sok₁ *vi.* To take a step, to set one's footing; to land, of anything capable of flight; in the water, to touch the bottom with one's feet; of kava, to begin to have an effect on one.

sok₂ *vi.* To become overgrown.

sok₃ *vt.* To bite, used only with reference to rats.

sohk₁ *vt.* To eat, drink, or smoke.

sohk₂ *n.* Chalk. [Eng.]

sokamah 1. *n.* The rhythmic pounding of the kava stones after the kava is prepared. 2. *vi.* To rhythmically pound a kava stone after the kava is prepared.

sohkatepe 1. *adj.* Useless. 2. *n.* Little finger.

Sokehs *n.* Name of a municipality in Ponape.

sohko *n.* Warehouse. [Jap.]

sokolahde *n.* Chocolate. [Span.]

sokolei *n.* Dwarf; leprechaun-like being said to dwell in the forest.

sokoled *n.* Chocolate. [Eng.]

sokoluhla *adj.* Impenitent.

sokon 1. *n.* Cane. 2. *vi.* To walk with a cane.

sokorohn *interj.* Never mind!

sokorohnki *vt.* To pay no attention to, to be unconcerned about. *E sokorohnki en ohlo ah koasoaio.* He paid no attention to that man's story.

sokko *interj.* That's admirable! [Jap.]

sokmwotou *vi.* To sit with one's legs dangling.

sohla, also solahr. *neg.* No longer. *I sohla soumwahu.* I'm no longer sick.

sohlap *adj.* Diluted, of a nature that it takes a lot to make a little.

solahr, also sohla. *neg.* No longer. *I solahr soumwahu.* I'm no longer sick.

sohmaleh *n.* Grass sp., *Cyrtococcum patens.*

sompihr *n.* Airplane. [*sohp*<Eng.]

sompihr en doulik *n.* Weather plane. [*sohp*<Eng.]

sohmw *n.* Mangrove sp., *Bruguiera conjugata.*

sohn *vt.* To soak; to plant yams.

song *vt.* To try, to attempt; to taste.

sohng 1. *vt.* To measure, to survey. 2. *n.* Measurement, pattern.

sohng karakar *n.* Temperature.

songaipwisi 1. *n.* An obstacle race. 2. *vi.* To run an obstacle race. [Jap.]

songosong *n.* Temptation.

songmar 1. *n.* Feast of preserved breadfruit. 2. *vi.* To prepare this feast.

songmaterek *vi.* To fish for the first time after someone's burial to test whether the spirit of the deceased will bring good or bad luck.

sop$_1$ *vi.* To stop by, to stop in on, to visit.

sop$_2$ *num. cl.* Used in counting stalks. *sehu silisop* three stalks of sugarcane.

sohp *n.* Ship. [Eng.]

sopa *n.* Soup. [Jap.]

sohpai *n.* Business. [Jap.]

sohpei- *vi.* To turn toward, to face. *Ohlo soupeido.* That man turned towards me.

Sohpeidi, also **Soupeidi**. *n.* Title holder in the *Nahnmwarki* line; member of the same clan as the *Nahnmwarki*.

sopin nanwehwe *n.* Rocket. [*sohp*<Eng.]

sopidu *n.* Submarine. [*sohp*<Eng.]

sopo *vi.* To flee.

sopohla *vi.* To run off with a woman, to elope.

sopuk *vt.* To intercept, to interrupt.

sopw *adj.* Saturated with pomade or hair lotion.

sohpw$_1$ *n.* A Japanese unit of measurement of area, approximately 100,000 square feet. [Jap.]

sohpw$_2$ *n.* Soap. [Eng.]

sopwou *n.* Fish sp., usually found in mangrove swamps.

sopwoupwou *adj.* Orphaned.

sohpwoson *adj.* Skeptical.

sohr *adj.* Transient.

sohrala *vi.* To vanish, to disappear.

sohrahn *n.* Pre-dawn morning hours.

sorapang *n.* Abacus. [Jap.]

sohri 1. *n.* Zories, thongs. 2. *vi.* To wear zories or thongs. [Jap.]

sos *adj.* Stinging.

Sohseng *n.* Korea. [Jap.<Korean]

soso *vi.* To burp, of a baby.

sohso *n.* Inheritance.

sosohng *n.* Practice, rehearsal; measurement.

sohdo 1. *n.* Shortstop, in baseball. 2. *vi.* To play shortstop. [Jap.<Eng.]

sohte *neg.* Not, none, nothing. *I sohte pahn mwadong.* I will not play. *Sohte rais wasaht.* There is no rice here.

sohte lipilipil *interj.* It makes no difference!

sohte pwerieng *interj.* It's really funny!; It's really good!

sohtik *adj.* Concentrated, of a nature that a little goes a long way, like pepper.

sohwar *adj.* Unworthy.

sohwawi *adj.* Lacking respect.

sowe$_1$ *vt.* To add liquid to a solid.

sowe$_2$ *n3s.* Back.

sowelihmw HONORIFIC. *n.* Broom made from the inner ribs of palm fronds.

sowuhk$_1$ *n.* An expert net maker.

sowuhk$_2$ 1. *n.* A type of net fishing, done by setting a net at high tide and trapping fish as the tide recedes. 2. *vi.* To do this type of fishing.

soai 1. *n.* Tale, story. 2. *vi.* To tell a tale or bedtime story. —**soaia**, *vt.*

soaia *vt.* See *soai.*

soaipoad *n.* Legend, story based partially on fact.

soakon, also **sakon**. *adj.* Self-centered, demanding; of children, spoiled; of an infant, always crying. —**sakone**, *vt.*

soakoa *n.* Hole among the rocks used as a place to defecate in.

soahl *n.* Salt. [Eng.]

soaloalekeng *adj.* Ignorant.

soallap *adj.* Crude, in manners or action.

soan *adj.* Aligned, arranged, settled, ordered.

soahn *vi.* To be wounded.

soanop *n.* Ball of sennit.

soahng *n.* Kind, sort, type.

soangiangi *adj.* Lethargic, listless.

soar *n (3s: soare).* Inner quality, of a person.

soahrong *n.* Ridgepole of a building.

su *vi.* Of two marbles, to be separated by the distance of an outstretched hand. [Jap.]

suika *n.* Watermelon, *Citrullus vulgaris.* [Jap.]

suk *vt.* To pound.

suke *n.* Sugar. [Eng.]

sukiaki *n.* Sukiyaki. [Jap.]

sukuhl 1. *vi.* To attend school. 2. *n.* School. [Eng.] —**sukuhlih**, *vt.*

sukuhlih *vt.* To teach. [*sukuhl*<Eng.]
—sukuhl, *vi.*

sukumei 1. *vi.* To masturbate. 2. *n.*
Masturbation.

sukuras *vi.* To scratch, in pool.
[Jap.<Eng.]

sukuru *n.* Screw. [Eng.]

sukuruhdi *vi.* To stay up and party all
night. [*sukuru*<Eng.]

sukrihn *n.* Screen. [Eng.]

sukweia *n.* Square, the carpenter's tool.
[Jap.<Eng.]

Sulai *n.* July. [Eng.]

suhmwong *vi.* To order. [Jap.]
—suhmwongih, *vt.*

suhmwongih *vt.* To order.
[*suhmwong*<Jap.] —suhmwong, *vi.*

sumwoak *vi.* To smoke. [Eng.]
—sumwoake, *vt.*

sumwoake *vt.* See *sumwoak.*
[*sumwoak*<Eng.]

sumwumw *n.* Trochus shell.

Suhn *n.* June. [Eng.]

sunname *n.* Surname. [Ger.]

supiran *vi.* To sing soprano. [Eng.]

suhpw *n.* Soup. [Eng.]

supwo *n.* A Japanese unit of
measurement of area, approximately
36 square feet. [Jap.]

suhpwu *n.* Innertube. [Jap.<Eng.]

supwuhn 1. *n.* Spoon. 2. *vi.* To eat
with a spoon. [Eng.] —supwuhnih, *vt.*

supwuhnih *vt.* To spoon.
[*supwuhn*<Eng.] —supwuhn, *vi.*

suhr *vi.* To sink in mud; to wade in
mud.

suhre *n.* Fish sp., barracuda, *Sphyraena
barracuda.* [?]

suripak *vi.* To jitterbug. [Eng.]

suhdo *vt.* To use judo on; to throw or
toss someone. [Jap.]

sut *n.* Suit, in cards. [Eng.]

suht 1. *n.* Shoes. 2. *vi.* To wear shoes.
[Eng.] —suhtih, *vt.*

suhtih *vt.* To wear shoes. [*suht*<Eng.]
—suht, *vi.*

suwaimwot HONORIFIC. *vi.* To whistle.

suwanawan *adj.* Attractive, excellent.

suwei *adj.* Boastful.

suwed *adj.* Bad.

skahdo 1. *n.* Skirt. 2. *vi.* To wear a
skirt. [Jap.<Eng.]

skengk *vi.* To skunk someone, to take
all the tricks in a card game. [Eng.]

skohso *n.* Airport, airfield. [Jap.]

skuhder *n.* Scooter, motorcycle. [Eng.]

skrudraipa *n.* Screwdriver.
[Jap.<Eng.]

spahk *n.* Spark plug. [Eng.]

speht *n.* Spade, in cards. [Eng.]

spihdpwoht *n.* Speedboat. [Eng.]

sdop *vi.* To stop. [Eng.]

swain *n.* Lace, attached to the bottom
of a slip for decoration. [?]

swangke *n.* Limeade, sugar water. [?]

D

da *interr.* What. *Pwuhk da?* What book?

-da *verb. suff.* Upwards; used with adjectives with an inchoative meaning; with verbs of cooking, detaching, wearing, and acquisition it signals the action has been carried through to its logical conclusion; with verbs of perception or thinking it indicates the thing being perceived or thought of has suddenly come into one's consciousness; with some verbs naming bodily activities it is used to indicate that an action was performed accidentally. *dou* climb, *douda* climb upwards; *katik* bitter, *katikada* get bitter; *kukih* cook (it), *kukihda* cook (it) up; *taman* remember, *tamanda* suddenly remember; *kang* eat, *kangada* accidentally eat.

dah *interr.* What. *Kowe me wahdo apeho? Dah?* Are you the one who brought that thing? What?

daia *n.* Tire. [Eng.]

daiasu *n.* Ship, usually one made of steel. [Jap.]

daiker *n.* Tiger. [Eng.]

daikong *n.* Radish. [Jap.]

daiksang, also deiksang. *n.* Carpenter, carpentry. [Jap.]

dail 1. *n.* Tile. 2. *vi.* To lay tile. [Eng.] —dailih, *vt.*

dailih *vt.* See *dail.*

daip 1. *n.* Typewriter. 2. *vi. neut.* To type. [Eng.]

daipih *vt.* See *daip.* [*daip*<Eng.]

daipraida *n.* Typewriter. [Jap.<Eng.]

dairuk, also pairuk₁. *vi.* To bend forward from the waist; to walk in a stooped position; to bow.

daidowa *n.* War, particularly the second world war; dispute. [Jap.]

daiwang *n.* A variety of banana.

dau *adj.* Overtired, as of a muscle.

dahu 1. *n.* Channel, canal, a passage in a reef. 2. POLITE. *n* (*3s: dowe*). Anus, vagina.

Dauk *n.* The third ranking title in the *Nahnmwarki* line.

daul *n.* Towel. [Eng.]

daulap *n.* Main channel.

daulih *vt.* To pass by, to go beyond; after, with reference to telling time. —douluhl, *vi.*

daur₁ *vt.* To weave a net. —dou₁, *vi.*

daur₂ *vt.* To climb; to follow laws, regulations, etc. —dou₂, *vi.*

dauso HONORIFIC. *n.* Anus.

dak *vi.* To rise, of the sun and the moon.

dahk *n.* Fish sp., a kind of needle fish.

daka, also dakadopi. *vi.* To high jump. [Jap.]

dakapahr HONORIFIC. *n3s.* Cane.

dakasingai *n.* Trochus shell. [Jap.]

dakadak dipenihd *n.* Feast given separately to the *Nahnmwarki* and *Nahnken* as sennit is prepared.

dakadakiso, also dakeiso. HONORIFIC. *n.* Stone placed in front of an entrance to a house, used to wipe one's feet on.

dakadopi, also daka. 1. *vi.* To high jump. 2. *n.* High jump. [Jap.]

dake₁ *vt.* To ride in or on a vehicle; to be the first or best, to top all others.

dake₂ HONORIFIC. *vt.* To drink.

dahkei *interr.* What things?, plural. *Dahkei men?* What are those?

dakeiso, also dakadakiso. HONORIFIC. *n.* Stone placed in front of an entrance to a house, used to wipe one's feet on.

daker *vt.* To shine on or in. *Ketepino daker nan meseiet.* The sun is shining in my face.

dahkihla *vt.* To watch intently. —dahla, *vi.*

dako *n.* Kite. [Jap.]

dahkot *interr.* What thing?, singular. *Dahkot men?* What is that?

dakuwang *n.* Pickled radish. [Jap.]

daks, also daksis. *n.* Tax. [Eng.]

daksi *n.* Taxi; slang for whore. [Eng.]

daksis, also daks. *n.* Tax. [Eng.]

dahl *n.* Coconut cup, dish, plate.

dahl sarawi *n.* Chalice.

dahla *vi.* To watch intently; to be spellbound, to be stupified. —dahkihla, *vt.*

daliere *n.* Fish sp., a kind of frog fish.

dahlimw *vi. neut.* To mop, to sponge off, to wipe. —**dahlimwih**, *vt.*

dahlimwih *vt.* See *dahlimw.*

dalok *n.* Food made from the meat of a sprouting coconut.

daldod *adj.* Said of one who drinks kava out of turn, one cup after another.

dahm 1. *n.* Outrigger of a canoe. 2. *n* *(3s: deme).* Directly possessed to mean (its) outrigger.

dama *n.* Lightbulb, bullet, pool ball. [Jap.]

damango *n.* Egg; zero, as a score. [Jap.]

damaski 1. *n.* The game of pool. 2. *vi.* To play pool. [Jap.]

dahme 1. *interr.* What. *Dahme ke wia aio?* What did you do yesterday? 2. *interr.* Used in combination with the suffix *-ki* to mean why. *Dahme ke kohkihdo?* Why did you come here?

dameni *vi.* To call interference in the marble game *anaire.* [Jap.]

dampangkot ARCHAIC. *vi.* A command to wipe the hibiscus bast well because of debris in the kava cup.

dampwo *n.* Rice paddy. [Jap.]

dampwulo *n.* Of a ship, the hold or the area below decks. [Eng.]

dahmwar HONORIFIC. *vi.* To give a title.

damwer *vt.* To caress, to rub, to pat affectionately; to pat the back end of a canoe on the outrigger side, a ceremonial action. —**demwidemw**, *vi.*

dana *n.* Shelf. [Jap.]

dane *n.* Seedling; small garden. [Jap.]

dahng *n (3s: denge).* Thigh.

dangaudek *adj.* Sluggish, lazy.

dangahnga *adj.* Lazy, to a great degree; lethargic.

dangapaur *adj.* Lazy to an extreme degree, wishing only to eat, sleep, and defecate.

dahnge *interr.* What, implying enumeration. *Dahnge me ke pahn wahdo?* What are you going to bring?

dangepel *adj.* Lame, crippled.

dangerei *adj.* Long-legged.

dangkaido *n.* Searchlight. [Jap.]

dangku *n.* A military tank. [Jap.<Eng.]

dap *vi.* To have the foreskin of the penis withdrawn.

dap- *vi.* To be pulled apart, to be pulled off. *Koakono dampeseng.* That box was pulled apart. —**dapeng**, *vt.*

dapadap *vi.* To catch, as a ball; to play catch; to play jacks; to juggle. —**daper**, *vt.*

dapeng *vt.* To pull apart, to pull off. —**dap-**, *vi.*

daper *vt.* To catch, as a ball. —**dapadap**, *vi.*

daperedi *vt.* To catch on, to learn; to tune in, as a radio station.

dapi 1. *n.* Tabi shoes. 2. *vi.* To wear tabi shoes. [Jap.]

dapiohka *n.* Cassava, manioc, tapioca. [Eng.]

dahpw, also **depw**. *n.* Tub. [Eng.]

dahpwohlin *n.* Tarpaulin. [Eng.]

dar₁ *vt.* To strike, of a fish. —**der**, *vi.*

dar₂ *vt.* To pick leaves or flowers. —**dender**, *vi.*

dahr 1. *vi.* To roll; of fish, to school during spawning season. 2. *adj.* Quick, in motion.

darai *n.* Washtub, basin. [Jap.]

darak *n.* Burial chant.

dararan *n.* Crumb, sleep, crust, a dry layer of a bodily secretion.

darop *n.* Fish sp., yellow eyed surgeonfish.

dahrkipene ARCHAIC. *vt.* To bring together, to assemble. *E dahrkipene aramas ekei.* He brought some people together.

dahda ARCHAIC. *n.* Omen, warning.

dadimai 1. *vi. neut.* To finish roofing a house, accompanied by a feast. 2. *n.* The name of the feast. [Jap.]

dahduwe *interr.* How, in what manner, possibly from *dahkot duwe.*

dawas, also **dowas**. HONORIFIC. *n (3s: dewese).* Mouth.

dawasi *n.* Japanese brush. [Jap.]

dawaspeseng HONORIFIC. *vi.* To open one's mouth to speak. —**dewesepeseng**, *vt.*

dawado HONORIFIC. *vi.* To rinse one's mouth, to gargle.

dawih *vt.* To inspect, examine, or check. —**dou₃**, *vi.*

de₁ *conj.* Or. *Ke pahn doadoahk de ke pahn meir?* Are you going to work or are you going to sleep?

de₂ *conj. adv.* Lest, when used in combination with *pwe. Kanaieng pwe* *ke de pwupwidi.* Be careful lest you fall.

deh, also **dehr.** *neg.* Not, used to negate commands. *Ke deh alu mwohn aramas.* Don't walk in front of people.

dei *adj.* Far, far along, unsurpassed.

deiad 1. *vi. neut.* To embroider. 2. *n.* Embroidery. —**deiadih,** *vt.*

deiadih *vt.* To embroider. —**deiad,** *vi.*

deied 1. *vi.* To eat breakfast. 2. *n.* Breakfast.

deikapwur 1. *n.* A type of embroidery. 2. *vi.* To do this type of embroidery.

deikenepeng *n.* Fish sp., castor-oil fish.

deikilelenwad 1. *n.* A type of embroidery, using x-stitches. 2. *vi.* To do this type of embroidery.

deiksang, also **daiksang.** *n.* Carpenter, carpentry. [Jap.]

deip 1. *n.* Tape, tape recorder. 2. *vi.* To record with a tape recorder. [Eng.] —**deipih,** *vt.*

deipih *vt.* To record something with a tape recorder. [*deip*<Eng.] —**deip,** *vi.*

deipin 1. *vi. neut.* To patch. 2. *n.* A patch. —**deipina,** *vt.*

deipina *vt.* See *deipin.*

deipw *n.* Pandanus sp., *Pandanus pulposus,* used for making baskets, hats, and sails, the fruit of which is edible.

deipwel *vi.* To move earth, as in the preparation of a house foundation.

deipwukuro, also **depwukuro.** 1. *n.* Glove. 2. *vi.* To wear gloves. [Jap.]

deisakau *vi.* To direct a kava ceremony.

deidei 1. *vi. neut.* To sew; to dig; to root, as a pig. 2. *n.* Needlework. —**dehk,** *vt.*

deitimw *vi. neut.* To put a ring in an animal's nose. —**deitimwih,** *vt.*

deitimwih *vt.* See *deitimw.*

dehu *n (3s: dewe).* Rank or station; area or location; place for sexual liaison.

deuk *vt.* To fill a container with food.

dek₁ *n.* Deck, of a ship. [Eng.]

dek₂ *n.* Bank of a taro patch.

dehk *vt.* To sew; to dig; to root, as a pig. —**deidei,** *vi.*

deke *n.* Island.

dekehnering HONORIFIC. *n (3s: dekehneringi).* Eyebrow.

dekilahr *n.* Fish sp., swordfish, sailfish, blue marlin.

dekking *n.* Concrete reinforcing bar. [Jap.]

del *vi.* To move in great numbers, to swarm.

deleurek *n.* Bush sp., *Jussiaea erecta* or *Jussiaea linifolia.*

delingek, also **elingek.** *vi. neut.* To carry something involving repeated trips, as numerous bags of copra.

dehm *vt.* To feel around for, when unable to see an object, to grope around for, to probe for. *I dehm masiso nanroto.* I felt around for the matches in the dark.

demma *n.* Small boat, usually one carried aboard a ship. [Jap.]

dempwa *interj.* I warned you!

dempwo₁ *n.* Dragonfly. [Jap.]

dempwo₂ *n.* Radio transmission, telegram. [Jap.]

dempwo- *vi.* To send a radio transmission or telegram. *I pahn dempwohla rehn lahpo.* I'll send a telegram to that guy. [Jap.]

dempwura *n.* Any food rolled in a batter and fried. [Jap.]

demwidemw *vi. neut.* To caress, to rub, to pat affectionately; to pat the back end of a canoe on the outrigger side, a ceremonial action. —**damwer,** *vt.*

dene 1. *vt.* To say. 2. *sent. adv.* It is said that, used to introduce reported speech. *Dene Kepina pahn kohdo lakapw.* It is said that the Governor will come tomorrow.

densi *n.* Battery. [Jap.]

densinpasura *n.* Telephone pole. [Jap.]

denso *n.* Ceiling. [Jap.]

dendenmwosi *n.* Land snail. [Jap.]

dender *vi. neut.* To pick, as leaves or flowers. —**dar₂,** *vt.*

deng₁ *adj.* Taut; stiff; tensed up, as of a muscle.

deng₂ *n.* Grade; score. [Jap.]

deng₃ *n.* Name of one of the holes in the marble game *anaire.* [Jap.]

dengideng *adj.* Straight, also used to describe eyes with an epicanthic fold.

dengk *n.* Tank, for containing liquids. [Eng.]

dengki *n.* Electricity, electric light, flashlight. [Jap.]

dengng *vi.* To ring, of one's ears; to whistle through the air, as a bullet.

dengwa *n.* Telephone. [Jap.]

dep *num.* Ten million.

dehpa *neg.* Not ever, used to negate commands. *Menlau ke dehpa kohkohla.* Please don't ever go.

depala *vi.* To be too much, excessive, more than enough. *E depala.* It's too much.

depe *interr.* How many; how much. *Aramas depe ke tuhweng?* How many people did you meet?

depelek *adj.* Tomboyish.

depehne *interr.* An interrogative noun meaning what relationship to (him, her, or it), used for family, body parts, and places. *Depehnen imwen Souliko?* Where is it in relation to Soulik's house? *Dehpenei?* Where is it in relation to me?

deppang *n.* Large sheet of iron used as a concrete trough. [Jap.]

depw, also **dahpw**. *n.* Tub. [Eng.]

depwala SLANG. *vi.* To drown.

depwe SLANG. *vt.* To bathe. —**depwedepw**, *vi.*

depweila 1. *vi.* To do something by chance; to commit a faux pas. 2. *n.* A chance occurrence.

depwek *n.* Cloud.

depwekinieng HONORIFIC. 1. *vi.* To greet. 2. *n.* Greeting.

depwen *adj.* Unhindered or unburdened by children or things.

depwedepw SLANG. *vi. neut.* To bathe. —**depwe**, *vt.*

depwukuro, also **deipwukuro**. 1. *n.* Glove. 2. *vi.* To wear gloves. [Jap.]

der *vi.* To strike, of a fish. —**dar₁**, *vt.*

dehr, also **deh**. *neg.* Not, used to negate commands. *Ke dehr alu mwohn aramas.* Don't walk in front of people.

derere *n3s.* Dried matter, crust on skin, as dried food on the face.

dereht *n.* Thread. [Eng.]

deriuhdang *n.* Hand grenade. [Jap.]

derinmwoarong *adj.* Said of one who takes advantage of others when they are distracted.

derir HONORIFIC. *vi.* To sleep.

deriwang *vi.* To limp.

derpwungedi *vi.* To be cut, of foliage. —**derpwungiedi**, *vt.*

derpwungiedi *vt.* To cut foliage. —**derpwungedi**, *vi.*

des 1. *n.* Test, examination. 2. *vi.* To take a test or examination. [Eng.]

dehde *adj.* Clear, evident.

dewen kainen *n.* Anus.

dewesepeseng HONORIFIC. *vt.* To open one's mouth to speak. —**dawaspeseng**, *vi.*

-di *verb. suff.* Downwards; used with verbs of confining or securing to indicate the action has been carried through to its logical conclusion. *pwupw* fall, *pwupwidi* fall down; *salih* tie (it), *salihdi* tie (it) down.

dih₁ *n.* Name of the letter *d.*

dih₂ *n.* Stick used for spreading stones in an *uhmw.*

dih₃ *n.* Generation, age group; litter, of animals; crop. *Kiht ehu dih.* We are the same age.

dih₄ *n.* Tea. [Eng.]

diapahd *vt.* To kick or shove with the bottom of the foot.

diar *vt.* To find. —**dierek**, *vi.*

die *vt.* To poke; to push or pull with a stick or the feet; to stir with an implement. —**diedihdi**, *vi.*

dierek *vi.* To be found. —**diar**, *vt.*

diedihdi *vi.* Of fruit, to be pulled down with a stick. —**die**, *vt.*

dik *vi.* To skip across a surface, as a stone skipping across water. —**dikih**, *vt.*

dikahk *vi.* To cackle, of a hen; idiomatically used to describe women's talk.

dikadik *n (3s: dikedike).* One's image.

dikeimwidi *vi.* To fall headfirst.

dikek 1. *n.* Needle; first shoot of a newly planted cutting. 2. *vi.* To sprout, to send forth the first shoots, said of a cutting.

dikeriker *adj.* Healthy looking, said of plants.

dikedik en eni *n.* Ancient Ponapean rituals, of a mystical nature.

dikih *vt.* To skip towards. —**dik**, *vi.*

dikou 1. *vi.* To bend forward, of people. 2. *adj.* Tilted.

dikoumoang *vi.* To dive headfirst.

dikseneri *n.* Dictionary. [Eng.]

dil *vi. neut.* To penetrate, go through, or pass into.

dihl₁ *n.* Dried palm frond; torch.

dihl₂ *n.* Nit, the egg of a louse.

dihl₃ *vi. neut.* To deal cards; to shuffle cards. [Eng.] —dihlih, *vt.*

dihlih *vt.* To deal cards; to shuffle cards. [*dihl*<Eng.] —dihl₃, *vi.*

dilin *vt.* To pull hair, as in a fight. —pidilin, *vi.*

dilin elimoang 1. *n.* A type of fishing for crabs, done in the mangrove swamps. 2. *vi.* To fish for crab in the mangrove swamps.

dilip *vt.* To mend a thatch roof; during the preparation of kava, to work water into the fibers by fluffing them; to shuffle, as of cards; to place a flower behind one's ear. —dilipek, *vi.*

dilipada *vt.* To store objects between cross pieces of thatch.

dilipek *vi.* To be patched, of a thatch roof; to be shuffled, of cards; to be placed behind one's ear, of flowers. —dilip, *vt.*

dillap *vi. neut.* To shuffle kava fibers before adding water. —dillepe, *vt.*

dillepe *vt.* See *dillap.*

dimwamwahi *n.* Spark.

dihn *n.* Large can, as for gasoline. [Eng.]

dinak *n.* One section of a thatch roof, from the eave to the peak one armspan in width.

dinapw 1. *n.* Board; the board in a canoe that covers the central part of the hull. 2. HONORIFIC. *n.* Tongue.

dindir 1. *vi.* To be barbed. 2. *n.* Barb, as of a hook. —dindirih, *vt.*

dindirih *vt.* To make a barb on something, as a hook. —dindir, *vi.*

ding *vi.* To drip or leak.

dihng *n.* Ti plant, *Cordyline terminalis.*

dingai *vi.* To giggle.

dingiding *n.* Drop.

dingiding en kepeirek *n.* Kava that flows from the upper side of the fist of the one preparing it.

dingngang *adj.* Hard working in feast activities.

dip 1. *n.* Grain, of wood; chip or slice, as of breadfruit or taro. 2. *num. cl.* Used in counting chips, slices, or shavings. *dipen mei riadip* two slices of breadfruit, *dipen pilein pahdip* four shavings from a plane.

dihp 1. *n (3s: dipe).* Sin, wrong doing. 2. *vi.* To sin, to commit adultery.

dipaniki *vt.* To be responsible for immoral behavior; to be guilty. —dipada, *vi.*

dipada *vi.* To be guilty. —dipaniki, *vt.*

dipe *vt.* To slice, as breadfruit or taro.

dipekelekel, also dipwekelekel. *vi.* To stumble, to stub one's toe.

dipen keleu 1. *n.* Hibiscus bast used for straining kava; one of the cups of kava in the kava ceremony. 2. *vi.* A command for the preparers of kava to take their turn to drink.

dipen rasaras *n.* Sawdust.

dipen wahn pwuro *n.* Original sin.

dipenihd *n.* Husk of a mature coconut; fiber of a green coconut, used for making sennit.

dipere *n3s.* Chip, flake.

dipeteu *adj.* Said of one who dislikes to get up in the morning.

diplohma *n.* Diploma. [Eng.]

dipw *n.* Exogamous, matrilineal clan.

dihpw *n.* Weed, grass.

dipwahk POLITE. 1. *vi.* To eat. 2. *n.* Food. —dipwahki, *vt.*

dipwahki *vt.* See *dipwahk.*

dipwekelekel, also dipekelekel. *vi.* To stumble, to stub one's toe.

Dipwilap *n.* A clan name.

Dipwinluhk *n.* A clan name.

dipwinmal *n.* Grass sp..

Dipwinmen *n.* A clan name.

Dipwinmen pwetepwet *n.* Name of a subclan of *Dipwinmen.*

Dipwinmen toantoal *n.* Name of a subclan of *Dipwinmen.*

Dipwinpahnmei *n.* A clan name.

Dipwinpehpe *n.* A clan name.

Dipwinwai *n.* A clan name.

dipwisou *n.* Thing, material, physical object of any kind. *Se kin kesempwaliki dipwisoun nan sahpw sang dipwisoun nan ihmw.* We value things of the land more than household goods.

dipwisou mweir *n.* Non-permanent crops, like yams as opposed to breadfruit.

dipwidipw *adj.* Weedy, grassy.

dipwoapw *n.* Tree sp., *Terminalia catappa.*

dipwtekatek *n.* Any thistle-like grass.

dir *adj.* Overcrowded, filled; plentiful.

diraht *n.* Barbed wire. [Ger.]

diremw *n.* Trump, in cards; the name of a card game. [Eng.]

direpw *adj.* Nosey, bothersome.

diromkang *n.* Drum, as an oil drum. [Jap.<Eng.]

diroap *n.* Drop pitch, in baseball. [Jap.<Eng.]

dihsek *n (3s: dihseki).* Storage area in the front of a feasthouse, where the porch roof extends inside.

dihsel *n.* Diesel. [Eng.]

did *vi. neut.* To build a wall. —**didih,** *vt.*

dihd *n.* Wall of a building.

didih *vt.* See *did.*

dihdi 1. *n3s.* Breast; baby bottle. 2. *vi.* To suckle, to nurse.

didmwerek 1. *n.* Phosphorescence. 2. *vi.* To sparkle; to be phosphorescent.

-do *verb. suff.* Here, toward the speaker. *pei* float, *peido* float here.

doh *adj.* Distant, far off. —**dohwan,** *vt.*

Dois *n.* Germany. [Ger.]

doismango *n.* Tree sp., a variety of mango.

dou₁ *vi.* To be woven, of a net. —**daur₁,** *vt.*

dou₂ *vi.* To climb. —**daur₂,** *vt.*

dou₃ *vi. neut.* To inspect, examine, or check; to patrol. —**dawih,** *vt.*

douiak 1. *n.* A type of spearfishing done in the mangrove swamp. 2. *vi.* To spearfish in this manner.

douleng *n.* A third *kehndou* for a yam vine, fastened higher than the first two.

doulong *n.* Stick of hibiscus wood, used to store kava cups.

douluhl 1. *vi.* To pass by, to go beyond. 2. *adv.* Thoroughly, completely. *E ese douluhl.* He knows it thoroughly. —**daulih,** *vt.*

doumwo *n.* A second *kehndou* for a yam vine, fastened higher than the first.

dok 1. *vi.* To be stabbed, to be speared, to be skewered, to be given an injection. 2. *n.* An injection. —**doakoa,** *vt.*

dokange *n.* Sp. of large green lizard. [Jap.]

dokapahini 1. *n.* Feast in which ripe breadfruit are employed. 2. *vi.* To prepare this feast.

dokawar *n.* Part of the outrigger support of a canoe.

doke *vt.* To concern, to be intended for.

dokia 1. *n.* A dance, done by females in a sitting position employing sticks which are tapped together rhythmically. 2. *vi.* To do this dance.

dokomei 1. *n.* Breadfruit, prepared by placing salt water or a rotten land taro stem in a hole in the core of the fruit and allowing it to age for at least one day. 2. *vi.* To prepare breadfruit in this manner.

dokomwomw 1. *n.* A type of spearfishing done from above the surface of the water. 2. *vi.* To spearfish in this manner.

dokoahs *vi.* To weave thatch.

doklaud 1. *vi.* To feed intravenously. 2. *n.* Intravenous feeding.

dol₁ *vi.* To mix, to add ingredients; to make yeast for drinking. —**doaloa,** *vt.*

dol₂ *vi.* To be severed.

dohl *n.* Small mountain, hill.

dolung *vt.* To pick, to remove from the stalk. —**dondol,** *vi.*

domahdo *n.* Tomato, ketchup. [Eng.]

dohming *n.* Native, used derogatorily. [Jap.]

dompiki *n.* Travois. [Jap.]

dompwuri *n.* Bowl. [Jap.]

dohnas *n.* Doughnut. [Eng.]

dondol *vi. neut.* To pick, to remove from the stalk. —**dolung,** *vt.*

dondorok, also **dorok.** *vi.* To cluck, of a hen; to grumble.

dohng *n.* Tree sp.; *Campnosperma brevipetiolata.*

dongodongki *vt.* To abhor.

dongki *n.* Donkey. [Eng.]

dopas *adj.* Fast, speedy. [Jap.]

dopasko *n.* Tabasco sauce.

dopwolong *vi.* To wash one's hair.

dohr *n.* Belt made of banana fiber, worn above a grass skirt; cloth made from breadfruit bark.

dohranai *vi.* Unacceptable, not well liked, only with reference to people. [Jap.]

doro *n.* The axle plus the wheels of a narrow gauge train, sometimes used as a barbell. [Jap.]

dorok, also **dondorok.** *vi.* To cluck, of a hen; to grumble.

doropwus *n.* Any small, round, hard candy that comes in rolls, as Lifesavers. [Jap.<Eng.]

dororo *n.* Grated, raw yam.

dorno 1. *n.* Japanese marble game. 2. *vi.* To play this game. [Jap.]

dod *adj.* Close together; frequent. *Uht kau nohn dod.* Those banana trees are too close together.

dohdai *n.* Lighthouse. [Jap.]

dohwan *vt.* To be far from. —**doh**, *adj.*

dowas, also **dawas**. HONORIFIC. *n (3s: dewese).* Mouth.

doahk *n.* Occupation, task, employment, responsibility, deed.

doahke *vt.* To touch or feel; to fight. —**poadoahk**, *vi.*

doahken sahpw *n.* Agriculture.

doakoa *vt.* To stab, to spear, to skewer, to give an injection. —**dok**, *vi.*

doakoadok *adj.* Bristly.

doaloa *vt.* To mix, to add ingredients. —**dol₁**, *vi.*

doar *adj.* Worse, of an ill person.

doare *vt.* To save from harm; to separate fighters; to steal or seize food at a feast. —**poadoandoar**, *vi.*

doarop *n.* Fish sp., surgeonfish.

doaropwe *n.* Paper, cardboard; something made of paper, as a ticket, diploma, certificate, etc..

doaropwehn rohng *n.* Newspaper.

doaropwehda *vi.* To predict with the assistance of magic.

doadoahk 1. *vi.* To work. 2. *n.* Work.

du *vi.* To go underwater; to dive. —**duhp₁**, *vt.*

duk *vi.* To be influenced, to give in, with a negative connotation. *Serepeino dukieng pwutako.* That girl was influenced by that boy. *Mehnda ke duk?* Why did you give in?

duhkihla *vt.* To be burdened with the support of. *Soulik duhkihla ah peneinei.* Soulik is burdened with the support of his family.

dukuru *n.* A variety of banana.

duhla *vi.* To be drowned, to be submerged.

dumpe *n3s.* Compensation.

dumwadumw *adj.* Hyperactive, of children.

dun *num. cl.* Used in counting bundles of things tied together. *dunen mei riadun* two bundles of breadfruit.

dune *vt.* To tie or attach together one after another, as breadfruit or flowers, to tie a bundle of things.

dunenilek *adj.* Given to sending others on repeated errands.

dundun₁ *n.* Penis, diminutive form.

dundun₂ *n.* A bunch, of anything.

duhp₁ *vt.* To dive for objects on the floor of the ocean or the bed of a stream. —**du**, *vi.*

duhp₂ *vt.* To bathe. —**duhdu**, *vi.*

duhpek 1. *adj.* Starved. 2. *n.* Starvation.

dupuk *vt.* To repay, to give back in recompense or reply.

duhr *vi.* Of a sound, to reverberate; to cause a ringing in one's ears; to make one's skin crawl.

duhrien *n.* Tree sp., durian, *Pangium edule*, edible fruit. [Malay]

durudara *n.* Fish sp., surgeonfish, *Acanthurus aliala*.

duhse 1. *n.* A type of net fishing, done by blocking off a pocket in the coral. 2. *vi.* To fish in this manner.

duhdu 1. *vi.* To bathe. 2. *n.* Bath. —**duhp₂**, *vt.*

duwau *num.* Nine; see *-u.*

duwaka *num.* Nine; see *ka₂.*

duwakap *num.* Nine; see *kap.*

duwakis *num.* Nine; see *kis₁.*

duwal *vi.* To squeeze through, to pass through in spite of an obstacle.

duwamwut *num.* Nine; see *mwut₂.*

duwapa *num.* Nine; see *pa₃.*

duwapak *num.* Nine; see *pak₁.*

duwapar *num.* Nine; see *par₂.*

duwapit *num.* Nine; see *pit₂.*

duwar *vi.* To stare, to be with one's eyes wide open.

duwara *num.* Nine; see *ra.*

duwarawar *adj.* Wide-eyed, staring.

duwasop *num.* Nine; see *sop₂.*

duwadip *num.* Nine; see *dip.*

duwadun *num.* Nine; see *dun.*

duwe *n3s.* Condition, nature, manner; used in combination with *ni* to mean according to. *Ia duwen omw kohdo?* How did you come? *Koaros pahn doadoahk niduwen me koasoandi.* Everyone will work according to the plan.

duweisek *num.* Ninety; see *eisek.*

duwehk *num.* Ninety; see *ehk.*

duwehl *num.* Nine; see *el*$_2$.

duwehla *vt.* To become the same as.

duwelep *num.* Nine; see *lep.*

duwemen *num.* Nine; see *men*$_3$.

duwemwodol *num.* Nine; see *mwodol.*

duwengoul *num.* Ninety; see *ngoul.*

duwepali *num.* Nine; see *pali*$_1$.

duwepenehte *vi.* To be the same. —**duwehte,** *vt.*

duwesel *num.* Nine; see *sel*$_2$.

duwesou *num.* Nine; see *sou*$_4$.

duwete *num.* Nine; see *te.*

duwehte *vt.* To be the same as, to be identical to. —**duwepenehte,** *vi.*

duwetumw *num.* Nine; see *tumw.*

duwewel *num.* Nine; see *wel*$_2$.

duwoumw *num.* Nine; see *umw*$_2$.

duwopwuloi *num.* Nine; see *pwuloi.*

duwoapoar *num.* Nine; see *poar.*

duwoapwong *num.* Nine; see *pwong.*

duwoapwoat *num.* Nine; see *pwoat.*

T

taimen *n.* Diamond. [Eng.]

tau *vi.* To fall in the water with a splashing sound.

taur *vt.* To weigh down.

tautawi, also toutowi. *n3s.* Weight.

takai *n.* Stone, rock.

takaimei *n.* Coral head.

takain nansed *n.* Coral head.

takain were *n3s.* Adam's apple.

takain wideh *n.* Stone placed in front of an entrance to a house, used to wipe one's feet on.

takainwel *vi.* To informally drink kava; to illicitly drink kava without inviting the *Nahnmwarki.*

takaipwet *n.* Coral head.

tal 1. *vi.* To make a click-like sound; Tsk Tsk! 2. *n.* Any click-like sound.

tala *n.* Dollar. [Eng.]

taman *vt.* To recall, to remember.

tahmw *n (3s: temwe).* Forehead.

tamwais *n.* Fish sp., a mature parrotfish.

tamwarok *n.* Fish sp., surgeonfish, *Acanthurus gahhm.*

tamwe *vt.* To lick.

tahmwel *n.* Ring finger.

tantal *adj.* Very popular, of a person.

tang *vi.* To run; to flee; to swim, of fish. —tenge, *vt.*

tapi *n3s.* Base of a tree; beginning.

tapiada, also tapihda. *vt.* To begin, to start. —tep₁, *vi.*

tapihda, also tapiada. *vt.* To begin, to start. —tep₁, *vi.*

tahpw *n.* Vine sp..

tapwi HONORIFIC. *n3s.* Head, temple.

tapwur *vi.* To roll, often of heavy objects.

tahr₁ *vt.* To attack in a hit and run fashion, of sharks, barracuda, and the sp. of bird *kutoahr.*

tahr₂ *vt.* To trim the fronds from a coconut palm.

tat₁ *vi. neut.* To lay a floor. —tete, *vt.*

tat₂ *vi.* To writhe, of a fish when poisoned; to be in a state of intense disgust or anger.

taht *n.* Floor.

tahta HONORIFIC. 1. *vi.* To be given a haircut. 2. *n.* A haircut.

te *num. cl.* Used in counting leaves or sheets of paper. *tehn tuhke riete* two leaves, *tehn doaropwe isite* seven sheets of paper.

-te *sent. adv.* Just, only; still (when suffixed to reduplicated verbs). *Ohlohte kangala rais koaros.* Just that man ate up all the rice. *E tangatangete.* He's still running.

teh *n3s.* Leaf; sheet, page.

tehap *n.* Owl.

tei₁ *num.* Other; functions like an ordinal numeral. *ohl teio* that other man.

tei₂ *vi.* To be torn. —tehr, *vt.*

tehi *n.* Sheet, as for bedding.

tehi mweinlikou *n.* Patchwork quilt.

teik *n.* Story, of a building.

teike *n.* Sheath knife, hunting knife, diving knife, dagger.

tein amwise *n.* Mosquito net.

teip *n.* Tape, braid, ribbon for sewing. [Eng.]

teirek *adj.* To be torn, to be worn out. —tehr, *vt.*

tek *n.* Horizontal pleats in a dress.

tehk₁ *vt.* To check; to keep an eye on. [Eng.]

tehk₂ *n.* Duck. [Eng.]

tekatek *adj.* Thorny, spiny.

teke₁ *n3s.* Thorn.

teke₂ *vt.* To make horizontal pleats in a dress.

tekemwer *n.* A variety of taro.

tekenwel *n.* Vine sp., *Antrophyum alatum.*

teki *n.* Turkey. [Eng.]

tekipwel *vi.* To have an infection under the nail.

tekitek *n.* Vine sp., *Hoya schneei.*

tel *vi.* To be lucky, to be fortunate, of one normally unlucky or of no consequence.

tehla *vt.* To line or cover with leaves.

tehlap *adj.* Wide, broad.

temenek *vi.* Of children, to become suddenly homesick.

tempel 1. *vi.* To rhythmically pound a kava stone. 2. *n.* Rhythmic pounding of a kava stone.

temwen ihmw *n.* Facade.

ten₁ *adj.* Congealed, colloidal, thick, viscous.

ten₂ *n.* Ton. [Eng.]

tehn₁ *adj.* Empty.

tehn₂ *n.* Ten, in cards. [Eng.]

tehn mwomwinsapw *n.* A feasthouse having three center posts, located inland.

tenek *vi.* To be hung up; to be weighed. —**teneki,** *vt.*

tenek kisinmei 1. *n.* A type of spearfishing done by baiting a line with a small breadfruit and then spearing the fish when they come to eat. 2. *vi.* To spearfish in this manner.

teneki *vt.* To hang; to weigh. —**tenek,** *vi.*

tener 1. *n.* Tenor. 2. *vi.* To sing tenor. [Eng.]

tenipei *n.* Fish sp., a sp. of shark.

tenihr *n.* Waterfall.

tehnihr *n.* Fan.

tenihrlap HONORIFIC. *n.* Saliva.

tehnkehl *n.* Stalk, of coconuts.

tehnkehs *n.* A playing card, a deck of playing cards.

tehnlap *adj.* Bully.

tehnlik *n.* Plant sp., *Asplenium nidus*, used for decorating yams and kava.

tehnpas HONORIFIC. *n. Nahs* or house of a chief.

tehnpese HONORIFIC. *poss. cl.* A possessive classifier used in honorific speech in place of the common language classifier *imwe.*

tehnpilei *n.* A playing card.

tehnpit *n.* Pandanus leaf.

tehnseu *n.* Fish sp., snapper, *Lutjanus kasmira.*

tentenihr HONORIFIC. *vi.* To cry, to weep.

tenter *n.* Cricket.

tehnwar HONORIFIC. *n.* Canoe, vehicle.

tehnwere HONORIFIC. *poss. cl.* A possessive classifier used in honorific speech in place of the common language classifier *were.*

teng *adj.* Tight.

tengala *vi.* To get stuck.

tenge *vt.* To run to. —**tang,** *vi.*

tenger *vi.* To contract the vagina during intercourse.

tep₁ *vi.* To begin, to start. —**tapihda** or **tapiada,** *vt.*

tep₂ *vi.* To kick. —**tepek,** *vt.*

tehp *n.* Fish sp., *Caranx.*

tehpahu HONORIFIC. *n.* Vagina.

tepek *vt.* To kick. —**tep₂,** *vi.*

tepel *n.* Devil. [Eng.]

tehpel 1. *n.* Table; party. 2. *vi.* To give a party. [Eng.]

tepinkasang HONORIFIC. *n.* Neck.

tepindang *n (3s: tepindenge).* Thigh.

tepinwer medek 1. *n.* Stiff neck. 2. *vi.* To have a stiff neck.

tepinwere *n3s.* Neck.

tepw *n.* A stage of growth of a yam in which many branches have developed.

tepwasang *vi.* To peel off, as of skin or paint.

tepwedi 1. *vi.* To have an abrasion or superficial wound. 2. *n.* An abrasion or superficial wound.

tepwtoal *n.* Growth period of a yam after the leaves turn dark green.

tehr *vt.* To tear; to criticize. —**tei** or **teirek,** *vi.*

tehrek *vi.* To creak or squeak; to make a tearing or grating noise.

tesin *n.* Dozen. [Eng.]

tete *vt.* To floor. —**tat₁,** *vi.*

tehte *n.* Any odorific substance added to coconut oil to give it a pleasant smell.

tehteh *vt.* To add any odorific substance to coconut oil to give it a pleasant smell.

tetempala HONORIFIC. *vi.* To be or become quiet.

tehtehn likamwada *interj.* An expression used when another attempts to cover up his embarrassment.

tehtehn peh *n3s.* Weapon; an implement; anything which determines wealth in Ponape.

tetensik HONORIFIC. *vi.* To stay awake.

tehtik *adj.* Narrow.

ti *vi.* Of a spirit, to possess or inhabit a human body.

tih₁ *n.* Name of the letter *t*.

tih₂ *n3s.* Bone.

tiak₁ *vt.* To step on.

tiak₂ *vt.* To start a song.

tiahk *n (3s: tiahke, tieke)*. Custom, manner, behavior, culture.

tiakidi *vt.* To interrupt some serious activity.

tiati 1. *n.* Earring. 2. *vi.* To wear earrings. —**tie₁**, *vt.*

tie₁ *vt.* To wear earrings; to hang from the ear. —**tiati**, *vi.*

tie₂ *poss. cl.* A possessive classifier for earrings.

tie₃ *n.* Deer. [Eng.]

tiekepe HONORIFIC. *n.* Child of a chief.

tiekopil *vi.* To gather *kopil*, a sp. of clam found in the mangrove swamp.

tiemwur *vi.* To arrive at someone's home just after he has departed for fishing or hunting, believed to bring bad luck. —**tiemwurih**, *vt.*

tiemwurih *vt.* See *tiemwur*.

tieng *vi.* To go first, to precede.

tiepene 1. *vi.* To meet, to convene, to confer. 2. *n.* Meeting, convention, conference.

tiepoans *n.* A kava plant, decorated with ornamental plants.

tiepwel HONORIFIC. 1. *n.* Feast given for a *Nahnmwarki* or *Nahnken* when he recovers from an illness. 2. *vi.* To prepare this feast.

tika SLANG. *adj.* Nonsensical, untruthful.

tikahp *n.* A variety of banana, *Musa tikap.*

tikel en neh *n3s.* Ankle bone.

tikelekelada *vi.* To protrude. *Kapehd en liho tikelekelada.* That woman's stomach protrudes.

tikida *vi.* To grow up in a location or condition. *I tikida semwehmwe.* I grew up poor.

tikitik *adj.* Small, little, young.

tile *vt.* To carry or lift something that can be lightly suspended with one hand. —**tintil**, *vi.*

tihle 1. *n.* Sty, swelling of the rim of the eyelid. 2. *vi.* To have a sty.

tihlepe *n3s.* Spinal column.

tihmw *n.* In the game *peisihr*, the area where the sticks are thrown against the ground.

tihmwe *n.* Middle finger.

tihn kahmam *n.* Food unworthy to be fed to guests.

tihn kopwou *n (3s: tihn kopwowi)*. Rib.

tihn moange *n3s.* Skull.

tihn mwaremware *n3s.* Breastbone.

tihn mwomw *n.* A hard core-like abnormal growth sometimes found in breadfruit.

tihnain *vi.* To recover, to grow healthy after an illness.

tihnsau *n (3s: tihnsewe)*. Backbone.

tihnsauriau *n.* A big pig or turtle.

tihnsautipw *n.* Humpback, as a consequence of a broken back.

tintil *vi.* To be carried or lifted, of something that can be lightly suspended with one hand. —**tile**, *vt.*

tip HONORIFIC. *vi.* To be full, after eating.

tipaker₁ *n.* Plant sp., tobacco, *Nicotrina sp.*; any rough-cut tobacco. [Eng.]

tipaker₂ *n.* Fish sp.

tipw₁ *vi.* To be broken, of any long object; to be interrupted, of a song. —**tipwang**, *vt.*

tipw₂ *vi.* To be cut with scissors or shears. —**tipwa**, *vt.*

tihpw *n.* The pair of sticks used for picking up hot rocks from an *uhmw*.

tipwa *vt.* To cut with scissors or shears; to pick up hot rocks from an *uhmw* with a pair of sticks. —**tipw₂**, *vi.*

tipwal *vi.* To make a slapping noise by striking two objects together.

tipwalapwal *adj.* Making a slapping or banging noise.

tipwang *vt.* To break any long object. —**tipw₁**, *vi.*

tipwatipw *adj.* Brittle, fragile.

tipwensapwasapw *n.* Yam tuber left in the ground for further growth.

tipwengen peh *n3s.* Crook of the arm.

tir *adj.* Funnel or hour glass shaped; narrowing.

tihrereng *adj.* Skinny, bony; strained.

Tihsempe *n.* December. [Eng.]

tiht *n.* Bird sp., gray in color.

tihti *adj.* Thin, skinny; of fish, bony.

titin *n.* Tree sp., *Messerschmidia argentea.*

tihwo *adj.* Frustrated, tense, worried.

toik *n.* Fish sp..

tou *n.* Contribution.

touk *vt.* To scoop out; to eat with a spoon. —**toutou$_2$**, *vi.*

toukihda *vt.* To contribute.

toulap HONORIFIC. *n.* Major activities of the *Nahnmwarki.*

toutik HONORIFIC. *n.* Minor activities of the *Nahnmwarki.*

toutou$_1$ *adj.* Heavy.

toutou$_2$ *vi. neut.* To scoop out; to eat with a spoon. —**touk**, *vt.*

toutouki *vt.* To be reluctant about.

toutowi, also **tautawi**. *n3s.* Weight.

tok$_1$ *vi.* To be ended, terminated, or stopped; to be amputated.

tok$_2$ *adj.* Old, of things; to be worn out.

tohk *n.* Stump, as a tree stump.

toki *poss. cl.* A possessive classifier for individuals with whom one has had sexual intercourse.

tokinmoang *vi.* To play tricks on people at a wake, done to cheer the family.

tokutok, also **tukutuk**. 1. *n.* Leprosy, leper; a breadfruit disease. 2. *vi.* To have leprosy; of breadfruit, to have the disease called *tokutok.*

tohl *n (3s: tole).* Clitoris.

tom *vi.* To stomp, to make a thudding noise. —**tomur**, *vt.*

tomur *vt.* To stomp on. —**tom**, *vi.*

tomw *vi.* To seek reconciliation or forgiveness.

tohmw *n.* Reconciliation, forgiveness.

tohn$_1$ *adj.* Crowded with people.

tohn$_2$ *n.* Member of; inhabitant of; participant of; this word is typically written attached to the word it precedes.

tohnkapar 1. *vi.* To attend a feast or party without contributing provisions. 2. *n.* A person attending a feast or party without contributing provisions. —**tohnkepere**, *vt.*

tohnkepere *vt.* See *tohnkapar.*

tohnleng *n.* Angel.

tohnmetei *vi.* To volunteer, to work without pay.

tohnmeteikihla 1. *vt.* To forgive and forget. 2. *interj.* Forget it!

tohnpadahk *n.* Disciple.

tohnsukuhl *n.* Student.

topwuk *n.* Tree sp., *Premna gaudichaudii.*

tohr$_1$ *sent. adv.* Only.

tohr$_2$ *vt.* To slide by pushing or pulling. —**tohrek**, *vi.*

tohrek *vi.* To be slid by pushing or pulling. —**tohr$_2$**, *vt.*

tohrohr *vi.* To be independent, to be different, to be excluded from the group.

tot *adj.* Overripe, of tuberous plants.

tohto *adj.* Many, much, numerous, plentiful.

totopai *n.* Bird sp., commonly found in swampy areas.

tohtowe *n3s.* Total amount.

towehla *vt.* To take up residence in.

towehda *vt.* To become a member, inhabitant, or participant of.

toai 1. *n.* Nasal mucus. 2. *vi.* To have a runny nose.

toahkoi *n.* Low cloud, touching the mountains; fog.

toahkte *n.* Doctor. [Eng.]

toahl$_1$ *n.* Doll. [Eng.]

toahl$_2$ *n.* Coal. [Eng.]

toamwoarok *n.* Fish sp., black surgeonfish.

toantoal *adj.* Black.

tu *vi.* To meet.

tuh *n.* Upright breather roots of the mangrove tree.

tuhke *n.* Tree, plant, lumber, wood.

tuhkehn kilin wai *n.* Tree sp., *Cassia alata.*

tuhkehn kopwopwoud *n.* Plant sp..

tuki *n3s.* Stub, stump.

tukutuk, also **tokutok**. 1. *n.* Leprosy, leper; a breadfruit disease. 2. *vi.* To have leprosy; of breadfruit, to have the disease called *tukutuk.*

tumw *num. cl.* Used in counting gusts of wind. *tumwenieng riotumw* two gusts of wind.

tumwe *n3s.* Nose.

tumwenieng *n.* Gust of wind.

tumwohki *vt.* To consider smelly; to be sick of.

tumwpak *adj.* Flat nosed.

tumwpwoar *n.* Nasal sound; cleft palate.

tungoal 1. *vi.* To consume, to eat or drink; to receive communion. 2. *n.* Communion; also used with *ah* possessive pronouns as a humiliative marker. —**tungoale**, *vt.*

tungoale *vt.* To consume, to eat or drink; to receive communion. —**tungoal**, *vi.*

tupweiklas   *n.* Spyglass, telescope, binoculars. [Eng.]

tutuwi   *n.* Bird sp., yellow in color.

tuwel   *vt.* To shake, of one's head; to sway. —**tuwelek**, *vi.*

tuwelek   *vi.* To shake, of one's head; to sway. —**tuwel**, *vt.*

tuwi   *n.* Firewood.

troahli   *n.* Narrow gauge train. [Jap.<Eng.]

W

wa₁ *vi.* To flower or bear fruit.

wa₂ *vt.* To carry.

wah *n3s.* Fruit, flower; offspring; result.

wai₁ 1. *vi.* To sneak; to prowl. 2. *adj.* Slow in movement. —**waine,** *vt.*

wai₂ *vi.* To be foreign, from abroad, now commonly used to mean American.

waik *vt.* To pull; to snatch; to stretch something.

wailes 1. *n.* Wireless telegraph, telegram. 2. *vi.* To send a telegram. [Jap.<Eng.]

wain *n.* Wine. [Eng.]

waine *vt.* To sneak up to. —**wai₁,** *vi.*

wair *n.* Bird sp., a land bird.

wahu *n.* Valley; respect, honor; a kava ritual.

waun *adj.* Respectful, respectable, honorable.

wak₁ *vi.* To be removed, of covers, lids, tops, etc.. —**waka,** *vt.*

wak₂ *vt.* To chop with an axe or knife, as foliage.

waka *vt.* To remove, as covers, lids, tops, etc. —**wak₁,** *vi.*

wahkahk *vi.* To call or cackle loudly, of a hen.

wakapw *n.* Fish sp., striped surgeonfish, *Acanthurus lineatus.*

wakar *n (3s: wekere).* Pubic hair.

wahkihla *vt.* To depend on someone or something, to rely on, with ill consequence.

wako, also **uwako.** *vi.* To gag.

waku *n.* Embroidery hoop. [Jap.]

wal *adj.* Able to fly far, of *sihr* in the game *peisihr.*

wahl₁ *n.* Jungle, forest, area overgrown with trees.

wahl₂ SLANG. *n (3s: wali).* Head.

walahileng HONORIFIC. *n.* A term used for the residence of the *Nahnmwarki.*

walek *adj.* Large, of any opening.

walimwut *num.* Eight; see *mwut₂.*

wahliniep *n.* Any woman in one's wife's clan except one the wife calls mother; any man in one's husband's clan except one the husband calls child.

walipit *num.* Eight; see *pit₂.*

waluh *num.* Eight; see *-u.*

wampwe *adj.* Putting on airs, showing off.

wahn ohl pirien *n.* Child of father's brother.

wahn lih pirien *n.* Child of mother's sister.

wahnedi *n3s.* Offspring.

wahnmeimei *n.* Two rear doors of a feasthouse.

wahnmwahng 1. *n.* The relationship that exists between an individual and the clan of his father's father. 2. *vi.* To be related in this way.

wahnmwahngih *vt.* See *wahnmwahng.*

wahnpei *n.* Pumice.

wahnpoaron *n.* Apostle, minister.

wahnpwuro *n.* Original sin.

wahnsakau *n.* A small branch of kava that can be planted.

wahnsahpw *n.* Agricultural products.

wahntal *n.* Vine sp., *Canavalia maritima.*

wahntuhke₁ *n.* Fruit, flower.

wahntuhke₂ 1. *n.* Arithmetic. 2. *vi.* To calculate. —**wahntuhkeih,** *vt.*

wahntuhkeih *vt.* To calculate. —**wahntuhke₂,** *vi.*

wangawang *adj.* Wide, of an opening, road, or channel.

wap *n.* Wharf, dock. [Eng.]

wapang *vi.* To lie crosswise.

war₁ *n (3s: were).* Body, of a person; seed, tumor, cyst.

war₂ *adj.* Worthy.

wahr *n (3s: were).* Canoe, vehicle; body, of a person.

wahr pei sakar *interj.* A greeting used by occupants of an arriving canoe.

warakih *vt.* To be a companion of; to associate with. —**werek,** *vi.*

waramwahu *adj.* Of coconut palms, bearing big nuts; of breadfruit, fecund.

warahr *adj.* Lumpy, grainy.

wahrar *n.* Fish sp..

warasapw *n.* A decoratively carved canoe.

118

warawar   n. Ditch, trench, groove.

warihmw   n. Ark.

was₁   adj. Obnoxious, discomforting.

was₂   n. Wristwatch. [Eng.]

wasa   n. Place, point.

Wasahi   n. The second ranking title in the *Nahnmwarki* line.

wasaile   HONORIFIC. n. Face.

wasahn alu   n. Aisle, sidewalk.

wasahn kilang kisinieng   n. Weather station.

wasahn pipihs   n. Urinal.

wasahn sompihr   n. Airport, airfield.

wasahn wailes   n. Wireless station, radio station. [*wailes*<Eng.]

wasapwong   vi. To get dark; to become night.

wasarahnpeseng   vi. To be dawn or daybreak.

wasas   vi. To stagger, to have difficulty keeping one's footing.

wahsek   adj. Of a hole or an opening, to be large enough so that something may pass through.

wasmelen, also watmelen.   n. Watermelon, *Citrullus vulgaris.* [Eng.]

wad   1. vi. Of mathematics, to multiply.   2. n. Multiplication. —wadiki, vt.

wahd   n. Fish sp., puffer fish.

wadawad₁   vi. To read; to count. —wadek₁, vt.

wadawad₂   adj. Admired; famous. —wadek₂, vt.

wadek₁   vt. To read; to count. —wadawad₁, vi.

wadek₂   vt. To admire. —wadawad₂, vi.

waderekerek   vi. To say something very fast.

wadiki   vt. Of mathematics, to multiply; to be counted among. —wad, vi.

wadilik   vi. To memorize, to know by heart. —wadilikih, vt.

wadilikih   vt. See *wadilik.*

waditik   vi. To be detailed.

watmelen, also wasmelen.   n. Watermelon, *Citrullus vulgaris.* [Eng.]

wahwah   poss. cl. A possessive classifier used to characterize the relationship between a man and the children of any person he would call sister.

wei   interj. An exclamation of surprise.

-wei   verb. suff. There, toward you. *kerep* creep, *kerepewei* creep there, toward you.

wehi₁   n. Turtle.

wehi₂   n. A political unit, as a municipality, district, state, country, or kingdom.

weia   vi. To laugh heartily, to howl with laughter.

wehia   n. Wire, spring. [Eng.]

weiapens   n. Barbed wire. [Eng.]

weikek   1. adj. Distressed, frustrated.   2. n. Frustration.

weingal   n. Mangrove sp., *Lumnitzera littorea.*

weipwul, also wempwul.   n. Tree sp., *Morinda citrifolia.*

weir₁   vt. To dig, to excavate. —weiweida, vi.

weir₂   vi. To race.

weirar   vi. To fish for *toik.*

weirek   adj. Painful, agonizing, torturous.

weirin kang donas   1. n. A race which involves eating a doughnut suspended from a string.   2. vi. To run this race.

weirin kerep   1. n. A race in which the participant runs on all fours.   2. vi. To run this race.

weirin meninrahn   1. n. A race in which a number of participants straddle a pole and run together.   2. vi. To run this race.

weirin pap   1. n. A swimming race.   2. vi. To participate in this race.

weirin pirene   1. n. A three-legged race.   2. vi. To run this race.

weirin tang   1. n. Track meet.   2. vi. To run a race.

weirin wilpahro   1. n. A wheelbarrow race.   2. vi. To run this race.

weid₁   n. A very high tide.

weid₂, also keid.   vi. To walk in a specific direction.

weid₃   ARCHAIC. adj. Heartless, without sympathy.

weidinpar   n. High tide during the trade wind season.

weitahta   1. adj. Red.   2. n. Red.

weiwei   1. n. Diaper, loincloth.   2. vi. To wear a diaper or loincloth.

weiweida   vi. To be dug out, to be excavated. —weir₁, vt.

wehk   vt. To confess, to reveal, to disclose.

wel₁, also nihdwel.   vi. To molt a shell.

wel₂   num. cl. Used in counting plants like bamboo which have a single root

but multiple stalks. *welin pehri
limewel five bamboo plants.

wel- *vi.* To be turned over, to be
flipped; to be bent back. *Pelien sereko
welidi.* The canvas is turned down.
—**welik,** *vt.*

wehl pwoht *n.* Whale boat. [Eng.]

welewel *num.* Eight; see *wel₂*.

weli *n3s.* The part of a yam that was
used in its propogation; a molted shell.

weliakan *num.* Eighty; see *ehk.*

weliel *num.* Eight; see *el₂*.

welik *vt.* To turn over, to flip; to bend
back. —**wel-,** *vi.*

welika *num.* Eight; see *ka₂*.

welikap *num.* Eight; see *kap.*

welikek *adj.* Agile.

welikis *num.* Eight; see *kis₂*.

welimen *num.* Eight; see *men₃*.

welimwodol *num.* Eight; see *mwodol.*

welingoul *num.* Eighty; see *ngoul.*

welipa *num.* Eight; see *pa₃*.

welipak *num.* Eight; see *pak₁*.

welipali *num.* Eight; see *pali₁*.

welipar *num.* Eight; see *par₂*.

welipoar *num.* Eight; see *poar.*

welipwong *num.* Eight; see *pwong.*

welipwoat *num.* Eight; see *pwoat.*

welipwuloi *num.* Eight; see *pwuloi.*

welira *num.* Eight; see *ra.*

welihsek *num.* Eighty; see *eisek.*

welisel *num.* Eight; see *sel₂*.

welisou *num.* Eight; see *sou₄*.

welisop *num.* Eight; see *sop₂*.

welidip *num.* Eight; see *dip.*

welidun *num.* Eight; see *dun.*

welite *num.* Eight; see *te.*

welitumw *num.* Eight; see *tumw.*

weliwel₁ *adj.* Bushy, full of foliage.

weliwel₂ ARCHAIC. *n.* Fish sp., tuna.

weluhmw *num.* Eight; see *umw₂*.

wellep *num.* Eight; see *lep.*

wempwul, also **weipwul.** *n.* Tree sp.,
Morinda citrifolia.

wen *vi.* To dance a Ponapean men's
dance.

wen- *vi.* To lie, to recline.

wehn *n.* Name of a Ponapean men's
dance.

wenakap *num.* Six; see *kap.*

weneisek *num.* Sixty; see *eisek.*

weneu *num.* Six; see *-u.*

wenehk *num.* Sixty; see *ehk.*

weneka *num.* Six; see *ka₂*.

wenekis *num.* Six; see *kis₁*.

wenemen *num.* Six; see *men₃*.

wenemwodol *num.* Six; see *mwodol.*

wenemwut *num.* Six; see *mwut₂*.

wenengoul *num.* Sixty; see *ngoul.*

wenepa *num.* Six; see *pa₃*.

wenepak *num.* Six; see *pak₁*.

wenepali *num.* Six; see *pali₁*.

wenepar *num.* Six; see *par₂*.

wenepit *num.* Six; see *pit₂*.

wenepoar *num.* Six; see *poar.*

wenepwong *num.* Six; see *pwong.*

wenepwoat *num.* Six; see *pwoat.*

wenera *num.* Six; see *ra.*

wenering *n.* Dried coconut meat after
the extraction of the oil.

wenesel *n.* Six; see *sel₂*.

wenedip *num.* Six; see *dip.*

wenetumw *num.* Six; see *tumw.*

wenewei *vi.* To continue on.

wenewel *num.* Six; see *wel₂*.

weniel *num.* Six; see *el₂*.

Wenik ARCHAIC. *n.* Ancient name for
Uh.

wenihmw *n.* Door.

wenihmw en lempahntamw *n.* Either
of the two rear doors of a feasthouse.

wenihmwtok *n.* Window.

wenoumw *num.* Six; see *umw₂*.

wenlep *num.* Six; see *lep.*

wenpwuloi *n.* Six; see *pwuloi.*

wens *n.* Crane, the machine; winch.
[Eng.]

wensakau *n.* Dried kava after the
extraction of the juice.

wensou *num.* Six; see *sou₄*.

wensop *num.* Six; see *sop₂*.

wendi *vi.* To lie down; to spend a night
at.

wendun *num.* Six; see *dun.*

wente *num.* Six; see *te.*

wengid *vt.* To wring, to squeeze with a
twisting motion. —**wengiweng,** *vi.*

wengidek *adj.* Twisted. —**wengid,** *vt.*

wengiweng *vi.* To wring, to squeeze
with a twisting motion. —**wengid,** *vt.*

wengkid *vi.* At the end of the kava
ceremony, to completely extract all
the juices from a batch of kava.

wenglopwon *vi.* To squeeze kava that has been set aside in anticipation of the arrival of titled guests.

wengmad *vi.* To squeeze kava until it is completely dried.

wengpoar *vi.* Of kava, to be processed for drinking for the final time.

wer *vi.* To shout, to scream, to howl, to yell, to holler. —**wering,** *vt.*

were₁ *n3s.* Neck.

were₂ *poss. cl.* A possessive classifier used for vehicles.

werei 1. *adj.* Lasting for a long time. 2. *n.* Duration.

werek HONORIFIC. 1. *vi.* To be companions; to be married. 2. *n.* Spouse, husband or wife; companion. —**warakih,** *vt.*

weren uhk *vi.* To fish with a net from a canoe or boat.

weren nansapw *n.* Automobile, car.

weren tuhke *n.* Seed.

werer *n.* Sp. of sea cucumber.

wering *vt.* To shout, to scream, to howl, to yell, to holler at. —**wer,** *vi.*

wes *n.* Any implement used for pulling weeds.

wese *vt.* To cut sugar cane or firewood.

wehsel *n.* Ship or work whistle. [Eng.]

wed *adj.* Puffed out, protruding, as of the stomach.

wehd, also **ohd.** *n.* Taro, *Alocasia macrorrhiza.*

wedei *adj.* Talkative.

wedin neh *n3s.* Calf, of the leg.

wehdpeseng *vt.* To rip open; to break into a house.

wet₁ 1. *vi.* To turn while in motion; to change direction; to stop along the way. 2. *n.* Bend or curve in a road or path.

wet₂ *vi. neut.* To eat raw. —**wete,** *vt.*

wete *vt.* To eat raw. —**wet₂,** *vi.*

wetih SLANG. *vt.* To whip, to spank. —**weweti,** *vi.*

wetikitik *adj.* Small in diameter, of holes, coconuts, or people.

wehwe 1. *vi.* To be understood. 2. *n* (*3s: wehweh*). Meaning; opening.

wehwepeseng *vi.* To be cleared out.

weweti *vi.* To be whipped or spanked. —**wetih,** *vt.*

wih₁ *n.* Name of the letter *w*.

wih₂ *n.* Tree sp., *Barringtonia asiatica.*

wih₃ *n.* Grease, fat.

wia *vt.* To do; occurs as *wie* when used with an incorporated object or when it marks durative aspect. *E wiemwangas.* He made copra. *E wie doadoahk.* He is working.

wiakau *adj.* Wasteful. —**wiakawe,** *vt.*

wiakawe *vt.* To waste; to mistreat. —**wiakau,** *adj.*

wiahla *vt.* To make, to become, to turn into.

wiahda *vt.* To make, to repair, to build.

wiawi *vi.* To occur, to happen; to have sexual intercourse.

wie See *wia.*

wiehni 1. *n.* The game of tag. 2. *vi.* To play tag.

wiedip *vi.* To have sexual intercourse.

wiewia *n.* Deed.

wik *n.* Trump, in cards.

wihk₁ *n.* Week. [Eng.]

wihk₂ *n.* Wick. [Eng.]

wikila *vi.* To be changed, to be transformed; to blush.

wikid *vt.* To turn over; to change, as in opinion.

wikidek *vi.* To turn, in direction.

wikidedi *vt.* To turn upside down; to drink an entire cup of kava.

wikpeseng *vi.* To be different.

wikwikin *adj.* Variable, inconsistent, changeable.

wil *n.* Will, the document. [Eng.]

wihl₁ *n* (*3s: wile*). Penis, of an adult.

wihl₂ *n.* Wheel. [Eng.]

wiliakapwala *vi.* To be repentant.

wiliali *vi.* To exchange; to be changed, to be substituted, to be replaced. —**wilian,** *vt.*

wilian *vt.* To change, to substitute, to replace, to represent. —**wiliali,** *vi.*

wilianter *n.* Bush sp..

wilie *n3s.* Substitute, successor.

wiliepe *n3s.* Replacement, representative.

wilpahro *n.* Wheelbarrow. [Eng.]

wihn 1. *vi.* To win; to profit. 2. *n.* Profit. [Eng.]

winakanak *adj.* Wet and matted, of hair.

winahni 1. *vi.* To cast a spell; to perform magic. 2. *n.* Spell, magic.

winapwehk SLANG. *adj.* Of bodily coverings, soaking wet.

wine *n3s.* Body hair, feathers, fur.

wini 1. *n.* Medicine. 2. *vi.* To take medicine. —**winie**, *vt.*

winie *vt.* To medicate; to treat with medicine. —**wini**, *vi.*

wihnmoar *n.* Tree sp., *Barringtonia racemosa.*

windeng 1. *vi.* To drive. 2. *n.* Driver. [Jap.]

wisekesek *adj.* Wet.

wisik 1. *n.* Burden, load. 2. *vi.* To be carried.

wisik pwehl 1. *vi.* To harvest a new planting of kava. 2. *n.* First harvest of a new planting of kava.

wisol *n (3s: wisole).* Testicle; baby boy.

wisol en kuloak *n.* Pendulum of a clock.

wisolmat *n.* Mature male pig; a derogatory term for filariasis; also used as an oath.

wisolpali *n.* A man or pig having only one testicle.

wisoar *vi.* To use a lotion or cream to hold one's hair in place; of a dog, to roll in something rotten. —**wisoare**, *vt.*

wisoare *vt.* See *wisoar.*

wideh *vi.* To wash one's feet.

widei *n.* Fish sp..

wideud *vi.* To be washed, of anything except clothing. —**widen**, *vt.*

wideudamwer HONORIFIC. *vi.* To cry, to weep.

widek *vi.* To be poured; to be spilled. —**wideki**, *vt.*

wideki *vt.* To pour; to spill. —**widek**, *vi.*

widen *vt.* To wash, of anything except clothing. —**wideud**, *vi.*

widengi, also **wudengi**. *vi.* To brush one's teeth.

widing 1. *vi.* To deceive, to lie, to defraud. 2. *n.* Deception, lie, fraud. —**widinge**, *vt.*

widinge *vt.* To deceive, to lie to, to defraud. —**widing**, *vi.*

widingek *adj.* Deceitful, fraudulent.

wounmei *n.* A door in the rear of a feasthouse used by the Nahnmwarki.

wohnohn *vi.* To lie down.

wonowei *vi.* To strive onward.

wonuhmw *n.* Cook house.

wowoki *vi. neut.* To whip, to spank, to beat. —**woakih**, *vt.*

woakih, also **poakih**. *vt.* To whip, to spank, to beat. —**wowoki**, *vi.*

woahkian *adj.* More than adequate.

woakida *vi.* To look up to and listen attentively, as of people in a feasthouse.

wudengi, also **widengi**. *vi.* To brush one's teeth.

ENGLISH-PONAPEAN FINDER LIST

abacus: *sorapang.*

abandon
to forget or abandon: *likidmeliehla.*

abbreviated
to be shortened, to be abbreviated: *kamwot.*

abdomen
lower abdomen: *pwere$_2$.*

abhor
to abhor: *akatantat, dongodongki.*

abnormal
abnormal, deformed, odd: *pakalong.*
abnormal sounding, as of the voice or an instrument: *par$_4$.*

aboard
to board, to step up onto, to climb aboard: *karada.*
to remain aboard a boat or canoe while others are diving for fish: *koluwar.*

abolish
to abolish: *kasohre.*

aboriginal
native, aboriginal: *pwilidak.*

about: *-seli.*

above
above, upon, on (him, her, or it): *powe.*
above, upper, upwind, windward side: *pohnangi.*

abrasion
to have an abrasion or superficial wound: *tepwedi.*

abroad
to be foreign, from abroad, now commonly used to mean American: *wai$_2$.*

absent-minded
absent-minded, forgetful: *limanokonok.*

absorb
to suck, to absorb: *mihk.*
to inhale, to breathe in deeply, to absorb: *ihk.*

abstain
to abstain, from anything: *likisang.*
to fast or abstain from food: *kalehk.*
to fast or abstain from food, voluntarily or on direction from a superior: *kaisihsol.*

abstemious
abstemious, temperate in eating and drinking: *ewetik.*

abundant
abundant, plentiful: *rek.*

abused: *mwou.*

accent
accent, dialect, tune, tone: *ngohr.*

to speak with an accent: *sis$_1$.*

accompany
to accompany, join, or go with, to participate, to attend: *iang.*
to accompany and assist: *likid$_2$.*

accomplish
to accomplish something: *keimwisak.*
to be accomplished: *keimwisek.*
to be finished, to be accomplished: *imwisekila.*

accordion: *kutian.*

account
debt, credit, account: *pweipwand.*

account
on account of: *pwehki.*

accurate
accurate, in shooting or throwing: *pehinen.*

accusation: *kadip, pakaraun.*

accuse
to accuse: *kadip, kadipa, karaunih.*
to make an accusation: *karaun, pakaraun.*
to falsely accuse: *karaun likamwih.*
to make a false accusation: *karaun likamw.*
to be falsely accused: *kangidirawi.*

accuser
prosecutor, accuser, tattletale: *sounkadip.*
false accuser: *sounkaraun.*

accustomed
to be used to or accustomed to: *ahn$_1$.*

ace
ace, in cards: *ehs$_2$.*

ache
to ache: *medek.*

acknowledge
to acknowledge: *pohnese.*
to formally acknowledge the presence of visitors, done as a respect gesture by individuals travelling after or with the recipients: *aluhmwur.*

acne
pimple, acne: *maht.*

acquainted
to be acquainted with one another: *pehse.*

acquiesce
to comply, to acquiesce, to do something against one's will: *seiren.*

acre: *eiker.*

acrophobic: *lengk.*

act
to demonstrate, to act as if: *akahk.*

action
to take immediate action on something because the opportunity is right: *isaniki.*

active
active, peppy: *pwahtiet.*

activity
major activities of the *Nahnmwarki*: *toulap.*
minor activities of the *Nahnmwarki*: *toutik.*
the final activity in a competition: *saingo.*

actually: *nahn₄.*

adage
talk, discussion, rumor, story, adage, parable: *koasoai.*

Adam's apple: *takain were.*

add
to add: *kapat.*
to add liquid to a solid: *sowe₁.*
to add or include: *iangahki.*
to add small stones to an *uhmw*: *kanai.*
to add water to pounded kava: *pwadik₂, pwed₂.*
to mix, to add ingredients: *doaloa, dol₁.*

addition: *kapat.*

adequate
to be enough, adequate, ample: *itar.*
more than adequate: *woahkian.*

adhere
to adhere to: *iangala.*

adherent
adherent, cohesive, gummy, sticky: *ngidingid.*

administrator
governor, district administrator: *kepina.*

admire
to admire: *wadek₂.*
admired: *wadawad₂.*

admit
to admit: *kapidolong₁.*

adopt
to adopt: *pwek₁.*

adore
to worship, to adore: *pwungih₁.*

adultery
to commit adultery, to fornicate: *nenek.*
to sin, to commit adultery: *dihp.*

advantage
to take advantage of: *engmwahukihla.*
said of one who takes advantage of

others when they are distracted: *derinmwoarong.*

advantageous
useful, worthwhile, valuable, advantageous: *katapan.*

Advent: *Adwendo.*

adventurous
daring, reckless, bold, adventurous: *loallap.*

adversary
adversary, enemy, feud: *imwintihti.*

advice: *peneu.*
advice taken to heart: *kepinwar.*

advise
to advise: *kaweid, panawih.*
to be advised: *peneu.*

advisor: *sounkaweid.*

adze
adze, axe: *sile₂.*
a kind of adze: *medeu, pairuk₂, sile moahl.*
shell adze, made from the shell of the giant clam: *kih₅.*

affection: *poakepoak.*
a term of affection used by parents with their children: *samwa₂.*

affiliated
to be affiliated with: *salih.*

affinity
having a special affinity for growing certain species of yams: *pwuwak.*

affix
to fasten, to affix: *kapasa.*

afraid
to be afraid of, to fear: *masak.*
afraid, frightened, cowardly, bashful: *masepwehk.*
afraid of ghosts: *lemmw, lommw.*

after
after, behind (him, her, or it): *mwuri.*
after, with reference to telling time: *daulih.*

again
to do again: *pwurehng, sapahl.*

age: *sounpar.*
old, aged: *mah.*
to age, of food: *kamat.*

agile: *welikek.*

agitated
of water, to be agitated: *pwungidekida.*

ago
a while ago: *ngkapwan, ningkapwan.*
long ago: *kawa₁, keilahn aio.*

agonizing
painful, agonizing, torturous: *weirek.*

agree
to agree, to like: *kupwurki.*
to heed, to pay attention to, to agree with: *ahne.*
to be settled, to be decided, to be agreed upon: *koasoandi.*

agreement
contract, promise, agreement, covenant: *inou₁.*
organization, structure, rule, plan, agreement: *koasoandi.*

agricultural fair: *impiokai.*

agricultural products: *wahnsahpw.*

agriculture: *doahken sahpw.*

aground
to run aground: *ser₂.*

ahead
ahead of, in front of, before (him, her, or it): *mwowe₁.*

aid
help, assistance, aid: *sawas.*
to help, assist, aid: *sawas, sewese.*

aim
to aim: *kainene.*

air
air, wind: *ahng₁, kisinieng.*
to be shut off from a source of air: *mwopw.*

air-raid shelter
man-made cave, air-raid shelter: *pwohkungo.*

airfield
airport, airfield: *skohso, wasahn sompihr.*

airplane: *sompihr.*

airport
airport, airfield: *skohso, wasahn sompihr.*

airy
breezy, airy: *engitik.*

aisle
aisle, sidewalk: *wasahn alu.*

akimbo
to stand with one's hands on one's hips, to stand with one's arms akimbo: *pedilukop.*

albatross: *kupwur₁.*

alcohol: *ahrkohl.*
initial effects of kava or alcohol: *litepw.*
to feel the initial effects of kava or alcohol: *litepw.*

alcoholic
alcoholic, always drunk: *nompe.*

alert
to disturb or alert by making a pounding noise: *kumw, kumwur.*

algae: *pwisehn ketipin.*

alight
to alight or step down: *keredi.*

align
to align, to equalize, to level: *kapahrek.*

aligned
aligned, arranged, settled, ordered: *soan.*

alive
alive, raw: *mour₂.*
to be alive: *ieias.*

all: *koaros.*

allergic
to be allergic to, to easily contract, as an illness: *kehieng.*

alligator
any large lizard, alligator, or crocodile: *kieil.*

allow
to allow or permit: *mweid₃, mweimwei.*

alone
to be alone: *kalapwuk, kelehpw.*

aloof
aloof, indifferent: *popohn.*

also: *pil₁.*

altar: *pehi₂.*
holy altar: *peisarawi.*
sacred place, altar, throne: *mwoahl.*

alternate
to alternate, to exchange, as a load or position: *peisipal.*

alto
to sing alto: *aldo.*

aluminum: *alminiom.*

always
incessantly, always: *poaden.*

amazed
to be surprised, astonished, amazed, or shocked: *pwuriamwei.*

amazement: *eimwolu.*
surprise, astonishment, amazement, shock: *pwuriamwei.*

ambush
to ambush: *rukihdi.*

amen: *ahmen.*

America
America, United States of America: *Amerika.*

amount
excessive amount: *mwuledek.*
total amount: *tohtowe.*

ample
to be enough, adequate, ample: *itar.*

amputated
to be amputated: *tok₁*.

amusing
amusing, pleasant, funny: *kaperen*.
funny, amusing: *kemenkouruhr*.

analogy
to make an analogy: *karasaras*.

ancestry
to trace one's ancestry, to recall past
history: *kadoudou, kodoudou*.
to trace one's ancestry according to
clan: *kadoukeinek, kodoukeinek*.

anchor: *angke, poudek*.
to be anchored or tied up, of a boat:
pei₅.
to weigh down, to anchor something in
place by placing an object on top:
koasuk.

and: *oh₂*.
and then: *apw*.
however, and: *ah₃*.

anemone
sea anemone sp.: *limwadong*.

angel: *tohnleng*.

angelfish
fish sp., angelfish: *senserek*.

anger
to be in a state of intense disgust or
anger: *tat₂*.
to speak in anger: *kahs₁*.

angle
corner, angle: *keimw*.

angry: *engieng, lingeringer*.
angry, furious: *mwehl₁*.
to be angry: *sall*.
to be angry at, to scold: *angiangih*.

animal
animal, insect: *mahn*.
any four-legged animal: *menkerep*.
castrated animal: *lekelek*.

ankle bone: *tikel en neh*.

annihilated
to be annihilated or destroyed:
mwomwsang.

announce
to notify, to announce: *pakair*.

announcement
notice, announcement: *pakair*.

annoying
irritating, bothersome, annoying:
kelingeringer.

anoint
to anoint: *kei, keie, marekeiso*.

answer
response, answer: *pasapeng*.
to respond to, to answer: *sapeng*.

to respond, to answer: *pasapeng*.

ant: *kaht₁*.
sp. of large black ant: *kakiles*.
sp. of small ant: *ketitik*.
sp. of small black ant: *ketitoal*.
sp. of small red ant: *ketiweita*.
sp. of small red ant, known for its bite:
ketkeikamedek.

antagonize
to antagonize: *kaloke*.

antenna: *andehna*.

anticipate
to anticipate, to expect: *awihala*.

anus: *dauso, dewen kainen, pwoaren
kahwe, pwoaren pwise*.
anus, vagina: *dahu*.

anxious
concerned, anxious, eager: *ngoang*.

anything
something, anything (singular): *mehkot,
okoteme*.
something, anything (plural): *mehkei*.

apart
apart, away from each other: *-peseng*.
far apart: *malau*.

apostle
apostle, minister: *wahnpoaron*.

apparently
apparently, it seems that: *likamw,
likamwete*.

appear
to appear: *pwar, pwer*.
to appear on the horizon, of land:
lingada.
to arrive at a specific location, to
appear on the scene: *loi-*.

appearance: *mwohmw*.
appearance, at a place: *moahl₂*.

appendage
appendage, finger, toe: *send*.

appendicitis: *mwohso*.

appetizing
of food, appetizing due to the manner
in which it is eaten by another:
otoht.

applaud
to applaud: *lopwor*.

apple: *apel*.
tree sp., mountain apple, *Syzygium
malaccense*: *apel*.

apply
to apply to the skin, as medicine: *kei*.

appoint
to appoint: *idihada*.
to be appointed: *idihdida*.

appropriate
appropriate, proper: *konehng.*

approval
to make official, to authorize, to give official approval to: *kamana.*
to be made official, to be authorized, to be given official approval: *kamanaman.*

April: *Epreil.*

arch
arch of the foot: *kapehden neh.*

archipelago: *kahndeke.*

area
area or location: *dehu.*
area between: *nanmadola-.*
area on the beach or along the reef where the waves break: *pohnlik.*

argue
to argue, to quarrel: *akamai.*

argument
argument, quarrel, dispute: *akamai.*

argumentative: *lokaia tohto.*

arithmetic: *wahntuhke$_2$.*

ark: *warihmw.*

arm
arm, hand: *lime, peh.*

armpit: *pahnpeh, pahnpwoal.*

army: *sounpei nansapw.*

aroma
smell, odor, aroma: *pwoh.*

around
to encircle, to go around: *kapil.*

arouse
to arouse any feeling, to arouse sexually: *inangih.*

arrange
to simplify, to arrange in a simple manner, to delete some part of task: *kamangaila.*

arranged
aligned, arranged, settled, ordered: *soan.*

arrest
to arrest: *parok.*
to be arrested: *poaridi$_1$.*

arrive
to arrive at a specific location, to appear on the scene: *loi-.*
to arrive at someone's home just after he has departed for fishing or hunting, believed to bring bad luck: *tiemwur.*
to arrive by sea: *pas$_1$.*
to arrive or depart early in the morning: *sangkenei.*

to arrive, by means of transportation: *peidi.*
to have arrived at or departed from an area: *samwodohr.*
to reach or arrive at: *lel$_1$.*

arrogant: *pohlemei.*

arrow
spear, arrow: *arep.*

arrow plant
plant sp., *Tacca leontopetaloides*, arrow plant: *mwekimwek.*

arthritis
arthritis, rheumatism: *nankoakonmedek.*

article
section or article: *ire$_2$.*

as
as if: *pala.*

ascend
to ascend: *piserwar.*

ash tray: *aisara, mehn loipehs.*

ashamed
bashful, embarrassed, ashamed: *liroaridi, namenek.*

ashes: *pehs$_1$.*

ask
to ask: *idek, keidek, keinemwe, peidek.*
to ask about, to inquire, to question: *kadeik.*
to ask for, to request: *peki.*
to check, to inquire, to ask: *kalelapak.*

asleep
asleep, as when one's leg falls asleep: *ketiket$_1$.*

aspirin: *aispiring.*

ass
ass, donkey: *ahs.*

assemble
to assemble, to put together: *kakonehda.*
to bring together, to assemble: *dahrkipene.*
to be assembled together in a crowd: *pokon.*

assist
to assist, to serve: *papah.*
to help, assist, aid: *sawas, sewese.*
to accompany and assist: *likid$_2$.*
to assist someone by carrying part of his load: *koade.*

assistance
help, assistance, aid: *sawas.*

associate
to associate with: *kapara$_1$, warakih.*

association
union, association, any cooperative
venture: *minimin.*

assume
to assume: *kihkieng.*

asthma
mild case of asthma: *nget.*
serious case of asthma: *lokulok,
lukuluk.*
serious case of asthma in which a
person gasps for breath: *eidak.*
to have a serious case of asthma:
lokulok, lukuluk.
to have a serious case of asthma in
which one gasps for breath: *eidak.*

asthmatic: *lokulok, lukuluk.*

astonished
to be surprised, astonished, amazed, or
shocked: *eimwolu, pwuriamwei.*

astonishment
surprise, astonishment, amazement,
shock: *eimwolu, pwuriamwei.*

at
at, to: *ni, nin.*

athlete
player, athlete: *sensuh, sounmwadong.*

athletic meet: *undohkai.*

attach
to tie or attach together one after
another, as breadfruit or flowers, to
tie a bundle of things: *dune.*
to be attached: *pakehng.*
loosely attached: *lisaimwer.*

attack
to attack in a hit and run fashion, of
sharks, barracuda, and the sp. of bird
kutoahr: *tahr$_1$.*

attempt
to try, to attempt: *song.*
to attempt to gain favor, to bribe:
natih.

attend
to accompany, join, or go with, to
participate, to attend: *iang.*
to attend a feast or party without
contributing provisions: *tohnkapar.*
to attend or serve a dignitary during a
feast: *aririh.*

attention
to pay attention to: *ahng$_3$.*
to pay no attention to, to be
unconcerned about: *sokorohnki.*
to bring to the attention of an
authority, to report: *leleki.*

attorney
attorney, lawyer, defender: *pengohsi,
sounsawas.*

attract
to employ magic to romantically
attract another: *mesehlih.*

attractive
attractive, attracting admiration or
interest: *mwongoungou.*
attractive, excellent: *suwanawan.*

augment
to augment, as a point in an argument:
ketihnain.

August: *Ahkos, Oakos.*

authority: *manaman.*
to make a display of magic, spiritual
power, or authority: *akmanaman.*

authorize
to make official, to authorize, to give
official approval to: *kamana.*
to be made official, to be authorized,
to be given official approval:
kamanaman.

automobile
automobile, car: *sidohsa, weren
nansapw.*

avenge
to avenge: *ikih.*

await
to await: *awihodo.*
to await an event: *koamwoadoaloan.*
to expect, to await: *kasik.*

awake
to stay awake: *pepehd, tetensik.*
to remain awake all night, as at a
wake: *kesihpwong, mwohdenpwong.*
easily awakened: *kehntik, kehnwasa.*
easily awakened, early rising: *pehmitik.*

awaken
to awaken: *pangin.*
to be awakened: *mpeng.*

award
to be awarded or to receive votes, a
degree, title, etc.: *alehdi.*

awkward
inappropriate, awkward because of
unfamiliarity, difficult to learn:
koasoakoahiek.

axe
adze, axe: *sile$_2$.*

baby bottle: *dihdi.*

baby-sit
to baby-sit: *epwelseri.*
to baby-sit, to pamper: *kamwait.*

back: *nantihnsewe, pelikiso, pohn sowe,
pohn tihn sowe, sowe$_2$.*

back of the head: *likinioar, likinleng, likinsekiri.*
back of the head or neck: *likinpaiki.*
back of the neck: *pohnihr.*
lower back, tailbone area: *sikinkihri.*
upper part of the back: *pelikie.*

backbone: *tihnsau.*

backslide
to backslide: *pweiek.*

backwards
to move backwards: *pweiek.*

bacteria
worm, bacteria, germ: *mwahs.*

bad: *sakanakan, suwed.*
very bad: *patukul.*
having a bad reputation: *adsuwed.*

bad breathed: *aumat.*

badge
metal, nail, badge, spear for a speargun: *mete.*

badmouth
to badmouth: *kehr.*

bag
bag, sack: *ehd₂.*

baggy: *pwoalosolos.*

bail
to bail: *limak, limalim.*

bailer: *lihm.*

bait
bait, lure: *pahn₂.*
bait arranged on the ocean floor to lure turtles: *kamwer.*
bait thrown around a canoe to attract fish: *kuroamw.*

bake
to bake in an *uhmw*: *umw₁, umwun₁.*

bald: *moangamad.*

ball: *mpwei.*
any soft object which is made into a ball: *lopwon.*
ball of sennit: *soanop.*
glass fishing ball: *ramwune.*
lightbulb, bullet, pool ball: *dama.*

ballast: *palas.*

balloon: *pwuhseng.*

bamboo
bamboo, *Bambusa vulgaris*: *pehri.*

banana
banana, *Musa paradisiaca*: *uht.*
banana, *Musa textilis*: *utisel.*
banana, *Musa tikap*: *tikahp.*
a variety of banana, from Fiji: *utin pihsi.*
a variety of banana, from Guam: *utin kuam.*

a variety of banana, from Manila: *utin menihle.*
a variety of banana, from Palau: *utin palau.*
a variety of banana, from Saipan: *utin seipahn.*
a variety of banana, from Truk: *utin ruk.*
a variety of banana, from Yap: *utin iap.*
a variety of banana, having a large trunk but small fruit: *poupoulap₂.*
a variety of banana, said to be native to Ponape: *uht mwot.*
a variety of banana: *akadahn, daiwang, dukuru, inasio, kaladahn, karat, karateniap, kudud, lakadahn, preisihl, utiak, utimwas, utin wai, utindol, utumwot.*
plantain: *mangat.*
banana flower: *kakipwel.*
breadfruit or grated banana cooked with coconut milk: *seipwok.*
grated green banana with coconut oil: *sampwil.*

band
marching band: *kakudai, mwusiko.*

band
to kill a tree by banding, to band a tree: *rehre.*

bandage
bandage, gauze: *ohdai.*

banish
to banish, to exile: *kalipe.*
to be banished, to be exiled: *kalipilip.*
to eject, to banish: *kaus.*
to be ejected, to be banished: *pokous.*

bank: *pangk₂.*

bank
bank of a taro patch: *dek₂.*

banyan tree
banyan tree, *Ficus carolinensis*, used in the treatment of tetanus and as a hemostatic in menstruation: *aiau.*

baptism: *pepdais.*

baptize
to baptize: *pepdaisih.*
to be baptized: *pepdais.*

bar
crowbar, bar: *pahru.*
concrete reinforcing bar: *dekking.*
bar, tavern: *pahr₄.*

barb
barb, as of a hook: *dindir.*
to make a barb on something, as a hook: *dindirih.*
to be barbed: *dindir.*

barbed wire: *diraht.*

barbell
the axle plus the wheels of a narrow gauge train, sometimes used as a barbell: *doro.*

barefoot
to go barefoot: *adasi.*

barge
raft, barge: *rahp.*

bark
to bark: *ngong.*
to bark at: *ngongih.*

bark
skin, bark, hide, any outer covering: *kihl₁.*

barnacle: *mpwun.*

barracuda
fish sp., barracuda: *nahliam.*
fish sp., barracuda, *Sphyraena barracuda*: *suhre.*
fish sp., barracuda, *Sphyraena langsar* or *Sphyraena bleekeri*: *sarau.*

barrel
bucket, barrel: *pekid.*

barren
barren female, usually of pigs: *iopwou.*

basalt
large boulder of basalt: *paip₁.*

base
base of a tree: *tapi.*
base of the stem of a palm: *pahle.*
first base, in baseball: *pahsdo.*
second base, in baseball: *sakando.*
third base, in baseball: *sahdo.*
home plate, in baseball: *ohmw.*

baseball: *iakiu.*
to play baseball: *iakiu.*
baseball field: *kurando.*

bashful
bashful, embarrassed, ashamed: *liroaridi, namenek.*
afraid, frightened, cowardly, bashful: *masepwehk.*

basin: *peisin.*
washtub, basin: *darai.*

basket: *ohdou, palang₂.*
basket, purse, handbag: *kopwou, kupwu.*
basket made from a palm frond: *kiam.*
a large basket made from a palm frond: *kelek.*
basket, suspended from a pole and carried by two or more people: *kiamoro.*
large basket carried by four or more people: *peikini.*

basket for the wives of the *Nahnmwarki* and *Nahnken* in which *lihli* is presented: *ilail en likend.*
basket in which *lihli* is presented to the pounder of the breadfruit: *ilail en sounlih.*
basket in which *lihli* is presented to the preparer of the coconut cream: *ilail en sounpiah.*

bass
to sing bass: *pas₃, peis, peisih.*

bass-grouper
fish sp., bass-grouper, *Cephalopholis argus*: *mwalusulus.*

bast
hibiscus bast used for straining kava: *dipen keleu.*
a command from the director of a *kamadipw* to bring more hibiscus bast for the kava: *koroikot.*

bat: *pwehk.*
a small sp. of bat: *kelemwed, kelimwed, limwehdi, liwair₂.*

bat
baseball bat: *padda.*

bath: *duhdu.*

bathe
to bathe: *depwe, depwedepw, duhdu, duhp₂, loakipil, loakiso.*

batter
batter, in baseball: *sounpok.*

battery: *densi, padiri.*

battle
war, battle: *mahwin.*
war, battle, dispute: *moromor.*

bawl
to bawl, to cry loudly: *rerehd wasa.*

bay
to bay, of dogs when hunting: *ngai.*

bayonet: *niondo.*
sword, cutlass, bayonet: *kedilahs.*

beam
beam of light: *linge.*
beam or rafter of a roof: *rehu.*
crossbeam in a house: *lohlo.*
girt, a beam connecting the corner posts of the exterior frame of a building at the roof level: *ndape.*

beans: *mame, pens, pihns.*

bear
to flower or bear fruit: *wa₁.*

bear: *pehr.*

beard
beard, mustache: *alis.*

beat
   to spank or beat: *apin, kamakam, keme.*
   to whip, to spank, to beat: *poakih, woakih, wowoki.*

beautiful
   beautiful, shiny: *lingan.*
   precious, beautiful, perfect, fine: *kaselel.*
   sensuous, beautiful: *pwuteletel.*

because
   because, since, but, so that: *pwe.*
   because of : *pwehki.*
   because, because of, in answer to a question: *ahki.*

become
   to make, to become, to turn into: *wiahla.*

bed: *peht.*
   bed of a river: *elen pillap.*
   seed bed: *kamwer.*
   to remain overnight, to go to bed, to bed down: *pweidi, pweiekidi.*

bed-ridden
   to become very ill, incapacitated, bed-ridden: *kehimwidi.*

bee
   honeybee: *loangen suke.*

beep
   to beep or honk a horn: *pihp, pihpih.*

beer: *pihe, pihru.*

before
   ahead of, in front of, before (him, her, or it): $mwowe_1.$

beg
   to request, to ask a favor, to beg: *pekipek.*

begging
   looking in a begging manner: *lipekekil.*

begin
   to begin, to start: *tapiada, tapihda,* $tep_1.$

beginning: *tapi.*
   in the beginning: *nintapi.*

behavior
   custom, manner, behavior, culture: *tiahk.*

behind
   after, behind (him, her, or it): *mwuri.*

behold
   to watch, to behold, to observe: *poudiahl, udiahl.*

behold : $nahn_3.$

belch
   to burp, to belch: *kirer.*

belief
   faith, belief, creed: *pwoson.*

believe
   to believe in, to have faith in: *pwoson.*
   to believe or suspect: *leme.*
   to believe to be true: *kamehlele.*
   to be verified, to be believed to be true: *kamehlel.*

bell: $pehl_2.$

belligerent
   belligerent, easily angered: *kotuhwahu.*
   cruel, belligerent, tough: *keses, lemei.*
   to be cruel, belligerent, or tough to: *lamai.*

belly: $ih_4.$
   belly, guts: *kapehd.*

bellyband
   bellyband, sash: *arimaki.*

beloved
   beloved, favored: *masamas.*

below
   below, under (him, her, or it): $pah_1.$

belt: *kateng, kengir, pirapir.*
   belt made of banana fiber, worn above a grass skirt: *dohr.*
   belt worn by women made of the bark of the *nihn* tree: *nihn.*
   belt buckle: *moangen kateng.*
   belt loop: $pwakel_2.$

bench: $pangk_1.$

bend
   to bend back: *welik.*
   to bend down to pick something up: *rekidi.*
   to bend forward from the waist: *dairuk,* $pairuk_1.$
   to bend forward, of people: *dikou.*
   to bend, of something rigid: *kupwel.*
   to bend, to bend to one's will: *kakosih, kakosih.*
   to bend, to droop: *itiek.*
   bend or curve in a road or path: $wet_1.$
   curve, bend: *mpwe.*

bent: $kos_2.$
   bent, crooked, curved: *pu.*
   bent, of something rigid: *kupwelek.*
   bent, smashed, mashed, dented: *limek.*

best
   to be the first or best, to top all others: $dake_1.$

bet
   to bet: *pet.*

betel nut
   betel nut, *Areca cathecu*: $pwuh_1.$

Bethlehem: *Pedlem.*

betray
to betray: *pangala.*
to be betrayed: *pengipengla.*

between
area between: *nanmadola-.*
location between: *nanpwunga-.*
space between things: *madol.*
time between events: *madol.*

beverage
any intoxicating beverage: *sakau.*
the liquid gathered from the coconut
flower, sometimes used to make
molasses or fermented to make an
intoxicating beverage: *sikaliwi.*

beyond
to pass by, to go beyond: *daulih.*

Bible: *Paipel, Pwuksarawi.*

bicycle: *pwaisikel.*

bid
to bid: *pet.*

big
big, old: *laud, likeilap.*

big mouthed
big mouthed, boastful: *oatalaud.*

bigness
bigness, greatness: *laud.*

bile
bile, of the liver: edi_2.

bill: pil_3.
bill, proposal, in legislative
proceedings: *mwomwadahn
kosonned.*

billion: lik_1.

binding
binding, wrapper: *pirepe.*

bingo: *pingko.*

binoculars
spyglass, telescope, binoculars:
tupweiklas.

bird: *menpihr.*

bird sp.
bird sp., Micronesian broadbill, *Myagra
oceanica*: $koikoi_3$.
bird sp., Pacific golden plover,
Pluvialis dominica: *kulu.*
bird sp., a land bird: *wair.*
bird sp., a sea bird: *sakier.*
bird sp., a sea bird having a twisted
beak: *lipoahrok.*
bird sp., a white sea bird: $sihk_1$.
bird sp., black and red in color:
pwiliet.
bird sp., black in color: *sioahk.*
bird sp., brown and white in color:
peluhs.

bird sp., commonly found in swampy
areas: *totopai.*
bird sp., crimson crowned fruit dove:
kiniwed.
bird sp., fairy tern: *kahke.*
bird sp., frigate bird: *kasap.*
bird sp., gray in color: *tiht.*
bird sp., heron-like: *kewelik, kowelik.*
bird sp., jungle fowl, *Gallus*:
malekenwel.
bird sp., resembling a parrot: *serehd.*
bird sp., with a wide fanning tail:
likepisir.
bird sp., with bluish wings: *kutoahr.*
bird sp., yellow in color: *tutuwi.*
bird sp.: *likedipwuhpwu.*

birth
to give birth: *naitikihdi, neitik.*
to give birth, used biblically:
kaipwihdi.
breech birth: $sileit_2$.

birthday: *ipwidi.*

birthmark
birthmark, any skin discoloration
present from birth: *mweinliroar.*

biscuit: *pwereht.*

bishop: *pisop.*

bit
a bit: *ekis, mwur.*
a little bit of, a small piece of, a
fragment of: *epwidik.*

bite
to bite: ke_2, *keikei, ngalis,
$ngelingel_1$.*
to bite, used only with reference to
rats: sok_3.
given to biting: *lingelingel.*

bitter
bitter tasting, of anything: $katik_1$.
bitter, of kava: *laikihk.*

bizarre
inappropriate, bizarre, incongruous,
not fitting: $sapa_1$.

black: *toantoal.*
pitch-black: *rotapwahk.*

blackboard: *plakpwoht.*

bladder: *edin kent, mpwein kent.*
swim bladder of a fish: *edinieng.*

blade
razor blade: *reise.*

blame
to blame: *keinahki.*
to blame, to lay the blame to: *ikidiki.*

bland
bland, tasteless, watery: *nampil.*

blanket: *pilangkes.*

blaspheme
to blaspheme: *lahlahwe.*

bleach: *sarasi.*
bleach, especially powdered bleach:
sarasko.
to bleach out: *sar.*

bleat
to bleat, of a goat: *meh.*

bless
to bless, to consecrate: *kasarawi*₁.

blessed
to be blessed, used biblically: *meid.*

blind: *masukun.*
to have blurred vision, to go blind:
ediedila.

blindness
temporary blindness induced by
excessive light: *mahl.*

blink
to blink: *limasaweirek, marep*₁.

blister: *mpwet.*
blister, from sunburn: *mpwel*₁.
blood blister: *korinta.*
to blister: *mpwet.*

block
to block: *pina.*
to be blocked: *pinapin.*

block
pulley, block, of a block and tackle:
piloak.

blood: *nta.*
blood blister: *korinta.*

blood brother
blood brother, one fed at the same
breast as a child: *souapwal.*

bloom
to blossom, to bloom: *masal.*

blossom
to blossom, to bloom: *masal.*
to blossom, of fruit trees: *pwer.*

blouse: *lepin seht.*

blow
to blow on, with air expelled from the
mouth: *peuk.*
to be blown on, with air expelled from
the mouth: *pepeuk.*
to blow with air expelled from the
mouth: *malimalih.*
to blow at: *ipir.*
to blow, as the wind: *ipihp.*
to spray or blow inside, of windblown
rain: *arer, sikarer.*
to blow one's nose: *pangid, pengidek.*

blue: *mei*₂.
blue, of the face as when cold:
*reirei*₂.

blue marlin
fish sp., swordfish, sailfish, blue marlin:
dekilahr.

blunt
dull, blunt: *kons.*

blurred
cloudy, blurred, smoky: *edied.*

blush
to blush: *pwukesok, wikila.*

boar
large boar with tusks: *ngihpwar.*

board: *dinapw.*
chopping board: *manaida.*

board
to board, to step up onto, to climb
aboard: *karada.*

boast
to boast: *kahs*₁, *uh*₄.

boastful: *aksuwei, akuh, kala*₁, *suwei.*
big mouthed, boastful: *oatalaud.*
pretentious, proud, boastful: *kerkala,
maskala.*

boat: *pwoht*₁.
a Japanese boat with a diesel engine:
*pwoampwoamw*₂.
small boat, usually one carried aboard
a ship: *demma.*
speedboat: *spihdpwoht.*
whale boat: *wehl pwoht.*

boat pole: *ketia*₂.

bobbin
bobbin, of a sewing machine:
*pwoht*₂.

bobbypin
pin, tack, bobbypin: *pihn.*

body
body, of a person: *erekiso, kahlap,
paliwar, wahr, war*₁.
the lower half of the human body:
kaipw.
the upper half of the human body, the
torso: *ihpwe.*

bog
taro patch, marsh, bog: *lehpwel.*

boil
to boil: *pwoail.*

boil
boil, swelling, infection: *mpwos.*

boisterous
to be boisterous: *ngis.*
given to exaggeration, loud mouthed,
boisterous: *aulaud.*

bold
 bold, brazen, insensitive: *soumahk.*
 daring, reckless, bold, adventurous:
  loallap.

bomb
 bomb, shell: *pakudang.*
 atomic bomb: *kinsipakudang.*

bone: *tih₂.*

bonfire: *isihs.*

bony
 skinny, bony: *tihrereng.*
 of fish, bony: *tihti.*

book: *pwuhk.*
 book, of the Bible: *iralaud.*

boom sheet
 boom sheet, sail rope: *lih₃.*

boot: *pwuht.*

border
 border or limit: *ire₂.*

bored
 to be bored or tired of something
  repetitious: *ngat-.*
 to be tired of, to be disinterested in, to
  be bored by: *pwangahki.*

boring
 tiresome, boring: *kapwang.*

born
 to be born: *ipwidi.*

boss: *pwohs.*
 ruler, boss, leader, director: *kaun.*
 to boss, to rule, to lead, to direct:
  kaun.

bossy
 bossy, demanding: *ilekitik.*

bother
 to bother: *kedirepwe.*
 to intentionally bother: *lidere.*

bothersome: *kedirepw.*
 irritating, bothersome, annoying:
  kelingeringer.
 nosey, bothersome: *direpw.*
 to be intentionally bothersome:
  lider₂.

bottle: *pwoatol.*
 sauce bottle, with a capacity of 1.8
  liters: *issohping.*

bottom: *kahu.*
 bottom, lower part, referring to the
  inside of an object: *nankapi.*
 bottom, the lowest part of yam or taro:
  kapi.

bougainvillia
 plant sp., bougainvillia: *pwukenwilia.*

boulder
 large boulder of basalt: *paip₁.*

bounce
 to bounce, to skip: *sik.*

bouncy: *sikasik.*

boundary
 land boundary: *pehs₂.*
 line, boundary: *lain.*
 boundary between the shallow and
  deep part of a lagoon: *mesenlam.*
 to reach a limit or boundary: *idi-.*

bow
 to bow: *dairuk, itiekidi, kerepwel,*
  pairuk₁.
 to bow or sit as a respect gesture:
  poaridi₂.

bow
 bow of a canoe: *mwohn wahr.*
 paddler who sits in the bow of a canoe:
  mwohnawar.

bow
 bow, of a bow and arrow: *kesingketieu.*

bowl: *dompwuri.*
 bowl, used in the preparation of food:
  kasak.
 soup bowl: *sawang.*

box
 box, chest, coffin, casket: *kohpwa₂.*
 small box: *koakon.*

boxing
 punch, boxing: *paker.*

boy: *pwutak.*
 baby boy: *wisol.*

bra
 brassiere, bra: *sispando.*

brace
 brace, bracket: *preisis₂.*
 drill, brace: *mehn pwuropwur.*

bracelet: *luwou.*

bracket
 brace, bracket: *preisis₂.*

braid: *ingihng₁.*
 tape, braid, ribbon for sewing: *teip.*
 to braid: *ingid, ingihng₁.*

brain: *mwahliel.*

brake
 brake, as on an automobile: *preik₂.*
 to brake: *preik₂.*

branch: *rah.*
 a small branch of kava that can be
  planted: *wahnsakau.*
 original branch of kava that is planted:
  kepinsinoangi.

brass: *pirahs.*

brassiere
 brassiere, bra: *sispando.*

brat: *ketipwehl.*

bratty: *ketipwehl.*

brave
brave, fierce: *kommwad.*

brazen
bold, brazen, insensitive: *soumahk.*

bread: *pilawa.*

breadfruit: *mahi.*
a variety of breadfruit: *kirimwot,
lehtemp, lipet, lukiamwas, lukielel,
lukuwal, meiais, meiapaup,
meiarepe, meikalak, meikidi,
meikimwer, meikole, meikuwet,
meimwed, mein padahk, mein
peimwas, mein pohn sakar, mein
pohnle, mein pwahr, mein pwuht,
mein sahrek, meinpwuhten sokehs,
meinuwe, meipa, meipwiliet,
meipwuhleng, meisaip, meise, meisei,
meiserihseng, meitehid, meiti,
meitoal, meiuhpw, meiweke,
nahnmwal.*
breadfruit or grated banana cooked
with coconut milk: *seipwok.*
breadfruit tree sprout: *perin mahi.*
breadfruit, prepared by placing salt
water or a rotten land taro stem in a
hole in the core of the fruit and
allowing it to age for at least one
day: *dokomei.*
feast of preserved breadfruit: *songmar.*
first breadfruit harvested, which are
taken to a chief: *mwohnmei.*
old preserved breadfruit: *maradahn.*
overripe breadfruit: *maikol.*
preserved breadfruit: *mahr₁.*
preserved breadfruit soaked in salt
water prior to placing it in the pit:
maresed.
ripe breadfruit: *mede.*
ripe breadfruit wrapped in leaves and
prepared in an *uhmw*: *mwehl₂.*
season of plenty, breadfruit season:
nanrek, rahk₁.
two or more breadfruit at the end of a
branch: *liteh.*

break
to break a long object by hand: *rihs.*
to break any long object: *tipwang.*
to break apart, of food: *piling.*
to break into a house: *wehdpeseng.*
to break into small pieces with the
hands, as breadfruit: *pilitikih.*
to break or shatter, especially of glass:
mwarahntik-.
to break, as a string: *mweid₁.*
to break, of waves: *pwungidek,
sawa₂.*

to break, to destroy, to ruin: *kawehla.*
to crack, to break, to come apart, of an
object fastened to something:
pwoapw.
in pool, to break, i.e. to shoot first:
preik₁.
to be broken into small pieces with the
hands, as breadfruit: *pilitik₁.*
to be broken, of a string: *mwei₂.*
to be broken, of any long object:
tipw₁.
to be broken, of anything containing
liquid, granular objects, or gas:
sawa₂.
to be broken, ruined, destroyed,
spoiled: *ohla.*
weak, soft, easily broken, fragile:
kopwukopw₁.

breaker
breaker, a wave that breaks into foam:
ilok sawa.

breakfast: *deied, kapwarsou,
kemenseng₁, mwengehn menseng.*
to eat breakfast: *deied, kapwarsou,
kemenseng₁, mwengehn menseng.*

breast: *dihdi.*
breast, as of a chicken: *kopwenadi.*

breastbone: *tihn mwaremware.*

breath: *esingek.*
to be out of breath, to be unable to
catch one's breath: *mwopw.*
to be unable to hold one's breath for a
long time under water: *sapeik₂.*

breathe
to breathe: *esingek.*
to breathe a sigh of relief: *esingekida.*
to breathe in an agitated manner:
lokulok, lukuluk.
to inhale, to breathe in deeply, to
absorb: *ihk.*

breech birth: *sileit₂.*

breed
to breed: *kapara₂.*
to be in heat, to be ready for breeding,
of female dogs and pigs: *mwetida.*

breezy
breezy, airy: *engitik.*

bribe
to attempt to gain favor, to bribe:
natih.

bride: *likamwohd.*

bridge: *piris.*

bright
bright, clear, shiny: *lingaling.*
bright, either with reference to light
or intelligence: *marain.*
excessively bright: *mahl.*

to burn brightly, of a source of light having a flame, as a lamp: *mpereng.*

bring
to bring along: *sehre.*
to bring together, to assemble: *dahrkipene.*

brittle
brittle, fragile: *tipwatipw.*

broad
wide, broad: *tehlap.*

broadcast
broadcast station: *proadkahs.*

broadjump
broadjump, longjump: *apadopi.*

broil
to cook, roast, broil, toast, etc.: *inihn.*

broke
to be broke, to be out of money: *pwurok$_2$.*

broken
to be broken into small pieces with the hands, as breadfruit: *pilitik$_1$.*
to be broken, of a string: *mwei$_2$.*
to be broken, of any long object: *tipw$_1$.*
to be broken, of anything containing liquid, granular objects, or gas: *sawa$_2$.*
to be broken, ruined, destroyed, spoiled: *ohla.*
to be smashed, to be broken: *marop.*

broom
broom made from the inner ribs of palm fronds: *kepennok, sowelihmw.*

brotherhood: *pirien.*

brown: *pohn pwehl.*

bruised: *mwou.*

brush: *piroas.*
Japanese brush: *dawasi.*
to brush one's teeth: *piroas, widengi, wudengi.*
to brush off: *siped.*
to be brushed off: *sipisip.*

bubble: *pwolol.*
to bubble: *pwolol.*

buck-toothed: *ngihpit.*

bucket
bucket, barrel: *pekid.*

buckle
belt buckle: *moangen kateng.*

bud
bud of a flower: *mpwek.*
bud of the coconut flower: *kowel.*

buddy
buddy, honey, pal, used in addressing one's spouse, or peers or children of the same sex: *nahn$_1$.*
dear friend, close buddy: *kompoakapah.*

buffalo
carabao, water buffalo: *karapahu.*

bugle: *rappa.*
cornet, trumpet, bugle: *koronihda.*

build
to make, to repair, to build: *wiahda.*
to build a wall: *did.*

builder
expert canoe builder: *soupal.*

building
building, house, home, dwelling: *ihmw.*

bulge
to bulge, of something covered, the shape of which is discernible: *mwemmwan.*

bulky
bulky, stocky, thick, large in girth: *ahlap.*

bulldozer: *pwuldohser.*

bullet
bullet, cartridge: *leht.*
lightbulb, bullet, pool ball: *dama.*

bully: *tehnlap.*

bump
to ring, to bump into: *sek.*

bumpy
bumpy, rough, not smooth: *mwangaingai.*

bun
to arrange one's hair in a chignon or bun: *lamisih, lemis.*

bunch
a bunch, of anything: *dundun$_2$.*
bunch, group, clump: *mwutumwut.*
bunch, of bananas: *ih$_3$.*
bunch, of palm nuts: *emwih.*
group, cluster of, bunch of: *uhn-.*

bundle
bundle, sheaf: *kapakap$_2$.*
large bundle: *pwoalos.*

buoy: *pwohi.*

buoyant: *mpei.*

burden: *katoutoupe.*
burden, load: *wisik.*

burdened
to be burdened with the support of: *duhkihla.*

burial chambers
stone burial chambers: *lolong.*

burn
to burn off: *isihs.*
to burn with a flame: *mpwul.*

to burn, of a light: *ok.*
to burn, to light, to set fire to, to burn off feathers or hair: *isik.*
to start or to burn, of a fire: *ngken, ok.*
to be burned, to be lit, to be set fire to: *isida.*
to be burned, of anything: *mwasik.*
burned, crisp, of something overcooked: *roang.*

burning landscape: *isihs.*

burp
to burp, to belch: *kirer.*
to burp, of a baby: *soso.*

burst
to burst forth, of something built up, as emotions or flood waters: *kiedek.*

bury
to bury: *saripidi.*
to bury in the mud, of crabs: *soudi.*
to bury, to put in a safe place: *nekidedi.*
to be buried: *seridi.*
to be buried, used Biblically: *nekinekidi.*

bush sp.: *pahtakai, pwisehn kou, pwishen karapahu, pwomakirant, wilianter.*
bush sp., *Allamanda cathartica*: *pahtou₂.*
bush sp., *Angelonia gardneri*: *karmihna.*
bush sp., *Coleus scutellarioides*: *koaramahd.*
bush sp., *Jussiaea erecta* or *Jussiaea linifolia*: *deleurek.*
bush sp., *Melastoma marianum*: *kisetikmei.*
bush sp., *Melastoma marianum*: *pisetikmei.*
bush sp., *Orthosiphon stamineus*: *elisenket.*
bush sp., *Psychotria carolinensis*: *kempenial.*
bush sp., used for poisoning fish: *uhpen palau.*

bushy
bushy, full of foliage: *weliwel₁.*

business: *pesnes, pisnis, sohpai.*
to do business: *pisnis.*

busy: *kedirepw, soupisek.*

busybody: *kedirepw.*

but: *ahpw.*
because, since, but, so that: *pwe.*

butt
butt, as of a cigarette: *paki₁.*

butt-in
butt-in, pesky: *liderewes.*

butter: *pwete.*
peanut butter: *pihnas pwete.*

butterfly: *lipahrourou.*

butterfly fish
fish sp., butterfly fish: *lierpwater.*

buttocks: *kahu.*

button: *pwaten, pwatin.*

buy
to buy: *natihada.*
to buy, sell, or trade, to shop: *net₁.*
to buy, to pay, to hire: *pwain.*
to be bought: *pweipwei₂.*

buzz
to buzz: *pwedehk.*

Bye
an informal greeting or leave taking expression, as Hi— or Bye : *kaselel.*

cabinet
cabinet, particularly one in which food is stored: *imwen padahk, sirangk.*
food cabinet: *aiso.*
locker, cabinet: *osihre.*

cable: *selmete.*

cacao
cacao, *Theobroma cacao*: *kakau.*

cackle
to cackle, of a hen: *dikahk.*
to call or cackle loudly, of a hen: *wahkahk.*

cafe: *kapwie.*

cage: *kelen mahn.*

cake: *keik.*

calabash
calabash, gourd: *pwilel.*
coconut shell container, calabash: *isek.*

calculate
to calculate: *wahntuhke₂, wahntuhkeih.*

calendar: *kalender.*

calf
calf, of the leg: *wedin neh.*

call
to call: *ediniei, likuwer, malipe.*
to call by shouting: *luwaikehk.*
to call in food, by a *Nahnmwarki* prior to a feast: *lohkinned.*
to call or cackle loudly, of a hen: *wahkahk.*
to call, as in to call someone a bad name: *kehr.*
to call, to summon: *eker.*

calm
calm and overcast, with no rain, used in describing the weather: *mahliok.*
calm, cool, not easily disturbed, of people: *mahnien.*

calm, of the weather: *mwele.*
to calm down: *rommwidi.*
to calm down after a time of
excitement, as after a fight:
rempwidi.

camel: *kamel.*

camera: *kamara₂.*
sign, mark, picture, camera, movie,
motion picture: *kilel.*

can: *kak.*

can
can, tin: *pwoaht.*
large can, as for gasoline: *dihn.*
milk can: *milikkang.*

canal
channel, canal, a passage in a reef:
dahu.

cancel
to postpone or cancel: *kapwowiala.*
to be canceled: *pweula.*

cancer: *kanser.*

candle: *kandehla.*

candy: *okasi.*
any small, round, hard candy that
comes in rolls, as Lifesavers:
doropwus.
candy, cookie, cracker: *kirahka.*
hard candy: *kanti.*

cane: *dakapahr, irar, rereiso, sokon.*
cane, of the *Nahnken*: *irareiso.*
cane, of the *Nahnmwarki*: *irareileng.*
to walk with a cane: *irar, sokon.*

cane grass
sp. of cane grass: *letek.*

cannibal
class of people of the past, believed to
be cannibals: *Liet₂.*

cannon: *kesik lapalap.*

canoe
canoe, vehicle: *tehnwar, wahr.*
a decoratively carved canoe:
warasapw.
large end of a canoe: *imwilap.*
small end of a canoe: *imwitik.*
outrigger side of a canoe: *palihdam.*
side of a canoe opposite the outrigger:
palikasa.
one of the outrigger supports on a
canoe: *rahk₂.*
the angular protrusion on either end of
the hull of a Ponapean canoe:
salenge.
to have something stuck between the
hull and the outrigger of a canoe:
koapwuroaloat.

canvas: *pelien serek.*

capable
competent, capable, well versed:
koahiek.

capacious
capacious, able to hold a lot: *liaudan.*
capacious, holding a lot: *audapan.*

cape
cape of land: *imwinsapw.*

capital
capital, of a place: *poasen kaun.*

capsize
to capsize or turn over, of any vehicle:
sepehlda.

captain: *kepin.*

capture
to be conquered, captured, overcome:
lohdi.

car
automobile, car: *sidohsa, weren
nansapw.*

carabao
carabao, water buffalo: *karapahu.*

caramel: *kiarameru.*

carbide
carbide, carbide lamp: *kahpaido.*

carbine: *karipin.*

card
a playing card: *tehnpilei.*
a playing card, a deck of playing cards:
tehnkehs.
playing cards: *pilei.*

cardboard
paper, cardboard: *doaropwe.*

care
to care about: *kupwurohki.*
to care for: *sounapwalih.*
to care for an invalid in the hospital:
kampio.
to take care of: *apwalih, nsenohki.*
to take care of, to watch out for:
kanaiehng.
able to take care of one's self: *koahiek.*

carefree
carefree, happy-go-lucky: *seukauti,
seukoahti.*

careless
careless with physical possessions,
likely to lose or misplace belongings:
peidlakid.
careless about where one defecates:
sehdokon.

caress
to caress: *likahde.*
to caress, to rub, to pat affectionately:
damwer, demwidemw.

carpenter
carpenter, carpentry: *daiksang, deiksang.*
master carpenter: *souse.*

carpentry
carpenter, carpentry: *daiksang, deiksang.*

carry
to carry: *wa₂.*
to carry a child on one's back: *palikir, pelikilik.*
to carry a number, as in the process of addition: *kataman.*
to carry in a bundle: *kepe-.*
to carry in a vehicle: *idan.*
to carry in one's arms: *sape.*
to carry in the mouth: *ila, ilail.*
to carry on a litter between forward and rear carriers: *rowe.*
to carry on one's shoulder: *kapaik, kepeik.*
to carry on one's side, to carry under one's arm: *apid.*
to carry or lift something that can be lightly suspended with one hand: *tile.*
to carry something involving repeated trips, as numerous bags of copra: *delingek, elingek, umpang.*
to carry two bundles of things with a pole across the shoulders: *ini.*
to pick up, to carry, to take along: *limehda.*
to be carried: *wisik.*
to be carried on a litter between forward and rear carriers: *ro.*
to be carried on one's side, to be carried under one's arm: *epid.*
to be carried or lifted, of something that can be lightly suspended with one hand: *tintil.*

cart: *kuruma.*
small two-wheeled cart, pulled or pushed by hand: *riahka.*

cartilage
gristle, cartilage: *kopwukopw₂.*

carton
carton of cigarettes: *pwohr.*

cartoon
cartoon, comic strip: *mangnga.*

cartridge
bullet, cartridge: *leht.*

case: *kehs₂.*

cash box
safe, cash box: *kingko.*

casing
empty casing, as of a coconut, cartridge, or shell: *powi.*
casing of a bullet: *pohnkares.*

casket
box, chest, coffin, casket: *kohpwa₂.*

cassava
cassava, manioc, tapioca: *dapiohka, kehp tuhke, menioak.*

cast
to cast a spell: *winahni.*

cast out
to send away, to cast out: *kasare, pakasar.*
to be cast out or damned: *lekidekla.*

castor-oil fish
fish sp., castor-oil fish: *deikenepeng.*

castrate
to castrate: *leke.*
to be castrated: *lek.*
castrated animal: *lekelek.*

cat: *kaht₂.*

cataract
cataract, opacity of the crystalline lens of the eye: *masomwomw.*

catch
to catch fish from holes in the coral by hand: *pwedipwed.*
to catch in the act: *rukihdi.*
to catch on, to learn: *daperedi.*
to catch something animate: *parok.*
to catch the kind of mangrove crab called *masaht*: *pikmasaht.*
to catch up to, to chase down, to overtake: *pwakihdi.*
to catch up with: *koanoa, pwekidi.*
to catch with a slip noose: *mol.*
to catch, as a ball: *dapadap, daper.*
to catch, as fish: *saik₁.*
to gather up, to catch with the hands: *rohk.*
to make a good catch with a net: *lohpwelipwel.*
to play catch: *dapadap.*
to be caught: *lo.*
to be caught, of something animate: *poaridi₁.*

catcher
catcher, in baseball: *kiassi.*

caterpillar: *limwehdi, mwehdi.*
a large sp. of caterpillar: *kidienleng.*

catholic: *kahdolik.*

cause
cause, reason, purpose: *kahrepe.*
to cause, to be the reason for: *kahrehda.*

cautious
cautious, hesitant, fearful: *per.*

cave
hole, cave: *pwoahr.*
man-made cave, air-raid shelter:
pwohkungo.

cease
to cease, resulting in a return to
normalcy: *mahkoneidi, sarada$_2$.*

ceiling: *denso.*

celebrate
to celebrate: *kasarawi$_1$.*

celebrated
famous, celebrated: *ndand.*

cement
cement, concrete, mortar: *simend,
siment.*

cemetery
grave, cemetery: *sousou.*

census: *nting en peneinei.*

cent
cent, money: *sens, sent.*

center
middle, center, or midst of (him, her,
or it): *nanwerenge.*

center field
center field, in baseball: *senda.*

centipede: *meninrahn.*

certainly
certainly, really, definitely, truly:
uhdahn.

chain: *sein, sihn.*

chair
chair, seat: *sehr$_2$.*

chalice: *dahl sarawi.*

chalk: *sohk$_2$.*

champion: *sampion.*

change
change, of money: *luhwe, sent
mwaramwer.*
to change direction: *wet$_1$.*
to change status: *kesepwil.*
to change the status of someone or
something, to graduate: *kasapwil.*
to change, as in opinion: *wikid.*
to change, to substitute, to replace:
wilian.
to rapidly change for the worse, of the
weather or emotions: *sawa$_2$.*
to transfer, to move or change
location: *kasau.*
of Micronesian canoes, to change
direction by repositioning the sail:
rop.
to be changed, to be substituted, to be
replaced: *wiliali.*

to be changed, to be transformed:
wikila.

changeable
variable, inconsistent, changeable:
wikwikin.

channel
channel, canal, a passage in a reef:
dahu.
main channel: *daulap.*
to channel a liquid into a container
with a trough, gutter, etc.: *paikere.*
of a liquid, to be channeled into a
container with a trough, gutter, etc.:
paiker.

chant
to chant: *ngis.*
chant, often one relating the oral
history of Ponape: *ngihs.*
burial chant: *darak.*

chaotic: *liseliping.*

chapel
chapel, used by protestants: *sinakoke.*

chapter
chapter, of a book: *iralaud.*

character
character, clown: *mangnga.*
to be a character: *kerlikamw.*
to be a character, to be a clown:
mangnga.

charcoal
cinder, ember, charcoal, coal of a fire:
mwoalus.

charitable: *mohngiong mwakelekel.*

charm
a love potion or charm: *mesehl.*

chase
to chase: *kowih, pwakih.*
to chase away: *karawan.*
to chase one another: *pwepweki.*
to catch up to, to chase down, to
overtake: *pwakihdi.*
to be chased: *pwek$_3$.*

chaser
food or drink employed as a chaser
after drinking kava: *lider$_1$.*

cheap
inexpensive, cheap: *pweitikitik.*

cheat
to cheat: *mwersuwedih.*
cheat, lie: *piht$_1$.*

check
to check: *tehk$_1$.*
to check on, to keep on eye on:
lehnmwese.
to check, to inquire, to ask: *kalelapak.*

to inspect, examine, or check: *dawih, dou$_3$.*

checkers: *seked.*

cheek: *likinmwoale, likinsap, sepe$_1$.*

cheese: *sihs.*

chela
chela, the claw of a crab, lobster, shrimp, etc.: *enge.*

chemise
slip, chemise: *semihs, simihs.*

cherish
to cherish: *kanai.*
cherished, well cared for: *keneinei.*

chest: *mwareiso, mwarmware, pahnadi, pahnkupwur.*
box, chest, coffin, casket: *kohpwa$_2$.*

chestnut
Polynesian chestnut, *Inocarpus fagiferus*: *mwoaroapw, mworopw.*

chew
to chew: *rukoa, rukoaruk.*
to chew into fine particles: *kangid.*

chewable
chewable, as of a soft bone: *rukoaruk.*

chewing gum: *kisinpwil, pwilis.*

chicanery
trickery, chicanery: *mwadik.*

chick
chick, just after hatching: *pwurok$_1$.*

chicken: *malek.*

chicken pox
smallpox, chicken pox: *kilitepw.*

chief
chief magistrate: *sihpw$_1$.*
lord, chief of the highest order: *Mwohnsapw.*

chignon
to arrange one's hair in a chignon or bun: *lamisih, lemis.*

child: *seri.*
child affianced by a parental arrangement: *kisinnin.*
child born of an adulterous relationship: *ipwin nenek, seri nenek, serien pirap.*
child of a chief: *tiekepe.*
child of father's brother: *wahn ohl pirien.*
child of mother's sister: *wahn lih pirien.*
child of the *Nahnmwarki* or *Nahnken*: *serihso$_1$.*
child, any person called child in the Crow kinship terminology: *nahi$_1$.*
first-born child: *mesenih.*
only child: *iehroas.*

youngest child: *pekindihdi.*

childless
childless woman: *liedepwen.*

chilly
cold, cool, chilly: *kopou, pwoaikentehine.*
feeling cold, cool, chilly: *pou.*

chin: *kaikai, kaiot.*

China: *Seini.*

Chinese cabbage: *nappa.*

chip
chip or slice, as of breadfruit or taro: *dip.*
chip, flake: *dipere.*

chisel: *sisel.*
to chisel: *sisel.*

chocolate: *sokolahde, sokoled.*

choice
to examine, to diagnose, to make a choice, to guess: *kasawih.*

choir: *kuair.*

choke
to choke on something: *piniwer.*
to choke, as a consequence of food lodging in the trachea: *ngat.*

choose
to choose, to pick out, to select: *pil$_2$, pilipil.*
to select or choose from a group of animate beings, to pick out an animal: *pwinik.*

choosy: *lipilipil.*
not choosy: *soulipilipil.*

chop
to chop with an axe or knife, as foliage: *wak$_2$.*

chopsticks: *asi$_2$.*

Christian: *Souleng.*

Christmas: *Kirismas.*

church: *ihmw sarawi.*

cigar: *nihkerehs.*
cigarette, cigar: *sika.*

cigarette
cigarette, cigar: *sika.*

cigarette lighter: *lait.*

cinder
cinder, ember, charcoal, coal of a fire: *mwoalus.*

circle: *pwonopwon.*
to circle: *kapil.*

circumcise
to circumcise: *sirkumsaisih.*
to be circumcised: *sirkumsais.*

circus: *sahkas.*

citrus
citrus plant or fruit: *peren$_2$*.
citrus, lime, lemon: *karer*.

city: *kahnihmw*.

civilization: *marain*.

civilized
civilized, enlightened: *marain*.

clam
the bitter part of a clam, used for medicine: *anihn*.

clam sp.: *kopil, lipwei, pahsu, sile$_2$*.
clam sp., giant clam: *ienlam*.

clamp
clamp, vise: *kilamp*.
to clamp, to crush: *ngidar*.

clan
a clan name: *Dipwilap, Dipwinluhk, Dipwinmen, Dipwinpahnmei, Dipwinpehpe, Dipwinwai, Lasialap, Ledek, Liarkatau, Lipitahn, Nahniek, Pwuton, Souniap, Sounkawad, Sounmaraki, Sounpelienpil, Sounpwok, Sounrohi, Sounsamaki*.
exogamous, matrilineal clan: *dipw, sou$_1$*.
lineage, extended family, clan: *keinek*.

clan deity: *enihwos*.

clap
to clap: *lopw$_2$, lopwor*.

claw
chela, the claw of a crab, lobster, shrimp, etc.: *enge*.
to claw: *rakih, rekirek*.

clay: *peiruhru*.

clean: *mwakelekel*.
neat, clean: *min, nei$_2$*.
to clean: *kamwakel*.
to clean and prepare kava for pounding: *mwatih, mwet*.

clear
bright, clear, shiny: *lingaling*.
clear, evident: *dehde*.
clear, evident, obvious: *sansal*.
cleared, as of vegetation: *mahsahs*.
to be cleared out: *wehwepeseng*.
to clear an area: *mwatih, mwet*.
to clear land by pulling up grass or weeds, to bare the earth: *rekipwel*.

clearing
clearing, field, plantation, garden, farm: *mwaht, mwetiwel*.
natural clearing in the forest, a grassy, unfertile area: *mall*.

cleft palate: *tumwpwoar*.

clerk
store clerk: *sounnet*.

clever
good at something, clever: *kadek$_2$*.

climax
to climax or ejaculate: *kus, nek$_1$*.

climb
to climb: *daur$_2$, dou$_2$*.

clipper
hair clipper: *parikang*.

clitoris: *tohl*.
having a large clitoris: *kaneng*.

clock
time, clock, watch, hour: *kuloak*.

clogged
stuffed up, clogged: *pon*.

clogs
Japanese clogs: *kedda*.

close
close together: *dod*.
close together, side by side: *paterek*.
near, close: *keren*.
to be close: *poak*.
to be near or close to: *karanih*.

close
to close one's mouth: *kakureiso*.
to close or to shut any round object, as a pipe or one's mouth: *kuhpene*.
to open or close anything hinged or attached, as a door or window: *riting*.
to be opened or closed, of anything hinged: *rit-*.
to be closed, of a charge account: *simekiri*.

cloth
cloth, anything made of cloth, material, clothes: *likou*.
material, cloth: *lepin likou*.
cloth made from breadfruit bark: *dohr*.
highly prized cloth made from breadfruit bark: *lakiot*.
a clothlike material made from the bark of breadfruit: *meimei*.
a cloth, used as a wrapper to carry objects: *piroski*.

clothes
cloth, anything made of cloth, material, clothes: *likou*.
dry clothes one puts on, extra clothes taken on a trip: *kemmad, kiemmad*.
old work clothes: *kihou*.
to give someone dry clothes: *kemmade*.
to put on dry clothes: *kemmad, kiemmad*.

clothesline: *selin peleng likou.*

cloud: *depwek.*
low cloud, touching the mountains: *toahkoi.*

cloudy
cloudy, blurred, smoky: *edied.*

clown
character, clown: *mangnga.*
to be a character, to be a clown: *mangnga.*

club
club, of cards: *klopis.*

cluck
to cluck, of a hen: *dondorok, dorok.*

clump
bunch, group, clump: *mwutumwut.*

cluster
group, cluster of, bunch of: *uhn-.*

coal: *toahl$_2$.*
cinder, ember, charcoal, coal of a fire: *mwoalus.*

coarse: *pisalap.*

coat
suit coat: *sekid welpeseng.*

cobweb
spider web, cobweb: *pesen likan.*

cock-eyed
to be tilted, crooked, cock-eyed: *pang.*

cocky
proud, self-assertive, cocky: *aklapalap.*

coconut
coconut palm, *Cocos nucifera*: *nih$_2$.*
a variety of coconut palm: *nihkengk, nihrir, nihtik.*
a variety of coconut palm, bearing green nuts: *nihtoal.*
a variety of coconut palm, bearing red nuts: *nihweita.*
a variety of coconut palm, having nuts with a sweet, juicy husk: *adohl.*
a variety of coconut palm, with round nuts: *nihkarat.*
immature coconut before reaching the growth stage called *uhpw*: *kurupw.*
drinking coconut: *pehn$_2$, pwihleng, uhpw.*
a stage of development of the coconut before it turns brown: *poupit.*
ripe coconut: *mwangas.*
ripe coconut, syn. with *mwangas*: *ering$_1$.*
coconut, containing no nut: *kengk.*
the soft upper part of the shell of the coconut, at a certain growth stage: *uhren uhpw.*
the spongy substance found in a

sprouting coconut in its early stage of development: *mpwein tenek.*
dried coconut meat after the extraction of the oil: *wenering.*
empty half of coconut shell: *ngarangar.*
sprouting coconut palm: *pahr$_3$.*

coconut crab: *emp$_1$.*

coffee: *koahpi.*

coffin
box, chest, coffin, casket: *kohpwa$_2$.*

cohesive
adherent, cohesive, gummy, sticky: *ngidingid.*

coil
coil of sennit: *sanek.*
mosquito coil: *kadorsingko.*
to gather up rope, to coil rope: *sim.*

coin: *sent mwaramwer.*

cold
cold, cool, chilly: *kopou, pwoaikentehine.*
cool, cold, damp: *lemwlemwur.*
feeling cold, cool, chilly: *pou.*
cold, flu: *soumwahu en wai.*

cold chisel: *kohl sisel.*

collapse
to collapse, of a pile of objects: *kiedek.*
to collapse with a crashing noise: *kioaroahr.*

collar: *kala$_2$.*

collide
to collide: *loi.*

colloidal
congealed, colloidal, thick, viscous: *ten$_1$.*

color: *mwahi, poh.*

comb: *kohmw.*
rooster's comb: *ropwe.*
to comb: *kar$_1$.*
to comb one's hair: *keriker$_2$.*

come
to come or go: *ape-, koh-.*
to come or go directly: *inen-.*
to come or go in a hurry, often in response to a leader's demands or an emergency: *piser-.*
to come or go in pairs: *mpwer-.*
to come or go, used in a derogatory way: *pwulahk.*
to come and go early in the morning: *sangk.*
to come from: *pwilisang.*
to crack, to break, to come apart, of an object fastened to something: *pwoapw.*

comeuppance
to receive one's comeuppance: *lesila.*
to take pleasure in seeing one receive
his comeuppance: *aniket.*

comfort
to comfort: *kaloalamwahu,*
kaloalamwahwih.

comic
cartoon, comic strip: *mangnga.*

comma: *kama₃.*

command
speech or command: *pahngok,*
poahngok.
to command: *poarone.*
to command, to order: *ruwes.*
to speak or command: *pahngok,*
poahngok.

common
common, useless, of no consequence:
mwahl.

commoner: *aramas mwahl.*

communion: *tungoal.*
to receive communion: *tungoal,*
tungoale.

commute
to commute: *sangk.*

companion: *werek.*
companion, follower, complement:
ienge.
to be a companion of: *warakih.*

company
company, corporation, group: *kaisa.*
company, friend: *kompani.*

compare
to compare: *karasapene.*
to equate, to compare in terms of size:
kasosohng.

compass: *kampos.*

compensation: *dumpe.*

compete
to compete: *uhpene.*
to compete with: *pelian.*

competent
competent, capable, well versed:
koahiek.

competition
contest, competition: *siai.*
yam raising competition: *siai en padok*
kehp.

competitive
proud, competitive, unwilling to be
humbled: *akutuhwahu.*

complain
to complain about the unfairness of
something: *akupwungki.*

complaint
criminal or civil complaint: *kadipadip.*
to file a complaint in court: *kampilein.*

complement: *peisenge.*
companion, follower, complement:
ienge.

complete
entire, whole, unanimous, complete:
unsek.
to complete by adding to: *kadokehla.*
to be complete, as a consequence of
being added to: *kadokodokala.*

completely
thoroughly, completely: *douluhl.*

completion
to bring to completion: *koadokehla.*
to be brought to completion:
koadokodokala.

complicated: *kasapwurupwur.*

comply
to comply: *menseiren.*
to comply, to acquiesce, to do
something against one's will: *seiren.*

composure
to lose one's composure: *patehla.*

conceal
hidden, concealed: *rir.*
to hide behind, to conceal: *ririh.*
to hide or conceal: *ekihla.*
to be hidden or concealed: *ekiek.*

conceited
impudent, conceited: *namaiki.*

concentrated
concentrated, of a nature that a little
goes a long way, like pepper: *sohtik.*

concern
to concern: *pid₂.*
to concern, to be intended for: *doke.*

concerned: *nsenoh.*
concerned, anxious, eager: *ngoang.*
to be concerned about, to be
interested in, to worry about:
nsenohki.

conch
conch shell, conch shell trumpet: *sewi,*
kederwahwa.

conclude
to be concluded: *erala.*

concrete
cement, concrete, mortar: *simend,*
siment.
to concrete: *kongkiri.*

condition
condition or state of a person or thing:
ire₁.
condition, nature, manner: *duwe.*

in good condition, young looking: *kot.*

conduct
to conduct music: *piht₃.*

confection
popsicle, frozen confection: *aiskehki.*

confer
to meet, to convene, to confer: *tiepene.*

conference
meeting, convention, conference: *tiepene.*

confess
to confess: *kansenoh₂, sakarada.*
to confess, to reveal, to disclose: *wehk.*

confession: *kansenoh₂.*

confirmation: *kakehlail.*

conflict
to come into conflict: *sekpene.*

confront
to confront: *eliwahki.*

confrontation
conflict, confrontation: *sekpene.*

confused
confused, disordered, messy: *ping.*
confused, said of one who misidentifies his possessions: *sas₂.*

confusing
to find something confusing, difficult to understand, or mysterious: *pwonopwoniki.*

confusion
confusion, disorder, mess: *pingiping.*

congealed
congealed, colloidal, thick, viscous: *ten₁.*

congregation
congregation, parish, a gathering in the presence of a *Nahnmwarki*: *mwomwohdiso.*

connect
to connect, to fasten together: *pouse.*
to be connected, to be fastened together: *pous.*

connection: *pous.*

conquer
to conquer: *alasapw, powehdi.*
to be conquered, captured, overcome: *lohdi.*

conscience: *kadeikpen loale.*

conscious: *kehnwasa.*

consecrate
to bless, to consecrate: *kasarawi₁.*

conservative
conservative, not wasteful, conserved: *kasohtik.*

conserve
to conserve: *kasohtikih.*
conservative, not wasteful, conserved: *kasohtik.*

consider
to consider most important: *mwohniki.*
to consider of no consequence: *kasohwe.*

consideration
to show consideration: *pohnese.*

constant
everlasting, constant, permanent: *poatoapoat.*

constellation
constellation, possibly the particular constellation Pleiades: *mwakereker.*

constipated
to be constipated: *iheteng.*

consume
to consume, to eat or drink: *tungoal, tungoale.*
to consume something, especially medicine, before kava: *kep₁.*

consumed
to be consumed or used up: *ros.*

contact
to come in contact with, to touch, to touch upon: *sair.*

contagious: *lusulus.*

container
coconut shell container, calabash: *isek.*
water container made of a leaf of *sepwikin*: *ngke₁.*

contempt
to hold in contempt: *sipwe.*
to hold in contempt, as in court: *kasohwe.*
to turn one's head in contempt: *kepirek.*

content
content, subject matter: *audepe.*

contented
happy, contented, enjoying the good life: *nsenamwahu.*

contents
inside of something, contents: *kanenge.*

contest
contest, competition: *siai.*
a throwing contest: *akedei.*
to engage in a throwing contest: *akedei.*

continuation: *uhsepe.*

continue
to continue on: *kanahng-, wenewei.*
to continue to completion: *uhse.*

contract
    to be allergic to, to easily contract, as
        an illness: *kehieng.*
    to contract: *nur.*
    to contract the vagina during
        intercourse: *tenger.*
contract: *kontirak.*
contradictive
    given to denial, contradictive:
        kahmahm.
contrary
    contrary to one's expectations: *rorok.*
contribute
    to contribute: *toukihda.*
contribution: *tou.*
    gift or contribution to a party: *mehn
        doadoahk.*
    sacrifice, offering, contribution:
        meiroang.
convene
    to convene, of a meeting: *keielekda.*
    to meet, to convene, to confer: *tiepene.*
convention
    meeting, convention, conference:
        tiepene.
converge
    to unexpectedly converge upon a
        place, of a large number of people:
        mpwelehdi.
convey
    to convey information: *uhsehiong.*
convulse
    to convulse: *pintat.*
cook
    to cook: *kuk, kukih.*
    to cook breadfruit or grated banana
        with coconut milk: *seipwok.*
    to cook fish with coconut milk and
        turmeric: *kourahpw.*
    to cook, roast, broil, toast, etc.: *inihn.*
    to finish cooking food not done:
        kalewiala.
    to be cooked: *leu.*
cookhouse: *imwen kuk.*
cookie
    candy, cookie, cracker: *kirahka.*
    a kind of sugar-coated cookie:
        karindong.
cooking pot: *ainpwoat.*
cool
    cool, cold, damp: *lemwlemwur.*
    cool, cooled off: *lou.*
    feeling cold, cool, chilly: *pou.*
    cold, cool, chilly: *kopou,
        pwoaikentehine.*

calm, cool, not easily disturbed, of
    people: *mahnien.*
to water, to cool with water: *kalamwir.*
to be cooled with water: *kelemwir.*
cooperation: *minimin.*
cooperative: *minimin.*
copper: *kapa.*
copra: *mwangas.*
copra drying platform: *pasapas.*
copra drying shed: *kansohpa.*
copulate
    to copulate with, to have sexual
        intercourse with: *kowarak.*
    to copulate, to have sexual intercourse:
        kowerek.
copy
    to copy, to imitate: *alasang.*
    to copy, to imitate, to mimic, to learn
        from: *alemengih.*
    said of one who copies or imitates
        fashions or behavior: *alemengi.*
coral: $pahi_1$.
    coral head: *takaimei, takain nansed,
        takaipwet.*
    finger coral: *rahr.*
    fire coral: *rarkapwudong.*
    large coral head: mad_1.
    large submerged coral head: *madepei.*
cord
    rope, cord, line, string: *sahl.*
    cord, looped around one's ankles and
        used for climbing: *liep.*
core
    core, as of breadfruit: *pwuri.*
    core, of a boil or pimple: edi_1.
cork: *kehpei.*
    cork-like wood: *usepehi.*
corn
    wart, corn: *mesenmwomw.*
corn: *kohn.*
corner
    corner, angle: *keimw.*
    corner of the mouth: *kepwil, pwekil.*
cornerstone: *pwukekeimw.*
cornet
    cornet, trumpet, bugle: *koronihda.*
corporation
    company, corporation, group: *kaisa.*
correct
    correct, right, just: $pwung_1$.
    petty, desirous of being correct at all
        times, disagreeable: *akupwung.*
correspondence
    letter, correspondence: *kisin likou.*
corroded
    rusty, corroded: *mer.*

cost: *pweine₁*.
 cost, wage, reward: *pweipwei₂*.

costly
 expensive, costly: *pweilaud.*

cotton: *koatun.*

cough: *kopokop.*
 to cough: *kohper, kopokop.*

could
 could, alternatively: *nek₂.*

count
 to count: *wadawad₁, wadek₁.*

counterpart
 counterpart, opponent: *pelie.*

country
 a political unit, as a municipality,
  district, state, country, or kingdom:
  wehi₂.

couple
 married couple: *pwopwoud, pwoton.*

course
 navigational course: *kohs.*

court: *mwoalen kopwung.*
 to court a man: *pwengwol.*
 to court a woman: *pwengilih.*

courthouse: *imwen kopwung.*

cove
 cove, inlet: *kosolong.*

covenant
 contract, promise, agreement,
  covenant: *inou₁.*

cover: *pere.*
 cover, wrapper: *kidikid, kidipe.*
 lid, cover: *pweine₂.*
 to cover: *pwaindi.*
 to cover an *uhmw* with leaves:
  kompwal, kompwel.
 to cover or shield oneself from the
  weather: *up, upuhp.*
 to cover picked, green bananas to
  hurry their ripening: *seipeng.*
 to cover up: *koduhpwal.*
 to cover, to screen from view: *pere.*
 to line or cover with leaves: *tehla.*
 to be covered: *pweipweidi.*
 to be covered up: *koduhpwel,
  komwaropwidi.*
 of an *uhmw*, to cover with hot stones:
  pai₁.
 of an *uhmw*, to cover with fresh
  leaves: *ngkoake.*
 of an *uhmw*, to be covered with fresh
  leaves: *ngkoak.*

covet
 to covet, to be greedy for: *noahroke.*

cow: *kou.*

cowardly
 afraid, frightened, cowardly, bashful:
  masepwehk.

cowrie: *pwili.*

crab
 coconut crab: *emp₁.*
 hermit crab: *mpwa.*
 mangrove crab: *elimoang.*
 rock crab: *likarahs.*
 small black mangrove crab: *masaht.*
 sp. of crab: *lisoapwoar, lisouduhdu,
  mpwel₅, pwor.*
 sp. of small crab: *lengen, limpwel,
  ngkopw.*
 sp. of small land crab: *rokumw.*

crack: *pwahl, pwalapwal.*
 slit, crack, small opening, empty space,
  outer space: *nanwehwe.*
 to crack, to break, to come apart, of an
  object fastened to something:
  pwoapw.

cracker
 candy, cookie, cracker: *kirahka.*

crackle
 to sizzle or crackle: *siar.*

cradle
 to cradle something in one's arms:
  roapoahnge.

crane
 crane, the machine: *wens.*

crater
 bomb crater: *mohn pakudang.*

crawl
 to crawl on all fours: *kerep.*
 to crawl on one's belly: *limwahdek.*
 to make one's skin crawl: *duhr.*

crayon: *kureiong.*

crazy
 crazy, mad, mentally retarded:
  kisingai.
 mentally disturbed, crazy, insane: *iahk.*

creak
 to creak or squeak: *tehrek.*

creased
 creased, as of trousers: *nok.*

credit
 debt, credit, account: *pweipwand.*

creed
 faith, belief, creed: *pwoson.*

creep
 to creep: *kerep.*
 to creep up to: *karapih.*

crevally
 fish sp., blue jack crevally, *Caranx
  melampygus*: *oarong.*

cricket: *tenter*.

crimson crowned fruit dove
  bird sp., crimson crowned fruit dove:
    kiniwed.

cringe
  to cringe: *roik*.

crippled
  lame, crippled: *dangepel*.

crisp
  burned, crisp, of something
    overcooked: *roang*.

critical
  critical, of people: *likesekeseu*.
  querulous, critical: *kaulim*.

criticism: *kaulim*.

criticize
  to criticize: *kawe, tehr*.
  to criticize or insult another, usually of
    women: *kapwai*.

crock: *sah*.

crocodile
  any large lizard, alligator, or crocodile:
    kieil.

crook
  crook of the arm: *tipwengen peh*.

crooked
  bent, crooked, curved: *pu*.
  crooked, off target, inaccurate: *pirek*.
  dishonest, crooked, malicious, wicked:
    mwersuwed, mworsuwed.
  to be dishonest or crooked to:
    mwersuwedih.
  to be tilted, crooked, cock-eyed: *pang*.

crop: *dih₃*.

cross
  cross or crucifix: *lohpwu*.
  cross or tough, of a person: *pwisinger*.
  to cross one's arms: *epidipe*.
  to cross over an obstacle: *sipal*.
  to cross to the other side: *kote*.

cross-eyed: *masapang*.

crossbeam
  crossbeam in a house: *lohlo*.

crosswise
  to lie crosswise: *pangapang, wapang*.

croton: *kurodong*.

crouch
  to crouch down: *karahkidi*.

crow
  to crow, of a rooster: *koakorot*.

crowbar
  crowbar, bar: *pahru*.

crowd
  crowd, fleet, school of fish: *polo*.

crowded
  crowded with people: *tohn₁*.
  crowded, lacking space: *koait*.

crown
  to give a title, to crown: *langilangih*.
  to be crowned with: *ninih*.

crucified
  to be crucified: *lohpwuala*.

crucifix
  cross or crucifix: *lohpwu*.

crude
  crude, in manners or action: *soallap*.
  displaying crude speech manners,
    foulmouthed: *ausuwed*.

cruel
  cruel, belligerent, tough: *keses, lemei*.
  to be cruel, belligerent, or tough to:
    lamai.

crumb
  crumb, sleep, crust, a dry layer of a
    bodily secretion: *dararan*.

crumple
  to crumple, to wrinkle: *amwer*.
  crumpled, wrinkled: *emwirek*.

crush
  to crush: *rukoa, rukoaruk*.
  to clamp, to crush: *ngidar*.

crushed
  pulverized, crushed, mashed: *mwut*.

crust
  crumb, sleep, crust, a dry layer of a
    bodily secretion: *dararan*.
  dried matter, crust on skin, as dried
    food on the face: *derere*.

cry
  to cry, to weep, to moan: *seng*.
  to cry, to weep: *mauk, tentenihr,
    wideudamwer*.
  to cry very softly: *ingihng₂*.
  to bawl, to cry loudly: *rerehd wasa*.
  always crying, of a child: *liseirkopw*.

cucumber: *kiuhri*.

culture
  custom, manner, behavior, culture:
    tiahk.

cup: *kep₂*.
  coconut cup used for drinking kava:
    ngarangar.
  coconut cup, dish, plate: *dahl*.
  first cup of kava in the kava ceremony:
    pwehl₁.
  second cup of kava in the kava
    ceremony: *arehn sakau*.
  third cup of kava in the kava
    ceremony: *esil*.
  depending on the municipality, the

fourth or the fifth cup of kava in the kava ceremony: *sapwe*.
one of the cups of kava in the kava ceremony: *dipen keleu, lopwon*.
the first four cups of kava in the kava ceremony: *nohpwei*.

cure
a cure for blindness caused by magic: *kapei*.

curled
closely twisted or curled, kinky, tangled: *pinipin*.

curly: *pikos*.

current: *ahd₂*.

curse: *riahla*.
to be cursed, resulting in illness or misfortune: *riahla*.
to curse, to use foul language: *peined*.

cursing
cursing, foul language: *peined*.

curtain: *kahdeng*.

curve: *kahp*.
bend or curve in a road or path: *wet₁*.
curve, bend: *mpwe*.
inside curve, in baseball: *inkahp*.
outside curve, in baseball: *audokahp*.

curved
bent, crooked, curved: *pu*.

custom
custom, manner, behavior, culture: *tiahk*.
custom, way of doing things: *ahnepe*.

cut
to cut a girl's hair straight across at the bottom: *kote*.
to cut crosswise: *lopuk*.
to cut down: *kote*.
to cut down vines: *kar₂*.
to cut foliage: *derpwungiedi*.
to cut grass: *passai*.
to cut into pieces: *sap, sepe₂*.
to cut ivory palm fronds for thatch: *uhwoas*.
to cut one's nails: *sarikik*.
to cut open, for the purpose of removing the contents: *kading₂*.
to cut or pull grass: *mwatih, mwet*.
to cut palm fronds for thatch: *uridi*.
to cut sugar cane or firewood: *wese*.
to cut with scissors or shears: *tipwa*.
to cut, to give a haircut: *sehk₁*.
to cut, trim, or sharpen with any large cutting tool: *par₁, periper*.
to pick, pull, or cut down in entirety: *amweredi*.
to slit, to cut open: *pwalang*.

to be cut crosswise: *lop*.
to be cut open, for the purpose of removing the contents: *ked*.
to be cut with scissors or shears: *tipw₂*.
to be cut, of foliage: *derpwungedi*.
to be picked, pulled, or cut down in entirety: *emwiemwidi*.
to be slashed, lanced, or cut: *lek*.
to be slit, to be cut open: *pwal*.
cut in a hill or mountain made for a road: *lopidi*.

cutlass
sword, cutlass, bayonet: *kedilahs*.

cylinder
cylinder, of an engine: *silinder*.

cyst
seed, tumor, cyst: *war₁*.

dad
father, dad, a term of familiarity: *ip, ipa*.

dagger
sheath knife, hunting knife, diving knife, dagger: *sihdnaip, teike*.

damage
ruin, damage, wound: *ohla*.

damned
to be cast out or damned: *lekidekla*.

damp
cool, cold, damp: *lemwlemwur*.

dance
dance: *kahlek, pwerik*.
a dance, done by females in a sitting position employing sticks which are tapped together rhythmically: *dokia*.
a marching dance: *kahlu, lehp*.
name of a Ponapean men's dance: *wehn*.
paddle dance: *kepir₁*.
woman's sitting dance: *sapei*.
dance master, one known for his knowledge of Ponapean dances: *soupwerik*.
to dance: *kahlek, pwerik, kahlu*.
to dance a marching dance: *lehp*.
to dance any Western style dance: *kahlek pwoaloapwoal*.
to dance the paddle dance: *kepir₁*.

dance paddle
paddle, dance paddle: *padil*.

dandruff: *kihl₁*.

dangerous: *keper*.

dangle
to dangle: *kamwatau*.

dare
don't dare: *kale*.

daring
daring, reckless, bold, adventurous: *loallap.*

dark: *rot.*
dark, of colors: *renged.*
in the dark, as of one who doesn't know something: *rotapwahk.*
to be in the dark without a source of light: *kepikirot.*
to become dark: *rotala.*
to get dark: *wasapwong.*
to have darkness descend upon one before reaching one's destination: *pwongiedi.*

darkness: *roht.*

dash
one hundred meter dash: *iakumehda.*
to run a one hundred meter dash: *iakumehda.*

dawn
to be dawn or daybreak: *wasarahnpeseng.*

day: *rahn.*
day before yesterday: *mandaken aio.*
yesterday: *aio.*
today: *rahnwet.*
tomorrow: *lakapw.*
next day: *manda.*
day after tomorrow: *pali₁.*
two days after tomorrow: *peilah.*

daybreak
to be dawn or daybreak: *wasarahnpeseng.*

deacon: *sounkohwa.*

dead
withered, dry, dead, of vegetation: *meng.*

deaf: *salengopon.*

deal
to deal cards: *dihl₃, dihlih.*

dear
dear, a term of affection used by parents with their children: *lao₁.*
Oh dear , Oh my : *oh tier.*

debris
garbage, waste, debris: *kihd.*
line of debris such as seaweed, twigs, leaves, etc. floating in the ocean: *rihr.*

debt
debt, credit, account: *pweipwand.*
to be in debt: *pweipwand.*

decayed
ripe, overripe, rotten, spoiled, decayed: *mat.*
decayed, of wood: *mwoasoahngot.*

to be decayed, of wood: *mwoasoangidi.*

deceitful
deceitful, fraudulent: *widingek.*

deceive
to deceive, to lie to, to defraud: *widinge.*
to deceive, to lie, to defraud: *widing.*
to fool or deceive: *mwalaunih.*

December: *Tihsempe.*

deception: *mwer₃.*
deception, lie, fraud: *widing.*

deceptive
devious, deceptive: *mwalaun.*

decide
to decide, to determine: *kupwurehda.*
to decide, to figure out: *lemehda.*
to settle, to decide: *koasoane.*
to be settled, to be decided, to be agreed upon: *koasoandi.*

decision
wish, intention, plan, decision, desire, heart: *kupwur₂.*

deck
a playing card, a deck of playing cards: *tehnkehs.*
deck of playing cards: *kahs₃.*
deck, of a ship: *dek₁.*

decorate
to decorate or ornament: *kapwat.*
to decorate, to give an elaborate description of: *ikidewe.*

decoration
decoration, ornament, or new outfit of clothing: *kapwat.*

decrepit
old, decrepit, of people: *likeilap.*

dedicate
to dedicate: *kusarawi₁.*
to be dedicated to: *peikieng.*

deed: *wiewia.*
occupation, task, employment, responsibility, deed: *doahk.*

deep: *loal.*
deep place within the barrier reef, lagoon: *nahmw, nehnamw.*
deep, of the hull of a canoe: *kepiloal₂.*

deer: *tie₃.*

defeat
to defeat: *kaluhsih.*
to defeat in competition: *kesepweke.*

defecate
to defecate: *kainen, loakewel, paur, pek, pidekila.*
to defecate on something: *pakad.*

to relieve oneself, to defecate or urinate: *kotala*.

defective
troublesome, hotheaded, defective: *lioakoahk*.

defendant
defendant, in a civil case: *mehn pahn repenpwung*.
defendant, in a criminal case: *mehn pahn kadip*.

defender
attorney, lawyer, defender: *pengohsi, sounsawas*.

deference: *mahk₁*.

definitely
certainly, really, definitely, truly: *uhdahn*.

deflower
to deflower, to cause a girl to lose her virginity: *kaped*.
to be deflowered: *pedala*.

deformed
abnormal, deformed, odd: *pakalong*.
deformed, of the eyelids: *likerwaite*.

defraud
to deceive, to lie to, to defraud: *widinge*.
to deceive, to lie, to defraud: *widing*.

delay
to delay, to impede: *koarompwa*.

delete
to simplify, to arrange in a simple manner, to delete some part of task: *kamangaila*.

delicious
sweet, delicious, tasty: *iou*.

delighted
delighted, overjoyed: *pohl*.

delirious
to be delirious: *liourehre*.

delirium: *liourehre*.

deliver
to send on an errand, to send to deliver a message: *ilakih*.

demanding
bossy, demanding: *ilekitik*.
easily bothered or upset by trivial matters, demanding, dependent: *inginsoi*.
self-centered, demanding: *sakon, soakon*.

demigod
demigod of canoe building and carpentry: *Nansehlang*.

demonstrate
a prefix meaning to demonstrate or demonstrating: *ak-*.
to demonstrate, to act as if: *akahk*.

demotion: *kesepwil*.

denial
denial, initial refusal out of politeness: *kahmahm*.
given to denial, contradictive: *kahmahm*.

denomination
religious denomination: *pelien lamalam, pelien pwoson*.

dense
dense, tightly woven or packed: *keirek*.

dent: *mek*.
dent, depression: *mwoaloal, pahd₁*.

dented: *mek, pad*.
bent, smashed, mashed, dented: *limek*.
to be dented: *mwoaloaldi*.

dentist: *sounwiengi*.

depart
to arrive or depart early in the morning: *sangkenei*.
to depart: *samwalahr*.
to have arrived at or departed from an area: *samwodohr*.
to leave or depart: *mwesel*.

depend
to depend on: *kawahki, pahsan*.
to depend on someone or something, to rely on, with ill consequence: *wahkihla*.

dependent
easily bothered or upset by trivial matters, demanding, dependent: *inginsoi*.

deprecative: *lipwoar*.

depression
dent, depression: *mwoaloal, pahd₁*.

derisive: *ngilekeng*.

descend
to descend from the sky, as thunder or an airplane: *karahkidi*.
to descend into, to fall into, to step into, as a hole: *pwuhr-*.

descendant
descendant, offspring, of humans: *kadaudok*.
descendant, offspring, usually of animals: *keperepere*.
paternal descendant: *ipwihpw*.

descended
to be paternally descended from: *ipwieng*.

description
to decorate, to give an elaborate description of: *ikidewe.*

desert: *sapwtehn.*

design
pattern or design, as of material: *mwahi.*

desire
desire or wish: *ineng₁.*
wish, intention, plan, decision, desire, heart: *kupwur₂.*
to desire or wish: *inengiada.*
to desire to have sexual intercourse: *inengida.*

despicable
unlikeable, obnoxious, despicable: *kadongodong.*

destroy
to break, to destroy, to ruin: *kawehla.*
to be broken, ruined, destroyed, spoiled: *ohla.*
to be annihilated or destroyed: *mwomwsang.*

destruction
destruction at the order of a chief: *oudek.*

destructive
to be destructive, to be wasteful: *koamwoamw.*

detail: *iretikitik, mengihtik, oaritik.*

detailed: *oaritik.*
to be detailed: *waditik.*
to give a detailed account of: *oaritikih.*

detain
to detain: *salihdi.*

determine
to decide, to determine: *kupwurehda.*

detonate
to detonate: *kapose.*

developed
well developed, of the tuber of a plant: *kaneng.*

devil: *ngensuwed, tepel.*
Satan, devil: *Sehdan.*

devious
devious, deceptive: *mwalaun.*

devoted
to be devoted, reliable, persevering: *loalehng, loalohng.*

dew: *pwoaik.*

diagnose
to examine, to diagnose, to make a choice, to guess: *kasawih.*
to be examined, to be diagnosed, to be figured out: *keseu.*

dialect
accent, dialect, tune, tone: *ngohr.*

diamond: *taimen.*

diaper: *osime.*
diaper, loincloth: *weiwei.*

diarrhea: *mehn tang.*

dictionary: *dikseneri.*

die
to die: *engila, matala, mehla, pweula, sipalla.*
to die while pregnant, also resulting in the death of the fetus: *lipahdopwonla.*

diesel: *dihsel.*

different
to be different: *wikpeseng.*
to be independent, to be different, to be excluded from the group: *tohrohr.*

difficult
difficult, hard, troublesome, impossible: *apwal.*
inappropriate, awkward because of unfamiliarity, difficult to learn: *koasoakoahiek.*
difficult to locate or understand: *rir.*
mischievious, naughty, difficult, frustrating: *ketihwo.*

difficulty
hard times, difficulty: *apwal.*
undesirable result, problem, difficulty: *kahpwal.*

dig
to dig: *dehk, deidei.*
to dig a hole for a yam: *pwahrih.*
to dig, to excavate: *weir₁.*
to penetrate, to sink, to dig in: *ir-.*
to be dug out, to be excavated: *weiweida.*

dilatory
dilatory, said of a child who stalls before carrying out instructions: *kataiau.*

diligent
diligent or persevering because of enthusiasm: *ngiangi.*
faithful, persevering, single-minded, diligent: *loaloapwoat.*
strenuous, diligent: *ngihtehte.*

diluted
diluted, of a nature that it takes a lot to make a little: *sohlap.*

dinner: *kasoutik, koduhsou, mwengehn soutik.*
to eat dinner: *kasoutik, koduhsou, mwengehn soutik.*

diploma: *diplohma.*

direct
  to boss, to rule, to lead, to direct:
    kaun.
  to direct a kava ceremony: *deisakau.*

director
  director of a feast: *menindeiuh,*
    soundeisakau.
  ruler, boss, leader, director: *kaun.*

dirt
  dirt, soil, earth, ground: *pwehl₁.*

dirty
  dirty, soiled: *pwelipwel.*

disadvantage: *kaupe.*

disagree
  to oppose, to disagree with: *uhweng.*

disagreeable: *ketiamau.*
  petty, desirous of being correct at all
    times, disagreeable: *akupwung.*

disappear
  to vanish, to disappear: *sohrala.*

disappointed
  disappointed, sorrowful: *pahtou₁.*
  to be disappointed: *pwuriamwei.*

disbelieve
  to disbelieve: *kelikemwe.*

discard
  to discard: *lakid.*
  to be discarded, to be neglected:
    lekidekla.

discern
  to see, discern, look at, observe,
    examine: *kilang.*
  to see, discern, look at, observe,
    examine, with a derogatory
    connotation: *ngar.*

discharged
  to be discharged, of a weapon: *pisel.*

disciple: *tohnpadahk.*

disclose
  to confess, to reveal, to disclose: *wehk.*

discomforted
  discomforted, by filth or something
    unpleasant looking: *malangalang.*

discomforting
  obnoxious, discomforting: *was₁.*

discourage
  to discourage: *katikala.*

discourteous
  rude, discourteous: *serekeileng.*

discuss
  to talk, to discuss, to tell a story:
    koasoai.

discussion: *kapwkapwung.*
  talk, discussion, rumor, story, adage,
    parable: *koasoai.*

disdain
  to disdain: *kalahdiki, kiles.*

disdainful: *kesileng, likirikirir.*

disease
  sickness, disease, illness: *luhmwuhmw,*
    soumwahu.
  a breadfruit disease: *semwek, tokutok,*
    tukutuk.
  a disease in which women bleed from
    the vagina: *ntahpwilipwil.*
  a disease of infants, attributed to the
    mother's becoming pregnant while a
    child is still nursing: *lohmwei.*
  a disease of taro, causing discoloration
    of the plant: *kilin kihs.*
  a disease of the skin, causing continual
    peeling: *kilin wai.*
  a disease of the skin, characterized by
    a light discoloration of the skin,
    usually on the trunk of the body:
    kilsarawi.
  breadfruit disease: *sakot.*
  skin disease caused by a fungus:
    sensen.
  yam disease, causing small black spots
    on the yam: *kil.*

diseased
  sick, diseased, ill: *soumwahu.*

disfigured
  to be disfigured by yaws: *kiauk.*

disgust
  an expression of disgust: *ahk₂.*
  to be in a state of intense disgust or
    anger: *tat₂.*

disgusting
  disgusting because of filthy or
    unsanitary conditions: *saut.*
  obnoxious, disgusting, irritating:
    limwesou.

dish
  coconut cup, dish, plate: *dahl.*

dishonest
  dishonest, crooked, malicious, wicked:
    mwersuwed, mworsuwed.
  to be dishonest or crooked to:
    mwersuwedih.

disinterested
  to be tired of, to be disinterested in, to
    be bored by: *pwangahki.*

disjointed
  limp, flexible, springy, disjointed, used
    to describe a manner of walking:
    kiahweliwel.

dislike
  to dislike, to refuse: *kahng₁.*
  to hate or dislike, of people: *kailongki.*

dislocated
to be dislocated, of a joint: *piselpeseng.*

dismiss
to dismiss, as a court case: *kasohre.*

disobedient: *lawalo, sapeik₁.*

disorder
confusion, disorder, mess: *pingiping.*

disordered
confused, disordered, messy: *ping.*

dispatch: *lokaia.*
dispatch or message: *ilek₂.*
to summon or dispatch: *poarone.*
to be summoned or dispatched:
   poaron.

display
to make a display of magic, spiritual
   power, or authority: *akmanaman.*

displeased
to be slighted, to be displeased:
   mwakar.

displeasure
to visibly show one's displeasure at a
   request: *koatoahnien.*

dispute: *daidowa.*
argument, quarrel, dispute: *akamai.*
war, battle, dispute: *moromor.*

disregard
to disregard: *kasohwe.*

disrespectful
disrespectful, usually said of children:
   laumwaumw.

distant
distant, far off: *doh.*

distressed
distressed, frustrated: *weikek.*

distribute
to divide, to distribute: *nehk.*
to formally distribute food at a
   kamadipw: *pwek₄, pwekipwek.*
to be divided, to be distributed: *ne.*
to be distributed, to be spread around:
   pahng₂.

district
a political unit, as a municipality,
   district, state, country, or kingdom:
   wehi₂.
district, precinct: *lopidi.*

distrustful: *soulikilik.*

disturb
to disturb: *mweseisei.*
to disturb or alert by making a
   pounding noise: *kumw, kumwur.*
to disturb with noise: *kataironge.*

disturbed
mentally disturbed, crazy, insane: *iahk.*

ditch
ditch, trench, groove: *warawar.*

dive
to dive: *du.*
to dive for objects on the floor of the
   ocean or the bed of a stream:
   duhp₁.
to dive headfirst: *dikoumoang.*

divide
to divide: *pwalang.*
to divide land: *pwalasapw.*
to divide land into large areas:
   pwallap.
to divide, to distribute: *nehk.*
to be divided: *pwal.*
to be divided into groups or sections:
   apalipeseng.
to be divided, to be distributed: *ne.*

diving knife
sheath knife, hunting knife, diving
   knife, dagger: *sihdnaip, teike.*

division
division of land: *pwalasapw.*
division, section: *pali₁.*
division, in arithmetic: *nehne.*
to do division: *nehne.*

divorce
to divorce: *kesehla.*
to grant a divorce: *mweidpeseng.*
to be divorced: *mwei₂.*

dizzy: *mwahliel, sahliel.*
giddy, dizzy: *mwahngieng.*

do
to do: *wia.*
to do something by chance: *depweila.*
to do something, either that one knows
   is wrong or that turns out to be
   wrong: *keluhla.*

dock
wharf, dock: *wap.*

doctor: *toahkte.*

dodge
to duck, to dodge: *sansar₂, sarek₁.*

dog: *kidi.*

dog-paddle
to dog-paddle: *pepen kairu, pepen
   lamwer.*

dogtuna
fish sp., dogtuna, *Gymnasarda
   unicolor*: *manguro.*

doll: *toahl₁.*

dollar: *tala.*

dolphin
fish sp., dolphin, *Coryphaena
   hippurus*: *kohko.*

donkey: *dongki.*
   ass, donkey: *ahs.*
door: *wenihmw.*
   a door in the rear of a feasthouse used
   by the Nahnmwarki: *wounmei.*
   either of the two rear doors of a
   feasthouse: *wenihmw en
   lempahntamw.*
   the two doors in the rear of a feast
   house, used by the *Nahnmwarki*
   and *Nahnken*: *kereilik.*
double
   to double, as roofing or paper:
   kamasriaparih.
double-cross
   to double-cross: *kamwahl.*
   to double-cross one member of a
   married couple, as a consequence of
   participation in an extra-marital
   affair: *kawehdi.*
douche
   to douche: *mwaur, mwoumwou.*
doughnut: *dohnas.*
downcast
   gloomy, downcast: *pohtou.*
downhill
   steep, downhill: *ukedi.*
downwards: *-di.*
downwind
   downwind, lower: *pahnangi.*
doze
   to doze: *lepalep.*
   to doze off, to nod when falling asleep:
   lisoi.
dozen: *tesin.*
drag
   to pull, to drag: *ruwahdeki, urahdeki.*
   to be pulled, to be dragged: *ruwahdek,
   urahdek.*
dragonfly: *dempwo₁, menin kahlipw.*
drain
   to drain: *kakus.*
   to be drained: *kokus.*
drama
   game, recreation, drama: *mwadong.*
drape
   to drape, as with a sheet or blanket:
   irepe.
draw
   to draw a line: *ele₁.*
   to draw back one's arm: *ngap.*
   to draw back one's arm as if to strike a
   blow: *ngapada.*
   to draw or fetch water: *idip, idipil.*
   to draw or paint, as a picture: *mahlen,
   mahlenih.*

to draw out, to pull out, of any string-
   like object: *air.*
to fetch or draw liquids: *ihd₃.*
to possess, to draw interest, of money:
   neitik.
drawer: *ikdasi.*
drawing
   painting, drawing: *mahlen.*
dream: *eliman, ouremen.*
   to dream: *eliman, ouremen.*
   to dream about: *elimene, ouraman.*
dress: *likouli.*
   muumuu, an ankle length dress:
   mwuhmwu.
   to dress: *likouda, pwuhrieng.*
   to dress oneself: *likawihada,
   mwoalehda.*
dried
   to be dried by heat, as of copra or
   tobacco: *kereng.*
   to be dried, as of copra or tobacco:
   reng.
drift
   to drift, to flow: *ahd-.*
driftwood
   very light driftwood: *kehpei.*
drill
   drill, brace: *mehn pwuropwur.*
   drill, training, exercise: *kaiahn.*
   to drill a hole: *pwuropwur.*
   to drill a hole in: *pwure.*
   to drill, to train someone: *kaiahne.*
   to drill, to train, to exercise: *kaiahn.*
drink
   to drink: *dake₂, nim, urak₃.*
   to drink an entire cup of kava:
   wikidedi.
   to drink directly from a container:
   kau₁.
   to drink kava from the same cup
   immediately after the
   Nahnmwarki: *kepin dowehlap.*
   to drink the first cup of kava: *pwelih.*
   to eat, drink, or smoke: *sohk₁.*
   to informally drink kava: *takainwel.*
   to take a drink and hold it in the
   mouth without swallowing:
   pwere₁.
   to consume, to eat or drink: *tungoal,
   tungoale.*
   soda, soft drink: *saida.*
drip
   to drip or leak: *ding.*
drive
   to drive: *undeng, windeng.*
   to drive fish into a net: *ihdak, kasare.*

driver: *windeng.*

droop
  to bend, to droop: *itiek.*

drop: *dingiding, mpwi.*
  drop pitch, in baseball: *diroap.*
  to drop: *kese, kesepweke, kos₁, lakid.*
  to drop into a hole, of a marble in the
    game *anaire*: *aida, airas.*
  to be dropped: *lekidek.*

drown
  to drown: *depwala.*
  to be drowned, to be submerged:
    duhla.

drum: *aip.*
  drum, as an oil drum: *diromkang.*
  to play the drum: *aip.*

drunk
  alcoholic, always drunk: *nompe.*
  to be intoxicated, to be drunk: *sakau.*

dry
  dry clothes one puts on, extra clothes
    taken on a trip: *kemmad, kiemmad.*
  dry, of something which commonly has
    a moisture content, i.e., wood, one's
    throat, dirt, but not clothing or
    dishes: *ngalangal.*
  dry, of the hair or skin: *marekeng.*
  very dry: *madekeng.*
  withered, dry, dead, of vegetation:
    meng.
  to dry by heat, as copra or tobacco:
    karang.
  to dry, to expose objects to the sun in
    order to dry them: *palang₁.*
  to give someone dry clothes: *kemmade.*
  to put on dry clothes: *kemmad,*
    kiemmad.
  of leaves, to turn or begin to dry:
    mahrdi.
  to be dried, to be exposed to the sun
    in order to be dried: *peleng.*
  to be dry: *mad₂.*

duck
  to duck, to dodge: *sansar₂, sarek₁.*

duck: *tehk₂.*

dug
  to be dug out, to be excavated:
    weiweida.

dull
  dull colored: *pohmarungurung.*
  dull or old-looking, of inanimate
    objects: *moarungurung.*
  dull, blunt: *kons.*

dumb
  mute, dumb, stuttering: *lohteng.*
  stupid, silly, idiotic, simple, dumb:

    kupwuropwon, loalopwon,
    pweipwei₁.
  extremely stupid, silly, idiotic, simple,
    dumb: *pweirengid.*

dump
  pile of debris, dump: *peinikid.*

dumpling
  a kind of dumpling stuffed with a red
    bean jam: *mansu.*

durable
  durable, having the ability to survive
    either time or circumstance: *koato.*

duration: *werei.*

duress
  force, duress: *itoit.*

durian
  tree sp., durian, *Pangium edule*, edible
    fruit: *duhrien, rawahn.*

during
  during the time, for a period of, while,
    within a distance: *erein.*

dust: *pwelipar.*
  dust covered: *pehsehs.*

duster: *lempweileng.*

dusty: *pwelipar.*

duty
  responsibility, obligation, duty:
    pwukoa.

dwarf: *sokolei.*

dwelling
  building, house, home, dwelling: *ihmw.*
  family dwelling: *ihmwalap.*

dye: *mehn kodu.*
  to dye: *reid.*
  to be dyed: *rei.*

dysentery: *mwesen ntahkereker.*

eager
  concerned, anxious, eager: *ngoang.*

eagle: *ikel.*

ear: *karonge, koarong, saleng.*

earache: *saleng medek.*

earring: *tiati.*

earth
  dirt, soil, earth, ground: *pwehl₁.*
  world, earth: *sampah.*

earthworm: *kamwetel.*

ease
  free, at ease in doing something:
    maledek.

easily: *kehn₁.*
  not easily: *sekeh, sekehn.*

east: *palimese.*

Easter: *Sarawihn Iasada.*

easy: *mengei.*

easygoing
    peaceful, easygoing, unenthusiastic, slow moving, passive, lethargic: *meleilei.*

eat
    to eat: *dipwahk, kang, lemwedek, mwenge, neminem, paun, sak.*
    to eat a late night snack: *mwengehn pwong.*
    to eat after drinking kava: *kenei sakau, pailol.*
    to eat before kava: *kepsakau.*
    to eat breakfast: *deied, kapwarsou, kemenseng$_1$, mwengehn menseng.*
    to eat dinner: *kasoutik, koduhsou, mwengehn soutik.*
    to eat lunch: *kasouwas, mwengehn souwas, pahnisou.*
    to eat meat or fish: *sali, selie.*
    to eat only meat, to eat only one thing: *ikoaik.*
    to eat raw: *wet$_2$, wete.*
    to eat raw fish or raw meat of any kind: *sasimi.*
    to eat with the *Nahnmwarki* or *Nahnken*: *pohnkoiohlap.*
    to eat, drink, or smoke: *sohk$_1$.*
    to eat, said only of infants: *mehme$_2$.*
    to eat, to taste, used derogatorily: *nam.*
    to consume, to eat or drink: *tungoal, tungoale.*

eave
    eave of a building: *ekipir.*

eavesdrop
    said of one who eavesdrops: *poarongorong.*

echo: *moahd.*

economize
    to economize on: *kirawih.*

edge: *keile.*
    edge of a reef: *mese.*
    seaward edge of the mangrove swamp: *pahniak.*
    to be on edge, of the teeth: *rer.*
    to sharpen, to put an edge on something: *adahd, ede$_2$.*

eel
    salt water eel, a generic term: *ihd$_4$, lapwed.*
    salt water eel, commonly found along the edge of mangrove swamps: *lapweden pahniak.*
    salt water eel, commonly found in deep water: *lapwedehlam.*
    salt water eel, commonly found in muddy areas: *limwahnsaleng.*
    salt water eel, commonly found on the barrier reef: *rap.*
    salt water eel, commonly found in mangrove swamps: *mwaso, mwesot.*
    fresh water eel: *kemisik.*

effect
    initial effects of kava or alcohol: *litepw.*
    of kava, to begin to have an effect on one: *sok$_1$.*

effective
    to be effective: *man.*
    having an impact, effective, efficient: *lipwan.*

effeminate
    of a man, effeminate: *piledek.*

efficient
    having an impact, effective, efficient: *lipwan.*

egg: *damango, kutohr.*
    nit, the egg of a louse: *dihl$_2$.*
    rotten egg: *pweisenwair.*

eggplant
    eggplant, *Solanum melongena*: *nasupi, pringihnas.*

Egypt: *Ekipten.*

eight: *ewel$_2$, walimwut, walipit, waluh, welewel, welidip, welidun, weliel, welika, welikap, welikis, welimen, welimwodol, welipa, welipak, welipali, welipar, welipoar, welipwoat, welipwong, welipwuloi, welira, welisel, welisop, welisou, welite, welitumw, wellep, weluhmw.*

eighty: *weliakan, welihsek, welingoul.*

ejaculate
    to climax or ejaculate: *kus, nek$_1$.*
    prone to premature ejaculation: *kehnek.*

eject
    to eject, to banish: *kaus.*
    to be ejected, to be banished: *pokous.*

elbow: *keimwinpeh.*

election
    election, raffle, lottery: *usuhs.*
    election, selection: *pilipil.*

electrician: *sounwielioal.*

electricity
    electricity, electric light, flashlight: *dengki.*
    lightning, electricity: *lioal.*

elegant
    to be elegant, to look good in one's clothing: *pahieng.*

elephant: *elipant.*

elevated: *ile.*

elevation: *ile.*

elope
to run off with a woman, to elope: *sopohla.*

embarrassed
bashful, embarrassed, ashamed: *liroaridi, namenek.*
embarrassed, usually of girls: *mwomwitik.*
to be embarrassed by the unexpected: *sihdiro.*
to be embarrassed or humiliated: *sarohdi.*

embarrassment
shame, embarrassment: *saroh.*

ember
cinder, ember, charcoal, coal of a fire: *mwoalus.*

embrace
to embrace, to hug: *pwoalehdi.*
to embrace, to hug each other: *pwoaloapwoal.*

embroider
to embroider: *deiad, deiadih.*

embroidery: *deiad.*
a type of embroidery: *deikapwur.*
a type of embroidery, using x-stitches: *deikilelenwad.*

employment
occupation, task, employment, responsibility, deed: *doahk.*

empty: *tehn$_1$.*
slit, crack, small opening, empty space, outer space: *nanwehwe.*

empty-handed
to be unburdened or empty-handed: *kahiep.*

empty-headed: *peunmoang.*

encircle
to encircle, to go around: *kapil.*

enclose
to surround, to enclose, to spread everywhere: *kipe.*

enclosure
enclosure, pen, fence, wall, as of a fort: *kehl$_2$.*

end
end of a canoe: *keimwinwar.*
end of kava ceremony, end, last one: *kodie.*
end, limit: *idi.*
large end of a canoe: *imwilap.*
small end of a canoe: *imwitik.*
tail, end, extreme: *iki.*
top, summit, end, outcome: *imwi.*
to be at the end of: *ikiala.*

to be ended: *erala.*
to be ended, terminated, or stopped: *tok$_1$.*

enemy
adversary, enemy, feud: *imwintihti.*

energetic: *angiangin.*

engine
machine, engine, outboard motor: *misihn.*

enjoy
to enjoy, of any intoxicating drink: *kamam.*

enlighten
to enlighten: *kamarainih.*

enlightened
civilized, enlightened: *marain.*

enough
to be enough, adequate, ample: *itar.*
to be too much, excessive, more than enough: *depala.*

enter
to enter: *pidolong.*

entertain
to entertain: *kamwait.*

entice
to tempt, to entice: *kasongosong.*

entire
entire, whole, as in *Pohnpeiuh:* *uh$_8$.*
entire, whole, unanimous, complete: *unsek.*
whole, entire, intact: *pwon.*

entry
gate, entry: *ewenkel.*

enumerate
to enumerate: *pahng$_1$.*

envelope: *pwuhdo.*

envious
jealous, envious: *luwak.*
extremely envious or jealous: *peirin.*

epicanthic
straight, also used to describe eyes with an epicanthic fold: *dengideng.*

equal
equal, even, flush: *pahrek.*
to be equal: *ras$_1$.*

equalize
to align, to equalize, to level: *kapahrek.*

equate
to equate, to compare in terms of size: *kasosohng.*

era
reign, era: *mwehi.*

erase
to erase: *iris.*
to be erased: *irihrla.*

erect
to erect, to raise: *kau₁*.
to be erected, to be raised: *kokou*.

erection
to have an erection: *kekel*.

errand: *poaron*.
always sending others on an errand: *pekehilek*.
to send on an errand, to send to deliver a message: *kautoke*.

errant: *saruwaru*.

erroneous
incorrect, wrong, erroneous: *sapwung*.

error
mistake, error: *sapwung*.

escape
to escape: *pit-*.

escorted
to be lead or guided, to be escorted: *pakahr*.

estimate
estimate, estimation: *kendo*.
to estimate: *kendo*.

estimation
estimate, estimation: *kendo*.

etcetera: *ape₁*.

even
equal, even, flush: *pahrek*.

evening: *soutik*.
this evening: *eten*.

event: *irair*.

everlasting: *soutuk*.
everlasting, constant, permanent: *poatoapoat*.

every: *koaruhsie*.

evident
clear, evident: *dehde*.
clear, evident, obvious: *sansal*.

exalt
said of one who tries to exalt himself by flattering or presenting gifts to his superiors: *alkeniken*.

exalted
to be exalted, to be promoted: *lapalapala*.

examination
test, examination: *des, sikeng*.
to take a test or examination: *des, sikeng*.

examine
to examine, to diagnose, to make a choice, to guess: *kasawih*.
to examine, to have a physical examination: *kensa*.
to inspect, examine, or check: *dawih, dou₃*.

to examine with a stethoscope: *rong*.
to be examined, to be diagnosed, to be figured out: *keseu*.
to see, discern, look at, observe, examine: *kilang*.
to see, discern, look at, observe, examine, with a derogatory connotation: *ngar*.

example: *karasepe*.
to give an example: *karasaras*.
to set an example for: *kaweid*.

excavate
to dig, to excavate: *weir₁*.
to be dug out, to be excavated: *weiweida*.

exceed
to go beyond, to exceed, to surpass, to overtake: *sipele*.

excellent
attractive, excellent: *suwanawan*.

excessive
excessive amount: *mwuledek*.
to be too much, excessive, more than enough: *depala*.

exchange
to alternate, to exchange, as a load or position: *peisipal*.
to exchange: *kohkang, wiliali*.
to exchange agricultural products for fish: *sewe*.
to exchange information: *kasahnwar*.
to exchange the lead, as in racing: *peiai*.
an exchange of agricultural products for fish: *sewen mwomw*.

excited
to get excited: *pwuriamwei*.

excluded
to be independent, to be different, to be excluded from the group: *tohrohr*.

excuse
Excuse me , Forgive me : *mahkehngie*.

execute
to kill, to execute: *kemehla*.
to be executed: *kamakamala*.

exercise
drill, training, exercise: *kaiahn*.
to drill, to train, to exercise: *kaiahn*.

exhaust
to exhaust a supply of something: *koamwoamwasang*.
to exhaust, of a supply: *kamwamw*.
to be exhausted, of a supply: *mwomwala*.

exhibited
to be exposed, to be exhibited: *kasansal.*

exhibition: *kasansal.*

exile
to banish, to exile: *kalipe.*
to be banished, to be exiled: *kalipilip.*

exist
to exist, a locative verb: *mi.*
to exist, an existential verb: *mie.*

exit
to exit: *pidohi.*

expand
to expand: *eirekpeseng.*

expect
to expect, to await: *kasik.*
to anticipate, to expect: *awihala.*

expensive
expensive, costly: *pweilaud.*

experience
to feel, to experience: *kehn₂.*
to have an experience for the first
time: *ehdila.*

expert: *semen, soupal.*
to be expert at: *samani.*

explain
to explain, to translate: *kawehwe.*

explode
to explode: *pos₂.*

expose
to show or expose: *kasale-.*
to dry, to expose objects to the sun in
order to dry them: *palang₁.*
to be dried, to be exposed to the sun
in order to be dried: *peleng.*
to be exposed: *salada.*
to be exposed, to be exhibited:
kasansal.
to accidentally expose one's genitals:
salla.

extend
to extend one's arms: *kapapeseng.*

extensive
extensive, large: *kowahlap.*

extinguished
to be extinguished: *kun.*

extract
at the end of the kava ceremony, to
completely extract all the juices
from a batch of kava: *wengkid.*

extreme
tail, end, extreme: *iki.*

extremely: *kodouluhl.*

eye: *edinperen, pwoarenmas.*
an eye condition caused by exposure

to glare, resulting in sensitivity to
light: *mahliel.*
black eye: *pilakai.*
cross-eyed: *masapang.*
large-eyed: *masduwarawar.*
to check on, to keep on eye on:
lehnmwese.
to have something in one's eye:
pwull₂.
to keep an eye on: *tehk₁.*

eyeball: *kutohr en mese.*

eyebrow: *dekehnering, padi.*

eyelash: *nihnihrek, ririnderihleng,
ririnmas.*

eyelid: *kilin mese.*

facade: *mese, temwen ihmw.*

face: *mahs₂, sihleng, wasaile.*
a derogatory term for face: *ker₂.*
to face, of inanimate objects: *salehng.*
to turn toward, to face: *sohpei-.*

fade
to fade, as of a color: *sar.*

faded: *marungurung.*

fail
to fail to complete a competitive
activity: *pwupwula.*
to fail, of a project: *pweula.*
to flunk, to fail: *rakudai.*

faint
to faint: *lipwongmas.*

fair
agricultural fair: *impiokai.*

fairy tern
bird sp., fairy tern: *kahke.*

faith
faith, belief, creed: *pwoson.*
faith, trust, hope: *koapwoaroapwoar.*
to believe in, to have faith in: *pwoson.*
to have faith, trust, or hope:
koapwoaroapwoar.

faithful
faithful, persevering, single-minded,
diligent: *loaloapwoat.*

fall
to fall: *kumwisekala, lempehdi,
pwupw.*
to fall down, of standing objects: *rauk,
sauk.*
to fall headfirst: *dikeimwidi.*
to fall in quantity, as rain or fruit:
mwer₂.
to fall in the water with a splashing
sound: *tau.*
to fall on, as of rain on leaves: *mwarak.*
to fall, of unripe fruit: *lempehdi.*

to descend into, to fall into, to step into, as a hole: *pwuhr-*.

to slide or fall, of a pile of non-living objects, as a landslide: *engkidi*.

false teeth: *ngih pasapas*.

falsetto
to shout in a falsetto voice, either when carrying kava or to challenge another to a fight: *kadekedek*.
to sing in a loud falsetto: *kadaileng*.

familiar
too familiar: *poupoulap₁*.

family
family, relative: *peneinei*.
lineage, extended family, clan: *keinek*.

famine
any period of famine: *lehk*.
scarcity, famine: *isol*.

famous: *wadawad₂*.
famous, celebrated: *ndand*.

fan: *irlapiso, tehnihr*.
to fan: *irihr, irip*.

fanning
ray-like, fanning, kinky: *sirang*.

far
distant, far off: *doh*.
far apart: *malau*.
far, far along, unsurpassed: *dei, dei*.
to be far from: *dohwan*.

farm
clearing, field, plantation, garden, farm: *mwaht, mwetiwel*.

farmer: *soumwet*.

farmstead
land, farmstead, homestead: *sahpw*.

fart
to fart: *nanmwoale, sing*.
to fart at: *singid*.
to want to fart: *menseker*.

fascinated
to be fascinated, by someone or something new: *pwerila*.

fast
fast, in bodily movement: *pitikan*.
fast, in the ability to perform actions: *pitipit*.
fast, in walking: *seimek*.
fast, speedy: *dopas, uk*.
fast, swift, of a moving object: *marahra*.
of a stream, rising and fast flowing: *ahdomour*.
speedy, fast: *sipihdo*.
fast growing: *pwed₁*.
to go fast: *pariki*.

to go fast, to be quick, to hurry: *mwadang*.

fast
to fast or abstain from food: *kalehk*.
to fast or abstain from food, voluntarily or on direction from a superior: *kaisihsol*.

fasten
to fasten, to affix: *kapasa*.
to connect, to fasten together: *pouse*.
to be connected, to be fastened together: *pous*.

fat
fat, healthy looking, of infants or young domestic animals: *sinopwunopw*.
fat, stout: *mworourou*.
grease, fat: *kirihs, wih₃*.

father: *pahpa₁, sahm₁*.
father, dad, a term of familiarity: *ip, ipa*.

fathom
fathom, the distance between outstretched arms, approximately six feet: *ngahp*.

faux pas
to commit a faux pas: *depweila*.

favor
to attempt to gain favor, to bribe: *natih*.
to request, to ask a favor, to beg: *pekipek*.

favored
beloved, favored: *masamas*.
favored, well-loved, of a child or pet: *soisoi*.

favorite: *keniken*.

fear
to be afraid of, to fear: *masak*.

fearful
cautious, hesitant, fearful: *per*.

feast
a feast: *kamadipw*.
death feast, given after the burial: *mwurilik, umwun mwurilik*.
family feast: *kamadipw en peneinei*.
feast for a new dwelling house: *kapidolong₂*.
feast for returning fishermen: *oulaid*.
feast given annually to pay tribute to the *Nahnmwarki*: *kamadipw en wahu*.
feast given at the end of the breadfruit season: *umwun luhwen mei*.
feast given at the end of the yam season: *keidisol*.
feast given at the time the

construction of a feasthouse is
initiated: *serida.*

feast given for a *Nahnmwarki* or
Nahnken when he recovers from an
illness: *tiepwel.*

feast given for one departing, a
farewell feast: *umwun kepinwar.*

feast given separately to the
Nahnmwarki and *Nahnken* as
sennit is prepared: *dakadak
dipenihd.*

feast given to celebrate the first fishing
trips with a new canoe: *katepeik.*

feast given upon completing the roof
of a new *nahs*: *editoal.*

feast given upon completion of a
building: *umwun edied.*

feast given upon completion of a new
feasthouse: *isimwas.*

feast in which ripe breadfruit are
employed: *dokapahini.*

feast involving yams, usually given in
December: *idihd₂.*

feast made for a fishing party: *kapas.*

feast of preserved breadfruit: *songmar.*

feast of public acceptance of a
koanoat title: *iraramwar.*

feast of public acceptance of a title:
kapasmwar.

feast of tribute, first fruits offering:
nohpwei.

feast to celebrate the first usage of a
new kava stone: *uramai.*

feast to welcome someone coming or
returning to Ponape: *kapel.*

first feast for a new canoe: *keting en
wahr.*

first feast of the breadfruit season:
kerismei.

first feast of the yam season, usually in
October: *kotekehp.*

second feast for a new canoe, when it
is lashed together: *keting en inou
wahr.*

second feast of the breadfruit season:
kehmei, pwutemei.

third feast given to celebrate the use
of a new net: *laid kapw.*

third feast of a new feasthouse: *keting
en taht.*

to feast: *kamadipw.*

to make a feast for: *kemedipwe.*

to make a small feast: *kamweng.*

to prepare a small informal feast or
party: *ainpwoat.*

hard working in feast activities:
dingngang.

feasthouse: *nahs.*

a feasthouse having five center posts:
koupahleng.

a feasthouse having three center posts
with pits for kava stones on the main
platform: *kehrourou.*

a feasthouse having three center posts
without pits for kava stones on the
main platform: *pahrourou.*

a feasthouse having three center posts,
located inland: *tehn mwomwinsapw.*

a feasthouse having three center posts,
located on the shore: *inen oaroahr.*

an informally built feasthouse:
nasepwel.

feather

body hair, feathers, fur: *wine.*

February: *Pepweri.*

feces: *pwise.*

fecund

to be fecund: *par₅.*

of breadfruit, fecund: *waramwahu.*

fee

fee, rental payment: *isepe.*

feeble

weak, feeble, sickly: *luwet,
luwetakahu.*

feed

to feed: *kamwenge.*

to feed intravenously: *doklaud.*

to be fed: *kamweng.*

feel

to feel around for, when unable to see
an object, to grope around for, to
probe for: *dehm.*

to feel the initial effects of kava or
alcohol: *litepw.*

to feel, think, or sense: *pehm.*

to feel, to experience: *kehn₂.*

to think, to feel: *kupwurehiong.*

to touch or feel: *doahke.*

feeling

feeling, thought: *pepehm.*

peace, tranquility, good feelings:
onepek.

will, feelings: *nsen.*

female

female of any species: *lih₂, pein₂.*

fertile female of any species: *lidep.*

female turtle: *asapein.*

female mangrove crab: *asapein.*

fence

enclosure, pen, fence, wall, as of a fort:
kehl₂.

fern sp.: *peipei eni.*

fern sp., *Cyathea ponapeana* or
nigricans, a tree fern: *katar.*

fern sp., *Cyclosorus adenophorus*:
mahrek.
fern sp., *Histiopteris incisa*: *peipei
aramas*.
fern sp., *Nephrolepis acutifolia*: *rehdil*.

ferocious
ferocious, rabid: *lipes*.

fertile
fertile female of any species: *lidep*.
fertile, of the soil: *pwelmwahu*.
fertile, procreating prolifically:
kaparapar.

fertilizer: *kamweng, koiasi*.

fetch
to draw or fetch water: *idip, idipil*.
to fetch or draw liquids: *ihd₃*.

feud
adversary, enemy, feud: *imwintihti*.

fever: *lusulus*.

few: *malaulau*.

fiber
fiber of a green coconut, used for
making sennit: *dipenihd*.
hibiscus fiber: *koht₂*.

field
baseball field: *kurando*.
clearing, field, plantation, garden,
farm: *mwaht*.
field, open area: *mohs*.

fierce
brave, fierce: *kommwad*.

fifth: *kelimau*.
depending on the municipality, the
fourth or the fifth cup of kava in the
kava ceremony: *sapwe*.

fifty: *limehk, limeisek, limengoul*.

fight
a fight: *pei₃*.
to fight: *doahke, pei₃*.
to fight each other: *poadoahk*.

figure
to decide, to figure out: *lemehda*.

filariasis: *liengimat*.

file: *pwail*.
file, sharpening stone, razor strop:
mehn adahd.
to file: *pwail*.

file
to file a complaint in court: *kampilein*.

fill
to fill a container with food: *deuk*.
to fill up with a liquid: *koadia*.
to fill, to load: *aude*.
to be filled, to be loaded: *audaud*.
to be filled: *koadiadi*.
overcrowded, filled: *dir*.

filling
filling, of a tooth: *simend, siment*.

film
photographic film: *pilim*.

filthy
messy, unsanitary, filthy: *samin*.

fin
pectoral fin of a fish: *ingi*.
top and bottom fins of a fish: *sike*.

final
to make a final statement or perform a
final action: *kemwurumwur*.

find
to find: *diar*.
to be found: *dierek*.
hard to find: *salong*.

fine
fine, not coarse: *pisetik*.
precious, beautiful, perfect, fine:
kaselel.

fine
fine, punishment: *pakking*.
to be fined, to be punished: *pakking*.

finger: *rekeleng, rekenleng, sendin peh*.
appendage, finger, toe: *send*.
index finger: *sendimesemese*.
little finger: *sohkatepe*.
middle finger: *tihmwe*.
ring finger: *tahmwel*.
thumb: *sendilepe*.

fingernail: *kikin peh*.

finish
to finish: *keimwisak*.
to finish cooking food not done:
kalewiala.
to finish defecating: *mwei₂*.
to finish, as of concrete: *kamadal*.
to be finished: *keimwisek, nek₁*.
to be finished, to be accomplished:
imwisekila.

fire: *ahi₁, kisiniei, mesiha*.
to add wood to an existing fire: *saun*.
to be burned, to be lit, to be set fire
to: *isida*.
to burn, to light, to set fire to, to burn
off feathers or hair: *isik*.
to make a fire: *saun*.
to make fire by rubbing a stick in a
trough of wood: *id₁*.
two large logs at the base of the fire
for an *uhmw*: *mpehn*.

firecracker: *anapi*.

firewood: *tuwi*.

first: *keieu, mahs₄*.
to be first in line or in order:
kohmwowe.

to be the first or best, to top all others: *dake*$_1$.

to visit a place for the first time: *pasakapw*.

first-born

first-born child: *mesenih*.

fish: *mwahmw*.

the meat or fish part of a meal: *irap, sali*.

to fish: *laid*.

to fish for: *laidih*.

to fish for *toik*: *weirar*.

to fish for *werer*, a sp. of sea cucumber: *kedwerer*.

to fish for crab in the mangrove swamps: *dilin elimoang*.

to fish for octopus: *seikihs*.

to fish for shrimp: *rohlikedepw*.

to fish for the first time after someone's burial to test whether the spirit of the deceased will bring good or bad luck: *songmaterek*.

to fish for the sp. of fish, *soupwou*: *rohsopwou*.

to fish with a net from a canoe or boat: *weren uhk*.

to fish with a throw line: *sipisip*.

to fish with a throwing net: *lekidek*.

to fish with line: *epiep*.

to fish by driving fish into the rocks on the reef: *pakatei*.

to taut line fish off the bottom: *kekihr*.

to torch fish: *ndil*.

fish sp.: *asimel, ehnta, epwel*$_2$*, ewen sawi, iht, ilek*$_1$*, inahme, kadek*$_3$*, katik*$_2$*, kendip*$_2$*, keriker*$_1$*, kih*$_2$*, kihrsal, kioakomwot, kohpwa*$_1$*, lisap, lisarapat, malekelek, marapat, masokod, maud, mmwen, moahk, mpwekin ripwiripw, mwanger, mwanger en mwoanipil, mwanger en nanipil, mwanger en nannamw, mwanger ripwiripw, nihtahta, pahini pokon, parakus, parapar, parapar en lik, pasete, pediped, pehris, peikopw, pidekilik, poros, poros en merer, pwerkidipw, pwuhn, ripwiripw*$_2$*, sakana, sammenip, sawi pwiliet, sengiseng, tipaker*$_2$*, toik, wahrar, widei*.

fish sp., *Caranx*: *tehp*.

fish sp., a kind of frog fish: *daliere, nehu*.

fish sp., a kind of mullet: *pehioang*.

fish sp., a kind of needle fish: *dahk, lidokodok pwise*.

fish sp., a kind of parrotfish: *kilikil,*

lida, mahuenmoar, mwomwmei, pahme, pedilik$_2$*, umwun*$_2$.

fish sp., a kind of parrotfish, *Scarus rubroviolaceus*: *lidoi*.

fish sp., a sp. of shark: *sahused, tenipei*.

fish sp., angelfish: *senserek*.

fish sp., any bluish parrotfish: *mahu*.

fish sp., barracuda: *nahliam*.

fish sp., barracuda, *Sphyraena barracuda*: *suhre*.

fish sp., barracuda, *Sphyraena langsar* or *Sphyraena bleekeri*: *sarau*.

fish sp., bass-grouper, *Cephalopholis argus*: *mwalusulus*.

fish sp., black surgeonfish: *toamwoarok*.

fish sp., blue jack crevally, *Caranx melampygus*: *oarong*.

fish sp., butterfly fish: *lierpwater*.

fish sp., castor-oil fish: *deikenepeng*.

fish sp., dogtuna, *Gymnasarda unicolor*: *manguro*.

fish sp., dolphin, *Coryphaena hippurus*: *kohko*.

fish sp., flying fish: *menger*.

fish sp., goatfish, *Mulloidichthys vanicolensis*: *epil*.

fish sp., goatfish, *Parupeneus cyclostomus*: *mwompwon, mwomwalis*.

fish sp., goatfish, *Parupeneus indicus*: *iomo*.

fish sp., goatfish, *Upeneus arge*: *marep*$_2$.

fish sp., grouper, *Plectropomus leopardus*, *Plectropomus melanoleucus*, or *Plectropomus truncatus*: *sawi*$_2$.

fish sp., half beak, *Hemiramphus guoyi*: *pwuwas*.

fish sp., halibut: *liper*$_1$.

fish sp., hammerhead shark: *pako lohpwu*.

fish sp., humphead parrotfish, *Bolbometopon muricatus*: *kemeik*.

fish sp., jack, *Atule mate*: *lahd*.

fish sp., jack, *Caranx sexfasciatus*: *oarong en pwong*.

fish sp., mackerel pike: *samma*.

fish sp., milkfish, *Chanos Chanos*: *eki*.

fish sp., mudskipper: *litak*.

fish sp., pompano, *Selar crumenopthalmus*: *pedihdi*.

fish sp., porcupine fish: *sei*$_2$.

fish sp., puffer fish: *wahd*.

fish sp., rabbitfish, *Siganus canaliculatus*: *umwule*.

fish sp., rabbitfish, *Siganus corallinus*: *seteu*.

fish sp., rabbitfish, *Siganus doliatus*:
kioak, pwerinmwomw.

fish sp., rabbitfish, *Siganus puellus*:
mahr$_2$.

fish sp., rabbitfish, *Siganus punctatus*: *palapal*.

fish sp., rabbitfish, *Siganus vulpinus*:
kompani.

fish sp., red snapper, *Lutjanus bohar*: *kihr en eiwel*.

fish sp., shark mullet: *ahpako*.

fish sp., silverfish, *Gerres abbreviatus*
or *Gerres kapas*: *kasapal*.

fish sp., skipjack tuna, *Katsawonus pelamis*: *kasuwo*.

fish sp., small and found in fresh
water: *kitel, palaiau*.

fish sp., snapper, *Lethrinus kallopterus*: *ikiepw*.

fish sp., snapper, *Lethrinus lentjan*:
medi.

fish sp., snapper, *Lethrinus ramak*:
samwei.

fish sp., snapper, *Lutjanus fulviflamma*: *likommwei*.

fish sp., snapper, *Lutjanus gibbus*:
pwahlahl.

fish sp., snapper, *Lutjanus kasmira*:
tehnseu.

fish sp., snapper, *Lutjanus malabaricus*: *kihr$_2$*.

fish sp., snapper, *Lutjanus semicinctus*: *pwehu$_1$*.

fish sp., squirrelfish, *Adoryx spinifer*: *sara$_2$*.

fish sp., squirrelfish, *Myripristis adustus*: *mwuhn*.

fish sp., striped surgeonfish,
Acanthurus lineatus: *wakapw*.

fish sp., surgeonfish: *doarop*.

fish sp., surgeonfish, *Acanthurus aliala*: *durudara*.

fish sp., surgeonfish, *Acanthurus gahhm*: *tamwarok*.

fish sp., surgeonfish, *Acanthurus xanthopterus*: *pakas*.

fish sp., surgeonfish, *Naso lituratus*:
pwulangking.

fish sp., sweetlips porgy,
Plectorhynchus goldmani or
Plectorhynchus chaetodontoides:
kehng.

fish sp., swordfish, sailfish, blue marlin:
dekilahr.

fish sp., trigger fish: *lioli*.

fish sp., trigger fish, *Rhinecanthus aculeatus*: *pwuhpw*.

fish sp., tuna: *weliwel$_2$*.

fish sp., unicorn fish, *Naso unicornis*:
pwulak.

fish sp., usually found in mangrove
swamps: *sopwou*.

fish sp., wahoo, *Acanthocybium solander*: *ahl$_2$*.

fish sp., wrasse, *Cheilinus undulatus*:
merer.

fish sp., yellow eyed surgeonfish:
darop.

fish sp., yellow-tailed brown parrotfish
Cetoscarus bicolor: *lawi*.

fish sp., yellowfin tuna, *Neothunnus macropterus*: *karangahp*.

shark mullet, at a growth stage of
approximately twelve inches: *ah$_4$*.

a small *ah*, a fish sp.: *epetik, limmwer*.

fish sp., a growth stage of *ah*:
moangtakai.

a large *ah*, a fish sp.: *siamwed*.

fish sp., an immature sweetlips porgy,
Plectorhynchus celebicus: *kakerepil*.

fish sp., a mature sweetlips porgy,
Plectorhynchus celebicus: *koail*.

a small *keriker*, a fish sp.: *kerilel*.

a large *keriker*, a fish sp.: *kertakai*.

fish sp., a small *pakas*: *peleu*.

a medium sized *ikem*, a fish sp.: *ikem asimel*.

a mature *mahu*: *mahulik*.

fish sp., a mature *pehioang*: *ikimweng*.

fish sp., a mature *samwei*: *samwei medi*.

fish sp., a mature parrotfish: *tamwais*.

fish trap: *uh$_6$*.
stone or coral fish trap: *mai$_1$*.

fisherman: *sounlaid*.
expert fisherman: *soused*.

fishy
fishy, greasy: *kideidei*.

fist: *kumwut*.
to make a fist: *roake*.

fit
to fit: *koakone, koakonokon*.
to fit together: *kakonepene*.
to fit, to go together well: *konpene*.

fitting
joint, fitting: *koakon*.

five: *alem, limadip, limadun, limakap,
limakis, limara, limatumw, limau,
limelep, limesel, limete, limewel,
limiel, limika, limisop, limisou,
limmen, limmwut, limoumw, limpa,
limpak, limpali, limpar, limpit,
limpoar, limpwoat, limpwong,
limpwuloi, limwomwodol*.

fix
  to repair, to fix: *apehne.*

flag: *pilaik.*

flake
  chip, flake: *dipere.*

flame: *lul, mpwul.*
  to burn with a flame: *mpwul.*
  to flame: *lul.*

flap
  to flap, as a bird flaps its wings:
    likepip.
  to flap, of a fish: *pitikek, pitirek.*

flash
  to flash: *pir$_2$.*

flashlight
  electricity, electric light, flashlight:
    dengki.

flat
  flat, of a surface: *patapat.*
  flat, of something normally rounded:
    pak$_2$.
  smooth and flat: *medendel.*
  wide and flat: *litehlapalap.*
  flat nosed: *tumwpak.*

flat tire: *pilat$_2$.*
  to have a flat tire: *pangku.*

flavor
  taste, flavor: *neme.*
  to flavor with coconut milk: *piah,*
    piahia.

flea
  louse, flea: *likarak.*
  sand flea: *menin lohsapw.*

flee
  to flee: *kereu, sopo, tang.*

fleet
  crowd, fleet, school of fish: *polo.*
  fleet of canoes: *sahi.*

flesh
  meat, flesh, muscle: *uduk.*

flexible
  limp, flexible, springy, disjointed, used
    to describe a manner of walking:
    kiahweliwel.

flick
  to flick: *let, leteng.*

flinch
  to flinch, to jerk away: *nur.*

flip
  to turn over, to flip: *welik.*
  to be turned over, to be flipped: *wel-.*

flirt
  to flirt: *pwangih, pwengipweng.*

float
  float, as for a fishing net: *uhs.*
  to float: *pei$_1$.*

flock
  flock of birds located over a school of
    fish: *ririnmen.*

flood
  a flood: *lapake.*
  a flash flood from the mountains:
    lewair, liwair$_1$.
  the Genesis flood: *nohlik.*
  flooded: *lapake.*
  to flood: *lapake.*
  to rise or flood, of a stream: *pwil$_2$.*

floor: *taht.*
  to floor: *tete.*
  to lay a floor: *tat$_1$.*

floor beam: *lohpwu.*

flour: *pilawa amas.*

flow
  to flow: *pwil$_2$.*
  to flow or trickle: *ker$_1$.*
  to spray, to cause to flow: *kakus.*
  to drift, to flow: *ahd-.*

flower
  flower, used generically: *kapwat.*
  flower, any flowering plant: *rohs.*
  flower of the breadfruit tree: *pehpe.*
  fruit, flower: *wah, wahntuhke$_1$.*
  flowering, of mango trees:
    moangepwet.
  to flower or bear fruit: *wa$_1$.*
  to flower, of mango trees: *pwet$_2$.*

flu
  cold, flu: *soumwahu en wai.*

flunk
  to flunk, to fail: *rakudai.*

flush
  equal, even, flush: *pahrek.*
  unequal, uneven, not flush: *sapahrek.*

flush
  to flush, of the face: *pwukesok.*

fly
  to fly: *pihr.*
  to start to fly, of a young bird:
    katengenei.

fly: *loahng.*
  a bluish colored fly: *loangen pwise.*

flying fish
  fish sp., flying fish: *menger.*

foam
  foam, scum: *pwudopwud.*

fog: *toahkoi.*

fold
  to fold: *lim.*
  to be folded: *limilimpene.*

foliage
  bushy, full of foliage: *weliwel$_1$.*

follow
to follow laws, regulations, etc:
*daur*₂.
to follow, to go after, to pursue, to obey: *idawehn*.

follower
companion, follower, complement:
ienge.

fontanel: *edin marer.*

food: *dipwahk, koanoat, lemwedek, mwenge, neminem, paun, sahk.*
any food prepared with grated coconut: *uter.*
any food rolled in a batter and fried: *dempwura.*
fermented pounded food: *lihli karer.*
food flavored with coconut milk: *piahia.*
food for the wives of all *koanoat* title holders: *pwenieu.*
food given to guests to take to their parents as a token of respect: *kadawahl.*
food made from the meat of a sprouting coconut: *dalok.*
food or kava served prior to a formal meal or kava ceremony: *ahmwadang.*
food provided for a hunting or fishing trip: *keting.*
food provided in return for labor: *keting.*
food unworthy to be fed to guests: *tihn kahmam.*
food, nourishment: *ketihnain, ketihnepe.*
ground food mixed with ripe bananas: *pihlohlo.*
leftover food: *luhweiso.*
pounded food, as breadfruit, taro, yams, and bananas: *lihli.*
premasticated food for infants: *mehme*₂.
to call in food, by a *Nahnmwarki* prior to a feast: *lohkinned.*
to go without food, or without feasting: *isol.*

fool
to fool: *kamwahl.*
to fool or deceive: *mwalaunih.*
to fool, to tease, to kid, to joke with: *ketewe.*

fool
Alas, you are a fool : *pakadanah.*
You fool : *pakehro.*

foot: *patehn neh.*
foot, measurement: *piht*₂.

footing
to stagger, to have difficulty keeping one's footing: *wasas.*

foppish
to be foppish: *mangnga.*

for
to, toward, in relation to, for: *-ehng, -ieng, ong.*

forbid
to forbid: *irehdi.*
to forbid or prohibit something taboo or illegal: *inapwih.*
to be forbidden: *irairdi.*

force
force, duress: *itoit.*
to force: *iding*₁, *iton.*
to force someone to do something, to impose one's will upon another: *sakone.*
to take by force: *angkehlail.*
to take by force, in a greedy manner: *pehdmour.*
to take by force, of any kind: *adih.*

forceful
to be forceful: *itoit.*

forearm: *uhnpeh.*

forehead: *isilap, tahmw.*

foreign
to be foreign, from abroad, now commonly used to mean American: *wai*₂.

foreleg
foreleg, as of a dog: *peh.*

foreskin
to have the foreskin of the penis withdrawn: *dap.*

forest
jungle, forest, area overgrown with trees: *nanwel, wahl*₁.

forest fire: *isihs.*

foretell
to foretell the future: *kosetipw.*
to foretell the future about: *kosetipwih.*

forever: *kohkohlahte.*

forget
to forget: *mankonehla, manokehla, meliehla.*
to forget or abandon: *likidmeliehla.*
to forgive and forget: *tohnmeteikihla.*
to be forgotten: *manokonokla.*
Forget it : *ieremen.*
Forget it , Better not : *eremen.*

forgetful
absent-minded, forgetful: *limanokonok.*

forgive
to forgive and forget: *tohnmeteikihla*.
to be forgiven, in a religious sense:
lapwada.
Excuse me , Forgive me : *mahkehngie*.

forgiveness
reconciliation, forgiveness: *tohmw*.
to ask for forgiveness: *sekenpwoud*.
to seek reconciliation or forgiveness:
tomw.

fork
fork, as of a tree, road, etc.: *kasang₁*.
fork, the eating utensil: *pwohk*.

form
form, for the pouring of concrete:
sekihda.

formal
reserved, containing one's feelings for
fear of self-embarrassment or
embarrassing others, constrained in
one's action by a social situation,
formal in one's relations with others:
mahk₁.

fornicate
to commit adultery, to fornicate:
nenek.

fortitude
guts, in the sense of fortitude or the
seat of the emotions: *nankapehd*.

fortunate: *iasenei, pai₂*.
to be lucky, to be fortunate, of one
normally unlucky or of no
consequence: *tel*.
to consider fortunate: *kepeia*.

fortunately
luckily, fortunately: *paiente*.

fortune
fortune, wealth, happiness, grace:
pai₂.

forty: *pahisek, pahngoul, pehk*.

forward
forward, uninhibited, outgoing:
limedramin.
outgoing, forward, of women: *limedek*.

foul
cursing, foul language: *peined*.
foul ball: *ahr₂*.
foul, in any sport: *ahr₂*.
to curse, to use foul language: *peined*.

foulmouthed: *lokaia suwed*.
displaying crude speech manners,
foulmouthed: *ausuwed*.

found
to be found: *dierek*.

foundation
foundation, purpose: *poahsoan*.

four: *epeng, pahdip, pahdun, pahiel,*
pahieu, pahka, pahkap, pahkis,
pahlep, pahmen, pahmwodol,
pahmwut, pahpa₂, pahpak, pahpali,
pahpar, pahpit, pahpoar, pahpwoat,
pahpwong, pahpwuloi, pahra,
pahsel, pahsop, pahsou, pahte,
pahtumw, pahumw, pahwel.

fourth: *kapahieu*.
depending on the municipality, the
fourth or the fifth cup of kava in the
kava ceremony: *sapwe*.

fowl
bird sp., jungle fowl, *Gallus*:
malekenwel.

fraction: *kisikis*.

fragile
brittle, fragile: *tipwatipw*.
weak, soft, easily broken, fragile:
kopwukopw₁.

fragment
a little bit of, a small piece of, a
fragment of: *epwidik*.

fragrant: *pwohtik*.

fraud
deception, lie, fraud: *widing*.

fraudulent
deceitful, fraudulent: *widingek*.

fray
to fray, as of ropes: *masal*.

freckle
freckle, mole, or any skin discoloration:
mwahi.

free
free from sin: *mohngiong mwakelekel*.
free, at ease in doing something:
maledek.
free, idle: *pisek*.
free, relieved, unrestrained, licentious:
saledek.
to be relieved, to be free from
encumbrances: *maiauda, maiouda*.

frequent: *dod*.

frequently: *kalapw, pwuwak*.

fresh: *mour₂*.

Friday: *Nialem*.

friend
company, friend: *kompani*.
dear friend, close buddy:
kompoakapah.

friendly
outgoing, friendly, knowing no
stranger, usually said of children and
pets: *liahn*.

friendship
to establish a close friendship: *pirien*.

frigate bird
bird sp., frigate bird: *kasap.*

frightened
afraid, frightened, cowardly, bashful: *masepwehk.*

frightening: *karerrer.*
any frightening thing or person, used with children: *kehkei.*

frog
toad, frog: *kairu.*

frog fish
fish sp., a kind of frog fish: *daliere, nehu.*

from
from, in opposition to: *-sang.*

frond
coconut palm frond: *pahini.*
dried palm frond: *dihl₁, pahdil.*

front
ahead of, in front of, before (him, her, or it): *mwowe₁.*

frown
frowning, unsmiling: *kounsup.*
to frown: *lolok.*

fruit
fruit, flower: *wah, wahntuhke₁.*
rotten fruit: *mwokuhr.*
unripe fallen fruit: *lempe.*

frustrated
distressed, frustrated: *weikek.*
frustrated, tense, worried: *tihwo.*

frustrating
mischievious, naughty, difficult, frustrating: *ketihwo.*

frustration: *weikek.*

fry
to fry: *pirain.*

fulfill
to fulfill: *kapwaiada.*

full
full moon: *maram mat.*
full of milk, of the breasts: *liet₁.*
to be full, after eating: *idier, itier, likier, med, tip.*
to be full, of a cup of kava: *pei₄.*
overcrowded, filled, full: *dir.*

fun
said of one who likes to tease or make fun of others: *kepit₂.*

fungus
fungus, fungus infection: *rihpw.*
covered by a fungus infection: *ripwiripw₁.*

funnel: *mehn koadi.*
funnel or hour glass shaped: *tir.*

funny
amusing, pleasant, funny: *kaperen.*
funny, amusing: *kemenkouruhr.*

fur
body hair, feathers, fur: *wine.*

furious
angry, furious: *mwehl₁.*

gag
to gag: *uwako, wako.*
to gag oneself with one's finger: *pwadik₁.*

gal
guy or gal: *lahp, sereu.*

gallon: *kalon.*

gamble
to gamble: *pilein mwohni.*

game
game, recreation, drama: *mwadong.*
a card game: *sakura.*
a game in which one attempts to pick up a bottle with a nail tied to a line which is attached to a stick: *empwoatol.*
a game, hide-and-seek: *pisirop.*
a game, hop-skip-jump: *sandangdopi.*
a game, involving teams in a game of catch: *rosotakai.*
a game, paper-scissors-stone: *saike, sangke.*
a game, similar to steal-the-flag: *alasapw, pansahi.*
a reed throwing game: *peisihr.*
a game involving bouncing a ball, usually played by girls: *isimome.*
the game of tag: *wiehni.*
the name of a card game: *diremw.*
the game, fly-take-a-bat: *rokupadda.*

gap-toothed
gap-toothed, having missing or broken teeth: *ngihtuk.*

garbage
garbage, waste, debris: *kihd.*

garden
clearing, field, plantation, garden, farm: *mwaht, mwetiwel.*
small garden: *dane.*

gardenia
gardenia, *Gardenia jasminoides*: *iohsep.*

gargle
to rinse one's mouth, to gargle: *dawado, mwukumwuk.*

garland: *ehl₁, kapwat, lengileng, mwaramwar.*
a garland worn by high title holders: *nihn.*

a type of garland worn by the nobility: *sedei*.

garland of *pwuhr*, *Fagraea sair*: *elinpwur*.

to wear a garland: *langilangih*.

to wear a garland, necklace, or lei: *mwaramwar*, *mware₂*.

gasoline: *kahs₂*, *kahsilihn*.

gate

gate, entry: *ewenkel*.

gather

to gather: *akerpene*.

to gather *iol* vines to be used as training ropes for yams: *eisel*.

to gather *kopil*, a sp. of clam found in the mangrove swamp: *tiekopil*.

to gather *lipwei*, a species of clam: *seilipwei*.

to gather *loangon*, a species of sea cucumber: *seiloangon*.

to gather *pahsu*, a species of clam: *seipahsu*.

to gather any non-swimming marine organism: *seimenihke*.

to gather material, in sewing: *ihkos*.

to gather palm fronds for thatch: *ur-*.

to gather reeds: *kar₂*.

to gather rope, to haul in a line: *sal*.

to gather up rope, to coil rope: *sim*.

to gather up, to catch with the hands: *rohk*.

to gather, as when a string is pulled in a piece of cloth: *eirekpene*.

to gather, of objects on the ground, or of people: *rik*.

gathering

congregation, parish, a gathering in the presence of a *Nahnmwarki*: *mwomwohdiso*.

gauze

bandage, gauze: *ohdai*.

gear: *kie₂*.

gecko: *lamwer*, *limwoahr*.

general

general, summarized: *oaralap*.

generation

generation, age group: *dih₃*.

generator: *misihn en lioal*.

generosity

kindness, generosity, mercy: *kalahngan*.

generous

generous, kind: *sapan*.

kind, generous: *kadek₁*.

kind, generous, merciful: *kalahngan*.

genitals: *kepwe*, *mesarawi*.

germ

worm, bacteria, germ: *mwahs*.

Germany: *Dois*, *Sehmen*.

get

to get around, as a problem: *kepidak*.

to get up: *kipada*, *pwourda*.

to get, to use: *kamangaida*.

to take or get: *ale*.

to be gotten around, as a problem: *kepidek*.

ghost: *eni*.

a ghost: *limaile*.

a ghost of the *Sounkawad* clan: *Inahs*.

a ghost of the sea, said to cause illness: *Nahnsahwinsed*.

a ghost, of the jungle: *Lipopohnwel*.

a ghost, said to take on various female forms, that dwells in the Kolonia area: *Limwohdeleng*.

a house ghost or spirit: *Nahnalosomw*.

a legendary male ghost, said to have dug the channel at *Sapwalap* with his penis: *Lapango*.

a net ghost or spirit: *Nahnullap*.

ancestral ghost: *eni aramas*.

ancestral ghost of a *Nahnmwarki*: *eni lapalap*.

ever-existing ghost: *enihwos*.

giant: *kodon*.

giddy

giddy, dizzy: *mwahngieng*.

gift

gift or contribution to a party: *mehn doadoahk*.

gift taken on a trip: *kepinwar*.

gift, present, prize: *kisakis*.

tribute, gift, reward: *isais*.

a party or gift given to a *sounwini* the fourth day of taking medicine: *koten wini*.

to give a gift, present, or prize: *kisakis*.

to give a party or gift to a medicine maker the fourth day of taking medicine: *ilisapw*.

gigantic

gigantic, spacious: *angahng*.

giggle

to giggle: *dingai*.

gill: *ede₁*.

ginger

any species of ginger plant: *sinter*.

ginger, *Eleocharis laxiflora*: *matamat₂*.

a variety of torch ginger, *Canna indica*: *iouioun wai*.

a variety of torch ginger, *Geocardia herbacea*: *kapehr*.

girl: *serepein*.

girt

girt, a beam connecting the corner posts of the exterior frame of a building at the roof level: *ndape*.

give

to give: *kih-*.

to give a gift, present, or prize: *kisikise*.

to give a title: *dahmwar, pwekmwar*.

to give a title, to crown: *langilangih*.

to give away, without motivation or compensation: *pangala*.

to give birth: *naitikihdi, neitik*.

to give out from exhaustion: *kehk*.

to give someone dry clothes: *kemmade*.

to give up: *lok*.

to repay, to give back in recompense or reply: *dupuk*.

to be given away, without motivation or compensation: *pengipengla*.

to be influenced, to give in, with a negative connotation: *duk*.

gizzard: *kataul*.

glance

to glance: *ikinteng*.

to glance at: *ikintangih*.

glare

to glare at: *keduwara*.

glass

glass, drinking glass, glasses, goggles, mirror: *kilahs*.

glasses

glass, drinking glass, glasses, goggles, mirror: *kilahs*.

sunglasses, dark glasses: *kilahs toantoal*.

glistening

shiny, glistening, polished: *melengileng*.

gloomy

gloomy, downcast: *pohtou*.

glove: *deipwukuro, depwukuro*.

baseball glove: *kuroap*.

glow

to glow as of embers: *ngken*.

glue: *kiluh, mehn kapas*.

gluttonous: *engidek*.

go

to accompany, join, or go with, to participate, to attend: *iang*.

to come and go early in the morning: *sangk*.

to come or go: *ape-, koh-*.

to come or go directly: *inen-*.

to come or go in a hurry, often in response to a leader's demands or an emergency: *piser-*.

to come or go in pairs: *mpwer-*.

to come or go, used in a derogatory way: *pwulahk*.

to encircle, to go around: *kapil*.

to fit, to go together well: *konpene*.

to go against: *uhweng*.

to go around: *pidakih, pidek*.

to go beyond, to exceed, to surpass, to overtake: *sipele*.

to go first, to precede: *tieng*.

to go on: *kadauluhl*.

to go through an entrance or opening: *pwed-*.

to go underwater: *du*.

to let go, to release: *kadar*.

to pass by, to go beyond: *daulih, douluhl*.

to penetrate, go through, or pass into: *dil*.

always bumming around, always on the go: *moahloahl*.

goat: *kout, kuht*.

goatfish

fish sp., goatfish, *Mulloidichthys vanicolensis*: *epil*.

fish sp., goatfish, *Parupeneus cyclostomus*: *mwompwon, mwomwalis*.

fish sp., goatfish, *Parupeneus indicus*: *iomo*.

fish sp., goatfish, *Upeneus arge*: *marep$_2$*.

god

a god of Ponapean religion: *Nahnsapwe*.

God: *Koht$_1$*.

goggles

glass, drinking glass, glasses, goggles, mirror: *kilahs*.

gonorrhea: *rimpio*.

to have gonorrhea: *rimpio*.

good: *kanakan, mwahu*.

good at something, clever: *kadek$_2$*.

good deeds, used biblically: *kepinwar*.

good news: *rongamwahu*.

good reputation: *rongamwahu*.

good-hearted: *loalamwahu*.

having a good reputation: *adamwahu*.

to like or love, to consider good, to desire sexually: *mwahuki*.

good-looking

good-looking, pretty, handsome: *masamwahu*.

goodbye
a formal greeting or leave taking
expression, as hello or goodbye:
kaselehlie.

goose: *kuhs.*

gore
to gore: *kodokod, kodom.*

gorilla: *korila.*

gospel
gospel, biblically: *rongamwahu.*

gossip: *lipahned, pilen pahnmweli.*
to gossip: *lipahned, pilen pahnmweli.*
to gossip about: *lipahnede.*

gourd
calabash, gourd: *pwilel.*

government
office, government: *ohpis.*

governor
governor, district administrator:
kepina.

grab
to grab, to seize: *kul, kulih.*
to grab at a woman's vagina:
pwedipwed.

grace
fortune, wealth, happiness, grace:
pai$_2$.

grade: *deng$_2$.*
group, team, grade level: *pwihn.*

graduate
to graduate: *kesepwil.*
to change the status of someone or
something, to graduate: *kasapwil.*

graduation: *kesepwil.*

grain
grain, of wood: *dip.*

grainy
lumpy, grainy: *warahr.*

grandfather
grandfather, spouse's grandfather,
father's mother's brother: *pahpa
kahlap, sahm kahlap.*

grandmother
grandmother, sometimes one's spouse's
grandmother: *ihn kahlap, nohno
kahlap.*

grass
grass, any of a number of grasses:
reh$_2$.
weed, grass: *dihpw.*
any thistle-like grass: *dipwtekatek.*

grass skirt: *koahl.*
to wear a grass skirt: *koal.*

grass sp.: *dipwinmal, liemeir, rehn
sehmen, sapasap$_2$.*

grass sp., *Andropogon glaber* or
Paspalum orbiculare: *rehnta.*
grass sp., *Axonopus compressus*:
rehmaikol.
grass sp., *Chrysopogon aciculatus* or
Eleusine indica: *rehtakai.*
grass sp., *Curcuma sp.*: *auleng$_1$.*
grass sp., *Cyperus javanicus*: *use.*
grass sp., *Cyrtococcum patens*:
sohmaleh.
grass sp., *Ischaemum chordatum*:
rehpadil.
grass sp., *Phyllanthus niruri*:
limeirpwong.
grass sp., *Thoracostachyum
pandanophyllum*: *pwoaki.*

grasshopper: *mensiek.*

grassy
weedy, grassy: *dipwidipw.*

grate
to grate: *iding$_1$.*
to grate on a coconut grater: *kohke,
koikoi$_2$.*
to grate, as taro: *idihd$_1$.*

grated
grated taro, yam, or banana mixed
with coconut milk and wrapped in
leaves: *idihd$_1$.*

grater
coconut grater: *pelik.*
any grater, other than a coconut
grater: *kisin ihr.*

grating
grating or unpleasant, of the voice:
ngilawas.

grave
grave, cemetery: *sousou.*

gravel
gravel, pebbles: *rakied.*
gravel, pebbles, crushed coral, any
rock-like material used as a ground
cover: *pwuker.*

gray
gray, grayish: *pehsehs.*
gray headed: *moangepwet.*

gray hair: *pwetepwet.*

grease
grease, fat: *kirihs, wih$_3$.*

greasy
fishy, greasy: *kideidei.*
oily, greasy: *moatoar$_1$.*

greatness
bigness, greatness: *laud.*

greed: *noahrok.*

greedy: *noahrok.*
  greedy, always wanting the biggest or
    the best: *pwinimas.*
  to covet, to be greedy for: *noahroke.*
green: *pohndihpw, pohntehndipw.*
  of breadfruit or bananas, still green but
    ready to eat: *ngkel.*
  of plants, to be a deep healthy green:
    molomol.
  undried or green, of wood: *mour₂.*
green thumb
  successful in growing things, having a
    green thumb: *pohnpe.*
greet
  to greet: *depwekinieng, rahnmwahu,
    rahnmwahwih.*
greeting: *depwekinieng, rahnmwahu.*
grenade
  hand grenade: *deriuhdang.*
grind
  to grind one's teeth: *ngihtehte.*
grinning
  grinning, without opening the mouth:
    pohkomwokomw.
gristle
  gristle, cartilage: *kopwukopw₂.*
gritty: *arekarek.*
groan
  to whisper, to hum, to groan: *ingitik.*
groin: *nandenge.*
groove
  ditch, trench, groove: *warawar.*
grope
  to feel around for, when unable to see
    an object, to grope around for, to
    probe for: *dehm.*
gross
  employing gross or inappropriate
    speech, speaking openly of sex,
    usually said of women: *ausaledek.*
ground
  dirt, soil, earth, ground: *pwehl₁.*
  ground level of a feasthouse: *nanras.*
grounder
  grounder, in baseball: *koro.*
group
  bunch, group, clump: *mwutumwut.*
  company, corporation, group: *kaisa.*
  group of islands: *kahndeke.*
  group of sizeable islands: *kahnsapw.*
  group, cluster of, bunch of: *uhn-.*
  group, team, grade level: *pwihn.*
  training group, kindergarten: *pwihnen
    kaiahn.*
  to go around in a group: *pelipelien.*

grouper
  fish sp., bass-grouper, *Cephalopholis
    argus*: *mwalusulus.*
  fish sp., grouper, *Plectropomus
    leopardus, Plectropomus
    melanoleucus,* or *Plectropomus
    truncatus*: *sawi₂.*
grow
  to grow up in a location or condition:
    tikida.
  to grow up, to progress: *keirida.*
  to sprout, to grow: *os.*
growl
  to growl or snarl at: *ngiringirih.*
  to growl or snarl, to quarrel: *ngiringir.*
growth
  a hard core-like abnormal growth
    sometimes found in breadfruit: *tihn
    mwomw.*
grumble
  to grumble: *dondorok, dorok.*
grunt
  to oink, to grunt, of a pig: *ngopw.*
guard
  guard, sentry: *kaiko.*
  security guard: *pampei.*
  to guard: *kaiko, pisilei, sile₁.*
  to be left behind to guard a house:
    sileimw.
guava
  guava, *Psidium guajava*: *kuahpa.*
guess
  to examine, to diagnose, to make a
    choice, to guess: *kasawih.*
guidance
  to provide guidance for children:
    kakairada.
guide
  to lead or guide: *kahluwa, kahre,
    kaweid.*
  to be lead or guided, to be escorted:
    pakahr.
guilty
  to be guilty: *dipada, dipaniki.*
guitar: *kida.*
gum
  chewing gum: *kisinpwil, pwilis.*
  gum, of a tree: *pwihl.*
gummy
  adherent, cohesive, gummy, sticky:
    ngidingid.
gums
  gums, of the teeth: *utun ngih.*
gun
  air gun: *kukusuh.*
  gun, as a rifle or speargun: *kesik.*

machine gun: *kikansu.*

gush
 to gush: *kus.*

gust
 gust of wind: *tumwenieng.*
 gust of wind containing rain: *einiar.*

guts
 belly, guts: *kapehd.*
 guts, in the sense of fortitude or the
  seat of the emotions: *nankapehd.*
 internal organs or guts of larger
  mammals: *kepwe.*
 internal organs or guts of smaller
  animals and fish: *pwise.*

gutter: *kereker.*

guy
 guy or gal: *lahp, sereu.*

hack
 to hack with a knife: *pal, pele.*

hair: *ihkosen iouiou, uliunleng.*
 abnormal hair, course and rapid
  growing: *ineng$_2$.*
 body hair, feathers, fur: *wine.*
 hair swirl, two of which are said to be
  the mark of a naughty child: *asiper.*
 hair, of the head: *pitenmoang,*
  pitentepwitepw.
 long hair of a woman: *pwilipeipei.*
 pubic hair: *wakar.*
 strand of hair: *pitenpeipei, pitenwel.*

haircut
 a haircut: *kotokot, seisei$_2$, tahta.*
 to cut, to give a haircut: *sehk$_1$.*
 to be given a haircut: *kotokot,*
  seisei$_2$, tahta.

hairy
 hairy, of the navel: *keidupwus.*

half
 half, of objects divided horizontally or
  by their width: *elep.*

half beak
 fish sp., half beak, *Hemiramphus*
  guoyi: *pwuwas.*

half-caste: *ainoko, apkahs.*

half-slip
 skirt, half-slip: *urohs.*

halibut
 fish sp., halibut: *liper$_1$.*

halt
 to halt, to stop: *ohlet.*

hammer: *ahmwe, ama.*
 to hammer: *pasur, poasur, pospos.*
 to be hammered: *pos$_1$.*

hammerhead shark
 fish sp., hammerhead shark: *pako*
  lohpwu.

hammock
 hammock for children: *mwek.*
 swing, hammock, seesaw: *likahs.*

hand
 arm, hand: *lime, limeiso, peh.*
 hands of a clock or watch: *rahn*
  kuloak.

handbag
 basket, purse, handbag: *kopwou,*
  kupwu.

handcuff
 handcuff, shackle: *ain$_2$.*
 to handcuff: *ainih$_2$.*
 to be handcuffed: *ainpene.*

handkerchief: *angkasi, angkesip,*
  limwinpwudo.

handle
 attached handle, as of a basket,
  suitcase, lamp, etc.: *ohntile.*
 handle of a tool: *mangil.*
 spear handle: *ihpw.*

handsome
 good-looking, pretty, handsome:
  masamwahu.

handwriting
 writing, handwriting, signature:
  menginpeh.

hang
 to commit suicide by hanging oneself:
  lusiam.
 to hang: *teneki.*
 to hang down: *mweteu.*
 to hang from the ear: *tie$_1$.*
 to hang up: *langa.*
 to hang, as the legs from a chair:
  kamwatau.
 to be hung up: *lang, tenek.*

happen
 happen to: *peien.*
 to happen to: *pisella, serala.*
 to occur, to happen: *wiawi.*

happiness: *nsenamwahu.*
 fortune, wealth, happiness, grace:
  pai$_2$.
 laughter, happiness: *uruhr.*

happy
 happy, contented, enjoying the good
  life: *nsenamwahu.*
 happy, joyful: *keremwel, keremweliso,*
  kupwur peren, peren$_1$.
 happy-looking, smiling: *likokouruhr.*

happy-go-lucky
 carefree, happy-go-lucky: *seukauti,*
  seukoahti.

harbor: *kepidau.*

hard
difficult, hard, troublesome, impossible: *apwal.*
hard to find: *salong.*
hard, not soft: *kekel, kekeluwak.*
industrious, hard working: *pwerisek.*

hard times
hard times, difficulty: *apwal.*

hardy
hardy, of crops and domesticated animals: *pwei.*

harelip: *aupwal.*
to have a harelip: *aupwal.*

harmonica: *keseng popouk.*

harpoon: *opohn.*
spear, harpoon: *ketieu$_1$.*

harsh
harsh acting: *lipwusinger.*

harvest
to harvest a new planting of kava: *wisik pwehl.*
to harvest, of bananas: *sapak.*
to be harvested, of bananas: *sapasap$_1$, sapidi.*

harvester: *soundolung.*

hasten
to hasten: *kapiser.*

hasty: *pwurur.*

hat: *lisoarop, ohpweisou, pweisou.*

hatch
to hatch: *kasawa.*

hate
to hate or dislike, of people: *kailongki.*

hatred: *kailok.*

haul
to gather rope, to haul in a line: *sal.*

have
to own, to have, used with nouns occurring with the classifier *ah*: *ahniki.*
to own, to have, used with nouns occurring with the classifier *nah*: *nainiki.*

hawksbill turtle: *sapwake.*

he
he, she, it: *e$_1$, ih$_2$.*

head: *kadokenmei, moahng$_1$, wahl$_2$.*
back of the head: *likinioar, likinleng, likinsekiri.*
back of the head or neck: *likinpaiki.*
head of a yam: *mesenpek.*
head, temple: *kodokenmei, peipei$_3$, tapwi.*
large coral head: *mad$_1$.*
large submerged coral head: *madepei.*

lower part of the back of the head: *kepinpaiki.*

headache: *moangmedek.*

headband
headband, worn to keep perspiration out of one's eyes: *asmaki.*

heal
to heal: *mo.*

healthy
fat, healthy looking, of infants or young domestic animals: *sinopwunopw.*
healthy looking, said of plants: *dikeriker.*
healthy, of human beings: *roson.*
strong, powerful, healthy: *kehlail.*
to recover, to grow healthy after an illness: *tihnain.*

hear
to hear: *elielpaidoke.*
to hear, to listen: *kapaidok, karonge, koaronge, rong.*
to witness, to observe or hear something with certainty, to testify: *kadehde.*

hearing
a hearing: *karongorong.*
to hold a hearing: *karongorong.*

heart: *mohngiong, ririnpaiso.*
heart, in cards: *aht$_2$.*
wish, intention, plan, decision, desire, heart: *kupwur$_2$.*

heartburn: *sohiahia.*

heartless
heartless, without sympathy: *weid$_3$.*

heartsick
heartsick, of a man who has lost his wife: *loaloh.*

heat: *kehl$_3$.*
final heat of a race: *kamehlel.*
of animals, to come out of heat: *lik$_2$.*
to be in heat, to be ready for breeding, of female dogs and pigs: *mwetida.*

heaven
sky, heaven: *lahng$_1$.*

heavy: *toutou$_1$.*

hectare: *ektahr.*

heed
to heed, to pay attention to, to agree with: *ahne.*

heel: *keimwinneh.*

hell: *ehl$_3$, nankisiniei.*

hello
a formal greeting or leave taking

helmet
  expression, as hello or goodbye: *kaselehlie*.

helmet: *erimeddo*.

help
  help, assistance, aid: *sawas*.
  to help, assist, aid: *sawas, sewese*.

hem
  to hem, as shirts, pants, dresses, etc.: *pwungih$_2$*.

hen: *litok*.

her
  his, her, its: *ah$_2$, nah*. *(See other possessive classifiers.)*

here: *me$_1$, met*.
  here and there, without definite direction: *-seli*.
  here, by me (plural): *iehkan, ietakan*.
  here, by me (singular): *ie$_2$, iet*.
  here, toward the speaker: *-do*.

hermit crab: *mpwa*.

hernia: *soumwahu en mwasahl*.

hesitant
  hesitant, indecisive: *peikasal*.
  cautious, hesitant, fearful: *per*.

hesitation
  hesitation, indecision: *peikasal*.

Hi
  an informal greeting or leave taking expression, as Hi__ or Bye : *kaselel*.

hibiscus pole
  hibiscus pole, after the bark has been stripped: *arepe, pwurien arepe*.

hibiscus sp.: *keleunleng, likidal, pehtakai, peren tikitik*.
  hibiscus sp., *Hibiscus rosa-sinensis*: *keleun wai*.
  hibiscus sp., *Hibiscus tiliaceus*, the inner bark of which is used as a bast in the preparation of kava: *keleu, kolou*.
  hibiscus sp., *Kleinhovia hospita*, used for making outriggers: *keleun and*.

hiccough
  to hiccough: *marer*.

hidden
  hidden, concealed: *rir*.
  to be hidden or concealed: *ekiek*.

hide
  to hide: *ruk$_2$*.
  to hide behind, to conceal: *ririh*.
  to hide one's feelings: *loalloale*.
  to hide or conceal: *ekihla*.
  to be hidden or concealed: *ekiek*.

hide
  skin, bark, hide, any outer covering: *kihl$_1$*.

hide-and-seek
  a game, hide-and-seek: *pisirop*.

high
  high ranking: *lapalap*.

high jump: *dakadopi*.
  to high jump: *daka, dakadopi*.

high language
  high language, respect forms of speech: *meing*.

hill
  rise, low hill: *mpwoampw*.
  small hill: *kumwukumw$_2$, uluhl*.
  small mountain, hill: *dohl*.

hinge: *insis*.

hint
  to hint: *karongorongki*.
  to hint about something: *serere*.
  to notify, to inform, to hint at, to let someone know: *kehsehki*.

hip: *lengelenge, pwone*.

hip toss
  to throw with a hip toss: *kadaur$_2$*.

hire
  to hire: *koadoadoahki*.
  to buy, to pay, to hire: *pwain*.

his
  his, her, its: *ah$_2$, nah*. *(See other possessive classifiers.)*

hiss
  to hiss at: *isih*.

historian
  historian, one known for his knowledge of Ponapean history: *soupoad*.

history
  history, sacred story: *poadoapoad*.

hit
  to be hit with an object: *pok*.
  to hit two marbles with one shot: *nireng*.

hoarse
  husky, hoarse, of the voice: *ngilekir*.

hoe: *kuwa*.
  hoe or any implement for digging: *ahk$_1$*.
  to hoe: *pokune*.

hold
  to hold: *kol*.
  to hold one's hands behind one's back: *pelikipe*.
  to hold the cup during the preparation of kava: *kolukol*.
  to hold, in a card game: *ohlet*.
  to take hold, to stick: *man*.
  to use a lotion or cream to hold one's hair in place: *wisoar*.

hold
of a ship, the hold or the area below decks: *dampwulo.*

hole: *pwoahr.*
hole among the rocks used as a place to defecate in: *soakoa.*
hole, for planting yams: *pwahr, pweriniak.*
large hole in the ground: *lihpw$_2$.*
mangrove crab hole: *sahr.*
to drill a hole: *pwuropwur.*
to drill a hole in: *pwure.*
to have a hole: *pwoar.*
to have a hole that results in a leak, as in a canoe, roof, or tire tube: *pate.*

holler
to shout, to scream, to howl, to yell, to holler: *wer.*
to shout, to scream, to howl, to yell, to holler at: *wering.*

hollow
hollow, ravine: *mweid$_2$.*

holy
holy, sacred: *sarawi.*

Holy Ghost: *Ngensarawi.*

home: *poahsoan.*
building, house, home, dwelling: *ihmw.*

home plate
home plate, in baseball: *ohmw.*

home run: *ohmwrang.*

homesick
of children, to become suddenly homesick: *temenek.*
to miss a person or a place, to be homesick: *loaleid, loaloid.*

homestead
land, farmstead, homestead: *sahpw.*
to homestead: *sapwasapw.*

honest
innocent, honest: *mwakelekel.*
true, honest: *mehlel.*

honestly
truly, honestly: *mehlel.*

honey
buddy, honey, pal, used in addressing one's spouse, or peers or children of the same sex: *nahn$_1$.*

honeybee: *loangen suke.*

honk
to beep or honk a horn: *pihp, pihpih.*

honor
biblically, to show respect, to honor: *kahka.*
respect, honor: *wahu.*

honorable
respectful, respectable, honorable: *waun.*

hoof: *patehn neh.*

hook: *kehs$_1$.*
to hook: *kehse.*

hoop
embroidery hoop: *waku.*

hop
to hop on one foot: *liwaisisik.*

hop-skip-jump
a game, hop-skip-jump: *sandangdopi.*

hope
faith, trust, hope: *koapwoaroapwoar.*
to have faith, trust, or hope: *koapwoaroapwoar.*

horizon: *pwetenleng.*
horizon at sea: *irepen sehd.*

horn
animal's horn: *kode.*
horn of an automobile: *pihp.*

horrible
horrible in appearance: *likamisik.*

horrify
to horrify: *likamisikih.*

horse: *oahs$_2$.*

hose: *ohs.*

hospital: *imwen wini, pioing.*

hot
peppery, spicy, hot: *kerengireng.*
red hot, of objects: *mwehl$_1$.*
very hot, of objects: *kehl$_3$.*
warm, hot: *karakar, kiriniol.*

hot pad
hot pad for pots: *inap.*

hotel: *ohtehl.*

hotheaded
troublesome, hotheaded, defective: *lioakoahk.*

hour: *awa.*
time, clock, watch, hour: *kuloak.*

house
building, house, home, dwelling: *ihmw.*
canoe house: *katauk.*
cook house: *wonuhmw.*
nahs or house of a chief: *tehnpas.*
temple, house of worship: *imwen kaudok.*
thatch house: *imwioas.*

how
how many: *depe.*
how much: *depe.*
how, in what manner, possibly from *dahkot duwe: dahduwe.*
How about that : *keti.*

however
however, and: *ah₃*.

howl
to laugh heartily, to howl with laughter: *weia*.
to shout, to scream, to howl, to yell, to holler: *wer*.
to shout, to scream, to howl, to yell, to holler at: *wering*.

hug
to embrace, to hug: *pwoalehdi*.
to embrace, to hug each other: *pwoaloapwoal*.

hull
to have something stuck between the hull and the outrigger of a canoe: *koapwuroaloat*.

hum
to whisper, to hum, to groan: *ingitik*.

human
people, person, human being, mankind: *aramas*.
biblically, human or sex: *uduk*.

humble
humble, unassuming, meek: *aktikitik, opampap*.
low, respectful, humble: *karakarahk*.
to be shamed, to be humbled: *lesikihla*.

humiliated
to be humiliated: *likamwada*.
to be embarrassed or humiliated: *sarohdi*.

humpback: *mpwokos*.
humpback, as a consequence of a broken back: *tihnsautipw*.

humped: *kos₂*.

humphead parrotfish
fish sp., humphead parrotfish, *Bolbometopon muricatus*: *kemeik*.

hundred
one hundred: *epwiki*.

hundred million: *sapw₂*.

hundred thousand: *lopw₁*.

hung
to be hung up: *lang, tenek*.

hung over: *ohn*.
hung over from kava or alcohol: *ohn sakau*.

hungry
always hungry: *owen mwenge*.
to be hungry: *menmwenge, pwongitik*.
to be hungry for meat: *menkumwo*.

hunting knife
sheath knife, hunting knife, diving knife, dagger: *sihdnaip, teike*.

hurdles
to run the hurdles: *kepir meliek*.

hurried
hurried, rushed: *karuwaru*.

hurry
always in a hurry: *saruwaru*.
to go fast, to be quick, to hurry: *mwadang*.
to hurry, to rush: *keruwa*.
Hurry up , Come on : *kanahng*.

hurt
irreconcilably or deeply hurt, of one's feelings: *likidek*.
to hurt: *medek*.

husband
spouse, husband or wife: *pwoud, werek*.

husk
husk of a mature coconut: *dipenihd*.
to husk with a stick: *kodokod, kodom*.

husky
husky, hoarse, of the voice: *ngilekir*.

hybrid
hybrid plant: *kiewek*.

hymn
Christian hymn: *koul sarawi*.

hyperactive
hyperactive, of children: *dumwadumw*.

hypocritical: *liksansalamwahu, lisalseliwi, liseliseliwi*.

I: *i, ngehi*.

ice: *ais₂*.

ice cream: *aiskurihm*.

icebox
icebox, refrigerator: *aispwoaks*.

idea
thought, idea, opinion: *lamalam*.

identical
to be the same as, to be identical to: *duwehte*.

identify
to point out, to identify: *idihada*.

idiotic
extremely stupid, silly, idiotic, simple, dumb: *pweirengid*.
stupid, silly, idiotic, simple, dumb: *kupwuropwon, loalopwon, pweipwei₁*.

idle
free, idle: *pisek*.
to be idle: *mwomwohdmwahl*.

if: *ma*.

ignorant: *soaloalekeng*.

ignore
said of one who ignores others: *sirangkau*.

to ignore: *pohnsehse, sirangkawe.*

ill
mentally ill or retarded: *sahliel.*
sick, diseased, ill: *soumwahu.*
to become very ill, incapacitated, bed-
ridden: *kehimwidi.*

ill intentioned: *moahng2.*

illegal
to be illegal, to do something illegal:
uweng kosonned.

illness
sickness, disease, illness: *luhmwuhmw,
soumwahu.*

image
one's image: *dikadik.*

imitate
to copy, to imitate: *alasang.*
to copy, to imitate, to mimic, to learn
from: *alemengih.*
to imitate: *kasosohng, mwomwehda.*
said of one who copies or imitates
fashions or behavior: *alemengi.*

immature
immature, of fruit: *pwul.*

impact
having an impact, effective, efficient:
lipwan.

impede
to delay, to impede: *koarompwa.*

impenitent: *sokoluhla.*

impertinent
impertinent, rude: *mwomwawas.*

implement
an implement: *tehtehn peh.*
any implement used for pulling weeds:
wes.
hoe or any implement for digging:
ahk1.
implement for drawing water: *idipen
pihl.*
wooden implement for splitting
breadfruit: *pwai1.*

impolite: *mwomwalap.*

importance
importance, value: *kesempwal.*

important: *kansenoh1.*
important or physically large: *lap.*
important, valuable: *kesempwal.*
to consider most important: *mwohniki.*

impose
to force someone to do something, to
impose one's will upon another:
sakone.

impossible
difficult, hard, troublesome, impossible:
apwal.

imprison
to imprison: *kakosih, salihdi.*
to be imprisoned: *selidi.*

improve
to improve: *kamwahwih.*

improvement: *kamwahu1.*

impudent
impudent, conceited: *namaiki.*
sassy, impudent, saucy: *pwisirek.*

in: *nan.*

inaccurate
crooked, off target, inaccurate: *pirek.*

inappropriate
inappropriate, awkward because of
unfamiliarity, difficult to learn:
koasoakoahiek.
inappropriate, bizarre, incongruous,
not fitting: *sapa1.*
employing gross or inappropriate
speech, speaking openly of sex,
usually said of women: *ausaledek.*

incapacitated
to become very ill, incapacitated, bed-
ridden: *kehimwidi.*

incense: *insens.*
incense holder: *rokpahs.*

incessantly
incessantly, always: *poaden.*

incest: *kilahpwada, kilahsoupwa,
kilikilengsuwed, likangkangenihmat,
ngengngersuwed.*

incestuous: *kilikilengsuwed,
likangkangenihmat,
ngengngersuwed.*

inch: *ins.*

incision: *lek.*
to have an incision made: *lek.*
to make an incision: *leke.*

incite
to incite: *pain.*

incline: *pangapang.*

include
to add or include: *iangahki.*

incompetent
unreliable, inept, incompetent:
salelepek.

incomplete
to be incomplete, as a consequence of
some part being removed: *luh.*

incongruous
inappropriate, bizarre, incongruous,
not fitting: *sapa1.*

inconsistent
variable, inconsistent, changeable:
wikwikin.

incorrect
incorrect, wrong, erroneous: *sapwung*.
incorrigible: *kidienwet.*
indecision
hesitation, indecision: *peikasal.*
indecisive
hesitant, indecisive: *peikasal.*
indecisive when confronted with a
number of appealing choices:
loalmasarang.
to be indecisive: *pwungiari.*
indeed: *iei.*
really, indeed: *pwa₁.*
independence: *uhtohr.*
independent: *uhtohr.*
to be independent, to be different, to
be excluded from the group:
tohrohr.
indifferent
aloof, indifferent: *popohn.*
indispensable
necessary, indispensable: *anahn.*
industrious
industrious, hard working: *pwerisek.*
inept
unreliable, inept, incompetent:
salelepek.
inexpensive
inexpensive, cheap: *pweitikitik.*
infant: *seri pwelel.*
infected
to be infected: *kens.*
to be infected by salt water: *kepised.*
infection: *paiking.*
a painful infection: *ingin.*
a pus filled infection: *kepinan.*
a skin infection resembling a burn:
kilin kutuwa.
boil, swelling, infection: *mpwos.*
fungus, fungus infection: *rihpw.*
to have an infection under the nail:
tekipwel.
infinite
unlimited, infinite: *soire.*
influence
to influence or prejudice another's
opinion: *kapihdi.*
to be influenced, to give in, with a
negative connotation: *duk.*
inform
to inform: *kairehki, sekerehki.*
to notify, to inform, to hint at, to let
someone know: *kehsehki.*
information
current news, recent information:
rongkapw.

to be given information: *pahudaud.*
to exchange information: *kasahnwar.*
inhabit
of a spirit, to possess or inhabit a
human body: *ti.*
inhabitant
inhabitant of: *tohn₂.*
to become a member, inhabitant, or
participant of: *towehda.*
inhale
to inhale, to breathe in deeply, to
absorb: *ihk.*
inheritance: *sohso.*
injection
an injection: *dok.*
to stab, to spear, to skewer, to give an
injection: *doakoa.*
to be stabbed, to be speared, to be
skewered, to be given an injection:
dok.
ink: *ingk.*
inland: *peilong-.*
inlet: *nankep.*
cove, inlet: *kosolong.*
inn: *imwen keiru.*
inner
inner side, inner surface: *masloale.*
innertube: *suhpwu.*
innocent
innocent, honest: *mwakelekel.*
inquire
to ask about, to inquire, to question:
kadeik.
to check, to inquire, to ask: *kalelapak.*
insane
mentally disturbed, crazy, insane: *iahk.*
inscribe
to inscribe: *ele₁.*
insect
animal, insect: *mahn.*
small green insect with a powerful
odor: *lioaroahrpwohtik.*
a tiny flying insect, commonly found in
the forest: *ahmw₁, liahmw,
omwinwel, serihso₂.*
insensitive
bold, brazen, insensitive: *soumahk.*
insert
to insert or retract: *kapwad.*
inside
inside (him, her, or it): *loale.*
inside of something, contents: *kanenge.*
insignia
insignia, sign: *mahk₂.*
insincere
insincere in the refusal of food,

prompted by the dictates of
hospitality: *kamadamad.*

insistent: *ketiket₂, ngidingid.*

insomnia
to be unable to sleep, to have
insomnia: *epwel₁.*

inspect
to inspect, examine, or check: *dawih,
dou₃.*
to inspect one's own appearance: *iroir,
irong.*

inspector: *sounkeseu.*

instruct
to teach, to instruct: *padahkih.*
to give instructions before leaving or
dying: *kehkehlik.*

instrument
anything capable of producing music, a
musical instrument, radio, tape
recorder, etc.: *keseng.*

insult: *kapailok.*
insulting: *kapailok.*
to insult: *kapailoke.*
to criticize or insult another, usually of
women: *kapwai.*

intact
whole, entire, intact: *pwon.*

intelligent
intelligent, smart: *loalekeng, loalokong.*
smart, intelligent: *simaht.*

intend
to intend: *mwomwehda.*
to concern, to be intended for: *doke.*

intention
wish, intention, plan, decision, desire,
heart: *kupwur₂.*

intercept
to intercept, to interrupt: *sopuk.*

intercourse
always willing to engage in sexual
intercourse, of a woman: *linenek.*
frequently engaging in sexual
intercourse: *lipwesepwes.*
sexual intercourse: *pwehs.*
to copulate with, to have sexual
intercourse with: *kowarak.*
to copulate, to have sexual intercourse:
kowerek.
to desire to have sexual intercourse:
inengida.
to have sexual intercourse: *ape₂, pwes,
wiawi, wiedip.*
to have sexual intercourse during
daylight hours: *uhrahn.*
to have sexual intercourse for the first
time, of a female: *pedala.*

to have sexual intercourse for the first
time, of a male: *edila.*
to have sexual intercourse with: *alehdi,
apehne.*

interested
to be concerned about, to be
interested in, to worry about:
nsenohki.

interfere
to interfere with: *lidere.*

interference
to call interference in the marble
game *anaire: dameni.*

intermediary
an intermediary for a boy and a girl:
sounkapahndil.

interpreter: *sounkawehwe.*

interrupt
to intercept, to interrupt: *sopuk.*
to interrupt some serious activity:
tiakidi.
to be interrupted, of a song: *tipw₁.*

intervene
to intervene: *lidere.*

intestine: *mwasahl.*
intestinal worm: *mwasenger.*
protrusion of the large intestine from
the anus: *pwuri.*

into
inwards, into: *-long.*

intoxicated
to be intoxicated: *keinihn.*
to be intoxicated by kava to the point
of losing one's self-control:
pwupwuda.
to be intoxicated to the point of being
immobile: *pilat₂.*
to be intoxicated, to be drunk: *sakau.*

intoxication
causing a feeling of intoxication, of
kava, alcohol, or sex: *kalitopw.*

introduce
to introduce or make something
known: *kasale-.*

inventory
to inventory: *kainen, kainene.*

invitation: *luhk₁.*

invite
to invite: *luke.*
to be invited: *luk.*

inwards
inwards, into: *-long.*

iron
an iron: *ain₁.*
large sheet of iron used as a concrete
trough: *deppang.*

to iron: *aine.*
to iron clothing: *ain₁.*
to press or iron: *kadangada.*
to be pressed, to be ironed: *kedengida.*

ironwood: *masinoki.*

irony
to employ irony: *serere.*

irrationally
to act irrationally: *rotala.*

irresponsible: *soepwel.*

irritating
irritating, bothersome, annoying:
kelingeringer.
itchy or irritating: *kapwudong.*
obnoxious, disgusting, irritating:
limwesou.

island: *deke.*
an island in a river or stream: *sineipw.*
any island off the coast of a main
island: *sampei.*

islander
any islander, Micronesian or
Polynesian, of non-Ponapean origin:
mehn namwanamw.
low islander: *mehn namwanamw.*

it
he, she, it: *e₁, ih₂.*

itchy
itchy or irritating: *kapwudong.*
to be itchy: *pwudong.*
to be itchy from something: *pitikihda.*

its
his, her, its: *ah₂, nah. (See other
possessive classifiers.)*

ivory nut palm
ivory nut palm, *Coelococcus
amicarum:* *oahs₁.*

jack
fish sp., jack, *Atule mate:* *lahd.*
fish sp., jack, *Caranx sexfasciatus:*
oarong en pwong.

jack
jack, as an automobile jack: *saki.*
to jack: *saki.*

jack
jack, in cards: *sehk₂.*

jacket: *sekid.*

jacks: *pispohra.*
to play jacks: *dapadap.*

jail
jail, prison: *imweteng, kalapwuhs.*

jam
jam, jelly: *sahm₂.*

January: *Senweri.*

Japan: *Sapahn.*

jasmine
plant sp., Arabian jasmine, *Jasminum
sambac:* *sampakihda.*

jaw: *pahrehre.*
jaw, of an animal: *aupah.*

jealous
jealous, envious: *luwak.*
jealous, usually with reference to one's
spouse: *luwakahk.*
extremely envious or jealous: *peirin.*

jelly
jam, jelly: *sahm₂.*

jellyfish: *liht.*

jerk
to flinch, to jerk away: *nur.*
to yank or jerk: *sereki.*
to be yanked or jerked: *peserek.*

Jesus: *Iesus, Sises.*

Jew: *mehn suhs.*

jiggle
to jiggle up and down, as of the fat on
a fat person: *mwenemwenei.*

jitterbug
to jitterbug: *suripak.*

join
to accompany, join, or go with, to
participate, to attend: *iang.*
to join: *koakone, koakonokon.*
to join the other side: *iangala.*

joint
joint, fitting: *koakon.*
knot, joint, as in a stalk of bamboo:
pwukel.

joist
joist, the timber to which floorboards
are attached: *ataut.*

joke: *kamwan, kepit₂.*
to fool, to tease, to kid, to joke with:
ketewe.
to joke or tease: *kamwan, kelipa.*
to joke with, to tease: *kapitih,
kemwene.*

joker
joker, in cards: *likaut.*

joy: *popohl.*

joyful
happy, joyful: *keremwel, keremweliso,
kupwur peren, peren₁.*

joyous
joyous, lusty: *pwut.*

judge
judge, except in court: *sounkamehlel.*
judge, in court: *sounkopwung.*
to judge: *kadeik.*

judgement: *sounkadeik.*

judgment
 a judgment: *kadeik.*

judo
 to use judo on: *suhdo.*

juggle
 to juggle: *dapadap.*

July: *Sulai.*

jump
 to jump: *lus, lusuk.*

jump rope
 to jump rope: *epini.*

June: *Suhn.*

jungle
 jungle, forest, area overgrown with
  trees: *nanwel, wahl₁.*

just
 correct, right, just: *pwung₁.*
 just, in a temporal sense: *ahpwtehn.*
 just, only: *-te.*

justice
 justice, right: *pwuhng.*

kangaroo: *kangkuru.*

Kapingamarangi
 Kapingamarangi, also known as
  Greenwich: *Kerenis.*

kapok
 kapok tree: *koatun.*

kava: *sakau, kalaidong.*
 a kava plant, decorated with
  ornamental plants: *tiepoans.*
 a kava plant, large enough that it
  requires being carried on a
  lohpwu: *sakau lohpwu.*
 a kava plant, large enough to be
  carried on a *pahs*: *sakau pahs.*
 a kava plant, requiring one person to
  carry it: *sakau kepeik.*
 a kava plant, requiring two persons to
  carry it: *sakau ro.*
 a kava planting: *kemenseng₂.*
 area where kava is planted:
  kemenseng₂.
 at the end of the kava ceremony, to
  completely extract all the juices
  from a batch of kava: *wengkid.*
 dried kava after the extraction of the
  juice: *wensakau.*
 first harvest of a new planting of kava:
  wisik pwehl.
 food or kava served prior to a formal
  meal or kava ceremony:
  ahmwadang.
 initial effects of kava or alcohol: *litepw.*
 kava that flows from the upper side of
  the fist of the one preparing it:
  dingiding en kepeirek.

 of kava, to be processed for drinking
  for the final time: *wengpoar.*
 small kava plant, one remaining after
  the larger plants have been
  removed: *mohr.*
 the first four cups of kava in the kava
  ceremony: *nohpwei.*
 the quantity of kava placed in the
  hibiscus bast: *ihn₂.*
 to feel the initial effects of kava or
  alcohol: *litepw.*
 to harvest a new planting of kava:
  wisik pwehl.
 to place kava in the hibiscus bast:
  ihnda.
 to squeeze kava that has been set aside
  in anticipation of the arrival of titled
  guests: *wenglopwon.*
 to squeeze kava until it is completely
  dried: *wengmad.*

keel: *kihl₂.*

keep
 to save, keep, store, put away:
  nekidala.

kerosene: *karisihn.*

ketchup
 tomato, ketchup: *domahdo.*

kettle: *ketel.*

key: *kih₃.*

khaki
 khaki, tan: *kahki, pohkahki.*

kick
 to kick: *kik₂, kikim, tep₂, tepek.*
 to kick or shove with the bottom of
  the foot: *diapahd.*

kid
 to fool, to tease, to kid, to joke with:
  ketewe.

kidney: *mwidihlihk.*

kill
 to kill, to execute: *kemehla.*
 to kill or finish off, of something
  wounded: *kadauluhl.*
 to kill a tree, by any method: *kamang.*
 to kill a tree by banding, to band a
  tree: *rehre.*
 to be killed: *kamakamala, kamala.*

kimchee: *kimsi.*

kind
 kind, generous: *kadek₁.*
 kind, generous, merciful: *kalahngan.*
 kind, loving: *limpoak.*
 kind, merciful: *kopwungloal.*
 generous, kind: *sapan.*

kind
  kind, sort, type: *kain, mwohmw, soahng.*

kindergarten
  training group, kindergarten: *pwihnen kaiahn.*

kindness
  kindness, generosity, mercy: *kalahngan.*

king
  king, in cards: *kihng$_2$.*

king post: *lepin keidu.*

kingdom
  a political unit, as a municipality, district, state, country, or kingdom: *wehi$_2$.*

kinky
  closely twisted or curled, kinky, tangled: *pinipin.*
  ray-like, fanning, kinky: *sirang.*

kiss
  to kiss: *kis$_2$, metik, mitik.*
  to kiss, to rub noses: *mehn$_2$, mpoake.*
  to French kiss, literally, 'to eat the tongue': *nemilo.*

kite: *dako.*

knead
  to knead, as of dough: *kapal.*
  to be kneaded, as of dough: *kepel.*

knee: *pohndele, pwukie.*

kneecap: *pohn delen pwukie.*

kneel
  to kneel: *kelepwiki.*

knife
  knife, machete: *kehpit, naip.*
  pocketknife: *naipokos.*
  sheath knife, hunting knife, diving knife, dagger: *sihdnaip, teike.*

knock
  to knock or rap: *letelet, leteng.*

knot: *pwukopwuk.*
  any non-slip knot: *pwuken eni.*
  knot, joint, as in a stalk of bamboo: *pwukel.*
  slip knot: *likoserek.*
  to knot: *pwuke, pwukopwuk.*

knotty: *pwukelekel.*

know
  to know: *mwahngih.*
  to know almost everything: *audaud.*
  to know thoroughly, to master: *ereki.*
  to know, to understand: *ese.*
  to memorize, to know by heart: *wadilik.*
  to not know: *sehse.*

knowledgeable: *audapan.*
  knowledgeable about many things: *eretik.*
  thoroughly knowledgeable: *er.*
  wise, knowledgeable: *eripit, kupwurekeng.*

knuckle: *koakon.*

Kool-Aid
  Kool-Aid, any similar drink: *kuhleid.*

Korea: *Sohseng.*

Kusaie: *Katau, Katau Peidak.*

labia
  labia, of the vagina: *pwehd.*

labor
  community improvement tax or labor: *kamwahu$_1$.*

lace
  lace, attached to the bottom of a slip for decoration: *swain.*
  ribbon, lace: *repen$_2$.*

ladder
  ladder, steps, stairs: *kehndake.*

lady: *lih$_2$.*

lagoon
  deep place within the barrier reef, lagoon: *nahmw, nehnamw.*

lake
  pool, lake: *leh$_2$.*

lame
  lame, crippled: *dangepel.*

lamp: *lamp.*
  bottle lamp, made with a wick in a bottle of kerosene: *lampwoatol, serpwoatol.*
  carbide, carbide lamp: *kahpaido.*

lance
  to be slashed, lanced, or cut: *lek.*

land
  division of land: *pwalasapw.*
  land under cultivation: *nansapw.*
  land, farmstead, homestead: *sahpw.*
  shore, land near the ocean, landing place for canoes or boats: *óaroahr$_2$.*
  to land, of anything capable of flight: *sok$_1$.*

landslide: *engk.*

language
  cursing, foul language: *peined.*
  high language, respect forms of speech: *meing.*
  language, speech: *lokaia, mahsen.*
  to curse, to use foul language: *peined.*

lantana
  lantana, *Lantana camara*: *landana, randana.*

lantern: *lanten.*

lap
the final lap in a race: *kesso.*
to run or swim the final lap in a race: *kesso.*

lap
to lap up: *urak₂.*

large: *kalaimwun.*
bulky, stocky, thick, large in girth: *ahlap.*
extensive, large: *kowahlap.*
important or physically large: *lap.*
large in stature: *lap.*
large or spacious, of inanimate objects: *koahiek.*
large, in quantity: *moron.*
large, of any opening: *walek.*
of clothing, too large at the waist: *pwoalosolos.*

lash
to lash: *inaur, inou₂.*
to lash with hibiscus bark for carrying: *paud₁.*

last
end of kava ceremony, end, last one: *kodie.*
to be last in a sequence: *ikmwir.*

lasting
lasting for a long time: *werei.*

late
late, slow: *pwand.*

later: *mwuhr.*

laugh
to laugh: *kouruhr, rarenei.*
to laugh heartily: *ngarahk.*
to laugh heartily, to howl with laughter: *weia.*
to laugh in a boisterous manner: *keseirahk.*
to laugh, to smile: *kiparamat.*

laughter
laughter, happiness: *uruhr.*

launch
a motor launch: *ransi.*

launder
to wash clothing, to launder: *lopwor.*

laundry
to wash clothing, to do laundry, literally the action of pounding clothing: *lopwolopw.*

lava-lava: *likoutei.*
lava-lava, made of the bark of the breadfruit tree: *likoumeimei.*

law: *kosonned.*

lawyer
attorney, lawyer, defender: *pengohsi, sounsawas.*

lay
to lay someone or something down: *kaunehdi, kawenehdi.*

lazy: *pohnkahke.*
lazy to an extreme degree, wishing only to eat, sleep, and defecate: *dangapaur.*
lazy, to a great degree: *dangahnga.*
sluggish, lazy: *dangaudek.*
tired, lazy: *pwang.*

lead
to boss, to rule, to lead, to direct: *kaun.*
to lead: *uhk₂.*
to lead one's aim when shooting birds: *kasamwoh, koasoamw.*
to lead or guide: *kahluwa, kahre, kaweid.*
to lead someone to do wrong: *kaweidsuwed.*
to be lead or guided, to be escorted: *pakahr.*

lead: *leht, namari.*

leader
in the Protestant church, a song leader: *sounkoul.*
prayer leader: *sounkapakap.*
ruler, boss, leader, director: *kaun.*

leaf: *teh.*
coconut leaves upon which food which is to be distributed at a feast is placed: *medehde.*
dried out leaves of the *uhmw*: *rihp.*
fresh banana, breadfruit, or taro leaves used to cover an *uhmw*: *ngkoak.*
leaf of any large leaved plant, such as taro or a palm: *pah₂.*
new leaf: *kupwud.*
pandanus leaf: *tehnpit.*
used leaves of the *uhmw*: *kulup.*

leak
to drip or leak: *ding.*
to leak, as a secret: *kapwadala.*

leaky
leaky, as of a roof: *mpwi.*

lean
to lean: *peng-.*
to lean, of animate beings: *idengek.*

learn
to catch on, to learn: *daperedi.*
to copy, to imitate, to mimic, to learn from: *alemengih.*

lease: *kohwa.*

leave
to leave a usual living area: *lip.*
to leave in haste because of
displeasure: *lip.*
to leave or depart: *mwesel.*

leeward: *lepdihla, peidi-.*

left
left field, in baseball: *lepdo.*
left side: *palimeing.*

left-handed
to be left-handed: *meingtoal.*

leftover
to be leftover: *luhwehdi.*

leg: *aluweluwe, neh.*
area of the leg just above the ankle:
ahtikitik en neh.

legend
legend, story based partially on fact:
soaipoad.

lei
garland, necklace, lei: *mwaramwar.*
to wear a garland, necklace, or lei:
mwaramwar, mware₂.

lemon
citrus, lime, lemon: *karer.*

Lent: *Pahsohpa.*

leper
leprosy, leper: *tokutok, tukutuk.*

leprechaun-like
leprechaun-like being said to dwell in
the forest: *sokolei.*

leprosy
leprosy, leper: *tokutok, tukutuk.*

lesson
lesson, teaching: *padahk.*

lest
lest, when used in combination with
pwe: *de₂.*

let
to let up: *sar.*
to let go, to release: *kadar.*
to be let go, to be released: *pekeder.*

lethargic: *dangahnga.*
lethargic, listless: *soangiangi.*
peaceful, easygoing, unenthusiastic,
slow moving, passive, lethargic:
meleilei.

letter
letter, correspondence: *kisin likou.*
letter, of the alphabet: *leter.*

level
level, a carpenter's tool: *lepel, mepel.*
to align, to equalize, to level:
kapahrek.

liaison
to go out at night for the purpose of a
sexual liaison: *eluwenpwong.*

liar
to be made a liar of: *likamwada.*

lice
louse, flea: *likarak.*
to look for lice: *litepwitepw, mpek,
pakid.*
to pick lice from one's own head: *liaid.*

license: *laisin.*

licentious
free, relieved, unrestrained, licentious:
saledek.

lichen
moss or lichen: *lihmw.*

lick
to lick: *tamwe.*

lid
lid, cover: *pweine₂.*

lie
to lie crosswise: *pangapang, wapang.*
to lie down: *engidi, kipedi, seidi,
wendi, wohnohn.*
to lie, to recline: *wen-.*

lie
cheat, lie: *piht₁.*
deception, lie, fraud: *widing.*
to deceive, to lie to, to defraud:
widinge.
to deceive, to lie, to defraud: *widing.*
to lie: *likamw.*
to lie to: *liepe, pitih.*
to make up a lie, to start a rumor:
kinehda.

life: *mour₁.*
life on earth as opposed to the
afterlife, literally this-side: *paliet.*

lift
to lift: *pwek₁.*
to lift up something hinged or
moveable on one side, as a page ,
lid, or hanging cloth: *pahk.*
to sail with the outrigger lifted from
the water: *neidam.*
to carry or lift something that can be
lightly suspended with one hand:
tile.
to be carried or lifted, of something
that can be lightly suspended with
one hand: *tintil.*

light
a portable light source, as a torch or
flashlight: *sehr₁, ser₁.*
electricity, electric light, flashlight:
dengki.
light, of a color: *merimer.*

source of light: *kampwul.*
to burn, to light, to set fire to, to burn off feathers or hair: *isik.*
to walk with a source of light: *ser₁.*

light
light, in weight: *marahra.*

lightbulb
lightbulb, bullet, pool ball: *dama.*

lighten
to lighten a burden, either physical or mental: *kamara₁.*

lighter
cigarette lighter: *lait.*

lighthouse: *dohdai.*

lightning
lightning without thunder: *ipihp.*
lightning, electricity: *lioal.*

like
to agree, to like: *kupwurki.*
to like or love, to consider good, to desire sexually: *mwahuki.*
to love, to like, to sympathize with: *poakpoake.*

lily
lily sp.: *kiepw.*

limber
supple, limber: *materek.*

limbo: *limpwo.*

lime: *laman.*
citrus, lime, lemon: *karer.*

lime
lime, made from coral: *pweht₁.*

limeade
limeade, sugar water: *swangke.*

limit
border or limit: *ire₂.*
end, limit: *idi.*
to reach a limit or boundary: *idi-.*

limited
limited, just sufficient: *itait.*

limp: *mwoator.*
limp, flexible, springy, disjointed, used to describe a manner of walking: *kiahweliwel.*
limp looking, of people: *lisaimwer.*
to limp: *deriwang, pilingek.*

line
a line or pole placed between a yam planting and the branches of a tree in order to direct the growth of the yam vine upward: *kehndou.*
line, boundary: *lain.*
road, street, trail, path, line: *ahl₁.*
rope, cord, line, string: *sahl.*
series, line: *irek.*
to draw a line: *ele₁.*

to line or cover with leaves: *tehla.*
to be lined up, to be ordered: *irekila.*

line fishing: *epiep.*

lineage
lineage, extended family, clan: *keinek.*

lion: *laiohn.*

lip: *kilinau.*
lower lip: *pahris.*
upper lip: *pohris.*

liquid
water, liquid: *pihl.*

listen
to hear, to listen: *kapaidok, karonge, koaronge, rong.*
to look up to and listen attentively, as of people in a feasthouse: *woakida.*

listing
tilted, listing: *keingihng.*

listless
lethargic, listless: *soangiangi.*

litter
carrying litter requiring two or more people to carry: *roh.*
carrying litter, for the *Nahnmwarki* or *Nahnken*: *rohpapiso.*
carrying litter, requiring four or more people to carry, used for carrying large yams, etc.: *pahs₂.*
litter, of animals: *dih₃.*
to litter, to make untidy: *kid-, kide.*

little
a little: *mwur.*
small, little, young: *tikitik.*
tiny, small, little: *pwidikidik.*

liver: *eh₂.*

lizard
any large lizard, alligator, or crocodile: *kieil.*
gecko: *lamwer.*
sp. of green lizard: *liseiseipahini, liteiteipahini.*
sp. of large brown lizard: *kieil.*
sp. of large green lizard: *dokange.*
sp. of lizard, light blue with dark blue stripes, *Perocheirus*: *limenimeninseri.*

load
burden, load: *wisik.*
to fill, to load: *aude.*
to be filled, to be loaded: *audaud.*

lobster: *uhr₁, urenna.*

locate
to locate lost objects through the use of magic: *kosetipw.*

location
area or location: *dehu.*

location between: *nanpwunga-*.
location of (him, her, or it): *reh₁*.
location some distance in relation to
(somewhere or something): *ile-*.

lock: *loahk.*
to lock: *loakehdi.*
to be locked: *loak.*

locker
locker, cabinet: *osihre.*

log
log, stick: *lepin tuhke.*

loincloth: *pwundosi.*
diaper, loincloth: *weiwei.*

lonely
lonesome, lonely: *sangat.*

lonesome
lonesome, lonely: *sangat.*

long
long, tall: *anged, reirei₁.*

long-legged: *dangerei.*

longjump
broadjump, longjump: *apadopi.*

look
to go look for someone or something
whose presence is expected: *sehng.*
to look for lice: *mpek, pakid.*
to look for wild mountain yams:
kapahr.
to look or peer in the distance: *iroir,
irong.*
to look out of the corner of one's eye:
ikinteng.
to look out of the corner of one's eye
at: *ikintangih.*
to look upwards: *sarada₁.*
to search for, to look for: *rapahki.*
to see, discern, look at, observe,
examine: *kilang.*
to see, discern, look at, observe,
examine, with a derogatory
connotation: *ngar.*
to watch out for, to look out for, to
observe: *mwasahn.*

loop
belt loop: *pwakel₂.*

loose
loose fitting: *pwull₁.*
loose, as of a knot or lashing: *mweir,
mwer₁.*
to rescue, to loose an animal or a
person: *kapit₃.*

lord
lord, chief of the highest order:
Mwohnsapw.
lord, used to refer to a number of
traditional Ponapean gods: *Luhk₂.*

lose
to lose: *luhs, pehrdi.*
to lose one's composure: *patehla.*
to lose one's footing: *katiasang.*
to lose one's will to succeed, to lose all
hope: *mwoarosala.*
to lose, in the card game *pilein
epwiki*: *pwoht₃.*
careless with physical possessions,
likely to lose or misplace belongings:
peidlakid.

lost
to be lost, of objects: *pwupwula.*

lot
a small plot of land, a house lot:
koakon.

lotion
oil, lotion: *kei.*

lottery
election, raffle, lottery: *usuhs.*

loud mouthed
given to exaggeration, loud mouthed,
boisterous: *aulaud.*

louse
louse, flea: *likarak.*
nit, the egg of a louse: *dihl₂.*

louver: *luhpes.*

love: *limpoak, poakepoak.*
a love potion or charm: *mesehl.*
to be in love: *limpoak, poak.*
to like or love, to consider good, to
desire sexually: *mwahuki.*
to love, to like, to sympathize with:
poakpoake.

loving: *poak.*
kind, loving: *limpoak.*

low
low, of the tide when the bottom is
exposed: *ngalangal.*
low, respectful, humble: *karakarahk.*
worn low on one's hips, as of trousers:
kirakahu.

lower
bottom, lower part, referring to the
inside of an object: *nankapi.*
downwind, lower: *pahnangi.*
to be lower than, to be younger or
smaller than: *peidihsang.*
to lower a sail: *lil.*
to sit down, to lower oneself:
keipwekidi.

lubricate
to oil or lubricate: *koamoatoare.*
to be oiled or lubricated: *koamoatoar.*

luck
luck, good fortune: *paiamwahu.*

luckily
luckily, fortunately: *paiente.*

lucky: *adaru, laki, materek, paiamwahu.*
to be lucky: *pwedila.*
to be lucky, to be fortunate, of one
normally unlucky or of no
consequence: *tel.*

lumber
tree, plant, lumber, wood: *tuhke.*

lumpy
lumpy, grainy: *warahr.*

lunch: *kasouwas, mwengehn souwas,*
pahnisou.
to eat lunch: *kasouwas, mwengehn*
souwas, pahnisou.

lung: *ngolungol.*

lure
bait, lure: *pahn$_2$.*

lush
lush, as of foliage: *losolos.*

lusty: *limwesou, mweseu, sengeu.*
joyous, lusty: *pwut.*

lying
lying, untruthful: *aulikamw,*
oatilikamw.
lying, untruthful, said of a person:
pitiniau.

macaroni: *makoroni.*

machete
knife, machete: *kehpit, naip.*

machine
machine, engine, outboard motor:
misihn.

mackerel
canned mackerel: *makirehl.*

mackerel pike
fish sp., mackerel pike: *samma.*

mad
crazy, mad, mentally retarded:
kisingai.

madam
sir, madam: *maing.*

maggot: *mwasakoil, mwesenloang.*

magic: *sarawi.*
a kind of magic applied to blood from
a wound, believed to cause death:
kadipw nta, kaluwenta.
a kind of magic that enables the user
to go unnoticed, as if invisible:
rotensowas.
a kind of magic to delay an action:
mwir.
a kind of magic used to halt an activity
or to inhibit an emotion: *pwehu$_2$.*
a kind of magic used to render

powerless one's opponent in a fight:
rihpe.
a kind of magic, employed to
romantically attract another: *mesehl.*
a kind of magic, performed to shorten
a distance, as when carrying a heavy
load: *kamwotial.*
a kind of magic, performed upstream
from a bather which results in
blindness: *siepil.*
a kind of magic, used to destroy
agricultural products: *siemen.*
harmful magic, sorcery: *kau$_3$.*
magic, mysterious or spiritual power:
manaman.
to employ a kind of magic used to halt
an activity or to inhibit an emotion:
pwewih.
to employ magic to romantically
attract another: *mesehl, mesehlih.*
to make a display of magic, spiritual
power, or authority: *akmanaman.*
to perform magic: *winahni.*
to take medicine or magic for
protection or to instill certain
qualities in the one taking it:
kepiloal$_1$.

magical
magical, mysterious, spiritual:
manaman.

magistrate
chief magistrate: *sihpw$_1$.*

magnet: *makinet.*

magnitude: *kalaimwun.*

mahogany: *maoakani.*

main
main part: *kahlap.*

majestic
majestic, inspiring fear and awe:
lammwin.

majority: *palimoron.*
the larger part, majority: *palilaud.*

make
to make, to repair, to build: *wiahda.*
to make, to become, to turn into:
wiahla.
to make a small *uhmw*: *paidi.*

maker
Lihli maker: *sounlih.*
maker of coconut cream for *lihli*:
sounpiah.

male
man, male: *mwahn, ohl.*
male turtle: *asamwan.*
male mangrove crab: *asamwan.*

malicious
  dishonest, crooked, malicious, wicked:
    mwersuwed, mworsuwed.

man
  man, male: *mwahn, ohl.*
  young man: *mwahnakapw.*
  good man: *olenei.*
  any man in one's husband's clan except
    one the husband calls child:
    wahliniep.
  a man or pig having only one testicle:
    wisolpali.

man-of-war
  man-of-war, an armed naval vessel:
    menuwa.

mandolin: *mandolihn.*

mango: *kehngid.*
  tree sp., a variety of mango:
    *doismango, kehngid en pohnpei,
    kiewek, sallong.*

mangrove crab
  female mangrove crab: *asapein.*
  male mangrove crab: *asamwan.*

mangrove jack: *ikem.*

mangrove sp.: *ahk₁, koatoa.*
  mangrove sp., *Bruguiera conjugata*:
    sohmw.
  mangrove sp., *Heritiera littoralis*:
    merepwinsed.
  mangrove sp., *Rhizophora apiculata*:
    akapa.
  mangrove sp., *Rhizophora
    mucronata*: *akelel.*
  mangrove sp., *Xylocarpus granatum*:
    pwulok.

mangrove swamp: *naniak.*
  seaward edge of the mangrove swamp:
    pahniak.

manifest
  to manifest itself, of a ghost:
    pwarosohs.

manioc
  cassava, manioc, tapioca: *dapiohka,
    kehp tuhke, menioak.*

mankind
  people, person, human being,
    mankind: *aramas.*

manly
  pretending to be manly: *popohnwol.*

manner
  condition, nature, manner: *duwe.*
  custom, manner, behavior, culture:
    tiahk.
  customary manner: *epweh.*

manta ray: *pehwehwe.*

many: *kidalap.*
  a great many, an uncountable number:
    ngeder.
  many, much, numerous, plentiful:
    tohto.

map: *map.*

marathon
  a marathon: *marosong.*

marble: *ramwune.*
  name of one of the holes in the marble
    game *anaire*: *deng₃, mannaka, naisi.*
  name of two of the holes in the marble
    game *anaire*: *iokoioko.*
  of two marbles, to be separated by the
    distance of an outstretched hand: *su.*
  to call interference in the marble
    game *anaire*: *dameni.*
  to drop into a hole, of a marble in the
    game *anaire*: *aida, airas.*
  to hit two marbles with one shot:
    nireng.
  to play marbles: *ramwune.*
  to shoot a marble into the wrong hole
    in the game *anaire*: *pannukas.*

marble game
  Japanese marble game: *dorno.*
  Japanese marble game, the object of
    which is to shoot a marble in proper
    order into five holes: *anaire.*

march
  a march or a procession: *kapar.*
  to march: *kapar, karis.*

March
  March, the month of the year:
    Mahs₅.

mark
  sign, mark, picture, camera, movie,
    motion picture: *kilel.*
  stain, mark: *mwahi.*
  to mark: *kilelehdi.*

marlin
  fish sp., swordfish, sailfish, blue marlin:
    dekilahr.

marry
  to be married: *werek.*
  to get married: *pwopwoud.*
  to marry: *pwoudiki.*
  to marry in the church: *inou sarawi.*

marsh
  taro patch, marsh, bog: *lehpwel.*

masculine
  of a woman, masculine: *piledek.*

mash
  to apply pressure to, to mash: *idang.*
  to be under pressure, to be mashed:
    idaid.

mashed
  bent, smashed, mashed, dented: *limek.*
  pasty, mashed: *pitakatak.*
  pulverized, crushed, mashed: *mwut.*

mask
  catcher's mask: *masuku.*

mass
  any mashed or pasty mass: *pitakatak.*

mass: *mihsa.*

massage
  to rub, to massage: el_1, *eliel.*

masseur
  masseur, masseuse, one who practices
    the art of massage for its healing
    powers: *souneliel.*

masseuse
  masseur, masseuse, one who practices
    the art of massage for its healing
    powers: *souneliel.*

mast
  mast, of a canoe or ship: *kehu.*

master
  to know thoroughly, to master: *ereki.*

masturbate
  to masturbate: *sukumei.*

masturbation: *sukumei.*

mat: *lirop, lohs, moatoar$_2$.*

match
  to match in competition: *peliali.*
  to be well matched in a competitive
    endeavor: *pwepwengi.*

match: *masis.*

mate
  to mate with, of animals: *kehsekih.*
  to mate, of animals: *kehsek.*

material
  a clothlike material made from the
    bark of breadfruit: *meimei.*
  cloth, anything made of cloth,
    material, clothes: *likou.*
  material, cloth: *lepin likou.*
  the fibrous, cloth-like material of the
    coconut palm: *inipal.*
  thing, material, physical object of any
    kind: *dipwisou.*

matted
  matted, of hair or feathers: *nokonokon.*
  wet and matted, of hair: *winakanak.*

mattress: *madires.*

maximize
  to maximize the volume of one's voice:
    mamahd.

May
  May, the month of the year: Mei_1.

maybe
  maybe, perhaps: *sekere.*

perhaps, maybe, possibly: ele_2.
probably, maybe, perhaps: *mwein.*

me: $-ie_1$.

meal
  meal after kava: *kenei sakau, pailol.*

mean: *mihn.*
  mean looking: *pohlemei.*

meaning: *wehwe.*

measles: *mehn kisetik.*
  to have the measles: *mehn kisetik.*

measure
  to measure with outstretched arms:
    ngepe.
  to measure, to survey: *sohng.*

measurement: *sosohng.*
  a Japanese unit of measurement of
    area, approximately 100,000 square
    feet: $sohpw_1$.
  measurement, pattern: *sohng.*

meat
  meat, flesh, muscle: *uduk.*
  the meat or fish part of a meal: *irap,
    sali.*
  to eat meat or fish: *irap.*

mechanic: *sounwiemisihn.*

medal
  medal, non-religious: *metel.*
  medal, usually a catholic religious
    medal: *medahlia.*

medicate
  to medicate: *winie.*

medicine: *wini.*
  medicine taken before eating food
    prepared by another to avoid the
    effects of magic: ais_1.
  medicine wrapped in coconut cloth:
    ihn wini.
  native medicine used for a jealous
    spouse: *kaloalamwahu.*
  practitioner of native Ponapean
    medicine: *sounwini.*
  to take medicine: *wini.*
  to take medicine or magic for
    protection or to instill certain
    qualities in the one taking it:
    $kepiloal_1$.

meek
  humble, unassuming, meek: *aktikitik,
    opampap.*

meet
  to meet: *mihding, mihting, tu.*
  to meet, to convene, to confer: *tiepene.*
  to meet, to meet by chance: *kasaing.*

meeting: *mihding, mihting, pokon.*
  meeting, convention, conference:
    tiepene.

melt
  to melt: *peipeseng.*

member
  member of: *tohn₂.*
  to become a member, inhabitant, or participant of: *towehda.*

memorial
  memorial, recollection, souvenir: *ketemenpe.*

memorize
  to memorize, to know by heart: *wadilik.*

mend
  to mend a thatch roof: *dilip.*
  to mend or repair, used principally with native objects: *one.*
  to be mended or repaired, used principally with native objects: *onohn.*

menstruate
  to menstruate: *soumwahu en lih.*

menstruation: *soumwahu en lih.*

meow
  to meow, the sound that a cat makes: *ngiau.*

merciful
  kind, generous, merciful: *kalahngan.*
  kind, merciful: *kopwungloal.*

mercy
  kindness, generosity, mercy: *kalahngan.*

mess
  confusion, disorder, mess: *pingiping.*

message
  dispatch or message: *ilek₂.*
  message from the *Nahnmwarki*: *ahng₁.*

Messiah: *Mesaia.*

messy
  messy, unsanitary, filthy: *samin.*
  confused, disordered, messy: *ping.*

metal
  metal, nail, badge, spear for a speargun: *mete.*

middle
  middle, center, or midst of (him, her, or it): *nanwerenge.*
  middle, either in a spatial or temporal sense: *lukope.*

midnight
  midnight, middle of the night: *lukepenpwong.*

midst
  middle, center, or midst of (him, her, or it): *nanwerenge.*
  midst, of an activity: *eilepe.*

midwife: *sounkeneitik.*

mildew
  mildew, stain caused by mildew: *enihep.*

mildewy
  mildewy, mildewed: *enihep.*

mile: *mwail.*

milk: *milik.*
  condensed milk: *milikten.*
  curdled coconut milk: *moakoan.*
  evaporated milk: *milikpil.*

milkfish
  fish sp., milkfish, *Chanos Chanos*: *eki.*

million: *rar₂.*

millipede: *limwakatantar.*

mimic
  to copy, to imitate, to mimic, to learn from: *alemengih.*

mingle
  to mix, to mingle: *patpene.*

minister
  apostle, minister: *wahnpoaron.*

minute: *minit.*

minute
  tiny, minute: *pwiningining.*

minutes
  minutes, as of a meeting: *minit.*

miracle: *manaman.*

mirror: *kilahsenirongin.*
  glass, drinking glass, glasses, goggles, mirror: *kilahs.*

miscarriage: *iohla.*

miscarry
  to miscarry: *iohla.*

mischievious
  mischievious, naughty, difficult, frustrating: *ketihwo.*

misplace
  careless with physical possessions, likely to lose or misplace belongings: *peidlakid.*

miss
  to miss a person or a place, to be homesick: *loaleid, loaloid.*
  to miss an event: *katiasang.*
  to miss one's chance: *pisel.*

mission
  Catholic mission: *misiohn.*
  Protestant mission: *misin.*

mist
  vapor, smoke, mist: *adi.*

mistake
  mistake, error: *sapwung.*
  to make someone realize his mistake: *kapehme.*

mistreat
to mistreat: *wiakawe.*

mitt
catcher's mitt: *middo.*

mix
mixed, of bananas and any other food: *repwirepw.*
to be of mixed blood lines, to be of a mixed breed: *ipwihpw.*
to mix liquids with non-liquids: *sewe.*
to mix, to add ingredients: *doaloa, dol₁.*
to mix, to mingle: *patpene.*
to prepare food with grated coconut, to mix things together: *uter, utere.*

moan
to cry, to weep, to moan: *seng.*

modest
submissive, modest, self-effacing: *mpahi.*

molar: *ngihlap.*

molasses
the liquid gathered from the coconut flower, sometimes used to make molasses or fermented to make an intoxicating beverage: *sikaliwi.*

mold: *kitei.*

moldy: *kitei.*
moldy or old tasting: *sensen.*
moldy smelling: *pwohsensen.*

mole: *mweinlihamwahu.*
freckle, mole, or any skin discoloration: *mwahi.*

molt
to molt a shell: *nihdwel, wel₁.*

mom
mother, mom, a term of familiarity: *in, ino.*

Monday: *Niehd.*

money: *mwohni.*
cent, money: *sens, sent.*

monkey: *mwengki.*

month: *sounpwong.*

moo
to moo, of a cow: *mwoh.*

moon: *maram, sounpwong.*
full moon: *maram mat.*
new moon: *maram pwul.*

moonlight: *maram.*

mop
to mop, to sponge off, to wipe: *dahlimw.*

morning: *menseng.*
early morning: *mentikitik.*
pre-dawn morning hours: *sohrahn.*

mortar
cement, concrete, mortar: *simend, siment.*

mosquito: *amwise.*

mosquito coil: *kadorsingko.*

mosquito net: *tein amwise.*

moss
moss or lichen: *lihmw.*

most: *keieu.*

mother: *ihn₁, nohno.*
mother, mom, a term of familiarity: *in, ino.*
wife's mother, all women one's wife calls mother: *soulap.*

mother-hen-like
protective, mother-hen-like: *lirohro.*

motion
a motion, as in a legislative proceeding: *kemwekid.*
to make a motion, as in a legislative proceeding: *kamwakid.*

motion picture
movie, motion picture: *kasdo, kilel mwekid.*

motor
machine, engine, outboard motor: *misihn.*

motorcycle
scooter, motorcycle: *odopai, skuhder.*

mound
to mound earth around the roots of a plant: *uhpwel.*

mountain: *nahna.*
mountain range: *kahng₂.*
small mountain, hill: *dohl.*

mountain apple
tree sp., mountain apple, *Syzygium malaccense*: *apel.*

mouse
rat, mouse: *kitik.*

mouth: *ahu, dawas, dowas, kaururi, oate.*
corner of the mouth: *kepwil, pwekil.*
having a large mouth: *oatwalek.*
mouth of a river: *kepinpil.*
upper part of the mouth: *pohrehre.*

mouthful
to have a mouthful: *inahpwed.*

move
to cause to move further: *kadauluhl.*
to initiate movement of the whole body, as when one starts to rise, walk, run, etc.: *mwusikek.*
to move: *kai-, kei-, mwekid, sepwil-.*
to move a group of things: *aker-.*
to move aside stones used for an

uhmw in the act of cleaning it: *paka*.

to move backwards: *pweiek*.

to move earth, as in the preparation of a house foundation: *deipwel*.

to move in great numbers, to swarm: *del*.

to move one's hips against another's in the manner characteristic of sexual intercourse: *kurih*.

to move one's hips in the manner characteristic of sexual intercourse: *kur*.

to move rapidly: *meliek, pitikek, pitirek*.

to move slowly, physically or mentally: *kamantik*.

to move something slowly and quietly: *kawai*.

to move swiftly up and down: *mesiek*.

to move to a cooler area: *kehngitik*.

to move vertically, of something flexible: *mwate*.

to move with a low profile, as in a squatting or bent over position: *karahk*.

to move, of covers, lids, tops, louvers, etc., generally of flat items parallel to the ground: *ripe*.

to move, to change residence: *sou₂*.

to move, to shake: *kamwakid*.

to transfer, to move or change location: *kasau*.

to be made to move or shake: *kemwekid*.

to be transferred, to be moved: *kosou*.

movie

movie, motion picture: *kasdo, kilel mwekid*.

sign, mark, picture, camera, movie, motion picture: *kilel*.

moving

emotionally moving, causing pity: *kompoake*.

much

many, much, numerous, plentiful: *tohto*.

to be too much, excessive, more than enough: *depala*.

mucus

nasal mucus: *toai*.

mud: *pwelmatak*.

muddy: *pwelmatak*.

muddy, sloppy: *pwakanakan*.

mudskipper

fish sp., mudskipper: *litak*.

mullet

fish sp., a kind of mullet: *pehioang*.

fish sp., shark mullet: *ahpako*.

shark mullet, at a growth stage of approximately twelve inches: *ah₄*.

multiplication: *wad*.

multiply

of mathematics, to multiply: *wad, wadiki*.

mummy apple

papaya, also called mummy apple: *memiap*.

mumps: *sampwo*.

municipality

a political unit, as a municipality, district, state, country, or kingdom: *wehi₂*.

name of a municipality in Ponape: *Kiti, Madolenihmw, Net₂, Sokehs, Uh₃*.

murderer

thief, murderer, rascal: *loallap*.

murky

murky, as of muddy water or a cloudy sky: *kiried*.

muscle

meat, flesh, muscle: *uduk*.

muscle of a clam, used for closing the shell: *uhre*.

mushroom: *saleng en eni*.

music

anything capable of producing music, a musical instrument, radio, tape recorder, etc.: *keseng*.

to play music: *keseng*.

mustache

beard, mustache: *alis*.

mute

mute, dumb, stuttering: *lohteng*.

mutter

to mutter indistinctly during sleep: *liourehre*.

muumuu

muumuu, an ankle length dress: *mwuhmwu*.

my: *ahi₂, ei₁, nei₁. (See other possessive classifiers.)*

mysterious: *kapwonopwon*.

magical, mysterious, spiritual: *manaman*.

to find something confusing, difficult to understand, or mysterious: *pwonopwoniki*.

nail

metal, nail, badge, spear for a speargun: *mete*.

nail, as a finger or toenail: *kihk*.
nail, spike: *nihl*.

naked
to be naked, to be nude: *kilisou, pohnkodoul*.

name: *ahd$_1$*.
a non-baptismal name: *adamwahl*.
affectionate name for baby girls: *pwohpwo$_1$*.
burial name given to a chief after his death: *edenpwel*.
common dog's name, from the Japanese word for black: *kuro*.
nickname, abbreviated name: *aditik*.
title, name: *mwahr, mwar*.
to name: *kahdaneki*.
to nickname: *aditikih*.

narrow: *tehtik*.

narrowing: *tir*.

nasal
nasal sound: *tumwpwoar*.

native
native, aboriginal: *pwilidak*.
native, one indigenous to an area: *uhdak*.
native, used derogatorily: *dohming, kinaka*.

nature
condition, nature, manner: *duwe*.

naughty
mischievious, naughty, difficult, frustrating: *ketihwo*.

nauseous: *pahnediwo*.

navel: *pwuhs$_1$*.

navy: *kaingun*.

near
near, close: *keren*.
to be near or close to: *karanih*.

neat
neat, clean: *min, nei$_2$*.

necessary
necessary, indispensable: *anahn*.

neck: *kasang$_2$, tepinkasang, tepinwere, were$_1$*.
back of the head or neck: *likinpaiki*.
back of the neck: *pohnihr*.
stiff neck: *tepinwer medek*.
the area between the collarbone and the neck: *peden were*.

necklace
garland, necklace, lei: *mwaramwar*.
to wear a garland, necklace, or lei: *mwaramwar, mware$_2$*.

necktie
necktie, tie: *nektait*.

need: *anahn*.
to need, to require: *anahne*.

needle: *dikek*.

needle fish
fish sp., a kind of needle fish: *dahk, lidokodok pwise*.

needlework: *deidei*.

neglected
to be discarded, to be neglected: *lekidekla*.

nerve-wracking: *kasaloh*.

nervous: *saloh*.
to cause another to be nervous: *kasalowe*.

nest: *pahs$_1$*.
to make a nest: *ilapas*.

net: *uhk$_1$*.
a large fishing net: *pwosou*.
a net ceremony given to the *enihlap*: *kapwusenleng*.
a net ceremony introduced from the East: *kapwusenmaraki*.
a net ceremony requiring the performance of sexual intercourse prior to use of the net: *kapwusenlimw*.
an expert net maker: *sowuhk$_1$*.
any of a number of ceremonies performed to bring luck to a fishing net: *kapwus*.
large seine or net: *ukalap*.
mosquito net: *tein amwise*.
small hand net: *lukouk*.
small seine or net: *uketik*.
throw net: *ukinlekidek*.

net fishing
a type of net fishing, done at night: *sehpwong*.
a type of net fishing, done by blocking off a pocket in the coral: *duhse*.
a type of net fishing, employing a net attached to a curved stick: *naik*.
a type of net fishing, where fish are chased into the net: *kasar*.
a type of net fishing, where the fisherman uses a *naik* in each hand: *ukouk*.

new: *kapw*.
to refurbish or make like new again: *kapwala*.

New Testament: *Kadehde Kapw*.

new year: *parakapw*.

news: *kair, nuhs, rohng*.
current news, recent information: *rongkapw*.

newspaper: *doaropwehn rohng, nuhspehpa, simpung.*

next
> next to (him or her), with animate relationships: *mpe.*
> next to (him, her, or it): *limwah.*
> to be next to: *peian.*

nickname
> nickname, abbreviated name: *aditik.*
> to nickname: *aditikih.*

night: *pahnkopwul, pwohng.*
> to spend the night with a woman: *engida.*

nine: *adu, duwadip, duwadun, duwaka, duwakap, duwakis, duwamwut, duwapa, duwapak, duwapar, duwapit, duwara, duwasop, duwau, duwehl, duwelep, duwemen, duwemwodol, duwepali, duwesel, duwesou, duwete, duwetumw, duwewel, duwoapoar, duwoapwoat, duwoapwong, duwopwuloi, duwoumw.*

ninety: *duwehk, duweisek, duwengoul.*

ninth: *kawaluh.*

nit
> nit, the egg of a louse: *dihl₂.*

no: *soh.*
> no longer: *soher, sohla, solahr.*

nod
> to doze off, to nod when falling asleep: *lisoi.*

noise
> a thudding noise: *kumwukumw₁.*
> making a slapping or banging noise: *tipwalapwal.*
> to disturb with noise: *kataironge.*
> to make a cracking, crunching, or static-like noise: *rar₁.*
> to make a slapping noise by striking two objects together: *tipwal.*
> to make a splattering noise: *pwirar.*
> to make a tearing or grating noise: *tehrek.*
> to make an explosive or slapping noise: *mweker.*
> to make noise: *mweseisei.*
> to stomp, to make a thudding noise: *tom.*

noisy: *mwoaroangoaroang.*
> to be noisy: *katairong, mwoaroang.*

nonbuoyant: *kihr₁.*

none
> not, none, nothing: *sohte.*

nonsensical
> nonsensical, untruthful: *tika.*

noodle: *udong.*

noon: *souwas.*

noose
> noose for snaring rats: *liapiap.*
> slip noose: *mol.*
> to catch with a slip noose: *mol.*
> to trap with a leg noose: *nsere.*
> to be trapped in a leg noose: *nsar.*

normal: *unsek.*

north: *paliepeng.*

nose: *keinuhnu, sisipwai, tumwe.*
> flat nosed: *tumwpak.*

nosebleed
> nosebleed, occurring spontaneously: *mehn rokumw.*

nosey
> nosey, bothersome: *direpw.*

nostril: *pworen timwe.*

not: *kaidehkin, kaidehn.*
> a negative prefix meaning not: *sa-.*
> a negative prefix meaning not or 'the opposite of': *sou-₂.*
> not at all: *soumwahn.*
> not ever, used to negate commands: *dehpa.*
> not yet: *kaik, kaikinte, saik₂, saikinte.*
> not, none, nothing: *sohte.*
> not, used in negative questions: *sou₅.*
> not, used to negate commands: *deh, dehr.*

notch
> a notch cut into a coconut tree, used as a step in climbing: *pelepel en sikaliwi.*

note
> musical note: *nohd.*
> to take note of: *kilelehdi.*

notebook: *pwuken nting.*

nothing
> not, none, nothing: *sohte.*
> to have nothing left: *pikipas.*

notice
> notice, announcement: *pakair.*
> signature, poster, sign, notice: *sain.*

notify
> to notify, to announce: *pakair.*
> to notify, to inform, to hint at, to let someone know: *kehsehki.*

noun: *ahd₁.*

nourish
> to revitalize, to nourish: *ketihnain.*

nourishment
> food, nourishment: *ketihnain, ketihnepe.*

November: *Nopempe.*

now: *me₁, met.*
o.k., so, well, now: *na.*

nude
to be naked, to be nude: *kilisou, pohnkodoul.*

numb: *ketiket₁.*

number: *nempe.*

numerous
many, much, numerous, plentiful: *tohto.*

nun: *lih kadek, mahdire.*

nurse
to suckle, to nurse: *dihdi.*

nymphomaniac: *lieraran.*

oath
to take an oath: *kahula.*

obedient
obedient, respectful: *peik₂.*

obligation
responsibility, obligation, duty: *pwukoa.*

obnoxious
obnoxious, discomforting: *was₁.*
obnoxious, disgusting, irritating: *limwesou.*
unlikeable, obnoxious, despicable: *kadongodong.*

observe
to observe a holiday: *kasarawi₁.*
to observe from a hidden position: *rukih.*
to see, discern, look at, observe, examine: *kilang.*
to see, discern, look at, observe, examine, with a derogatory connotation: *ngar.*
to watch out for, to look out for, to observe: *mwasahn.*
to watch, to behold, to observe: *poudiahl, udiahl.*
to witness, to observe or hear something with certainty, to testify: *kadehde.*

obstacle
to run an obstacle race: *songaipwisi.*

obvious
clear, evident, obvious: *sansal.*

occupation
occupation, task, employment, responsibility, deed: *doahk.*

occur
to occur, to happen: *wiawi.*

occurrence
occurrence, time: *pak₁.*
a chance occurrence: *depweila.*

ocean
ocean, beyond the reef: *madau₁, nanmadau.*
ocean, sea: *nansed, sehd.*
ocean, sea, as the Pacific Ocean, or the Philippine Sea: *lepin sed.*

October: *Oakotope.*

octopus: *kihs.*
a large octopus-like creature, said to live in the mouth of rivers, possibly mythical: *lupwoluwo.*

odd
abnormal, deformed, odd: *pakalong.*

odor
smell, odor, aroma: *pwoh.*

of: *-n₁, en₁.*

offensive
employing an offensive tone of voice: *ngilawas.*

offer
to make an insincere offer of food, prompted by the dictates of hospitality: *kemwetemwet.*
to offer a drinking coconut to someone before tasting it: *pwurepwur en eni.*
to offer as a first fruit: *mwowe₂.*

offering
sacrifice, offering, contribution: *meiroang.*

office
office, government: *ohpis.*

official: *manaman.*
to make official, to authorize, to give official approval to: *kamana.*
to be made official, to be authorized, to be given official approval: *kamanaman.*

offspring: *wah, wahnedi.*
descendant, offspring, of humans: *kadaudok.*
descendant, offspring, usually of animals: *keperepere.*
having many offspring: *nain.*

Oh : *ah₅.*

oil: *oail.*
coconut oil for the hair: *lehn wisoar, lehnawahu.*
coconut oil for the skin: *lehn kei, lehnkalangi.*
oil, for cooking or as a lotion: *leh₁.*
oil, lotion: *kei.*
oil, perfume: *kisin leh.*
to oil or lubricate: *koamoatoare.*
to be oiled or lubricated: *koamoatoar.*
to be oiled, to be shiny with oil: *keimwoale.*

oily
    oily, greasy: *moatoar₁*.

oink
    to oink, to grunt, of a pig: *ngopw*.

okay: *okei*.

old
    big, old: *laud*.
    dull or old-looking, of inanimate
      objects: *moarungurung*.
    moldy or old tasting: *sensen*.
    old, aged: *mah*.
    old, decrepit, of people: *likeilap*.
    old, of inanimate objects: *mering*.
    old, of things: *tok₂*.

Old Testament: *Kadehde Mering*.

omen
    omen of death: *kihlenuwo*.
    omen, warning: *dahda*.
    to perform some action or to say
      something that is interpreted as an
      omen of death: *kihlenuwo*.

on
    above, upon, on (him, her, or it): *powe*.

one: *aka₂, akap, apa, apak, apali, apar,*
    ara₂, edip, ehd₁, ehl₂, ehu, ekis, elep,
    emen, emwodol, emwut, epit, esel,
    esou, ete, ewel₁, ih₃, me₂, oapoar,
    oapwoat, odun, opwong₁, opwuloi,
    osop, otumw, oumw.
    one of, thing of: *mehn₁*.

one-eyed: *maspali*.

onion: *anien*.
    green onion: *nengi, ningi*.

only: *tohr₁*.
    just, only: *-te*.

open
    to open at the top, of a drinking
      coconut: *pwuremas*.
    to open one's eyes: *pehdpeseng*.
    to open one's mouth: *sara₁*.
    to open one's mouth to speak:
      dawaspeseng, dewesepeseng.
    to open or close anything hinged or
      attached, as a door or window:
      riting.
    to open or untie, as a bag: *lapwa,*
      lapwad, lawad.
    to be opened or closed, of anything
      hinged: *rit-*.
    to be opened or untied, as of a bag:
      lawadek.

opening: *wehwe*.
    slit, crack, small opening, empty space,
      outer space: *nanwehwe*.

operate
    to operate on: *pwalang*.
    to be operated on: *pwal*.

operation
    medical operation, in which the body
      cavity is entered: *pwal*.
    medical operation, on the legs or arms:
      lek.

opinion
    thought, idea, opinion: *lamalam*.

opponent
    counterpart, opponent: *pelie*.

oppose
    to oppose, to disagree with: *uhweng*.

opposite
    a negative prefix meaning not or 'the
      opposite of': *sou-₂*.

opposition
    from, in opposition to: *-sang*.

opressive: *limeidihd*.

or: *de₁*.

orange
    Mandarin orange, tangerine:
      manterihn, manterihng.
    orange, the fruit: *orens*.

orchid
    plant sp., *Galeola ponapensis*, a kind
      of orchid: *lamwahk*.
    plant sp., a kind of orchid: *lamwahk en*
      wai.

order
    aligned, arranged, settled, ordered:
      soan.
    to be lined up, to be ordered: *irekila*.
    to command, to order: *ruwes*.
    to order: *oaht, oahte, suhmwong,*
      suhmwongih.

organ: *keseng tiati*.

organization
    organization, structure, rule, plan,
      agreement: *koasoandi*.

organize
    to organize, to structure: *koasoane*.
    to be organized, to be structured:
      koasoandi.

original: *kahlap*.

originate
    to originate from, of a person:
      pwilisang.

ornament
    decoration, ornament, or new outfit of
      clothing: *kapwat*.
    to decorate or ornament: *kapwat*.

ornamented: *ipwerek*.
    ornamented, outfitted in new clothing:
      kapwatapwat.

orphaned: *sopwoupwou*.

other: *tei*.

otherwise: *mahkete.*

ouch
ouch, an exclamation of pain: *ehk₂, esse.*

our
our, dual: *ata, neita.*
our, exclusive: *aht₁, nait.*
our, plural: *atail, neitail. (See other possessive classifiers.)*

out
outside (him, her, or it): *liki.*
to be out of breath, to be unable to catch one's breath: *mwopw.*
to be out, in baseball: *aud.*

outboard motor
machine, engine, outboard motor: *misihn.*

outcome
top, summit, end, outcome: *imwi.*

outer
outer side, outer surface: *masliki.*

outgoing
forward, uninhibited, outgoing: *limedramin.*
outgoing, forward, of women: *limedek.*
outgoing, friendly, knowing no stranger, usually said of children and pets: *liahn.*
talkative, outgoing: *medakahn.*

outhouse: *imwen kainen.*

outrigger
outrigger of a canoe: *dahm.*
outrigger platform: *parap.*
outrigger side of a canoe: *palihdam.*
outrigger support, extending from the side of the hull to the ends of the outrigger: *apis.*
part of the outrigger support of a canoe: *dokawar, kehnti.*
side of a canoe opposite the outrigger: *palikasa.*
to have something stuck between the hull and the outrigger of a canoe: *koapwuroaloat.*
one of the outrigger supports on a canoe: *rahk₂.*

outside
outside (him, her, or it): *liki.*

outwards: *-iei.*

oval: *lipeiahk, peiahk.*

oven
a traditional Ponapean oven made of loose stones which are heated and placed around the food to be baked: *uhmw.*

overalls
bib overalls: *rausis preisis.*

overcast
calm and overcast, with no rain, used in describing the weather: *mahliok.*

overcome
to overcome: *powehdi.*
to be conquered, captured, overcome: *lohdi.*

overcrowded
overcrowded, filled: *dir.*

overgrown
to become overgrown: *sok₂.*

overjoyed
delighted, overjoyed: *pohl.*

overripe
overripe, of breadfruit: *semwek.*
overripe, of tuberous plants: *tot.*
ripe, overripe, rotten, spoiled, decayed: *mat.*

overtake
to catch up to, to chase down, to overtake: *pwakihdi.*
to go beyond, to exceed, to surpass, to overtake: *sipele.*

overtired
overtired, as of a muscle: *dau.*

owl: *likoht, tehap.*

own
to own land: *sapwasapw.*
to own, of land: *sapweniki.*
to own, to have, used with nouns occurring with the classifier *ah*: *ahniki.*
to own, to have, used with nouns occurring with the classifier *nah*: *nainiki.*

oyster: *lingkiri, pelekenna, pwai₂.*

Pacific golden plover
bird sp., Pacific golden plover, *Pluvialis dominica*: *kulu.*

packed
dense, tightly woven or packed: *keirek.*

paddle
paddle, dance paddle: *padil.*
rice paddle: *samusi.*
steering paddle: *ilihl.*
to paddle: *sei₁.*
to paddle from the bow of a canoe: *mwohnawar.*
to paddle from the stern of a canoe: *mwurinwar.*
to paddle or pole against the wind: *pediang.*
to paddle to: *saih.*

paddler
   paddler who sits in the bow of a canoe: *mwohnawar*.
   paddler who sits in the stern of a canoe: *mwurinwar*.

paddy
   rice paddy: *dampwo*.

pagan
   pagan, uncivilized, uneducated, uncultured: *rotorot*.

page
   sheet, page: *teh*.

painful
   painful, agonizing, torturous: *weirek*.
   painful, physically or mentally: *kamedek*.
   to be painful: *medek*.

paint: *litepw*.
   to draw or paint, as a picture: *mahlen, mahlenih*.
   to paint: *litapwih, litepw*.

painter: *sounmahlen*.

painting
   painting, drawing: *mahlen*.

pair
   member of a matched pair: *pelie*.
   to be a member of a matched pair: *peliali, pelian*.
   to come or go in pairs: *mpwer-*.

pal
   buddy, honey, pal, used in addressing one's spouse, or peers or children of the same sex: *nahn$_1$*.

pale
   pale, of the face as after a sudden shock: *reirei$_2$*.

palm
   a variety of coconut palm: *nihkengk, nihrir, nihtik*.
   a variety of coconut palm, bearing green nuts: *nihtoal*.
   a variety of coconut palm, bearing red nuts: *nihweita*.
   a variety of coconut palm, having nuts with a sweet, juicy husk: *adohl*.
   a variety of coconut palm, with round nuts: *nihkarat*.
   a variety of palm: *apwraiasi, koatop, mpwel$_3$*.
   a variety of palm, *Ponapea ledermanniana*: *kedei*.
   coconut palm, *Cocos nucifera*: *nih$_2$*.
   ivory nut palm, *Coelococcus amicarum*: *oahs$_1$*.
   nipa palm, *Nipa fruticans*: *parem*.
   sprouting coconut palm: *pahr$_3$*.

pamper
   to baby-sit, to pamper: *kamwait*.

pan: *pan*.
   frying pan, skillet: *pirain, piraipang*.

pancake: *pankeik*.

pancreas: *keisar*.

pandanus
   any of a number of varieties of pandanus: *kipar, mwatal*.

pandanus sp.: *rara*.
   pandanus sp., *Humata banksii*: *mwataliniak*.
   pandanus sp., *Pandanus pulposus*, used for making baskets, hats, and sails, the fruit of which is edible: *deipw*.
   pandanus sp., *Pandanus tolotomensis*: *kiparenwel*.

pant
   to pant: *nget*.

pants
   short pants, shorts: *lepin rausis, rausis mwotomwot*.
   trousers, pants: *rausis*.

papaya
   papaya, also called mummy apple: *memiap*.

paper
   paper, cardboard: *doaropwe*.

parable
   talk, discussion, rumor, story, adage, parable: *koasoai*.

paradise: *paradais*.

paradox
   to point out a paradox: *karasaras*.

paralyzed: *mwoator*.

parcel: *koruk*.

pardon
   pardon me , used when one passes in front of another: *ihieng*.

parent
   to be a parent: *neitik*.

parish
   congregation, parish, a gathering in the presence of a *Nahnmwarki*: *mwomwohdiso*.

park
   to be parked, of a car: *pei$_5$*.

parlaysis: *lisongapwo*.

parole
   parole, probation: *parohl*.
   to parole, to place on probation: *parohlih*.
   to be on parole or probation: *parohl*.

parrot
   bird sp., resembling a parrot: *serehd*.

parrotfish
fish sp., a kind of parrotfish: *kilikil,
lida, mahuenmoar, mwomwmei,
pahme, pedilik₂, umwun₂.*
fish sp., a kind of parrotfish, *Scarus
rubroviolaceus*: *lidoi.*
fish sp., a mature parrotfish: *tamwais.*
fish sp., any bluish parrotfish: *mahu.*
fish sp., humphead parrotfish,
Bolbometopon muricatus: *kemeik.*
fish sp., yellow-tailed brown parrotfish
Cetoscarus bicolor: *lawi.*

part
part, in the hair: *elenwel.*
part, side: *pali₁.*
the larger part, majority: *palilaud.*
to part, of the hair: *elenwel.*

participant
participant of: *tohn₂.*
to become a member, inhabitant, or
participant of: *towehda.*

participate
to accompany, join, or go with, to
participate, to attend: *iang.*

party: *tehpel.*
a party or gift given to a *sounwini* the
fourth day of taking medicine: *koten
wini.*
feast, party: *kamadipw.*
to give a party: *tehpel.*
to give a party or gift to a medicine
maker the fourth day of taking
medicine: *ilisapw.*
to prepare a small informal feast or
party: *ainpwoat.*

pass
to pass along: *kadauluhl.*
to pass along physical objects from one
person to another: *ahng₂.*
to pass around, to pass indirectly:
kepidak.
to pass by: *moahl₂.*
to pass by, to go beyond: *daulih,
douluhl.*
to pass in the traditional manner of
respect: *loange.*
to pass on verbal information: *pouse.*
to pass, in a card game: *iranai,
pahs₃.*
to pass, in a race: *pwar.*
to penetrate, go through, or pass into:
dil.
to squeeze through, to pass through in
spite of an obstacle: *duwal.*
to be passed around, to be passed
indirectly: *kepidek.*

to be passed in the traditional manner
of respect: *loang.*
to be passed on, of verbal information:
pous.

pass
large pass in the outer reef and the
area inside the lagoon adjacent to
the pass: *kepidau.*

passage
channel, canal, a passage in a reef:
dahu.

passenger: *pahsinse.*

passive
peaceful, easygoing, unenthusiastic,
slow moving, passive, lethargic:
meleilei.

past
in the past, a long time ago: *mahs₁.*

paste
bean paste: *miso.*

pasty
pasty, mashed: *pitakatak.*

pat
to pat: *pikipik, pikir.*
to pat the back end of a canoe on the
outrigger side, a ceremonial action:
damwer, demwidemw.
to caress, to rub, to pat affectionately:
damwer, demwidemw.

patch
a patch: *deipin.*
to patch: *deipin, pina.*
to be patched: *pinapin.*
to be patched, of a thatch roof: *dilipek.*

path
road, street, trail, path, line: *ahl₁.*
side path, a small path off the main
one: *alesop.*

patient: *kanengamah.*

patrol
to patrol: *dou₃.*

pattern
measurement, pattern: *sohng.*
pattern or design, as of material:
mwahi.

pay
to buy, to pay, to hire: *pwain.*
to heed, to pay attention to, to agree
with: *ahne.*
to pay tribute, to repay a service or
good deed: *isais, ise.*
to be paid: *pweipwei₂.*

payment
payment or reward: *keting.*
fee, rental payment: *isepe.*

peace: *meleilei.*
  desiring peace and quiet while under
    the influence of kava: *kahka.*
  peace, tranquility: *popohl.*
  peace, tranquility, good feelings:
    onepek.

peaceful
  peaceful, easygoing, unenthusiastic,
    slow moving, passive, lethargic:
    meleilei.

peak
  top, peak, summit, ridge: *koadoke.*

peanut: *pihnas.*

peanut butter: *pihnas pwete.*

pearl: *menemen en pahsu.*

pebbles
  gravel, pebbles: *rakied.*
  gravel, pebbles, crushed coral, any
    rock-like material used as a ground
    cover: *pwuker.*

peck
  to peck, of birds or of fish nibbling
    bait: *palih$_1$, pel$_1$.*

peel
  to peel off: *kirehdi.*
  to peel off, as of skin or paint:
    tepwasang.
  to peel, as a banana: *kaup, kokoup.*
  to peel, of the skin after being
    sunburned: *sar.*
  to skin or peel: *rar$_3$, rere.*
  to slice, to peel with an instrument:
    sere$_1$.
  to uproot, to peel, to pry: *sarek$_3$.*
  to be sliced, to be peeled: *sansar$_1$.*

peep
  to peep at: *mwoanok, rukih.*
  to peep at people bathing in a river:
    mwoanipil.

peer: *pelie.*
  to look or peer in the distance: *iroir,
    irong.*

pen
  enclosure, pen, fence, wall, as of a fort:
    kehl$_2$.

pen
  pen, for writing: *pehn$_1$.*

pencil: *pinsel.*

pencil sharpener: *mehn seipinsel.*

pendulum
  pendulum of a clock: *wisol en kuloak.*

penetrate
  to penetrate, go through, or pass into:
    dil.
  to penetrate, to pierce: *sinom.*
  to penetrate, to sink, to dig in: *ir-.*

penis: *kiresek, kurupdoloina.*
  penis of an infant: *sihk$_2$.*
  penis, diminutive form: *dundun$_1$.*
  penis, of an adult: *lahk, wihl$_1$.*

people
  people, person, human being,
    mankind: *aramas.*
  people of olden times: *mehn kawa.*

pepper: *peper.*
  chili pepper, *Capsicum frutescens*:
    sele.
  sp. of pepper plant, the leaves of
    which are used as a wrapping for
    betel nut: *kapwoi.*

peppery
  peppery, spicy, hot: *kerengireng.*

peppy
  active, peppy: *pwahtiet.*

perceive
  to perceive: *pehm.*

percent
  percentage, percent: *persent, piresent.*

percentage
  percentage, percent: *persent, piresent.*

perfect
  perfect, just right: *lel$_2$, leltih, pwakan.*
  precious, beautiful, perfect, fine:
    kaselel.

perform
  to cause or perform some action or
    motion: *ape$_2$, apehne.*

perfume: *leh$_1$, lehn wai.*
  oil, perfume: *kisin leh.*

perhaps
  maybe, perhaps: *sekere.*
  perhaps, maybe, possibly: *ele$_2$.*
  probably, maybe, perhaps: *mwein.*

permanent
  everlasting, constant, permanent:
    poatoapoat.

permission: *mweimwei.*

permit
  to allow or permit: *mweid$_3$,
    mweimwei.*

persevering
  diligent or persevering because of
    enthusiasm: *ngiangi.*
  faithful, persevering, single-minded,
    diligent: *loaloapwoat.*
  to be devoted, reliable, persevering:
    loalehng, loalohng.

person
  people, person, human being,
    mankind: *aramas.*
  person, Catholic biblical term, one of
    the trinity: *persona.*

perspiration
perspiration, sweat: *pwudau, pwudo.*

persuade
easily persuaded: *materek.*
to cautiously persuade: *kamantik.*

pertain
to pertain to: *pid₂.*

pesky
butt-in, pesky: *liderewes.*

pestle
pestle, for pounding breadfruit: *peinar.*

petty
petty, desirous of being correct at all times, disagreeable: *akupwung.*

Pharisee: *Parisehr.*

phlegm: *kapatau, kopatau.*

phonograph: *sikongki.*

phosphorescence: *didmwerek.*

phosphorescent
to be phosphorescent: *didmwerek.*

photograph
to photograph: *kilel, kilele.*

pick
a pick used for the ear, as a Q-tip: *mehn ersaleng.*
to choose, to pick out, to select: *pil₂, pilipil.*
to pick fruit with a pole: *pile, pilede.*
to pick leaves or flowers: *dar₂.*
to pick lice from one's own head: *liaid.*
to pick up hot rocks from an *uhmw* with a pair of sticks: *tipwa.*
to pick up, to carry, to take along: *limehda.*
to pick, as leaves or flowers: *dender.*
to pick, pull, or cut down in entirety: *amweredi.*
to pick, to remove from the stalk: *dolung, dondol.*
to select or choose from a group of animate beings, to pick out an animal: *pwinik.*
to be picked, pulled, or cut down in entirety: *emwiemwidi.*

pickaxe: *pihkahkis.*

picture
picture, snapshot: *pikser.*
sign, mark, picture, camera, movie, motion picture: *kilel.*

Pidgin
Pidgin, as Pidgin English: *pisin.*

piece
a little bit of, a small piece of, a fragment of: *epwidik.*
section, piece: *lepi-.*

pierce
to penetrate, to pierce: *sinom.*

pig: *pwihk.*
a big pig or turtle: *tihnsauriau.*
a man or pig having only one testicle: *wisolpali.*
female pig before it is bred: *mpwel₄.*
mature male pig: *wisolmat.*

pigeon: *mwuroi.*
female pigeon: *ledin.*
male pigeon: *sapa₂.*

pigheaded
pigheaded, refusing to accept advice or follow instructions: *sarongorong.*

pike
fish sp., mackerel pike: *samma.*

pile
pile: *koaskoasok, pehi₂.*
pile of debris, dump: *peinikid.*
pile of leaves or banana stems placed on the ground to cushion the fall of breadfruit being picked: *katep₁.*
to pile up: *koasok, koasoke.*

pillow: *rerinpehiso, uluhl.*
to use a pillow: *uluhl, ulung.*

pilot: *pwailet.*

pimple
pimple, acne: *maht.*

pin
pin, tack, bobbypin: *pihn.*

pinch
to pinch: *kinih, kinikin.*

pineapple
pineapple, *Ananas comosus*: *pweinaper.*

ping-pong: *pimpong.*

pink: *mpwulapwul.*

pipe
pipe, as a water pipe: *paip₂.*
pipe, for smoking: *paip₃.*
to tap ashes from a cigar, cigarette, or pipe: *loipehs.*

pistol
pistol, revolver: *pisdor.*

piston
piston, of an engine: *pisdong.*

pit
pit, area for storing preserved breadfruit: *kahlipw.*
pit, formerly the pit in the middle of the main platform of a *nahs* where a fire was kept burning from which the first of the *uhmw*s were lit: *nanparas.*

pitch
  pitch, tar: *pis.*

pitch
  in baseball, an underhand pitch:
  andasiro.

pitch-black: *rotapwahk.*

pitcher: *pissa.*

pitiful
  pitiful, saddening: *kempoake.*

pity
  emotionally moving, causing pity:
  kompoake.
  to pity: *poakehla.*

place
  place for sexual liaison: *dehu.*
  place for wrestling or fighting: *merei.*
  place of the *uhmw*: *pahpei, rahs.*
  place, point: *wasa.*
  sacred place, altar, throne: *mwoahl.*
  sandy place inside the barrier reef:
  se$_2$.
  to place a cup under the hibiscus bast
  during the process of preparing
  kava: *pel$_4$.*
  to place a wrap over one's shoulders so
  that the front of the torso is covered:
  liapwahpw.
  to place in successive order: *irekidi.*
  to place one thing across another
  thing: *loange.*
  to be placed across another thing:
  loang.
  to be placed behind one's ear, of
  flowers: *dilipek.*

placenta: *iengen seri.*

plain
  a plain, level ground: *patapat.*

plan: *pilahn.*
  organization, structure, rule, plan,
  agreement: *koasoandi.*
  wish, intention, plan, decision, desire,
  heart: *kupwur$_2$.*
  to plan: *pilahn, pilahne.*

plane
  plane, a carpenter's tool: *pilein.*
  to plane: *pilein, pileinih.*

plane
  airplane: *sompihr.*
  fighter plane: *sendohki.*

plant
  to plant: *poadok.*
  to plant yams: *sohn.*
  to be planted: *poad.*
  tree, plant, lumber, wood: *tuhke.*
  replantable part of a plant: *paki$_1$.*

plant sp.: *ihd$_2$, paiwed, tuhkehn
  kopwopwoud.*
  plant sp., *Alpinia carolinensis*: *ieuieu,
  iouiou.*
  plant sp., *Asplenium nidus*, used for
  decorating yams and kava: *tehnlik.*
  plant sp., *Celosia argentea*: *ropwen
  malek.*
  plant sp., *Clerodendrum inerme*: *ilau.*
  plant sp., *Derris elliptica*, used for
  poisoning fish: *uhp.*
  plant sp., *Enhalus acoroides*, found in
  fresh water: *oaloahdenpil.*
  plant sp., *Galeola ponapensis*, a kind
  of orchid: *lamwahk.*
  plant sp., *Lycopodium cernuum* or
  phlegmaria: *limpahr.*
  plant sp., *Plumeria rubra*, plumeria:
  pwohmaria.
  plant sp., *Selaginella kanehirae*:
  kidienmal.
  plant sp., *Tacca leontopetaloides*,
  arrow plant: *mwekimwek.*
  plant sp., *Taeniophyllum
  petrophilum*: *patehn nehn kewelik.*
  plant sp., Arabian jasmine, *Jasminum
  sambac*: *sampakihda.*
  plant sp., a flowering plant: *pauwehs.*
  plant sp., a kind of orchid: *lamwahk en
  wai.*
  plant sp., a kind of vine:
  pwoampwoamw$_1$.
  plant sp., bougainvillia: *pwukenwilia.*
  plant sp., having a sticky sap: *luwehs.*
  plant sp., the leaves of which are used
  as a spice: *kadiring.*
  plant sp., the leaves of which cause
  itching: *leles.*
  plant sp., tobacco, *Nicotrina sp.*:
  tipaker$_1$.
  plant sp., useful in starting fires: *kehid.*
  plant sp., with a pink flower:
  kehoaroahr.

plantain: *mangat.*

plantation
  clearing, field, plantation, garden,
  farm: *mwaht, mwetiwel.*

planting
  a kava planting: *kemenseng$_2$.*
  a yam planting: *pwahr, pweriniak.*
  individual planting, of any plant:
  poahd.

plastic: *pilasdik.*
  rubber, plastic: *komi, kumi.*

plate: *pileit.*
  coconut cup, dish, plate: *dahl.*

platform: *pasapas.*
  main rear platform of a feasthouse:
    lempahntamw.
  outrigger platform: *parap.*
  platform upon which the
    Nahnmwarki and *Nahnken* sit, in a
    nahs.: *mwoalehlap.*
  side platform of a *nahs*: *mwengintik.*

play
  to play: *mwadong.*
  to play a dirty trick: *pokaraun,*
    pokaraunih.
  to play cards: *pilei.*
  to play music: *keseng.*
  to play the drum: *aip.*
  to play tricks on people at a wake,
    done to cheer the family:
    tokinmoang.
  to play with: *mwadonge.*
  to play with a toy canoe or boat: *kape.*

player
  player, athlete: *sensuh, sounmwadong.*
  last player in playing marbles:
    isipangpiri.

pleasant
  amusing, pleasant, funny: *kaperen.*

please: *mahs$_3$.*

pleasure
  to take pleasure in seeing one receive
    his comeuppance: *aniket.*

pleat
  horizontal pleats in a dress: *tek.*
  to make horizontal pleats in a dress:
    teke$_2$.
  to pleat, as a dress: *ihkos.*

plentiful: *dir.*
  abundant, plentiful: *rek.*
  many, much, numerous, plentiful:
    tohto.

plenty
  season of plenty, breadfruit season:
    nanrek, rahk$_1$.

pliable
  pliable, resilient: *matamat$_1$.*

pliant: *eirek.*

pliers: *plaias, pwuraia.*
  needle nose pliers: *pensi.*

plot
  a small plot of land, a house lot:
    koakon.

pluck
  to pull out, to pluck: *us$_1$.*
  to scale or pluck: *kahwin, kahwina,*
    kauna, kederwin, kederwina.
  to pluck out whiskers: *kameimeiso.*

plum
  pickled plum: *umepwosi.*

plumeria
  plant sp., *Plumeria rubra*, plumeria:
    pwohmaria.

plywood: *peniaida.*

pocket: *pwekid.*

pocketknife: *naipokos.*

point
  place, point: *wasa.*
  to point: *id-.*
  to point at: *idih.*
  to point out, to identify: *idihada.*
  to turn or point into the wind when
    sailing: *sempwe.*
  to be pointed out, to be identified:
    idihdida.

poison: *poisin.*
  to poison fish: *uhpaup.*

poke
  to poke: *die, pwahrih.*

pole
  a line or pole placed between a yam
    planting and the branches of a tree
    in order to direct the growth of the
    yam vine upward: *kehndou.*
  fishing pole: *pwou.*
  hibiscus pole, after the bark has been
    stripped: *arepe, pwurien arepe.*
  pole for picking breadfruit: *piled.*
  pole, used to train yam vines: *palodou.*
  telephone pole: *densinpasura.*
  to paddle or pole against the wind:
    pediang.
  to pole a boat or canoe: *ketia$_2$.*

pole-vault
  to pole-vault: *pwohdaka.*

policeman: *pilisimen, pwolismasda.*

polished
  shiny, glistening, polished:
    melengileng.

polite: *akpapah.*

polygamy: *pekehi.*

pomade: *pahro.*

pompano
  fish sp., pompano, *Selar*
    crumenopthalmus: *pedihdi.*

Ponape: *Pohnpei, Pohnpeiuh.*

pond: *kisin leh.*
  pool, pond, puddle: *lepin pil.*

pool
  pool of money, the combined wagers
    of betters: *mwusing.*
  pool, lake: *leh$_2$.*
  pool, pond, puddle: *lepin pil.*

pool
lightbulb, bullet, pool ball: *dama.*
the game of pool: *damaski.*
to play pool: *damaski.*

poor: *semwehmwe.*

pop
to pop, as a balloon: *kapose.*

pope: *pahpa sarawi.*

popsicle
popsicle, frozen confection: *aiskehki.*

popular
very popular, of a person: *tantal.*

porch: *kengkang, palangk.*

porcupine fish
fish sp., porcupine fish: *sei$_2$.*

porgy
fish sp., a mature sweetlips porgy,
Plectorhynchus celebicus: *koail.*
fish sp., an immature sweetlips porgy,
Plectorhynchus celebicus: *kakerepil.*
fish sp., sweetlips porgy,
Plectorhynchus goldmani or
Plectorhynchus chaetodontoides:
kehng.

pork
pig, swine, pork: *pwihk.*

porpoise: *laidiniki.*

portion: *irair.*

portrait: *sansal.*

Portugal: *Pwohtiki.*

Portuguese man-of-war
Portuguese man-of-war, the jellyfish:
lilikoio.

possess
of a spirit, to possess or inhabit a
human body: *ti.*
to possess, to draw interest, of money:
neitik.

possession
thing, possession: *kepwe.*

possibly
perhaps, maybe, possibly: *ele$_2$.*

post: *uhr$_2$.*
central post of a *nahs*: *keidu.*

post office: *pwohsdo.*

poster: *sansal.*
signature, poster, sign, notice: *sain.*

postpone
to postpone or cancel: *kapwowiala.*
to postpone: *kasau.*
to be postponed: *kosou, pweula.*

pot: *kama$_1$.*
cooking pot: *ainpwoat.*

potato
potato, sweet potato *Ipomea batatas*:
pedehde.

potion
a love potion or charm: *mesehl.*

pound
to pound: *suk.*
to pound food: *lihli.*
to pound or press something into a
thick, heavy mass: *kangid.*
to pound with rhythmical beats prior
to the pounding of kava: *pedidi.*
to rhythmically pound a kava stone:
tempel.
to rhythmically pound a kava stone
after the kava is prepared: *sokamah.*
to rhythmically pound a kava stone at
the beginning of the kava ceremony:
reidi.

pound: *paun.*

pour
to pour: *wideki.*
to pour in: *koadia.*
to be poured: *widek.*

pout
to pout: *eikek.*

powder
baby powder: *osiroi.*
powder of any kind: *paute.*
powder of any kind, tooth powder or
tooth paste: *kona.*

power
magic, mysterious or spiritual power:
manaman.
said of one who shows off his power or
strength: *angkehlail.*
to make a display of magic, spiritual
power, or authority: *akmanaman.*

powerful
strong, powerful, healthy: *kehlail.*

powerless
a kind of magic used to render
powerless one's opponent in a fight:
rihpe.

practice
practice, rehearsal: *sosohng.*
to practice for an athletic event, to
warm up for an athletic event:
rensuh.

practitioner
practitioner of: *soun.*
practitioner of native Ponapean
medicine: *sounwini.*

praise
to praise: *kepinga.*

pray
to pray: *kapakap₁, kasakas, loulou.*
to worship, to pray: *kaudok.*

prayer: *kapakap₁, kasakas, loulou.*
worship, religion, prayer: *kaudok.*

preach
to preach: *padahk.*

preacher: *sounpadahk.*

precede
to go first, to precede: *tieng.*

precinct
district, precinct: *lopidi.*

precious
precious, beautiful, perfect, fine: *kaselel.*

predict
to predict the success of an activity while it is still in progress, believed to bring bad luck: *sepwere.*
to predict with the assistance of magic: *doaropwehda.*

pregnant: *liseian.*
to become pregnant: *ahpada.*

prejudice
to influence or prejudice another's opinion: *kapihdi.*

prepare
to prepare: *kaunop-.*
to prepare a small informal feast or party: *ainpwoat.*
to prepare an *uhmw*, so that it is ready to be lit: *soumaleu.*
to prepare food in a pot: *ainpwoat.*
to prepare food with grated coconut, to mix things together: *uter, utere.*
to prepare, to get ready: *onopada.*
to study, to prepare: *onop.*

present
gift, present, prize: *kisakis.*
to give a gift, present, or prize: *kisakis, kisikise.*

preserved breadfruit: *mahr₁.*
old preserved breadfruit: *maradahn.*
preserved breadfruit soaked in salt water prior to placing it in the pit: *maresed.*

press
to pound or press something into a thick, heavy mass: *kangid.*
to press or iron: *kadangada.*
to squeeze or press, to push, as a switch: *padik.*
to be pressed, to be ironed: *kedengida.*
to be squeezed or pressed, to be pushed, as a switch: *ped.*

pressure
to apply pressure to, to mash: *idang.*
to be under pressure, to be mashed: *idaid.*

pretend
to pretend: *mwomwehda.*

pretentious: *lioasoahs.*
pretentious, proud, boastful: *kerkala, maskala.*

pretty
good-looking, pretty, handsome: *masamwahu.*

priest
a traditional high priest: *Samworo, Soumwaroh.*
a traditional lesser priest: *Laiap.*
Catholic priest: *pahdire.*

prison
jail, prison: *imweteng, kalapwuhs.*

prisoner: *kalapwuhs.*

prissy: *malangalang.*

prize
gift, present, prize: *kisakis.*
to give a gift, present, or prize: *kisakis, kisikise.*

probably
probably, maybe, perhaps: *mwein.*

probation
parole, probation: *parohl.*
to parole, to place on probation: *parohlih.*
to be on parole or probation: *parohl.*

probe
to feel around for, when unable to see an object, to grope around for, to probe for: *dehm.*
to probe: *erier.*
to probe the earth to find yams: *nsoange.*
to stir, to probe: *arih.*

problem
undesirable result, problem, difficulty: *kahpwal.*

proceed
an interrogative verb meaning 'to proceed by what means': *ed-.*

procession
a march or a procession: *kapar.*

profit: *wihn.*
to profit: *wihn.*

program
program, especially a radio program: *pwurokiram.*

progress
to grow up, to progress: *keirida.*

prohibit
to forbid or prohibit something taboo
or illegal: *inapwih.*
to prohibit: *keinapwih.*
to be prohibited: *keinepwi.*

prominence
the prominence of anything: *pwuki.*

promise
contract, promise, agreement,
covenant: *inou₁.*
to promise: *inou₁, pilerehre.*

promoted
to be exalted, to be promoted:
lapalapala.

promotion: *kesepwil.*

proof
final proof: *kamehlel.*

prop
to prop: *utung.*
to be propped: *utuht.*

propeller: *pirepira.*

proper
appropriate, proper: *konehng.*

property
a piece of property: *lain.*

prophesy
to prophesy: *kohp.*

prophet: *soukohp.*

propitiator: *sountomw.*

proposal
bill, proposal, in legislative
proceedings: *mwomwadahn
kosonned.*

prosecution
the prosecution, a court term: *pelien
kadip.*

prosecutor
prosecutor, accuser, tattletale:
sounkadip.

prostitute
prostitute, used biblically: *liedipan.*

protect
to protect: *uhpoar.*

protection: *pere.*
magical protection against another's
harmful magic, medicine, or spirits:
silasil.
protector, protection: *poadoarepe₁.*

protective
protective, mother-hen-like: *lirohro.*

protector
protector, protection: *poadoarepe₁.*

Protestant: *Prohs.*

protrude
to protrude: *sik-, tikelekelada.*

protruding
puffed out, protruding, as of the
stomach: *wed.*

protrusion
the angular protrusion on either end of
the hull of a Ponapean canoe:
salenge.

proud
pretentious, proud, boastful: *kerkala,
maskala.*
proud, competitive, unwilling to be
humbled: *akutuhwahu.*
proud, self-assertive, cocky: *aklapalap.*
proud, with a negative connotation:
pohnmwahso.

proverb
saying, proverb: *lepin kahs.*

provide
to provide a source of light for:
sere₂.
to provide bedding or clothing for
someone: *kinte.*
to provide food: *kamweng.*
to provide food to be prepared in the
uhmw at a *kamadipw*: *kaneng en
uhmw.*

provisions
provisions taken on a trip: *kepinwar,
ngke₂.*

prowl
to prowl: *wai₁.*

pry
to pry out: *kapit₂, kepit₁.*
to pry out, to pry off, as a nail or
bottle cap: *pwisik.*
to uproot, to peel, to pry: *sarek₃.*

pubic hair: *wakar.*

puckered
puckered up, of the mouth as after
eating unripe bananas: *reirei₂.*

puddle: *lehn pwelmatak, pahd₁,
pedenpil.*
pool, pond, puddle: *lepin pil.*

puffed
puffed out, protruding, as of the
stomach: *wed.*
swollen or puffed up as a consequence
of a wound or blow: *pwuwalok.*

puffer fish
fish sp., puffer fish: *wahd.*

pull
to pull: *waik.*
to pull apart, to pull off: *dapeng.*
to pull down an eyelid, a lip, or the
foreskin of the penis: *kirehdi.*
to pull each other's hair, as in a fight:
pidilin.

to pull hair, as in a fight: *dilin.*
to pull in a net: *kom.*
to pull out, to pluck: *us₁.*
to pull something, usually with a rope: *apih.*
to pull, to drag: *ruwahdeki, urahdeki.*
to push or pull with a stick or the feet: *die.*
to pick, pull, or cut down in entirety: *amweredi.*
to draw out, to pull out, of any string-like object: *air.*
to cut or pull grass: *mwatih, mwet.*
to be picked, pulled, or cut down in entirety: *emwiemwidi.*
to be pulled apart, to be pulled off: *dap-.*
to be pulled, to be dragged: *ruwahdek, urahdek.*
to be pulled, usually with a rope: *ep.*
of fruit, to be pulled down with a stick: *diedihdi.*

pulley
pulley, block, of a block and tackle: *piloak.*

pulverized
pulverized, crushed, mashed: *mwut.*

pumice: *wahnpei.*

pump
to pump: *pwoamwih.*
to be pumped: *pwoamw.*

pumpkin: *pwengkin.*

punch: *pilakai.*
punch, boxing: *paker.*
to punch: *paker, pakere, pilakai.*
to throw or punch forcefully: *likimwei, mweilik.*

punish
to punish: *kaloke.*
to be punished: *kalokolok.*
to be fined, to be punished: *pakking.*

punishment: *kalokolok, oudek.*
fine, punishment: *pakking.*

pupil
pupil, of the eye: *limarepeileng.*

pure
virgin, pure, undefiled: *meipwon.*

purgatory: *pwurkadorio.*

purple: *pohn ntahn mwell.*

purpose
cause, reason, purpose: *kahrepe.*
foundation, purpose: *poahsoan.*

purse
basket, purse, handbag: *kopwou, kupwu.*
wallet, purse, valise: *pilihs.*

pursue
to follow, to go after, to pursue, to obey: *idawehn.*

pus: *nahn₂.*
a pus filled infection: *kepinan.*
full of pus, pussy: *kepinan.*

push
to push: *pwuhs₂, siken.*
to push each other: *pisiken.*
to push or pull with a stick or the feet: *die.*
to push with one's foot: *pahd₂.*
to squeeze or press, to push, as a switch: *padik.*
to be squeezed or pressed, to be pushed, as a switch: *ped.*

pussy
full of pus, pussy: *kepinan.*

put
to assemble, to put together: *kakonehda.*
to bury, to put in a safe place: *nekidedi.*
to put aside, of one's beliefs or emotions: *pwil₁.*
to put down: *pwil₁.*
to put on dry clothes: *kemmad, kiemmad.*
to save, keep, store, put away: *nekidala.*
to store, to put away: *nekinek.*
to be put aside, of one's beliefs or emotions: *pwilidi.*
to be put down: *pwilidi.*

putting on airs
putting on airs, showing off: *kakko, wampwe.*

putty: *pwati.*

quadrangle
quadrangle, square: *permasepeng.*

quadrangular
to be quadrangular, to be square: *permasepeng.*

quality
inner quality, of a person: *soar.*

quarrel
argument, quarrel, dispute: *akamai.*
to argue, to quarrel: *akamai.*
to growl or snarl, to quarrel: *ngiringir.*

querulous
querulous, critical: *kaulim.*

question: *peidek.*
to ask about, to inquire, to question: *kadeik.*
to be questioned: *pakadeik.*

question mark: *kilel en peidek.*

quick
  quick, in motion: *dahr.*
  quick, in performing an action: *setik.*
  to go fast, to be quick, to hurry:
    mwadang.

quickly
  quickly, suddenly: *mwadangete.*

quiet
  desiring peace and quiet while under
    the influence of kava: *kahka.*
  quiet, not talkative, passive in a
    confrontation: *sepeimwekid.*
  quiet, silent: *nennen.*
  to be or become quiet: *tetempala.*

quilt
  patchwork quilt: *tehi mweinlikou.*

rabbit: *rapit.*

rabbitfish
  fish sp., rabbitfish, *Siganus
    canaliculatus*: *umwule.*
  fish sp., rabbitfish, *Siganus
    corallinus*: *seteu.*
  fish sp., rabbitfish, *Siganus doliatus*:
    kioak, pwerinmwomw.
  fish sp., rabbitfish, *Siganus puellus*:
    mahr$_2$.
  fish sp., rabbitfish, *Siganus
    punctatus*: *palapal.*
  fish sp., rabbitfish, *Siganus vulpinus*:
    kompani.

rabid
  ferocious, rabid: *lipes.*

race
  a race in which a number of
    participants straddle a pole and run
    together: *weirin meninrahn.*
  a race in which the participant runs on
    all fours: *weirin kerep.*
  a race which involves eating a
    doughnut suspended from a string:
    weirin kang donas.
  a swimming race: *weirin pap.*
  a three-legged race: *weirin pirene.*
  a wheelbarrow race: *weirin wilpahro.*
  to race: *weir$_2$.*
  to run a race: *weirin tang.*
  to run a relay race: *rerei.*

rack
  to rack, as in pool: *rak.*

radio: *redio.*
  radio transmission, telegram:
    dempwo$_2$.
  to send a radio transmission or
    telegram: *dempwo-.*

radio station
  wireless station, radio station: *wasahn
    wailes.*

radish: *daikong.*
  pickled radish: *dakuwang.*

raffle
  election, raffle, lottery: *usuhs.*

raft
  raft, barge: *rahp.*

rafter: *reulap.*
  a minor rafter to which pieces of
    thatch are attached: *rahu.*
  beam or rafter of a roof: *rehu.*

rail: *rehl.*

rain: *keteu.*
  to rain: *keteu.*

rainbow: *ahia, iahia.*

raise
  to erect, to raise: *kau$_1$.*
  to be erected, to be raised: *kokou.*

rake: *rehki.*
  to rake: *rehki.*

rank
  rank or station: *dehu.*

rap
  to knock or rap: *letelet, leteng.*

rape
  to rape: *angkehlail.*

rapid
  to move rapidly: *meliek.*

rascal
  thief, murderer, rascal: *loallap.*

rash: *pwudong.*

rat
  rat, mouse: *kitik.*

ration: *aikiu.*
  to ration: *aikiu, aikiuih.*

rattan
  rattan, *Flagellaria indica*: *idahnwel.*

ravine
  hollow, ravine: *mweid$_2$.*

raw
  alive, raw: *mour$_2$.*
  raw fish, raw meat of any kind: *sasimi.*
  raw, uncooked: *amas.*
  to eat raw: *wet$_2$, wete.*

ray
  a large ray: *pehpoahrok.*
  manta ray: *pehwehwe.*
  stingray: *likendinkep.*

ray-like
  ray-like, fanning, kinky: *sirang.*
  ray-like, pointing in all directions:
    sirangarang.

razor: *reise.*
 razor blade: *reise.*

reach
 to reach for: *eng-.*
 to reach or arrive at: *lel₁.*

read
 to read: *wadawad₁, wadek₁.*

realize
 to make someone realize his mistake:
 kapehme.
 to suddenly realize: *saliokda.*

really: *apw.*
 certainly, really, definitely, truly:
 uhdahn.
 really, indeed: *pwa₁.*

reason
 cause, reason, purpose: *kahrepe.*
 to cause, to be the reason for:
 kahrehda.

reassemble
 to reassemble: *kakonepene.*

recall
 to recall the past history of: *kadaur₁.*
 to recall, to remember: *taman.*
 to trace one's ancestry, to recall past
 history: *kadoudou, kodoudou.*

receipt: *risiht.*

receive
 to be awarded or to receive votes, a
 degree, title, etc.: *alehdi.*

reckless
 daring, reckless, bold, adventurous:
 loallap.

recline
 to lie, to recline: *wen-.*

recognize
 to recognize: *kilelehdi.*

recollect
 to remember or recollect: *kataman.*

recollection: *kataman.*
 memorial, recollection, souvenir:
 ketemenpe.

reconciliation
 reconciliation, forgiveness: *tohmw.*
 to seek reconciliation or forgiveness:
 tomw.

record
 record, a sound recording: *pilat₁,
 rekohdo.*
 to record something with a tape
 recorder: *deipih.*
 to record with a tape recorder: *deip.*

recover
 to recover, to grow healthy after an
 illness: *tihnain.*

recreation
 game, recreation, drama: *mwadong.*

rectangle: *keimwpahieu.*

rectangular
 to be rectangular: *keimwpahieu.*

red: *weitahta.*
 reddened, of the skin: *pwukapwuk.*

red snapper
 fish sp., red snapper, *Lutjanus
 bohar*: *kihr en eiwel.*

reduce
 to reduce in number: *kamalaulawih.*
 to be reduced in number: *kamalaulau.*

reduction: *kamalaulau.*

reed sp.
 reed sp., *Miscanthus floridulus*:
 sapeleng.
 reed sp., *Phragmites karka*: *rahu.*
 reed sp., *Saccharum spontaneum*, used
 as a building material and for
 medicinal purposes: *ahlek.*
 reed sp., a variety of *ahlek* with
 reddish spots on the stem:
 litokmwanger.
 reed sp., used for weaving: *lirau.*

reef: *mad₁, oht.*
 barrier reef: *pahina.*
 deep place within the barrier reef,
 lagoon: *nehnamw.*
 edge of a reef: *mese.*
 reef, deep below the surface, but
 visible: *ohio.*
 reef, with many large stones or coral
 heads protruding above the surface
 of the water: *nahri.*

refill
 to refill: *audsapahl.*

reflection
 to see one's own reflection: *iroir,
 irong.*

refrigerator
 icebox, refrigerator: *aispwoaks.*

refurbish
 to refurbish or make like new again:
 kapwala.

refusal
 denial, initial refusal out of politeness:
 kahmahm.
 insincere in the refusal of food,
 prompted by the dictates of
 hospitality: *kamadamad.*

refuse
 to dislike, to refuse: *kahng₁.*
 to politely refuse an offer: *soik.*
 to refuse to obey: *sipwe.*

region
region, large area of land: *pwallap.*

rehearsal
practice, rehearsal: *sosohng.*

reheat
to reheat, to warm over, as food: *pehl₁, pehle.*

reign
reign, era: *mwehi.*

related
to be related: *peneinei.*
to be siblings: *pirien.*

relation
to, toward, in relation to, for: *-ehng,*
-ieng, ong.

relationship
the relationship that exists between an
individual and the clan of his father's
father: *wahnmwahng.*

relative
family, relative: *peneinei.*

relax
to relax a wire or stick under tension:
kapit₂, kepit₁.

relay
to run a relay race: *rerei.*

release
to let go, to release: *kadar.*
to release: *lapwahda, pweisang.*
to be let go, to be released: *pekeder.*
to be released: *lapwada.*

reliable: *lelepek.*
to be devoted, reliable, persevering:
loalehng, loalohng.

relieve
to relieve another of his burden:
sarek₂.
to relieve oneself, to defecate or
urinate: *kotala.*
to be relieved, to be free from
encumbrances: *maiauda, maiouda.*

relieved
free, relieved, unrestrained, licentious:
saledek.

religion
worship, religion, prayer: *kaudok.*

religious
religious belief: *lamalam.*
religious service: *sarawi.*

reluctant
to be reluctant about: *toutouki.*

rely
to depend on someone or something,
to rely on, with ill consequence:
wahkihla.

remain
to remain aboard a boat or canoe
while others are diving for fish:
koluwar.
to remain overnight, to go to bed, to
bed down: *pweidi, pweiekidi.*

remaining
the one remaining: *luhwe.*

remains
remains, remnant: *luhwe.*

remember
to recall, to remember: *taman.*
to remember or recollect: *kataman.*

remind
to remind: *katamaniki.*
to warn, to remind: *kaunop-.*

reminder: *mehn kataman.*

remnant
remains, remnant: *luhwe.*
remnant of cloth: *pingin likou.*
remnants, small pieces of cloth:
mweinlikou.

remove
to pick, to remove from the stalk:
dolung, dondol.
to remove a yam by cutting it below
the vine so that another yam will
develop: *kapwude.*
to remove gray hair: *uskomwkomw,*
uspwetepwet.
to remove some part of something so
that it is no longer whole or
complete: *kaluwanda.*
to remove whiskers: *usalis.*
to remove, as covers, lids, tops, etc.:
waka.
to be removed, of covers, lids, tops,
etc.: *wak₁.*

repair
to make, to repair, to build: *wiahda.*
to repair, to fix: *apehne.*
to mend or repair, used principally
with native objects: *one.*
to be mended or repaired, used
principally with native objects:
onohn.

repay
to repay, to give back in recompense
or reply: *dupuk.*
to pay tribute, to repay a service or
good deed: *isais, ise.*

repeat
to repeat: *pwurehng.*
to repeat an activity: *sapahl.*

repent
to repent: *keluhla, koluhla.*

repentance: *koluhla.*

repentant
  to be repentant: *wiliakapwala.*

replace
  to change, to substitute, to replace:
    wilian.
  to be changed, to be substituted, to be
    replaced: *wiliali.*

replacement
  replacement, representative: *wiliepe.*

replantable
  replantable part of a plant: *paki₁.*

report
  to bring to the attention of an
    authority, to report: *leleki.*

repound
  to repound kava: *kapwur, kapwure.*
  to repound kava with a small stone:
    kapwur moahl.
  to repound kava with the fist: *kapwur
    peh.*

representative
  replacement, representative: *wiliepe.*

reprimand
  to scold or reprimand: *kidahwe.*

reputation
  having a bad reputation: *adsuwed.*
  having a good reputation: *adamwahu.*

request
  to ask for, to request: *peki.*
  to make an insincere request for
    assistance: *koasoamwoasoamw.*
  to request: *kamangaida.*
  to request permission to leave:
    sakarada.
  to request, to ask a favor, to beg:
    pekipek.

require
  to need, to require: *anahne.*

requisition: *pekipek.*

rescue
  to rescue, to loose an animal or a
    person: *kapit₃.*

resent
  to resent something, as a critism or a
    jest taken seriously: *akupwungki.*

reserved
  reserved, containing one's feelings for
    fear of self-embarrassment or
    embarrassing others, constrained in
    one's action by a social situation,
    formal in one's relations with others:
    mahk₁.

reside
  to reside: *kousoan.*

residence: *kousoan.*
  to take up residence in: *towehla.*

residue: *uwe₂.*
  residue at the bottom of a cup of kava:
    mwoarok en sakau.

resilient
  pliable, resilient: *matamat₁.*

resist
  to resist: *pelianda.*

resound
  to resound: *ngirisek.*

respect
  respect, honor: *wahu.*
  biblically, to show respect, to honor:
    kahka.
  lacking respect: *sohwawi.*
  not respected: *mwamwahl.*

respectable
  respectful, respectable, honorable:
    waun.

respectful
  low, respectful, humble: *karakarahk.*
  obedient, respectful: *peik₂.*
  respectful, respectable, honorable:
    waun.

respond
  to respond to, to answer: *sapeng.*
  to respond, to answer: *pasapeng.*

response
  response, answer: *pasapeng.*

responsibility: *pwais, pwukepe.*
  occupation, task, employment,
    responsibility, deed: *doahk.*
  responsibility, obligation, duty:
    pwukoa.

responsible
  to be responsible for immoral
    behavior: *dipaniki.*
  to be responsible for providing
    something or doing a task:
    pweisaniki.

rest
  to rest: *kommoal, nanmwoalehdi,
    rahnmwoalehdi.*

restaurant: *imwen mwenge.*

restless: *lokalok, selitilit.*
  restless, with reference to a child:
    lierikik.

result: *wah.*
  result of one's work: *menginpeh.*
  undesirable result, problem, difficulty:
    kahpwal.

resurrected
  to be risen, to be resurrected, used
    biblically: *iasada.*

retarded
crazy, mad, mentally retarded:
kisingai.
mentally ill or retarded: *sahliel.*

retract
to insert or retract: *kapwad.*

retrieve
to retrieve from a hole with one's
hand: *pwadik₁.*

return
to return: *pwur, sapahl.*
to return an action in kind: *kasapahl.*
to return from fishing: *pas₁.*
to return to the wild state, of animals:
arewella.

reveal
to reveal: *kapwadala.*
to reveal verbally: *ketia₁, ketihti.*
to confess, to reveal, to disclose: *wehk.*

revelation
revelation, used biblically: *koudiahl.*

reverberate
of a sound, to reverberate: *duhr.*

reverse
to put in reverse, of a vehicle:
kosdang.

revitalize
to revitalize: *ketihna.*
to revitalize, to nourish: *ketihnain.*

revolver
pistol, revolver: *pisdor.*

reward
cost, wage, reward: *pweipwei₂.*
payment or reward: *keting.*
tribute, gift, reward: *isais.*

rheumatism
arthritis, rheumatism:
nankoakonmedek.

rib: *tihn kopwou.*
main rib of the stem of a palm frond:
nohk.

ribbon
ribbon, lace: *repen₂.*
tape, braid, ribbon for sewing: *teip.*

rice: *rais.*
rice paddy: *dampwo.*

rich
rich, wealthy, having many possessions:
kepwehpwe.
to make one rich: *kepeiahda.*

rid
to throw away, to get rid of: *kesehla.*

riddle: *kahk₂.*
to ask a riddle: *kahk₂.*

ride
to catch a ride with: *lusuk.*

to ride a bicycle: *pwaisikel.*
to ride in or on a vehicle: *dake₁.*

ridge
ridge area of a house or land: *pweleng.*
top, peak, summit, ridge: *koadoke.*

ridge cap: *pwarapwar.*

ridgepole
ridgepole of a building: *soahrong.*

right
correct, right, just: *pwung₁.*
justice, right: *pwuhng.*
perfect, just right: *lel₂, leltih, pwakan.*
right side: *palimaun.*
right?: *kaud.*

right field
right field, in baseball: *raido.*

right-handed
to be right-handed: *maun.*

ring
to ring, as a bell: *seker.*
to ring, of one's ears: *dengng.*
to ring, to bump into: *sek.*
to ring a bell: *leser.*
to be rung, of a bell: *les₂.*

ring
ring, as for the finger: *rihng.*
to put a ring in an animals's nose:
deitimw.

ringing
to cause a ringing in one's ears: *duhr.*

rinse
to rinse one's mouth, to gargle:
dawado, mwukumwuk.

rip
to rip open: *wehdpeseng.*

ripe: *mah.*
almost ripe, as of bananas and
mangoes: *merimer.*
almost ripe, ready to harvest:
seringiring.
ripe, before the stage called *mat*:
kanu.
ripe, overripe, rotten, spoiled, decayed:
mat.
ripe, ready to eat, of fruit: *matenei.*
to let get ripe: *kamat.*

rise
rise, low hill: *mpwoampw.*
to rise or flood, of a stream: *pwil₂.*
to rise, as of bread: *mpwosada.*
to rise, of the sun and the moon: *dak.*
to rise, of the tide: *id₂.*
to be risen, to be resurrected, used
biblically: *iasada.*

rising
  of a stream, rising and fast flowing:
    ahdomour.
ritual
  a traditional ritual to maintain the
    fertility of the soil: *pwungen sahpw.*
  ancient Ponapean rituals, of a mystical
    nature: *dikedik en eni.*
river: *pillap.*
roach: *koll, kull.*
road
  road, street, trail, path, line: ahl_1.
  main road, usually one for vehicular
    traffic: *allap.*
roast
  to cook, roast, broil, toast, etc.: *inihn.*
rock
  stone, rock: *takai.*
rock slide: *rengk.*
rocket: *sopin nanwehwe.*
rocky
  rocky area: *mweli.*
roguish: *pwidingeu.*
roll
  to roll: *dahr.*
  to roll a cigarette: pid_1.
  to roll a toy wheel: *kadahr.*
  to roll, of objects too heavy to lift: *uke.*
  to roll, often of heavy objects: *tapwur.*
  to slide or roll, as a toy wheel:
    kadahre.
  to be rolled over, of inanimate objects:
    piruwek.
  of a dog, to roll in something rotten:
    wisoar.
roof
  area below the peak of a roof:
    mweleng.
  roof of the mouth: *ngetengete.*
  roof, thatch: $oahs_1$.
  to finish roofing a house, accompanied
    by a feast: *dadimai.*
  to roof a building: *ngkad.*
  to roof a building with thatch: *ngked.*
roofing
  tin roofing: *oasmete, pelien mete.*
room: *pere.*
roomy: *maledek.*
rooster: $kihng_1$.
root: *kaleu, kalo.*
  hair roots of kava: *kamwetel.*
  hanging roots, as of a banyan tree:
    kik_1.
  newly sprouted roots: kik_1.
  roots of kava or of the wild yam,
    kehpineir: *sarang.*

upright breather roots of the
    mangrove tree: *tuh.*
root
  to root, as a pig: *dehk, deidei.*
  to root, while looking for something:
    sarip, $senser_1$.
rope
  a jump rope: *epini.*
  boom sheet, sail rope: lih_3.
  rope used for tying boats or canoes:
    poudek.
  rope, cord, line, string: *sahl.*
rosary: *rosario.*
  to say the rosary: *rosario.*
rotten
  ripe, overripe, rotten, spoiled, decayed:
    mat.
  rotten egg: *pweisenwair.*
  rotten, of fruit: *mwokuhr.*
  rotten, of wood: *mwasod, mwosod.*
rough
  bumpy, rough, not smooth:
    mwangaingai.
round: *pwonopwon.*
  a round of kava: *lakohn.*
rounds
  to make the rounds: *raun.*
row: $kahng_2$.
  mounded row, as in a garden: *une.*
  row, always appears with the construct
    suffix: *kah-.*
royalty: *oloiso.*
rub
  to rub: *iris.*
  to rub to make a fire: $iding_2$.
  to rub, to massage: el_1, *eliel.*
  to caress, to rub, to pat affectionately:
    damwer, demwidemw.
  to kiss, to rub noses: $mehn_2$, *mpoake.*
  to be rubbed: *irisek.*
rubber
  rubber, plastic: *komi, kumi.*
rucksack: *ruksaku.*
rude
  impertinent, rude: *mwomwawas.*
  rude, discourteous: *serekeileng.*
rug: *pingin likou.*
ruin
  ruin, damage, wound: *ohla.*
  to break, to destroy, to ruin: *kawehla.*
  to be broken, ruined, destroyed,
    spoiled: *ohla.*
ruins
  scar, trace, ruins: *mowe.*

rule
  organization, structure, rule, plan,
    agreement: *koasoandi.*
  to boss, to rule, to lead, to direct:
    kaun.

ruler
  ruler, boss, leader, director: *kaun.*
  ruler, for measuring: *ruhl.*
  ruler, tape measure: *mehn sohng.*

rum: *roam.*

rumble
  to rumble, as of one's stomach:
    kioaroahr.

rumor
  talk, discussion, rumor, story, adage,
    parable: *koasoai.*
  to make up a lie, to start a rumor:
    kinehda.
  to start a rumor: *kakonehda.*

run
  to run: *kereu, tang.*
  to run a one hundred meter dash:
    iakumehda.
  to run a relay race: *rerei.*
  to run aground: *ser$_2$.*
  to run off with a woman, to elope:
    sopohla.
  to run or swim the final lap in a race:
    kesso.
  to run the hurdles: *kepir meliek.*
  to run to: *tenge.*
  to run, as of water: *ker$_1$.*
  to run, said of a machine: *lallal.*

runners
  of a yam vine, to put out runners in all
    directions: *kepeira.*

runny
  runny, of colors in materials: *reirei$_2$.*

runt
  runt, of a litter: *kapwer.*

rush
  to hurry, to rush: *keruwa.*
  hurried, rushed: *karuwaru.*

rusty
  rusty, corroded: *mer.*

Sabbath
  Sunday, Sabbath: *Rahn en Sapwad.*

sack
  bag, sack: *ehd$_2$.*

sacred
  holy, sacred: *sarawi.*
  sacred place, altar, throne: *mwoahl.*
  anything peculiarly sacred: *likamisik.*

sacrifice
  sacrifice, offering, contribution:
    meiroang.

sad: *kapahtou.*
  sad-looking: *massuwed.*
  sad, sorry: *nsensuwed.*

saddening
  pitiful, saddening: *kempoake.*

sadness: *nsensuwed.*

safe
  safe, cash box: *kingko.*
  to be safe, in baseball: *sehp.*

sail
  a sail: *serek.*
  to lower a sail: *lil.*
  to sail: *serek.*
  to sail with the outrigger lifted from
    the water: *neidam.*

sailfish
  fish sp., swordfish, sailfish, blue marlin:
    dekilahr.

sailor: *sehla.*

saint: *aramas sarawi.*

saliva: *pilen dawas, pilen ewe, tenihrlap.*

salt: *soahl.*

salt water: *rensed.*

salvage
  to salvage: *kapit$_3$.*

same
  to be the same: *duwepenehte.*
  to be the same as: *ras$_1$.*
  to be the same as, to be identical to:
    duwehte.
  to become the same as: *duwehla.*

sand: *pihk.*

sandpaper: *sandepehpa.*

sandy: *pikapik.*

sardine: *saip.*

sash
  bellyband, sash: *arimaki.*

sassy
  sassy, impudent, saucy: *pwisirek.*

Satan
  Satan, devil: *Sehdan.*

sated
  to be sated, to have had it with
    something or someone: *lokala.*

satisfied
  to be satisfied: *lik$_2$.*

saturated
  saturated with pomade or hair lotion:
    sopw.
  to be saturated: *so.*

Saturday: *Nikaunop, Rahn Kaunop.*

saucy
  sassy, impudent, saucy: *pwisirek.*

save
  to save from harm: *doare.*

to save, keep, store, put away:
nekidala.

savior: *soundoar, sounkomour.*

saw: *rasaras.*
to saw: *rasaras, rese.*

sawdust: *dipen rasaras.*

say
to say: *dene, nda, paud₂, pwa₂.*
to say good things about someone:
kamwahwih.
to say something under one's breath:
ingitingkihdi.
to say something very fast:
waderekerek.
to say, to see: *idawarih, mahsanih.*

saying
saying, proverb: *lepin kahs.*

scale
to scale or pluck: *kahwin, kahwina,
kauna, kederwin, kederwina.*

scalp: *kilin moange.*

scapegoat
to be a scapegoat: *kangidirawi.*

scar: *mohn ohla.*
a large scar by the mouth caused by
yaws: *auselpat.*
a scar by the mouth caused by yaws:
aupwet.
a scar inflicted to demonstrate one's
manhood: *lekelek.*
light colored scar: *pwet₁.*
scar, trace, ruins: *mowe.*
scarred: *pat₂.*
scarred around the mouth by yaws:
aupwet.
scarred at the corner of the mouth by
yaws: *kepwilipwet.*
scarred severely around the mouth by
yaws: *auselpat.*

scarcity
scarcity, famine: *isol.*
season of scarcity, when yams and
breadfruit are not bearing: *nanisol.*

scare
to scare: *kamasak.*
to scare off: *kalawahda.*
to scare someone by surprising him:
kapwuhr.

scavenge
to scavenge, of people: *likidere.*

scavenger-like: *likidar.*

school
crowd, fleet, school of fish: *polo.*
school of fish: *ririnmwomw.*
of fish, to school during spawning
season: *dahr.*

school: *sukuhl.*
to attend school: *sukuhl.*

schoolhouse: *imwen sukuhl.*

scissors: *siset.*

scold
to scold: *lipwoar, lipwoare.*
to scold or reprimand: *kidahwe.*
to be angry at, to scold: *angiangih.*

scoop
to scoop out: *touk, toutou₂.*

scooter
scooter, motorcycle: *odopai, skuhder.*

score: *deng₂.*

scorpion: *eskorpion, ikimwang.*

scramble
to scramble, to put out of order: *kied.*

scrape
to scrape the surface of something:
kalupwur, koalupwulupw.
to scrape together and pick up a pile
of something, such as dirt, kava, etc.:
oare, oaroahr₁.
to scrape together with the hands:
koahre₂.
to scrape, as the meat out of a
coconut: *korehd, koroiroi.*

scratch
to scratch with the fingernails: *rakih,
rekirek.*
to scratch, as of a chicken: *senser₁.*
to scratch, as when itching: *karipwude,
keripwud.*
to scratch, in pool: *sukuras.*

scream
to shout, to scream, to howl, to yell, to
holler: *wer.*
to shout, to scream, to howl, to yell, to
holler at: *wering.*

screen: *ami, sukrihn.*
to cover, to screen from view: *pere.*

screw: *sukuru.*

screwdriver: *skrudraipa.*

scum
foam, scum: *pwudopwud.*

sea
ocean, sea: *nansed, sehd.*
ocean, sea, as the Pacific Ocean, or the
Philippine Sea: *lepin sed.*

sea anemone
sea anemone sp.: *limwadong.*

sea cucumber
sp. of sea cucumber: *katop, kemed,
koid, loangon, madep, penipen,
werer.*

sea level: *iren sehd.*

sea urchin: *lidik.*
   small black sp. of sea urchin: *peipei₁.*

seal
   to seal a bottle or end of a tube: *pina.*
   to be sealed: *pinapin.*

seal
   seal, the sea mammal: *sihl.*

search
   to search: *repen₁.*
   to search for, to look for: *rapahki.*

searchlight: *dangkaido.*

seasick
   to be seasick: *mehn madau.*

season
   season of plenty, breadfruit season:
     nanrek, rahk₁.
   season of scarcity, when yams and
     breadfruit are not bearing: *nanisol.*
   trade wind season: *nanpar.*

seat
   chair, seat: *sehr₂.*
   seat, in a canoe: *loh₃, lohnwar.*

seated
   of commoners, to be seated facing the
     main platform in a *nahs*: *salada.*
   of nobles, to be seated facing the
     commoners: *saledi.*

seaward: *peiei-.*

seaweed sp.
   seaweed sp., *Blyxa muricata*: *oaloahd.*

second
   second, as a unit of time: *seken.*

second: *kariau.*
   second cup of kava in the kava
     ceremony: *arehn sakau.*

secretary: *sekteri.*

secretion
   crumb, sleep, crust, a dry layer of a
     bodily secretion: *dararan.*

section
   division, section: *pali₁.*
   one section of a thatch roof, from the
     eave to the peak one armspan in
     width: *dinak.*
   section or article: *ire₂.*
   section, piece: *lepi-.*

secure
   to secure a canoe by placing a pole
     between the outrigger and the hull
     and sticking it into the ocean bed:
     ilewe.

see
   to say, to see: *idawarih, mahsanih.*
   to see one's own reflection: *iroir,*
     irong.

to see, discern, look at, observe,
   examine: *kilang.*
to see, discern, look at, observe,
   examine, with a derogatory
   connotation: *ngar.*
to strain one's neck to see: *usuwer.*

seed: *weren tuhke.*
   a big seed, as in a mango: *pehi₁.*
   seed bed: *kamwer.*
   seed, tumor, cyst: *war₁.*

seedling: *dane.*

seem
   apparently, it seems that: *likamw,*
     likamwete.
   to seem to have the attributes of:
     likamwala.

seesaw
   swing, hammock, seesaw: *likahs.*

segregate
   to segregate: *katohrepeseng.*
   to be segregated: *katohrohr.*

seine
   large seine or net: *ukalap.*
   small seine or net: *uketik.*

seize
   to grab, to seize: *kul, kulih.*
   to seize food at a feast, done by a large
     group of people: *simw, simwih.*
   to steal or seize food at a feast: *doare.*

select
   to choose, to pick out, to select:
     pil₂, pilipil.
   to select or choose from a group of
     animate beings, to pick out an
     animal: *pwinik.*

selection
   election, selection: *pilipil.*

self: *pein₁.*

self-assertive
   proud, self-assertive, cocky: *aklapalap.*

self-centered
   self-centered, demanding: *sakon,*
     soakon.

self-conscious
   short-tempered, self-conscious:
     likotkotuhwahu.

self-effacing
   submissive, modest, self-effacing:
     mpahi.

selfish: *lehk.*
   selfish with food: *ewen mwenge.*
   selfish with food, used in an extremely
     derogatory sense: *ewen neminem.*
   uncooperative, unsociable, acting
     alone, selfish: *liakotohrohr.*

sell
to buy, sell, or trade, to shop: *net₁*.

send
to send: *kadar*.
to send a dispatch or message: *ilek-*.
to send a radio transmission or
telegram: *dempwo-*.
to send away, to cast out: *kasare,
pakasar*.
to send on an errand, to send to
deliver a message: *ilakih, kautoke*.
to be sent: *pekeder*.

sennit: *kepeukuhk, pwehl₂*.
an ornamentally wrapped ball of
sennit: *koansop*.
ball of sennit: *soanop*.
coil of sennit: *sanek*.
to make sennit: *koale, ngkoal*.

sense
common sense: *lamalam*.
to feel, think, or sense: *pehm*.
to sense: *pepehm*.

sensitive
sensitive, susceptible to stimuli: *ner*.
sensitive, temperamental:
limwakarakar.

sensuous
sensuous, beautiful: *pwuteletel*.

sentry
guard, sentry: *kaiko*.

separate
to separate: *irepeseng, katohre*.
to separate a fight: *poadoandoar*.
to separate fighters: *doare*.
to sort or separate: *katohrepeseng*.
to be separated: *katohrohr*.
to be sorted or separated:
katohrohrpeseng.

September: *Septempe*.

series
series of long objects placed together
side by side: *pasapas*.
series, line: *irek*.

sermon
speech or sermon: *kapahrek*.
to give a speech or sermon: *kapahrek*.

servant
female servant, either politically or
domestically: *lidu*.
male servant, either politically or
domestically: *ladu*.

serve
to assist, to serve: *papah*.
to attend or serve a dignitary during a
feast: *aririh*.
to serve: *uhpa*.

to serve as a cup bearer in the
drinking of kava: *erir*.
to serve as a slave: *lidu, liduih*.

service
service, as in a restaurant: *sahpis*.

settle
aligned, arranged, settled, ordered:
soan.
to settle a quarrel: *kamwahu₂,
kamwahwih*.
to settle, to decide: *koasoane*.
to be settled, to be decided, to be
agreed upon: *koasoandi*.

seven: *eis, isidip, isidun, isiel, isika,
isikap, isikis, isilep, isimen,
isimwodol, isimwut, isipa, isipak,
isipali, isipar, isipit, isipoar,
isipwoat, isipwong, isipwuloi, isira,
isisel, isisop, isisou, isite, isitumw,
isiwel, isuh, isuhmw*.

seventh: *keisuh*.

seventy: *isiakan, isihsek, isingoul*.

sever
to be severed: *dol₂*.

several: *ekei₁*.

sew
to sew: *dehk, deidei*.

sewing machine
treadle operated sewing machine:
misihn tiati.

sex
biblically, human or sex: *uduk*.

shackle
handcuff, shackle: *ain₂*.

shade: *mweteh*.

shadow
soul, spirit, shadow: *ngehn*.

shake
to shake: *itik*.
to shake hands: *itipe*.
to shake out with a snapping motion:
siped.
to shake, of one's head: *tuwel, tuwelek*.
to move, to shake: *kamwakid*.
to tremble or shake: *rer*.
to be made to move or shake:
kemwekid.
to be shaken: *itiht*.
to be shaken out with a snapping
motion: *sipisip*.

shaky: *rer*.
shaky, wobbly: *itikek*.

shallow: *pedeped*.
shallow as a consequence of being flat-
bottomed, as a canoe: *kempak*.

shaman
  shaman, sorcerer: *sounwinahni*.

shame
  shame, embarrassment: *saroh*.
  to be shamed, to be humbled:
    lesikihla.

share
  share of food: *pwais*.
  share of food formally received at a
    kamadipw: *pwekidah*.
  share, as of stock: *sehr₃*.
  to share, either food or advice:
    kepinwarih.

shark: *pako, poake*.
  fish sp., a sp. of shark: *sahused, tenipei*.
  fish sp., hammerhead shark: *pako
    lohpwu*.

sharp
  sharp, of an edge or point: *keng*.

sharp-tongued: *kepweikeng*.

sharpen
  to sharpen, to put an edge on
    something: *adahd, ede₂*.
  to cut, trim, or sharpen with any large
    cutting tool: *par₁, periper*.
  to sharpen to a point: *saim*.
  to be sharpened to a point: *seisei₁*.

sharpening stone: *uh₇*.

shatter
  to break or shatter, especially of glass:
    mwarahntik-.
  to shatter, as glass: *pwalang*.

shave
  to shave: *koahkoa, koakoahk, sihp₁,
    sihpih₁*.
  to shave one's head: *moangkoikoi*.
  to be shaved, of the head: *koikoi₁*.

shave ice
  shave ice, snow cone: *kohri*.

shaving
  small wood shavings for starting a fire,
    dry wood for the *uhmw*: *kodourur*.

she
  he, she, it: *e₁, ih₂*.

sheaf
  bundle, sheaf: *kapakap₂*.

sheath knife
  sheath knife, hunting knife, diving
    knife, dagger: *sihdnaip, teike*.

shed
  copra drying shed: *kansohpa*.

sheep: *sihpw₂*.

sheet
  large sheet of iron used as a concrete
    trough: *deppang*.
  sheet, as for bedding: *tehi, uhrelleng*.

shelf: *dana, pasapas*.

shell
  a molted shell: *weli*.
  any species of sea shell: *pwili*.
  bomb, shell: *pakudang*.
  coconut shell: *pohndal*.
  conch shell: *kederwahwa*.
  conch shell, conch shell trumpet: *sewi*.
  empty half of coconut shell:
    ngarangar.
  empty shell, as of a coconut, a crab,
    etc.: *pewi*.
  the shell of the clam sp. called
    lipwei: *pelik*.
  the soft upper part of the shell of the
    coconut, at a certain growth stage:
    uhren uhpw.
  tortoise shell: *pweht₂*.
  trochus shell: *dakasingai, sumwumw*.

shellfish
  sp. of shellfish: *kemei, likid₁, lisop*.
  sp. of shellfish, black in color:
    lingkorot.
  sp. of shellfish, found in fresh and salt
    water: *kataur*.
  sp. of shellfish, found in fresh-water:
    kalemwei.

shelter
  to take shelter: *ruk₂*.

shield
  to cover or shield oneself from the
    weather: *up, upuhp*.

shifty-eyed: *ikinteng*.

shin
  upper shin bone: *ululin neh*.

shine
  to shine on or in: *daker*.

shiny
  beautiful, shiny: *lingan*.
  bright, clear, shiny: *lingaling*.
  shiny with oil or grease: *mwoalehle*.
  shiny, glistening, polished:
    melengileng.
  to be oiled, to be shiny with oil:
    keimwoale.

ship: *sohp*.
  ship, usually one made of steel: *daiasu*.
  warship: *menuwa*.

shirt: *seht*.

Shit
  Shit , a mild explicative in Ponapean:
    set.

shiver
  to shiver: *sis₂*.
  to shiver, to shudder: *mwusihrer*.

shoal: *resires.*

shock

surprise, astonishment, amazement, shock: *pwuriamwei.*

to be surprised, astonished, amazed, or shocked: *pwuriamwei.*

shocked

to be shocked, as by bad news: *kesehkida.*

to be surprised, astonished, or shocked: *eimwolu.*

shoes: *suht.*

leather shoes: *kawa₂, kawakusu.*

tabi shoes: *dapi.*

shoo

to shoo: *karawan.*

shoot

first shoot of a newly planted cutting: *dikek.*

new shoot or sprout of a tuber: *ose.*

shoot, of a plant: *poans.*

to shoot: *kasikih, kesik.*

to shoot a marble into the wrong hole in the game *anaire*: *pannukas.*

to shoot, to perform the action which discharges a weapon: *kapisel.*

shop

to buy, sell, or trade, to shop: *net₁.*

shore

shore, land near the ocean, landing place for canoes or boats: *oaroahr₂.*

short: *mwotomwot.*

anything short or stubby: *latok.*

short legged: *karahk.*

short of a competitor's distance, as in throwing or jumping: *pwek₂.*

very short: *mwotkoloi.*

short-tempered: *pwuriemwot.*

short-tempered, self-conscious: *likotkotuhwahu.*

shorten

to be shortened, to be abbreviated: *kamwot.*

shorts

short pants, shorts: *lepin rausis, rausis mwotomwot.*

shortstop

shortstop, in baseball: *sohdo.*

shoulder: *apere, pwopwe.*

shoulder joint: *kepin tihn peh.*

to carry on one's shoulder: *kapaik, kepeik.*

shout

to shout, to scream, to howl, to yell, to holler: *wer.*

to shout, to scream, to howl, to yell, to holler at: *wering.*

to shout at someone to stop him from doing something: *siring.*

to shout in a falsetto voice, either when carrying kava or to challenge another to a fight: *kadekedek, kowet, se₃.*

shove

to kick or shove with the bottom of the foot: *diapahd.*

shovel: *sapwel.*

to shovel: *sapwel, sapwele.*

show

to show or expose: *kasale-.*

to make a show of doing something: *kihkieng.*

showing off

putting on airs, showing off: *kakko, wampwe.*

shrimp

freshwater shrimp: *likedepw.*

small sp. of shrimp: *luhr.*

shrink

said of something which will shrink, as cloth: *nur.*

to shrink: *eirekpene.*

shudder

to shiver, to shudder: *mwusihrer.*

shuffle

to shuffle cards: *dihl₃, dihlih.*

to shuffle kava fibers before adding water: *dillap.*

to shuffle, as of cards: *dilip.*

to be shuffled, of cards: *dilipek.*

shut

a command to Shut up__ or Be quiet : *katairong.*

to be shut off from a source of air: *mwopw.*

to close or to shut any round object, as a pipe or one's mouth: *kuhpene.*

shutdown

to be shutdown as a consequence of being in violation of the law: *selidi.*

shy: *mwomwitik.*

sibling: *pirien.*

a possessive classifier used for siblings or any person called sibling in the Crow kinship terminology: *rie.*

older sibling relationship: *pohnangi.*

the sibling of the opposite sex by whom one would swear: *pedeli.*

sic

to sic an animal: *kisim.*

sick
  sick, diseased, ill: *soumwahu.*
  sick, weak: *liper$_2$.*
  to be sick: *luhmwuhmw.*
  to be sick of: *tumwohki.*
  to be sickened by too much greasy
    food: *mangarangar.*

sickle: *kama$_2$.*

sickly: *luhmwuhmw.*
  weak, feeble, sickly: *luwet,*
    luwetakahu.

sickness
  sickness, disease, illness: *luhmwuhmw,*
    soumwahu.
  sickness of a pig after giving birth:
    lidangalangal.
  a kind of sickness, producing dizziness:
    mehnsahk.

side: *pengepenge.*
  inner side, inner surface: *masloale.*
  outer side, outer surface: *masliki.*
  outrigger side of a canoe: *palihdam.*
  part, side: *pali$_1$.*
  side exposed to: *palisal-.*
  side of a canoe opposite the outrigger:
    kasah, palikasa.

sideburn: *menipinipi.*

sidewalk
  aisle, sidewalk: *wasahn alu.*

sieve
  a sieve: *sihp$_2$.*
  to strain in a sieve: *sihp$_2$, sihpih$_2$.*

sigh
  to sigh: *likelikad.*
  to sigh in one's sleep: *lipengipeng,*
    rerinmwoalu.

sign
  insignia, sign: *mahk$_2$.*
  sign, mark, picture, camera, movie,
    motion picture: *kilel.*
  signature, poster, sign, notice: *sain.*
  to sign: *sain.*

signal
  to wave, to signal: *oale, oaloahl.*

signature
  signature, poster, sign, notice: *sain.*
  writing, handwriting, signature:
    menginpeh.

silent
  quiet, silent: *nennen.*

silk: *silik.*

silly
  extremely stupid, silly, idiotic, simple,
    dumb: *pweirengid.*
  silly, given to monkeying around:
    mwengki.

stupid, silly, idiotic, simple, dumb:
  kupwuropwon, loalopwon,
  pweipwei$_1$.

silver: *siliper.*

silverfish
  fish sp., silverfish, *Gerres abbreviatus*
    or *Gerres kapas*: *kasapal.*

simple
  extremely stupid, silly, idiotic, simple,
    dumb: *pweirengid.*
  stupid, silly, idiotic, simple, dumb:
    kupwuropwon, loalopwon,
    pweipwei$_1$.

simplify
  to simplify, to arrange in a simple
    manner, to delete some part of task:
    kamangaila.

sin
  sin, wrong doing: *dihp.*
  original sin: *dipen wahn pwuro,*
    wahnpwuro.
  to sin, to commit adultery: *dihp.*

since
  because, since, but, so that: *pwe.*
  since (contrary to expectations): *pa$_1$.*

sing
  to sing: *koul, melikahka.*
  to sing a Christian hymn: *koul sarawi.*
  to sing a love song: *koulin sampah.*
  to sing a song to soothe a restless child:
    kadawado.
  to sing a song written in memory of a
    deceased person or a person who has
    permanently left Ponape:
    kedepwidepw.
  to sing alto: *aldo.*
  to sing bass: *pas$_3$, peis.*
  to sing in a loud falsetto: *kadaileng.*
  to sing soprano: *supiran.*
  to sing tenor: *tener.*

singer: *sounkoul.*

single
  to be single, to be unmarried: *kiripw.*

single-minded
  faithful, persevering, single-minded,
    diligent: *loaloapwoat.*

singlet
  T-shirt, singlet: *singiles, sipiring$_2$.*

sink
  to penetrate, to sink, to dig in: *ir-.*
  to sink in: *sinom.*
  to sink in mud: *suhr.*

sir
  sir, madam: *maing.*

siren
> siren, as on a police car or ambulance: *saireng.*

sit
> to sit: *mwoalehdi, mwohd.*
> to sit down: *mwohndi.*
> to sit down, to lower oneself: *keipwekidi.*
> to sit in on, as a meeting: *mwohdang.*
> to sit up from a supine position: *pwourda.*
> to sit with one's legs dangling: *sokmwotou.*
> to bow or sit as a respect gesture: *poaridi₂.*
> of a hen, to sit on eggs just prior to their hatching: *kompwel.*

six: *aun, oun, wenakap, wendun, wenedip, weneka, wenekis, wenemen, wenemwodol, wenemwut, wenepa, wenepak, wenepali, wenepar, wenepit, wenepoar, wenepwoat, wenepwong, wenera, wenesel, wenetumw, weneu, wenewel, weniel, wenlep, wenoumw, wenpwuloi, wensop, wensou, wente.*

sixth: *keweneu.*

sixty: *wenehk, weneisek, wenengoul.*

size: *uwe₁.*
> size, as of clothing: *sais.*
> to be the right size: *sais.*

sizzle
> to sizzle or crackle: *siar.*

skeptical: *sohpwoson.*

skewer
> to stab, to spear, to skewer, to give an injection: *doakoa.*
> to be stabbed, to be speared, to be skewered, to be given an injection: *dok.*

skill
> navigational skill: *pali₂.*

skillet
> frying pan, skillet: *pirain, piraipang.*

skillful: *mai₂.*
> skillful as a batter in baseball: *adaru.*
> skillful in making sennit: *pohn kepehmwahu.*
> skillful in tree climbing: *palek, palesek.*
> skillful, of a diver able to go deep or hold his breath for a long period of time: *peik₁.*

skin: *kihl₁, ihrekiso.*
> skin, bark, hide, any outer covering: *kihl₁.*
> dried skin from drinking too much kava: *mwelengen sakau.*

> to skin or peel: *rar₃, rere.*

skinny
> skinny, bony: *tihrereng.*
> thin, skinny: *tihti, liper₂.*

skip
> to bounce, to skip: *sik.*
> to skip across a surface, as a stone skipping across water: *dik.*
> to skip an object at something: *eidikih.*
> to skip towards: *dikih.*
> to skip, as a grade in school or a title: *sipal.*
> to throw an object so that it will skip, as on the surface of the water: *eidik.*

skipjack tuna
> fish sp., skipjack tuna, *Katsawonus pelamis:* *kasuwo.*
> dried skipjack tuna: *kasuwopwisi.*

skirt: *skahdo.*
> skirt, half-slip: *urohs.*

skull: *tihn moange.*

skunk
> to skunk someone, to take all the tricks in a card game: *skengk.*

sky
> sky, heaven: *lahng₁.*

slack
> slack, as of a rope: *mwerek.*

slap
> to slap affectionately: *pikipik, pikir.*
> to slap someone's face: *pohr.*
> to be slapped in the face: *popohr.*

slash
> to be slashed, lanced, or cut: *lek.*
> to slash: *leke.*

slate: *sileit₁.*

sleek
> of the skin, sleek: *molomol.*

sleep
> crumb, sleep, crust, a dry layer of a bodily secretion: *dararan.*
> deep in sleep: *meirkelik.*
> sleep, the crust around the eyes formed during sleep: *pwunan.*
> to be unable to sleep, to have insomnia: *epwel₁.*
> to put to sleep: *kamair.*
> to sleep: *derir, meir, seimwoak.*
> to sleep, of children: *nenne, rorong.*
> to stir in one's sleep: *koahnek.*

sleeping place: *moatoar₂.*

sleepy
> to feel sleepy during the daytime as a result of staying up at night: *ihkenpwong.*

slender
thin, slender, of small girth: *ahtikitik.*

slice
chip or slice, as of breadfruit or taro: *dip.*
to slice, as breadfruit or taro: *dipe.*
to slice, to peel with an instrument: *sere₁.*
to be sliced, to be peeled: *sansar₁.*

slick
slippery, slick: *likeikiris, likekiris.*

slide
to slide by pushing or pulling: *tohr₂.*
to slide into or out of: *nihd.*
to slide or fall, of a pile of non-living objects, as a landslide: *engkidi.*
to slide or roll, as a toy wheel: *kadahre.*
to slide, as on a cable: *kakihr.*
to slide, of rocks: *rengk.*
to slide, usually of light objects: *peieki.*
to slip, to slide: *kiris.*
to be slid by pushing or pulling: *tohrek.*
to be slid into or out of: *nihdek.*
to be slid, usually of light objects: *peiek.*

slighted
to be slighted, to be displeased: *mwakar.*

slimy: *meteitei.*

sling
sling, for throwing: *pahi₂.*

slingshot: *kesingkomi.*
forked stick part of a slingshot: *mada.*

slip
slip, chemise: *semihs, simihs.*
to slip off, to lose one's grip when climbing: *pisel.*
to slip, to slide: *kiris.*

slip noose
slip noose or snare for catching animals: *ahm.*

slippery
slippery, slick: *likeikiris, likekiris.*
smooth or slippery, as of silk: *kitentel.*

slit
slit, crack, small opening, empty space, outer space: *nanwehwe.*
to slit, to cut open: *pwalang.*
to be slit, to be cut open: *pwal.*

slope: *niaul.*

sloppy
muddy, sloppy: *pwakanakan.*

slow
late, slow: *pwand.*

peaceful, easygoing, unenthusiastic, slow moving, passive, lethargic: *meleilei.*
slow in maturing: *kot.*
slow in movement: *wai₁.*
slow, referring to long intervals between some repetitious activity: *malamal.*
unhurried or slow at an activity: *sepitipit.*

sluggish
sluggish, lazy: *dangaudek.*

small
small in diameter, of holes, coconuts, or people: *wetikitik.*
small, little, young: *tikitik.*
smallest one, as of a bunch of coconuts: *kapwer.*
thin, slender, of small girth: *ahtikitik.*
tiny, small, little: *pwidikidik.*
to be lower than, to be younger or smaller than: *peidihsang.*
to be the smallest: *kapwer.*

small-hipped: *ikipak.*

smallpox
smallpox, chicken pox: *kilitepw.*

smart
intelligent, smart: *loalekeng, loalokong.*
smart, intelligent: *simaht.*

smash
bent, smashed, mashed, dented: *limek.*
to be smashed, as of a fallen ripe fruit: *pak₂.*
to be smashed, to be broken: *marop.*

smegma: *kirek.*

smell
smell, odor, aroma: *pwoh.*
strong smelling, stinking: *pwohpwo₂.*
moldy smelling: *pwohsensen.*
to smell: *ingir, lel-, ned.*

smelly: *ingirek, pwohlap.*
to consider smelly: *tumwohki.*

smile
to smile: *sirei.*
to laugh, to smile: *kiparamat.*

smiling
happy-looking, smiling: *likokouruhr.*

smoke: *ediniei.*
vapor, smoke, mist: *adi.*
to smoke: *sumwoak.*
to eat, drink, or smoke: *sohk₁.*
to have smoke in one's eyes: *kehd.*

smoky
cloudy, blurred, smoky: *edied.*

smooth
smooth and flat: *medendel.*

smooth or slippery, as of silk: *kitentel.*
smoothed: *nok.*
to smooth out: *kamadal.*

smudged
smudged, faultily washed: *ramin.*

snack
a late night snack: *mwengehn pwong.*
to eat a late night snack: *mwengehn pwong.*
to eat a late night snack, usually of a woman who is breastfeeding a child: *ienpwong, lesihpwong.*

snail
land snail: *dendenmwosi.*

snake: *sinek.*

snap
to snap off: *karihs.*
to snap, of dogs or pigs: *ngoapwur.*
to be snapped off: *kerihri.*

snapper
fish sp., red snapper, *Lutjanus bohar*: *kihr en eiwel.*
fish sp., snapper, *Lethrinus kallopterus*: *ikiepw.*
fish sp., snapper, *Lethrinus lentjan*: *medi.*
fish sp., snapper, *Lethrinus ramak*: *samwei.*
fish sp., snapper, *Lutjanus fulviflamma*: *likommwei.*
fish sp., snapper, *Lutjanus gibbus*: *pwahlahl.*
fish sp., snapper, *Lutjanus kasmira*: *tehnseu.*
fish sp., snapper, *Lutjanus malabaricus*: *kihr₂.*
fish sp., snapper, *Lutjanus semicinctus*: *pwehu₁.*

snapshot
picture, snapshot: *pikser.*

snare
slip noose or snare for catching animals: *ahm.*
to snare with a slip noose: *nsehn.*

snarl
to growl or snarl at: *ngiringirih.*
to growl or snarl, to quarrel: *ngiringir.*

snatch
to snatch: *waik.*
to snatch, to steal, to do something illegal: *kawai.*

sneak
to sneak: *wai₁.*
to sneak up to: *karapih, waine.*

sneer
to sneer: *kumwutik.*

sneeze
to sneeze: *asi₁, sihpek.*

sniff
to sniff, to draw in air sharply through the nose: *ngutoar.*

snore
to snore: *moamoar, nono.*

snow: *sino.*

snow cone
shave ice, snow cone: *kohri.*

so
o.k., so, well, now: *na.*
then, so: *eri.*

soak
to soak: *sohn.*

soap: *sohpw₂.*
powdered soap: *rinso.*

sob
to sob: *makiaki.*

sober: *amas.*

socks
stockings, socks: *sidakin.*

soda
soda, soft drink: *saida.*

soft: *mwuterek.*
soft, easy to sink in, as a swampy place: *lususuhr.*
weak, soft, easily broken, fragile: *kopwukopw₁.*

soil
dirt, soil, earth, ground: *pwehl₁.*
overused, unproductive soil: *pekinpwel.*
black soil: *pweltoal.*
red soil: *pwelweita.*
said of a plant which leaches all nutrients from the soil: *kik suwed.*

soiled
dirty, soiled: *pwelipwel.*

solar plexus: *kopwkopwenadi, mesenedi.*

soldier: *sounpei.*

sole
sole of the foot: *pahnepwel, pahnneh.*

some: *ekei₁.*

something
something, anything (singular): *mehkot, okoteme.*
something, anything (plural): *mehkei.*

song: *koul, melikahka.*
a love song: *koulin sampah.*
song to soothe a restless child, often one which tells a story of a child of antiquity: *kadawado.*

soothe
to sing a song to soothe a restless child: *kadawado.*

soprano
  to sing soprano: *supiran.*

sorcerer
  shaman, sorcerer: *sounwinahni.*

sorcery
  harmful magic, sorcery: *kau₃.*

sorrowful
  disappointed, sorrowful: *pahtou₁.*

sorry
  sad, sorry: *nsensuwed.*
  to be sorry: *pwuriamweikihla.*

sort
  kind, sort, type: *kain, mwohmw,*
    soahng.
  to sort or separate: *katohrepeseng.*
  to be sorted or separated:
    katohrohrpeseng.

soul
  soul, spirit, shadow: *ngehn.*
  soul, spiritual side of a being:
    palingehn.

sound
  any click-like sound: *tal.*
  any very soft sound: *ingihng₂.*
  barely discernable sound from a
    distant source: *moahd.*
  sound made by the rubbing of crossed
    branches: *pesenkoahte.*
  voice, sound: *elinge.*
  to make a sound: *lal.*

soup: *sopa, suhpw.*
  Chinese-style noodle soup: *ramen.*

sour: *karer.*

source
  source of light: *kampwul, ndil.*
  source, of a river or a stream: *utuhn*
    pihl.

soursop
  soursop, *Annona muricata*: *sei₃.*

south: *palieir.*

souvenir
  memorial, recollection, souvenir:
    ketemenpe.

sow
  to sow, as seed: *kamwarak.*

soy
  soy sauce: *soiu₁.*

space
  slit, crack, small opening, empty space,
    outer space: *nanwehwe.*
  space between things: *madol.*

spacious
  gigantic, spacious: *angahng.*
  large or spacious, of inanimate objects:
    koahiek.

spade
  spade, in cards: *speht.*

Spain: *Sipein.*

spank
  to spank or beat: *apin, kamakam,*
    keme.
  to whip, to spank: *wetih.*
  to whip, to spank, to beat: *poakih,*
    woakih, wowoki.
  to be whipped or spanked: *weweti.*

spark: *dimwamwahi.*

spark plug: *spahk.*

sparkle
  to sparkle: *didmwerek.*

speak
  to speak: *kapit₁, lokaia, mahsen.*
  to speak in anger: *kahs₁.*
  to speak incessantly: *lallal,. pimpip.*
  to speak or command: *pahngok,*
    poahngok.
  to speak to another using respect
    forms of speech: *maingih.*
  to speak using respect forms of speech:
    meing.
  to speak with an accent: *sis₁.*

spear
  spear, arrow: *arep.*
  spear, harpoon: *ketieu₁.*
  metal, nail, badge, spear for a
    speargun: *mete.*
  spear handle: *ihpw.*
  to stab, to spear, to skewer, to give an
    injection: *doakoa.*
  to be stabbed, to be speared, to be
    skewered, to be given an injection:
    dok.

spearfishing
  a type of spearfishing done by baiting
    a line with a small breadfruit and
    then spearing the fish when they
    come to eat: *tenek kisinmei.*
  a type of spearfishing done from above
    the surface of the water:
    dokomwomw.
  a type of spearfishing done in the
    mangrove swamp: *douiak.*

spectacular
  to be spectacular: *koudiahl.*

speech
  language, speech: *lokaia, mahsen.*
  speech of a chief: *ririnpaiso.*
  speech or command: *pahngok,*
    poahngok.
  speech or sermon: *kapahrek.*
  high language, respect forms of
    speech: *meing.*
  employing gross or inappropriate

speech, speaking openly of sex,
usually said of women: *ausaledek.*
to give a speech or sermon: *kapahrek.*

speedboat: *spihdpwoht.*

speedy
speedy, fast: *sipihdo.*
fast, speedy: *dopas, uk.*

spell
to spell: *sipel, sipelih.*

spell
to cast a spell: *winahni.*

spellbound
to be spellbound, to be stupified:
dahla.

spend
to spend a night at: *seidi, wendi.*
to spend the night with a woman:
engida.

sphere: *mpwei.*

spicy
peppery, spicy, hot: *kerengireng.*

spider conch sp.: *lahng₃.*

spider sp.: *likan, nahluhk₁.*

spider web
spider web, cobweb: *pesen likan.*

spike
nail, spike: *nihl.*

spill
to spill: *wideki.*
to be spilled: *widek.*

spin
to turn, to spin, to twist: *pir₁, pirer.*

spinal column: *tihlepe.*

spiny
thorny, spiny: *tekatek.*

spirit
soul, spirit, shadow: *ngehn.*

spiritual
magical, mysterious, spiritual:
manaman.

spit
to spit: *kendip₁, likidi.*
to spit out: *pwurak.*

splash
to splash: *pwung₂, pwungidek,
pwungur.*
to splash water towards an object:
usup, usupih.

splatter
to make a splattering noise: *pwirar.*

spleen: *ehtik.*

split
to split: *pwaik.*
to split a husked coconut: *leser.*
to be split: *pwepweik.*

to be split, of a husked coconut:
les₂.

splotched
spotted, splotched: *mwangerenger.*

spoil
to spoil, of cooked food: *poula.*

spoiled
of children, spoiled: *sakon, soakon.*
ripe, overripe, rotten, spoiled, decayed:
mat.
to be broken, ruined, destroyed,
spoiled: *ohla.*

spokesman: *sounlokaia.*

sponge: *lihmw.*
to mop, to sponge off, to wipe:
dahlimw.
to sponge off, to wipe dry: *limwih,
limwilimw.*

spongy
spongy center of a sprouting coconut:
pahr₃.

spoon: *supwuhn.*
to eat with a spoon: *touk, toutou₂.*
to spoon: *supwuhnih.*

spot
spot, stain: *mwei₁.*

spotted
spotted, splotched: *mwangerenger.*

spouse
spouse, husband or wife: *pwoud,
werek.*
spouse, married in church: *inou
sarawi.*
the opposite sex sibling of one's spouse,
the spouse of one's opposite sex
sibling: *mwah.*

sprained
to be sprained: *ruwek.*

spray
to spray or blow inside, of windblown
rain: *arer, sikarer.*
to spray, to cause to flow: *kakus.*
to be sprayed: *kokus.*

spread
to spread: *kihpeseng.*
to spread from one area to another:
par₅.
to spread gravel or coral, as on the
road: *pwukere.*
to spread news around: *lohk.*
to spread out, as a mat: *kamwarak.*
to spread the stones of an *uhmw* too
thin, so that the earth shows: *erpehs.*
to spread, as a sheet or blanket: *irepe.*
to surround, to enclose, to spread
everywhere: *kipe.*

to be distributed, to be spread around:
*pahng$_2$.
to be spread, as a sheet or blanket:
iraparap.

spring
spring of water: *pwoarukus.*
spring, as a coil spring: *sipiring$_1$.*
well, spring: *pwarer.*
wire, spring: *wehia.*
to spring back: *pit$_1$.*

springy
limp, flexible, springy, disjointed, used
to describe a manner of walking:
kiahweliwel.

sprinkle
to sprinkle water, as on clothing prior
to ironing: *kaurere.*

sprout
breadfruit tree sprout: *perin mahi.*
new shoot or sprout of a tuber: *ose.*
sprout of a yam: *oh$_3$.*
to sprout, of coconuts: *par$_6$.*
to sprout, to grow: *os.*
to sprout, to send forth the first shoots,
said of a cutting: *dikek.*

spur
spur of a chicken: *ose.*

spy
to spy: *lipahrok.*
to spy on: *lipahroke.*

spyglass
spyglass, telescope, binoculars:
tupweiklas.

square
quadrangle, square: *permasepeng.*
square, the carpenter's tool: *sukweia.*
to be quadrangular, to be square:
permasepeng.

squat
to squat: *kohntutuk.*
to squat down in the water:
mwoaloaldi.

squeak
to creak or squeak: *tehrek.*

squeeze
to squeeze: *ingidpene.*
to squeeze kava that has been set aside
in anticipation of the arrival of titled
guests: *wenglopwon.*
to squeeze kava until it is completely
dried: *wengmad.*
to squeeze or press, to push, as a
switch: *padik.*
to squeeze through, to pass through in
spite of an obstacle: *duwal.*
to wring, to squeeze with a twisting
motion: *wengid, wengiweng.*

to be squeezed or pressed, to be
pushed, as a switch: *ped.*

squid: *nuhd.*

squirrelfish
fish sp., squirrelfish, *Adoryx
spinifer*: *sara$_2$.*
fish sp., squirrelfish, *Myripristis
adustus*: *mwuhn.*

stab
to stab: *katuk.*
to stab, to spear, to skewer, to give an
injection: *doakoa.*
to be stabbed, to be speared, to be
skewered, to be given an injection:
dok.

stacked
to be stacked: *posoke.*

stagger
to stagger: *sas$_1$.*
to stagger, to have difficulty keeping
one's footing: *wasas.*

stain
stain, mark: *mwahi.*
mildew, stain caused by mildew:
enihep.
to stain: *reid.*
to be stained: *rei.*

stairs
ladder, steps, stairs: *kehndake.*

stalk
stalk, of coconuts: *tehnkehl.*

stamp
a stamp, trademark: *sidamp.*
to stamp: *sidampih.*
to be stamped: *sidamp.*

stand
always standing: *likekehu.*
to stand: *kesihnen, ninlengida, uh$_2$.*
to stand for: *uhki.*
to stand with one's hands on one's
hips, to stand with one's arms
akimbo: *pedilukop.*

stanza
stanza of a song: *pwuloi.*

staple
large staple, as used in building:
kasingai.

star: *usu.*
Venus, the morning star: *Usuhn Rahn,
Usuhrahn.*

star fruit
tree sp., star fruit tree: *ansu.*

starch: *sidahs.*

stare
to stare: *kakil.*
to stare at one another: *pekekil.*

to stare, to be with one's eyes wide
open: *duwar.*

starfish

crown of thorns starfish: *rarahni.*

New Guinea starfish: *ulungen wehi.*

staring

wide-eyed, staring: *duwarawar.*

start

to begin, to start: *tapiada, tapihda,
tep₁.*

to start a song: *tiak₂.*

to start an activity: *kohmwowe.*

to start or to burn, of a fire: *ngken, ok.*

to start over, as in the preparation of
kava: *audsapahl.*

to start, of a court case: *keielekda.*

to start, of an engine: *kamaurada.*

starvation: *duhpek.*

starved: *duhpek.*

state

a political unit, as a municipality,
district, state, country, or kingdom:
wehi₂.

condition or state of a person or thing:
ire₁.

station

broadcast station: *proadkahs.*

rank or station: *dehu.*

station of the cross: *esdasion.*

wireless station, radio station: *wasahn
wailes.*

status

to change status: *sepwil-.*

stay

to stay temporarily: *keiru.*

to stay up and party all night:
sukuruhdi.

to stay up late: *pehdinpwong.*

steal

to steal: *pirap.*

to steal or seize food at a feast: *doare.*

to snatch, to steal, to do something
illegal: *kawai.*

steamboat: *pwoht kisiniei.*

steamer: *sidihma.*

steep

steep, downhill: *ukedi.*

steep, uphill: *ukada.*

steer

to steer a canoe with a paddle: *pel₃.*

to steer a vehicle: *ilihl.*

steering wheel: *mehn windeng.*

stem: *kirikir.*

stem of a fruit: *kehke.*

stem of the ivory nut palm, used for
mending thatch roofs: *ida.*

of cane-like plants, the part of the
stem between the joints: *pwuloi.*

step

to step: *kahk₁.*

to step on: *tiak₁.*

to take a step, to set one's footing:
sok₁.

to alight or step down: *keredi.*

to board, to step up onto, to climb
aboard: *karada.*

to descend into, to fall into, to step
into, as a hole: *pwuhr-.*

steps

ladder, steps, stairs: *kehndake.*

stern

stern-faced, unsmiling: *likokohunsop.*

stern, of parents or spouses: *koakos.*

to be stern with: *koakose.*

stick

log, stick: *lepin tuhke.*

stick of hibiscus wood, used to store
kava cups: *doulong.*

stick used for spreading stones in an
uhmw: *dih₂.*

the pair of sticks used for picking up
hot rocks from an *uhmw*: *tihpw.*

a throwing stick, typically a reed, used
in the game *peisihr*: *sihr.*

stick

to take hold, to stick: *man.*

sticky: *pas₂, pwilipwil.*

adherent, cohesive, gummy, sticky:
ngidingid.

stiff: *deng₁.*

stiff neck: *tepinwer medek.*

still

still (when suffixed to reduplicated
verbs): *-te.*

stimulated

to be sexually stimulated by petting:
kararanda.

sting

to sting, as of jellyfish: *pitik.*

stinging: *sos.*

stingray: *likendinkep.*

stink

You stink , derogatory exclamation
used principally by women:
pwohmat.

stinking

stinking, foul-smelling: *ngelingel₂.*

strong smelling, stinking: *pwohpwo₂.*

stir

to stir: *erier.*

to stir in one's sleep: *koahnek.*

to stir with an implement: *die.*

to stir, to probe: *arih.*

stockings
stockings, socks: *sidakin.*

stocky
bulky, stocky, thick, large in girth: *ahlap.*

stomach: *edin mwenge, kupwuriso, mpwei.*
stomach, of certain fish like tuna: *pwuri.*

stomp
to stomp on: *tomur.*
to stomp, to make a thudding noise: *tom.*

stone: *takai.*
file, sharpening stone, razor strop: *mehn adahd.*
kava pounding stone: *ketia₃, moahl₁.*
large flat pounding stone employed in the preparation of kava or pounded foods: *peitehl.*
one of the principal kava stones in a *nahs*: *uhpeileng, uhpeimwahu, uhpeiuh.*
small stones used for making an *uhmw*: *rahs.*
stone placed in front of an entrance to a house, used to wipe one's feet on: *dakadakiso, dakeiso, takain wideh.*
the principal kava stone in a *nahs*, from which the *Nahnmwarki* is served: *soumoahl.*
the stones used in an *uhmw*: *pai₁.*
to stone, to throw rocks at: *kate.*

stoop
covered stoop of a Japanese style house: *kengkang.*

stooped
to walk in a stooped position: *dairuk, pairuk₁.*

stop
to halt, to stop: *ohlet.*
to stop: *katokiedi, sdop.*
to stop along the way: *wet₁.*
to stop by, to stop in on, to visit: *sop₁.*
to stop some action: *kapweiek.*
to stop suddenly: *pweiek.*
to stop, of a mechanical object: *mehla.*
to stop, of moving objects: *uhdi.*
to stop, of rain: *mahkada.*
to be ended, terminated, or stopped: *tok₁.*

stopper: *pinapin, pinepe.*

storage area
storage area in the front of a

feasthouse, where the porch roof extends inside: *dihsek.*

store: *imwen net, sidohwa.*
wholesale store: *ohlsehl.*
to save, keep, store, put away: *nekidala.*
to store objects between cross pieces of thatch: *dilipada.*
to store, to put away: *nekinek.*

storeroom
storeroom, storage area: *nahk.*

storm
windstorm, typhoon: *melimel.*
to be struck by a windstorm or typhoon: *melimel.*

story
history, sacred story: *poadoapoad.*
legend, story based partially on fact: *soaipoad.*
tale, story: *soai.*
talk, discussion, rumor, story, adage, parable: *koasoai.*
to talk, to discuss, to tell a story: *koasoai.*

story
story, of a building: *posoke, teik.*

stout
fat, stout: *mworourou.*

stove: *sidohp.*

straight: *inen.*
straight, also used to describe eyes with an epicanthic fold: *dengideng.*

straighten
to straighten: *kainen, kainene.*

strain
to strain in a sieve: *sihp₂, sihpih₂.*

strained: *tihrereng.*

strake
canoe part, the vertical sheer strake that ordinarily extends above the central portion of the leeward gunwale: *pedilik₁.*

strand
strand of hair: *pitenpeipei, pitenwel.*
strand, as of sennit, hair, etc.: *ainkot, angkot.*

stranded
to be stranded in shallow water: *pindi.*

stream: *pilitik₂.*
small stream: *kahng₂.*
bathing spot in a stream: *kereiso.*

street
road, street, trail, path, line: *ahl₁.*

strength: *kehl₁.*
said of one who shows off his power or strength: *angkehlail.*

strengthen
to strengthen: *kakehle.*

strenuous
strenuous, diligent: *ngihtehte.*

stretch
to stretch something: *waik.*
to stretch, to make taut: *kadang,*
kedengideng.
to be stretched: *kedeng.*

stretcher: *mehn roh.*

strike
strike, in baseball: *siraik.*
to strike or hit something that makes
noise: *seker.*
to strike, of a fish: *dar₁, der.*

strike-out
to strike-out, in baseball: *sansing.*

string: *kisinsel.*
a string of something, as of flowers or
fish: *ihr₂.*
rope, cord, line, string: *sahl.*
string of flowers or beads: *ehl₁.*
to string, as flowers or fish: *ihr₂.*

strip
to strip off clothes: *kakihr.*
to strip off water, to strip the leaves
off a vine: *ehd₃.*

striped: *alahl.*

strive
to strive onward: *wonowei.*

strong
strong, powerful, healthy: *kehlail.*
strong, capable of moving steadily and
with force: *idipek.*

strop
file, sharpening stone, razor strop:
mehn adahd.

structure
organization, structure, rule, plan,
agreement: *koasoandi.*
to organize, to structure: *koasoane.*
to be organized, to be structured:
koasoandi.

struggle
to struggle: *pwurur.*

strut
a strut supporting the outrigger of a
canoe: *kiai.*

stub
stub, stump: *tuki.*
to stumble, to stub one's toe:
dipekelekel, dipwekelekel.

stubborn
very stubborn: *keptakai.*

stubby
anything short or stubby: *latok.*

stuck: *kot.*
to get stuck: *tengala.*
to have something stuck in one's
throat: *loh₂.*

student: *tohnsukuhl.*

study
to study, to prepare: *onop.*

stuffed: *it.*
stuffed up, clogged: *pon.*

stumble
to stumble, to stub one's toe:
dipekelekel, dipwekelekel.

stump
stub, stump: *tuki.*
stump, as a tree stump: *tohk.*

stupid
stupid, incapable of learning: *makunai.*
stupid, silly, idiotic, simple, dumb:
kupwuropwon, loalopwon,
pweipwei₁.
extremely stupid, silly, idiotic, simple,
dumb: *pweirengid.*
stupid, stupified: *lampwon.*

stupified
stupid, stupified: *lampwon.*
to be spellbound, to be stupified:
dahla.

stutter
mute, dumb, stuttering: *lohteng.*

sty
sty, swelling of the rim of the eyelid:
tihle.

style: *sidail.*

subclan
name of a subclan of *Dipwinmen*:
Dipwinmen pwetepwet, Dipwinmen
toantoal.

subject
content, subject matter: *audepe.*

submarine: *sopidu.*

submerge
to submerge: *kaduh, kakihr.*
to be drowned, to be submerged:
duhla.

submissive
submissive, modest, self-effacing:
mpahi.

submit
to submit: *kapidolong₁.*

subpoena
subpoena, summons: *pehkiek.*

substance: *kanenge.*
any odorific substance added to
coconut oil to give it a pleasant
smell: *tehte.*

substitute
  substitute, successor: *wilie.*
  to change, to substitute, to replace:
    wilian.
  to be changed, to be substituted, to be
    replaced: *wiliali.*
subtract
  to subtract: *katohre, katohrohr.*
subtraction: *katohrohr.*
successful
  successful in growing things, having a
    green thumb: *pohnpe.*
  successful in seeking a spouse: *pohnpe.*
  successful, in fishing or hunting:
    seikan.
  to be successful: *pweida.*
successor
  substitute, successor: *wilie.*
suck
  to suck on, as a cigarette or sugar
    cane: *kuhl.*
  to suck, to absorb: *mihk.*
sucker
  sucker of banana, breadfruit, taro, etc.:
    ili.
suckle
  to suckle, to nurse: *dihdi.*
suddenly: *pa₁.*
  quickly, suddenly: *mwadangete.*
suffer
  to suffer, physically or mentally: *lok.*
suffering: *lokolok.*
sufficient
  limited, just sufficient: *itait.*
sugar: *suke.*
sugar cane
  sugar cane, *Saccharum*
    officinarum: *sehu.*
  a variety of sugar cane: *seualahl, seun*
    nta, seun nukini, seun palau, seun
    wai, seuneir, seupwet, seutoal.
sugar water
  limeade, sugar water: *swángke.*
suicide
  to commit suicide by hanging oneself:
    lusiam.
suit
  suit coat: *sekid welpeseng.*
  suit, in cards: *sut.*
suitcase: *kapang.*
sukiyaki: *sukiaki.*
summarized
  general, summarized: *oaralap.*
summary: *oaralap.*
summit
  top, peak, summit, ridge: *koadoke.*

  top, summit, end, outcome: *imwi.*
summon
  to call, to summon: *eker.*
  to summon or dispatch: *poarone.*
  to be summoned or dispatched:
    poaron.
  to be summoned: *pehkiek.*
summons
  subpoena, summons: *pehkiek.*
sun: *ketipin, sou₆.*
Sunday: *Rahn Sarawi, Rahn en Santi.*
Sunday, Sabbath: *Rahn en Sapwad.*
sunglasses
  sunglasses, dark glasses: *kilahs*
    toantoal.
superstition: *ketieni.*
superstitious
  to be superstitious: *ketieni.*
supple
  supple, limber: *materek.*
support
  to support: *irere, uhki.*
suppress
  to suppress, as a cry of pain, a cough,
    laughter, or a bowel movement:
    koatoanehng.
surface
  inner side, inner surface: *masloale.*
  outer side, outer surface: *masliki.*
surgeonfish
  fish sp., black surgeonfish: *toamwoarok.*
  fish sp., striped surgeonfish,
    Acanthurus lineatus: *wakapw.*
  fish sp., surgeonfish: *doarop.*
  fish sp., surgeonfish, *Acanthurus*
    aliala: *durudara.*
  fish sp., surgeonfish, *Acanthurus*
    gahhm: *tamwarok.*
  fish sp., surgeonfish, *Acanthurus*
    xanthopterus: *pakas.*
  fish sp., surgeonfish, *Naso lituratus*:
    pwulangking.
  fish sp., yellow eyed surgeonfish:
    darop.
surgery: *pwal.*
surname: *sunname.*
surpass
  to go beyond, to exceed, to surpass, to
    overtake: *sipele.*
  to surpass previous performance or
    behavior: *sik-.*
surprise
  surprise, astonishment, amazement,
    shock: *pwuriamwei.*
  an exclamation of pleasant surprise:
    akka.

surprised
   to be surprised: *lusida.*
   to be surprised, astonished, amazed, or
      shocked: *eimwolu, pwuriamwei.*

surround
   to surround: *pidakihpene.*
   to surround, to enclose, to spread
      everywhere: *kipe.*

survey
   to measure, to survey: *sohng.*

survive
   durable, having the ability to survive
      either time or circumstance: *koato.*

suspect
   to suspect: *mwelekih.*
   to believe or suspect: *leme.*

suspend
   to suspend from one shoulder or both
      with a strap or rope, as a bag or
      purse or knapsack: *lipwene,
      lipwanapwan.*

suspenders: *preisis*$_1$.

suspicious: *lemelemehk.*

swallow
   to swallow: *kadall, kadalle, kadanle.*

swamp
   large swamp: *lehpwel.*
   mangrove swamp: *naniak.*

swamped
   to be swamped, of canoes and boats:
      mwowihdi.

swarm
   to swarm: *simw.*
   to swarm on: *simwih.*
   to move in great numbers, to swarm:
      del.

sway
   to sway: *tuwel, tuwelek.*
   of women, to sway the body and head
      while dancing: *mwahkohko.*

swear
   I swear : *pedeli.*

sweat
   perspiration, sweat: *pwudau, pwudo.*

sweaty: *pwudowado.*

sweep
   to sweep: *koahkoa, koakoahk.*

sweet: *mem.*
   sweet, delicious, tasty: *iou.*

sweet potato
   potato, sweet potato *Ipomea batatas*:
      pedehde.

sweetheart
   sweetheart (with *ah*): *lahp.*
   secret sweetheart: *kerir.*

swell
   to swell: *mpwosada.*
   to swell, of waves: *pwung*$_2$.

swelling
   boil, swelling, infection: *mpwos.*
   sty, swelling of the rim of the eyelid:
      tihle.
   a swelling wave: *pwuki.*

swift
   fast, swift, of a moving object:
      marahra.

swim
   to swim, of people, non-marine
      animals, and turtles: *pap.*
   to swim to, of people, non-marine
      animals, and turtles: *pepe.*
   to swim, of fish: *kereu, tang.*
   to run or swim the final lap in a race:
      kesso.

swine
   pig, swine, pork: *pwihk.*

swing
   swing, hammock, seesaw: *likahs.*
   to swing: *likahs.*

swollen
   swollen or puffed up as a consequence
      of a wound or blow: *pwuwalok.*

sword
   sword, cutlass, bayonet: *kedilahs.*

swordfish
   fish sp., swordfish, sailfish, blue marlin:
      dekilahr.

sympathize
   to love, to like, to sympathize with:
      poakpoake.

synagogue: *sinakoke.*

T-shirt
   T-shirt, singlet: *singiles, sipiring*$_2$.

tabasco
   tabasco sauce: *dopasko.*

tabi
   tabi shoes: *dapi.*

table: *tehpel.*

taboo: *kepelipel, sarawi.*
   to be in a taboo relationship with
      someone or something: *pel*$_2$.
   to be taboo: *kasarawi*$_2$.

tack
   pin, tack, bobbypin: *pihn.*

tagged
   to be tagged, as in the game of *wie
      eni*: *pas*$_2$.

tail: *katwelwel, pwadai, pwadaiki.*
   tail, end, extreme: *iki.*

tailbone
   lower back, tailbone area: *sikinkihri.*

tailbone area: *sikihr.*

tailor: *soundeidei.*

take

to take by force: *angkehlail.*

to take by force, in a greedy manner: *pehdmour.*

to take by force, of any kind: *adih.*

to take care of: *apwalih.*

to take immediate action on something because the opportunity is right: *isaniki.*

to take in handfulls: *roake.*

to take in, as clothing: *katikala.*

to take one's turn to: *ihd₁.*

to take or get: *ale.*

to take sides: *poupoar.*

to take sides with: *uhpal.*

to take someone to some place: *kahre.*

to take advantage of: *engmwahukihla.*

to pick up, to carry, to take along: *limehda.*

to be taken in, as clothing: *ketikila.*

to be taken or gotten: *alahldi.*

tale

tale, story: *soai.*

talk

talk, discussion, rumor, story, adage, parable: *koasoai.*

to talk back: *kapeilokaia.*

to talk someone into doing something: *koangoangehki.*

to talk to oneself: *mengiloal.*

to talk, to discuss, to tell a story: *koasoai.*

to talk, to speak: *kapit₁, lokaia.*

talkative: *owen wedei, wedei.*

overly talkative, protesting too much, all talk and no action: *ngihnwer, ngoatamah.*

talkative, outgoing: *medakahn.*

tall

long, tall: *anged, reirei₁, reisuwan.*

tame: *mand.*

to tame: *kemenda.*

tan

khaki, tan: *kahki, pohkahki.*

tangerine

Mandarin orange, tangerine: *manterihn, manterihng.*

tangled

closely twisted or curled, kinky, tangled: *pinipin.*

tank

tank, for containing liquids: *dengk.*

a military tank: *dangku.*

tantrum

to throw a temper tantrum: *pwusukoal.*

tap

to tap ashes from a cigar, cigarette, or pipe: *loipehs.*

tape

tape, braid, ribbon for sewing: *teip.*

tape, tape recorder: *deip.*

tape measure

ruler, tape measure: *mehn sohng.*

tape recorder

tape, tape recorder: *deip.*

to record something with a tape recorder: *deipih.*

to record with a tape recorder: *deip.*

tapioca

cassava, manioc, tapioca: *dapiohka, kehp tuhke, menioak.*

coarsely grated tapioca: *ruhdo.*

tar

pitch, tar: *pis.*

target: *mehn akinen.*

taro

a variety of dry land taro: *mwahngin moar.*

a variety of mountain taro, *Alocasia macrorrhiza*: *sepwikin.*

a variety of swamp taro: *simihden.*

a variety of taro from Hawaii, *Xanthosoma saittifolium*: *sawahn awai.*

a variety of taro from Meir: *mwahngin meir.*

a variety of taro from Ngatik: *mwahngin ngetik.*

a variety of taro from Nukuoro: *mwahngin nukuwer.*

a variety of taro from Palau: *mwahngin palau.*

a variety of taro from the outer islands: *mwahngin namwanamw.*

a variety of taro with a stalk colored like the sp. of lizard *kieil*: *mwahng kieil.*

a variety of taro with lacy edged leaves: *mwahng suwain.*

a variety of taro, *Colocasia esculenta*: *sawa₁.*

a variety of taro, *Xanthosoma sp.*: *sawahn wai.*

a variety of wet land taro: *sounpwong weneu.*

a variety of wet land taro, *Cyrtosperma chamissonis*: *mwahng.*

a variety of taro, *Alocasia macrorrhiza*: *ohd, wehd.*

a variety of taro: *pahnta, saleng walek, tekemwer.*

bank of a taro patch: *aek$_2$.*

grated taro mixed with bananas and sweetened: *rotama.*

taro leaves placed around the base of a kava stone to catch fallen pieces of kava: *pweikoar.*

taro patch
taro patch, marsh, bog: *lehpwel.*

tarpaulin: *dahpwohlin.*

task: *poaron, pwais.*
occupation, task, employment, responsibility, deed: *doahk.*

taste: *namanam.*
moldy or old tasting: *sensen.*
taste, flavor: *neme.*
to taste: *song.*
to eat, to taste, used derogatorily: *nam.*

tasteless
bland, tasteless, watery: *nampil.*

tasty
sweet, delicious, tasty: *iou.*

tattletale
prosecutor, accuser, tattletale: *sounkadip.*

tattoo: *pelipel.*
to tattoo: *nting, ntingih, palih$_2$, pelipel.*
a sacred tattoo placed just above the knee of females: *nting sarawi.*

taut: *deng$_1$.*
to stretch, to make taut: *kadang, kedengideng.*
to be made taut: *kedeng.*

tavern
bar, tavern: *pahr$_4$.*

tax: *daks, daksis.*
community improvement tax or labor: *kamwahu$_1$.*

taxi: *daksi.*

tea: *dih$_4$.*

teach
to teach: *sukuhlih.*
to teach, to instruct: *padahkih.*

teacher: *sounpadahk.*

teaching
lesson, teaching: *padahk.*

teachings
Christian teachings: *padahk en lamalam.*

team
group, team, grade level: *pwihn.*

tear
to tear: *tehr.*

to tear easily, to wear out easily, of clothing: *sepwurek.*
to be torn: *tei.*
to be torn, to be worn out: *teirek.*

tear
tear, teardrop: *pilen mese.*

teardrop
tear, teardrop: *pilen mese.*

tease
to tease: *kumwus.*
to joke with, to tease: *kapitih, kemwene.*
to joke or tease: *kamwan, kelipa.*
to fool, to tease, to kid, to joke with: *ketewe.*
said of one who likes to tease or make fun of others: *kepit$_2$.*

technician
laboratory technician: *sounkeseu.*

telegram
radio transmission, telegram: *dempwo$_2$.*
wireless telegraph, telegram: *wailes.*
to send a radio transmission or telegram: *dempwo-.*

telegraph
wireless telegraph, telegram: *wailes.*

telephone: *dengwa.*

telescope
spyglass, telescope, binoculars: *tupweiklas.*

tell
to tell the history of something, to tell a sacred story: *poadoapoad.*

temper
to throw a temper tantrum: *pwusukoal.*

temperamental
sensitive, temperamental: *limwakarakar.*

temperate
abstemious, temperate in eating and drinking: *ewetik.*

temperature: *sohng karakar.*

temple
head, temple: *kodokenmei, peipei$_3$, tapwi.*

temple
temple, house of worship: *imwen kaudok.*

tempt
to tempt, to entice: *kasongosong.*

temptation: *songosong.*

ten: *ehk$_1$, eisek, koadoangoul, ngoul.*
ten, in cards: *tehn$_2$.*

ten million: *dep.*

ten thousand: *nen.*

tenor: *tener.*
    to sing tenor: *tener.*

tense
    frustrated, tense, worried: *tihwo.*
    tensed up, as of a muscle: *deng₁.*
    to tense, of the muscles: *kadang.*

tent: *impwal.*

tentacle
    tentacle, as of an octopus: *rah.*

tenth: *keisek.*

terminated
    to be ended, terminated, or stopped:
        tok₁.

termite: *lohng, longenmwet.*
    termite ridden: *mwoasoahngot.*

tern
    tern, a black sea bird: *paret.*

test
    test, examination: *des, sikeng.*
    to take a test or examination: *des,*
        sikeng.

Testament
    New Testament: *Kadehde Kapw.*
    Old Testament: *Kadehde Mering.*

testicle: *wisol.*

testify
    to witness, to observe or hear
        something with certainty, to testify:
        kadehde.

testimony: *kadehde.*

thank you: *kalahngan en komwi.*
    thank you, used only with younger
        people: *mehn sahmwa.*

thanks
    thanks, informal: *menlau.*

that
    that one, away from you and me: *mwo.*
    that one, by you: *men₂.*
    that, away from you and me: *-o.*
    that, by you: *-en.*
    That's it , from *Ih men*: *men₂.*

thatch
    roof, thatch: *oahs₁.*
    to weave thatch: *dokoahs.*

their
    their, dual: *ara₁, neira.*
    their, plural: *ahr₁, arail, nair, neirail.*
        (See other possessive classifiers.)

them
    them, dual: *-ira.*
    them, plural: *-irail.*

then
    then, so: *eri.*
    and then: *apw.*

there
    there, away from you and me: *-la,*
        mwo.
    there, away from you and me (plural):
        iohkan.
    there, away from you and me
        (singular): *io.*
    there, by you: *men₂.*
    there, by you (plural): *ienakan.*
    there, by you (singular): *ien₁.*
    there, toward you: *-wei.*
    here and there, without definite
        direction: *-seli.*

these
    these, by me: *aka₁, akat, ka₁, kat,*
        mehkan, metakan.
    these here, by me (emphatic): *pwuka,*
        pwukat.

they
    they, dual: *ira.*
    they, plural: *ihr₁, irail, re.*

thick: *mosul.*
    bulky, stocky, thick, large in girth:
        ahlap.
    congealed, colloidal, thick, viscous:
        ten₁.
    thick, as a coat of hair: *losolos.*

thief: *pehsas.*
    thief, murderer, rascal: *loallap.*

thievish
    thievish, given to stealing: *lipirap.*

thigh: *dahng, kepe, kepehiso, tepindang.*

thin
    thin, of flat objects as paper:
        menipinip.
    thin, skinny: *tihti.*
    thin, slender, of small girth: *ahtikitik.*

thing: *ape₁.*
    one of, thing of: *mehn₁.*
    thing, material, physical object of any
        kind: *dipwisou.*
    thing, possession: *kepwe.*

think
    to think: *madamadau, medewe,*
        mwuserehre.
    to think, to feel: *kupwurehiong.*
    to feel, think, or sense: *pehm.*

third: *kesiluh.*
    third cup of kava in the kava
        ceremony: *esil.*

thirsty
    to be thirsty: *mennim.*

thirty: *siliakan, silihsek, silingoul.*

this
    this one, by me: *me₁, met.*
    this, by me: *-e, -et.*

thongs
zories, thongs: *sohri.*

thorn: *teke₁.*

thorny
thorny, spiny: *tekatek.*

thoroughly
thoroughly, completely: *douluhl.*

those
those there, away from you and me (emphatic): *pwukau, pwuko.*
those there, by you (emphatic): *pwukan.*
those, away from you and me: *akau, kau₂, ko, mwohkan, oko.*
those, by you: *akan, kan, menakan.*

thought: *madamadau, madau₂.*
feeling, thought: *pepehm.*
thought, idea, opinion: *lamalam.*

thousand: *kid.*

thread: *dereht.*

three: *esil, silidip, silidun, siliel, silika, silikap, silikis, silimen, silimwodol, silimwut, silipa, silipak, silipali, silipar, silipit, silipoar, silipwoat, silipwong, silipwuloi, silira, silisel, silisop, silisou, silite, silitumw, siliwel, sillep, siluh, siluhmw.*

throat: *kepinwer.*

throe
the throes of death: *ahdin mehla.*

throne
sacred place, altar, throne: *mwoahl.*

throw
to throw: *kese, kos₁.*
to throw at: *katepweke.*
to throw away, to get rid of: *kesehla.*
to throw bait around a canoe to attract fish: *kuroamw.*
to throw or punch forcefully: *likimwei, mweilik.*
to throw underhanded: *andasiro.*
to throw with a hip toss: *kadaur₂.*
to stone, to throw rocks at: *kate.*

throwing contest
a throwing contest: *akedei.*
to engage in a throwing contest: *akedei.*

thud
to thud: *kumwusek.*

thumb: *sendilepe.*

thunder: *nahnsapwe.*

Thursday: *Niepeng.*

thus
well, then, thus: *eri.*

ti
ti plant, *Cordyline terminalis*: *dihng.*

tickle
to tickle: *kading₁, kediked.*

tickling
given to tickling others: *likediked.*
having a tickling effect: *kararan.*

tide: *uh₅.*
a very high tide: *weid₁.*
high tide during the trade wind season: *weidinpar.*
of the tide or of bodies of fresh water, to reach a low point where much of the bottom is exposed: *ras₂.*

tie
necktie, tie: *nektait.*
to tie: *pirapir, pire, salih.*
to tie or attach together one after another, as breadfruit or flowers, to tie a bundle of things: *dune.*
to tie up: *salihdi.*
to tie, with any knot other than a slipknot: *pwuken eni.*
to be tied: *sel₁.*
to be tied, with any knot other than a slipknot: *pwukeneu.*
to be anchored or tied up, of a boat: *pei₅.*

tiger: *daiker.*

tight: *teng.*
too tight, as of clothing: *it.*

tightrope
to walk on a tightrope: *sahkas.*

tile: *dail.*

tilted: *dikou.*
tilted, listing: *keingihng.*
to be tilted, crooked, cock-eyed: *pang.*

time
in the past, a long time ago: *mahs₁.*
time between events: *madol.*
time, a period of time: *ansou.*
time, clock, watch, hour: *kuloak.*
to be on time for an event: *koanoa.*

times: *pahn₃.*

tin
can, tin: *pwoaht.*
tin roofing: *oasmete, pelien mete.*

tingly
tingly, as when the circulation is shut off in one's leg: *ketipinipin.*

tiny
tiny, minute: *pwiningining.*
tiny, small, little: *pwidikidik.*

tip
tip, in baseball: *sippwu.*
tip, of anything high: *kadoke.*

tiptoe
to tiptoe: *sikel.*

tire: *daia.*
  flat tire: *pilat₂.*
  to have a flat tire: *pangku.*

tired
  tired, lazy: *pwang.*
  to be tired: *lok, ngir.*
  to be tired of, to be disinterested in, to be bored by: *pwangahki.*
  to be bored or tired of something repetitious: *ngat-.*

tiresome
  tiresome, boring: *kapwang.*
  tiresome, physically: *kadau.*

title: *mwahr.*
  a title: *Isohlap, Isohpahu, Kaniki, Kanikihn Sapawas, Kiroulikihak, Kiroun, Kiroun Dolehtik, Kuloap, Lempwei Ririn, Lepen, Lepen Madau, Luhennos, Luhk Pohnpei, Mwarekehtik, Mwarikihtik, Nahluhk₂, Nahmadau, Nahmadoun Oare, Nahn Kirou, Nahn Kirou Ririn, Nahnawa Iso, Nahniau, Nahnkei, Nahnmadaun Pehleng, Nahnpei Ririn, Nahnsaumw en Ririn, Nahnsaumw en Wehi, Nahnsou, Nahnsou Sed, Nahnsou Wehi, Nahntu, Oaron Maka, Oaron Pwutak, Ou, Oun Sapawas, Oundol, Oundol en Ririn, Sapwetan, Soulik, Soulikin Dol, Soulikin Sapawas, Soulikin Soledi, Soumadau, Soumaka, Soupwan, Souwel en Wasai, Souwene.*
  a title, in the *Nahnken* line: *Kaniki Ririn, Lepen Ririn, Nahn Pohnpei, Nahnku, Nahnmadaun Idehd, Ou Ririn, Oun Pohnpei, Souwel Lapalap.*
  a title, in the *Nahnken* line, formerly of the second highest priest: *Nahnapas.*
  a title, in the *Nahnmwarki* line: *Lempwei Lapalap, Nahlik Lapalap₁, Nahn Kiroun Pohn Dake, Nahnawa, Nahnihd Lapalap, Nahnpei, Noahs, Oundolen Ririn, Saudel.*
  rank of the highest chief in one of the two title lines: *Nahnmwarki.*
  the second ranking title in the *Nahnken* line, formerly the highest priestly title: *Nahlaimw.*
  the second ranking title in the *Nahnmwarki* line: *Wasahi.*
  the third ranking title in the *Nahnken* line: *Nahnsahu Ririn.*

the third ranking title in the *Nahnmwarki* line: *Dauk.*
title of a *Nahnmwarki*: *nainai.*
title of the *Nahnmwarki* of Kiti: *Soukise.*
title of the *Nahnmwarki* of Madolenihmw: *Isipahu.*
title of the *Nahnmwarki* of Uh: *Sahngoro.*
title of the highest chief in one of the two title lines: *Nahnken.*
title of the wife of a *Dauk*: *Nahnte.*
title of the wife of a *Kaniki Ririn*: *Kanep.*
title of the wife of a *Kiroun Pohn Dake*: *Nahlikiroun Pohn Dake.*
title of the wife of a *Kuloap*: *Kedinikapw.*
title of the wife of a *Lempwei Lapalap*: *Pweipei Lapalap.*
title of the wife of a *Lepen*: *Lampein.*
title of the wife of a *Lepen Ririn*: *Lampein Ririn.*
title of the wife of a *Mwarekehtik*: *Nahnkar.*
title of the wife of a *Nahlaimw*: *Nahnkulai.*
title of the wife of a *Nahlik Lapalap*: *Nahlikiei Lapalap.*
title of the wife of a *Nahn Pohnpei*: *Kadipwan.*
title of the wife of a *Nahnapas*: *Nahnapasepei.*
title of the wife of a *Nahnawa*: *Nahleo.*
title of the wife of a *Nahnihd Lapalap*: *Nahnidipei Lapalap.*
title of the wife of a *Nahnken*: *Nahnkeniei.*
title of the wife of a *Nahnku*: *Nahnkuhpei.*
title of the wife of a *Nahnmadaun Idehd*: *Nahnkedin Idehd.*
title of the wife of a *Nahnmwarki*, in Net, Kiti, and Sokehs: *Nahnalek.*
title of the wife of a *Nahnmwarki*, in Uh and Madolenihmw: *likend.*
title of the wife of a *Nahnpei*: *Nahnpweipei.*
title of the wife of a *Nahnsahu Ririn*: *Nahlisahu Ririn.*
title of the wife of a *Nahntu*: *Nahntuhpei.*
title of the wife of a *Noahs*: *Nahnado.*
title of the wife of a *Saudel*: *Kedindel.*
title of the wife of a *Soupwan*: *Kedipwan.*

title of the wife of a *Souwel Lapalap*:
Eminalau Lapalap.
title of the wife of a *Wasai*: *Nahnnep.*
title of the wife of an *Isohlap*:
Likendlap.
title of the wife of an *Ou*: *Liou.*
title of the wife of an *Ou Ririn*: *Liou Ririn.*
title of the wife of an *Oun Pohnpei*:
Liounpei.
title of the wife of an *Oundol*:
Lioundol.
title holder in the *Nahnmwarki* line:
Sohpeidi, Soupeidi.
alternative title: *pelikilik.*
any high title: *lengileng.*
old title of the *Nahnmwarki* of Sokehs:
Isoeni.
title, in the legal code: *iralaud.*
to give a title: *dahmwar, pwekmwar.*
to give a title, to crown: *langilangih.*

to
at, to: *ni, nin.*
to, toward, in relation to, for: *-ehng,
-ieng, ong.*

toad
toad, frog: *kairu.*

toast
to cook, roast, broil, toast, etc.: *inihn.*

tobacco: *kereng.*
any rough-cut tobacco: *tipaker₁.*
plant sp., tobacco, *Nicotrina sp.*:
tipaker₁.

today: *rahnwet.*

toe: *rekenpwel, rekepwel, sendin neh.*
appendage, finger, toe: *send.*

toenail: *kikin neh.*

together
to be together: *pat₁.*
together, toward each other: *-pene.*

tomato
tomato, ketchup: *domahdo.*

tomboyish: *depelek.*

tomorrow: *lakapw.*
day after tomorrow: *pali₁.*
two days after tomorrow: *peilah.*

ton: *ten₂.*

tone
accent, dialect, tune, tone: *ngohr.*

tongue: *dinapw, lahu, loh₁.*

too: *nohkin, nohn.*
to be too much, excessive, more than
enough: *depala.*

tool: *kepwehn doadoahk, mehn
doadoahk.*

a barbed piece of wood, used as a tool
for tying thatch onto a roof: *koahr.*

tooth: *ering₂, eseng, inadi, ngih₂.*
buck-toothed: *ngihpit.*
gap-toothed, having missing or broken
teeth: *ngihtuk.*

tooth paste
powder of any kind, tooth powder or
tooth paste: *kona.*

tooth powder
powder of any kind, tooth powder or
tooth paste: *kona.*

toothless: *aupwahpw.*

toothpick: *loangenmeiso, mehn eringi.*

top
top, peak, summit, ridge: *koadoke.*
top, summit, end, outcome: *imwi.*
to be the first or best, to top all others:
dake₁.

topic: *irair.*

torch: *dihl₁.*
palm frond torch: *ser pahdil.*
torch made of dried coconut palm
fronds: *ndil.*
to torch fish: *ndil.*

torn
to be torn: *tei.*
to be torn, to be worn out: *teirek.*

torso
the upper half of the human body, the
torso: *ihpwe.*

torturous
painful, agonizing, torturous: *weirek.*

total
total amount: *tohtowe.*

touch
to touch or feel: *doahke.*
to come in contact with, to touch, to
touch upon: *sair.*
in the water, to touch the bottom with
one's feet: *sok₁.*

tough
cross or tough, of a person: *pwisinger.*
cruel, belligerent, tough: *keses, lemei.*
tough, as of meat: *kekeluwak.*
to be cruel, belligerent, or tough to:
lamai.

tourist party: *kangkohdang.*

tow
to tow: *luke.*
to be towed: *luk.*

toward
to, toward, in relation to, for: *-ehng,
-ieng, ong.*

towel: *daul.*

toy: *mehn mwadong.*

toy wheel: *kadahr.*
    to roll a toy wheel: *kadahr.*

trace
    scar, trace, ruins: *mowe.*
    trace or track: *lihpw₁.*
    trace of movement either seen or
      heard, as made by a person sneaking
      around: *mwand.*
    to trace or track, as the spoor of an
      animal: *kadipw.*
    to trace one's ancestry according to
      clan: *kadoukeinek, kodoukeinek.*
    to trace one's ancestry, to recall past
      history: *kadoudou, kodoudou.*

track
    to trace or track, as the spoor of an
      animal: *kadipw.*
    trace or track: *lihpw₁.*

track meet: *weirin tang.*

trade
    to buy, sell, or trade, to shop: *net₁.*

trade wind: *enginpar.*
    trade wind season: *nanpar.*

trademark
    a stamp, trademark: *sidamp.*

trail
    road, street, trail, path, line: *ahl₁.*

train: *kisa.*
    narrow gauge train: *troahli.*
    the two wheels and the axle of a
      narrow gauge train: *nehn troahli.*
    to drill, to train someone: *kaiahne.*
    to drill, to train, to exercise: *kaiahn.*
    to train a hibiscus tree in order to
      direct the growth of a yam vine:
      kapapeseng.
    to train for an athletic event: *kassoku.*
    to train not to do something:
      kalikasang.

training
    drill, training, exercise: *kaiahn.*

tranquility
    peace, tranquility: *popohl.*
    peace, tranquility, good feelings:
      onepek.

transfer
    to transfer, to move or change
      location: *kasau.*
    to be transferred, to be moved: *kosou.*

transform
    to be changed, to be transformed:
      wikila.
    to be transformed by supernatural
      power: *pikila.*

transient: *sohr.*

translate
    to explain, to translate: *kawehwe.*

transport
    to transport in a vehicle: *peidaid.*

transportation: *peidaid, peidepe.*

trap
    an animal trap: *lidip.*
    to trap: *lidip, lidipih.*
    to trap with a leg noose: *nsere.*
    to be trapped in a leg noose: *nsar.*
    to build a fish trap of coral or stone on
      a reef: *kasokamai.*

travel
    to go on a trip, to travel: *seiloak.*
    to travel: *luwaruhru.*
    to travel without provisions: *kahiep.*

travois: *dompiki.*

tray
    carrying tray: *opwong₂.*

treasurer: *sounkanekid.*

treat
    to treat with medicine: *winie.*

treatment
    heat treatment: *umwulap.*

tree
    tree, plant, lumber, wood: *tuhke.*

tree fern
    fern sp., *Cyathea ponapeana* or
      nigricans, a tree fern: *katar.*

tree sp.: *dohng, kahkirek, kehpei, komou,*
    mamenoki, pwuhr, remek, soiu₂.
    tree sp., *Abrus precatorius*: *kaikes.*
    tree sp., *Aglaia ponapensis*: *marasau.*
    tree sp., *Barringtonia asiatica*:
      wih₂.
    tree sp., *Barringtonia racemosa*:
      wihnmoar.
    tree sp., *Calophyllum inophyllum*,
      used for lumber: *isou.*
    tree sp., *Cananga odorata*, having
      fragrant flowers: *pwurenwai, seirin*
      wai.
    tree sp., *Cassia alata*: *tuhkehn kilin*
      wai.
    tree sp., *Cinnamomum*: *madeu.*
    tree sp., *Elaeocarpus carolinensis*:
      sadak.
    tree sp., *Erythrina*: *pahr₂.*
    tree sp., *Exorrhiza ponapensis*: *kotop.*
    tree sp., *Fagraea sair*, having fragrant
      flowers: *seirin pohnpei.*
    tree sp., *Ficus tinctoria*: *nihn.*
    tree sp., *Garcinia ponapensis*:
      kehnpwil.
    tree sp., *Glochidion ramiflorum*, the
      terminal buds of which are used for

increasing the appetite of young
children: *mwehk.*

tree sp., *Heritiera littoralis*:
mworopwinsed.

tree sp., *Ixora casei*: *ketieu₂.*

tree sp., *Macaranga carolinensis*, used
for medicinal purposes: *apwid.*

tree sp., *Messerschmidia argentea*:
titin.

tree sp., *Morinda citrifolia*: *weipwul,*
wempwul.

tree sp., *Myristica hypargyraea*:
karara.

tree sp., *Northiopsis hoshinoi*, known
for its strong wood: *koahre₁.*

tree sp., *Palaquium karrak*: *kalak.*

tree sp., *Parinarium glaberrimum,*
used for poles, paint, and caulking
canoes: *ais₁.*

tree sp., *Pemphis acidula*: *ngih₃.*

tree sp., *Poinciana pulcherrima*:
sehmwida.

tree sp., *Premna gaudichaudii*:
topwuk.

tree sp., *Randia cochinchinensis*:
kehnmant.

tree sp., *Syzygium carolinense*:
kehnpap.

tree sp., *Terminalia carolinensis*:
kehma.

tree sp., *Terminalia catappa*:
dipwoapw.

tree sp., *Thespesia populnea*: *pone.*

tree sp., a variety of mango:
doismango, kehngid en pohnpei,
kiewek, sallong.

tree sp., acacia: *pilampwoia.*

tree sp., durian, *Pangium edule*, edible
fruit: *duhrien, rawahn.*

tree sp., flame tree: *pilampwoia*
weitahta.

tree sp., known for its hard wood,
commonly found on the low islands:
kih₄.

tree sp., malay apple, *Syzyguim*
stelechanthum: *kirekinwel.*

tree sp., mountain apple, *Syzygium*
malaccense: *apel.*

tree sp., star fruit tree: *ansu.*

tremble
to tremble or shake: *rer.*

trench
ditch, trench, groove: *warawar.*

trial: *kopwung.*
to go to trial: *kopwung.*

triangle: *keimwsiluh.*

triangular
to be triangular: *keimwsiluh.*

tributary
tributary of a stream: *kesengenpil.*

tribute
tribute, gift, reward: *isais.*

trick
a trick, as a card trick: *akmanaman.*
to trick: *liepe, pitih.*
to play a dirty trick: *pokaraun,*
pokaraunih.

trickery
trickery, chicanery: *mwadik.*

trickle
to flow or trickle: *ker₁.*

trigger fish
fish sp., trigger fish: *lioli.*
fish sp., trigger fish, *Rhinecanthus*
aculeatus: *pwuhpw.*

trim
to cut, trim, or sharpen with any large
cutting tool: *par₁, periper.*
to trim hair at or below the base of the
neck: *sipuwer.*
to trim the fronds from a coconut
palm: *tahr₂.*

trip: *seiloak.*
trip by sea, ocean voyage: *sahi.*
to go on a trip, to travel: *seiloak.*

trochus
trochus shell: *dakasingai, sumwumw.*

troll
to troll for fish: *luk.*
to troll while paddling: *seiloakoaloak.*

troublesome
difficult, hard, troublesome, impossible:
apwal.
troublesome, hotheaded, defective:
lioakoahk.

trousers
trousers, pants: *rausis.*

true
true, honest: *mehlel.*

Truk: *Ruk₁.*

truly: *meid.*
truly, honestly: *mehlel.*

trump
trump, in cards: *diremw, wik.*

trumpet
conch shell, conch shell trumpet: *sewi.*
cornet, trumpet, bugle: *koronihda.*

trunk
waist or trunk of the body: *lukope.*

trust
faith, trust, hope: *koapwoaroapwoar.*

to have faith, trust, or hope:
koapwoaroapwoar.
to trust: *likih.*

Trust Territory of the Pacific Islands:
*Kahn Sapwen Kohwa Likilik en
Dekehn Pacific.*

trusteeship: *kohwa.*

trustworthy: *likilik.*

try
to try, to attempt: *song.*
said of one who tries hard: *nanti.*

tub: *dahpw, depw.*

tuber
main tuber of a yam plant: *inoande.*
smaller tuber of a yam plant: *seuseu.*

tuberculosis: *limengimeng.*

Tuesday: *Niare.*

tug-of-war
to engage in a tug-of-war: *epini,
pehdsel.*

tumor
seed, tumor, cyst: *war*$_1$.

tuna
fish sp., dogtuna, *Gymnasarda
unicolor*: *manguro.*
fish sp., skipjack tuna, *Katsawonus
pelamis*: *kasuwo.*
fish sp., tuna: *weliwel*$_2$.
fish sp., yellowfin tuna, *Neothunnus
macropterus*: *karangahp.*
dried skipjack tuna: *kasuwopwisi.*

tune: *ngihl.*
accent, dialect, tune, tone: *ngohr.*
to tune in, as a radio station: *daperedi.*

turkey: *teki.*

turmeric: *oahng.*

turmeric sp.: *oangalap, oangen palau.*
turmeric sp., *Zingiber zerumbet*:
oangen pelle.
turmeric sp., a variety of *Curcuma*:
oangitik.
turmeric sp., edible: *kisinioang.*

turn
to capsize or turn over, of any vehicle:
sepehlda.
to make, to become, to turn into:
wiahla.
to take one's turn to: *ihd*$_1$, *uhd.*
to turn a canoe away from the
outrigger: *kasahi.*
to turn a canoe in the direction of the
outrigger: *idemei.*
to turn away from the wind when
sailing: *koaik.*
to turn one's head: *pirekek.*

to turn one's head in contempt:
kepirek.
to turn or point into the wind when
sailing: *sempwe.*
to turn or twist: *kapir.*
to turn over: *wikid.*
to turn over, to flip: *welik.*
to turn toward, to face: *sohpei-.*
to turn upside down: *wikidedi.*
to turn while in motion: *wet*$_1$.
to turn, in direction: *wikidek.*
to turn, to spin, to twist: *pir*$_1$, *pirer.*
to be turned or twisted: *kepir*$_2$.
to be turned over, to be flipped: *wel-.*
of leaves, to turn or begin to dry:
mahrdi.

turtle: *wehi*$_1$.
hawksbill turtle: *sapwake.*
Pacific green back turtle: *kalahp.*
female turtle: *asapein.*
male turtle: *asamwan.*
a big pig or turtle: *tihnsauriau.*

tusk: *ngihpwar.*

twenty: *riehk, rieisek, riengoul.*

twins: *mpwer.*

twist
to turn or twist: *kapir.*
to turn, to spin, to twist: *pir*$_1$, *pirer.*
to twist off breadfruit with a pole and
let it fall to the ground: *pilloak.*
to twist or wind together: *mwulepene.*
to be turned or twisted: *kepir*$_2$.
twisted: *wengidek.*
closely twisted or curled, kinky,
tangled: *pinipin.*

twitch
to twitch: *nur.*

two: *are, ari, riadip, riadun, riai, riaka,
riakap, riakis, riapa, riapak, riapali,
riapar, riara, riasop, riau, riehl,
rielep, riemen, riemwodol, riemwut,
riepit, riesel, riesou, riete, riewel,
rioapoar, rioapwoat, rioapwong,
riopwuloi, riotumw, rioumw.*

type
kind, sort, type: *kain, mwohmw,
soahng.*

type
to type: *daip.*

typewriter: *daip, daipraida.*

typhoon
windstorm, typhoon: *melimel.*
to be struck by a windstorm or
typhoon: *melimel.*

ugly: *kersuwed, massuwed.*
ugly, matted looking, as wet feathers:
piokiok.

ukulele: *ukulehle.*

ulcerate
to ulcerate: *kens.*

ulcers: *soumwahu en mpwei.*

umbrella: *amper.*

umpire: *ampaia, ampangia.*

unacceptable
unacceptable, not well liked, only with
reference to people: *dohranai.*

unaccustomed
to be unaccustomed to: *sahn.*

unanimous
entire, whole, unanimous, complete:
unsek.

unassuming
humble, unassuming, meek: *aktikitik,
opampap.*

unattractive
sexually unattractive: *sapakaris.*

unaware
to be unaware of: *sasairiki.*

unburdened
to be unburdened or empty-handed:
kahiep.
unhindered or unburdened by
children or things: *depwen.*

uncivilized
pagan, uncivilized, uneducated,
uncultured: *rotorot.*

uncle
uncle, of the same clan: *ullap.*

uncomfortable
uncomfortable, causing minor
discomfort: *lokalok.*

unconcerned: *soukautih, sounsenoh.*
unconcerned about imposing on
others: *salamalam.*
unconcerned, untroubled: *pisek.*
to pay no attention to, to be
unconcerned about: *sokorohnki.*

uncooked
raw, uncooked: *amas.*

uncooperative: *saminimin.*
uncooperative, unsociable, acting
alone, selfish: *liakotohrohr.*

uncultured
pagan, uncivilized, uneducated,
uncultured: *rotorot.*

undefiled
virgin, pure, undefiled: *meipwon.*

under
below, under (him, her, or it): *pah₁.*

underestimate
to underestimate: *katik₃.*

undershirt: *ranning.*

understand
to know, to understand: *ese.*
to completely understand: *eruwahn.*
to be understood: *wehwe.*

underwear: *sarmada.*
to go without underwear: *neipi.*

underworld
underworld, below the ocean: *pahsed.*

undress
to undress: *pwuhrsang.*

undried
undried or green, of wood: *mour₂.*

uneducated
pagan, uncivilized, uneducated,
uncultured: *rotorot.*

unenthusiastic
peaceful, easygoing, unenthusiastic,
slow moving, passive, lethargic:
meleilei.

unequal
unequal, uneven, not flush: *sapahrek.*

uneven
unequal, uneven, not flush: *sapahrek.*
uneven, of an edge: *madap.*

unfortunate
unlucky, unfortunate: *maiai.*

unhindered
unhindered or unburdened by
children or things: *depwen.*

unhurried
unhurried or slow at an activity:
sepitipit.

unicorn fish
fish sp., unicorn fish, *Naso unicornis*:
pwulak.

uninformed: *keinimek.*
to be uninformed about: *sasairiki.*

uninhibited: *eimah.*
forward, uninhibited, outgoing:
limedramin.

union
union, association, any cooperative
venture: *minimin.*

unit
a political unit, as a municipality,
district, state, country, or kingdom:
wehi₂.

United States
America, United States of America:
Amerika.

unlikeable
unlikeable, obnoxious, despicable:
kadongodong.

unlimited
unlimited, infinite: *soire.*

unloving: *sempoak.*

unlucky: *paisuwed.*
unlucky, unfortunate: *maiai.*

unmarried
to be single, to be unmarried: *kiripw.*

unpleasant
unpleasant, always in a bad mood: *lipwusinger.*
grating or unpleasant, of the voice: *ngilawas.*

unreliable
unreliable, inept, incompetent: *salelepek.*

unrestrained
free, relieved, unrestrained, licentious: *saledek.*

unroll
to unroll, as a mat: *perek, pereki.*

unsanitary
messy, unsanitary, filthy: *samin.*

unsheathe
to unsheathe a knife or hidden weapon: *kakihr.*

unsmiling
stern-faced, unsmiling: *likokohunsop.*

unsociable
uncooperative, unsociable, acting alone, selfish: *liakotohrohr.*

unstable
unstable, as of a canoe: *sepehl.*

unsurpassed
far, far along, unsurpassed: *dei.*

untangle
to untie, to untangle: *sapwad.*
to be untangled: *sapwedek.*

untie
to open or untie, as a bag: *lapwa, lapwad, lawad.*
to untie, to untangle: *sapwad.*
to be opened or untied, as of a bag: *lawadek.*
to be untied: *lapwedek, sapwedek.*

until: *lao$_2$.*

untroubled
unconcerned, untroubled: *pisek.*

untrustworthy: *kesoulikilik.*

untruthful: *likamw.*
lying, untruthful: *aulikamw, oatilikamw.*
lying, untruthful, said of a person: *pitiniau.*
nonsensical, untruthful: *tika.*

unworthy: *sohwar.*

uphill
steep, uphill: *ukada.*

upland
upland, land to the east: *peidak.*

upon
above, upon, on (him, her, or it): *powe.*

upper
above, upper, upwind, windward side: *pohnangi.*

upright
a large upright in the framing of the walls of a building: *mesendid.*

uproot
to uproot, to peel, to pry: *sarek$_3$.*
to be uprooted: *sansarada, saretep.*

upset
easily bothered or upset by trivial matters, demanding, dependent: *inginsoi.*

upstream: *utuwi.*

upwards: *-da.*

upwind
above, upper, upwind, windward side: *pohnangi.*

urge
to urge: *uhk$_2$.*

urinal: *wasahn pipihs.*

urinate
to urinate: *koamwosod, pipihs.*
to urinate on: *pihs.*
to relieve oneself, to defecate or urinate: *kotala.*

urine: *kent.*

us
us, dual: *-kita.*
us, exclusive: *-kit.*
us, plural: *-kitail.*

use
to use: *doadoahngki, ius.*
to use wisely: *kirawih.*
to get, to use: *kamangaida.*
to be used to or accustomed to: *ahn$_1$.*

used
to be consumed or used up: *ros.*

useful
useful, worthwhile, valuable, advantageous: *katapan.*

useless: *sohkatepe.*
common, useless, of no consequence: *mwahl.*
It's useless , It's in vain : *kapwkapwewasa.*

uterus: *poahsoan.*

uvula: *lohtik.*

vagina: *pie, pihpi, pwalapwal, tehpahu.*
anus, vagina: *dahu.*
slang for vagina: *pahsu.*

vague: *rir*.

vain: *lipopohn*.

valise
    wallet, purse, valise: *pilihs*.

valley: *wahu*.

valuable
    important, valuable: *kesempwal*.
    useful, worthwhile, valuable,
    advantageous: *katapan*.

value
    importance, value: *kesempwal*.

vanish
    to vanish, to disappear: *sohrala*.
    to make vanish: *kasohre*.

vapor
    vapor, smoke, mist: *adi*.

variable
    variable, inconsistent, changeable:
    wikwikin.

vegetable: *iasai*.

vehicle
    canoe, vehicle: *tehnwar, wahr*.

veil: *koduhpwel*.

Venus
    Venus, the morning star: *Usuhn Rahn,
    Usuhrahn*.

verify
    to verify: *kamehlele*.
    to be verified, to be believed to be
    true: *kamehlel*.

verse
    verse of the Bible: *iretikitik*.

very: *inenen*.

vessel
    blood vessel: *selin nta*.
    major blood vessel: *selin mour*.
    man-of-war, an armed naval vessel:
    menuwa.

victory: *pansahi*.

vigil
    to maintain a vigil: *pisilei*.

vine
    vine, of a yam: *ohn kehp*.

vine sp.: *iol, nokonok, sellap, tahpw*.
    vine sp., *Antrophyum alatum*:
    tekenwel.
    vine sp., *Canavalia maritima*:
    wahntal.
    vine sp., *Davallia solida*: *ulungen
    kieil*.
    vine sp., *Hoya schneei*: *tekitek*.
    vine sp., *Ipomoea digitata*: *likehmw*.
    vine sp., *Ipomoea gracilis*: *emp$_2$, omp*.
    vine sp., *Passiflora foetida*:
    pwompwomw.

vine sp., *Piper ponapense*, used in the
    treatment of toothache: *konok*.
vine sp., *Polypodium phymatodes*:
    kideu.
vine sp., used for poisoning fish: *uhp
    kitik, uhpen iap, upenei*.

vinegar: *pinike*.

violin: *paiolihn*.

virgin
    virgin, pure, undefiled: *meipwon*.

viscous
    congealed, colloidal, thick, viscous:
    ten$_1$.

vise
    clamp, vise: *kilamp*.

vision
    to have defective vision: *rotala*.

visit
    to visit: *lawarourou, moahl$_2$,
    mwemweit, pwarek*.
    to visit a church for the purpose of
    praying, used by Catholics:
    pasdohng.
    to visit a place for the first time:
    kapwala, pasakapw.
    to visit door by door: *kahng$_3$*.
    to stop by, to stop in on, to visit:
    sop$_1$.

visor
    sun visor made from coconut fronds,
    used while fishing: *pweisou*.

voice: *ngihl*.
    voice, sound: *elinge*.

volcano: *pwolkeno*.

volleyball: *palepwohl*.
    to play volleyball: *palepwohl*.

volunteer
    to volunteer, to work without pay:
    tohnmetei.

vomit
    to vomit: *kaluhlu, keliali, kiliali,
    mmwus*.

voracious: *mehwo*.

vote
    to vote: *usuhs*.
    to vote by a show of hands: *koupe*.
    to vote for: *us$_2$*.

voyage
    trip by sea, ocean voyage: *sahi*.

voyeuristic: *limwasahsa*.

waddle
    to waddle: *eluwentek*.

wade
    to wade, as in water or tall grass: *ur,
    urak$_1$*.
    to wade in mud: *suhr*.

, reward: *pweipwei₂*.

wahoo, *Acanthocybium*
der: *ahl₂*.

l, at a funeral: *mwahiei*.

st or trunk of the body: *lukope*.

wait: *awih, sepit*.
wait for an event: *uhran*.
to wait for high tide: *kaidih*.
to wait on: *pahsan*.

wake
to have a wake: *pehdinpwong*.
to remain awake all night, as at a
wake: *kesihpwong, mwohdenpwong*.
to wake someone up: *kapirada*.
to wake up: *ohpalawasa, pirida,
pwourda*.

walk
to walk: *alu*.
to walk backwards: *kahsekir*.
to walk in a specific direction: *keid,
weid₂*.
to walk in a stooped position: *dairuk,
pairuk₁*.
to walk together with physical contact:
kapara₁.
to walk with a cane: *irar, sokon*.
to walk, implying to a destination a
considerable distance away: *sapal*.

walking
walking with swinging hands: *eipahi*.

walking stick
insect sp., walking stick: *menin
douioas*.

wall
wall of a building: *dihd*.
enclosure, pen, fence, wall, as of a fort:
kehl₂.
stone wall: *koaskoasok*.
back wall of a feast house: *pelik wahu*.

wallet
wallet, purse, valise: *pilihs*.

wandering
wandering, of speech: *lusulus*.

want
to want: *men₁*.

war
war, battle: *mahwin*.
war, battle, dispute: *moromor*.
war, particularly the second world war:
daidowa.
to be at war: *mahwin*.

warehouse: *imwen kepwe, sohko*.

warm
warm, hot: *karakar, kiriniol*.
to warm oneself by a fire:
karakaramwahu, rengireng.
to reheat, to warm over, as food:
pehl₁, pehle.
to practice for an athletic event, to
warm up for an athletic event:
rensuh.

warn
to warn, to remind: *kaunop-*.

warning
omen, warning: *dahda*.

warrior
Japanese warrior: *samurai*.

warship: *menuwa*.

wart: *mehme₁, pwudoniap*.
wart, corn: *mesenmwomw*.

wash
to wash clothing, to do laundry,
literally the action of pounding
clothing: *lopwolopw*.
to wash clothing, to launder: *lopwor*.
to wash one's face: *apwin, epwinek,
mahlengida*.
to wash one's feet: *wideh*.
to wash one's hair: *dopwolong*.
to wash one's hands: *amwin,
emwiemw, sikamwerada*.
to wash up on the reef or shore:
pwungur.
to wash, of anything except clothing:
widen.
to be washed up on the reef or shore:
pwungidekida.
to be washed, of anything except
clothing: *wideud*.
smudged, faultily washed: *ramin*.

washtub
washtub, basin: *darai*.

wasp: *loangalap*.

waste
garbage, waste, debris: *kihd*.
to lay waste to: *koamwoamwala*.
to waste: *kaluhsih, wiakawe*.

wasteful: *koluhs, sekerou, wiakau*.
to be destructive, to be wasteful:
koamwoamw.

watch
to take care of, to watch out for:
kanaiehng.
to watch intently: *dahkihla, dahla*.
to watch out for, to look out for, to
observe: *mwasahn*.
to watch, to behold, to observe:
poudiahl, udiahl.

time, clock, watch, hour: *kuloak*.
wristwatch: *was₂*.

watchman: *kandoku*.

water: *pihl*.
water for bathing: *loakiso*.
water for the *Nahnmwarki*: *ngke₂*.
water taken on a trip: *auleng₂*.
to water, to cool with water: *kalamwir*.
to be watered: *kelemwir*.
of the tide or of bodies of fresh water,
     to reach a low point where much of
     the bottom is exposed: *ras₂*.

water buffalo
carabao, water buffalo: *karapahu*.

waterfall: *tenihr*.
a small waterfall: *koropwung*.

watermelon
watermelon, *Citrullus vulgaris*: *suika*,
     wasmelen, watmelen.

waterspout: *lahpweseisei*.

watery
bland, tasteless, watery: *nampil*.

wave
wave, as in the ocean: *ilok*.
to wave, to signal: *oale, oaloahl*.

way
custom, way of doing things: *ahnepe*.

we
we, dual: *kita*.
we, exclusive: *kiht, se₁*.
we, plural: *kitail*.

weak
weak, feeble, sickly: *luwet,*
     luwetakahu.
weak, soft, easily broken, fragile:
     kopwukopw₁.
sick, weak: *liper₂*.

wealth
fortune, wealth, happiness, grace:
     pai₂.
anything which determines wealth in
     Ponape: *tehtehn peh*.

wealthy
rich, wealthy, having many possessions:
     kepwehpwe.

wean
to wean: *kalikasang*.

weapon: *tehtehn peh*.
any weapon employing gun powder:
     kesik pos.

wear
to wear: *likawih*.
to wear a diaper or loincloth: *weiwei*.
to wear a garland: *langilangih*.
to wear a garland, necklace, or lei:
     mwaramwar, mware₂.

to wear a grass skirt: *mwoalehda*.
to wear around the waist, of a weapon:
     pipih.
to wear clothing: *likou*.
to wear earrings: *tie₁*.
to wear shoes: *suht, suhtih*.
to be worn around the waist, of a
     weapon: *pip*.

wear out
to tear easily, to wear out easily, of
     clothing: *sepwurek*.
to be worn out: *tok₂*.

weather
bad weather: *lahng₂*.

weather plane: *sompihr en doulik*.

weather station: *wasahn kilang*
     kisinieng.

weave
to weave: *pa₂, peipei₂*.
to weave a net: *daur₁*.
to weave reeds or cane, as for a fish
     trap: *senser₂*.
to weave thatch: *dokoahs*.
to be woven, of a net: *dou₁*.

web
spider web, cobweb: *pesen likan,*
     pesen likan.

Wednesday: *Niesil*.

weed
weed, grass: *dihpw*.

weedy
weedy, grassy: *dipwidipw*.

week: *wihk₁*.

weep
to cry, to weep: *mauk, tentenihr,*
     wideudamwer.
to cry, to weep, to moan: *seng*.

weigh
to weigh: *teneki*.
to weigh down: *taur*.
to weigh down with stones: *pai₁*.
to weigh down, to anchor something in
     place by placing an object on top:
     koasuk.
to be weighed: *tenek*.

weight: *tautawi, toutowi*.

welcome
to welcome: *kasamwoh, koasoamw*.

welcoming
a welcoming: *koasoamw*.

weld
to weld: *inimpene*.

well
o.k., so, well, now: *na*.
well, then, thus: *eri*.

Well then?, Then what?, So what?:
ahn₂.
well: *ido*.
well, spring: *pwarer*.
west: *palikapi*.
wet: *wisekesek*.
of bodily coverings, soaking wet:
winapwehk.
wet and matted, of hair: *winakanak*.
to be wet under the arms from sweat,
or in the crotch from urine or sweat:
pworou.
whale: *roahs*.
wharf
wharf, dock: *wap*.
what: *da, dah, dahme*.
an interrogative noun meaning what
relationship to (him, her, or it), used
for family, body parts, and places:
depehne.
what thing?, singular: *dahkot*.
what things?, plural: *dahkei*.
what, implying enumeration: *dahnge*.
what, in response to being called: *e₃*.
where, what: *ia*.
Well then?, Then what?, So what?:
ahn₂.
What else? What other alternative is
there? Why not?: *apweda*.
wheel: *wihl₂*.
steering wheel: *mehn windeng*.
toy wheel: *kadahr*.
to roll a toy wheel: *kadahr*.
wheelbarrow: *wilpahro*.
when: *iahd*.
where: *iawasa*.
where, plural: *iahnge*.
where, what: *ia*.
which: *mehnia*.
while: *nindokon*.
during the time, for a period of, while,
within a distance: *erein*.
whip: *pohk*.
to whip, to spank: *wetih*.
to whip, to spank, to beat: *poakih,
woakih, wowoki*.
to be whipped: *popoki*.
to be whipped or spanked: *weweti*.
whirlpool
whirlwind, whirlpool: *elipip*.
whirlwind: *einiar, engipip*.
whirlwind, whirlpool: *elipip*.
whisper
to whisper: *ingihng₂, loiloitik,
mwenginingin, mwokuhku,
mwoluhlu*.

to whisper, to hum, to groan: *ingitik*.
whistle
police whistle: *kisin metehn popouk*.
ship or work whistle: *pwuh₂, wehsel*.
to whistle: *kuwai, suwaimwot*.
to whistle through one's fingers:
peukpe.
to whistle through the air, as a bullet:
dengng.
white: *pwetepwet*.
who
who, whoever: *ihs₁*.
who, plural: *isinge*.
whoever
who, whoever: *ihs₁*.
whole
whole, entire, intact: *pwon*.
entire, whole, unanimous, complete:
unsek.
entire, whole, as in *Pohnpeiuh*: *uh₈*.
wholesale
wholesale store: *ohlsehl*.
whore
slang for whore: *daksi*.
why
used in combination with the suffix
-ki to mean why: *dahme*.
why, to what purpose: *mehnda*.
Why?: *pwekida*.
wick: *wihk₂*.
wicked
dishonest, crooked, malicious, wicked:
mwersuwed, mworsuwed.
wide
wide and flat: *litehlapalap*.
wide, broad: *tehlap*.
wide, of an opening, road, or channel:
wangawang.
wide-eyed
wide-eyed, staring: *duwarawar*.
widow: *liohdi*.
widower: *olohdi*.
wife
spouse, husband or wife: *pwoud,
werek*.
wife, usually referring to wives of high
chiefs: *likend*.
any wife besides the principal wife:
pekehi.
wild
wild, not domesticated: *lawalo*.
to return to the wild state, of animals:
arewella.
will
will, feelings: *nsen*.
will, the document: *wil*.

to make a will: *kehkehlik*.

wilt
to wilt, to lose muscular control: *mwoator*.

win
to win: *kana, wihn*.

winch: *wens*.

wind
air, wind: *ahng*₁, *kisinieng*.
gust of wind: *tumwenieng, tumwunieng*.
gust of wind containing rain: *einiar*.
south wind, shifting wind, believed to bring bad weather: *engeir*.
trade wind: *enginpar*.
whirlwind: *einiar, engipip*.
whirlwind, whirlpool: *elipip*.

wind
to twist or wind together: *mwulepene*.

window: *wenihmwtok*.

windstorm
windstorm, typhoon: *melimel*.
to be struck by a windstorm or typhoon: *melimel*.

windward: *lepdahla, peidak*.
above, upper, upwind, windward side: *pohnangi*.

windy: *engieng*.
windy with accompanying rough seas: *engimah*.

wine: *wain*.
Japanese rice wine: *sake*.

wing
wing, of a bird: *peh*.

wink
to wink: *men*₄.
to wink at: *manih*.

wipe
to mop, to sponge off, to wipe: *dahlimw*.
to sponge off, to wipe dry: *limwih, limwilimw*.
to wipe, after defecation: *poahr*.
a command to wipe the hibiscus bast well because of debris in the kava cup: *dampangkot*.

wire
wire, spring: *wehia*.
barbed wire: *diraht, weiapens*.

wise
wise, knowledgeable: *eripit, kupwurekeng*.

wish
desire or wish: *ineng*₁.
wish, intention, plan, decision, desire, heart: *kupwur*₂.

to desire or wish: *inengiada*.

withdraw
to appear withdrawn: *rommwidi*.
to have the foreskin of the penis withdrawn: *dap*.

withered
withered, dry, dead, of vegetation: *meng*.

within
during the time, for a period of, while, within a distance: *erein*.

witness: *sounkadehde, sounkamehlel*.
to witness, to observe or hear something with certainty, to testify: *kadehde*.

wobbly
shaky, wobbly: *itikek*.

wolf
wolf, used biblically: *kidilipes*.

woman: *lih*₂, *pein*₂.
any woman in one's wife's clan except one the wife calls mother: *wahliniep*.
childless woman: *liedepwen*.
good woman: *lielehle*.
woman desiring sexual intercourse: *liesengou*.
woman who goes aboard visiting ships for sexual reasons: *lienseisop*.
young woman: *peinakapw*.

womanly
pretending to be womanly: *popohnli*.

wonder
to wonder: *eimwolu*.

wood
tree, plant, lumber, wood: *tuhke*.
small wood shavings for starting a fire, dry wood for the *uhmw*: *kodourur*.

word: *lepin lokaia, lepin mahsen*.

work: *doadoahk*.
hard working in feast activities: *dingngang*.
to work: *doadoahk*.
to work on: *koadoahke*.
to do community improvement work: *kamwahu*₁.
to volunteer, to work without pay: *tohnmetei*.

world
world, earth: *sampah*.

worm
worm, bacteria, germ: *mwahs*.
earthworm: *kamwetel*.
intestinal worm: *mwasenger*.

worn out
to be torn, to be worn out: *teirek*.

worried: *pwunod.*
frustrated, tense, worried: *tihwo.*

worry
to be concerned about, to be
interested in, to worry about:
nsenohki.

worse
worse, of an ill person: *doar.*

worship
worship, religion, prayer: *kaudok.*
to worship, to adore: *pwungih₁.*
to worship, to pray: *kaudok.*

worth: *katep₂.*

worthwhile
useful, worthwhile, valuable,
advantageous: *katapan.*

worthy: *war₂.*

wound
to be wounded: *soahn.*
to be wounded, as a consequence of
fighting: *lel₃.*
to have an abrasion or superficial
wound: *tepwedi.*

woven
dense, tightly woven or packed: *keirek.*
to be woven, of a net: *dou₁.*

wrap
to wrap: *kidikid, kidim.*
to wrap around: *lukom, pid₁, pinpene.*
to wrap kava in a bast with a minimal
number of twists: *limrei.*
to wrap kava in a bast with many
twists: *limmwot.*

wrapper
wrapper, cover: *kidikid, kidipe.*
binding, wrapper: *pirepe.*

wrasse
fish sp., wrasse, *Cheilinus undulatus*:
merer.

wreath
the royal wreath placed on the head of
a *Nahnmwarki* at his coronation:
elin katieu.

wrench: *rens.*

wrestle
to wrestle: *poadoar.*
to arm wrestle: *poadoarepe₂.*

wrestling: *poadoar.*
arm wrestling: *poadoarepe₂.*

wring
to wring, to squeeze with a twisting
motion: *wengid, wengiweng.*

wrinkle
to crumple, to wrinkle: *amwer.*
to wrinkle up one's nose: *konuhr.*

wrinkled: *mwerek, mwerekirek.*
crumpled, wrinkled: *emwirek.*
wrinkled, as the face of an old person:
mwalekuluk.

wrist: *kumwut en peh.*

wristwatch: *was₂.*

write
to write: *nting, ntingih.*

writhe
to writhe, of a fish when poisoned:
tat₂.

writing
writing, handwriting, signature:
menginpeh.

wrong
incorrect, wrong, erroneous: *sapwung.*
sin, wrong doing: *dihp.*

yam: *kehp.*
a variety of yam: *kait, kehmmarepe,*
kehmmarepehn kehpwetik,
kehmmeirkelik, kehmmwot en
namwanamw, kehmmwot en
pohnpei, kehmmwuterek,
kehmpahini, kehmpekehi,
kehmpwedawel, kehp kos, kehp
lapwed, kehp send, kehpenei,
kehpeneikesu, kehpin dolen pohnpei,
kehpin lupwu, kehpin na kitik,
kehpin namwo kepeu, kehpin
namwo kepsu, kehpin peisaper,
kehpin wai, kehpineir en wai,
kehpinou, kehpwetik en
kehmpwalap, kiewek en kakonehp,
kiewek en kehpin kipar, kiewek en
kehpin namwu pwetepwet, kiewek
en kehpin namwu weitahta, kiewek
en mahnd, kiewek en pasahnpwehk,
kilimenip en kakonehp pwetepwet,
kilimenip en kakonehp weitahta,
kilimenip en kehmmeirkelik,
kilimenip en kehmmwuterek,
kilimenip en kehpenei, kilimenip en
kehpinamwu pwetepwet, kilimenip
en kehpinamwu weitahta, kilimenip
en kiewek en mahnd, kilimenip en
lukenaisais, kilimenip en
pasahnpwehk, kilimenip en pohnpei,
koakonehp, lukenaisais, nahlik en
sokele, nahlik lapalap₂, neinsokihn,
ngisingisido, ohpwet, ohpwet en
pohnpei, ohpwet en wai, ondol en
luwi, ounsouna, pahmaru,
pasahnpwehk.
a variety of yam, bearing seeds:
kehmmwot.
a variety of yam, cigar-shaped: *kehp*
tipaker.

a variety of yam, from And: *kehpin and.*

a variety of yam, from China: *kehpin seini.*

a variety of yam, from Fiji: *kehpin pisi.*

a variety of yam, from Hawaii: *kehpin awai sohkatepe.*

a variety of yam, from Japan: *kehpin sapahn.*

a variety of yam, from Kipar, fruit-bearing: *kehpin kipar.*

a variety of yam, from Lohd: *kehpin lohd.*

a variety of yam, from New Caledonia: *nuhkaledohnia.*

a variety of yam, from Palau, having red flesh: *kehpin palau weitahta.*

a variety of yam, from Palau, having white flesh: *kehpin palau pwetepwet.*

a variety of yam, from Peilam: *kehpin nanpeilam.*

a variety of yam, from Penieu: *kehpin penieu.*

a variety of yam, from Saipan: *kehpin seipahn.*

a variety of yam, from Tomwara: *kehpin tomwara.*

a variety of yam, having a sweet flavor: *kehpin pwahr.*

a variety of yam, having fibrous flesh: *kehpsel.*

a variety of yam, having no particular season: *kehpwallal, kehpwetik.*

a variety of yam, having red flesh: *kehp silik, kehpin dolen wai weitahta, kehpin kipar weitahta.*

a variety of yam, having sweet-smelling, red flesh: *kehpin namwo weitahta.*

a variety of yam, having sweet-smelling, white flesh: *kehpin namwo pwetepwet.*

a variety of yam, having white flesh: *kehpin dolen wai pwetepwet.*

a variety of yam, non-native: *kehmpuwalap, kehmpuwetik.*

a variety of yam, producing fruit on the vine: *kehmpalai.*

a variety of yam, red: *koakonehp weitahta.*

a variety of yam, slow in maturing: *kehmmeirkelik mwotomwot.*

a variety of yam, slow in maturing, having red flesh: *kehmmeirkelik weitahta.*

a variety of yam, slow in maturing,

having white flesh: *kehmmeirkelik pwetepwet.*

a variety of yam, surface rooted: *kehpineir.*

a variety of yam, sweet-smelling: *kehpin mweli.*

a variety of yam, thin, with fibrous roots: *kehmmwas.*

a variety of yam, white: *koakonehmpwetepwet.*

a yam that develops on the vine, not edible: *mwehmwe.*

a variety of the yam *kehpineir*, shaped like a dog's paw: *kumwitin kidi.*

a variety of wild yam, *Dioscorea bulbifera*: *palahi.*

a large yam tied to a pole, requiring two men to carry it: *kehi.*

a small yam that can be carried by hand: *kutohr.*

a growth stage of a yam: *kehpwel.*

a stage of growth of a yam in which many branches have developed: *tepw.*

growth period of a yam after the leaves turn dark green: *tepwtoal.*

head of a yam: *mesenpek.*

the part of a yam that was used in its propogation: *weli.*

vine, of a yam: *ohn kehp.*

yam tuber left in the ground for further growth: *tipwensapwasapw.*

small yam: *mwaramwer.*

of a yam vine, to put out runners in all directions: *kepeira.*

grated, raw yam: *dororo.*

first feast of the yam season, usually in October: *kotekehp.*

yam disease, causing small black spots on the yam: *kil.*

yam raising competition: *siai en padok kehp.*

having a special affinity for growing certain species of yams: *pwuwak.*

yank

to yank or jerk: *sereki.*

to be yanked or jerked: *peserek.*

Yap: *Iap, Katau Peidi.*

yard

yard, the unit of measurement: *iaht.*

yawn

to yawn: *maudel, moaralap.*

yaws: *kens.*

yeah

yeah, an informal affirmative response: *ehng.*

year: *pahr₁, sounpar.*
  new year: *parakapw.*

yeast
  yeast, the alcoholic beverage prepared
    from yeast: *ihs₂.*
  to make yeast for drinking: *dol₁.*

yell
  to shout, to scream, to howl, to yell, to
    holler: *wer.*
  to shout, to scream, to howl, to yell, to
    holler at: *wering.*

yellow: *oangoahng.*

yellowfin tuna
  fish sp., yellowfin tuna, *Neothunnus*
    macropterus: *karangahp.*

yen
  yen, Japanese currency: *ien₂.*

yes: *ei₂.*
  yes, as a response to a negative
    question: *iei.*

yesterday: *aio.*
  day before yesterday: *mandaken aio.*

yet
  not yet: *kaik, kaikinte, saik₂, saikinte.*

yolk
  yolk, of an egg: *oange.*

you: *-iuk, -uhk, ihr₁, ke₁, koh, komw,*
  komwi, kowe, re.
  you, dual: *-kumwa, kumwa.*
  you, plural: *-kumwail, kumwail.*

young: *pwulopwul.*
  in good condition, young looking: *kot.*
  small, little, young: *tikitik.*
  young, of females: *peinakapw.*
  young, of males: *mwahnakapw.*
  to be lower than, to be younger or
    smaller than: *peidihsang.*

your
  your, dual: *amwa, noumwa.*
  your, plural: *amwail, noumwail.*
  your, singular: *ahmw₂, noumw, omw,*
  omwi. (See other possessive
  classifiers.)

zero: *sero.*
  zero, as a score: *damango.*

zipper: *seper.*

zories
  zories, thongs: *sohri.*